PENGUIN
COMPASS

THE ALPHABET VERSUS THE GODDESS

Leonard Shlain is the author of *Art & Physics: Parallel Visions in Space, Time, and Light,* and a contributor to *The Encyclopedia of Creativity* (Academic Press, 1999). He has written for many publications and lectures. Chief of laparoscopic surgery at California-Pacific Medical Center in San Francisco, he lives and writes in Mill Valley. His e-mail address is lshlain@aol.com, and the book's Web site is www.alphabetvsgoddess.com.

Praise for *The Alphabet Versus the Goddess*

"Every once in a while, during middle age, we come upon a book we wish we'd had the chance to read when we were much younger. So it is for me with this bold and fascinating investigation of the 'dark side of literacy.' Shlain . . . makes the startling claim that the advent of literacy ushered in the demise of goddess societies, and shifted the balance of power from women with their intuitive and holistic, right-brain orientation to the more concrete, linear-focused, left-brain men. . . . Both hemispheres of my cerebrum . . . remained stimulated throughout."
—Bart Schneider, *The Washington Post Book World*

"Shlain invites us to do nothing less than re-examine the vast history of humankind on planet earth . . . he mounts an argument that is . . . persuasive and entertaining."
—*The Baltimore Sun*

"Give Leonard Shlain credit for giving the commonplace practice of reading its full cultural importance. In exploring the elusive psychology of literature, he reaches some ambitious conclusions."
—*San Francisco Chronicle*

"A stimulating read . . . Shlain has produced a lively, readable and often suggestive tract. The ground traversed is immense, the horizons uncovered are often intriguing."
—George Steiner, *The Observer* (London)

"As provocative as anything published in the last decade. . . . Shlain's thesis is shocking . . . *The Alphabet Versus the Goddess* is fascinating, vexing, provocative, and sometimes maddening."
—Clay Evans, *Boulder Camera*

"Leonard Shlain may himself be the quintessential fusion of word and image. With superb writing, he draws for us a fascinating account of the evolution of our male and female ways of knowing, of the curses—not just the blessings—of reverence for the word alone. As a history and science lesson, this book is a vivid, breathing page-turner. As a threshold to a new perception of our history and our future, it offers both chilling reminders and great hope."
—Clarissa Pinkola Estés, author of *Women Who Run with the Wolves*

"A tour de force, with stunning new insights about gender relations, language and consciousness."
— Michael Murphy, author of *The Future of the Body*

"*The Alphabet Versus the Goddess* is as brilliant as it is well-wrought, an intricate weaving of past and present told in a story that is never less than absorbing."
— Richard Selzer, author of *Mortal Lessons*

"A fascinating, thought-provoking and original contribution to the literature on the goddess and her disappearance from our world."
— Jean Shinoda Bolen, M.D., author of *Goddesses in Everywoman*

"This is a bomb of a book—a highly original, titillating thesis that will delight, infuriate, challenge and enlighten."
— Larry Dossey, M.D., author of *Healing Words* and *Prayer Is Good Morning*

"A bold and courageous work."
— Fritjof Capra, author of *The Tao of Physics*

"Moving rapidly from the mists of prehistory to the glow of the PC screen, Shlain offers an ambitious interpretive account of the entirety of human culture: a well-written, daring work of the imagination, worthy of debate—and likely to generate plenty."
— *Publishers Weekly*

"Engrossing, occasionally poetic, and sure-to-be controversial."
— *Booklist* (starred review)

"Continually engaging . . . a monumentally ambitious work that treats all history as a great struggle between the written word and the visual. . . . A fascinatingly elaborate idea for readers to chew over."
— *Kirkus Reviews*

"An absorbing, provocative, and, ironically, highly literate work."
— *Library Journal*

LEONARD SHLAIN

THE ALPHABET VERSUS THE GODDESS

THE CONFLICT BETWEEN WORD AND IMAGE

PENGUIN/COMPASS

PENGUIN COMPASS
Published by the Penguin Group
Penguin Group (USA) Inc., 375 Hudson Street, New York, New York 10014, U.S.A.
Penguin Books Ltd, 80 Strand, London WC2R 0RL, England
Penguin Books Australia Ltd, 250 Camberwell Road, Camberwell, Victoria 3124, Australia
Penguin Books Canada Ltd, 10 Alcorn Avenue, Toronto, Ontario, Canada M4V 3B2
Penguin Books India (P) Ltd, 11 Community Centre, Panchsheel Park, New Delhi – 110 017, India
Penguin Group (NZ), cnr Airborne and Rosedale Roads, Albany, Auckland 1310, New Zealand
Penguin Books (South Africa) (Pty) Ltd, 24 Sturdee Avenue,
Rosebank, Johannesburg 2196, South Africa

Penguin Books Ltd, Registered Offices: 80 Strand, London WC2R 0RL, England

First published in the United States of America by Viking Penguin,
a member of Penguin Putnam Inc. 1998
Published in Compass 1999

15 17 19 20 18 16 14

Portions of this work first appeared in *The Utne Reader*.

Illustration credits
Title page, pages 139 (both), 228 (both), 313 (all): Alinari/Art Resource, New York; 31: Musée
d'Aquitaine, Bordeaux; 38 (top): Gift of Mrs. W. Scott Fitz. Courtesy, Museum of Fine Arts,
Boston; 38 (bottom): Archaeological Museum of Heraklion, Crete; 48, 56, 267: Réunion des
Musées Nationaux Agence Photographique, Paris; 60, 359 (top): Giraudon/Art Resource, New
York; 62 (both): © The British Museum; 123: © 1998 Estate of Pablo Picasso/Artists Rights Soci-
ety (ARS), New York. *Seated Bather*, Paris (early 1930). Oil on canvas, 64-1/4 x 51". The Museum
of Modern Art, New York. Mrs. Simon Guggenheim Fund. Photograph © 1998 The Museum of
Modern Art, New York; 126 (left), 179: Mark Reynolds; 126 (right): © 1998 The Georgia O'Keeffe
Foundation/Artists Rights Society (ARS). New York, The Metropolitan Museum of Art, The
Alfred Stieglitz Collection, 1949. (52.203) ; 134 (left): Scala/Art Resource, New York; 134 (right):
Gift of Edward Perry Warren and Fiske Warren. Courtesy, Museum of Fine Arts, Boston; 166:
The Metropolitan Museum of Art, Florance Waterbury Fund, 1970. (1970.44); 201 (left) The
Metropolitan Museum of Art. Purchase, Bequest of Florance Waterbury, 1969. (69.222); 201
(right): Courtesy of the author; 359 (bottom), 373 (both): Dover Pictorial Archives; 382: *Joseph—
Nez Perce, 1903* by Edward S. Curtis (published in *The North American Indian,* Volume VIII),
courtesy of Lois Flury, Flury & Company Ltd., Seattle, Washington; 410 (left): Courtesy of the Los
Alamos Historical Museum Archives, Los Alamos, New Mexico; 410 (right): NASA

THE LIBRARY OF CONGRESS HAS CATALOGED THE HARDCOVER EDITION AS FOLLOWS:
Shlain, Leonard.
The alphabet versus the goddess: the conflict between word and image/Leonard Schlain.
p. cm.
includes bibliographical references and index.
ISBN 0-670-87883-9 (hc.)
ISBN 0 14 01.9601 3 (pbk.)
1. Written communication—Social aspects.   2. Literacy—Social aspects.   3. Alphabet—
History.   4. Language and culture   5. Patriarchy.   6. Misogyny.   I. Title.
P211.7.S57   1998
302.2'244—dc21   98–21673

Printed in the United States of America
Set in Minion
Designed by Francesca Belanger

To my mother, Frances Shlain

PREFACE

The thesis of this book occurred to me while I was on a tour of Mediterranean archaeological sites in 1991. Our group had the good fortune to have for its guide a knowledgeable University of Athens professor. At nearly every Greek site we visited, she patiently explained that the shrines we stood before had originally been consecrated to a female deity. And, later, for unknown reasons, unknown persons reconsecrated them to a male one.

We then traveled to Crete to wander among the impressive remains of Knossos. Elegant palace murals depicted festive court women, girl acrobats, and snake-holding priestesses—mute evidence of women's seemingly high status in Bronze Age Minoan culture.

The trip ended at Ephesus on the Anatolian coast—the site of the ruins of the Temple of Artemis, the largest shrine to a female deity in the Western world. Until Christian authorities closed it in the late fourth century, a woman (or a man) could officially worship a goddess and priestesses could officially perform major sacraments. As our group contemplated these facts, our guide told the legend of Jesus' mother, Mary, coming to Ephesus to die. The guide then pointed out the hillside on which Mary's remains were purported to have been buried.

On the long bus ride back to the airport, I asked myself why Mary would have chosen a place sacred to a "pagan" goddess as her final resting place. Even if the legend was a fiction, why did it gain credence? This led me to ponder a larger question hovering over the entire trip—what caused the disappearance of goddesses from the ancient Western world?

There is overwhelming archaeological and historical evidence that during a long period of prehistory and early history both men and women worshiped goddesses, women functioned as chief priests, and property commonly passed through the mother's lineage. What in culture changed to cause leaders in all Western religions to condemn goddess worship? Why were women forbidden to conduct a single significant sacrament in these religions? And why did property begin to pass only through the father's line? What event in human history could have been so pervasive and immense that it literally changed the sex of God?

I was familiar with the current, most commonly accepted explanation: just before recorded history began, invading horsemen sweeping down from the north imposed their sky gods and virile ethics on the peaceful goddess cultures they vanquished. Somehow, this answer seemed to me inadequate to explain a worldwide social phenomenon that occurred everywhere civilizations emerged and which took a millennium to unfold.

My Mediterranean journey coincided with the publication of my first book, *Art & Physics: Parallel Visions in Space, Time, and Light,* which put forth the idea that innovations in art prefigure major discoveries in physics. Art and physics are two different languages; the artist uses image and metaphor; the physicist uses numbers and equations. To sharpen the ideas I put forth in *Art & Physics,* I had immersed myself in the study of how different communication media affect society.

While on that bus ride, and perhaps because of my heightened interest in how we communicate, I was struck by the thought that the demise of the Goddess, the plunge in women's status, and the advent of harsh patriarchy and misogyny occurred around the time that people were learning how to read and write. Perhaps there was something in the way people acquired this new skill that changed the brain's actual structure. We know that in the developing brain of a child, differing kinds of learning will strengthen some neuronal pathways and weaken others. Extrapolating the experience of an individual to a culture, I hypothesized that when a critical mass of people within a society acquire literacy, especially alphabet literacy, left hemispheric modes of thought are reinforced at the expense of right hemispheric ones, which manifests as a decline in the status of images, women's rights, and goddess worship. The more I turned this idea over in my mind the more correlations appeared. Like a dog worrying a bone, I found this connection compelling and could not let it go until I had superimposed it on many different historical periods and across cultural divides. The book that you now hold in your hand is the result of my teeth-gripping, head-shaking, magnificent obsession.

By profession, I am a surgeon. I head a department at my medical center and I am an associate professor of surgery at a medical school. As a vascular surgeon operating on carotid arteries that supply blood to the brain, I have had the opportunity to observe firsthand the profoundly different functions performed by each of the brain's hemispheres. My unique perspective led me to propose a neuroanatomical hypothesis to explain why goddesses and priestesses disappeared from Western religions.

My hypothesis will ask readers to reconsider many closely held beliefs and open themselves up to entirely new ways of looking at familiar events. In an effort to prevent factual errors from detracting from my ideas, I enlisted many experts to help me along the way, and the manuscript continually became smoother and finer as it sifted through the collective sieve of their multiple intelligences.

Because there is patriarchy even in non-alphabetic Eastern cultures, I felt compelled to make a brief detour into their history to see if it would fit within the framework of my thesis. The result is a book covering many centuries and many belief systems, a few of which, unfortunately, received short shrift. My mission was to present my reasoning in a manageable space while providing a panoramic view of the human condition. I am aware that numerous other respected explanations have been given for the dramatic events I recount. I could not in this book present accounts of all other historical theories, and chose to focus on the relationship between literacy and patriarchy.

I am by nature a storyteller. I have tried to make this book a lively read devoid of technical jargon. I had to balance this goal with my love for the luxuriant diversity of English. At times, I could not restrain myself from trying to rescue a few of my favorite words from what I fear may be their impending extinction due to neglect. Therefore, in the following pages the reader may occasionally sight an unfamiliar member of an endangered species of the English language. I ask the reader's indulgence.

As I sit here on a beautiful spring day thumbing through the freshly printed, hefty cube of manuscript that sits upon my desktop, I realize that my part in this engaging, maddening, wonderful, complicated, exciting writing project is complete. Now it is your turn. Have a good read.

Leonard Shlain
Mill Valley, California, 1998

ACKNOWLEDGMENTS

This book covers a broad expanse of intellectual territory and took seven years to complete. During its gestation, I continually refined my ideas by asking for and receiving help from a diverse group of people. Some were specialists whom I needed to read specific sections; others were generalists with varying political and social persuasions from whom I desired an overall assessment. Some read it in its earliest raw form and others had the benefit of seeing a more polished version. To all these stalwart individuals I wish to express my sincere gratitude.

Those in particular I wish to thank for their substantive comments are the following: Maria Watts, Larry Garlington, Jerold Lowenstein, Earl Saunders, David Nelson, Harrison Sheppard, Diane Roche, Duane Elgin, Edward Tamler, Pamela Nelson-Munson, Elinor Gadon, Fritjof Capra, Marion Diamond, Andrew Rosenblatt, Toghra Ghaem Maghami, Jim Schultz, Dorothy Donnely, Fr. Alvaro de Silva, Mogid Algar, Francis Dubose, Jennifer Ross, Marc Lieberman, Bernie Millman, Tiffany Shlain, Ken Goldberg, Laurel Airica, Clint and Cheryl Brown, Harry Newman, Hannah Hirsch, Dean Echenberg, Fred Miller, Phyllis Andreae, Jennifer Loeb, Pat Fobair, Caroline Garrett, Michael Parker, Mark Jackson, Adolphus Wong, Clifford Wong, Sheldon Levin, Karen Sirota, Carole Pecorrini, Terry Horrigan, J. Humphrey, Benjamin Fleck, Yong Lam, Mickey Bourne, Sam Gray, Ann Nadel, Linda Clever, Cheryl Haley, Nathan Siegal, Michael and Lynn Braverman, Kimberly Brooks, and Jordan Shlain.

Several readers deserve special thanks because of their very professional comments concerning style and syntax. In the manuscript's early stage, Cynthia Stern and Barbara Szerlip both made invaluable suggestions. The attention to detail that William Henkin put into his very specific queries and his many thoughtful recommendations early on helped immensely and greatly strengthened the book. My good friend Robert Stricker was steadfast in his support for this project from the very beginning and I wish to express my gratitude to him.

My agent, Elaine Markson, was skillful shepherding both me and my manuscript through the publishing canyons of New York and I am grateful for her enthusiastic support. I had the good luck to have David Stanford at Viking then take on the final editing and I feel privileged to have worked side by side with him. David's diligence, skill, and good humor throughout this next phase in the process made this usually onerous task a pleasurable one. I also appreciate the work of David's colleagues Kate Griggs, the book's production editor, and Francesca Belanger, who designed its interior.

I wish to thank Judy Snyder, who was so helpful in the tedious labor of translating into type my nearly illegible corrections in numerous revisions. I also want to thank Mark Reynolds for his excellent artwork that graces the pages in the text and Kimberly Brooks for her design of the book's Web site. And I wish to thank the great stickler for accuracy, Connie Goffreddi. Her forays into libraries to research my many obscure footnotes proved invaluable.

Lastly, I wish to express my deepest gratitude to Ina Gyemant, my wife, who so generously and patiently acted as my sounding board and gave me the gift of time to pursue this goal, and whose thoughtful edits pruned some of my unrulier sentences.

CONTENTS

THE
ALPHABET
VERSUS
THE
GODDESS

CHAPTER I

IMAGE/WORD

But of all other stupendous inventions, what sublimity of mind must have been his who conceived how to communicate his most secret thoughts to any other person, though very far distant either in time or place? And with no greater difficulty than the various arrangement of two dozen little signs upon paper? Let this be the seal of all the admirable inventions of man.

—Galileo[1]

Even a positive thing casts a shadow. . . . its unique excellence is at the same time its tragic flaw.

—William Irwin Thompson[2]

Of all the sacred cows allowed to roam unimpeded in our culture, few are as revered as literacy. Its benefits have been so incontestable that in the five millennia since the advent of the written word numerous poets and writers have extolled its virtues. Few paused to consider its costs. Sophocles once warned, "Nothing vast enters the life of mortals without a curse."[3] The invention of writing was vast; this book will investigate the curse.

There exists ample evidence that any society acquiring the written word experiences explosive changes. For the most part, these changes can be characterized as progress. But one pernicious effect of literacy has gone largely unnoticed: writing subliminally fosters a patriarchal outlook. Writing of any kind, but especially its alphabetic form, diminishes feminine values and with them, women's power in the culture. The reasons for this shift will be elaborated in the coming pages. For now, I propose that a *holistic, simultaneous, synthetic,* and *concrete* view of the world are the essential characteristics of a feminine outlook; *linear, sequential, reductionist,* and *abstract* thinking defines the masculine. Although these represent opposite perceptual modes, every individual is generously endowed with all the features of both. They coexist as two closely overlapping bell-shaped curves with no feature superior to its reciprocal.

These complementary methods of comprehending reality resemble the ancient Taoist circle symbol of integration and symmetry in which the tension between the energy of the feminine yin and the masculine yang is exactly balanced. One side without the other is incomplete; together, they form a unified whole that is stronger than either half. First writing, and then the alphabet, upset this balance. Affected cultures, especially in the West, acquired a strong yang thrust.

In the 1960s, Marshall McLuhan proposed that a civilization's principal *means* of communication molds it more than the *content* of that communication. McLuhan classified speech, pictographs, ideographs, alphabets, print, radio, film, and television as distinctive information-conveying media, each with its own technology of transmission. He declared that these technologies insinuate themselves into the collective psyche of any society that uses them, and once embedded, stealthily exert a powerful influence on cultural perceptions.

McLuhan's aphorism, "the medium is the message," is the leitmotif of this book. Robert Logan, the author of *The Alphabet Effect*, expounded on this idea:

> A medium of communication is not merely a passive conduit for the transmission of information but rather an active force in creating new social patterns and new perceptual realities. A person who is literate has a different world view than one who receives information exclusively through oral communication. The alphabet, independent of the spoken languages it transcribes or the information it makes available, has its own intrinsic impacts.[4]

While McLuhan, Logan, and others have explored many of the effects that alphabetic literacy has had upon Western history, I wish to narrow the focus to a single question: how did the invention of the alphabet affect the balance of power between men and women?

The proposition that the alphabet has hindered women's aspirations and accomplishments seems, at first glance, to be antithetical to historical facts. Western society, based on the rule of law and constitutional government, has increasingly affirmed the dignity of the individual, and in the last few centuries Western women have won rights and privileges not available in many other cultures. Most people believe that the benefits that have accrued to women are due primarily to a high level of education among the populace. But a study of the origins of writing in less complex times thousands of years ago reveals how writing, first, and then the alphabet, altered the balance of power to women's detriment.

Anthropological studies of non-literate agricultural societies show that, for the majority, relations between men and women have been more egalitarian than in more developed societies. Researchers have never proven beyond dispute that there were ever societies in which women had power and influence greater than or even equal to that of men. Yet, a diverse variety of preliterate agrarian cultures—the Iroquois and the Hopi in North America, the inhabitants of Polynesia, the African !Kung, and numerous others around the world—had and continue to have considerable harmony between the sexes.

Anthropologist Claude Lévi-Strauss was one of the very few scholars to challenge literacy's worth.

> There is one fact that can be established: the only phenomenon which, always and in all parts of the world, seems to be linked with the appearance of writing . . . is the establishment of hierarchical societies, consisting of masters and slaves, and where one part of the population is made to work for the other part.[5]

Literacy has promoted the subjugation of women by men throughout all but the very recent history of the West. Misogyny and patriarchy rise and fall with the fortunes of the alphabetic written word.

The key to my thesis lies in the unique way the human nervous system developed, which in turn allowed alphabets to profoundly affect gender relations. The introductory chapters will explore why and how we evolved in the manner we did. In later chapters, I will reinterpret a number of myths and historical events, making correlations based on circumstantial evidence. Correlation, however, does not prove causality—the disappearance of the stars at dawn does not cause the sun to rise. As we examine various sets of facts, I will appeal, therefore, to the court of what archaeologists call *competitive plausibility,* and I will ask the reader to consider with me which of the hypothetical explanations of historical events is the most plausible.

Although each of us is born with a unique set of genetic instructions, we enter the world as a work-in-progress and await the deft hand of the ambient culture to sculpt the finishing touches. Among the two most important influences on a child are the emotional constellation of his or her immediate family and the configuration of his or her culture. Trailing a close third is the principal medium with which the child learns to perceive and integrate his or her culture's information. This medium will play a role in determining which neuronal pathways of the child's developing brain will be reinforced.

To observe an enthralled four-year-old mastering the letters of the alphabet is to witness the beginning of a lifelong method central to the acquisition of knowledge. Literacy, once firmly rooted, will eclipse and supplant speech as the principal source of culture-changing information. Adults, for so long enmeshed in the alphabet's visual skein, cannot easily disentangle themselves to assess its effect on culture. One could safely assume that fish have not yet discovered water.

Imagine that you came of age in a non-literate culture and were unaware of the impact the written word could have on your life. Suppose that as an adult you then found yourself in a literate society confronted by others who seemed to possess magical powers. Your reaction probably would not differ much from that of Prince Modupe, a young West African who, in his autobiography, related his encounter with the written word:

> The one crowded space in Father Perry's house was his bookshelves. I gradually came to understand that the marks on the pages were *trapped words*. Anyone could learn to decipher the symbols and turn the trapped words loose again into speech. The ink of the print trapped the thoughts; they could no more get away than a *doomboo* could get out of a pit. When the full realization of what this meant flooded over me, I experienced the same thrill and amazement as when I had my first glimpse of the bright lights of Konakry. I shivered with the intensity of my desire to learn to do this wondrous thing myself.[6]

The prince could not know that in his attempt to free the *doomboo*, the pit itself would trap him in an unforeseen way: written words and images are entirely different "creatures." Each calls forth a complementary but opposing perceptual strategy.

Images are primarily mental reproductions of the sensual world of vision. Nature and human artifacts both provide the raw material from the outside that the brain replicates in the inner sanctum of consciousness. Because of their close connection to the world of appearances, images approximate reality: they are *concrete*. The brain simultaneously perceives all parts of the *whole* integrating the parts *synthetically* into a gestalt. The majority of images are perceived in an *all-at-once* manner.

Reading words is a different process. When the eye scans distinctive individual letters arranged in a certain *linear sequence,* a word with meaning emerges. The meaning of a sentence, such as the one you are now reading, progresses word by word. Comprehension depends on the sentence's syntax, the particular horizontal sequence in which its grammatical elements appear. The use of analysis to break each sentence down into its component words, or each word down into its component letters, is a prime example of *reductionism*. This process occurs at a speed so rapid that it is below awareness. An alphabet by definition consists of fewer than thirty meaningless symbols that do not represent the images of anything in particular; a feature that makes them *abstract*. Although some groupings of words can be grasped in an *all-at-once* manner, in the main, the comprehension of written words emerges in a *one-at-a-time* fashion.

To perceive things such as trees and buildings through images delivered to the eye, the brain uses wholeness, simultaneity, and synthesis. To ferret out the meaning of alphabetic writing, the brain relies instead on sequence, analysis, and abstraction. Custom and language associate the former characteristics with the feminine, the latter, with the masculine. As we examine the myths of different cultures, we will see that these linkages are consistent.

Associating images with the feminine would seem to fly in the face of numerous scientific studies that demonstrate that males are better at mentally manipulating three-dimensional objects than their female counterparts. Also, numerous other studies reveal that young females are more facile with words, spoken and written, than are their male peers. Despite these studies attributing different image and word skills to each sex, I will present many cultural, mythological, and historical examples that will solidly connect the feminine principle to images and the masculine one to written words. Again, I will use the terms "masculine" and "feminine" in their transcendent sense. Every human is a blend of these two principles.

The life of the mind can be divided into three realms: inner, outer, and supernatural. The inner world of experienced emotions and private thoughts is essentially invisible to others. The outer, concrete world of nature constitutes our environment: it is objective reality. There exists also a third realm: some call it spiritual, some call it sacred, and some call it supernatural. Humans have acknowledged and incorporated this third realm into every culture ever created.

The cosmology of any given culture is analogous to the psyche of an individual. Its myths and religion reveal how the group psyche arrives at its values concerning sex, power, wealth, and gender roles. In hunter-gatherer societies, members generally worship a mixture of male and female spirits. In general, virile spirits tend to be more prestigious in societies that place a high value on hunting; nurturing ones are more highly esteemed wherever gathering is the primary strategy of survival.

Humankind discovered horticulture approximately ten thousand years ago. In the Mediterranean, the most extensively studied region, archaeologists have uncovered strong suggestive evidence that in all emerging agrarian civilizations surrounding the basin, a mother Goddess was a principal deity. From the outer rim of history, we begin to learn Her name. In Sumer, She was Inanna; in Egypt, She was Isis; in Canaan, Her name was Asherah. In Syria, She was known as Astarte; in Greece, Demeter; and in Cyprus, Aphrodite. Whatever Her supplicants called Her, they all recognized Her as the Creatrix of life, nurturer of young, protector of children, and the source of milk, herds, vegetables, and grain. Since She presided over the great mystery of birth, people of this period presumed She must also hold sway over that great bedeviler of human thought—death.

Prior to the development of agriculture, male spirits embodied the attributes of bold, courageous hunters. But in the iconography of the Great Goddess, male imagery paled. Her consort was a companion who was smaller, younger, and weaker than She. A conflation of a son She loved in a motherly way, and a lover She discarded after he consummated his duties of impregnation, he was so dispensable in these ancient myths that he frequently died, either by murder or by accident. In many agrarian cultures, the yearly sacrifice of a young male surrogate in the consort's honor was a common ritual. The participants then plowed the victim's seed blood into the earth as "fertilizer" to ensure that the following year's crop would be bountiful. The clearest demonstration of the Goddess's power was Her ability to bring him back to life each spring. Whether She was resurrecting Her consort or regenerating the earth, Her adherents stood in awe of Her fecundity. For several thousand years, every people throughout the Fertile Crescent venerated a deity who personified the Great Goddess. When we speak of this area as the "cradle" of civilization, we tacitly acknowledge the superior role the feminine principle played in the "birth" of modern humankind.

Then, the Great Goddess began to lose power. The barely legible record of the earliest written accounts beginning about five thousand years ago provides intimations of Her fall. Her consort, once weak and inconsequential, rapidly gained size, stature, and power, until eventually he usurped Her sovereignty. The systematic political and economic subjugation of women followed; coincidentally, slavery became commonplace. Around 1500 B.C., there were hundreds of goddess-based sects enveloping the Mediterranean basin. By the fifth century A.D. they had been almost completely eradicated, by which time women were also prohibited from conducting a single major Western sacrament.

In their attempts to solve the mystery of the Goddess's dethronement, various authors have implicated foreign invaders, the invention of private property, the formation of archaic states, the creation of surplus wealth, and the educational disadvantaging of women. While any or all of these influences may have contributed, I propose another: the decline of the Goddess began when some clever Sumerian first pressed a sharp stick into wet clay and invented writing. The relentless spread of the alphabet two thousand years later spelled Her demise. The introduction of the written word, and then the alphabet, into the social intercourse of humans initiated a fundamental change in the way newly literate cultures understood their reality. It was this dramatic change in mind-set, I propose, that was primarily responsible for fostering patriarchy.

The Old Testament was the first alphabetic written work to influence future ages. Attesting to its *gravitas*, multitudes still read it three thousand years later. The words on its pages anchor three powerful religions: Judaism, Christianity, and Islam. Each is an exemplar of patriarchy. Each monotheistic religion features an imageless Father deity whose authority shines through His revealed Word, sanctified in its written form. Conceiving of a deity who has no concrete image prepares the way for the kind of abstract thinking that inevitably leads to law codes, dualistic philosophy, and objective science, the signature triad of Western culture. I propose that the profound impact these ancient scriptures had upon the development of the West depended as much on their being written in an alphabet as on the moral lessons they contained.

Goddess worship, feminine values, and women's power depend on the ubiquity of the image. God worship, masculine values, and men's domination of women are bound to the written word. Word and image, like masculine and feminine, are complementary opposites. Whenever a culture elevates the written word at the expense of the image, patriarchy dominates. When the importance of the image supersedes the written word, feminine values and egalitarianism flourish. In this book we will explore what this has meant throughout the human past, and in later chapters will consider what it says about the present and portends for the future.

CHAPTER 2

HUNTERS/GATHERERS

The social relations of all mammals are determined primarily by the physiology of reproduction.
                                                    —Sir Solly Zuckerman[1]

From the available evidence it appears that the most egalitarian societies are . . . hunting/gathering tribes, which are characterized by economic interdependency. A woman must secure the services of a hunter . . . to be assured of a meat supply for herself and her children. A hunter must be assured of a woman who will supply him with subsistence food for the hunt and in the event the hunt is unsuccessful.   —Gerda Lerner[2]

As primates differentiated from other mammals, they evolved three distinguishing modifications for living in tree branches. These ultimately affected the relations between the sexes of the human species. First, primates developed forelimbs with delicate hands sporting a versatile new appendage, the opposable thumb, a configuration that enabled them to effectively grasp, hold, and manipulate objects. Their arboreal habitat affected the ratio of their senses. Their olfactory sense, crucial to a ground dweller, atrophied. Once-grand snouts shrank into puny nostrils. But what primates, like birds, lost in their diminished sense of smell, they gained by evolving spectacular eyes. Sight became their most important sense. Lacking wings, primates risked their lives whenever they left the safety of one branch and leapt across empty space to the security of another. They needed to judge the tensile strength of vines, assess the direction and force of the wind, and operate the muscles of their complex forelimbs and hands with split-second timing. Natural selection bestowed upon primates their third distinguishing characteristic—a big, complex brain.*

---

*The evolution of life forms is impelled by three factors: changing environmental demands, the organisms' adaptations to these demands, and the mutation of genes that creates the adaptations. While the radiation into diverse species appears to have been

Due to changes in the earth's crust five million years ago, the climate in the Great Rift Valley in Africa changed drastically. In some areas, a thinning of the canopy of trees occurred. This development brought the local tree dwellers to a critical juncture. Some larger apes climbed down to the ground. Among the latter, one species literally took the first step by evolving another crucial adaptation. The smooth, round, tough heel was as stolid and boring as the hand was intricate and interesting. Yet, the heel was instrumental in permitting the first hominids to walk upright. The bipedalism that resulted was a boon to survival. With hominids' feet firmly planted on terra firma and their forelimbs freed from having to maneuver through the trees, their delicate hands could now be put to other uses.

Ethologists hypothesize that hominids began to scavenge the carcasses of dead animals killed by the big cats. To get to these leftovers, they first had to scare off other dangerous scavengers such as hyenas. The protohumans polished a skill their ancestors had used crudely—throwing. Eventually, practice led to a new method for killing small game. The primate that walked became the hominid that killed—the first higher animal capable of murder-from-a-distance. By freeing the hands, bipedalism enabled hominids to compress the journey from hunted vegetarian to scared scavenger to tentative hunter to accomplished killer in a mere million years.

Hominid brain size increased in response to the needs of nature's newest predators. Bigger brains meant longer childhoods. Needing to care for her children, who were progressively smarter but slower to develop past the stage of vulnerability, put new pressures on the hominid female. In addition to being born naked, hominid infants lost the ability to locomote at birth and were too weak to cling to their mothers. Absorbed in feeding, toting, and keeping her offspring warm, the hominid female became the first

---

carefully orchestrated by some supreme intelligence, many scientists do not believe any super-conscious effort is actually involved. They theorize that the orderly progression of life forms results from constant friction among the three above listed factors. Exercising a writer's artistic license, I will anthropomorphize the random process of evolution in the coming pages and I will use the terms "nature," "natural selection," "evolution," and "life" interchangeably. Further, since this is a book intended for the general public and these first few chapters must cover a vast amount of scientific terrain, I will focus on what are currently considered to be the most plausible speculations of how we came to be as we are. I will not include many interesting—but diverting—alternative hypotheses.

mother of any animal species who could not easily take care of herself in the postpartum period. She needed help. Food sharing evolved as a distinguishing trait of the hominid line, and its collateral attributes—altruism, kindness, generosity, and cooperation—also increased.

The growing human brain consumes great quantities of energy. A mother nursing her baby for as long as two years has an insatiable appetite. With the females increasingly busy taking care of their young, the males had to assist both mothers and their children and began to do something other predators rarely do. Hunters resisted the urge to consume game where it had fallen and instead undertook the arduous task of dragging their prizes back home. There, elders, women, and children would share the meat. The increasing importance of hunting induced changes in female sexuality.

Ethologists have observed that on the rare occasion when chimpanzee and baboon males kill and consume other animals for food, females form a circle around the noisily eating males. By their body stance and gesture, the females appear to be pleading for a share. Males most often bestow their meat upon those females who are in estrus.[3] Ethologists inferred from this behavior that all the males had something the females wanted—meat. But only a few of the females had something all the males desired—sex.

As meat consumption increasingly became a staple of the hominid's diet, so, too, did the exchange of meat for sex. Researchers such as Geza Teleki, Helen Fischer, and Jane Goodall believe that over time, natural selection favored females whose estrus was longer than average. Eventually, estrus disappeared in the hominid female altogether, with far-reaching implications. Sexuality and reproduction became uncoupled. The human female can, if she chooses, be receptive to a male 365 days of the year, including during menstrual periods and pregnancy. She can maintain her sexuality even after menopause. In the transition from hominid to human, this radical change in sexual programming gave her something of immense value to barter with male hunters.

Other primate groups and most mammalian species are organized as monarchies. The alpha male has first, and in most cases exclusive, access to the females at the height of their heat. But his intense passion for any one female wanes as she leaves estrus. The disappearance of estrus in the hominid line made it possible for a lower male in the hierarchy to secure sexual access to a female without having to challenge the alpha male. If he could return from a hunt with a portion of the spoils, he could attract a female, provided, of course, that he wooed her. Hunting prowess alone was not enough because the female was very selective about choosing her mate.*

The acquisition of meat involves a considerable expenditure of effort. A potential quarry will always put up a spirited defense. Meat, therefore, is associated with danger. The hunter who consistently brought meat back displayed daring and courage, two qualities that females desired in a potential mate. Thus hunting possessed an erotic overtone: meat was an aphrodisiac.

In her signature work, *The Second Sex*, Simone de Beauvoir asserts that the thrill of the hunt caused the divergence of human sexes by transforming the male. Killing made him *transcendent*, elevating him above his previous existence, giving him purpose, meaning, and an exciting task. The female, on the other hand, performed repetitive routines that had little glory or reward and kept her *immanent*. Women's work was not inspiring because it was not dangerous, even though everyone tacitly recognized its value to the tribe's overall well-being. Because hunting was not always successful, gathering edibles remained a vital source of nutrition. In general, the men hunted, and the women continued to gather.

As estrus disappeared from the hominid females, a new sexual feature, menses, became prominent. Shedding the lining of her uterus every twenty-eight days resulted in the loss of blood containing the crucial element iron. Other large mammals experience infrequent periods of estrus and minimal menstrual flow. They conserve iron by repeatedly licking themselves when they bleed, an anatomically impossible task for the human female. Human menstrual flow, by far the heaviest among all mammals, predisposes females to iron-deficiency anemia, which in turn can lead to lack of vigor, and increased susceptibility to all diseases. The infants of iron-deficient mothers are sickly from birth and are less likely to survive.

There is little iron in most vegetables, and in the north, winter made procuring iron-rich vegetables problematic. The food consistently rich in iron is meat. Males have no particular need for iron, but females absolutely must have it. If sex-for-meat was the unspoken exchange that rewired the female's physiologic responses, then her appetite for iron would motivate her to be ever more sexy. This, in turn, would increase meat's value to the male. His sexual drive would goad him into taking greater risks to kill game in order to impress the female he desired. Menses was the prod that inspired

*Loss of estrus was also responsible for the disturbing fact that among mammals rape is common only in our species and orangutans.

males to become audacious hunters. The pair bonding we now call marriage has its taproot sunk into this primitive transaction.

At about this point in the story a new problem arose. As the need for hominid intelligence steadily increased, the brain size of hominid babies continued to enlarge. But hominid mothers needed to continue to walk upright. Increasing the size of her pelvis to accommodate bigger-brained babies caused the distance between the heads of her femurs, the long bones of the thighs, to stretch apart. To compensate, the female began to walk with a distinctive swivel to her hips. Enlarging the birth canal beyond a certain diameter was impractical, as it would cause her to waddle rather than stride, seriously impairing her mobility. If the femurs were spread too far apart they could no longer support the upright body above them for purely mechanical reasons. Going back to the trees was not an option because the heel now deprived hominids of their former climbing agility.

The single most important factor limiting hominid intelligence became the diameter of the female pelvis, because the ever enlarging neonatal head made childbirth, an act of great simplicity for other viviparous animals, a dangerous ordeal for hominids. Birth became increasingly traumatic. For the first time among mammals, childbirth became the greatest cause of death for females. Nature tried to solve the problem by bringing forth an immature protohuman with a head so large that the creature couldn't support it and legs so short that they were useless for walking, but hominid females continued to die in large numbers during birthing. The eventual solution further divided the sexes.

Hominid neonates' brains became more immature than those of other mammalian species' neonatal brains. Major neuronal pathways such as the instinctual instructions that automatically inform all other mammals how to survive at birth disappeared. To compensate, the missing pieces of the hominid neonatal brain were added after the infant was safely on the other side of the mother's pelvic ring of bone. Much later we would name these pieces "culture."*

Culture was ladled into the baby's brain through the agency of a stunning evolutionary innovation—language. The advent of speech fissured

---

*While many other social animals, such as geese, lions, and monkeys, have rudimentary group behavioral responses that they learn as they mature, in no other species has culture taken on such a vital role as it has in ours.

humans away from the hominids. In earlier species, changes in behavior were primarily a function of waiting for beneficial mutations to affect chromosomes, a process that took millions of years. Using speech, one member of a clan, learning a lesson that would enhance survival, could pass it on to the others within hours instead of eons. Further, the clan could preserve wisdom in the net of language for successive generations yet unborn. Culture was the solution to the brain size problem imposed by bipedalism. The new corporate brain called culture hovered like a friendly poltergeist over each tribe of hunter-gatherers.

Language had to start somewhere. There had to have been a single moment when symbolic thinking insinuated itself into the stolid mentation of the animal world. Perhaps it began with that most basic of all human gestures—pointing. Humans are the only animals that convey information in this manner.* The outstretched arm and finger of the pointer demanded that the pointer's audience roll their eyes along the line of the pointer's arm and then continue off into empty space in the direction indicated by the index finger. Because there is nothing to see at the end of the finger, this gesture urges people to take a visual leap of faith, and look in the direction of the outstretched arm. If they do they will be rewarded—they will see what the pointer wanted them to see. The space between the tip of the first pointer's finger and the intended object was humankind's progenitor synapse.

In one of the most famous paintings in Western culture—Michelangelo's Sistine Chapel ceiling—God reaches out his finger to touch the finger of Adam. The artist implies that with this contact, the human adventure began. Part of this image's power lies in the fact that because God is stretching to touch Adam, He is pointing. So, too, is Adam. The viewer's eye jumps across the small but significant gap between God's finger and Adam's. To make the journey across the small break between their fingers is to recapitulate the leap across the immense chasm crossed by our hominid ancestors in the distant past—from concrete mentation to abstract thinking—a leap that transformed *them* into *us*.

Pointing led to other, more sophisticated, symbolic gestures. Soon hominids waved their hands and fingers at each other in increasingly complex gesticulation. There were, however, distinct limitations to gestural language. It did not work in the dark. It monopolized the receiver's vision

---

*Dogs can be taught to point with their bodies, but, like walking on their hind legs, it is not an activity they do naturally. A few primates also point.

because one had to watch the gesturer. And gesture occupied the gesturer's hands, making them unavailable for other tasks. A language based on gesture placed too many demands on valuable survival resources.

Casting about for a replacement, evolution came up with the economical idea of using the human tongue for communication. While virtually every other muscle group in the body engaged in a vital activity fairly regularly, the tongue just sort of lay in the mouth between meals, doing little except help with swallowing saliva. The brain, like a patient Olympics coach, taught the tongue to perform a wide range of acrobatic gymnastics. Complex maneuvers shaped exhalation into distinctive sounds. The *langue* (tongue) in language became the indispensable shaper of speech.

Speech freed both hands and eyes, and it worked in the dark. Once there was agreement that the sound of the spoken word "tree" symbolized the image of a tree, early people could refer to trees when none were in sight. This ability, which humans take for granted, is so profound that it forms the great divide between all other animals and us. Ants and bees can *signal* limited information about the direction and distance to food. Monkeys can *inform* the other members of the troop that danger is near. But only humans can *ask* a compound question and, further, *discuss* and *dispute* the answer.

For the hunting hominid, language became an important weapon. For example, a hunting party coming upon the footprints of prey could discuss the paw print with considerable sophistication. How long ago did the animal pass by? How large is it? How far away is the animal? How many of us will it take to locate it? How many to kill it? Shall we divide up? What is our strategy? This ability to compare and analyze information with others does not exist in any other predator.

Speech also added another dimension to nurturing. Besides providing her young with breast milk, a mother became responsible for imparting the knowledge of the culture, imprinting upon the infant's mind essential lessons regarding love, honor, respect, courage, loyalty, honesty, curiosity, playfulness, and self-esteem. Communication between a mother and her child begins while her fetus is in utero and increases dramatically at birth. Though separated by the severing of the umbilical cord, mother and baby remain attached by the enmeshing web of language, both verbal and nonverbal, including cooing and singing, babble and banter. The two are strongly tied through their eyes—the mother's face is as compelling to her baby as the baby's face is to her. Each learns to instantly recognize the nuances in the expression of the other. In this manner, mothers become skilled at caring, and children begin the long road to humanhood.

The increasingly burdensome task of raising their young required that women form cooperative alliances with other women. To enhance their off-spring's chances of survival, the females also reached across the growing divide separating the sexes and engaged the males of the tribe in the job of socializing children. Adult males had already learned love and the concept of sharing from their mothers when they were small boys; these emotional responses proved invaluable in the new adventure they were undertaking, one with which few other mammals had experimented—fathering.

The prolonged childhood of their progeny precluded most women from hunting. A mother could not leave her young for long and a crying baby could not accompany a hunting expedition. Among other social predators such as wolves, lions, and killer whales, the females actively participate in both hunting and killing. Humans became the first group of social predators in which females left this critical task to the males. While the men refined the technology of killing, women made other life-enhancing cultural contributions. Learning how to convert dead skin into warm clothing, weave cloth, and shape pottery were activities as essential to a tribe's survival as the development of slings and spears. Since gathering required a thorough knowledge of plants, women would have been more likely than men to ferret out their medicinal and nutritional secrets.*

In the northern latitudes, hunting skills were more important than gathering skills. In winter, fruits and grains disappeared for months at a time. The necessity of hunting larger and more dangerous animals in these regions meant that hunters had to be bolder. Cave paintings and butchering tools from the Paleolithic period attest to the importance of meat among northern European cultures. Nevertheless, a tribe's survival was as dependent on the female's nurturing skills as on the hunter's daring. Ongoing generations of healthy children were as vital as a constant source of protein. A strong interdependence cemented the sexes together even as their skills diverged.

Hunting demands "cold-bloodedness" tinged with cruelty; nurturance requires emotional generosity combined with warmth. A hunter must maintain a singularity of purpose when focused on prey; a mother must keep a field awareness of all that is going on around her. While scouting for edibles, she cradled her infant in the crook of her left arm and had to monitor constantly the activity of her other children, playing at the periphery of

*Women most likely discovered that the foxglove (digitalis) contained a powerful cardiac stimulant; sucking on willow bark (aspirin) relieved inflammation; poppies (morphine) relieved pain, and specific molds (penicillin) cured some infections.

her vision and consciousness. She could rarely carry out a task without, at the same time, remaining vigilant. Failure to do so often meant the death of, or serious injury to, her offspring.

Because of their different roles, evolution, in time, equipped men and women emotionally to respond differently to the same stimuli. This resulted in men and women having different perceptions of the world, survival strategies, styles of commitment, and, ultimately, different ways of *knowing*: the way of the hunter/killer and the way of the gatherer/nurturer. In accommodating these differences, nature redesigned the human nervous system, radically breaking with all that had gone before.

CHAPTER 3

RIGHT BRAIN/LEFT BRAIN

In each of us two powers preside, one male, one female; and in the man's brain, the man predominates over the woman, and in the woman's brain, the woman predominates over the man. . . . If one is a man, still the woman part of the brain must have effect; and a woman also must have intercourse with the man in her. Coleridge perhaps meant this when he said that a great mind is androgynous. It is when this fusion takes place that the mind is fully fertilised and uses all its faculties.

—Virginia Woolf[1]

For the first two million years, both the hominid's body and brain slowly enlarged. And then over the next one million years, a remarkable change occurred: while its stature increased only minimally, its brain acquired one extra pound of neural tissue, primarily in the neocortex. At the same time, the brain's functions split in two—a revolutionary development made necessary because evolution had to rewire one lobe to accommodate speech.

To place this event in context, a brief review of the brain is in order. All vertebrates, beginning with fish, have a bilobed brain. And each of these anatomically mirror-image hemispheric lobes perform the *same* type of tasks. The human brain lobes, while appearing symmetrical, are *functionally different*. This specialization is called hemispheric lateralization. There is evidence of this feature in some other vertebrates, but its manifestations in behavior (speech and handedness) are far more striking in humans than in any other species. A bridge of neuronal fibers called the *corpus callosum* connects and integrates the two cortical lobes so that each side knows what the other is thinking.

The popular press has widely disseminated the essential features of right/left brain asymmetry. Most well-informed people know that each hemisphere of the brain controls the muscles of the body's opposite side.

Most people also understand that the hemispheres work closely in concert with one another.

But scientists have only recently discovered the attributes distinctive to each hemisphere. While poets and mystics have long alluded to sharp divisions within our psyche, it was not until the late nineteenth century that clinicians began systematically to take note of these differences. Patients who had traumatic injuries and strokes provided the most dramatic examples. In the last few decades, neuroscientists examining split-brain patients and using sophisticated brain mapping scanners on normal people have been able to study each hemisphere in relative isolation.

The dysfunction that occurs as a result of a left-brain injury in right-handers is so calamitous that neuroscientists traditionally call the left cerebral hemisphere the dominant lobe.* While some have objected to over-simplifying the brain's lateralization scheme, certain facts remain beyond dispute. If a right-handed person has a major stroke in the controlling left hemisphere, with few exceptions, a catastrophic *deficit of speech, right-sided muscle paralysis and/or dysfunction in abstract thinking* will occur. Conversely, damage to the right brain will impair the afflicted person's ability to *solve spatial problems, recognize faces, appreciate music,* besides *paralyzing the left side of the body.*

Of the twin human hemispheres, the right side is the elder sibling. In utero, the right lobe of a human fetus's brain is well on its way to maturation before the left side begins to develop. The old, wise, right side, more familiar with the needs and drives stemming from earlier stages of evolution, can be better relied upon to negotiate with them than the younger left side. The right hemisphere integrates feelings, recognizes images, and appreciates music. It contributes a field-awareness to consciousness, synthesizing multiple converging determinants so that the mind can grasp the senses' input *all-at-once.*

The right brain is nonverbal, and has more in common with earlier animal modes of communication. It comprehends the language of cries, gestures, grimaces, cuddling, suckling, touching, and body stance. Its emotional

---

*In the following discussion, I will use the brain organization of someone who is right-handed and left-brain dominant. I do not mean to slight the 8 to 9 percent of the population who are left-handed and right-brain dominant. Rather, I wish to use the most common mode and avoid bogging my discussion down in qualifiers. Most of what follows is true in reverse for left-handers, but a left-hander's brain is not simply a right-hander's mirror image. Their brains are less strictly divided into a speech and non-speech lobe, as are those of right-handers.

states are under little volitional control and betray true feelings through fidgeting, blushing, or smirking.

The right brain, more than the left, expresses *being*—that complex meshing of competing emotions that constitutes our existential state at any given moment. In English, we ask someone, "How are you?" The answer begins, "I am . . ." The verb "to be" frames both question and answer.

The right brain more often than the left generates feeling-states, such as love, humor, or aesthetic appreciation, which are *non-logical*. They defy the rules of conventional reasoning. When Blaise Pascal wrote, "The heart has its reasons which reason knows nothing of," he was referring to the kind of knowing that goes on in the emotional right brain, and distinguishes it from that which occurs in the cerebral left.

The right brain's feeling-states are *authentic*. Once a person has experienced love or ecstasy, he or she *knows* it. An internal voice verifies the experience beyond debate. Feeling-states allow us to have faith in God, to grasp the essence of a joke, to experience patriotic fervor, or to be repulsed by a painting someone else finds beautiful. These states all possess a *non-discursive* quality. Standing in the shadows of our ancient beginnings, feeling-states overwhelm the brain's more recently evolved glib facility with words. No crisp nomenclature exists to describe them. When pressed to explain their emotional experiences, people, in exasperation, commonly fall back upon tautology—"It is because it is!" The things one loves, lives, and dies for cannot easily be expressed in words.*

Feeling-states do not ordinarily progress in a linear fashion, but are experienced *all-at-once*. "Getting" the punch line of a joke results in an explosion of laughter. An intuitive insight arrives in a flash. Newton and Einstein both reported examples of what the poet Rilke called "conflagrations of clarity." Love at first sight, such as what Dante experienced when he encountered Beatrice, happens in an instant. Religious conversions, such as the one that overwhelmed Paul on the road to Damascus, strike like lightning.

A feature of nonverbal communication is that no symbolization interferes with the direct appreciation of reality. The right brain perceives the world *concretely*. For example, a facial expression is "read" without any attempt to translate it into words.

The right hemisphere is also the portal leading to the world of the invisible. It is the realm of altered states of consciousness where faith and mystery

---

*Recently, researchers have identified the feeling-states of happiness, optimism, and cheerfulness to be in the left frontal lobe, indicating that not all emotions reside in the right hemisphere.

rule over logic. There is compelling evidence that dreaming occurs primarily in the right brain.[2]

When people find it necessary to express in words an inner experience such as a dream, an emotion, or a complex feeling-state, they resort to a special form of speech called *metaphor* that is the right brain's unique contribution to the left brain's language capability. The word *metaphor* combines two Greek words—*meta,* which means "over and above," and *pherein,* "to bear across." Metaphors allow one to leap across a chasm from one thought to the next. Metaphors have multiple levels of meaning that are perceived simultaneously. They supply a plasticity to language without which communication would often be less interesting, sometimes difficult, and occasionally impossible. The objective world can be described, measured, and catalogued with remarkable precision, but to communicate an emotion or feeling-state we employ metaphors. To tell another that one's heart is "soaring like an eagle" or "as cold as ice" reveals the synergy between the right brain's concrete images and the left brain's abstract words. Metaphors beget poetry and myth, and are essential to the parables of religion and the wisdom of folktales.

The right brain is also distinguished by its ability to cognate images. It can simultaneously integrate the component parts in the field of vision, synthesizing incongruous elements *all-at-once.* The human face is the most compound image the right brain must decipher. Fluctuating facial expressions and the infinite variety of human faces adds to the complexity of the task, as does the possibility that the person behind the face is engaging in an act of deception. The right brain takes all these factors into account and usually turns in a virtuoso performance instantly.

One demonstration of this right-brain skill is the ease with which people can recognize the faces of others. An old friend's countenance may have been altered dramatically by wrinkles and baldness, yet we are still able to pick out that childhood pal in a crowd decades after we last saw him. But some unfortunate individuals, having suffered damage to their right hemispheres, cannot recognize even their own family and friends; a few are even unable to recognize their own faces in the mirror.

The right brain does not speak, yet it actively participates in the comprehension of the spoken word. By listening carefully to the *forms* of speech while the left brain is deciphering speech's *content,* the right hemisphere is expert at ferreting out hidden messages by interpreting inflection and nuance. It is aware of the speaker's posture, facial expression, and gesture. Just below conscious awareness, it registers pupil size and hand tremors. This skill is not particularly useful when the information being transmitted is factual, such as legal, scientific, economic, or academic topics. But, when the conversation is personal, facial gestalts and vocal inflection can give the listener substantial insight into what is *really* going on, sometimes even more than whatever words are being said. Since it is virtually impossible to describe how the right side deciphers nonverbal language, most people refer to this skill as "intuition."

Another major right-brain feature is its ability to appreciate music; the perception of sounds which the right lobe integrates into an *all-at-once* harmonious feeling state. Though extremely difficult to define scientifically, each of us is quite sure we can distinguish music from noise. During World War I, doctors observed many soldiers who had sustained traumatic injuries to their dominant left hemispheres and as a result could not speak a word. This select group could, however, sing many songs they knew before they were injured. Alexander Luria, the Russian neurologist, reported the case of a composer who created his best work after he was rendered speechless by a massive stroke in his left hemisphere.[3] These case histories lend credence to the tale that Mozart asked his wife to read stories to him while he composed. By distracting his left brain with spoken language, the stories may have freed his music-oriented right brain to compose.

The right brain is better than the left in perceiving space and making judgments as to balance, harmony, and the composition of gestalts, from which we make aesthetic distinctions between ugly and beautiful. Since the right hemisphere processes input instantaneously, it is the better side for appreciating dimensions and judging distances. Driving, skiing, and dancing are its province. The right brain's principal attributes concern *being, images, holism,* and *music.*

The left brain's primary functions are opposite and complementary to the right's. The right side is concerned with *being,* the left with *doing.* The left lobe controls the vital act of *willing.* Its agent, the right hand, picks berries, throws spears, and fashions tools. The left lobe knows the world through its unique form of symbolization—speech. In right-handed people, 90 percent of language skills reside in the left hemisphere. Speech gave the left brain the edge to usurp the sovereignty of the mind from its elder twin.

Speech and action are closely related. Words are tools: the very essence of action. We use them to abstract, discriminate, analyze, and dissect the world into pieces, objects, and categories. But speech is not only outer-directed; within the self, words are the implements of thought.

Analysis—reducing the components of sentences into their separate parts—is essential to understanding speech, especially if the content of the message concerns objective facts. This key left brain task depends upon *linear* progression, in contrast to the holistic perception of the right brain.

Speech itself is also *abstract* and depends upon the left brain's unique ability to process information without the use of images. The mind arranges words, as children assemble Legos, as image substitutes, building concepts that allow us to think about *freedom, economics,* and *destiny* without needing to conjure images for these words. The ability to conceptualize that the abstract words *crime, virtue, punishment,* and *justice* are all related is supremely human. To be able to leap from the *particular* and *concrete* to the *general* and *abstract* has allowed us to create art, logic, science, and philosophy. But this skill tore us out of the rich matrix of nature. The part torn away became the ego. The left brain cleaved the right brain's integrated sense of wholeness into a duality that resulted in humans creating a distinction between *me-in-here* and *world-out-there.* The ego requires duality to gain perspective. Dualism also enhanced the human penchant for objective thinking, which in turn increased our reasoning skills and eventually led to logic.

Logic is not holistic, nor is it conceived as a gestalt. It click-clacks along the left brain's linear railway of sequence. *If–then* syllogisms, the basis of logic, have become the most reliable method of foretelling the future. They have all but replaced omens, visions, and intuition. The rules of logic form the foundation of science, education, business, and military strategy.

Along with *doing, speech,* and *abstraction,* the fourth characteristic unique to the left hemisphere is *numeracy.* Although the ability to count began in the visio-spatial right brain, the ability to permutate larger numbers allows the left brain to build towering computations. While other animals are capable of distinguishing among *one, two,* and *many,* we alone can conceive of algebra and Boolean logic. The close association between abstract speech and abstract numeracy is evident among small children who learn the alphabet and learn to count at the same stage of development.

All the innovative features of the left hemisphere—*doing, speech, abstraction,* and *numbers*—are linear. To develop craft, logic, strategy, and arithmetic, the mind must range back and forth along the line of past, present, and future. The survival and then success of humans required that evolution set aside an area in the newly enlarging brain in which the concept of time could be contemplated free of the holistic and gestalt spatial perceptions of the earlier mammalian and primate brains. An appreciation of linear time was the crucial precondition for linear speech.

A conversation can be understood only when one person speaks at a time. In contrast, one's right brain can listen to the sounds of a seventy-piece orchestra and hear them holistically. Time and sequence are the very crux of the language of numbers; it is impossible to think of arithmetic outside its framework. I propose that the left hemisphere is actually a new sense organ designed by evolution to perceive time.

Researchers have discovered that women have between 10 percent and 33 percent more neuronal fibers in the forward part of their corpus callosum than do men.[4] The higher the number of connecting neurons, the greater must be the integration between the two sides. Women and most men freely concede that women are more aware of and can better express their feelings than men. The extra connecting neurons seem to enhance the communication of emotions and increase global awareness, field perception, and understanding of the moods of offspring. Generally, women can perform multiple tasks simultaneously better than men.

Although the male paid a price for his relative isolation from his right-brain emotions, he gained the ability to shut out feelings that might otherwise have distracted him while he was engaged in the dangerous activity of hunting. The ability to focus on a single task and remain emotionless is a more desirable attribute for a hunter than are gestalt awareness and emotional depth. A detached subject/object split also allows a hunter to separate himself from the hunted. The dispassion inherent in dualism, a viewpoint indispensable for killing, is the opposite of a mother's binding love for her child.

Like the male and female members of a gatherer/nurturer–hunter/killer society, each hemisphere of the brain executes the tasks for which it is best suited. To ensure versatility in case of injury, each hemisphere has some capacity to perform the other side's functions. So, too, can each sex of the human species assume the other's principal labors. Women not burdened with small children could and did hunt: they, too, could kill quarry dispassionately. And men were resourceful gatherers; they, too, could love. Nevertheless, in general, the majority of men excelled at hunting and killing, and the majority of women excelled at gathering and nurturing.

Over one hundred thousand years ago *Homo sapiens sapiens*, the wise human, appeared. Despite our present civilization's far remove from the caves of Lascaux, we remain strongly influenced by the original neurodesign that bred eminently successful nomadic gatherer-hunters. The dichotomy between the left and right hemispheres mirrors the differences between hunter/killer and gatherer/nurturer strategies. Metaphorically, time is the masculine coordinate, and space is the feminine one. The poet William Blake wrote, "Time & Space are Real Beings, a Male & a Female. Time is a Man and Space is a Woman."[5]

The new human dual brain conferred upon early Homo sapiens an enormous evolutionary advantage. The right and left hemispheres can, on occasion, behave nearly independently, each one able to solve problems differently, each capable of its own decisions, memories, judgments, and actions. Intelligence is defined as a flexible response to varying stimuli. Splitting the brain into two separate functional units did not simply double the potential number of responses a human might have to a situation. Because of the constant feedback between the two lobes, hemispheric lateralization led to an almost *infinite* variety of responses, making our forebears supremely intelligent among animals. To many thoughtful people, it also seems to have created two subspecies of Homo sapiens—Woman and Man.

Like the brain, the human eye also evolved opposite but complementary functions. Each human eye is a perfect mirror image of the other, yet within each retina there reside two functionally different types of cells. With elegant symmetry, the contrasting functions of the rods and cones correspond to the division of tasks between the right and the left brain.

Rods, named for their cylindrical shape, are extremely light sensitive. Like trip wires, they detect the slightest movement in a visual field. Distributed evenly throughout the periphery of each retina, they see in dim light and appreciate the totality of the visual field, seeing images as gestalts. Rods share with the right brain the ability to perceive reality *all-at-once.*

Cones, in contrast, congregate densely in a small spot in the central part of the retina, called the *macula.* The *fovea centralis* at the macula's center has the highest concentration of these cone-shaped cells and, accordingly, is vision's focal point. Cones have two attributes. They appreciate color and intensify clarity. Concentrating on one aspect of reality at a time, cones view the visual field as if through a tunnel. Like rods, cones report to both hemispheres, but the left is metaphorically best suited to process their input.*

The eye divides every scene into two major elements: figure and ground. Figure is visualized sharply and in detail; ground provides the context within which the figure resides. The cones best see figure; the rods best visualize ground.

Because rods supply the big picture, they are the key component of a visual, physical, and mental state known as *contemplation.* The rods enlist the entire individual to help them perform. Muscle tension diminishes. The brow becomes unfurrowed. The pupil dilates. The skeletal muscles of the

*There are no specific neuronal pathways yet identified that connect the periphery of vision with only the right brain or the cones preferentially with the left brain.

eyes relax, unfocusing vision. These actions serve to let maximum light into the eye. In this right-hemispheric mode, the individual is better able to see the entire visual field rather than any one detail. Looking at nothing, the eye in this state sees everything. This receptivity affects the whole body. Consciousness idles and a person slides into the integrated mental state of *being*.

Rods have an older ancestry than cones; all vertebrate eyes have them. But only a few animals possess cones in abundance. The evolutionary history of the rods and cones is telescoped in infants. Babies can see with rod vision within days of birth. Cone vision (color and detail) does not fully develop until many months later. As a legacy of our primate heritage, humans have one of the highest ratios of cones to rods among mammals. And because of the left brain's expanded sense of linear time, humans greatly refined this propitious gift. The need for cones is particularly acute in predatory birds, predatory mammals, and the only truly predatory primate, the human. Herbivores rarely need them: plants cannot run away. But predators must be able to observe not only where their potential dinner is, but also where it might be going. Cones allow an animal to *scrutinize*.

Scrutiny corresponds to the mental state of *concentration*. The body's sense of alertness is heightened. Skeletal muscles tense. The brow furrows. The pupil of the eye constricts. These actions reduce the amount of light entering the eye, effectively shutting down the light-sensitive rods. It is not unlike theater technicians dimming the house lights so that the audience can see the stage more clearly. Intense concentration upon a colored detail, the special gift of the cones, is the opposite of holistic contemplation, the relaxed, open-eyed activity of the rods.

The left brain's discriminatory, analytic mode is better suited for focused vision than the right's holistic one. The cones isolate sections of the visual field, then inspect each one *in sequence*. This focusing ability of the fovea centralis creates the illusion of time passing because the images seen within this narrow circle of the eye can only be processed *one-at-a-time*. Because macular vision examined *what was* and then moved on to *what is,* it forced the emerging human brain to consider the possibility of what might come *next*. Cone vision, I suggest, created the necessary parameters for the left brain to invent the all-important idea of *next*, which led, inexorably, to foresight (or *next*-sight)—a sense of the future.

An illustration of how this works: imagine walking into a theater, your eyes not yet adjusted to the dark. The usher leads you down the aisle, stops, and then turns on a flashlight. As the beam scans a row, one person after another appears within the light's circular field. As the flashlight's glare leaves each person, he disappears, and the next person magically emerges.

The constricted cone of the flashlight's beam resembles the macula's tunnel vision. Although everyone in the theater row is already there in space, searchlight vision isolates them, creating the *illusion* that they exist only in an orderly sequence of time.

The specialization of visual functions within each human eye corresponded to the lateralization of the cerebral hemispheres and the bifurcation of the human sexes. The holistic vision of the rods assisted the right brain in gathering and nurturing. Tunnel vision was primarily subordinated to the unique demands of the hunting left brain. Women have more rods in their retinas than men, and as a result, have better peripheral vision. They can see better in the dark and take in more at a glance than men. Men have more cones than women, allowing them to see one segment of the visual field in greater detail and with better depth perception than women.[6]

Not only brains and eyes, but human hands, too, specialized. The left hand, controlled by the right brain, is more protective than the right. The left hand is the one that commonly holds a baby regardless of the hand preference for other tasks, and the left arm wards off blows.[7] Its movements are grosser, that is, less coordinated than the right's. Hunters and warriors carry their shields with their left hand. Hand preference became more prominent when hominids advanced from foraging to gathering. Whereas the forager consumes on the spot whatever can be easily picked, the gathering hominid postponed eating in order to *carry* what had been collected back to a home base. The right hand selected what the left hand carried. Carrying, gathering, and defending evolved as left upper extremity tasks. Shielding, holding, and toting are maternal functions necessitated by the helplessness of human infants.

Many cultures use the left hand exclusively to aid in elimination of feces and urine and consider it unclean, reserving the right hand for eating.* The evidence that these prejudices still persist resides in our language. To be *left* out, to be served *left*-overs, to receive a *left*-handed compliment, or to be *left* in the lurch reflects the negative connotation associated with this side, and by extension, the right hemisphere. The word for left in Italian is *sinistra*. The word *sinister* in English comes from the same root. In French, left is *gauche*, which also means clumsy. *Droit*, the right, means correct.

---

*Until fairly recently, left-handed children were often beaten in school in an effort to force them to write with their right hands, as the left was often believed to be under the control of the devil.

The dominant right hand is the agent of action. It throws the spear, picks the fruit, or flakes the flint. Its movements are more precise. The right hand actively wields the hammer; the left hand passively steadies the nail. The right hand reaches; the left hand holds.

The high degree of preferential handedness is a trait unique to the human line. To help Homo sapiens adapt in its struggle for survival, natural selection divided the cortex of the brain, differentiated the two functions of the retina of the eye, and specialized the hands. The divisions between right and left also reflect the differences between the primary perceptual modes of men and those of women.

All animals depend on a dominant mode of survival. Most ungulates (horses, cows, zebras) congregate in herds and eat grass. Some predators (sharks, eagles, tigers) hunt alone, while others, social predators (lions, wolves, wild dogs), hunt in packs and cooperate closely with one another to bring down large quarry. Trying to emulate the precision of carnivores, humans were not always successful: unlike other predators, we had to learn how to do it. As we stepped away from the herbivore life, it was necessary to retain our skills at gathering. Thus, we became one of a handful of species that can survive either way.

These two mirror-image strategies, gather/nurture and hunt/kill, are combined in each of us. In society at large, there are females who manifest predominantly masculine traits, and there are males who display feminine traits. The lateralization of brain, eye, and hand affects how each person perceives, manipulates, symbolizes, and, ultimately, thinks about the world. Herein lies the secret of our success. Each man has a gatherer/nurturer aspect to his personality, psyche, and mind, just as each woman has hunter/killer aspects to hers. Every individual has encased in his or her skull both a feminine brain and a masculine one. Any particular society can accentuate one or the other of these two ways of interacting with the world, depending on the demands of the environment or the shaping influences of its inventions.

CHAPTER 4

MALES:DEATH
FEMALES:LIFE

Anxiety is the result of the perception of the truth of one's condition. What does it mean to be a self-conscious animal? The idea is ludicrous, if it is not monstrous. It means to know that one is food for worms. This is the terror: to have emerged from nothing, to have a name, consciousness of self, deep inner feelings, an excruciating inner yearning for life and self-expression—and with all this yet to die.

—Ernest Becker[1]

Fear was the first mother of the gods. Fear, above all, of death.

—Lucretius[2]

An increasing appreciation of linear time stretching back into the past and projecting far into the future led humans to two profound insights, one involving death and the other, sex. Pondering their personal longevity, eventually all humans realized that they would live for only a limited time. Animals witness death as an event happening to another—a dog may grieve for its master, but it is unlikely the dog knows it, too, will die. All humans came to understand that one day each person will experience death personally, inevitably, and with a finality that brooks no compromise, rejects all cajoling, and has no alternatives. Once the implications of this dark thought sank in, a disquieting anxiety began to gnaw, different from the sudden fear that all animals experience when confronted by immediate danger.*

---

*This Paleolithic epiphany occurs afresh in every generation when it dawns on each child, usually at around seven years of age, that his or her parents are mortal. Extrapolating this time-knowledge, the child then realizes in a life-changing insight that he or she, too, will someday die.

To ameliorate death's crushing finality, humans conceived of an afterlife. Observing that the bodies of the dead decayed, the living imagined the self as an ectoplasmic soul capable of leaving the visible world to live on, and they established elaborate rituals to assist the soul's transmigration into the next realm. Archaeologists have excavated reverential burials dating back sixty thousand years, and funerary rites became a defining characteristic among all human cultures.

At about the same time that humans were coming to grips with this morbid subject, no doubt men made another profound discovery—they finally grasped their personal role in the birth process. Women most likely understood this connection earlier than men. Their close and constant association with their offspring would have helped them recognize the similarities in both features and character of children and their fathers sooner. The thought dawned on men, previously unaware of this vital link and still lamenting their inevitable demise, that they, too, played an indispensable role in bringing forth children. Then, these two towering insights, one concerning death and the other sex, intersected in the male mind.*

A male's discovery that he could have heirs meant that he could wrest a small victory from death's maw by siring a child to whom he could pass on his name, wisdom, and weapons. This made urgent his need to be certain a newborn was the result of his copulatory efforts. A mother *never* has to doubt her kinship to her progeny: her infants literally come from and through her. A man, however, can never be completely sure. The male's heavy-handed solution was to demand virginity in his bride and absolute chastity in his wife thereafter. Making babies, an unfettered and essentially joyous process in less time-aware animals, turned deadly serious for humans. Whether willingly or reluctantly, the female acquiesced to this restrictive arrangement. In some ways, it was in her interest, and that of her present or future children, to enjoy one man's loyalty. The sex-for-meat exchange developed by earlier hominids now became considerably more complicated. The new social contract exchanged male fealty for female chastity, and eventually formed the basis of marriage. A woman sacrificed her sexual freedom in exchange for aid, companionship, and, perhaps, love.

*All children recapitulate this evolutionary crossroad around the age of seven. They usually understand how babies originate about the same time they come to realize they will not live forever. Perhaps this is why the Roman Catholic Church recognizes age seven as the onset of moral consciousness and why the Confucian Chinese consider age seven the onset of maturity. There remained, until very recently, some peoples (the Trobrianders of the Pacific, for example) who had not made the sex-birth connection. The date these insights occurred to our ancestors is presently unknown.

A man pledged himself and his accumulated property to one woman and their combined issue in the expectation that the children she bore would be his. Chastity and fidelity became the two foundation stones underpinning all future patriarchies.

The alpha male primate is extremely possessive of his females when the latter are at the height of their estrus; his need to control them does not, however, intrude into every aspect of their lives. When human males realized that they could achieve a kind of immortality *only* through their heirs, they imposed a menarche-to-menopause tyranny over females. Much of what is vigorously debated in our culture right up to the present has its roots in the archaic dichotomy between males/death and females/life.

Fear of death lies behind another trait peculiar to humans—guilt. It begins with having to kill another creature in order to eat. Roberto Calasso, the classicist, wrote,

> The primordial crime is the action that makes something in existence disappear: the act of eating. Guilt is thus obligatory and inextinguishable. And, given that men cannot survive without eating, guilt is woven into their physiology and forever renews itself.[3]

In the Old Testament, guilt enters the world by way of a bite from a fruit.

Once Paleolithic hunter/gatherers viewed life as finite, then all life became sacred. Yet to eat, hunters had to kill prey, and this act tore the weft of life in which they, too, were wrapped. Somehow, the spirits of their victims had to be appeased every time a hunter extinguished another life to feed his family. The herds of bulls, bison, aurochs, and horses that thunder across the ceilings of Altamira or Lascaux exude a sense of the sacred.

Evidence found by archaeologists at cave painting sites suggests that Paleolithic people also revered the feminine principle. The entrances to some caves are guarded by sculpted female figures. Found also at Paleolithic living sites, these figures' exaggerated breasts, buttocks, and protuberant bellies glorify pregnancy. In southern France, over 130 of these artifacts have been identified.[4*]

Archaeologists speculate that in the minds of early people, death was but an unseen phase of the cycle of life. Because the female gave birth, early peoples reasoned that a divine female was also inextricably associated with

---

*Curiously, archaeologists have never discovered a painted image of these female figures and, conversely, have rarely discovered sculpted animals.

The 22,000-year-old *Venus of Laussel*, discovered in a cave in southern France. She is representative of the mother figures found throughout the world in both present-day and archaic preliterate cultures.

death (even though the mortal male was often the agent who brought death). All things that die return to life through the agency of the female: the earth is both womb and tomb. Anne Baring and Jules Cashford in their book *The Myth of the Goddess* have eloquently expressed this relationship.

> Can we understand from this that there were originally not one but two basic myths: the myth of the goddess and the myth of the hunter? The pregnant figures of the statues suggest that the myth of the mother goddess was concerned with fertility and the sacredness of life in all its aspects, and so with transformation and rebirth. By contrast, the myth of the hunter was concerned above all with the drama of survival—the taking of life as a ritual act in order to live. The first story is centred on the goddess as the eternal image of the whole. The second story is centred on humanity, who, as hunter, has continually to rupture this unity in order to live the daily life of time. These two stories, both essential to human experience, pull apart in response to two apparently different human instincts: the instinct for relationship and meaning, and the instinct to survive. They seem, then, to tell different and even mutually exclusive stories: one where life and death are recognized as phases of an eternal process; the other, where the death of animal and human being loses its connection to the whole and is no longer sacred. Here death becomes final, and our experience of life tragic.[5]

In many myths a Great Mother wields the twin powers of life and death. Ereshkigal in Sumerian mythology was the Mother Goddess of the Underworld. Demeter was a Greek fertility and earth goddess and the Mother of the Dead. These beliefs are also present in remaining hunter/gatherer tribes.

The archaeologist André Leroi-Ghouran, who extensively studied the Paleolithic period, believed that the feminine divine played an important role in its belief systems. Joseph Campbell wrote:

> So, from the Pyrenees to Lake Baikal, the evidence now is before us of a Late Stone Age mythology in which the outstanding single figure was the Naked Goddess. . . .[6]

Among Stone Age peoples, a core hunting group comprised approximately ten adult males in their prime. Modern society still depends on the cooperation of approximately ten adults, male or female, to accomplish major undertakings. There are ten soldiers in a squad, eleven players on a football team, nine on a baseball team, twelve members on a jury, ten to twelve on a board of directors, and nine Supreme Court justices. Ten vigorous adults usually assure inspiration, leadership, cooperation, and purpose.

Accordingly, there would have been about the same number of women in their childbearing years, caring for an additional thirty to forty children. Adding adolescents and the elderly, the most economical and efficient size of a human hunter/gatherer group was approximately eighty to one hundred individuals. Familiarity among members made understanding one another's moods commonplace. Contact with strangers was relatively rare. New wives (or husbands) came or went, depending on social mores, but the tribe maintained a tight cohesiveness. The gatherer/nurturer–hunter/killer tribe provided a successful template for human society, and it remained essentially unchanged for some 2,990,000 years.

Then, somewhere, sometime, someone noticed that where seeds had fallen around the kitchen midden, grain consistently appeared the following season. This observation led inevitably to the insight that if seeds were *intentionally* planted and tended, they could ensure a reliable food supply.

More or less concurrently, people discovered they could domesticate and breed herds of some animals. Husbandry was a marked improvement over the risky occupation of the hunter. As the practice spread, the hunter's skill was no longer necessary to bring home the bacon: it was already home, gently rooting and multiplying in a corral. Instead of endangering his life trying to slay a dangerous wild boar, a man could saunter down to the yard, select a pig for dinner, and slaughter it in safety.

The skills and knowledge necessary for gathering and nurturing segued into farming. Horticulture accentuated the feminine attributes of both men and women.* A seed placed in the ground in the spring, attended to with patience and care, became a stalk heavy with grain ripening in the fall. Farmers needed to gather their harvests; herders needed to nurture their herds. Fecundity and fertility became society's highest values. Women easily adapted to the new way of life. Caring for young plants and animals were nurturing tasks that they had been performing all along in their role as mothers.

Animals, especially dogs, cats, and horses, had been receiving scraps from kitchen middens since Paleolithic times. At the dawn of history, all had become established pets. The bond of love, a maternal principle, now extended beyond humans to these other species.

Agriculture unbalanced the gatherer/hunter equilibrium as hunting's importance to survival plummeted. The swiftness with which men struck their spears and converted them into pruning hooks caught their nervous systems off guard. Hair-trigger "fight or flight" neural pathways, cocked to pump adrenaline the instant that danger appeared, had shored up hunters' courage in the face of charging bison. Farming was not very exciting compared to the chase. Suddenly, the male was required to fend off *other* predators who were determined to eat *his* ripening harvests and cull *his* flocks. For men, the farmer's life required a drastic psychological reprogramming.

Nevertheless, farming and husbandry were such dramatic advances that whenever hunter/gatherer cultures brushed up against agrarian ones, the former often adopted the revolutionary new lifestyle, and over time, agriculture doomed the ancient way of life. Tribes of a hundred or so individuals, roaming as one large organism from hunting ground to hunting ground, became increasingly rare. Compared to the length of time humans had lived nomadically, the wandering way of life all but disappeared in a blink. Beginning some seven thousand years ago, farming societies began to sprout all across the Mediterranean and southern Europe.

The process of planting seeds and waiting for the earth to bring forth its bounty became the symbol of impregnation and gestation. The need to encourage herds to be fertile reinforced the imagery of the female as lifegiver. The shift from gatherers/hunters to farmers/herders manifested symbolically in the religions of the new culture. There was a winnowing of the

*Horticulture is small-scale gardening. Agriculture is large-scale farming. While the strength necessary to handle large animals is a masculine trait, the principle behind farming remains feminine.

gatherer/hunters' multiple hunting and vegetative spirits, in favor of a powerful female deity known as the Earth Mother. It was not only women who
prayed to her. Men, whose hunting prowess had once sustained whole tribes,
readily acknowledged her power. Since the cornucopian abundance that
flowed from farming and husbandry reduced to a trickle whenever blight,
drought, or pestilence stifled the land, early agrarians believed that it was in
their best interests to placate the motherly Creatrix rather than the fierce
gods of the huntsmen. Mircea Eliade writes of this era,

> Woman and feminine sacrality are raised to the first rank. Since women
> played a decisive part in the domestication of plants, they become the
> owners of the cultivated fields, which raises their social position.[7]

As the size of settled communities continued to grow, large irrigation
schemes and rudimentary administrative functions developed. These structures and institutions took the place of now unnecessary male cooperative
hunting ventures, but these bloodless activities could not satisfy the hunter's
craving for marrow sucked out of the splintered bones of fresh red kill. The
male's pent-up aggression began its toxic accumulation. Sport hunting, contests of courage, ritual killings, and human sacrifices came into being
because of men's need to replace the excitement of the hunt. Eventually, war-
to-the-death superseded the hunt as the principal means of periodically
lancing the boil of the men's innate combativeness.

Nevertheless, farming progressively reined in the male's predatory
impulses by yoking his killer instincts to the plow. His disposition became
softer as his calluses grew harder. Archaeologists have uncovered intriguing
evidence from the period between 7000 and 4000 B.C., suggesting a muting
of violence in many early farming communities. Settlers frequently located
their villages in the rich bottomlands of valleys, and many of these communities lacked fortifications, suggesting that these people were not concerned
about attackers.[8] Sifting through the artifacts of such settlements, archaeologists do not find the preponderance of war weapons over domestic utensils
characteristic of later civilizations. Their deities are not depicted carrying
spears or hurling thunderbolts, and their gravesites do not include elaborate
tombs of warrior kings buried with their retinues and great material
wealth.[9] Women were often buried in more favorable locations than men.
There is little evidence confirming the domination of the many by the few.
While archaeologists cannot know with certainty what transpired in the
day-to-day lives of these prehistoric peoples, these clues suggest an existence
relatively free from the strife that seems to have characterized most of

recorded history. And everywhere in the ruins of these cultures there are statue fragments of a female deity.[10]

Archaeology as a profession only began in earnest in the last century and has been dominated since its inception by Caucasian Christian males. With a patronizing arrogance characteristic of Victorian times, these early pioneers usually dismissed the plentiful female statues as relics of a minor "fertility cult." The idea that there was once a time when the newly settled world prayed to a Goddess was simply too fanciful for serious consideration. In the late 1890s Arthur Evans excavated Knossos, the staggeringly sophisticated Minoan palace on Crete that flourished from 3500 B.C. to 1500 B.C. In 1957, James Mellaart reported on his excavation of the earlier farming communities in southern Turkey, Çatal Hüyük and Hacilar, extant between 7000 B.C. and 5000 B.C. His and Evans's work broke new ground, forcing other archaeologists to reassess their views.

Mellaart concluded that women had created Neolithic religion, developed agriculture, and controlled its products. He believed these factors explained the absence of military castes, central authority, and a science of warfare in Neolithic times.[11] Archaeologists have not unearthed positive proof that Neolithic people ever fought organized wars.[12]

Evidence has steadily mounted that the fertile female statues were not part of a "cult"—they were icons of the Neolithic culture's major religion extant between 10,000 and 5,000 years ago. Then, over the course of the next 2,000 years, the Goddess's power and status rapidly eroded. Warrior sky gods were everywhere on the rise. Cultures that had been guided by a preponderance of right-brain values came to be dominated by those of the left brain, and the reign of patriarchy began, despite the societies' remaining agricultural. Elinor Gadon, a feminist historian, mused, "When we look back across the historical time of patriarchy . . . there seems to be some terrible inevitability, a relentless desire to crush the female essence, human and divine. The question of why is among the most puzzling of our time."[13]

In answer to Gadon's query, Marija Gimbutas, an archaeologist, speculated in the 1960s that a semi-pastoral people called the Kurgan culture domesticated the horse in southern Russia around 5000 B.C. and mounted the first cavalry.[14] Gimbutas asserts that these horsemen swept down out of the steppes of Russia beginning in 4500 B.C. and fell upon peaceful agricultural settlements, killing the men, enslaving the women, and appropriating wealth and land. The Kurgan people, Gimbutas speculates, then repressed Earth Goddess worship, supplanting Her with their sky gods.

History books tell of similar brutal invasions elsewhere, and Gimbutas's Kurgan hordes theory seemed a plausible explanation to account for the

precipitous decline of the Goddess. Riane Eisler, Merlin Stone, Jules Cashford, and Anne Baring, among others, accepted the Kurgan theory. But there
are serious problems with Gimbutas's theory. Historians know very little
about the Kurgan culture. There is scant hard archaeological data to support
her arguments. Most persuasively, historical precedent argues against it.

Wherever a primitive people have come in contact with a more sophisticated culture, the transmission of values has inevitably flowed from the
advanced to the primitive. The Goddess people were more advanced than
the pastoral Kurgan people. Agriculture had led the Goddess cultures to create permanent settlements, providing the stimuli for further economic
diversification, and increasingly innovative progress in craft, metallurgy,
invention, architecture, and knowledge.

According to Gimbutas, the Kurgan herdsmen astutely appreciated the
advantages of agricultural life and relinquished their nomadic ways, settling
down to lord over the conquered farm folk. But since, by this act of imitation, they tacitly acknowledged the superiority of their vassals, why did not
the Kurgan people pay homage to the Goddess?

History offers many examples of unsophisticated victors being cultur-
ally absorbed by the more advanced people they have vanquished. When
Rome conquered Greece, it co-opted the Greeks' sophisticated ways. A few
centuries later, after Visigoth and Ostrogoth warriors stormed the gates of
Rome, they readily abandoned their polytheistic beliefs to embrace the new
Christian religion of their enemies. Mongol hordes, resembling those in
Gimbutas's Kurgan hypothesis, thundered off the Asian steppes to attack
advanced Muslim cities in the fourteenth century. Baghdad, a great center of
Islamic culture and learning, was thoroughly destroyed in the sack of 1348.
And yet, Baghdad remained Muslim after the conquest, and Islam has
become the majority religion in Outer Mongolia. The theory that Kurgan
horsemen dethroned the Goddess does not adequately explain the pervasive
onset of the subsequent five-thousand-year reign of patriarchy.

Anthropologist Claude Lévi-Strauss believed the decline of feminine
values began as a result of the much earlier practice of *bride barter*. Inspired
by the taboo against incest, *exogamy* served two purposes: it prevented the
inherited congenital defects that occur with inbreeding and it strengthened
inter-tribal alliances. Since adolescent girls can conceive at an earlier age
than when boys are ready to take their place alongside full-fledged hunters,
young grooms, then as now, were usually several years older than their
brides. Consequently, the tribe's elders more often exchanged their very
young girls, rather than their older boys. Lévi-Strauss proposes that once
men began to think of women as commodities, men also began to appropri-

ate women's power.[15] His hypothesis does not explain the dramatic zigzag from masculine to feminine and then back to masculine principles that occurred before, during, and after the first five thousand years of agriculture. Why did most societies have such a strongly feminine orientation immediately after the arrival of agriculture, even though elders were still exchanging brides?

In 1974, anthropologist Sherry Ortner asserted that gender roles between men and women diverged because there is a universal societal tendency to align the male with *culture* and the female with *nature*. Every human group strives to rise above nature by mastering it, tacitly placing a higher value on culture.[16] Ortner reiterated what Freud and others had said regarding the important difference between the upbringing of boys and girls: every boy loves the first woman in his life, his mother. However, in order to become a man, he must reject her values so that he can be free to identify with manly ones. A girl does not experience this ambivalence; she can love and continue to identify with her mother since she aspires to emulate her. This inescapable male dilemma has led to the devaluation of women in every society Ortner studied.

Ortner's thesis does not account for the prevalence of female imagery in the mythology, statuary, symbolism, and ritual of Goddess societies, imagery that appears to have venerated nature over culture.

Friedrich Engels, the cofounder of Marxism, believed that the demise of the Great Goddess and "the world historic defeat of the female sex" resulted from the rise of private property. Hunters, he argued, had a tenuous connection to the land, due to their nomadic ways. Agriculture introduced the concept of land ownership and also resulted in food surpluses, which in turn created excess wealth, which translated into power. The concept of owning land, wrote Engels, facilitated the idea of "owning" women, and it replaced the gatherer/hunter ethic of women-as-partners with the dominator shibboleth of women-as-chattels. The "invention" of private property does not, however, convincingly explain the wrenching change from Goddess to God worship.* William Irwin Thompson and Jane Jacobs more recently proposed that the agrarian revolution's creation of surplus wealth so reduced the status of hunters that they resorted to conquest which in turn led to the downfall of egalitarian societies and ultimately the defeat of the Goddess.

---

*Engels's argument, of course, ignores the possibility that males in hunter-gatherer societies also coveted property. In fact, nearly every male mammal, including our primate ancestors, exhibits intense feelings of territoriality.

Gerda Lerner, a modern feminist historian, posits that the downfall of the Goddess was due to the formation of archaic states. Emerging governments required complex organization. In order to effectively regulate trade, store surpluses, defend the cities, and design irrigation projects, power necessarily became concentrated in the hands of the few. This centralized authority of the early archaic state favored the strong, and the alpha male was now called a king. To justify his authority, he invoked divine parentage. Slavery became an integral part of the economy of those archaic states.

Hunter/gatherers had little use for slaves; captured warriors could not

The art of Bronze Age Minoan culture suggests a high status for Minoan women. Minoan snake-priestess (left) and Minoan court women (below)

be counted on to be loyal during the hunt, and they were too dangerous to leave behind with the women and children. Agriculture made slavery feasible, since a few guards could oversee the work of many slaves coerced to perform the backbreaking tasks of farming. Captured women could be forced to submit sexually, thus furthering their dehumanization. Brute strength and cruelty, two attributes of the hunter/killer, were much admired by the rulers of these early civilizations. Dr. Lerner proposes that the elevation of these values, at the expense of gatherer/nurturer ones, was the decisive factor in the dethronement of the Goddess.

While this hypothesis is suggestive, it doesn't account for the numerous Goddess-based archaic societies that were extant between seven thousand and five thousand years ago. One has only to view the joyful murals at the palace of Knossos to appreciate the feminine nature of the Minoan culture. King Minos, the Greek myths tell us, demanded that other fiefdoms under his sway send healthy young slaves as tribute. If the formation of archaic states brought patriarchy into being, then why were there many slave-owning Goddess-based archaic states in the period following the invention of agriculture but few after the beginning of recorded history?

Rather than patriarchy resulting from an invasion from the *outside,* I propose that this radical shift from the feminine to the masculine, from the values of the caring mother to the ways of the domineering patriarch, was brought about by forces subtly at work on the *inside.* Something happened five thousand years ago that was as significant to its time as the discovery of agriculture had been five thousand years earlier to its age. It was not the Kurgan horsemen from the north who ended the reign of the Goddess, nor was it the creation of private property, nor surplus wealth. While these events may have played a role, I propose that the central factor in the fall of the Goddess was a revolutionary development which occurred during the same period—literacy. First writing, and then its more sophisticated refinement, the alphabet, tolled the death knell of feminine values both metaphorically and, as we shall see, quite literally. Alphabets are the reason that Western culture's perception of reality radically shifted. This is literacy's hidden cost. The patriarchal warrior-dominator that plays so prominent a role in all Western history books succeeded *because of the invention of books themselves.*

CHAPTER 5

NONVERBAL/VERBAL

In oral communication the eye, ear, brain, senses and faculties acted together in busy co-operation and rivalry, each eliciting, stimulating, and supplementing the other. —Harold Innis[1]

The evidence indicates that learning to read and write a language in youth influences the way the hemispheres work. —Robert Ornstein[2]

T o speak, we need the cooperation of *both* hemispheres of the brain, and we use *both* areas of the retina and we employ *both* hands. Although speech is generated primarily from the dominant left brain, articulation requires the activation of muscles controlled equally by both hemispheres. Retinal cones and rods both engage when we speak and listen; in many instances, the listener's eye gathers more about the meaning of the speaker's message than does his ear. Gesture is also a bicameral activity with both hands participating. Their role varies, depending on the emotional content of the conversation and the ethnic background of the speakers, but gestures are always present.

When written words began to supersede spoken words, the left brain's dominance markedly increased. To write and read, an individual uses *primarily* the left hemisphere, *only* the hunting cones and *only* the killing hand. With the strokes of a thousand chisels, styli, brushes, and pens, literacy diminished the right brain's complementary role in creating and deciphering language, dismissing with it the importance of both the rods of the retina and the left hand.

While no one knows exactly when speech began, enough scientific data has accumulated to engage in cautious speculation. Gestures probably preceded vocalizations. A few milliseconds before the vocal cords begin to vibrate, the muscles of the hands and face begin to twitch.[3] Of the 408 muscles in our bodies, a disproportionately high number are located in the face, and many exist primarily for expressing emotions.

Another human feature that developed in conjunction with gesture is the peculiar color of our hands. Among the varied species of primates, only humans—including highly melanotic native Africans—lack pigment on their palms. One explanation of this unique feature is that it once served the hands' function in communication. Before the full development of spoken language, our ancestors sat around the fire speaking and gesturing to each other. It would have been a distinct advantage for the palms to be pale and thus more visible in dim light.[4]

Gesture is such a vital component of speech that it is nearly impossible to have a conversation without it. In some cases it is the more expressive mode. Anyone asked to describe a spiral staircase will inevitably accompany the spoken answer with a corkscrew motion of the hand. This pantomime is far more descriptive than words could be.

Hearing is the most important sense for understanding speech, but while listening one also continually monitors the speaker's facial expressions and body language visually. The retina's rods allow an appreciation of gestalts and slight movements in the periphery; more than cones, they are expert at gathering subtle visual clues. The speaker's fingers nervously drumming on a desktop may not be heard by the listener's ear, but peripheral vision does not "lose sight" of this revealing information. Nor does it miss him shaking his head from side to side (indicating his rejection) while he is saying that he agrees wholeheartedly with your position. (Of these two contradictory messages, the listener intuitively knows that the nonverbal one is more accurate.)

Vision is also important to the speaker. While talking, he constantly watches the listener for nonverbal feedback. If he believes that his message is producing a desired (or undesired) effect, he can switch his mode of speech in mid-sentence. He can also reduce what he says to a kind of oral shorthand if he is confident that the listener's nods of assent mean his unfinished sentences and incomplete thoughts are being anticipated and understood.

Millions tune in to watch presidential debates. Asked why they feel it necessary to observe the candidates on television when they have already read their positions in the newspaper, many reply that they want to *see* how each candidate comports himself. Ignoring speech's content, the viewer's right brain evaluates the candidate's sincerity, cleverness, honesty, cunning, and forthrightness. The conduct of a conversation is, in many cases, more illuminating than its content, reinforcing the wisdom of the Chinese aphorism, "Let us draw closer to the fire so that we may better see what we are saying."

Some time in our distant past, speech supplanted gesture as the principal means of human communication. However, the left brain's speech centers never completely eliminated the influence that the older right brain has on both the creation and comprehension of oral language. If the spoken word was the result of delicately balanced assignments of the feminine and the masculine sides of the brain, then the invention of writing completely upset this balance.

A letter writer has no instant visual feedback to assess the impact of his words on the recipient, and a letter deprives the reader of the body language, facial expression, and other clues she would normally garner from the letter writer. "Reading between the lines" is a far more difficult exercise than evaluating the nonverbal clues of speech. Ferdinande de Sassure, an early researcher in the field, noted, "Writing veils the appearance of language; it is not a guise for language but a disguise."[5]

Speech and writing differ significantly in a purely mechanical aspect. All spoken languages fall within a narrow range of meter: too rapid, and the listener will have difficulty comprehending; too slow, and the listener will be bored; too monotonic, and the listener will tune out; too histrionic, and the listener will become overburdened. The speaker sets the pace and the listener must follow. In reading, the opposite is the case: the reader's left brain is in complete control.

Music appreciation resides principally in the right hemisphere. Inflection and rhythm are musical qualities that are crucial components of speech. A change in the enunciation and emphasis of certain phrases and words can subtly redirect the entire meaning of the speaker's message. A speaker can imply or exaggerate double entendres, puns, and humorous interpretations simply by varying his inflection. The written word, in contrast, is silent. Writers use punctuation marks in an attempt to overcome this serious disadvantage, but while these symbols enliven prose, a question mark is a pallid substitute for an arched eyebrow above a mocking smirk.

With speech, both speaker and listener must occupy proximate physical spaces at the same moment for any interaction to take place.* Speech generation and listener comprehension are *simultaneous* events. The written

---

*For the vast majority of humankind's history, this condition held true. Recent technological developments, such as the telegraph, radio, telephone, etc., have added new caveats.

word's message is deciphered sometime in the future and usually in another location. It is *linear*. Speech is framed in the *here* and *now*. Writing's context is *there* and *then*.

Speech is the consummate act of improvisation and everyone, at one time or another, has been surprised by her or his own eloquence. Every day, we speak complex sentences that we did not plan in advance. Somehow, in the interstices of Broca's left-brain speech center, grammatically correct phrases are hurriedly stitched together and emerge as relatively seamless diction. In most conversations, there is little editorial interference. This helps the listener evaluate the speaker's message. Slips of the tongue cannot be retrieved. In contrast, a writer has far more control than the speaker, more time to "collect his thoughts" and calculate their effect, allowing him to edit and revise what the reader sees.

Also missing from the written word is the aesthetic quality of the speaker's voice. Different people's voices—dull, sexy, forced, slippery, seductive, earnest, convincing, or stentorian—evoke different emotional responses. While consciously attending to the content of spoken language, the listener is also evaluating speech's emotional tenor subliminally.*

While the right brain can sometimes evaluate the nonverbal content of handwriting, this paltry amount of nuance pales when compared to the nonverbal clues available from the full panoply of facial expression. And in modern times, the printing press and then the typewriter further diminished the right brain's participation by replacing the individuality of handwriting with standardized and impersonal type.

While speakers and listeners fully engage both their rods and cones during conversation, reading requires *only* a small circle of tunnel vision to follow the linear progression of words on a page. Information contained in the paragraph further down the page is of no interest until the reader gets there.

The writer's eye uses only cone vision to follow the trail of ink emerging from the pen tip as it advances across a page. Handwriting, like reading, proceeds in a linear, sequential fashion, and like all cone vision tasks, requires a high level of concentration. If we are writing (or reading) in a room where there are distracting peripheral stimuli, we generally will rise to turn off a television or move to a quieter place. In contrast, our conversational skills

---

*Listening to radio supplies us with only auditory clues. We imagine how the radio personality looks based solely on voice quality. When we actually see photographs of someone we have known only through his or her voice, the image jars as it is usually quite different from the face we had imagined.

allow us to banter at crowded cocktail parties, oblivious to the welter of incoming visual and competing auditory information.

The font of the print on this page contains serifs. They are the horizontal "finishes" at the top and bottom of most letters. Serifs form what amounts to a set of rails, marking out tracks that the cones of the eye can easily follow. They serve to keep the reader's visual train of thought rolling smoothly over the print. They accentuate the sequential nature of the written word. There are no serifs in a frown or a smile.

Speech requires the active participation of both halves of the paired somatic muscles of vocalization. The formation of the word *tree* involves an equal effort of right and left sides of the diaphragm, both vocal cords, cooperation between the tongue's opposite sides, and the pursing of both halves of the lips. Anyone who has ever returned from the dentist's office after having one side of the tongue and lips paralyzed with anesthetic is acutely aware that the articulation of words depends on the musculature of both sides of the mouth.

Writing involves the muscles of *only* one side of the body. Pure writing, using stylus, quill, pencil, or pen, engages the dominant hand, which the dominant hemisphere controls. Right-brain participation is markedly reduced. The left hand has no role during this activity. Evolution selected the dominant hand to be the aggressor, the hand that wields the club, swings the sword, and pulls the trigger. Placing the pen in the fighting hand etches aggression into the written word differentiating it from speech, which depends more on a bicameral cooperative effort.

Nonverbal clues, concrete gestalts, music, inflection, spontaneity, simultaneity, aesthetics, emotion, slips of the tongue, gesticulation, and *peripheral vision* are all features best processed by the right brain. Speech—and its reciprocal, listening—are hemispheric activities requiring a large amount of traffic in both directions across the corpus callosum.

The written word issues from *linearity, sequence, reductionism, abstraction, control, central vision,* and the *dominant hand*—all hunter/killer attributes. Writing represented a shift of tectonic proportions that fissured the integrated nature of gatherer/hunter communication and brain cooperation. Writing made the left brain, flanked by the incisive cones of the eye and the aggressive right hand, dominant over the right. The triumphant march of literacy that began five thousand years ago conquered right-brain values, and, with them, the Goddess. Patriarchy and misogyny have been the inevitable result.

CHAPTER 6

CUNEIFORM/MARDUK

In the history of *Homo sapiens,* the book is an anthropological development, similar essentially to the invention of the wheel.

—Joseph Brodsky[1]

If a woman speaks out against her man, her mouth shall be crushed with a hot brick.[2]   —First Mesopotamian written law code, ca. 2350 B.C.

Before there was writing there were pictures. The desire to control the forces of nature led Paleolithic humans to create images of the world around them. If the gods made the world, then graphic imitation was a godlike act that carried with it the illusion of power.

Pictographs, humankind's first attempt to preserve communication, were the precursors of writing. Preschoolers recapitulate this early artistry when they begin to draw stick figures with crayons. Because images drawn from life require that the brain first establish key elements like shape, size, and the relationship of the parts to the whole, pictographs and every other visual art form that followed fall primarily under the right brain's purview.

Petroglyphs (stone pictographs or rock art) appear wherever humans have lived. Virtually indecipherable, these simple representations are the garbled record preliterate people left for posterity. The arrival of agriculture changed this artistic activity. Around 3000 B.C., two centers of civilization began to flourish in the Fertile Crescent—Mesopotamia and Egypt—and each of them developed a distinctive form of writing.

The first Mesopotamians were Sumerians, a loose federation of communities on the rich plain between the Tigris and Euphrates Rivers. The Sumerians' irrigation system led to bountiful harvests and burgeoning towns. The twin settlements of Uruk and Ur became large enough to be called cities. As commerce expanded, the thorny problems of keeping track of transactions (sheep for barley, oats for goats) created the need for better record keeping. In devising a solution, the Sumerians took the first step in a process that would reconfigure all human relations. By gouging tiny wedge-shaped marks with sharp sticks into wet clay tablets, they invented the first written language. Beginning in 3100 B.C., the first cuneiform figures appeared.

At first heavily pictographic, cuneiform's ideograms became progressively more abstract until each of its visual signs was a stylized symbol that represented an idea, concept, object, or action. This process of abstraction, associated with the left side of the brain, was offset by a distinctly right-sided one: the pictures built up from these wedge-shaped marks were not arranged in linear fashion. Early Sumerian writers placed their characters haphazardly within the confines of the writing tablet's surface.[3] Scribes had to rely heavily on pattern recognition—the simultaneous appreciation of all the symbols—to make sense of messages.

The earliest Sumerians never quite appreciated the potential of their written language. For them, writing served mainly as a means of recording how many jars of olive oil a worshiper offered to a particular temple deity or the number of rams he sacrificed. Eventually, Sumerians began to transcribe their literature, but it constitutes a small percentage of surviving Sumerian writings. Recognizing the importance of their innovation, the Sumerians created schools to teach it. Soon, a highly influential class of scribes emerged, and as Sumerian cities grew in complexity, the scribes' status grew.

The Akkadians, a northern people, conquered Sumer five centuries after its founding. They were astute enough to discern the value of the Sumerians' tiny triangles impressed in clay. Since the Akkadians spoke a language different from the Sumerians', they adapted cuneiform by inventing *phonograms,* symbols that stand for syllables of speech. These abstractions increasingly replaced the earlier image-inspired *ideograms.* Cuneiform characters now served two purposes: a single character often represented both the *image* of a noun and the *sound* of a word. Thus, necessity, the mother of invention, forced the Akkadians to create the father of all abstractions—phonetic writing. Akkadians jettisoned most of the pictorial content of cuneiform within a century of their Sumerian conquest. The Akkadian feat of transliterating their spoken words using the Sumerian script pointed the way for other cultures to do the same. Soon, variations of cuneiform appeared in all the neighboring countries.

Influenced by the abstractness of their writing system, the Akkadians invented words for such abstract concepts as justice, destiny, and truth. They also began to create a rich literature. Religious epics previously passed along only orally were baked in clay. It was during the Akkadian assimilation of Sumerian culture that cuneiform became a supple language and written documents began to proliferate.

Akkadians intuited that meaning would be more accessible if the cuneiform figures were arranged linearly. At first, words were sometimes written right to left, and sometimes left to right—and in a few cases, up and down. But by about 2300 B.C., the direction had stabilized. Cuneiform would henceforth exhibit the left hemispheric characteristic of linearity and be written from left to right.

Despite these refinements, cuneiform remained difficult to learn, read, and write because scribes had to master a large number of characters. To ensure that they would be understood, scribes often wrote their message redundantly. The system confounded all but an extremely small group of literate cognoscenti, who formed a highly specialized elite.

The Sumerians had believed that cuneiform was a gift from Nisaba, the goddess of grain and storage. Since cuneiform is essentially a clever way to store thoughts, it was a fitting attribution. After the conquest of Sumer, with the changeover from a pictorial script to a more abstract, sequential, linear one, she was superseded by Nabu, the Akkadian god of writing.

In the Sumerians' polytheistic pantheon, goddesses possessed considerable power. In their oldest stratum, the Sumerians venerated a supreme female deity. In one tradition, the Great Goddess Nammu, representing water, the universe's primordial element, created the sky god An and the earth goddess Ki. The premier position of Mother Nammu corresponded to the high status of women in Sumerian society. Excavations of royal tombs of Ur reveal that ruling queens shared status, power and wealth with kings.

Besides the written record, there are rich pictorial remnants that show women in a respectful light. Wisdom and authority emanate from many of the female figures. The first distinct literary voice that can be identified in the Sumerian record belongs to the woman author Enheduanna.[4]

An and Ki mated and produced the early Mesopotamian divine family, whose most important member was Inanna. She was the sexual goddess who bestowed fertility and fecundity on mortals. Her consort, Dumuzi, was a lesser god whose only function seems to have been to serve patiently as her husband and die each winter so Innana could resurrect him in the spring. But Inanna was not a woman who stayed near the hearth. Unlike Dumuzi, she had many adventures. Inanna controlled the fates of mortals. She ruled from the highest heavenly throne, rendering judgments and meting out destinies. Her totem was the owl, and she was also the goddess of wisdom. She had no domestic duties and lived like a young man.

Inanna holding her breasts, ca. 2000 B.C.

Inanna was the sexual partner in the Sumerians' most important ritual—the *hiero gamos*, the sacred marriage. A Sumerian king's chief religious duty was to consummate his vows to Inanna in the sanctified wedding chamber. Through this act, eagerly anticipated by all his subjects, a king legitimized his reign. A comely surrogate, chosen from the people, ensured that the king would not be disappointed. Sumerians considered this ritual essential to a successful harvest and it was also necessary to guarantee the fertility of human unions and animal matings. Not unexpectedly, the agricultural Sumerians revered the feminine principle, as should have the agrarian Akkadians. The creation myth that the Akkadian priests conjured, therefore, is shocking for its misogynist virulence.

The Seven Tablets of Creation replaced previous creation myths around 1700 B.C. and was recited every spring in Babylon for the next thousand years as the most plausible explanation for how the physical world came into existence. With the rise of Babylon, power previously wielded by first the Sumerians and then the Akkadians now shifted to the Babylonians.

The beginning of this 170-line poem introduces the Great Goddess Tiamat. Her essence was the saltwater of the oceans and she could manifest herself either in human form or as a sea serpent. Her male consort was Apsu, a lesser being. The story begins with a rowdy party taking place in Tiamat's primordial womb. The celebrants are a group of young gods under her protection. "Indeed, they upset Tiamat's belly by song in the midst of the divine abode."[5] Their boisterousness disturbed Tiamat but angered Apsu. After many sleepless nights, he informed her that he planned to slay all the young gods. Tiamat admonished Apsu, urging him to consider the young gods' age and to be more tolerant. This led to a heated argument.

The young gods, privy to this thunderous discord and fearing for their lives, murdered Apsu. At the site of his death, the god Marduk was born. Given the winds as a plaything, he used them to roil Tiamat's waters. This, along with the continued disruptive activities of the other young gods, made Tiamat furious, and she vowed to wreak vengeance on her consort's murderers. Alarmed by the mobilization of Tiamat's forces, the young gods were terrified: "Nowhere is there a god who will attack Tiamat. He would not escape from Tiamat's presence with his life."[6] Marduk, now fully grown, volunteered, but before accepting such a suicidal mission, he demanded that should he win, the other gods must make him chief.

Marduk prepared for his encounter with the Great Mother by sneaking into her womb to reconnoiter. (This passage of the epic illustrates the confusion between Tiamat as a female deity with a human form and as an all-enveloping maternal entity.) The battle began with Tiamat's wily attempt to disarm Marduk by flattering him. When her ruse failed, both protagonists began hurling insults. She accused the young god of being too big for his britches. Marduk sneered and taunted Tiamat that she was too haughty and needed to be cut down to size. Insults led to physical blows and a mighty struggle ensued. The other gods cowered, holding their breath.

Just when it appeared that Tiamat would defeat Marduk, she opened her mouth widely to devour him. At this desperate juncture, he unleashed his secret weapons. Marduk was, after all, the god of gale and storm. Seven whirlwinds flew into Tiamat's mouth, whistled down her gullet, and greatly distended her abdomen. With Tiamat distracted by the sudden inflation of her girth, Marduk recovered sufficiently to string an arrow and then quickly loosed it, rupturing her bloated stomach and splitting her heart. The god Marduk was victorious; he had slain the Great Goddess Tiamat.

Contemplating Tiamat's enormous corpse, Marduk decided to create the universe by dismembering her. Tiamat's buttocks became the mountains and her breasts the foothills. He pierced her eyes with his spear, and the tears welling up from within her sockets formed the two great rivers, the Tigris and Euphrates. He then pricked her breasts in many places, creating all the tributaries that flowed into these two main rivers, and in a final indignity used the Great Mother's pubic mound to support the sky.[7]

Soon his vassal gods complained to Marduk that their existence was dreary because they lacked worshipers to make them offerings. Marduk responded by creating mortals. He began by pardoning all of Tiamat's allies. Singling out Kingu, Tiamat's favorite son who had ruled with her after Apsu's death, Marduk accused the youth of instigating his mother's attack. In a ritual murder witnessed by all, Marduk forced one victim to expiate everyone else's crimes. He ordered Ea (Marduk's father) to knead the flesh and blood of his hapless sacrifice, like a potter manipulating raw clay. After creating the multitudes of mortals from this gory pastiche, Marduk condemned these puny creatures to crawl across the surface of Tiamat's carcass. They must spend their brief allotment of life toiling to provide food and wine for the gods. Babylonians embracing this myth would forever be burdened by guilt; they owed their very existence to the martyrdom of a god. Kingu, the divine son, suffered and died for the sins of others.

Virtually all societies invent creation stories to explain the presence of the physical universe, the puzzle of human existence, and the reasons for death and evil. Because of the obvious association between beginnings and births, the vast majority of them revolve around the union of male and female deities. But in the Babylonian version, an allegory of death has replaced the metaphor of birth. Stripped of its convoluted subplots, this is the story of a rebellion against a mother by her male children. The powerful woman who has created their life is murdered by one of them. He kills her at the moment her abdomen is massively distended, resembling a woman in her ninth month of pregnancy. Her killer then creates the universe from the anatomical remains of her body. In a portentous move, the Babylonians elevated to the supreme position a god who had conquered and then mutilated a goddess.

In the Freudian lexicon, sons are supposed to wrest power from their fathers—not their mothers. Unless, of course, the mother originally held the power. Alongside the thousands of creation myths of other cultures, *The Seven Tablets of Creation* stands starkly alone. Three features distinguish it. First, in the field of comparative religion, there does not exist a more misogynist and macabre story. Second, this is the first creation myth to appear in written form. And third, this myth originated in a proto-Western culture.*

*The literate Mitanni, Hittites, Aryans, and even the Indians also adopted it.

. . .

The worship of Marduk began in the early 1700s B.C. This approximate date coincides with the life of the Babylonian chieftain Hammurabi, who composed a written law code in cuneiform. Written laws became a new and important feature of Western civilization at just the moment that the Babylonian Goddess suffered defeat and dismemberment. This peculiar pairing of events—the ascendancy of written laws and the decline of feminine power—can be traced to a feature unique to writing.

Speech is a skill that toddlers master with delight and speed. Linguist Noam Chomsky has argued that humans are born with an innate ability to learn oral language. The complicated rules of syntax appear to be genetically encoded. Any mother can attest to her child's amazing ability to string words together in their proper sequence, even though the toddler has never heard the sentences she effortlessly speaks. Young children learning to talk handle case endings, plurals, and pronouns with relative aplomb.

But this ease does not extend to writing. Writing is not genetically encoded. No one writes as he speaks. Judging from the many tablets devoted to teaching it, grammar was a most tedious part of the curriculum in the first scribal schools and took years to master. It still is difficult. Small children can communicate effectively by the time they are four; lucid writing is an achievement high school English teachers seldom see.

Forced to learn the rules of grammar, scribes introduced into culture a novel concept: the transcription of codes of human conduct, or The Law. For the unlettered, conduct is regulated by taboos that are acknowledged by everyone in the tribe. Elders and shamans pass down these conventions through oral teaching. Tribal mores discourage individuality; everyone is inextricably enmeshed in the community at large, and in general, violating a *taboo* brings misfortune on everyone. Breaking a *law,* however, singles out an individual. This significant distinction encourages individuality and ego development in literate societies. Customs organically grow with the maturing of a community; laws press down upon the people and can be initiated and manipulated by a privileged literate elite.

Scribes transferred the authority previously vested in the shaman's chanted spells to the written word. Now, an abstraction called a law was in effect even when no one of influence was present. Posted throughout the kingdom on stone stelae, these abstractions took on a life of their own, outliving the lawgivers themselves. Civil laws bear the unmistakable imprint of the rules of grammar. They are abstract, authoritative, and elude an ordinary individual's ability to tamper with them.

Grammar and laws are unique to the left brain. Abstract, they are the antithesis of spontaneity and intuition, and they inherently reinforce masculine principles.* The dreary record of the written law's overt discrimination against the female gender, with the exception of very recent history, is testimony to the masculine bias of this innovation.

The earliest Mesopotamian law code (2350 B.C.), attributed to King Urokagina of Lagash, begins with a proscription against polyandry. "The women of the former days used to take two husbands, but the women of today (if they attempt to do this) must be stoned."[8] Patriarchy is the dominant theme of Hammurabi's Code, which was promulgated at the moment in Mesopotamia's history when written documents increased a thousand-fold (and we can safely assume, so, too, did literacy).[9] Hammurabi's Code contained one very crucial flaw: it did not apply equally to Hammurabi and his subjects. One-fourth of the code relates to women's rights, or more accurately, restrictions on women's rights. The code commands that sons honor their fathers. No similar exhortation applies to their mothers. Although the code confirmed certain rights accorded to women of the upper class, pertaining to property, business, and religious participation, overall, women's sexual rights and freedom were sharply restricted. Eunuch chaperones and veiling became commonplace. Tiamat's downfall coincided with the erection of Hammurabi's stela.

*For example, complex rule books dominate boys' sports; they are relatively unimportant in most traditional female games, e.g., hopscotch, jump rope, etc.

CHAPTER 7

HIEROGLYPHS/ISIS

The Egyptologist knows that never was there a race more fond of life,
more light-hearted, or more gay. A lovable trait is the evident equality
of the sexes: both in the reliefs and in the statues the wife is seen clasp-
ing her husband round the waist, and the little daughter is represented with the same tenderness as the little son.   —Sir Alain Gardner[1]

O what miserable and perfect copies have they grown to be of Egyptian ways! For there the men sit at home and weave while their wives
go out to win the daily bread.
                —Oedipus despairing over his sons in Sophocles' *Oedipus at Colonus*

The Egyptians founded their civilization in the Nile River Valley.
Evolving a writing system entirely different from cuneiform, the
Egyptians invented a pictorial script we call hieroglyphs. The ap-
pearance of these distinctive figures in 3000 B.C. marked the beginning of
Egyptian civilization.

Though based on images, Egyptian script was more than a sophisticated
form of picture-writing. Each picture/glyph served three functions: (1) to represent the image of a thing or action, (2) to stand for the sound of a syllable,
and (3) to clarify the precise meaning of adjoining glyphs. Writing hieroglyphs
required some artistic skill, limiting the number chosen to learn it. Despite its
complexity, hieroglyphs were a surprisingly expressive writing system.

The aesthetic sense guided the arrangement of the icons more often
than did the dictates of grammar. For example, a tall icon had to precede a
short squat one, even if the thought order suggested that they should be
transposed.[2] In many instances, the reader grasped the meaning of the sentence by recognizing the patterns of all the icons in it simultaneously.[3]

While hieroglyphs were able to express most ideas, some concepts presented a challenge for a language based on pictures. To solve the problem,

the Egyptians invented twenty-five icons to represent each of their language's spoken consonants and thus allow the reader to sound out a word-concept anacrostically. This is the principle of the alphabet. Although the Egyptian scribes had developed the first rudimentary alphabet, they used this new shorthand sparingly. They failed to recognize how useful and economical a small number of signs corresponding to the individual phonemes of their spoken language could be.

As would be expected of a people whose writing system was based on concrete images, rather than abstract figures, Egyptian mythology featured benign creation stories compared to those of the Babylonians. In one of the oldest, dating back to the Early Dynastic period (3100–2680 B.C.), two primordial female deities—Nekhbet, the vulture goddess of Upper Egypt, and Wadjet, the cobra goddess of Lower Egypt—emerged out of chaos. After cooperatively bringing forth the world, they created the Egyptian people, who were linked by their dependence on the Nile River.[4]

While the vulture may not seem a very appropriate symbol of the female essence, the ancient Egyptians believed that all vultures were exclusively female (the hieroglyph for mother and vulture are one and the same). Vultures, a divine manifestation of death, represented an important aspect of the Goddess. And vultures seemed to possess foresight, as evidenced by their circling a potential meal long before dinner was a certainty.

Western culture has long reviled the snake, associating it with evil and temptation. But at the dawn of civilization the snake was a positive symbol of feminine energy. Egyptians perceived the snake as a beneficent, vital creature intimately associated with female sexuality, and, by extension, with life. A snake's sinuous mode of locomotion is evocative of a nubile woman's walk and dance. Her movements in the throes of lovemaking are serpentine in contrast to the mechanical pumping of the male. In some cultures, orgasm has been likened to releasing the latent energy of a coiled snake.

Snakes also resembled three other important life-affirming images: the meander of rivers, the roots of trees and plants, and the umbilical cord of mammals. There can be no structure that better symbolizes the idea of a mother/nurturer than an umbilical cord. Its form resembles two snakes entwined about each other. Rising out from a placenta's sinuous blood vessels, the umbilical cord might easily inspire the notion that snakes were vital to life.* Further, snakes live in deep crevices and fissures in the earth, tying

---

*Confirming that two entwined snakes are the perfect image to represent life, in 1953 James Watson and Francis Crick discovered DNA's configuration to be a double helix, the crucial molecule basic to all life.

them to the Great Mother. And, because a snake regularly sheds its skin to begin anew, it can easily be imagined as an immortal creature that does not die, and is thus a potent symbol of rebirth. The *ouroboros,* the snake forming a circle to bite its own tail, was a recurrent theme in Neolithic art and occurs in almost all early cultures. Many archaeologists believe that this symbol represents the cyclical constancy of the feminine. Snakes' association with vitality is so embedded in our psyches that the caduceus—two entwined snakes—remains as the symbol of the healing art.

Finally, the snake is associated with wisdom. Its eye is the opening to mystic insight and foresight. So connected in the Egyptian psyche were beneficent serpents and goddesses that the hieroglyph for goddess was the same as the one for serpent. The *uraeus,* the coiled cobra atop every pharaoh's headdress, was the crowning symbol of Egyptian royal power.

By the time of the Middle Kingdom (2040–1600 B.C.), when literacy became more firmly established, several masculine-based creation myths rapidly gained in popularity alongside the feminine-based ones, which conjoined scales and feathers. Gradually a single god began to differentiate away from the others. Amon began his divine career as a local deity of Thebes. As Thebes grew in stature, Amon began to arrogate the power of Ra, the sun god, to become Amon-Ra, a god who could manifest his solar identity in the form of a ram-headed human. During Amon's ascent, female deities continued to exercise jurisdiction in their respective domains, but they were steadily losing their preeminence.

During the transition from the Early Dynasty to the Middle Kingdom, Egyptian society remained rooted in agriculture. Fellahs tilled the rich delta loam and brought their produce to market as they still do today. The system of government remained a hereditary kingship balanced by a feudal aristocracy. Despite the constancy of the society's economic and political systems, the gender of its principal deities shifted. The only truly revolutionary innovation that occurred during this period was the invention and increasing importance of written communication.*

A creation story illustrating the rise of masculine power is the one concerning Atum. As Creator, Atum masturbated into existence the *Ennead,* a family of eight potent gods and goddesses. Fifteen hundred years after the Nekhbet/Wadjet story of two females intertwining to bring forth life, Atum manages the task single-handedly.

---

*Even though the Egyptian icon-based system remained more right-brained than the Mesopotamians' cuneiform, I maintain that any written method of communication skews society toward masculine values.

Each of the nine members of the Ennead (Atum plus the other eight) represented an important force of nature. Two of them, Nut, the sky goddess, and Geb, the earth god, mated to create the physical world and all its inhabitants. Nut and Geb went on to produce three important offspring. Isis, their daughter, became Egypt's principal fertility goddess. She was the rich black soil that lined the sacred river, and Egyptians believed she taught them the art of agriculture. Her brother, the river deity Osiris, became both her lover and her husband. The third, Seth, was in some traditions an evil brother who was jealous of Osiris. Osiris was handsome, virile and admired by all. Seth murdered Osiris in his prime, hacked his corpse to pieces, and hid the parts. Isis, tearing at her hair and scratching her face, searched for his remains. After many trials, she located them in the east. She bore his remains back to Egypt in a chartered boat, and then brought him back to life, establishing her reputation as the goddess who can resurrect both life and the land. In this myth, feminine love conquered masculine death.

Osiris's rebirth occurred in the spring, and Egypt celebrated this miracle as its most important religious ceremony. But each fall he had to return to the netherworld. Osiris died again and again, and during the dark segment of his annual passage, he ruled as Lord of the Dead.

Isis nurturing
Horus

Amidst this triumph and tragedy, and (in one version of the myth) without the aid of male insemination, Isis gave birth to her son, Horus. The many statues of Isis nursing her infant son presaged by many centuries the tender love evident between the Madonna and her infant Jesus. As mortals' closest relative, Horus was the intermediary between ordinary humans and the divine. By claiming to be the incarnation of Horus, pharaohs legitimized their right to rule.

These gods and goddesses supplied the foundation for Egyptian religion for the first fifteen hundred years of its dynastic tradition. While Isis and Osiris occupy center stage in the wall paintings, the solitary Amon gradually accumulated power in the written texts. Then sometime between 1700 and 1550 B.C. significant changes occurred in Egyptian culture.

After several millennia of pharonic civilization, a mysterious group of invaders swept into or infiltrated the valley from the east and wrested control of the eastern part of the kingdom. For the first time in Egypt's history, foreigners ruled the natives. Most experts identify these hated kings, known as the *Hyksos,* as northern Semitic Canaanites. It is likely that the Hyksos knew cuneiform. Writing had been in existence for fifteen hundred years in Mesopotamia, and conquerors boring in from this direction would have been familiar with it.*

After little more than a century, the Egyptians drove out the Hyksos, and beginning in the seventeenth century B.C., were once again in control. During the Hyksos interregnum, however, the foreigners surely exposed the Egyptians to ideas they brought from Mesopotamia. During the New Kingdom (1550–700 B.C.) that followed the expulsion of the Hyksos, Egyptian arts and architecture broke out from the conservative conventions that had typified old pre-Hyksos Egypt. Great military pharaohs such as Thutmose I, Thutmose III, and Ramses II extended Egyptian influence far beyond the eastern and southern borders of the Nile River Valley. These pharaohs commemorated their reigns with magnificent monuments.

All these dramatic changes occurring in the New Kingdom coincided with a major change in the Egyptians' style of writing. In a trend that accelerated after the overthrow of the Hyksos, scribes increasingly used an older alternative form called *hieratic script,* which began to supplant hieroglyphics. Nearly abandoning the iconic principle of classical hieroglyphs, hieratic relied on the principle of phonetic pronunciation. Aesthetic considerations

*Yet little in the way of a written record has come down from them. It is likely that they left one, but it would not be surprising if the Egyptians had destroyed such reminders of this ignominious chapter in their history.

no longer influenced the arrangement of written characters. Earlier scribes sometimes arranged hieratic vertically but New Kingdom scribes wrote the script horizontally. Scribes also converted the glyphs representing the uniconsonants into abstract letters. Although this step presaged a true alphabet, they inexplicably did not advance to the next obvious step, which would have been to jettison everything else and keep only the abstract letters.

During the period in which a linear and abstract hieratic gained over the classical Egyptian iconic script, the culture experienced a rise in patriarchy. At the outset of the New Kingdom, Thutmose III (1490–1436 B.C.) elevated Amon's status above all other deities by decree.* Prior to Amon, most Egyptian gods and goddesses were chimeras with both animal and human characteristics. In the New Kingdom, deities increasingly assumed human form. In a significant departure from Egyptian convention, one of Amon's manifestations was invisible. That is, he didn't have an image. Amon became the god-with-no-face at the moment Egyptian writing passed from icons based on images to symbols based on abstraction.

During the same period, Egypt's principal female deities also experienced a reordering. In the earlier dynasties, Nekhbet, Wadjet, Nut, or Hathor, had been paramount. Half-human and half-vulture, cobra, sky, or cow, these early goddesses were the protectresses of birth, children, and fecundity. Isis, the principal goddess of the next generation, was more a consort, wife, mother, sister, and lover. Her most distinguishing characteristics were sexuality, fertility, and maternity. Nature personified, she also embodied the theme of resurrection.

In the New Kingdom, priests elevated a previously obscure goddess to a superior position over all the others, but in a departure from tradition as startling as the ascension of an imageless god, she was completely divorced from nature: her name was Maat and she represented Truth. Like Amon, Maat originally had been a minor fertility and nature deity. She did not reach the zenith of her sway over people until Amon lost his face. Her physical form then became human, and her symbol was an ostrich feather. In another departure, she was not a god's lover: instead of sexuality and fecundity, she personified the abstractions of law, truth, order, and justice. When a man died, his heart was weighed on one side of the scales of justice, with Maat's ostrich feather on the other. If the deceased had led a righteous life, the scales balanced. Occasionally, Maat was represented in the form of a hermaphrodite. Despite Maat's rise among the literati of the court, the largely

---

*At the time of Amon's ascent, Egypt's empire was expanding. Local gods no longer sufficed to satisfy Egypt's enlarging national ego.

illiterate people continued to revere Isis and eagerly anticipated her compelling act of resurrection each spring.

Against this backdrop, a strange perturbation occurred in the Eighteenth Dynasty of the New Kingdom, when a most unusual person became pharaoh. Amenhotep IV inherited the throne on a fluke of genetic roulette. Sickly as a child and disfigured as an adult, this teenager who ascended to high office eschewed the usual pharaonic pastime of hunting and cared little about the strategy of war or politics. He held court with his beautiful wife, Nefertiti. His two passions were reforming Egypt's religion and its writing system.

The young regent was contemptuous of the worship of Amon. Excess power and wealth had accrued to temple priests. Spurning the advice of his counselors, he set about dismantling the trappings of the encrusted Egyptian pantheon. He declared that his subjects should worship only Aton, an obscure god, whom Amenhotep IV himself had elevated to be the Supreme Being. Like his rival Amon, Aton also had no image. But unlike Amon, Aton was so sublime and potent that he was all that there was.

Wishing to make a clean break with tradition, Amenhotep IV renamed himself Akhenaton, in deference to his newly conjured Supreme Being. He then made it a crime for anyone in the kingdom to worship the old deities. But in a telling concession, Akhenaton revealed to the people that Aton had chosen Maat to be his consort. Many historians have hailed Akhenaton as the first monotheist. Even though Maat lacked the fleshy buttocks of a Neolithic Goddess figure and she personified abstract principles, she was, nevertheless, a complementary feminine principle operating within a supposedly masculine monotheistic system. Maat's presence in the service of Aton invalidates the claim that Akhenaton was history's first monotheist.*

The entrenched Egyptian priesthood chafed under Akhenaton's fiats. The young pharaoh's decrees were decried by many as heresy. To further his reformation, Akhenaton forbade artists from making any images of Aton and in related edicts he ordered that scribes use the simplified non-iconic hieratic form of writing promoting the use of a new variant, what Egyptologists would later call the Late Egyptian.[5] There is evidence that his new religion met resistance—wall paintings portray armed guards increasingly surrounding him, presumably to protect him.[6]

---

*Late in Akhenaton's reign, he ordered the erasure of Maat's icon from temple walls and stelae, leaving only her name spelled phonetically.

Unfortunately, Akhenaton had not completely thought through all the ramifications of his new religion. He had banished by edict both Isis's presence and Osiris's Land of the Dead from ordinary citizens' lives. Rich cultic rites and beliefs, refined over many centuries, disappeared almost overnight. Akhenaton had not invented a mythology to accompany the worship of Aton. Also, since hieroglyphs were dependent on images, Akhenaton confronted the first of many problems his spare reform had raised: If Aton did not have an image, how were the folk to worship him? Akhenaton conceded that artists could portray this faceless, featureless god as an empty circle representing the solar disk with rays streaming down.*

Akhenaton, Nefertiti, and their daughter worship Aton.

The people grumbled. Gone were the pomp, circumstance, and imagery associated with the older myths. All that remained was a stiff offering to an empty sun disk and a hymn of praise written in the spare new hieratic script. Religious art, the traditional outlet for creativity, was dammed up by the severe and restrictive new state religion. Perhaps for this reason, other arts flourished. The Eighteenth Dynasty was the only period in ancient Egypt's long history when art departed from the rigid conventions of its more familiar angular style. The royal couple commissioned many portraits of themselves and their family in attitudes of repose and worship. The fluid lines of these paintings and sculptures are sinuous and lively.

---

*At the end of each ray was a small hand holding the "ankh," the Egyptian symbol for life which Western culture adopted as the symbol for a female.

In 1908, archaeologists discovered at Tel el Amarna a large cache of ancient correspondence pertaining to Akhenaton's reign. Satraps, loyal to Akhenaton and ruling for him on the edges of Egypt's eastern empire, wrote the pharaoh imploring him to send military aid to help them keep Egypt's enemies at bay. The consternation evident in the tone of these letters indicates that Akhenaton did not respond to their pleas. The Tel el Amarna letters graphically depict Egypt as a headless giant stumbling toward a fall. After ruling repressively for seventeen years, Akhenaton died and the scepter passed to Tutankhamen, a pharaoh of questionable parentage. Pressed by dissident advisers, the youth ordered the entire apparatus of Aton's worship dismantled and Amon reinstated.

A comparison of Mesopotamia and Egypt, two neighboring civilizations that invented the written word nearly simultaneously, affords a unique opportunity to test the hypothesis of this book. Despite their geographic proximity, these two first civilizations' attitudes toward women were as widely divergent as were their forms of writing.

The Egyptians had many joyous festivals and created the first truly erotic art. Pictures of startling anatomical accuracy have been unearthed in some temples and crypts. On occasion, they even supplied the deceased with sexual aids to enliven their afterlife.[7] Their religion was based more on magic and pageantry than on obligation and morality. Premarital customs were free and easy compared to those of the Mesopotamians. Their gods were plentiful and their images, half-animal and half-human, appeared everywhere. While Amon and Aton were the chief deities among the priests and aristocracy, the common people preferred Isis, the Great Mother. Isis was *not* a goddess of war, and Osiris was *not* a warrior but rather a victim.* There is no Egyptian counterpart to the matricidal Marduk story.

While women in Mesopotamia progressively lost power, they maintained their high position in ancient Egypt. The historian Max Mueller commented, "No people ancient or modern has given women so high a legal status as did the inhabitants of the Nile Valley."[8] Wall paintings depict unself-conscious women eating and drinking in public, strolling the streets unattended, and freely engaging in industry and trade. Classical Greek his-

---

*The lioness-headed goddess Sekhmet was a goddess of war but she was minor compared to Isis.

torians who visited Egypt commented upon the extraordinary power Egyptian wives exerted over their husbands.*

Among royalty, Egyptian men married their sisters, not because familiarity had heightened romance, but because they desired to partake in their family's inheritance—which in many instances passed from mother to daughter.[9] The words *brother* and *sister* in Egyptian have the same significance as *lover* and *beloved*.

In courtship, women often took the initiative, and in the majority of Egyptian love poems and letters the woman addresses the man. She suggests assignations, she presses her suit, and she is the one to propose marriage.[10]

The Mesopotamians excelled in war, laws, cruelty, science, morality, conquest, commerce, and abstract concepts. They made it a law that sons honor their fathers. Sensuality, gaiety, and respect for motherhood were more often Egypt's chief characteristics. The Egyptians were notable for their pictorial arts, sculpture, and architecture. In general, the Babylonians hammered swords in their foundries and the Egyptians turned out exquisite jewelry in theirs. The Mesopotamian Ishtar was the goddess of strife and sexuality; Isis was maternal, loving, and fertile. Marduk was harsh and remote; the polytheistic menagerie of the Egyptians was intimate and fanciful. Women began the descent into servitude in Mesopotamia; Egyptian women maintained the highest status in the entire historical West.

LEFT: Loving Egyptian family

BELOW: Marduk pursues Tiamat before mutilating her.

---

*The Greek tourist Diodorus Siculus reported in the second century B.C. that Egyptian husbands had to promise obedience to their wives at the time of marriage vows.

What could account for these diametrically opposing differences? While there are many possible answers, one clear distinction between the two cultures was their form of writing: the Mesopotamians invented abstract, linearly placed wedges; the Egyptians evolved a form of script dependent on concrete, simultaneously perceived images. These choices, I propose, in turn profoundly affected the thinking processes of each culture.

Egyptian women fared better than their sisters in Mesopotamia. Nevertheless, as Egypt's literacy rate increased, feminine authority suffered a decline. In every society that learned the written word, the female deity lost ground to the male deity. Before the invention of writing, these two powerful forces had remained entwined in sexual union. In every Mediterranean society that embraced literacy, women lost their hold and fell from grace—economically, politically, and spiritually. Writing was a gift eagerly accepted by the ancients. Unfortunately, hiding among the neat rows of carefully incised script was an unwelcome demon—misogyny. In trying to understand what went wrong between the sexes, these two cultures are at the pivot of history.

The perceptions of anyone who learned how to send and receive information by means of regular, sequential, linear rows of abstract symbols were wrenched from a balanced, centrist position toward the dominating, masculine side of the human psyche. This radical shift produced a revolution in gender relationships that was so subtle and insidious that no one noticed what was happening. But the writing styles that had been introduced so far were only hieroglyphs and cuneiform. The most dramatic changes for women were yet to come; the coming storm was brewing in the lands between Mesopotamia and Egypt.

CHAPTER 8

ALEPH/BET

It is only as language is written down that it becomes possible to think about it. The acoustic medium, being incapable of visualization, did not achieve recognition as a phenomenon wholly separable from the person who used it. But in the alphabetized document the medium became objectified. There it was, reproduced perfectly in the alphabet . . . no longer just a function of "me" the speaker but a document with an independent existence.

—Eric Havelock, classicist[1]

As one would expect, the scripts that surfaced in the lands between the Mesopotamian and Egyptian empires were hybrids of cuneiform and hieroglyphs. In those times, Midianites, semi-nomadic camel caravaneers, roamed the inhospitable terrain of the Sinai Peninsula; Serite miners worked the copper quarries near the Gulf of Aqaba; Phoenician sea traders established enclaves along the curving Levantine coast. Inland lay Canaan, a land the Bible later characterized as "flowing with milk and honey." Terraces honeycombed with vineyards and trees ripe with olives attested to its temperate climate and fertile soil. To the north lay the kingdom of the fierce Assyrians. Ugarit, one of its principal provincial cities, became a thriving center for a brief period and then suffered the inevitable fate of any community that lay in the path of armies on their way to somewhere else. The fabled city of Jericho anchored the southern end of this region, astride key intersecting trade routes. Standing on the ramparts of this fortress, shading his eyes against the sun's glare, a lookout would have seen only desert to the south and west. To the east, the hills fell sharply away into the Jordan Valley.

Wandering throughout these lands were groups of herders seeking pastures for their goats and sheep. These people are referred to in both ancient Mesopotamian and Egyptian texts as Habiru which means "dusty travelers."[2] The similarity between "Habiru" and "Hebrew" has led many scholars to speculate that these Habiru may have been the precursors of the Israelites.

In the first two millennia after the founding of Egypt and Mesopotamia, the patchwork quilt of clans inhabiting this region never came close to achieving the grandeur, sophistication, or prosperity of their two powerful neighbors. Their architecture was unoriginal, its scale unimpressive. Their science was nonexistent. Museum curators have relegated their crafts to the alcoves of present-day museums—reserving the main halls for Egyptian and Mesopotamian exhibits. Their forms of government were primitive. The petty satraps who ruled their provincial city-states proved forgettable. And their priests plagiarized unabashedly from the religions of the colossi to either side of them.

The motley collection of proto-nations occupying the area bounded by present-day Israel, Jordan, Lebanon, Syria, and the Sinai Peninsula would all have sunk into obscurity except for one stunning discovery. Someone, or some group among them, invented a greatly simplified method of written communication that shifted the perceptual mode by which people understood their reality, deflected the thrust of gender politics, and changed the course of history. This new scrivening was the alphabet.

What made the alphabet so revolutionary was the ease with which people could learn to use it. Because it was in their interest to keep others ignorant, the scribes of Egypt and Mesopotamia guarded the secrets of the written word. One who was literate had an immense advantage over those who were not, whether they were powerful or poor.

The alphabet ended the hegemony of the literate elite. Instead of a complex syllabary of over six hundred cuneiform characters, or six thousand hieroglyphs coupled with rules of grammar that would daunt the most eager student, an alphabet contained a mere twenty-odd letters.* Four-year-olds could, did, and do master the alphabet's essentials. People with below-average intelligence could, did, and do learn to read and write alphabets. Thus an empowering skill that had been guarded by a favored few was now accessible to the multitudes. The religions that henceforth spiraled outward from unwinding reams of written scrolls demanded that acolytes be literate. Until that time, to know the deity one had only to *see* Her image or observe Her rituals. With the advent of the alphabet, to know the deity demanded that one must first *read* His written words.

Despite the power of the empires that stood behind them, the two pillars of ancient literacy, cuneiform and hieroglyphics, eventually crumbled and were buried by the blowing sands of antiquity. Where once they had

*An alphabet by definition is any form of writing that contains fewer than thirty signs.

towered, the humble, vigorous, people's alphabet emerged. Over time, the cultures taking advantage of this new writing tool glorified monotheism, used the Rule by Law to reorganize society, instituted democracy, hallowed individualism, invented money, and created prose, drama, and philosophy. And this list is by no means complete. These same cultures, especially the later ones, also abused nature, glorified war, perfected imperialism, and held deep-seated sexist attitudes. And despite the advantages conferred upon them by alphabetic literacy, they all eventually tore themselves apart; for the first time in recorded history, civilizations foundered over purely internal ideological disputes. This innovation and frenzy was caused by the profound change in perception wrought by the alphabet.

A crucial collateral benefit springing from the alphabet was that it allowed people to systematize knowledge. Compendia, dictionaries, encyclopedias, filing systems, indices, telephone books, stock market quotes, and libraries are almost unthinkable without the alphabet. The alphabet's simplicity made it possible to store and retrieve data with ease, which in turn laid the foundation for the alphabet's most portentous gift to those who learned it—theoretical science.

The abstract alphabet encouraged abstract thinking. People who used an alphabet began to see beyond what was particular in nature and sought out what was universal. Divining the laws that unite seemingly disparate events is the essence of theoretical science. Combined with the alphabet's simple means of classifying and recording observations, people began to investigate the workings of nature.

The small group of theoretical scientists appearing first in classical Greece, and succeeded by other scientists in every subsequent culture that has embraced the alphabet, have done more to transform the human condition than any other single group or factor. If, as has been said, "The past is prologue," then the alphabet's appearance in the archaeological record marks the preface to the drama known as Western civilization. Simply put, the invention of the alphabet reconfigured the world.

Aside from the obvious benefits that derived from their ease of use, alphabets produced a subtle change in cognition that redirected human thinking. For sophisticated neurolinguistic reasons the early practitioners could not have known, alphabets reinforced only half of the dual strategy that humans had evolved to survive. As we have seen, this strategy had three components: left brain/right brain, cone/rod, and right hand/left hand. Each tripartite half of this duality perceived and reacted to the world in a different way; a unified response emerged only when both complementary halves were used.

All forms of writing increase the left brain's dominance over the right. As civilization progressed from image-based communication, such as pictographs and hieroglyphs, to non-iconic forms, such as cuneiform, written communication became more left-brain oriented. An alphabet, being the most abstract form of writing, enhances left-brain values the most. Each letter stands only for a singular sound; meaning emerges only when letters are strung together in a row. Unlike icons, which often evolved from images of things, an alphabetic word bears no resemblance to the object or action it symbolizes. Nowhere in the word *dog* can we discern a dog. There remain some trace correlations, as with the word *water,* which begins with the letter *w*. The ancient Egyptians created a hieroglyph for water that resembles our letter *w* and to indicate water on a map, or in a cartoon, we still use a series of wavy lines. This iconic symbol for water became the alphabetic letter *w* and is a component of many words associated with the liquid state of matter (e.g., wet, wave, wash, wade, wallow, winnow, womb, and woman). However, we no longer connect the letter *w* with water directly. When we see *w* in print as part of a word, the brain issues complex directions that instruct the lips to purse so that we can pronounce the phonetic sound of *w*. Alphabets have long divorced themselves from the images of concrete things. They have washed out of the written language iconic patterns that were apparent in earlier forms of writing. All that remains are letters that stand starkly like rows of pier posts at ebb tide.

The versatility of letters becomes evident when they are placed in regular, linear, consensually agreed upon arrangements. Aligning three letters to spell *d-o-g* results in the English reader instantly seeing a dog in the mind's eye. Yet the mental image of a dog was once attached only to a real dog, or to the invisible spoken word, *dog*. The induction of any member of society (usually a young child) into alphabet arcana numbs her to the fact that she supplants *all-at-once* gestalt perception with a new, unnatural, highly abstract *one-at-a-time* cognition. In this fashion, alphabets subliminally elevated, within each alphabet user, the influence of the left hemisphere at the expense of the right. Rods were not as important as cones for reading this new form of writing. As more and more people could read and write, the dominant pen-wielding right hand played an increasingly critical role in communication, masculinizing culture. It made no difference if the writing hand belonged to a female or male: both sexes were inexorably brought to heel by the left brain within each individual.

Any form of writing dramatically changes the perceptions of those who use it. In cuneiform and hieroglyphic-based cultures, these changes manifested as a slippage of right-brain feminine values below conscious awareness. If the effect of earlier scripts on human development is likened to a significant mudslide, the advent of the alphabet produced a thundering avalanche.

The sexual orientation of the alphabet can be unmasked by studying the myths of the peoples who used it. Upon learning the alphabet, both women and men turned away from the worship of idols and animal totems that represented the *images* of nature, and began paying homage to the abstract *logos*. A God with no face replaces the sacred images that had hitherto transfixed the faithful. The alphabet-people's god became indisputably male and he would become disconnected from the things of the earth. He was abstract, nowhere, and yet everywhere, at once.

Who deserves credit for inventing the alphabet? Textbooks traditionally cite the Phoenicians. In the fifth century B.C., Herodotus, Greece's first historian, wrote, "The Phoenicians who came with Cadmus introduced into Greece . . . a number of accomplishments, of which the most important was writing, an art till then, I think, unknown to the Greeks."[3] Many centuries later, archaeologists uncovered evidence for an earlier alphabet in Canaan, circa 1600 B.C. As Canaan was intimately associated with Phoenicia, this evidence seems to confirm Herodotus's assertion.

Who were the Phoenicians and Canaanites? The name Phoenicia means "purple" in Greek, and derives from a much-coveted dye the inhabitants of the coastal region harvested from an indigenous mollusk. The Phoenicians sold the dye chiefly to the royalty of other Mediterranean nations, and purple became universally associated with rulers. The "purple people," as the Greeks referred to them, became sailors, traders, and explorers. Their cities of Tyre, Sidon, Byblos, and Acre jutted from a narrow strip of coastline that is now part of Lebanon and Israel. Their territory never extended more than ten miles inland, primarily because the Phoenicians disdained agricultural pursuits. From their homeports, they established outposts to expand and extend their burgeoning trade, and their cities eventually dotted the Mediterranean coastline. Strolling along the wharves in Cadiz, Marseilles, or Malta, one could hear Punic, their spoken language. In the fifth century B.C., the Phoenicians founded a satellite empire on the shores of North Africa. Centered around the city of Carthage, the thriving community eventually dwarfed all of the original Phoenician cities.

Across the Mediterranean to the north, the nation-state of Rome was on the rise. Three Punic wars, fought between Rome and Carthage between 264 and 146 B.C., ended in Roman victory. When the Roman general Scipio conquered Carthage, he ordered every building reduced to rubble. The besieged populace who survived were sold into slavery. After this crushing defeat, the Phoenicians disappeared from the stage of history, and Punic became a dead language.

One might expect that the inventors of the alphabet would have excelled culturally, or that the creativity that inspired the alphabet would lead to other significant advances. Yet, the only area in which the Phoenicians can be credited with innovation is in the art of naval design. One would certainly expect a literary legacy of some sort from the inventors of the alphabet. Significantly, none survives, even though the word *book* itself derives from the name of the Phoenician city of Byblos. The contrast between their writers and those of the other major Mediterranean seagoing culture, Greece, is stark.* Only two Phoenicians' names can be found in most general history books—King Hiram from the tenth century B.C. with whom Solomon formed an alliance, and the brilliant general Hannibal of second-century Carthage. The most vivid descriptions of the Phoenicians come not from their own pens but from their enemies, the Romans. In the final stages of the Roman siege of Carthage, the Phoenicians threw several hundred children, drawn from their finest families, onto the stoked fires within the bronze belly of their god Moloch. This cruel deity could be appeased only by human sacrifice. If the sacrifice happened to be a loved child, so much the better.[4] The city authorities ordered their children burned alive to save their own skins. Numerous sacrificial funerary urns unearthed at Carthaginian sites, containing the bones and ashes of children, lend credence to this report.[5] The immolation of children suggests that the Phoenicians had not achieved a very advanced level of religion and morality. A contributor to the first issue of the *American Journal of Archaeology* in 1885 summed up the Phoenicians thus:

> The Phoenicians, so far as we know, did not bring a single fructifying idea into the world . . . their arts . . . hardly deserve to be called arts; they were for the most part only traders. Their architecture, sculpture, painting were of the most unimaginative sort.

In a century of excavation since this harsh indictment was written, little that is substantive has turned up to alter this judgment.

---

*When the Romans destroyed Carthage, they set fire to its large library. Some might argue that the Phoenician literary legacy disappeared in the conflagration, yet Phoenician colonies studded the Mediterranean. If there had been a Phoenician Euripides, would not his works have survived elsewhere?

In both contemporaneous as well as subsequent cultures, as we shall see, the introduction of alphabetic literacy had a profound impact on religion. Yet the Phoenicians instituted no religious reforms. Their key dieties were the Harsh-Storm-Ruler-God and Fierce-Warrior-Sexual-Goddess, similar to others throughout the Fertile Crescent. The early Phoenician El and his consort Asherah, and the later couple Baal and Astarte, were indistinguishable from other regional celestial pairs.

There have been four scripts that had monumental impact on historical development: cuneiform, hieroglyphics, Chinese, and the alphabet. The cultures that developed from the first three were distinctive and creative. Phoenician culture was not. The paucity of cultural innovation suggests the possibility that the Phoenicians did not in fact invent the alphabet.

Were the Canaanites, then, the inventors? Did they pass it along to the Phoenicians? There is little in the archaeological or historical record to encourage the idea. The Tel el Amarna cache from 1450 B.C. contains many letters from Canaanite leaders to Akhenaton: all are written in cuneiform. The very few alphabetic inscriptions that have been identified as Canaanite do not indicate a high level of literary, ethical, religious, or philosophical thought.

Many credit the Egyptians with "discovering the alphabet," because they invented the *principle* of the alphabet. But there was not a single Egyptian alphabetic document until their adoption of Coptic, almost two thousand years *after* the introduction of the Semitic alphabet.

Phoenicia, Canaan, and Egypt are advanced as the three most likely sources of the alphabet. Yet, most archaeologists acknowledge that the oldest alphabet discovered is the one found in the Sinai desert. In 1905, Sir William Flinders Petrie found a script resembling Hebrew letters, at the site of an Egyptian temple dedicated to a goddess. Surrounding the area were rocks upon which Petrie found further evidence of this alphabet. Petrie called these precursor letters, dated at around 1800 B.C., the Proto-sinaitic alphabet. Few challenge the fact that the sinaitic inscriptions are the oldest known alphabet script. Petrie discovered them in one of the most moon-like, barren places in the world. There are no cities to speak of in Sinai, no crumbled remains of empires, few water sources and hardly any vegetation; yet, evidence of the oldest alphabet stared at him across the millennia from the craggy surfaces of sun-baked rocks.

The numerous exotic place-names of the ancient world are redolent with oriental opulence and stirring events. Egyptian wall paintings and hieroglyphs sumptuously record the grand pageantry of Thebes, Memphis, and Karnak. The Babylonian cities of Ur, Uruk, and Nineveh call to mind scenes of intrigues, battles, and coronations.

There is only one major event associated with the name "Sinai." It was here that Yahweh gave Moses the Ten Commandments for the Hebrew people. It seems like an extraordinary coincidence and a striking intersection of myth and science that the oldest alphabet was found in the place where *the* seminal episode in the history of the ancient Hebrews occurred.

The biblical version of what transpired in the Sinai recounts the rededication of an entire people to their solitary God. Monotheism was a revolutionary idea, and many believe it is the primary legacy of the Hebrews to future generations.

The other revolutionary idea emerging in the Sinai shaped the future of all human aspirations: Yahweh proclaimed that there exists a code of morality that stands above human intercourse. The Ten Commandments applied *universally* to everyone. No king, pharaoh, or potentate was above the law. If human society was to be organized on a principle other than "might makes right," all would have to submit. The codes of Draco, Solon, and Justinian, the Magna Carta, the United States Constitution, and the Miranda rights can all be traced back to what happened in the Sinai.

But how did a landless, powerless, nomadic people, wandering in a dusty, rock-strewn environment, come to two such ideas by themselves? The key is that Yahweh expected all His chosen people to *read* what He had written. To mandate this new approach to religion, He forbade anyone from visualizing any feature of His person or from trying to imagine the form of another god. From Sinai forward, He proscribed the making of all images— He sanctioned only written words. It is not mere coincidence that the first book written in an alphabet is the Old Testament. There is none earlier.

Previously, Akhenaton and Hammurabi each took tentative steps toward introducing monotheism and the Law to their people. These abstract concepts initially failed to take hold because both monarchs ruled over barely literate societies. The mystery of why not one but *both* these incredible ideas should appear shimmering together in a mirage in the middle of the desert, to a group of escaped slaves teetering on the edge of survival far from centers of learning, is one of the great puzzles of all time. Perhaps the transforming event that transpired so long ago at the foot of Mount Sinai was the invention of the alphabet.

CHAPTER 9

HEBREWS/ISRAELITES

I am the Lord, and there is none else, there is no god besides me.

—Isa. 44:6

The occurrence of monotheism, codified law, and the alphabet all at the same moment in history cannot have been coincidental. . . . The abstractness of all three innovations were mutually reinforcing.

—Robert Logan[1]

The Bible is the oldest influential written record, and it is the primary source of information concerning the birth of Judaism. Besides immortalizing the story of the origin of monotheism, it has underpinned the religious, mythological, and moral framework of Western civilization. It speaks so eloquently to the human condition that its spiritual truths have resonated across many diverse and tumultuous historical periods. Most of the world calls these sacred scriptures the Old Testament, distinguishing them from the New Testament. To the Jews, they are simply the Bible—the Book. The first five sections of the Bible comprise the Torah—the deepest gnarled root of Western literature and tradition.

The oldest sections of the Torah were first transcribed between 1,000 and 900 B.C.,[2] and subsequently underwent three major revisions, with later sections added over the next millennium. Analyzing the first five books, biblical scholars have identified four different voices speaking to us across the centuries; J, E, P, and R are the letters they have assigned to each distinctive author (or authors). J composed the most ancient sections, and is called the Yahwist, because this author identifies God by the singular noun Yahweh. E, called the Elohist, refers to God using the plural noun Elohim, and E tells a different version of Genesis and Exodus than J; E also includes sections chronicling the rise and fall of the kingdom of Judea. P, the Priestly author(s), is so named because of the liturgical nature of his (their) writings.

Scholars believe these sections were completed by the seventh century. R, the Redactor, made the last major revisions in the Torah sometime between 430 and 400 B.C. Circumstantial evidence strongly suggests that the Redactor was the Prophet Ezra. Whoever this person was, he or she edited the previous versions, interweaving the distinct voices of J and E so that their often contradictory stories appear to be one. Modern biblical scholars have teased apart the two different versions and estimate that J predates E by one hundred[3] to five hundred years.[4]

In the turmoil following the fall of Judea to the Romans around the time of Christ, rabbis, desperately trying to preserve Jewish identity, refused to sanction any further revisions in the Old Testament. But new generations needed to reinterpret the Scriptures in light of new situations, and scholars subsequently added rich compendia to the original document. The most familiar of these post-Diaspora writings is the Talmud.

In A.D. 367, Christians canonized the New Testament, acknowledging the ancient book of the Hebrews as an integral part of their own story. Subsequently, the Muslims did so too. The Old Testament's triad of monotheism, Rule by Law, and the command to live ethically eventually became universal Western values.

To best examine the circumstances surrounding the origins of the Old Testament, let us keep in mind the hypothesis that alphabetic literacy may not only have shaped its unique message but dictated that it should emerge precisely when and where it did. The conversion of what had been a mixture of oral traditions and written segments into the cohesive and eloquent Torah occurred around the time of King David. No fragment of the original document exists. We surmise its existence because it was mentioned in subsequent Old Testament editions. Every tradition states that the Torah was written using letters. The Septuagint Bible was translated into Greek by a team of seventy rabbis working from an earlier Aramaic manuscript in the second century B.C., nearly a millennium *after* the first King David version, which was itself written many centuries after the events described in the Old Testament's earliest sections. The passage of so many centuries between the events and their recording must have profoundly affected their retelling. It is likely that a strong oral tradition kept the stories alive while the Hebrews wrestled with the evolution of alphabetic grammar until a true literary genius finally wrote them down in a style so eloquent that the work continues to command respect. The archaeological record suggests that by the seventh century B.C. the Israelites, unlike their neighbors, were substantially alphabet literate. Hebrew alphabetic letters routinely appeared on cylinder seals used in everyday commerce from this date forward, instead of the far more common iconic symbols present on the cylinder seals of surrounding cultures.[5] Rising Israelite alphabet literacy, I propose, was behind the most striking features of the Old Testament distinguishing them from the history, religion, and literature of other contemporary societies.

The purpose of all historical or mythical accounts concerning the founding of a nation was to glorify that nation. It is unlikely that any people would fabricate a story of their defeat and servitude unless its telling dignified their heritage. Yet the Exodus begins with the Hebrews shackled in slavery. This departure from self-aggrandizement is most unusual.

A strong argument can also be made that the Exodus never occurred. Egyptian pharaohs had scribes record in stone the milestones of their reigns. Except for a few dark periods, Egyptologists have been able to reconstruct the chronology of Egyptian dynasties. Despite the compulsive documenting of their history, the Egyptians remained silent on the subject of the Exodus. It would seem that either the Exodus and the founding of an Israelite nation were events blown out of all proportion by a semi-nomadic tribe given to exaggeration, or the Egyptians put the best face on an ignoble episode of their history by ignoring it.

How is it that the Hebrews were the singular champions of monotheism and Rule by Law in a period drenched in polytheism and the divine rights of kings? Are not great ideas usually associated with settled communities? How could the concept of a God who was supreme because there *were* no other gods occur to a culture that had no distinctive art, craft, architecture, innovative weaponry, and, most significantly, no homeland? Why would a lofty and abstract principle such as the Rule by Law arise in a people whose principal activity was herding goats and sheep? Does there exist a parallel to a pastoral people coming in off the desert carrying in their gunnysacks the key staples of Western civilization?

In the Hebrews' new conception of religion, God chose a particular people to be His subjects rather than the other way around. In the ancient world, gods had always been local: their jurisdiction extended over a finite space. Upon moving to another locale, a prudent worshiper did well to learn the names and rituals of the new divine landlords, though choosing from the surfeit was left entirely up to the individual.

Another enigma: why did Yahweh give the Hebrews the Ten Commandments in alphabetic form instead of in hieroglyphs? Moses had been raised and educated as an Egyptian prince. If Moses knew any written language well, it would have been the one he learned as a child. How could the Hebrews, slaves in Egypt for the preceding 430 years and not possessing their own written language, have been able to read Yahweh's instructions?

Another shimmering idea, rising like heat from the desert, was the Israelites' emphasis on justice. What distinguishes the Book from other belief systems of that era is its dominating theme of righteousness. Living a pious life and obeying written laws were more important than winning battles, honoring the king, or sacrificing to a local god. Justice for All was a unique community standard in a time when the dominant principle was that of the raised fist. Along with right living, or perhaps because of it, a novel type of leader appeared among the Israelites—the prophet. Biblical prophets were self-appointed witnesses and critics of Israelite behavior, constantly battling with the people's baser urges.

In other contemporary cosmologies, the heroes were hunters, adventurers, warriors, magicians, and kings. The Bible's key characters, in contrast, were dour men who railed against injustice and impiety. They constantly upbraided the Israelites, reminding them that Yahweh—unlike all previous and contemporary deities, with the possible exception of the Egyptian goddess Maat—cared *only* that His people lived in truth. Prophets did not achieve their position by birthright, appointment, election, or dominance, but rather because they were inspired and just. By sheer force of their personalities, these charismatic men enforced the laws of the Covenant. Kings humbled themselves before them and commoners feared their pronouncements. Prophets railed against apostasy, image-worship, and backsliding. They inveighed against the contumely of the rich and the plight of the poor. They shored up the Israelites' resistance against the many opulent temptations of less demanding religions that wafted in from surrounding cultures. Prophets accomplished these tasks without an army, police force, or sanctions—they managed to keep their young nation on the straight and narrow using exhortation alone because they could speak with authority about the principles set forth in a book that had been written by God.

Perhaps the most unusual deviation from the convention of those times was that the new Hebrew faith did not subscribe to an afterlife. The Land of the Dead played a pervasive role in the Egyptian belief system, and though Moses and the Hebrews emerged from Egyptian culture, there is no mention of an existence after death *anywhere* in the Torah. Relinquishing the idea of immortality no doubt posed a thorny problem for prophets. An Egyptian priest could warn supplicants that, upon their demise, Maat would weigh their worldly actions on the divine scale of justice in the presence of the jackal-headed Anubis, the fearsome sheriff of the underworld. An Israelite prophet could not invoke the specter of a similar reckoning in the next world because, according to Israelite beliefs, *there was no next world*. Yet the Israelites were, by all accounts, the most pious of the ancient peoples.

Israelite prophets cajoled and compelled their followers to observe the Law by instilling in their people the belief that an omniscient, stern judge was constantly observing their every action in the here and now. A personal sense of guilt emerged among the Israelites.

The Egyptians, Babylonians, Greeks, and Romans had no word in their language for sin; the Israelites introduced both the word and the concept into the stream of Western civilization and by so doing, diverted it. The Babylonians and Egyptians believed that one's entire destiny was in the hands of the gods. The biblical prophets convinced each Israelite that every decision was theirs to make. The prophets introduced the idea of Free Will and left the agonizing choice between right and wrong to rest, ultimately, on the conscience of the individual.

The Egyptians never developed a code of laws that spelled out moral expectations. For most of Egyptian history, the people depended on the priesthood to make the requisite number of sacrifices and conduct important ceremonies to appease the gods.* The Mesopotamians and archaic Greeks believed their pantheon was populated by gods and goddesses who had better things to do than spend their days keeping track of their mortal subjects' failings. Since their deities were often occupied with their own peccadilloes, the people believed their immoral actions might also escape detection. Cunning was held in exceptionally high regard. In the *Odyssey*, Athena praised Odysseus:

> Cunning must he be and knavish, she tells him, smiling, and stroking him with her hand, who would go beyond thee in all manner of guile, aye, though it were a god that met thee. Bold man, crafty in counsel, insatiate in deceit, not even in thine own land, it seems, wast thou to cease from guile and deceitful tales, which thou lovest from the bottom of thine heart.[6]

Besides his courage and cleverness, Odysseus's dishonesty was a key trait that made him a hero. In the Israelite system, such duplicity was reclassified as evil. Had Odysseus been Jewish, he would have been a sinner.

With no consorts or relatives to distract His attention, Yahweh could fret over the actions of every single one of His chosen people. And fret He did. Compassion was a characteristic notably lacking in the pantheons of other cultures. Unlike the diffident polytheistic gods, Yahweh actually *cared*. If someone was cheating widows and orphans, or not being hospitable to

---

*The afterlife trial of the individual was a late convention in the Egyptian religion. It gained prominence as Maat became ascendant and hieratic script supplanted hieroglyphics.

strangers, Yahweh knew and became wrathful. Each ancient Israelite established a personal relationship with Yahweh. Unlike the distant Marduk,
Amon, and Baal, Yahweh operated on the plane of everyday life, and He was
not above intervening in the daily affairs of ordinary people. He had spelled
out in excruciating detail exactly what He wanted from each Israelite. All of
His laws were written down and everyone knew them, since it was an
absolute Judaic condition that *every* male be literate. Ignorance of the Law
was no defense.

Friedrich Nietzsche proclaimed "God is dead" in 1888, because he
observed that God had become only marginally relevant. Nietzsche noted
that science, philosophy, psychology, and constitutional laws had diminished God's role in the daily lives of most people. But in the Fertile Crescent
thirty-eight hundred years ago, worship was a critical human activity. Little
happened to an individual that was not related to supernatural forces. There
was not even a word for *religion* in the Mesopotamian, Egyptian, or Hebrew
languages of that period, because religion was not a separate category of
daily living. Any innovation that changed the way people worshiped, therefore, constituted nothing less than a revolution.

As far back as we know anything about the emergence of humankind,
people have created sacred sanctuaries. Local populations have at one time
or another identified trees, rocks, caves, woods, groves, copses, rivers, and
mountains as the dwelling places of deities, and have consecrated these sites
by building shrines to gods, goddesses, or other spirits who hovered there.
Hallowed haunts have been an enduring feature of all religions. But the
Hebrews did not have this attachment to or reverence for sacred places.
Considering the miraculous nature of what occurred at the foot of Mount
Sinai, one might expect that the Hebrews would have marked the place with
a shrine or temple. Yet to this day, theologians and archaeologists have not
been able to determine the location of this legendary site.

From a practical standpoint, the Israelites considered no place holy
because they had no homeland and were constantly on the move. And
because no single place was holy to them, the God they worshiped could not
be tied to a single locale. Part of what made Yahweh a new idea, therefore,
was that unlike previous deities, He was *everywhere*.

Even though they did not designate any particular *place* as holy, the
Israelites believed that the Ten Commandments Yahweh gave them at
Mount Sinai were their tribe's most precious possession. To honor this
divine gift they constructed a wooden box in which to carry Yahweh's written words during their years of wandering. They called this box the Ark of
the Covenant and considered it to be their Holy of Holies.

When Moses or a Levite priest periodically opened it before the faithful, the assembled congregation trembled with awe knowing they were in the presence of the deity. But unlike every other inner sanctum, this one contained *no* likeness of a god: inside the Ark were written words. For the first time in the historical record, people revered not the *image* of a deity but His *written words*, and for the first time ever, religion demanded that followers be literate: "Moses commanded . . . thou shalt read this law before all Israel" (Deut. 31:10-11). The reading of Torah remains the most sacred obligation of every Jew.* Reading about the deity instead of gazing upon his form was such a radical break with past practices that at first, words shared the stage in the Ark with a few icons, notably a bronze serpent fashioned by Moses himself. Later, the Israelites would destroy every image. The Word would not deign to consort with a single other relic, statue, symbol, or mandala.†

Elsewhere, *every other people* continued to invest images of deities with divine powers, creating fertility amulets, totem poles, and diorite statues. Only in the Sinai was this practice abandoned. What factor, we might ask, allowed the ancient Hebrews to make the leap from concrete statue worship to the abstraction of the Divine Logos?

The answer lies in the pages of the Old Testament, which many believe to be a reasonably accurate historical account of a people enveloped by a miraculous nimbus. I propose that neither their deliverance from slavery nor the parting of the Red Sea was the miracle. Neither was the emergence of monotheism and Rule by Law the miracle; nor was the enthronement of righteousness. All these epiphanies were *results* of the miracle. The miracle, I believe, was the reduction of graphic symbols from thousands to two dozen. All the questions posed and innovations puzzled over in the previous

---

*In every culture of the world, elders design a rite of passage for young men entering adulthood. In virtually all other contemporaneous cultures, the task was physical—killing a lion, fasting, surviving in the wilderness, or enduring painful scarification. Only the Hebrews made their young men prove they had conquered the complexities of literacy. The Bar Mitzvah requires a reading of Torah before the assembled congregation by a thirteen-year-old male. In Judaism, it is as important a ritual as a wedding or a funeral. Until recently, only a male could be a Bar Mitzvah. Now, girls too can participate and be a Bat Mitzvah. Although an ancient ritual, it is not mentioned in the Torah. Records in the second century mention thirteen as the age of religious manhood but the practice did not become widespread until the Middle Ages.

†Josephus, in his history of the Jewish War, recounted how the Roman general Pompey looked forward to being the first gentile to ever enter the inner sanctum of the Temple when Jerusalem fell to the Romans in 63 B.C. Rumor had it this room contained a monstrous idol of the Jews' deity. Upon his profane trespass, Pompey recoiled; the room contained *absolutely nothing*.

pages can be answered and understood if it is assumed that the ancient Hebrews were the first to embrace alphabetic writing.

The Ten Commandments were most likely transmitted in an alphabetic form not very different from the modern English you are now reading. The abstract letters, grammatical sequence, and uniconsonantal phonemes of ancient Hebrew share the same principles. The alphabet introduced the possibility of universal literacy. A radical new communication technology would so change cultural perceptions that the first people to utilize it would introduce the fundamental features underpinning Western civilization.

The sound of spoken words can have great power. For example, there is a deeply felt resonance in the sonorous recitation of Catholic Mass or Hindu chant. The introduction of Jewish sacred scripture meant that the written, silent word superseded the authority and the sanctity of the spoken one, thus reducing the importance of liturgical sound and concrete images in worship.

To the ancients, writing was wizardry. Literacy is so pervasive in modern Western society that most people find it impossible to imagine what it must have been like for those who first encountered this culture-changing tool. The written word has a heft, gravity, and authority not present in the spoken one; a signature more than an oath puts one's honor on the line; hearsay cannot contend with a deposition; talk is cheap.

The written word is essentially immortal. To a hyper-conscious primate who had become aware that death was inevitable, the discovery of a method to project one's self beyond a single life span seemed nothing less than miraculous. Perhaps this feature of the written word explains the absence of an afterlife in the revolutionary Israelite belief system.

In other religions of the day, priests resplendent in brightly colored robes conducted ceremonial sacrifices and processional rituals. The air was redolent with incense, and the rhythmic pulse of music and dance contributed to an overload of sensory input. These kaleidoscopic religious events, involving all the senses and experienced in a group, were best integrated by the right brain.

The new Israelite faith required of its male followers that they *read* a sacred written text, and reading is decidedly a left-brain function. Indeed, the first religion based on the alphabet, and those subsequently growing from it, would eventually banish bright colors altogether, as they would also eliminate idols, bells, drums, dance, incense, cymbals, and imagery of any kind. Eventually, even though he might be part of a larger group, the orthodox Jew (early Christian, orthodox Muslim or early Protestant), dressed only in black and white, communed with his invisible deity by reading from a black-and-white text. All prayer shawls and yarmulkes would be restricted to the colors of scroll and ink.*

Compared to the religious epics of Canaan, Egypt, and Mesopotamia, the Torah adopted many compassionate and enlightened ethical positions. For example, an Israelite warrior was forbidden to rape or enslave the women of a defeated enemy: widows of fallen foes were allowed to mourn for their dead husbands. All those who were not married to Israelite warriors were to be set free (Deut. 21:10–14). An Israelite slave owner had to grant freedom to a slave after a period of bondage lasting seven years (Deut. 15:12).

Despite these improvements in ethical behavior in the ancient world, the new Israelite religion introduced the first examples of *religious* intolerance in human history. The Israelites' ideological xenophobia served to preserve their unique identity, for without it they would have intermarried, in adversity left their faith, and most likely disappeared from the pages of history. As it was, their zeal brooked no compromise. Yahweh despised the worship of images, and by making faith in monotheism the paramount criterion of human worth, the Israelites took the stance that they were superior to those people who continued to worship idols.

The Israelites' sectarian prejudice stood in sharp contrast to other religions of those times. Polytheism had many hierarchical layers. There were national gods, local gods, family gods, and even personal gods. A kind of golden rule existed among the ancients. Each person respected the gods of other peoples and expected that their own gods would be respected in return.† To everyone except the Israelites, it was self-evident that there were large numbers of gods and goddesses, and it was common for a culture to sample other religions and incorporate foreign features into its own. There is not a single recorded case of Egyptian followers of the god Thoth sacking the temples of those who honored Ptah. Adherents of Marduk did not kill those who worshiped Baal. Devotees of the militaristic Ares never attacked the followers of warlike Apollo. By their very nature, polytheistic religions fostered tolerance. Piety did not lead ineluctably to religious hatred as it has so often in history. Although there were many bloody conflicts fought over land, women, booty, or to avenge a perceived wrong, there were *no* religious wars in the ancient world before monotheism.

---

*For reasons that will be explained in later chapters this trend is now reversing.

†After the conquest of an enemy's lands, it was not uncommon for the victors to topple the statues of the gods of the vanquished. This desecration was a heavy-handed demonstration of who was in charge. These wars, however, were *never* fought because of differing religious beliefs.

One plausible explanation: monotheism does not mirror human society. Humans are first and foremost social animals. A deity who was alone, not by choice but because there were no other companions for Him, was a concept without parallel in human society. The God of the Israelites did not have a wife, a son, a daughter, a father, or a mother.

Monotheism encouraged people to think in new ways. A monotheistic God not tied to a concrete image is a highly abstract concept. Abstraction is a crucial component of logical reasoning and its use can set people free from superstition. But there is a terrible price to pay for devotion to an abstract God. If everyone agrees that only one God exists, and different groups conceive of Him in different ways, then whose perception of that deity is the correct one? This question has goaded monotheists to wage war with an intensity and purpose never witnessed in polytheistic cultures. Outside the monotheistic West, people have killed each other because they looked, dressed, spoke, or gestured differently; but killing solely because someone *believes* in a different *abstract idea* loosed into the world an odious impulse. Raiding another village because one aspired to steal horses has a practical logic. Killing each other over religious, philosophical, or economic abstractions is folly.

If the skulls of the people who have been killed in the name of God, Jesus, and Allah in religious wars and persecutions could be piled in one place, they would form an immense mountain. If we tallied the cost in human suffering for the belief in monotheism, we might not think of the other religions of the world as primitive. Monotheism was a major advance along the road to enlightenment, but its cost was steep.

How to explain this singular feature of the revolutionary Hebraic faith? What factor or factors inspired its extremism? One effect of a new abstract, linear, sequential, and reductionist means of communication would have been to move people who learned it into a left-brain, masculine mode. And is not one expression of this lurch to the left great certainty in the right-eousness of one's cause? Monotheism was a very abstract idea. The alphabet subliminally coaxed users to be intolerant of other iconic systems of belief. As this narrative proceeds through history, I will present other examples of this dark side of alphabet literacy.

The Ten Commandments are the core of the Israelite faith, and the ethics they embody were more sophisticated than those of other contemporary cultures. The Commandment to honor both father *and* mother, for example, recognized the importance of the mother in family relations. And yet, to the twentieth-century reader something appears to be missing. Yahweh did not make loving others a Commandment. The instruction is, however, buried in Leviticus 19:18, ". . . thou shalt love thy neighbor as thyself."

The last six Commandments are not unusual. It would be a rare society that could sustain itself without its members obeying the strictures to honor parents and to refrain from killing, stealing, lying, coveting, slandering, and adultery. The first four Commandments, however, are unique. Each one seems to encourage alphabetic literacy by rejecting the right brain's way of knowing.

The First Commandment, "I *am* the Lord thy God. Thou shalt have no other gods before me" (Exod. 20:2–3), announces the disappearance of the Goddess. The meta-message of the Commandment is, "I am the only deity. I am a man, and I do not have nor do I need a wife or consort." While it is never explicitly stated in the Old Testament that Yahweh is male, all Yahweh's titles—Lord, Host, King, Ruler, and Master—are indisputably masculine. Furthermore, the two biblical names for him, Yahweh (Adonai) and Elohim, are both masculine nouns. The Shekina, a much later Jewish feminine aspect of spirituality, is nowhere mentioned in the Torah.*

The First Commandment declares that Yahweh will not tolerate mention of a Goddess. Given that the Hebrews and Moses emerged from Egypt, the most goddess-worshiping culture in the ancient world, the First Commandment represented a sharp rupture with the past. And given that all people acknowledge that life is a conjoining of masculine and feminine principles, the exclusion of any feminine presence from the First Commandment makes it the most radical sentence ever written.

The Second Commandment is equally remarkable: "Thou shalt not make unto thee any graven images, or any likeness of *any thing* that *is* in heaven above, or that *is* in the earth beneath, or that *is* in the water under the earth" (Exod. 20:4). This proscription against making images is repeated throughout the Torah.

> Take ye therefore good heed unto yourselves . . .
> Lest ye corrupt yourselves, and make you a graven image, the
> similitude of any figure, the likeness of male or female.
> The likeness of any beast that is on the earth, the likeness of any
> winged fowl that flieth in the air.
> The likeness of any thing that creepeth on the ground, the likeness of
> any fish that is in the waters beneath the earth. (Deut. 4:15–19)

---

*Later Jewish writers identified the Shekina as the feminine force. Her name does not appear until the first century A.D.

The traditional explanation for the Second Commandment is that it turns people away from worshiping other gods. This might be reasonable if Yahweh had only proscribed making graven images, but His injunction is all-encompassing: no likeness of *anything*. Why would drawing a bird in flight or a fish leaping in sunlight represent a threat to Him? The Second Commandment forbids Israelites from conveying *any* iconic information: no illustrations, no colorful drawings, and no art. So far as we know, there had never before existed a culture that forbade representative art. Why should a prohibition against making images be the second most important rule for righteous living? If the Ten Commandments were listed in order of their relative significance to society today, the Second would most assuredly be ranked last by most people, and the second place would be given to the Sixth, which states, "Thou shalt not murder." According to the Ten Commandments, art, therefore, is more dangerous than murder.

In the Old Testament, religious intolerance manifested itself primarily in an abhorrence of images. The word *idol* comes from the Latin *idolum*, which in turn derives from the Greek word for image, *eidōlon*. It wasn't the pagan *belief* in their gods or the *ritual* of their worship that inflamed Hebrew passions as much as their attachment to the images of gods. Throughout the Old Testament, all the major prophets and pious Israelites inveigh against the sin of idolatry. For example, in 2 Kings 10:30, Yahweh praises Jehu for murdering the priests of Baal because they worship idols; when the Israelites are ready to invade Canaan, He instructs them:

> Then ye shall drive out all the inhabitants of the land from before you, and destroy all their pictures, and destroy all their molten images, and quite pluck down all their high places. (Num. 33:52)

One explanation for the Israelites' intense hostility toward images is that, having discovered the immense utility of alphabetic writing, they considered iconic information to be a threat to their newfound skill. Learning to think without resorting to images is indispensable to alphabet literacy. "Make no images" is a ban on right-brain pattern recognition. All who obey it will unconsciously begin to turn their backs on the art and imagery of the Great Mother and, reoriented a full 180 degrees, will instead seek protection and instruction from the written words of an All Powerful Father.

The Third Commandment prohibits the utterance of the name of Yahweh. "Thou shalt not take the name of the Lord thy God in vain; for the Lord will not hold him guiltless that taketh His name in vain." Placed directly after the proscription of images, this Commandment reinforces the importance of words over icons. While images *of any kind* have been banned in the Second Commandment, Yahweh emphasizes the importance of words by forbidding the use of only one: His name. Since a worshiper cannot use images to honor Him, the only way to glorify Him is to use all the other words available. These reside in the domain of the left brain.

In Genesis, Yahweh's first instruction to Adam is not something practical such as how to make a fire or fashion a weapon. He teaches the first man to name all of His creatures. By this act, Yahweh emphasizes that naming is the most potent power He will confer on mortals. Through naming, Adam gains "dominion over all the earth."* Naming confers meaning and order. To name is to know. To know is to control.

The Fourth Commandment is a directive to keep track of time, "Remember the Sabbath day, to keep it holy. Six days shalt thou labor, and do thy work: but the seventh day is a sabbath . . ." Seven days are not a natural break point in any rhythmic cycle of nature except the quarter moon. Cloudy skies and the three days of the lunar cycle when the moon is not visible make moon watching a problematic method of reckoning seven days.[†7]

Counting off the days between Sabbaths was the simplest of the time-dependent Commandments contained in Deuteronomy. The math computations grow in complexity, and some require considerable rigor to calculate. For example,

> Six years thou shalt sow thy field . . . But in the seventh year shall be a sabbath of rest unto the land . . . And thou shalt number seven sabbaths of years unto thee, seven times seven years; and the space of the seven sabbaths of years shall be unto thee forty and nine years.
>
> Then shalt thou cause the trumpet of the ju-bi-lee to sound on the tenth day of the seventh month . . .
>
> And ye shall hallow the fiftieth year, and proclaim liberty through all the land unto all the inhabitants thereof. (Lev. 25:3–10)

---

*Visitors to prehistoric cave painting sites rarely come away without a feeling of awe. With consummate skill, Paleolithic artists imbued their images of bison, reindeer, and horses with the spirit of these animals and in some mysterious way gained a measure of control over them. But Yahweh did not teach Adam how to draw the likeness of animals. In this new word-based religion, the power previously imputed to the image has been transferred to the word.

†Modern researchers tell us that seven is the highest number in an arithmetic sequence that a majority of people can recall with consistency. This is the reason that telephone numbers contain only seven digits.

Since a jubilee was a joyous event and slaves were set free, even the down-trodden took a keen interest in this arithmetical exercise. No other culture at that time in history had ever instructed *all* its followers, not just a priestly class, to compute such complex time periods.

The Time Commandment lays the groundwork for the idea of justice, since a well-developed sense of linear time is necessary to conceive of pun-ishment delayed and reward postponed. Non-literate peoples are not as pre-occupied with the notion of justice as their alphabet-literate counterparts, because they do not conceive of time only as linear. A Judgment Day occurs *only* in literate cultures. Non-literate people tend to conceive of death as a passage to another world, *not* as a day in court. Alphabets stretch out the sense of time and make its users more aware of the possibility of retribution at a date far in the future.

People who became alphabet-literate also became aware of the possibil-ity of writing history: the chronological sequencing of events. Ahimaoz, the author of the Book of Samuel, preceded Herodotus by several centuries. Without any previous guides, he wrote a historical masterpiece that had dra-matic power, literary style, and psychological insight.

The Fourth Commandment would seem to have little to do with living an ethical life. Yahweh is really instructing his people to be aware of passing time, to count time, to celebrate time. Awareness of abstract time will be of crucial interest to all subsequent alphabet-based cultures. They will invent and then become mesmerized by sundials, water clocks, pendulums, escape mechanisms, cogs, gears, and calendars. Eventually a manacle wristband that tells the time—all the time will enslave them. Time, as I have pointed out, is the key feature of the left brain.

Each of the first four Commandments reinforces the ability of a people to think abstractly, linearly, and sequentially. Together, they encourage a mindset that enhances the use and facility of alphabet literacy. Learning the *aleph-bet* in turn strengthens the belief in the absolute rectitude of the first four Commandments. There have been other rules for conduct set down in other cultures. The first four Commandments cannot be found in the top ten of any other ethical list outside the West.

Suppose you were Moses, the leader of a small group of people who had discovered a technology you surmised could help weld them into a cohesive nation. Suppose you were a visionary and recognized that this new method of perception would have far-reaching effects on any culture that employed it. And, suppose you were confronted with the problem of how to persuade others to learn this new method. If you could invest written words with magic, you would substantially increase ordinary people's interest in them. Written words to the newly initiated are magical to begin with; it is only a short step to proclaim that they were the creation of an omniscient, omnipotent God. His message was in a secret code. Those who desired to be let in on the secret and release the supernatural power contained within the words had to learn to read and write. To eliminate any options, you would declare that the worship of images, the other principal means of perceiving information, was forbidden. God was stripped of any image. In fact, it was a terrible sin even to *try* to visualize Him. As Yahweh warned Moses, "Thou canst not see my face; for there shall no man see me and live" (Exod. 33:20). An Israelite could know Him *only* by reading what He had written. The written letter had replaced the graven image.

The Old Testament was a powerful social instrument that realigned culture. Many groups benefited; others suffered. The winners were the common folk, the poor, widows, orphans, slaves, Levite priests, the literate, warriors, lawyers, judges, prophets, farmers, businessmen, sons, fathers, husbands, and bigamists. Also celebrating were alphabet literacy, law, logic, justice, ethics, morality, dualism, democracy, conscience, and individualism. The losers were wives, prophetesses, queens, artists, daughters, female slaves, rape victims, sexually adventuresome persons, and priestesses. Images, beauty, nature, wholeness, tolerance, and intuition also experienced a decisive setback. Judaism was, and always has been, based on the steadfast worship of God through the medium of the written word. The Hebrews founded the first religion based on literacy, and for the first time in history, a people repudiated both the Goddess and the making of images in their art.

CHAPTER 10

ABRAHAM/MOSES

Deep within them I will plant my Law, writing it in their hearts.

—Jer. 31:33

Of all the great hybrid unions that breed furious release of energy and
change, there is none to surpass the meeting of literate and oral cultures. The giving to man of an eye for an ear by phonetic literacy is,
socially and politically, probably the most radical explosion that can
occur in any social structure.   —Marshall McLuhan[1]

The beginnings of Judaism mark a new chapter in the historical
record. What transpired before seems remote and disconnected
from Western sensibilities. Hurrian conquests, Mitanni quarrels,
and Egyptian rites do not speak to our hearts. The ancient Hebrews brought
into the human conversation a series of ideas that others had only tentatively
or briefly explored, and they also introduced some startlingly original concepts. The Hebrews shepherded these constructions of the mind through
the centuries until they spread out widely and eventually permeated Western consciousness.

Alphabetic literacy profoundly reconfigured the relationship between the
Hebrews and their deity and between the Hebrews and their neighbors. Their
sacred scriptures imbued them with such an unshakable faith that among the
Sumerians, Hittites, Hurrians, Cretans, Babylonians, Mitanni, Assyrians, Persians, Canaanites, Egyptians, Greeks, Phoenicians, and Romans, they are the
only people of antiquity whose fundamental belief system has survived the
scouring of subsequent centuries.* This occurred despite a litany of calamities
that should have extinguished them.

---

*There are still Egyptians, Greeks, and Romans but their current belief systems do
not resemble those they held long ago.

The origins of Judaism are important to this book's thesis because of the exclusionary First Commandment, proclaimed at a time when the Goddess still held a place of high regard in people's hearts and lives. That a religion was founded on the precept that a masculine deity created life without *any* female participation signaled that something had changed radically.*

One of the chief reasons that the Old Testament has retained its hold over the generations is its sheer readability. Even a nonbeliever can appreciate the text as literature. The concerns, predicaments, and responses of its characters reveal a deep understanding of human nature. When the ninety-year-old Sarah overhears God promising her husband Abraham that the elderly childless couple's progeny will become the multitudes of a new nation, she mocks God's assurance. Twenty-four years have passed since Yahweh first brought up the subject, and Sarah resents that her gullible spouse still believes. If Nefertiti scoffed at Akhenaton's obsession, or Hammurabi's wife thought her husband's "Eye for an eye and a tooth for a tooth" code was too harsh, neither history nor literature records such exchanges.

Other contemporaneous literate cultures did not reveal people's inner feelings. A stilted, sycophantic tone informs their writings. Royal scribes did not record the flaws and foibles of their leaders. The braggadocio of the pharaohs and the self-puffery of their minions and priests fail to elicit our sympathy. Unlike the legends and myths of Mesopotamia and Egypt, the Old Testament is as much about ordinary people as it is about exalted beings. What commends the ancient Hebrews to us is their unflinching honesty when reporting their leaders' and their own failings.

The young future patriarch Joseph, we are told, tattled on his brothers. Jacob's deceit, Noah's drunkenness, and David's perfidy diminish the reader's respect for each one. If the purpose of a national founding document is to engender reverence, why does the Old Testament include such debunking anecdotes? Perhaps the reason that these flaws have been so faithfully preserved throughout the ages is because they are true. The Old Testament's often critical portrayal of its protagonists makes it history's first relatively objective literary work. Objectivity depends on rational analysis. Use of an alphabet increases the left brain's ability to be objective.

The Old Testament is an anthology of disparate literary pieces ranging from poetry, proverbs, and wisdom literature to prophecy, revelation, and explicit laws. Its core, however, is its historical narrative. In this chapter, I will arbitrarily divide its chronicles into myth, legend, and history and look for

---

*Both the Egyptian gods Atum and Ptah created life without a female consort, but goddesses played prominent roles in their worship.

evidence of the alphabet's role as the Bible's éminence grise. The first part of Genesis—the story of Creation, the trials and tribulations of the progenitor family of Adam and Eve, through to the story of Noah—I will designate as mythological. Many of its themes, including key elements in the stories of the Garden of Eden, the Flood, and the Tower of Babel, were fables apparently appropriated from Mesopotamian culture.

The Book of Judges through the Book of Samuel provides a detailed account of the rise and fall of the Kingdom of Judea between 900 and 400 B.C. and has the true ring of history. The author(s) spin out compelling stories about the reigns of, among others, Saul, David, and Solomon. While the tales contain many moral lessons, the dramatis personae were most assuredly real people, and there is little question in the minds of most historians that these late narratives are based on real, not fictional characters.

The intermediate section of the Old Testament, between later Genesis and Judges, tells the stories of the patriarchs, the Egyptian Bondage, the Exodus, Sinai, the Covenant, the Wandering, and the Conquest of Canaan. Because none of these stories has yet been corroborated by any hard supporting evidence, I will designate these passages as legends.

Imagine that you were charged with compiling the founding story of your people. Undoubtedly, you would begin with the seminal events that distinguish your culture from others. A creation myth, inserted before the main story line, would be conjured *after* the crucial events that stimulated the need for a unique cultural document had been recorded. Biblical scholars believe the poetic first chapters of Genesis were composed by the Priestly author ca. 600 B.C.

The unknown authors of the Old Testament conjoined myth, history, and legend so artfully that it is impossible to tell where one ends and another begins. The legendary Abraham, Joseph, and Moses seem as real as the historical Saul, David, and Solomon. The distinction between the two narratives is that the earlier characters experience miracles; the later ones do not. Beginning with the account of Abraham, the story appears fresh, vivid, intricate, and does not seem mythological. Let us assume, for argument's sake, that the crossover from myth to legend begins with Abraham.

The Jewish people originated as an identifiable group in approximately 1800 B.C. in "Ur of the Chaldees." It was a period of prosperity and advances in all the arts and sciences. Through conquest and military alliances, Hammurabi was piecing together a flourishing empire of which Ur was a major part. Hammurabi honored learning and used the written word to declaim his famous legal code.

Among the polyglot of peoples living in Ur was a man named Terah who made his living crafting idols. Given the melange of religions practiced in Ur—Babylon was, after all, the model for the story of the Tower of Babel—Terah prospered. His artistic skill and political acumen brought him considerable respect. His profession involved carving sacred images onto blocks of wood, a calling that may have militated against Terah's developing a strong allegiance to any one particular cult. (An idol-maker working among competing deities most assuredly would be among history's first skeptics.)

The Old Testament fails to reveal the name of Terah's wife when reciting all the "begats." This seems a strange omission because Terah had three sons, one of whom was an imposing youth named Abram, who would later become Abraham, patriarch of all the religions of the West. The efflorescence of the arts in Ur would have exposed Abram to its rich offerings. Exercising an author's right to poetic license, I will speculate on what life would have been like for Abram growing up in Ur.

Because of his father's position, the precocious youth was able to learn how to write cuneiform. Sitting in his father's atelier practicing his syllabary lessons on clay tablets, Abram watched with bemused interest as foreigners with thick accents placed talismanic orders with his father. His perception altered by his learning, he was perhaps disdainful of the stacked idols in his father's shop, and looked down on those who believed that something man-made could emanate the spirit of the divine. Witnessing daily the transformation of mute timber into gods and goddesses, Abram might have experienced a growing aversion for idolatry.

At some point and for reasons unclear, Terah gathered up his family and departed Ur for Canaan to the west. Included in his little tribe was Sarai, the wife of Abram. The Old Testament tells us early on that "Sarai was barren, she *had* no child" (Gen. 16:1). Shortly after arriving in Canaan, Terah died, leaving Abram to head the small clan.

With his herds, Abram began a nomadic life as a merchant leader. From time to time, he rented grazing land for his cattle from Canaanite landlords, and by most accounts Abram and his hosts coexisted peacefully. Because of a drought, there was soon a famine in Canaan. He did not return to Ur but instead drove his herds in the opposite direction toward Egypt.

The cross-fertilization of cultures has always been the busy work of travelers, adventurers, and pilgrims, who carry the ideas of one culture to another like honeybees carrying pollen. While residing in Egypt, Abram would have been intrigued by his hosts' written language, so different from the cuneiform he had learned as a child. As the son of an artist, he marveled at the ability of hieroglyphs to convey ideas using aesthetically composed images. After an indeterminate amount of time, he returned with his wife and clan to live in Canaan.

Abram's travels afforded him the opportunity to observe the customs of different peoples and their religious idiosyncrasies. People who develop a cosmopolitan outlook become less loyal to parochial religions and tend to embrace more universal ones. Perhaps Abram's abstract theological musings, stimulated by his familiarity with the written word, persuaded him that there was, after all, only one God and He did not have an image.

Perhaps Abram took to the art of writing, having experienced two diametrically opposite methods to achieve the same end. Perhaps he played with the idea that there could be an even better way to write. Other Canaanites were also tinkering with a simpler means of written communication. Despite the efforts of these innovators, the entrenched Canaanite aristocracy did not acknowledge the value of their experiments. Canaanite scribes, having taken the trouble to learn the cumbersome Akkadian language, were reluctant to relinquish the power that accrues from restricting the flow of information. The archaeological record from Tel el Amarna indicates they continued corresponding in cuneiform.

Many epigraphers have argued that it is unlikely that the Hebrews used an alphabet before the Canaanites or Phoenicians because they have not uncovered concrete evidence. The small family of Hebrews and other, similar out-of-power groups had no loyalty to hieroglyphic and cuneiform scripts. Because they were constantly on the move, they controlled no cities, commissioned no monuments, and built no stone structures, so they did not chisel any writing for the future. It is worth noting that there is no lapidary form for the Hebrew alphabet. Whatever writing they inscribed was committed to parchment and animal skins, none of which survived. The absence of evidence, it must be remembered, is not evidence of absence.

After a long and prosperous life as a trader, mercenary, and herder, the ninety-nine-year-old Abram experienced an epiphany: he heard the voice of Yahweh. The Old Testament informs us that Yahweh "appeared" to Abram (Gen. 17:1) suggesting that he was a transitional character between image worship and word worship. At the time, Canaan was replete with religious cults. The principal ones worshiped the goddesses Anath, Asherah, and Astarte: well over 90 percent of votive figures recovered from Iron Age Canaan are representations of a female.[2] By 1500 B.C., the written record begins to indicate a shift in loyalty to a god called El who shared many of Yahweh's attributes but who ruled with a female consort, Asherah. At the time that the solitary Yahweh addressed Abram, there were no known living followers of Yahweh. Noah and even Methuselah, Yahweh's earlier champions, were long dead. Nothing in the historical or archaeological record of Canaan or anywhere in the Fertile Crescent indicates that any people worshiped Yahweh.

When He spoke to Abram, Yahweh (the god with no followers) informed the childless Abram (the man with no god) that one day his seed would grow into a multitude and his heirs would possess the land of Canaan. Twenty-four years passed and neither of these promises had come to pass. Again Yahweh appeared to Abram and this time He proposed a contract (Covenant). If Abram would give Yahweh unswerving allegiance, Yahweh would fulfill his earlier pledges. Yahweh told Abram that his issue will be ". . . as the dust of the earth: so if a man can number the dust of the earth, *then* shall your dust be numbered" (Gen. 13:16).

To seal the covenant, Yahweh demanded that males of this new faith set themselves apart by sacrificing the foreskin of their penises. The order must surely be the strangest quid pro quo in religious history, but seen in the context of a cultural and psychological shift to masculine values and patriarchy, this demand made cruel sense. By requiring circumcision, Yahweh eliminated the possibility that any females could actively participate in the Covenant. With no foreskin to offer, women became accessories, their power and influence effectively neutered. The aged Abram must have winced when he learned that a condition of the Covenant was for him to set the example. He agreed to the two conditions: fealty and circumcision, in exchange for Yahweh's two promises: nationhood and homeland. Abram assembled his clan and told them of the agreement he had just concluded. One can only imagine what went through the minds of his male relatives, farmhands, and slaves when they learned that circumcision was part of their obligation to their new deity, but biblical history suggests that everyone of consequence submitted. Yahweh told Abram and Sarai to change their names to Abraham and Sarah to mark their changed status, and they became the first Israelites.

Surprisingly, the Covenant between Yahweh and Abram was an oral agreement. Nothing was written either in stone or on parchment, although cuneiform had been in use for more than a thousand years in nearby Ur. Considering that contracts concerning such mundane matters as shipments of olive oil were routinely set in writing, it seems anomalous that neither Yahweh nor Abram legitimized their Covenant with such a document.

To Sarah's delight, Yahweh finally delivered on the first part of the pact. Upon learning that she was with child, Sarah became Yahweh's second enthusiastic convert. She exulted, "God hath made me laugh, *so that* all that hear me will laugh with me. Who would have said unto Abraham that Sarah should have given children suck? For I have borne him a son in his old age."

Abraham and Sarah doted on Isaac, their newborn son. Seeing what this child meant to his new worshipers, Yahweh decided to test Abraham's commitment by ordering him to sacrifice his son. Sarah was not consulted. Abraham felt compelled to do this terrible duty for his God, telling himself that fealty to Yahweh superseded his loyalty either to his only son or to his wife. As he tearfully prepared to slit his beloved child's throat, Yahweh stayed his hand, revealing that His order was but a test. Implicit in the story is Sarah's powerlessness in so grave a matter.

While repugnant to the modern mind, child sacrifice had an intrinsic, if grim, logic. Humankind had always striven to maintain some semblance of control over the random forces of nature by frequently petitioning the gods for favors. In the more prosaic congress between mortals, everyone understood that barter was necessary: if you coveted someone else's beads, you had to offer an item of equal value. When asking a god or goddess for a dispensation, barter was also appropriate but the stakes were higher. At the pinnacle of the scale of value would be one's firstborn child; no one could imagine anything more precious. If a family wanted to deflect its destiny in a truly propitious manner, they knew what they were expected to give up in exchange. The Yahweh of Genesis often appears harsh, yet on this crucial issue he held an extremely civilized view. *Thou shalt not commit human sacrifice* is but one of His many enlightened positions.

Isaac grew to manhood, married Rebecca, and together they had twin sons. Esau emerged from Rebecca's womb first. As the oldest, he would inherit his father's blessing. Jacob, the Old Testament tells us, followed Esau out of the birth canal clutching his brother's heel, and displayed a similar tenacity as an adult. While Esau grew into a vigorous outdoorsman, Jacob was a "sitter in tents" (Gen. 25:27), a peculiar phrase suggesting that Jacob preferred domestic and scholarly pursuits to the thrills of the hunt. In one story Jacob used his cooking skills to convince Esau to trade his birthright for a "mess of pottage." Jacob later deceived his dying father into bestowing his patriarchal blessing upon him, pretending to be his brother, the elder son. Jacob, therefore, not Esau, presided over the descendants promised to Abraham by Yahweh.

Jacob left home and journeyed to Haran and there he fell in love with Rachel. At the time, custom demanded that a man had to buy a bride (later, in the patriarchal world, a girl's family would give the groom a dowry). Because Jacob had no dowry, he labored many years for Rachel's father to earn her hand. Haran was influenced by the culture of Ur, the sophisticated center of Babylonian learning. Jacob would have been aware of the diverse offerings of this great city. Being Abraham's grandson, he most likely evinced a curiosity commensurate with his heritage.

Jacob returned to Canaan with two wives, tricked by Rachel's father into marrying her sister, Leah, as well. Leah bore him six sons and a daughter. Only after Leah's childbearing was over did Rachel bear him two sons, Joseph and Benjamin. Rachel died during Benjamin's childbirth. Tradition relates that young Joseph disdained physical labor. While his brothers worked in the fields as farmers and herders, Joseph preferred to stay home and dress in fine clothes. Despite this seemingly unmanly behavior, Joseph was his father's favorite. In an agricultural society, fathers need sons to plow and milk. Why dote on one who did neither? A scholarly father, himself a "sitter in tents," might be partial to a son who also enjoyed intellectual pursuits.

Jacob's preferential treatment of this one son, combined with Joseph's overweening arrogance toward his siblings, turned his brothers against him. When Jacob gave Joseph a magnificent coat of many colors, they became so enraged that they conspired to kill him. One day, they found Joseph alone in the fields far from home, and cast him into a pit. At the last minute, they decided not to kill him as planned, but instead left him to die of thirst and exposure. Returning home, the conspirators poured goat's blood over the coat of many colors, and told Jacob that Joseph had been eaten by a beast. Grief-stricken, the old man rent his own garments.

Joseph, meanwhile, had been rescued by Midianites who sold him to a caravan on its way to Egypt. Upon arriving in Egypt, Joseph was purchased by Potiphar, a minister of the royal family, who most assuredly would himself have been literate. Joseph's intellectual acumen soon became evident to his master, who rapidly elevated Joseph to the position of overseer of his entire estate. Although the Old Testament never mentions it, it would be safe to assume Joseph was skilled in the art of writing—Potiphar would not have put an illiterate in charge of his business affairs. Just when things were going quite well for Joseph, his good looks and intelligent mien entranced Potiphar's wife, who tried to seduce him. Joseph's rejection of her advances almost cost him his life.

Cast into the royal dungeons, Joseph extricated himself by his wits. His uncanny ability to interpret his fellow prisoners' dreams attracted the jailer's attention. He, in turn, mentioned Joseph's clairvoyance to someone connected to the pharaoh's court, and in an amazing change of fortune, Joseph soon found himself a trusted adviser to the pharaoh. His soothsaying and sagacious judgment so impressed the pharaoh that he eventually made Joseph the second most powerful ruler in Egypt.

And Pharaoh said unto his servants, Can we find such a one as this is, a man in whom the Spirit of God is?

And Pharaoh said unto Joseph, Forasmuch as God hath shewed thee all this, there is none so discreet and wise as thou art:

Thou shalt be over my house, and according unto thy word shall all my people be ruled: only in the throne will I be greater than thou. (Gen. 41:38–42)

Joseph warned the pharaoh that Egypt would enjoy seven years of plenty followed by a severe seven-year drought, and advised him to lay away a surplus in the state's granaries in anticipation of the famine. As he predicted, a grievous drought gripped the land after the bountiful years passed. As their food supplies ran low, the harried Egyptian farmers beseeched the pharaoh for relief. In return for the ownership of the farmers' lands, Joseph dispensed the prior years' largesse to the people.

And there was no bread in all the land; for the famine was very sore, so that the land of Egypt and all the land of Canaan fainted by reason of the famine (Gen. 47:13)

Wherefore shall we die before thine eyes, both we and our land? Buy us and our land for bread, and we and our land will be servants unto Pharaoh: and give us seed, that we may live, and not die, that the land be not desolate.

And Joseph bought all the land of Egypt for Pharaoh; for the Egyptians sold every man his field, because the famine prevailed over them: so the land became Pharaoh's. (Gen. 47:19–20)

Though the Egyptians were forced to trade their land for grain, they still fared better than the starving population of Canaan. The now aged Jacob sent his sons to Egypt to buy grain from Joseph, whom they did not recognize. Joseph had forgiven his brothers and bore them no enmity. Joseph's family moved to Egypt, and Joseph "nourished" them.

Joseph lived a long and prosperous life. Soon after his death, the pharaoh who had been his patron also died. The new pharaoh loathed the influence Joseph's relatives enjoyed and issued successive decrees that gradually eroded the Hebrews' status. Seeking to humiliate them further, he did nothing as the Egyptians robbed them of their possessions. Still not content, he ordered the Hebrews rounded up and deported to slave camps, where they could be worked to death. Despite these draconian punishments, the Egyptian aristocracy and throne continued to fear the Hebrews.

Why? This question has never been satisfactorily answered. The Egyptian masters outnumbered and thoroughly dominated their slave population. What special skill did the Hebrews possess that would so intimidate their masters? Let us contemplate this story. Theologians use it as a parable containing moral lessons. Historians and archaeologists have, for the most part, dismissed it as a fable. I propose an additional interpretation.

No one knows in what historical period the story of Joseph in Egypt took place, if indeed it took place at all. Nowhere in Egyptian chronology is there a record of a minister named Joseph or of influential Hebrews who were stripped of their power and enslaved. The Old Testament maddeningly omits the names of the two pharaohs, friend and foe respectively, who played pivotal roles in Joseph's story. Modern biblical scholars estimate that Joseph lived between the thirteenth and tenth century B.C. but these are speculations based on uncertain evidence.

In Chapter 11, I discuss the seventeenth century B.C. Hyksos invasion of Egypt. Let us assume that the Ishmaelite caravan that deposited Joseph in Egypt arrived during the reign of one of the Hyksos pharaohs who was better at conquest than administration. In a stroke of good fortune, the skills that the Hebrews had been nurturing in relative isolation proved extremely useful. Like the Hyksos, who originated in northern Canaan, Joseph was a Semite and an exceptionally gifted one at that. A Hyksos usurper would have been more inclined to trust one of his own ethnic kinsmen than a conquered Egyptian native. Throughout their history, the Egyptians were extremely condescending toward anyone unfortunate enough not to have been born an Egyptian. Joseph's meteoric rise from slave to vizier would have been highly unlikely in an Egyptian regime. The Old Testament story gains plausibility if Joseph's patron was a Hyksos king.

Joseph's extraordinary rise to power also suggests that he had excelled at some skill besides foresight and good sense. Mastery of the written languages of Mesopotamia and/or of Egypt would have increased his usefulness to the pharaoh. A stranger in a strange land who could converse with foreign emissaries and write in several different scripts was a valuable asset.* If Joseph served a Hyksos pharaoh, the date of the Exodus is three or four cen-

*The family of Joseph experienced the same heady success followed by calamity that adumbrated the Jewish viziers to the caliphs in the eighth century, the Jewish ministers to the Spanish kings in the fifteenth century, and the German Jews in the twentieth century. In every case, it was the Jews' facility with literacy that propelled them to the forefront of these cultures.

turies earlier than most scholars have speculated. A few specialists, such as Martin Bernal, Cyrus Gordon, and Donald Redford, have indeed proposed that the Exodus was coterminous with the Hyksos rule in Egypt.

The Old Testament records that the Egyptian people effusively loved Joseph. Human nature being what it is, they might have experienced a different emotion. Throughout history, losing one's farm to the government has engendered only bitterness. Joseph's role in the expropriation of private lands for the throne effected a massive transfer of Egypt's wealth. In the hardship of the drought, the seeds of revolution were planted, aggravated no doubt by a pharaoh who was also a Hyksos conqueror. Also, in caring for his brothers, Joseph would have likely made enemies. Resentment and envy always attend nepotism by those outside the family circle.

If Joseph was a contemporary of the Hyksos, we can understand why the Egyptians turned on the Hebrews so viciously after the death of the pharaoh. A powerful foreign minister serving under a Hyksos pharaoh would have inevitably accumulated enemies among the subjugated native population. If Joseph's death coincided with the revolt of the populace against the Hyksos rule, the Hebrews would quite suddenly have experienced an ominous turn of the wheel. After their triumph, the new Egyptian pharaoh and his loyal officers would surely have focused their fury on the Hyksos' alien advisers. Yet, even after enslaving the Hebrews, the pharaoh and his advisers still feared them. Urged by his court advisers, the pharaoh issued an edict that all firstborn sons of Hebrew women must die.

News of the pharaoh's decree leaked to the slave camp. One desperate Levite mother put her baby in a basket and set it afloat down the Nile River. The infant's cries from the basket, entangled in some bulrushes, attracted the attention of the pharaoh's daughter and her retinue. The princess claimed the child and named him Moses.

Moses spent his childhood among princes in the royal compound where they were taught the art of war and the skill of reading and writing hieroglyphs. Moses excelled in athletic competitions because of his imposing stature and strength, but the Old Testament reveals that he had two flaws: one was a speech impediment; the other was a hot temper. His stuttering made him avoid public speaking. By Moses' own admission, "I *am* slow of speech and of a slow tongue" (Exod. 4:10). Speech defects stimulate in those people who suffer from them an interest in alternative forms of communication, such as writing. There is no stammer in the written word.

One day, the young prince witnessed an overseer whipping a Hebrew worker and ordered him to stop. The taskmaster, angry that a member of the royal house would intervene on behalf of a slave, told Moses to mind his own business. A fight ensued and Moses killed the overseer. Fearing repercussions from this event, Moses fled the kingdom. Eventually he reached the homeland of the Midianites, the same people who had rescued Joseph.

Soon after Moses' arrival he came upon a watering hole where he encountered a group of men accosting women trying to draw water. A fight ensued and Moses prevailed. Upon learning of a stranger who had fought on behalf of Midianite women, Jethro, a high-ranking Midianite priest, encouraged Moses to wed his daughter Zipporah.* Moses cast off his royal upbringing and settled down to a pleasant life tending herds and helping Jethro, who would have likely initiated Moses into the Midianite worship of their fierce volcano god Jahve.†3

Midianites were caravaneers. They traveled through many lands and had a firsthand opportunity to observe and learn from the customs of others. Like the surrounding peoples, the Midianites were most likely experimenting with a new way of writing not unlike what Joseph may have learned from his father in Canaan. Epigraphers agree that the alphabet began somewhere in this area and the Midianites' home was the Sinai Peninsula, the same region where Petrie had discovered evidence of the oldest alphabet.

Out walking one day, Moses came upon a preternatural sight: a bush was burning on a hillside, yet the flames did not consume it. Suddenly, the thunderous voice of Yahweh addressed Moses from the fire. His divine voice had been strangely silent during the long suffering of His chosen people, who were still in Egypt, being punished by the Egyptians for, among other things, their unbending loyalty to Him. Indeed, this was the first pronouncement Yahweh had made to mortals since Joseph's death; according to the Old Testament, 430 years had passed.

Yahweh informed Moses that He had chosen him to liberate the Hebrews. Their suffering and contrition now made the time ripe for their deliverance. When asked by the astonished herdsman how he was to accomplish this feat, Yahweh told him to walk into the pharaoh's court and demand the Hebrews' release. If the pharaoh did not comply, Yahweh would intervene. As an added incentive, He assured Moses that He would make good on His promise to Abraham to provide a homeland for the Israelites. A reluctant Moses packed his things, left his wife, and set out on a hero's journey.

---

*This interfaith marriage involved a Hebrew patriarch and so goes against the religious tenets of the Hebrew faith, that the fact that it was recorded suggests it was true.

†Freud, among others, has pointed out the many similarities between Jahve and Yahweh.

An older and bearded man by now, Moses was not immediately recognized at court. Upon gaining an audience with the pharaoh, Moses ordered him to let his people go and warned of dire consequences if their freedom was not immediately granted. The court's surprise was followed by derision. If Yahweh was a proper god, the Egyptians asked, why did He let His people languish for so long, ignoring their supplications? Why should Egypt, the most powerful empire the world had ever seen, have anything to fear from this invisible desert god who, up to then, had not performed a single miracle known to them. Furthermore, they asked, what kind of god would send a speech-defective litigant to represent Him? The Hebrew's petition seemed ludicrous in the extreme, and the pharaoh refused it.

Yahweh then unleashed a series of increasingly troublesome plagues upon the land—vermin, frogs, boils, cow disease, darkness, and a blood-stained Nile—and still the pharaoh refused to free his slave-labor force. Finally, Moses warned the pharaoh that the Angel of Death would pass over the city at night, killing all the Egyptians' firstborn sons. Although fast becoming convinced he was dealing with something supernatural, the pharaoh still refused to relent. Moses then hurried down to the slave camps, where he instructed the Hebrews to sacrifice a lamb, drain its blood, and use the blood to daub an X on the doors of their own dwellings. Yahweh's Angel of Death would *pass-over* each marked house, sparing their firstborn sons.

In the morning, a terrible communal wail rose up throughout the kingdom, as Egyptian parents discovered their children dead in their beds. A grim pharaoh, whose family had not been spared, summoned Moses and commanded him to gather his people and depart immediately. Exultant, Moses hastily assembled the Hebrews and the Exodus began.

After traveling for some days, they came to the Sea of Reeds, which blocked their passage. The Hebrews' growing anxiety concerning their new leader's sense of direction was compounded when they saw that an army, led by the pharaoh, was closing in on them. Pharaoh was determined to recapture his former slaves. Caught between the impassable sea and an onrushing army, Moses appealed to Yahweh, who responded by parting the waters, allowing the Hebrews to cross the seabed. When the pharaoh's army attempted to follow, Yahweh caused the walls of waters to rush back together, drowning both the pharaoh and his troops.

Following this harrowing escape, the Hebrews embarked upon their forty-year journey through the inhospitable terrain of the desert. When they arrived at the base of Mount Sinai, Moses asked his brother Aaron, a man noted for his oratorical gifts, to be his spokesman in his absence.

Moses himself ascended the mountain for his second audience with the imageless God. In return for Moses' faith and because of His love for His people, Yahweh bestowed a precious gift upon the Hebrews: Ten Commandments engraved on two stone tablets written by the finger of Yahweh* (Exod. 32:15–16).

After his dialogue with Yahweh, Moses descended the mountain with the tablets under his arms. Arriving back at the camp, he discovered to his great consternation his people genuflecting before a statue of a heifer. During Moses' long absence the Hebrews had become restless without their leader and had besieged Aaron with requests to fashion an idol for them to worship. They pooled their gold jewelry and, after melting it down, had crafted a golden calf.

Enraged that his feckless charges had reverted to the worship of an image—a practice that Yahweh had expressly forbidden—Moses raised his arm as if to strike, and the stone tablets clattered to the ground and shattered. Furious, Moses destroyed the golden calf, rebuked Aaron, and reprimanded the people. When the Hebrews' first written words confronted their last image, the resulting collision destroyed them both. The allegorical conflict between word and image could not have been more dramatically expressed. Observing this commotion, Yahweh took Moses aside and instructed him to make a duplicate set of tablets. For the next forty days and forty nights, pausing neither to "eat bread or drink water," Moses wrote while Yahweh dictated (Exod. 34:27–28). This important passage implies that Yahweh taught Moses how to write the alphabet.[†]

Chastised, the Hebrews pledged themselves to honor Yahweh's Commandments, and changed their name to the Israelites. They placed the precious tablets in the wooden Ark and carried these linear abstract markings deep into the desert. The Covenant Yahweh first struck with Abraham was now committed to writing, as befits all binding contracts. At Moses' direc-

---

*Yahweh's choice of the *uleph-bet* in the writing of the Ten Commandments is the first acknowledgment of an alphabet's existence in the literature of the region. There are no references in Canaanite or Phoenician alphabetic writings to suggest that they considered the use of this new form of communication revolutionary. Neither does the introduction of the alphabet play any significant role in their myths.

†The people noticed that after Moses' return from his fateful meeting with Yahweh, his face had changed so that none dared look upon him. He wore a veil for the next forty years. The man credited with giving the Word to his people, like his solitary deity, lost his most identifying image—his face.

tion, the Ark was set before the people and its doors were periodically opened. The Hebrews adopted a reverential stance in the presence of Yahweh's divine words.*

The Hebrews remained in the desert for forty years, preparing for their conquest of Canaan. Since the distance between Egypt and Canaan can be crossed by car in two and one-half hours, the question arises—what took them so long? Talmud scholars interpret this question as follows: Yahweh understood that after generations of captivity the Israelites had developed a slave mentality. They would have to shed this mind-set if they were ever to conquer the well-entrenched Canaanites. Yahweh instructed Moses to keep his people in the Sinai for two generations, long enough to breed a third generation, which would not have known the shackles of slavery. These youths would constitute the nexus of an army that would build a new nation. When at last the Israelites could see the distant ramparts of Canaan's southernmost outposts, the aged Moses transferred his command to Joshua, a child of the new generation.

Exhausted from old age, Moses' last act was to write down on a scroll all the important events that had happened to the Hebrew people. He then ordered them to *read* the entire scroll, section by section, in sequence and on a regular basis, so that this written document would be burned into memory.† Moses died within sight of the land of Canaan and was buried in the desert. His popularity was so great, and he was so grievously mourned, that Yahweh took measures to ensure that the Israelites could not worship him as a god: his remains were interred at an unknown and unmarked site.

Assuming the mantle of leadership, Joshua led the desert-hardened Hebrews across the border, and they successfully attacked the well-defended Canaanite settlements. Despite his youth, Joshua's military tactics were brilliant. As each Canaanite bastion fell, Yahweh told Joshua to put all the men, women, and children to the sword, sparing only the virgin girls, who were to be absorbed into the Israelite nation.

---

*After four thousand years, the tradition continues. On every Jewish sabbath and religious holiday, the Ark is opened and the rabbi removes the sacred scrolls, carrying them through the midst of the congregation. Each worshiper has the duty (and the chance) to kiss the written word as it passes.

†In the reign of Josiah (421 B.C.) these long lost directions were rediscovered and were used to form the basis of modern Jewish ritual. Some historians believe that the temple priest Ezra actually wrote this section and attributed it to Moses.

In many passages from the Old Testament, the Canaanites had not been hostile to the Israelites: they had rented grazing lands to Abraham, had desired to marry Jacob's daughters, and in a friendly gesture, had sold the cave at Hebron to the foreigner Abraham so that he might bury Sarah. Yet, because the Canaanites worshiped images, Yahweh commanded His Israelites to slaughter them.

On one level this war was about the possession of territory—nothing new to the student of history. The massacre of the defeated was also nothing particularly extraordinary in the bloodstained chronicles of the human race. What distinguished this episode of savagery is that for the first time in recorded history, an innocent people was exterminated because another people were consumed with religious zeal.

The ostensible rationale for the war between the Canaanites and the Israelites can be simply put: the former worshiped their gods through their use of images, the latter worshipped their God through the medium of written words. Words triumphed in this first of many confrontations between pictures and text.

CHAPTER II

THERA/MATZAH

Why is it continually inferred that the age of the "pagan" religions, the time of the worship of female deities (if mentioned at all), was dark and chaotic, mysterious and evil, without the light of order and reason that supposedly accompanied the later male religions, when it has been archaeologically confirmed that the earliest law, government, medicine, agriculture, architecture, metallurgy, wheeled vehicles, ceramics, textiles and written language were initially developed in societies that worshiped the Goddess? —Merlin Stone[1]

Let us return to the enigma surrounding the date of the Exodus. The first mention of Israel in the Egyptian record is by the pharaoh Merneptah, whose reign began in 1219 B.C. His scribes recorded how he laid waste its many city-states in Canaan, including one they identified by the name Israel. The Exodus, therefore, must have occurred earlier.

In most academic circles, dates for the Exodus oscillate between the thirteenth and eleventh centuries B.C., but many of the mysterious events surrounding the birth of the Hebrew nation can be explained in scientific terms if the Exodus is moved back several centuries.

Perhaps the crucial clue in establishing the correct date is the cluster of miracles recorded in Exodus. For the sake of argument, let us assume they occurred but were *not* the result of divine intervention. We have no reason to doubt that the Hebrews faithfully recorded what they saw, but because of their lack of sophistication in scientific matters, we should examine with care their *interpretation* of what they observed. When Aborigines in Australia first saw an airplane overhead, they accurately described it but imputed to the aircraft a preternatural spirit. A similar confusion may have affected the ancients of the Mediterranean.

If we assume that the events described by the Hebrews in the Bible are real, we need to identify a cataclysm in the historical and archaeological records that could explain the strange happenings in the natural world that occurred in conjunction with the Exodus. Plato passed along a story he heard from even older sources about an ancient civilization they called "the lost continent of Atlantis." According to legend, there was once a very advanced island culture that suffered a sudden, devastating calamity and disappeared under the waves.[2]

Recent research by geologists has provided corroborating evidence that an enormous natural disaster occurred in the ancient Mediterranean. A volcanic eruption that dwarfed the combined might of Mount Saint Helens, Mount Etna, and Krakatoa engulfed the Mediterranean's eastern region. This cataclysm spewed ash, ore, rock, and flaming cinder high into the atmosphere and is believed to have consumed the island of Thera southwest of Greece and seventy miles north of Crete. The present-day cliff town of Santorini, perched on the caldera's rim, looks down on what remains of the archaic island. Geologists surveying the remnants of Thera—a five-mile-diameter water-filled crater surrounded by a circle of smaller islands—have reconstructed what happened as a result of this immense volcanic event they are convinced occurred in 1628 B.C.[3]

During the eruption, tsunamis (tidal waves) and earthquakes brought an abrupt end to many civilizations in the area.* Low-lying deltas, such as the one at the mouth of the Nile, were particularly vulnerable. Chaos and anarchy in the aftermath of the devastation toppled rulers from Minos to Mycenae. People trembled under skies that turned dark at noon. As the ash and smoke blocked out the sun, crops withered. Falling sulfuric ash produced pestilence and boils among herds and humans, and cattle fell dead in their pastures. The circadian rhythms and reproductive cycles of frogs and "vermin," such as locusts, are set in most cases by solar cycles, and could have been completely upset by the sun's sudden dimming, resulting in massive swarms. The high iron ore content of the raining cinders would oxidize upon contact with water, turning rivers red and killing all marine life; it could well appear that the waters had turned to blood.

There would have been nothing in the affected people's collective memory that would allow them to put the largest natural disaster in recorded history in its proper context. If a stable government such as the Minoan one on nearby Crete came to an abrupt end, as it is presumed it did because of

*The Mount Saint Helens eruption, small compared to that on Thera, dimmed the sky over areas 700 miles away. Krakatoa's blow in Indonesia in 1888, also much less powerful than Thera's, produced tidal waves 100 feet high, killed thirty-six thousand people, and its blast could be heard 2,000 miles away.

Thera's blow, how would people living in Egypt, 500 miles downwind, interpret the earthquake(s) and dark clouds of pumice that harried them?[*][4]

Many archaeologists are convinced that Thera and mythical Atlantis were one and the same.[†][5] Volcanic eruptions are associated with increased earthquake activity and the loss of life is much higher among people who live in stone dwellings than among those who live in wooden houses. It would not be surprising that royal Egyptians, including their firstborn sons, would perish in an earthquake that reduced their palatial stone structures to rubble, while an enslaved population, huddling in humble thatched huts made of papyrus reeds and mud, would survive. The people of Egypt could not have witnessed the destruction of Thera directly and its fallout could have been thought to be the action of a vengeful Hebrew God.

There is no mention in official Egyptian chronicles of a disaster on such a violent scale, but an Egyptian papyrus fragment, the Ipuwer Parchment, of an uncertain date, describes just such a natural calamity.

2:8 Forsooth, the land turns round as does a potter's wheel.

3:13 All is ruin!

7:14 The residence is overturned in a minute.

2:5–6 Plague is throughout the land. Blood is everywhere.

2:10 The river is blood.

6:1 No fruit nor herbs are found . . .

6:3 Forsooth grain has perished on every side.

5:5 All animals, their hearts weep. Cattle moan. . . .

4:3, and 5:6 Forsooth, the children of princes are dashed against the walls.[6]

If Exodus occurred at the end of the Hyksos rule, and the eruption of Thera occurred at the same time, the biblical account is explainable as history. Such a scenario also accounts for the Egyptians' failure to corroborate the Hebrews' dramatic narrative. Applying this chronology, it would have been a few centuries *after* the overthrow of the Hyksos and the escape of the Hebrew nation that Akhenaton instituted his sun-centered monotheism. In his monograph *Moses and Monotheism*, Freud speculated that the Hebrews had received their idea of monotheism from a former priest still loyal to

---

*Leon Pomerance, a retired executive and amateur historian, was one of the first to connect the events during Exodus and Thera's eruption.

†Interest in the lost continent of Atlantis is so pervasive that there have been 21,000 relevant articles, including 7,000 books, written on the subject.

Akhenaton's vision of one god. "Moses" is, as Freud pointed out, an Egyptian name, not a Semitic one.[7]

But suppose it was the other way around—suppose it was the Hebrews who inspired the Egyptians. Soon after the reign of the Hyksos, Egyptian writing underwent its first major revision in fifteen hundred years. Could the simplified hieratic script that emerged at the beginning of the Eighteenth Dynasty have been the result of Egyptians' becoming familiar with a new abstract writing form introduced by the Hebrew Hyksos advisers? Alphabets predate the Hyksos reign. Why wouldn't a pharaoh, familiar with a new method of writing and the single-god worship of foreign advisers, be influenced by these trends?*

Akhenaton, whose word was literally law and whose birth was divine, could not impose monotheism on his people. How, then, did the stammering leader of a wandering desert tribe manage to persuade his flock to worship one, nameless and invisible god? How did he generate a love and respect for the written word that would lead his people to embrace a democratic, universal code of laws based on righteousness and justice? The answer, I believe, is the edge given to them by their knowledge of the alphabet.

The similarities between Moses' character and his exploits and those of Abraham suggest the possibility that the Old Testament contains two distinct stories characterizing two distinct Hebrew nations, annealed so that they seem to be one. It is as if there were once twin brothers who lived in Canaan. One departed to go down into Egypt while the other stayed home. The first twin experienced unimagined success and then bitter travail, climaxing in a burst of miracles and epiphanies. Returning to Canaan he rejoined his long-lost brother and together they defeated the Canaanites, appropriated their land, and renamed the conquered portion, Israel.

But something profound had happened to the wandering twin during his time in Egypt, and the twin who had stayed behind in Canaan no longer felt at ease with him. The adventuresome twin was proficient in a new form of written communication, was imbued with radical ideas, and had a new sacred book that told his story. To assuage the discontent felt by the stay-at-home twin, his brother incorporated into their life story a, perhaps fictional, narrative about a man called Abraham. This Abraham was acclaimed as the leader of the people who had remained in Canaan: in this metaphor he rep-

*It is telling that of all the names Akhenaton must have considered for his new deity, he chose Aton. The Semitic name for Lord was Adon. The Jews continue to refer to God as Adonai.

resents the twin who is the equal of the twin who had left to go to Egypt. In this alternative interpretation of an ancient story, Abraham represented Yahweh's promise, Moses His fulfillment.

This twin theory becomes one credible way to understand the history of the early Israelites. The melding of these two political entities, Canaanite Hebrews (Abraham) and Egyptian Hebrews (Moses), into a single nation eventually failed. They soon split into two contentious tribal entities. The southern kingdom, closer to Egypt and the Sinai Desert, adhered to the radical implications of pure monotheism. The northern kingdom, based more on the religion and ethics of Canaan, maintained a relaxed attitude toward polytheism and goddess worship. Perhaps this division explains the two distinct early voices in the Bible: J, extolling a strict monotheist point of view, and E, expressing a pluralist one. These irreconcilable differences may have sundered and polarized the kingdoms. And perhaps it explains why Abraham appears to be the doppelgänger of Moses.

The essential feature that divides these two patriarchs is alphabet literacy. The art of writing is not mentioned in the Old Testament until the appearance of Moses. Statements about writing and reading dominate the narrative thereafter, and the crucial characteristic distinguishing Moses from Abraham is that one lives by the written word and the other relies on the spoken oath.* Considering that the defining experience of Moses' reign was the introduction of a complex code of laws written in alphabetic form, many subtle morality tales could have been expected to accompany his story, the purpose of which was to reduce the power of the Goddess, women, and images. Indeed, these tales proliferate as soon as the Israelites begin their protracted desert trek.

One of the most hallowed traditions concerning the Wandering is that while journeying for forty years under the searing Sinai sun, the Hebrews ate matzah, a dry, flat, and all but tasteless unleavened cracker known as the "bread of affliction." Matzah has the corrugated, scorched appearance of desiccated desert wadis through which the Hebrews undoubtedly passed. The Hebrews were forced to eat matzah because, according to the Old Testament, they left Egypt so precipitously that the women did not have time to secure a supply of yeast to leaven bread (Exod. 11:39).

Yet, as the Hebrews were leaving Egypt, Moses instructed them to visit the homes of the wealthy Egyptians and ask for their jewels and clothes.

---

*Elohim is the name of God until writing enters the story. Not until then does God reveal to Moses his Yahwist name in the form of the Tetragrammaton YHWH (pronounced Yahweh) (Exod. 3:13–14).

> And the Egyptians were urgent upon the people, that they might send them out of the land in haste; for they said, We be all dead men.
>
> And the people took their dough before it was leavened, their kneading-troughs being bound up in their clothes upon their shoulders.
>
> And the children of Israel did according to the word of Moses; and they borrowed of the Egyptians jewels of silver, and jewels of gold and raiment . . . (Exod. 12:33–36)

If there was time for gathering jewelry, it would appear a dereliction of a woman's duty not to secure yeast, an essential staple.

Yeast is a metaphor for things of the earth that rise and grow: children maturing, grain stalks shooting up, the tumescence that signifies male sexual desire—all rise. Growth is implicitly associated with the female. Dough, composed of four elemental feminine symbols—water, salt, grain, and yeast—becomes the quintessential foodstuff called "the staff of life." Dough rising slowly in an oven is metaphorical for a baby growing in a mother's womb; "a bun in the oven" in modern parlance. In all emerging agricultural societies, kneading dough and baking bread were acts symbolic of fertility. Made of grain—the sacred gift of agriculture—bread baked by a mother for her family combined earth, hearth, and love.*

Jewish communities around the world have slightly different versions of the Passover ceremony, but eating matzah and forgoing leavened bread is an unbroken tradition harkening back millennia. The symbolism of unleavened bread subtly devalues an important female contribution to culture, and indirectly demotes the role of the Goddess.

Virtually every cult, sect, culture, and religion has a spring ritual that celebrates the female themes of fertility, birth, resurrection, renewal, and the return of nature's gifts. The Exodus marks the beginning of the Hebrew people's rebirth and their rededication to the principles of their religion. Yet, the leitmotifs of the Passover story are deprivation, deliverance by a male deity, swearing fealty to Him alone, and the hardships of the Wandering, all of which glorify male ethics and values. This most important myth surrounding the birth of a distinct culture contains neither a single major female participant nor any statement of the themes of resurrection, fertility, sexuality, and the fruitfulness of the land.† Even the fact that the Ten Commandments were given to the Hebrews when they were wandering supports

---

*The Greek Goddess Demeter revealed the secret of bread to mortals.

†Miriam is the only female character in this drama. Despite her early heroism and courage, Yahweh turns her into a leper for speaking her mind (Num. 12:10).

a patriarchal ethos: the lands that honored the Goddess were agricultural and, by necessity, settled; nomadic societies, made up of herders and hunters, lived more by an ethic based on virility.

Another tradition that has survived these many centuries also has to do with grain, though obliquely. For many people, a bounteous waving field of ripening wheat is associated with a healthy, wavy head of hair, just as long, thick, lustrous hair and dense vegetation are both connected with sensuality and are associated with the mystery of a woman. Waves of grain and waves of hair merge together in our dreams, poetry, and unconscious. Young women devote considerable time and energy to their hair, intuiting that a gorgeous crown will enhance their sexual attractiveness.* The mirror image of this phenomenon can be observed when many women past menopause crop their hair. Hair length is entwined with sexuality and she who possesses long hair signals her fertility to potential mates.

In the Old Testament's tale of Samson and Delilah, Samson derives his extraordinary strength from his long mane. Delilah, a Philistine, robs him of his strength by having his hair cut while he sleeps. One could well imagine that something other than his hair was being metaphorically clipped. Castration neutralizes manhood. Curiously, Samson's hair has been invested with the power usually attributed to testosterone. However, a woman's power lies not in her physical prowess but in her sexuality, which holds both the promise of male pleasure and the ability to bring forth new life.

If Samson had shaved Delilah's head, her womanhood and allure would have been severely compromised, and she would have been profoundly humiliated. Women undergoing chemotherapy leading to baldness have uniformly reported that they experience a precipitous loss of self-esteem principally because their sexual identity as women has been damaged. After the Liberation in World War II, citizens loyal to the Free French shaved the heads of young women who had collaborated or cohabited with the Nazis during the Occupation; the punishment fit the women's crime, which had been to grant sexual favors to foreign invaders.

What, then, are we to make of the ancient Israelite demand that a bride shave her head immediately upon becoming a man's wife? No similar convention applies to the bridegroom. After shaving her scalp, a married woman must wear wigs or scarves for the rest of her life. Would not a young

---

*Any parent of a teenage girl will attest to the simultaneous appearance of pubescent hormones and a teenager's obsessive self-absorption with the appearance of her hair. While similar changes occur in boys, this preoccupation is more pronounced in young women.

woman submitting to this practice while in the full flush of her sexuality feel like Samson? Wouldn't this symbolic castration place her at a disadvantage in the inevitable power struggle that occurs during the establishment of a new relationship? The shock over the loss of something as personal and vital as her entire head of hair would certainly make her more dependent and compliant. Cut off both literally and figuratively from a source and potent symbol of her woman-strength, the new bride would be malleable to her husband's will. The men of the first culture based on the alphabet were also the first in history to demand that their married women shave their heads.*[8] Like eating matzah, this strange rite has a very long history and has survived to the present day among Orthodox Jews.

The great Earth Mother's most generous act had been to generate food from seeds placed in the ground. There was little food in the story of the Wandering but the Israelite people did not go hungry in the wilderness. In one of the weirdest miracles recorded in the Old Testament, Yahweh providentially rained *manna* down from the sky. Manna was delicious and sustaining, and was born of a complete inversion of normal biological ordering. Instead of food pushing up from beneath the ground, manna fell to earth from the sky. A male sky god that can nourish an entire population from above usurps a principal function previously performed by the Goddess. And as Yahweh displaced the very earth that had been responsible for sustaining them, soil, also previously associated with the Goddess, came to be reviled. The new Israelite religion became very concerned with cleanliness, with an aversion to dirt and other "unclean" things.

Pigs are smart, friendly animals that thoroughly enjoy wallowing in the dirt. Deuteronomy forbids members of the Israelite faith from eating or keeping pigs, which is the first time in history a group had, using the force of religious doctrine, collectively condemned this member of the swine family. Apologists have claimed that the Old Testament was protecting the Israelites from eating an animal that commonly carried the trichinosis parasite, but the many other cultures that based their diet on pig meat did not suffer decline. Halfway around the world, the people of the Pacific Rim considered pigs to be sacred because they were so plentiful in sustaining them. The Germanic tribes that overran Rome thrived on ham. The Israelites' intense animosity toward this domesticated animal cannot be explained on the basis of hygiene alone.

---

*The second alphabet culture, the Greeks, had a similar rite. In the fourth century B.C. the goddess Artemis, in Euripides' play *Hippolytus*, orders young women to "cut off their hair" on the eve of their marriage.

Across the spectrum of cultures, soil has been associated with the Earth Mother.* Animals that enjoy immersing themselves in dirt have traditionally been under the aegis of the Goddess. The pig, a symbol of fertility in many cultures, was Demeter's favorite animal; a sow often appeared at her side. Artists portrayed Isis, the Egyptian goddess of fertility, giving birth on the back of a pig. In the wild, packs of roaming pigs are led by the oldest sow, making pigs one of the few animal societies that are organized as a matriarchy. A rotund animal that thrives in mud, grows quickly, and is very fertile can serve as an appropriate metaphor for pregnancy. Proscribing the pig was yet another way to diminish female power.

Prior to the Old Testament, there did not exist any society that prevented women from conducting significant sacraments, but the first religion based on a book, and all subsequent Western literate religions, banned women from officiating over important ceremonies.† With the sudden rise of literacy, the requisite spirituality necessary to conduct a religious ritual became the sole province of males.

Before the appearance of the Old Testament, sexuality played *the* central role in virtually all creation stories. Tiamat and Apsu, Uranus and Gaia, El and Asherah all coupled. Even the Egyptian god Atum masturbated in order to create the world. But Yahweh went about His act of creation with no mention as to how He did it. No kneading of raw material, no conjoining of sexes: it was a *creatio ex nihilo*—a creation from nothing.

All the words and metaphors associated with creation—*conception, gestation, ingenuity, labor, prolific, seminal, prodigious, genesis, genius, profligate,* and *productive*—evoke sexuality or a woman giving birth, but Yahweh replaces sexuality with an act of will encoded in words. The very first lines of the very first lesson of this revolutionary religion, when Yahweh commands "Let there be . . . ," concern the overarching importance of *logos.*

---

*The Goddess's association with freshly turned earth is revealed in an episode from Greek mythology. During the marriage festivities of Cadmus and Harmony, Demeter, the original agricultural Earth Goddess and the mother of Zeus, pulled Iasion, a handsome youth, out into a freshly plowed field. Lying on her back in a damp furrow, she urgently coupled with him. When the two lovers tried to rejoin the other revelers, pretending that nothing had happened, Zeus, seeing his mother's mud-caked flanks and buttocks, surmised what had occurred and killed Iasion on the spot. Besides the Greeks, many early cultures had rituals where couples copulated in furrows prepared for planting, to ensure that the Goddess would bless them with fertility.

†There were a minuscule number of exceptions to this skewing: Deborah, Huldah, and Miriam, for example.

CHAPTER 12

ADAM/EVE

Because Adam and Eve are characterized as they are, human history
and social relationships are set in order in such a way that certain possibilities are excluded.
—John Phillips[1]

The innovations of monotheism and Rule by Law, combined with the
abrupt repudiation of *all* female deities, created considerable confusion concerning the relationship between men and women. The
Bible reflects this disarray. The obligation to create a society in which every
individual, including a slave, must be treated with a new sense of dignity had
to be balanced against the need to eradicate female power, epitomized by
Goddess worship.

The women who appear in the Old Testament are notable for their mul-
tifaceted personalities. For example, Sarah, Rachel, Miriam, Deborah,
Judith, Jezebel, and Delilah exhibit real-life traits common to the human
condition. Nevertheless, in a seminal book over seven hundred pages long,
the demolition of women's status begins on page 2 and is essentially completed on page 3. Gender relations is the *first* issue raised *and settled* after the
creation of the universe, which suggests its priority for the author(s). J and
E, the earliest authorial voices in Genesis, represent two diametrically
opposing views. In the E version, written one hundred to five hundred years
after J, the Supreme Being created man and woman in His image at the same
moment—affirming that the sexes are equal. Since the Old Testament makes
monotheism and anti-iconism the subject of the first two Commandments,
the allusion to creating mortals in Elohim's image instead of His nature
reveals E's inclination toward an older, iconic polytheism.

J, the uncompromising monotheist, informs us that Yahweh created
woman only as an afterthought because Adam could not find a suitable
"helpmeet" among the animals. According to J, Yahweh molded her from
one of Adam's ribs. In a survey of human anatomy a single rib is superflu-

ous. Each human is born with twenty-four to twenty-six of them; removing any one has little or no effect on the health or muscular function of the individual so inconvenienced. Had Yahweh chosen to fashion woman out of an eye, a lung, or a right hand, her value would certainly have been enhanced. That Yahweh should make a woman from an inconsequential rib does not augur well for this gender under the new alphabet regime.

Virtually all buildings, from tepees to temples, contain a structural element that resembles the human rib. From struts and studs to pillars and posts, they all serve to hold up and strengthen the grand features of the edifice. A single rib's function contributes a small part to the strength of the entire rib cage.

By using Adam's rib as raw material for Woman, the Yahwist author influenced, however subliminally, all subsequent readers of the Bible. They could not help but deduce from this familiar story that a woman's function in life was to support a man. Earlier, in the more egalitarian Sumerian culture, the word for life, *ti*, also meant "rib." In the new alphabet-based culture, an alternative meaning for the biblical Hebrew word for rib, *Tsela,* was "stumbling," which seems to debase women further.[2]

After woman has been created, J tells the story of the forbidden fruit, which further diminishes women's place in society. Yahweh instructs the first couple to make themselves at home in His Garden of Eden and to enjoy its delights—with one exception: they are not to eat of the fruit of the Tree of Knowledge "lest they die." Enter the Serpent, cast as a villain, but actually the only character in this morality play who speaks the truth. The Serpent tells Eve that partaking of the Tree of Knowledge's fruit will *not* cause her death; instead, the Serpent says, "In the day ye eat thereof, then your eyes shall be opened, and ye shall be as gods, knowing good from evil." Intrigued by the prospect of such a wondrous gift, Eve "took of the fruit thereof, and did eat, and gave also unto her husband with her; and he did eat."

The omniscient Yahweh pretends not to know what has transpired. When He confronts the first man with his breach of discipline, Adam blames the first woman. She confesses, but claims that the Serpent had beguiled her. Faced with the three culprits, Yahweh first curses the Serpent, pronouncing, "I will put enmity between thee and the woman." In every earlier culture, the snake was one of the Goddess's most potent power symbols: Yahweh's first disciplinary act was to sever this ancient connection.

Turning to Eve, Yahweh pronounces, "I will greatly multiply thy sorrow and thy conception, in sorrow thou shalt bring forth children and thy desire shall be to thy husband and he shall rule over thee." Eve's lot and that of all women thereafter was to suffer pain and possible death in childbearing, and irrevocably *lose her freedom for life.* Later, in the Decalogue, the last Commandment would list her among her husband's property, along with his ass and house. The biblical Hebrew word for wife, *beulah*, meant "owned."[3]

Lastly, Yahweh sentences Adam and all his descendants to labor for their food, and tells him that they will die, "for dust thou *art* and unto dust shalt thou return." The message is clear. Because of Eve's transgression, humans would know pain, hardship, suffering, and death. In a turnabout with far-reaching consequences for Western womanhood, woman who had been primarily associated with life in all previous cultures, was now blamed for the death of every mortal.

Of the three, Eve's punishment was the most severe. She alone, among the planet's myriad creatures, would bear children with great difficulty and high mortality, and she lost her freedom permanently.* The Old Testament dictates that masters must emancipate their slaves after seven years of servitude (Deut. 15:12) but women are to serve a lifetime of subjugation. This sentence appears excessive in light of the circumstances under which Adam and Eve disobeyed God. Eve's decision to transgress was made *before* she had eaten the magic fruit, when she could not even have known the difference between good and evil. A few passages later, Cain kills Abel. Cain knew good from evil (due to his mother's actions), yet Yahweh treats him with the unmistakable compassion of a parent disciplining a wayward but beloved child. Yahweh banishes Cain, but when the youth protests, Yahweh reconsiders and marks Cain's forehead to protect him from harm. In these two morality tales less than one page apart, Yahweh judges murder by a man a less egregious crime than disobedience by a woman.

Yahweh knew that Adam and Eve were childlike in their innocence. Confronted by a minor, a judge will take into consideration the offender's inexperience. Why didn't Yahweh temper his punishment for Adam and Eve to more appropriately fit their crimes? Had Eve let her fear of retribution overcome her desire *to know,* then the travail and triumph called the human experiment would have never begun. Curiosity is indispensable for the acquisition of wisdom, the search for which is at the heart of the Jewish culture that arose from the Old Testament. Yet in the very first interaction between mortals and their deity, Yahweh branded female curiosity the greatest sin. Much later, in the New Testament, there would be a listing of the seven deadly sins—curiosity is not among them.

*In Chapter 5, I pointed out that one of the turning points in human development was precipitated by the limitation on intelligence imposed by the size constraints of the bipedal hominid's female pelvis. The increasing need for bigger-brained babies resulted in mothers dying during childbirth; it also produced the most intelligent animals. Higher consciousness was traded for high death rates among mothers.

After Yahweh expels the first couple from Eden because of the woman's "stumbling," Adam, exercising the power invested in those who name, renames Woman "Eve," which means "Mother of all Living." This was an honorific used to describe the Great Mother. Unlike the Great Mother, however, Eve is clearly not divine: she is the *mortal* mother of all living *mortals*. By this subtle artifice, the feminine is stripped of its sacrality.

Woman's new name, Eve, is also rich with meaning. Eve's name in Hebrew, *Haweh*, and J's biblical tetragram of God's name, *Yahweh*, both derive from the Hebrew verb *to be*.[4] Haweh also closely resembles *Hewya*, which is Hebrew for serpent, and *Hawa* is the Hebrew verb *to instruct*.[5]

Although She is never mentioned, the Goddess—the missing consort of God—is an unseen presence in Genesis. When Yahweh states that He is a jealous god, a reader might be prompted to ask, "of whom?" And when Yahweh refers to Himself as "Us," to whom does He refer?* The entire thrust of monotheism is that there is only one god; why then does the *One* speak of *Himself* in the plural? Who is the other divine presence that would comprise an "Us?" One alternative possibility: perhaps the figure is the Great Mother.

Throughout the Old Testament, Yahweh and His prophets inveigh repeatedly against the goddess Asherah. Asherah was the original, all-powerful *Magna Mater* of archaic Canaan. While she continued to maintain a prominent place in Canaanite religion, El, her male consort, gradually appropriated her power until by the start of the third millennium B.C., he became Canaan's chief deity. Their daughter, Astarte, then ruled with Baal, and they became the succeeding female and male consorts. They were also the reigning Canaanite sacred couple in the time of the Old Testament. The people's devotion to Astarte did not anger Yahweh as much as their worship of the older, more primordial Asherah: there are forty entries in the Old Testament condemning the worship of Asherah but only nine for Astarte.[6]

The story in Genesis of the creation of woman and the trouble she caused seems designed to convert those members of the Israelite nation who still held the Goddess in high regard. Archaeologists have recovered many female talismanic figurines from Iron Age Israel; male figures are almost nonexistent.[7] Their presence suggests the deep entrenchment of feminine values in Israelite culture and the impediments a new religion, based on the written word, would have encountered in eradicating feminine influences, images, and worship. A sacred book that details how mischievous and

---

*For example, after learning that Adam and Eve have partaken from the fruit of the Tree of Knowledge, Yahweh exclaims, "Behold, the man is become as one of us, to know good and evil."

worthless women are would be a powerful means of advancing, at women's expense, the fortunes of both the left brain and literacy.

After He expelled Adam and Eve from Eden, Yahweh performed a series of destructive miracles—heavy rains, floods, and firestorms—feats other male storm gods in the region could also do. But beginning with the story of Abraham, Yahweh crossed over the line that had previously separated divine masculine and feminine functions. Yahweh assured the Patriarchs that their seed would populate the earth with heirs who would be as numerous as the sand at the seashore or the stars in the heavens. And yet the first three Hebrew patriarchs, Abraham, Isaac, and Jacob, all married women who, initially, were barren. Disappointed with their inability to fulfill their destiny as mothers, Sarah, Leah, and Rachel encouraged their husbands to mate with their handmaids. These successful couplings produced children, confirming that it was not the males who were the cause of the women's infertility. The Scriptures make it very clear that the future mothers of the Hebrew nation, not the fathers, were deficient.

In every other culture of that time, barren women appealed to a goddess to heal their blight, but in the Old Testament Yahweh took over the task. Beginning with Sarah's improbable pregnancy, J continues to hammer home the point. "And Isaac entreated the Lord for his wife [Rebekah] because she was barren. And the Lord let himself be entreated of him and Rebekah conceived" (Gen. 25:21). "And the Lord saw that Leah was hated, and he opened her womb" (Gen. 29:31). "And God remembered Rachel . . . and opened her womb (Gen. 30:22–23). Even Eve acknowledges Yahweh's role in her conception, "I have gotten a man with the help of the Lord" (Gen. 4:1). Conception, that most invisible and mysterious act, previously associated with woman and the Goddess, was henceforth deemed a male's job.

In every earlier and contemporaneous religion, the principal male deities ruled with principal female consorts. If coupling was the normal state of affairs between gods and goddesses, who then, we may ask, was Yahweh's consort? As historian Tikva Frymer-Kensky points out, she was the nation of Israel itself. Beginning with Moses and continuing with the Prophets, conjugal metaphors are used over and over again to describe the relationship between Yahweh and His chosen nation. Both Jeremiah and Deutero-Isaiah identify *Zion* as the mystical spirit of the Israelite nation; she is personified by the beautiful city of Jerusalem. Many times they use "Israel," "Zion," and "Jerusalem," interchangeably with "bride," "wife," "spouse," "harlot," "beloved," "adulterer," "mother," and "daughter." Jeremiah calls Israel by turns "lovely and delicate," "my people-girl," and the "wanton wife." The prophet Amos, lamenting the destruction of the Northern Kingdom, refers to it as "Israel-maid." Expressing Yahweh's wrath at Israel's "adulterous" liaisons with foreign gods, Hosea writes,

> Plead with your mother, plead: for she is not my wife, neither am I her husband: let her therefore put away her whoredoms out of her sight, and her adulteries from between her breasts. Lest I strip her naked, and set her as in the day that she was born, . . . For she has played the harlot. (Hosea 2:4-7)

Prophets attribute the catastrophes visited upon Israel as retribution for Israel's metaphorical "whoredom" with other gods.

For five generations beginning with Abraham, Yahweh actively participated in the lives of His chosen People, but after Joseph's death, for reasons that are never made explicit, He abandoned them to slavery. The Egyptians enslaved the Hebrews chiefly because they refused to be assimilated into the Egyptian religion. This steadfastness should have pleased Yahweh, but despite the Hebrews' supplications, He remained indifferent for 430 years before finally selecting Moses to secure the freedom of His chosen people.

This is one example of how the metaphorical relationship between Yahweh and Israel resembles what Frymer-Kensky calls ". . . a nightmare of domination in a punitive relationship."[8] The husband is demanding, controlling, and capricious; the woman is long-suffering, obedient, and loyal. Yahweh lavishes his wife, Israel, with promises and attention, only to abandon her without explanation. In the period of Egyptian bondage, she becomes prey to merciless foreign predators. This scenario has been repeated throughout history. The agents who bring woe, rapine, and enslavement to the hapless, wifely nation of Israel do not even believe in Yahweh. They worship strange gods, yet Israel never asks why Yahweh, who claims to love her, does not avenge her or destroy them; instead, she patiently accepts the convoluted explanations of Yahweh's prophets and rabbis and blames herself. In His turn, Yahweh tolerates the Assyrians, Egyptians, and Romans so that they can properly punish His chosen nation for violating His tenets for worshiping strange gods. The atrocities committed by these dark forces against the people of Israel are grossly disproportionate to her petty sins.

If the Goddess reemerged in the Hebrew patriarchal system in the person of the Israelite nation, what happened to Her sexuality? Under the new regime of alphabet literacy, men learned to sublimate; they projected their sexual desire onto *Sophia,* a feminine noun meaning "wisdom." Appearing in the fourth century B.C., after Hellenizing influences had infiltrated into Judaic culture, men begin writing with passion about their desire for knowledge, using metaphors referring to male-female relationships. The author of the first century B.C. Wisdom of Solomon aches to mate with Wisdom.

> I loved her above health and beauty, and chose to have her instead of light, for the light that cometh from her never goeth out.
> For she is more beautiful than the sun, and above all the order of stars: being compared with light, she is found before it.
> I loved her, and sought her out from my youth, I desired to make her my spouse, and I was a lover of her beauty. (Wisd. 7:7, 10, 21–27, 29; 8:2)[9]

So, too, the author of Proverbs 4:5–6, 8–9:

> Acquire wisdom, acquire discernment;
> do not forget and do not swerve from my words.
> Do not forsake her and she will guard you,
> love her and she will protect you.
>
> Hug her to you and she will exalt you;
> she will bring you honor if you embrace her.
> She will adorn your head with a graceful wreath;
> crown you with a glorious diadem.

Tikva Frymer-Kensky comments,

> The figure of Wisdom as a woman expresses the profound pull of devotion to scholarship. Desire for learning is a lust: it is a compelling attraction that can absorb a person deeply, that can consume a person's life and desires, and can (in our language) supplant or suppress the libido. The male scholars of antiquity expressed the magnetism of this drive by representing wisdom as a female. But the erotic metaphor is aimed at *men,* as Wisdom states explicitly in Proverbs 8:4: "To you, O men, I call, and my voice is towards the sons of Adam."[10]

While Wisdom is always feminine, none of these writers seeks feminine wisdom. None aspires to intuition, prophecy, or woman-knowing; they all long for book learning! With the rising importance of alphabet literacy in Jewish culture, young men are instructed to turn their eyes away from desirable young women and instead, pore over written words. In one of the strangest aberrations to occur in the 3,000,000-year-old human condition, men substituted dry scrolls in place of a woman's beauty.

The subtle and not so subtle metaphors of the Old Testament and the wisdom literature that followed suggest that Canaan was not the only entity the Israelites conquered: the *aleph-bet* broke the spirit of women and banished the Goddess.

Let us now step back and review these last six chapters concerning the Jews. Throughout history, a new way of communicating has precipitated a major upheaval in the way people perceive reality. Anthropologists mark the advent of speech as the dividing line between hominids and humans; I have proposed that the introduction of writing completely reconfigured early agricultural civilizations. The printing press and, more recently, the photograph, telegraph, telephone, radio, television, and computer have profoundly transformed civilization. Yet, with the exception of speech, while all the improvements in information transfer changed and continue to change the direction of human enterprise, they were and are *not* as revolutionary as the alphabet was to its time. The ability of large numbers of ordinary working people to learn reading and writing formed the basis of Western civilization. Accurately identifying the alphabet's inventors can explain much of what transpired at the beginning of our history.

The Hebrews were older than the Greeks; the Old Testament is older than the *Iliad*. Moses was not only a great lawgiver and champion of Yahweh, he appears to have been the first wordsmith. Because of Moses' trials and achievements, the Hebrews imprinted the future with their history, their unique concept of monotheism, and their Rule by Law. I propose it was they who bequeathed the alphabet to the Canaanites, who then taught it to the Phoenicians, who then transmitted it to the Greeks. And the rest, as they say, is *his*tory.

CHAPTER 13

CADMUS/ALPHA

Knowing letters is the best beginning of understanding.
—Ancient Greek student's tablet[1]

There is no such thing as an isolated mythical event, just as there is no
such thing as an isolated word. Myth, like language, gives all of itself
in each of its fragments.   —Roberto Calasso[2]

The surge in law, art, ethics, knowledge, and philosophy that has characterized Western culture resulted from the confluence of two very
different sources. The first emerged from the Sinai Desert; the second from the widely separated islands of an archipelago sprinkled across the
Aegean Sea. The extreme contrast in topography between these two sites,
and their immensely differing political circumstances, determined that they
would be opposed on many issues. Concerning one, however, they were in
full agreement: the need to usurp the power invested in female deities.

Israel and Greece were the first two cultures that unreservedly embraced
the alphabet. Like the Israelites, the Greeks revised their mytho-history to
disempower women. Since alphabets tend to disorient a culture coming in
contact with this revolutionary new means of communication, the Greek
mythomania was no more a conscious effort than had been the Hebrews'.
There is a certain sexist symmetry between Homer and Hesiod on the one
hand and the Hebrews on the other. Rather than begin by searching their
creation story for clues about the Goddess's downfall, the place to start is
with a more fundamental myth: the story of Prince Cadmus, the mythical
hero who introduced the alphabet to the Greeks.

The tale begins with a rape. Europa, the daughter of the Phoenician king
of Sidon, disappeared while picking flowers along the seashore. Attracted by
her beauty and purity, Zeus, the chief Olympian god, had lusted after her.
Using one of his protean ploys, the god of gods disguised himself as a white

bull. Dazzling Europa with his magnificence and feigning docility, Zeus lured her into the shallow water, where he enticed her to mount his broad back. Once she sat astride him, Zeus bellowed out his true intentions and plunged into the deep water with Europa clinging precariously to his neck. Indifferent to her cries of alarm and entreaties he carried her off to Crete, where he ravished her. Europa's anguished father, knowing only that his daughter had been abducted, dispersed his five sons all across the Mediterranean in search of her. Prince Cadmus sought her in Greece.

According to the myth, Cadmus, while searching for Europa, stumbled on a cosmic altercation. Zeus and Typhon, the terrible serpent, were engaged in a battle to the death; the winner would rule the universe. Typhon had overcome Zeus by tearing out the Olympian's sinews, and the other Olympians fled in terror when they saw their leader disabled. Enter the puny mortal, Cadmus. Distracting Typhon with flattery and music, he allowed Zeus to regain his sinews, and then stood back while Zeus slew the monster with his awesome thunderbolts. Unprecedented in a Greek myth, a mere mortal, lacking the superhuman strength of a Hercules (and a foreigner no less), intervened in a battle of titanic proportions, saved the day for the Olympians, and earned for himself their respect and gratitude.

In a variation of the story, Cadmus spent months wandering all over Greece seeking his sister. In despair, he consulted an oracle that advised him to abandon his quest and acquire a cow instead. He was told to whip this creature to keep it moving, and at the place where the cow would drop from fatigue, he was told to sacrifice it. The oracle predicted that at this spot Cadmus would become a mighty king. Distracted from the original purpose for his journey, Cadmus did as he was advised.

The exhausted cow collapsed near a spring at a place called Thebes; there, Cadmus slit her throat. He soon learned that a dreaded serpent guarded the city's water source, keeping the local inhabitants in constant fear. In this version of the story, Cadmus slew the terrible serpent himself. Then, surveying the monster's sinuous body, he opened its mouth and extracted its fangs, sowing them in a nearby field. From each tooth (allegorically each letter) sprang a fierce warrior. The people of Thebes, reveling in their deliverance, rewarded the Phoenician prince by making him king.

This story contains the essential facts about the alphabet's arrival in Greece. Herodotus retold the same story in the fifth century B.C., but without its mythic trappings. Modern epigraphic researchers have confirmed that the Phoenicians brought the alphabet to the Greeks. The Cadmus myth, however, contains embellishments that underscore the letters' alliance with patriarchy.

In Cadmus's tale, as in the Old Testament, the serpent plays the villain's role. Remember that until the appearance of the written word, a writhing snake had been a graphic symbol of female sexual energy and power. Shortly after writing's acceptance across the ancient world, male heroes dispatched serpents in order to acquire knowledge or to gain power. Marduk became omnipotent by defeating Tiamat, whose form was a sea snake. In Egypt, Ptah defeated the loathsome serpent, Apophsis. In Canaan, El defeated the dreaded sea monster, Yam. Later, Baal slew Lotan, another sea serpent. Apollo, the god whose sacred gift was the alphabet, gained control of the important function of foresight by slaying the terrible she-snake Python, guardian of the Delphic Oracle. Perseus killed Medusa, a sorceress with a head of snakes instead of hair. Medusa's most powerful weapon was her image: any man who gazed on her turned to stone. But at the dawn of literacy, Medusa met the fate reserved for all she-serpents.

Biblical scholars have identified Psalms 74 and 89 as the two oldest passages in the Old Testament. Each psalm tells a Creation story that predates Genesis in which Yahweh gains dominion over the universe by killing Leviathan (or Rahab), both sea serpents. The universe, therefore, must have been created by some other entity, perhaps Leviathan.

To all these myths, Cadmus adds a peculiar refinement. He extracts the serpent's teeth. Fear of castration has given rise to many men's speculation that lurking just beyond the lips of a woman's vulva lies a row of sharp teeth. *Vagina dentata* have appeared in Picasso's art and Freud's psychology, and they crop up in numerous coarse jokes men tell among themselves in an attempt to alleviate their own neurotic anxieties. That these teeth do not exist is irrelevant; men, in their nightmares, fear that they do. In the Greek myth, the hero who brought the alphabet to Greece also extracted the dreaded fangs of the female's totem.

A human has twenty-eight teeth, plus four wisdom teeth that erupt later in life. There is approximately the same number of letters in any alphabet. A line of soldiers on parade, a row of finely aligned teeth, and the neatly arranged letters of an alphabet marching across a page all resemble one another enough to be connected in our myths and dreams.

Metaphorically, letters perform the same function as teeth. Writing can tear the wholeness of nature into small bites. Scientists use words to dissect and digest the universe. Lawyers and judges hone words to tease apart minute distinctions in the law. The proliferation of Western laws, science, and philosophical inquiries are rooted in the alphabet's incisive features. Incisors perform a similar function during mastication.

Alphabet-induced thought patterns permeate every facet of the culture

Vagina dentata in Picasso's
Seated Bather (1930)

adopting this form of writing, even those aspects seemingly far removed. For example, a key innovation in Greek warfare was the phalanx. Instead of rushing pell-mell at the enemy, a typical method of attack, Greek hoplites lined up in a horizontal row in which the shield of one warrior protected the flank of the soldier beside him. They marched in rehearsed unison, appearing to the enemy as a clanking, armor-jointed centipede walking sideways, bristling with spears. A single metal shield bears a striking resemblance to a single tooth—a row of abutting shields (as in a phalanx) resembles both a row of teeth and a line of letters.

The Cadmus myth also reaffirms another feminine connection. The Phoenician hero intuited that the serpent's fangs were the source of its wisdom and power. At a deep level, our psyches associate rooted teeth and profound wisdom. The people of most alphabet cultures refer to the late-erupting back molars as "wisdom teeth." Enamel is the hardest substance any living thing produces. Why is one of the most abstract of concepts— wisdom—attached to the most adamantine body part? Many would attribute this colloquialism to the late appearance of these molars—at the age of eighteen or so, when one may arguably be ready to acquire wisdom. On the other hand, many parents might think it more appropriate to call these molars the "impetuous teeth," or the "messy-bedroom teeth," or "sex-crazed teeth." Wisdom is rarely conferred on teenagers, and is more likely to be attained by those who are old enough to be losing their teeth.

The connection between teeth and wisdom concerns the intuitive wisdom of women. At the Delphic Oracle in ancient Greece, the always-female Pythian priestesses ingested venom extracted from the fang of a poisonous snake. In modulated doses, this poison induced an altered state of consciousness, otherwise inaccessible to ordinary mortals.[3] The tooth of the serpent, often combined with other mind-altering drugs, enabled these women to tap into something mysterious, and prophecize. The serpent in Genesis, remember, is coiled around the Tree of Knowledge. The association among teeth, serpents, women, and wisdom is a very old one.*

Cadmus "planted" the teeth in the ground, and in so doing, inverted the life-affirming growing cycle to be death-dealing instead. Rather than food that would have replenished Thebes, these "seeds" grew soldiers who sprang from the ground eager to kill. In this myth, the male obsession with death substituted warriors for stalks of the Great Mother's sustaining grain: hunter/killers had infiltrated the chthonic realm of gatherer/nurturers.

After Cadmus became the king of Thebes, the gods presented him with a goddess to marry. Harmony was the beautiful daughter of Ares and Aphrodite. That the gods gave Cadmus an immortal wife speaks to the importance the Greeks attached to his immortal gift, the alphabet. There were many mortal heroes in ancient Greece: Hercules, Perseus, Jason, Odysseus, and Theseus, to name a few. But the gods rewarded only Cadmus in this way. During the festivities that followed Cadmus's and Harmony's vows, Zeus humiliated his mother, Demeter, by killing Iasion, the youth with whom she had lain in a freshly plowed furrow. Zeus degraded the goddess of the earth at a celebration of the alphabet's triumph.

Recall that the Cadmus myth begins with a bull raping Europa. This is another instance of the remything that occurred in the wake of the alphabet. Along with the snake, the bull was the Goddess's other most potent totem. To the modern mind, this may seem odd: a bull's capacious chest and virility seem the essence of masculinity. His snorting and pawing the ground when squaring off before macho matadors, and chasing young men keen to test their courage down Pamplona's narrow streets, seems to affirm the bull's masculinity. But when a bull's head is viewed frontally, its horns and skull together bear a striking resemblance to a female mammal's reproductive organs—a uterus with its two fallopian tubes each extending to a side.

---

*Part of an initiation ritual among some American southwestern Indians is to be bitten by a venomous snake. Those who survive are reputed to have gained great wisdom about the workings of the world.

Long ago, the slaughtering of animals was a common activity. Disembowelling, cleaning, and dressing a fresh kill were among the first skills elders taught their young. It is unlikely anyone remained unfamiliar with the wondrous, convoluted system of hidden tunnels and secret openings secreted in the female's pelvis.* Animistic cultures sought to connect the mysterious womb so central to their lives with a totem they could venerate. The bull became the Goddess's totem.

In ancient myths, bulls often lived underground or under the sea—both locations associated with goddesses. Pasiphae, the daughter of King Minos of Crete, fell in love with a white bull the gods had given her father for the purpose of sacrifice. After engineering a reprieve for the handsome beast, she had Daedalus, the master craftsman, design a hollow, cow-shaped contraption into which she wedged herself. She enticed the bull to copulate with her, but the gods cursed the result of their union. The Minoan Minotaur was a frightful creature, half-man and half-bull. Confined to a labyrinth deep below the palace at Knossos, it was fed live human sacrifices. The association between the dark passageways that line the female's reproductive tract and mazes such as the Minotaur's labyrinth is ancient.

Poseidon, the Olympian god of the sea, presided over what had traditionally been considered the quintessential feminine essence: water. Many bulls inhabited his home in the deep. The image of a bull inside a body of water or in an underground labyrinth is evocative of the female's reproductive organs. In the myth that precipitates Cadmus's fateful journey to Greece, a bull carries a terrified young woman out to sea on his back. Initially, she trusted the intentions of a creature that had been associated with her gender for eons. Zeus chose to rape her at Crete, the island culture consecrated to the Goddess. Europa's violation by a feminine totem is allegorical: it is the incident that initiates the mythical transfer of the alphabet from Phoenicia to Greece. With the beginning of alphabetic writing, women would have reason to fear the bull, which came to represent lustful virility. In Picasso's twentieth-century rendering of the Minotaur, his monster was more interested in ravishing women than he was in devouring men.

Georgia O'Keeffe, the twentieth-century artist, is best known for two distinctly different images. Her sensual flowers resemble women's external genitalia—luxuriant orchids and black irises are anatomically correct renderings of the labia majora, labia minora, and clitoris. Her other most familiar image is her head-on view of a steer's skull and horns. At first glance,

---

*The exact opposite condition holds today. Most people in an urban society have only the vaguest idea of the location of their internal organs.

these bone paintings seem unrelated to her sensual, vulvar flowers. But on reflection, the bull's skeletal cranial remains with its bone splinters outlining a tubular oral chamber hollow intake that leads to a swelling pear-shaped skull, from which protrude two horns—is strikingly similar to the female mammalian reproductive tract with its vagina, womb, and two fallopian tubes. The evocative imagery of both Georgia O'Keeffe's bleached bulls' skulls and her lurid floral vulvas can be interpreted as the modern artist's rendering of the ancient connection between the bull and the feminine.

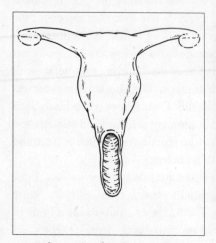 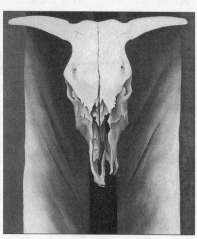

Schematic of vagina, uterus,   Georgia O'Keeffe's *Cow's Skull—Red,*
fallopian tubes, and ovaries   *White, and Blue,* 1931

The Semitic alphabet represented an advance over the earlier Linear A and B syllabary scripts with which the Greeks had haltingly experimented.* Still, letters remained difficult to read because of ambiguity concerning pronunciation. The Greeks refined the consonantal Semitic alphabet by inventing seven new letters to stand for vowels and reduced the number of letters to twenty-four. The new Greek alphabet was extremely user-friendly and it enabled the Greeks to achieve very high literacy rates.[†]

In the eighth century B.C., Homer transcribed the oral epic *The Iliad.*[‡] Homer's work glorifies masculine values and denigrates feminine ones. Its main focus is the deeds of men, and the story line is drenched in male-death

---

*In a syllabary, signs signify individual syllables of words rather than letters that signify single phonemes.

[†]Some historians believe the Semites invented the vowels.

[‡]Milburn Parry has explained how this oral poem became a written one.

consciousness. Male heroism, deceits, and travails are told crisply with frequent descriptions of death and battle scenes. Mortal women play minor roles and seem unable to influence events. The covenant stated throughout is this: if men are willing to die a hero's death, their names will be immortalized in poems that will be retold long after they are gone. As every college freshman is well aware, the terms of this contract have been fulfilled.

The *Iliad* begins in the middle of a war between the Achaean Greeks and the Trojans. Achilles and Agamemnon argue over whom shall have exclusive sexual rights to a young girl captive, Briseis. A high-born Trojan, she was now merely a spear bride, to be given or taken away at Agamemnon's whim. The ostensible reason the Greeks attacked Troy was because of another woman. Paris, a Trojan prince, abducted Helen, who was the wife of Menelaus, the Spartan chieftain. Menelaus entreated his brother Agamemnon to help him rescue her.* Many historians believe the real reason for the war was for the control of Troy, which was situated along a trade route leading to the lucrative East. But Homer does not cast the story in *Realpolitik*. Instead he blames the conflict on the *image* of a woman. Helen, Christopher Marlowe later penned, had "the face that launched a thousand ships."

The argument between Achilles and Agamemnon betrays the Greeks' frustration and frayed tempers. After ten long years of fighting, the war is at a stalemate. To break it, Odysseus proposes tricking the Trojans into believing that the Greeks have wearied of the fight and left. The Greeks pretend to lift their siege, board their ships, and appear to set sail for home. But they leave a massive, wooden horse as a peace offering in front of the Trojan gates. Hidden inside are Greek warriors.†

Cassandra, the Trojan king's daughter, urges her father not to let the horse into the city, but he ignores her warning.‡ Convinced that they have won the long war, the Trojans take in the horse. A huge celebration follows. The Greeks listen quietly until the silence outside assures them that the Trojans have fallen into a drunken sleep. When they slip out and open the gates to admit the Greek army, pandemonium ensues.

The image of warriors waiting silently and patiently within the belly of

*There are several conflicting versions of how Helen was abducted.

†The stories of the Trojan horse, the end of the war, and the enslavement of the Trojan women are not told in the *Iliad* but they were part of a cycle of stories. Virgil's *Aeneid* gives the best accounting of the rest of this very ancient tale.

‡A sacred serpent at the Oracle of Delphi darted its tongue into Cassandra's ear when she was a child, endowing her with the ability to foretell the future. Fearful of a mortal who possessed this skill, Apollo cursed her. Cassandra retained her clairvoyance, but Apollo's hex ensured that mortals would never follow her advice.

a wooden horse is a peculiar literary construction. Living beings within the abdomen is the fundamental image of pregnancy. Instead of fetuses nourished within a mother's womb, these are armed warriors who become agents of death upon their "birth."

There are other sexual metaphors. The Trojans, who can be perceived as the "women" of the story, open their "gates" to allow in the huge, stiff, wooden horse which turns out not to be a gift but a rude conqueror who "rapes" Troy. From Achilles's pout over being denied the slave girl, Briseis, to the enslavement of the Trojan women after the city's destruction, much of the *Iliad* can be seen as a story about men's need to control women and their reproductive organs.

In the beginning of the *Iliad*, Agamemnon sacrifices his daughter, Iphigenia, to obtain a favorable wind for the Greek armada's sail to Troy. Homer neatly balances Iphigenia's sacrifice at the beginning of the *Iliad* with the sacrifice of Polyxena, the daughter of the Trojan king Priam, at the end. Iphigenia's death keeps alive the tragic destiny that haunts the House of Atreus: Orestes, her brother, will murder his mother Clytemnestra to avenge his mother's axe-murder of his father. This long epic begins with a father sacrificing his daughter and ends when a son kills his mother.*

Within a hundred years of the *Iliad*, a dour farmer named Hesiod composed the *Theogonis*, which was a genealogy of the gods.† This third book written in an alphabet has a virulent misogynist bias. An example is Hesiod's tale of Pandora, the Greek counterpart of Eve. As Hesiod tells it, Zeus brooded over Prometheus's unauthorized gift of fire to mortals and sought revenge. He created women as malevolent, irritating companions for men.

> The deadly race and tribes of womankind,
> Great pain to mortal men with whom they live,
> Helpmeets in surfeit—not in dreadful need.
> Just as in ceilinged hives the honeybees
> Nourish the drones, partners in evil deeds,
> And all day long, until the sun goes down,
> They bustle and build up white honeycombs,
> While those who stay inside the ceilinged hives
> Fill up their bellies from the others' work,

---

*Homer's *Odyssey*, transcribed later, deals more sympathetically with women than does the *Iliad*.

†There are some classicists who believe Hesiod predated Homer.

> So women are a curse to mortal men—
> As Zeus ordained—partners in evil deeds.
> For fire's boon he made a second curse.[4]

This second curse was Pandora. Zeus gave her as a wife to the slow-witted Titan, Epimetheus, and then entrusted him with a box containing the ills of the world. Disobeying her husband's orders to leave the box untouched, Pandora opened the lid and released a collection of evil spirits, which, from that day forward, wreaked havoc on the world.* In punishment for her disobedience, Zeus sentenced Pandora and all her daughters to experience difficult childbirth. Having demonstrated the untrustworthiness of her gender, she—and all women yet unborn—were to be dominated by their fathers and then by their husbands.

Pandora disobeyed the order not to open the box because she desired knowledge. Her crime and punishment mirror Eve's in Eden. Both stories have the same purpose: to denigrate women, demote the Great Mother, and create a myth that enables men to dominate women. Women must have possessed power prior to the creation of these stories, or it would not have been necessary for mythmakers to try to alter cultural perceptions.[†]

The following myth is another example of cultural perceptions being altered. Hera, goddess of power and prosperity and wife of Zeus; Athena, goddess of wisdom and victory in war; and Aphrodite, goddess of love and sexual desire, quarrel among themselves as to who is the prettiest. Unable to settle the dispute, they solicit the opinions of Paris, a young prince of Troy. Each goddess then privately attempts to influence his decision with the promise of a gift: Hera pledges power and possessions, Athena, knowledge and military prowess, and Aphrodite, sexual delight. Paris, being a callow youth, chooses Aphrodite, and for his vote is awarded Helen, the most beautiful and sexually desirable woman in the world.

Demeter, the goddess of grain and the oldest of the four, was conspicuous by her absence in this first beauty contest. Splitting her off from the others significantly devalued the regeneration of the earth and the remaining three diminish their stature by behaving like a clique of spiteful schoolgirls who fritter away the grave powers they embody.

The birth stories of these three goddesses—remnants of the Magna

*Since the Greek word for box, *pyxis,* was also slang for a woman's vagina, Hesiod's myth also contained an unflattering pun.

†Pandora is an ambiguous name. It can mean "bearer of all gifts" (an honorific frequently used to address the Great Mother in prayer) or it can mean "taker of all gifts." In Hesiod's telling, her name assumes the second, mean-spirited, definition.

Mater—are so peculiar that they could only have been devised by a male mind intent on changing the perceptions of society. Each goddess emerged from the insides of a male, though this required convoluted plot twists. Hera was the daughter of two Titans, Demeter and Cronus. An oracle warned Cronus that one of his children would murder him, to avenge his murder and castration of *his* father, Uranus. To avoid this fate, Cronus devoured his children at the moment of their birth.

Hera had hardly drawn her first breath before her father gulped her down. Each of her siblings, Poseidon, Hephaestus, Pan, and Hades, suffered a similar fate. But Demeter outwitted her husband, substituting a nine-pound rock wrapped in swaddling clothes when Zeus was born. Failing to notice the difference, Cronus swallowed the stone, believing it to be his son.

Demeter spirited Zeus away and raised him in secret. Upon reaching manhood, Zeus assassinated Cronus, then slit open the old man's belly. Out sprang Hera and her siblings, unharmed. The goddess of power, although born of a woman, entered the world from the innards of a man.

Athena's birth was equally unusual. Zeus's original consort was Metis, the ancient goddess of Mind, Measure, and Order. Zeus coveted her power, and to satisfy his urge, he devoured her whole.* Unbeknownst to him, Metis was pregnant with their daughter, Athena. Although Metis died, the embryonic Athena continued to grow in Zeus's brain until her size caused him terrible pain. Prometheus applied a wedge to Zeus's brow and hit it with a great hammer. From out of the resulting deep fissure sprang Athena, fully grown and fully armed. The goddess of wisdom emerged from the brain of a man.

Aphrodite's birth was no less strange. After Cronus killed his father, Uranus, he castrated him and flung the royal genitals into the ocean. Uranus's sperm and blood spattered upon contact with seawater, and the resulting brew sank and coalesced in the depths to form Aphrodite. Bursting through the surface in a shower of mist, the goddess of sexual desire emerged fully formed—a nubile adolescent. Gestating in Poseidon's watery domain, Hesiod presents Aphrodite as forming from a mixture of sperm, male blood, and foam without needing a placenta or womb.

Not only did all three goddesses, Hera, Athena, and Aphrodite, enter the world by way of a man instead of through the birth canal of a woman, but none of these exemplars of the Great Mother was nurtured during childhood by a mother. This resulted in the paradox that these three representa-

---

*Metis in Greek has two different meanings. One is "mind" or "wisdom"; the other is "nobody." One might suspect that the first meaning was the true one and the second one was a later sexist revision.

tives of the Great Mother were themselves motherless! New myths are frequently imposed on a culture by the needs of a dominant ruling class. What better way to discredit women's roles in the creation of life, and by extension, the Great Goddess, than to have your goddesses born of gods? The *Iliad*, the *Theognis* and the Old Testament turn barnyard commonsense upside down by asserting that birthing is a man's job.

The Old Testament and the *Iliad* cycle are the West's oldest literary anchors. Virtually all educated Western adults know the story of Adam and Eve and the Serpent, and the tale of the Trojan horse. Hesiod's stories, while less well known, are also familiar to many. What effect, one might ask, would these seminal tales have on the psyches of young girls and boys learning them? Would not a young girl's sense of self-worth be diminished by them? Would not they encourage the concept of patriarchy in the minds of young boys? The death throes of the Great Mother can be read between the lines of these sexist credos.

CHAPTER 14

SAPPHO/GANYMEDE

Kallignotos swore to Ionis that no one, man or woman, would ever be dearer to him than she . . . But now he is heated by male fire, and the poor girl . . . isn't in the picture any more.
—Meleagros, fourth century B.C. Greek poet[1]

Boys' sweat has a finer smell than anything in a woman's makeup box.
—Achilles Tatius, second century A.D. Greek writer[2]

T he first two cultures in which the alphabet took hold were, in many respects, radically different. The Israelites despised images because they were convinced representative art polluted the purity of Yahweh's written words. The Israelites were the only significant historical culture to leave no trace of a national art style. The Greeks elevated images to a state so sublime that they became the standard by which the Western world judged the merits of art for most of its history.

The Israelites tried to channel sexuality into the narrowest of furrows—the Old Testament condemned any variation other than the sanctified coupling of a husband and wife; all other expressions were proscribed and almost all were punishable by stoning. Sexuality, on the other hand, played a vital role in Greek religious rituals, and it was generally given free rein. Their graphic depictions of copulatory acts are without shame or false modesty. By contemporary standards, many of their vase paintings would be considered pornography. No other people in antiquity recorded their sexual proclivities as candidly as did the ancient Greeks. Because we are so indebted to Classical Greek poets, jurists, athletes, sculptors, dramatists, physicians, scientists, debaters, generals, biologists, geometers, engineers, botanists, architects, politicians, historians, astronomers, mythographers, philosophers, cartographers, and mathematicians we generally turn a blind eye to the Greek culture's sheer riot of sexual excesses.

Yahweh and Zeus were at opposite ends of the spectrum on this vital subject. Yahweh exhibited no sexual urges whatsoever and He never impregnated a mortal woman. Zeus, in contrast, was the most lascivious of celestial beings. The Greeks seemed to take a perverse delight in his sexual peccadilloes. By comparison, El, Amon, Baal and Marduk were paragons of sexual restraint. Yahweh professed love but was unmoved by lust; Zeus, on the other hand, was incapable of love, and yet constantly indulged his lusts. As Zeus, the seducer, he often used soft words and gentle actions, but if the object of his desire repulsed his advances, he readily resorted to deceit and was quite willing to impose his will by sheer brute force. By contemporary standards, Zeus was a serial rapist. Zeus also raped boys, as in his rough abduction of the beautiful youth Ganymede. In the study of comparative religions, does there exist another chief deity who was a rapist? Why would a society honor a god whose principal activities include actions, which, if imitated by a mortal, would be punishable by imprisonment or worse? If Zeus were a minor character in the mythodrama of Mount Olympus, then allowances could be made for his persistent priapism. But he was the revered ruler of the Olympian pantheon. The ascension of a regent god whose principal activity seems to have been to despoil beautiful young women could only have been in response to an urgent cultural need.

Another feature of Greek society exaggerated this skewing. The Greeks were the first to encourage sexual intercourse between members of the same sex. Homer considered the relationship between men (for example, the love between Achilles and Patroclus) to be on a higher, purer plane than any existing between a man and a woman. Homosexuality was the theme of Plato's *Symposium*. Sappho of Lesbos was the first historical figure to extol sexual attraction and love between women. Because of its implications for birth rates, any society openly embracing homosexuality could be expected to wane, yet, during the period between the eighth century and the fourth century B.C., the Greeks bequeathed a distinctive and vigorous culture which was, and remains, *sui generis*. Given the high mortality rates among its males due to constant internecine warfare, why did homosexuality become so acceptable at this particular time and in this particular place?

Although the causes of homosexuality remain unknown, increasingly modern scientists consider sexual preferences to be based on genetic predispositions.[3] Whatever are its causes, it is most unusual that the Greeks went against the evolutionary grain—especially when their predilection would have such debilitating consequences for their continuity. Some extremely powerful force would have to have been present for a culture to stake out a position so at variance from the majority of other cultures.

Among the Israelites, homosexuality was not tolerated. Mosaic law declared it an "abomination," a biblical term reserved for acts considered to be beyond the pale. The suppression of any forms of sexuality that did not result in children was understandable among a fledgling people trying to forge a national identity in a hostile environment. Why did not the Greeks adopt a similar attitude? Perhaps it was because the Greeks did not have to obey a Second Commandment that banished images.

The Greeks valued images so highly that they could not bring themselves to interdict this potent right hemispheric mode of perceiving information. Alphabetic writing had released a surge of Greek creativity that resulted in an uncontainable artistic flood. Unlike the Israelites, pictorial illustration blossomed in parallel with the Greek written word. Unwilling to disparage image cognition, the Greeks (unconsciously) sought another way to undermine the Goddess. Installing a rapist as their chief deity and extolling the virtues of homosexual love were two alternate ways to achieve this goal.

The replenishment of the ranks of their warriors suggests that despite the theme of homosexuality in their art and literature, the Greeks practiced *bisexuality*. Married Greek men often found another man or young boy as desirable as a woman. Husbands cohabited with their wives and sired children, but their wives had to live with the unsettling knowledge that they were not their husband's only choice. A woman knows in her bones how to compete with another woman for a man's affection, but she will become demoralized if she must also compete with men.

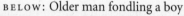

LEFT: Zeus abducts Ganymede.

BELOW: Older man fondling a boy

The bloody downfall of Greek culture in the fourth century B.C. was exacerbated by the very attributes that had made it burgeon in the first place. From the exaltation of battles in the *Iliad* to the removal of women from public life, the glorification of masculine values over feminine ones proved to be the Greeks' undoing. Had they been able to overcome their petty ethnic hatreds and join forces with one another, they might have been able to resist the Macedonians who invaded from the north and easily conquered their strife-weakened city-states. After the conclusive Macedonian/Greek battle of Chaeronea Plain outside Thebes in 339 B.C., pairs of Theban corpses littered the plains. The warriors were male couples who had gone to their deaths fighting at each other's sides, trying to protect the city that Cadmus had made famous by bringing to it his precious letters.[4]

No one has yet provided a satisfactory explanation for the prevalence of homosexuality and bisexuality in Greek society. The phenomenon has never been repeated to the same extent in any other culture.* It appeared just when intellectual pursuits became transcendent in Greek society and when the Goddess was relegated to the culture's periphery. I suggest that the masculinizing effects of alphabet literacy were responsible for all these phenomena.

One would have expected the first two alphabet cultures to develop a certain affinity for each other. The opposite occurred. The Greeks' love of both sexuality and imagery clashed with the Israelites' repudiation of sexual freedom and visual beauty and set the stage for a centuries-old enmity between these two principal contributors to Western culture. Our civilization is the schizophrenic only child of these two "fathers," each of whom brought unique aspects to the union.

---

*The only one that came close was the Italian Renaissance of the *quattrocento*. Again, the same mix of necessary elements was present: an explosion in alphabet literacy, a male zenith of creativity, and a near total absence of female participants.

CHAPTER 15

DIONYSUS/APOLLO

A God who is mad! A God part of whose nature it is to be insane.
What did they experience or see—these men upon whom the horror
of this concept must have forced itself?   —Walter Otto[1]

The major advances in civilization are processes that all but wreck the
societies in which they occur.   —Alfred North Whitehead[2]

When Homer transcribed the *Iliad* cycle into alphabetic script in
the eighth century B.C., a distinct oral Greek culture had existed
for seven hundred years. During that time, Greeks worshiped a
plethora of deities, each of whom exemplified specific traits of human
behavior. In addition to the Olympian Golden Circle of twelve key deities,
their pantheon included myriad naiads, satyrs, and nymphs, all of whom
engaged in convoluted adventures and inventive liaisons. Out of this divine
crush the Greeks wove a grand mythological tapestry.

Yet, despite this protean variety, after the introduction of the alphabet,
the Greeks lamented that Mount Olympus was short one god embodying
one type of behavior. The Greeks broke the Golden Circle in the fifth century B.C. and ejected Hestia, goddess of the hearth, family, and children. Her
replacement was Dionysus, god of wine, sexuality, and dance. The missing
behavior was madness. The dynamic growth of his cult coincided with the
rise of alphabet literacy, Greek rationality, and the flowering of classical art.

Dionysus was born of the union between Semele, a virgin princess, and
Zeus. The story of his conception and birth is an allegory of the rise of patriarchy in Greece. Semele's beauty attracted Zeus's attention. Sensing a bout of
spousal infidelity, Hera disguised herself as an old crone and visited Semele
to warn her of her impending ravishment. She advised the young princess to
insist that Zeus grant her one wish—to see him in his god form, complete

with flashing thunderbolts. Hera smiled to herself, confident that the girl's request would be her death sentence.

As expected, Zeus descended to Semele's bedchamber in the heat of rut and urged her to participate willingly in what would otherwise be another of his forced conquests. Taking advantage of the paradoxical fact that a man is never softer than when he is hardest, Semele followed the crone's advice and asked him to grant her one wish. Zeus readily acquiesced and then began his seduction. He transformed himself into a serpent and slithered along Semele's body, licking her with his forked tongue. Flummoxed by Zeus's unusual foreplay, Semele forgot her request. Watching from above, Hera stamped her foot in consternation. Her stratagem had gone awry.

Seven months later, with the boy-god Dionysus growing within her womb, Zeus visited Semele again. Unwittingly, Semele sealed her doom by requesting that Zeus appear before her as the mighty chief of Mount Olympus. Zeus tried to dissuade her from such folly, protesting that no mere mortal could gaze upon him in his full glory and survive. But Semele insisted that Zeus comply. Resigned, he reverted to the majesty of his true form— and the bolts of lightning that accompanied this transformation incinerated the hapless Semele on the spot. Seeing her once fair form burned and disfigured, Zeus, experiencing an uncharacteristic surge of remorse, split open her pregnant belly and snatched the fetus, Dionysus, who had narrowly survived this maternal conflagration.

Summoning Hermes, the god of trickery, Zeus had the fetus sewn under the skin of his groin in close proximity to the royal genitals swaying gently above the fetus's inguinal cocoon. These unusual neighbors would strongly influence the essential character of Dionysus. When the full nine months were up, Dionysus was born . . . again. The Greeks would call him the "twice born" or the "born again." As with the birth of Hera, Athena, and Aphrodite, a male arrogated the female's most central function.

Hera hated the child at first sight. Correctly gauging her murderous intent, Zeus spirited Dionysus away, to be raised in the household of a distant king and queen. Hera discovered his hiding place and bewitched Dionysus and his foster parents with madness. The royal couple died. Dionysus survived, but lived thereafter with the knowledge that Hera and her allies would be his eternal enemies. Furthermore, he would not always be in control of his destiny since he would be, periodically, out of his mind.

Dionysus was the god of the moon, night, the fig tree, moisture, guiltless sexuality, altered states of consciousness, and the orgiastic celebration of dance and music. Under his aegis were the bull and the serpent. He taught mortals how to cultivate the vine, leading them blindfolded to be initiated into the mysteries of fermentation, which has been both the balm and bane of people ever since. He was the god of the lucky hunch, the flash of insight, the divine epiphany, and intuitive knowledge. Plutarch ascribed to Dionysus the gift of divination.[3] He could prick the imagination of mortals and tear open a minute hole out of which would gush creative inspiration. But this touch was but a hair's breadth away from the inundation of insanity.

Madness is extreme irrationality. When someone is mad, we say they are "unbalanced." The alphabet, through its emphasis on linearity and sequence, caused the left side of the brain of those who learned it to hypertrophy, resulting in a marked cerebral dominance of one lobe over the other. Metaphorically, the mind listed to one side, as one carrying an unevenly distributed load. It seems more than coincidence that the Greeks, who codified logic, would at the same time elevate madness to a place of honor. Dionysus (madness) and Apollo (reason) alternated in presiding over the sacred oracle of Delphi.* Previously, irrationality had traditionally been associated with the feminine. The ancients revered prophecy, intuition, and altered states of consciousness. That the god of irrationality, Dionysus, was a now a man cloaked in feminine garb is but another awkward artifice enabling a male god to usurp feminine attributes.

Another revealing clue concerning Dionysus's true gender lineage was the composition of his ever-constant entourage. The followers of the persecuted, eternally young boy-god were chiefly women who called themselves *menders;* the Greek word for nurses (Il.6.132.) His fanatical priestesses were called *maenads.* His retinue also included all the *Muses* of the arts, every one of whom was female.

Drama, the art form combining poetry, music, gesture, and spectacle, arose from Dionysian ritual and is best appreciated by the right brain. The art of tragedy expresses the irrational nature of Dionysus. Plays like *Antigone* and *Hamlet* end with the stage littered with corpses, yet tragedy is a most exhilarating form of entertainment. Why do audiences feel ennobled after witnessing the anguished destinies of *Medea, Oedipus,* or *King Lear*? Why does the hero's or heroine's despair transmute into the audience's exultation? This paradox is at the heart of the Dionysian enigma.

The first actors to perform on a stage covered their faces with huge masks exaggerating each character's face. The twin masks of tragedy and

*One tradition states that Delphi became Apollo's shrine after he usurped it from its original goddess, Themis. According to Plutarch, Apollo presided over Delphi for nine months, then, during the winter, it was Dionysus's principal shrine.

LEFT: The multi-breasted Goddess Artemis

RIGHT: Dionysus as a cluster of grapes

comedy that symbolize the theater in modern times can be traced back to the worship of Dionysus, who represented the duality in human nature. Greek vase painters often depicted the faces of all the other gods in profile; Dionysus was the one they represented frontally.[4] He was the god of confrontation—the god who startled. He was further distinguished from other gods by his red face and red body makeup.[5] His persona has enlivened cavorting maskers in celebrations up through the Renaissance, and lives on today in the masked revelers of Mardi Gras and Halloween.

Apollo was the source of pithy proverbs. "Know Thyself" and "Nothing in Excess" were engraved on his temples. No statements attributable to Dionysus appear at his shrines. Although words, spoken or written, played little role in his cult, images did. All other deities were invisible when they arrived at the festivals given in their honor: Dionysus alone was always represented by a concrete image, an effigy carried on a palanquin by his exuberant intoxicants.[6] Preceding his statuary form in these corybantic processions were usually one or more huge phalli. Dionysian revelry celebrated the lubricious sexuality of youth in bloom. Virtually all the Dionysian characteristics mentioned: figs, bulls, Muses, the moon, dance, music, moisture, serpents, sexuality, regeneration of the earth, the cultivation of plants, and the nonverbal expressiveness of the mask, were originally under the aegis of the Goddess.

Archaic peoples considered irrationality coequal with reason. In many preliterate cultures, the shaman was held in higher esteem than the chieftain. With few exceptions, subsequent literate societies have demonized irrationality. Because of this prejudice against irrationality, it would be salutary to list some of the human activities that belong to its realm.

Laughter is irrational. Faith is irrational. Watching a sunset is an irrational act: there is no demonstrable "purpose" involved. The appreciation of both art and beauty are irrational: logic cannot completely explain why a work of art is compelling; the experience is essentially ineffable. Sexual arousal is irrational: who has not been set aquiver by a particular person, in a particular social setting that is totally inappropriate? Love is irrational. Many forms of dancing and music fall under the rubric of irrationality.

The lump in our throat when reciting the Pledge of Allegiance is irrational, as is the exhilaration we experience when our hometown team wins. All acts of altruism are inherently irrational. Yet who among us would want to eliminate art, sex, love, faith, music, dance, altruism, patriotism, or laughter from our lives? Like irrationality itself, they contribute to the sumptuous, variegated texture of the human condition.

Dionysus drove some men mad when they incurred his wrath, but his mind-reeling touch more often afflicted women. Imagine the mental state of women in cock-of-the-walk Greek classical culture, in which many men both despised and feared women. Greek myths abound with tales of scary women. The wives of Lemnos killed their husbands; the Danaides did the same to their suitors right after they married them; the Amazons hated men and the maenads tore them apart. There were far more female mythical creatures to give men the heebie-jeebies, such as griffins, chimeras, and sphinxes, than there were mythical male creatures to frighten women. The disparity between the power ascribed to Greek mythical femme fatales, and the plight of ordinary women in Greece, was enormous. Not surprisingly, Greek women suffered a high rate of depression. In Greek myths, many women associated with Dionysus committed suicide. Erigone, the daughter of the first mortal to whom Dionysus taught the cultivation of the vine, hanged herself. Ariadne, the Cretan princess abandoned by Theseus on the Isle of Naxos, hanged herself after becoming Dionysus's bride. Her daughter Phaedra did the same. Suicide was so common among classical Greek women that Plutarch reported that it had reached epidemic proportions in the city-state of Miletus. To control the outbreak, the king posted a proclamation that any woman who died by her own hand would have her naked corpse carried through the streets.[7]

It was the women more than the men who actually experienced the pain, terror, and death of the god's dark side in Dionysian rituals. At the Agrionia festival in Orchomenus, a trumpet blast signaled a group of young girls to begin running, literally for their lives. A Dionysian priest chased after them brandishing a sword. Any girl he overtook, he struck dead.[8] In Arcadian Alea, the festivities began with the flogging of women.[9] At Tenedos, child sacrifice was carried out in the god's name.[10]

Before the rapid expansion of the cult of Dionysus, the Greeks had acknowledged the dual nature of the human psyche through their veneration of Apollo and his twin sister, Artemis. They were the nascent West's first yang and yin. Apollo quickly became Zeus's favorite son. God of light and reason, he was the patron of judges, lawyers, architects, engineers, physicians, and philosophers. Known as the Sun God, the "Luminous One" protected both the *polis* and culture. He gave to humankind the clarity of an ordered mind. Plato extolled the Apollonian ideal.

But Apollo's insensitivity and aloofness did not endear him to women. Try as he might, he could not entice maidens to accept his sexual advances; neither could he make them love him. The mortal woman Coronis cuckolded him. The nymph Daphne turned herself into a tree rather than let Apollo touch her. Apollo, the god of the alphabet, reserved his greatest sexual passions for boys and men like Hyacinth and Admetus, relationships characterized by sadomasochism. The Olympian in charge of acquired knowledge, Apollo never laughed. Intelligent, aggressive, humorless, and imperious, he personified the left brain.

Artemis was as reserved as her brother. A fiercely independent huntress, she ruled over all the wild things in the forest and was a virgin by choice. Besides protecting women in childbirth, she was responsible for making sure all young ones grew up healthy and straight-limbed. With the rise of Dionysus, Artemis became less important to men, but increasingly women looked to her for consolation and inspiration. She shared the famous shrine at Eleusis with Demeter, and her Eleusinian mysteries initiated women into the secret rites of her worship. Very little is known of these rites because they were not committed to writing.

Over time, Dionysus, the new, effeminate god of madness, appropriated many of Artemis's aspects. By the fourth century, Apollo/Dionysus supplanted Apollo/Artemis as the pair personifying the dual nature of the human condition. When Dionysus was admitted to Mount Olympus, the upstart god was seated next to Apollo.

We associate Dionysian revelry with a carnival atmosphere, but men, too, had reason to fear Dionysus; carnival and carnivore derive from the same Latin root—to eat flesh. Enveloped by the vegetation of the forest in the dark of night, his maenads, after drinking wine or taking other mind-altering drugs, danced themselves into a frenzy. They suckled the young of wild animals and sometimes engaged in bestiality. Driven to a state of ecstasy, they sought out a sacrifice—usually a lamb or a goat that had been tied to a stake beforehand, but sometimes it was a man who had haplessly wandered into their celebrations. Possessing the superhuman strength that can accompany such delirious trances, the maenads pounced on their victim and tore it, or him, limb from limb, scratching off its (or his) flesh with their fingernails. Still in an altered state, they drank the victim's blood and devoured what was left of the body parts. The sunrise found them exhausted and besotted; slowly they returned to their senses.

The savagery of this aspect of the Dionysian cult has few parallels among oral peoples. The height of Dionysus's popularity coincided with the zenith of the Greek Golden Age. The civilized Classical Greeks, who bequeathed to us the likes of Solon, Pericles, and Xenophon, at the same time paid homage to a cannibal god, for Dionysus, too, participated in his rites. He, too, ripped apart his victims' bodies and drank their blood. But, paradoxically, Dionysus himself was the hunted as well as the hunter.

Besides being the suffering Olympian persecuted by other gods, Dionysus was also the only member of the Golden Circle who died. As Dionysus Zagreus, one of his alter egos, he was attacked and brutally dismembered by the Titans, Hera's allies.* But in a novel twist on the archaic Goddess story, he possessed the power to resurrect himself each spring. This single feature distinguished him from previous dying gods.

Dionysus was the master magician of pleasure and pain, beauty and cruelty, ecstasy and terror, and creativity and madness. He was the enigmatic spirit of the dual-yet-opposing natures of human existence. He represented the complementarity between intuition and reason, sacred and profane, feminine and masculine. He is the closest we have come in the West to the Eastern symbol of the yin/yang. He was both the exultant god who brings his devotees indescribable joy and encourages them to indulge their sensual urges, and the suffering, dying god whose death holds out the promise of salvation through rebirth. In an age in which the Greeks refined intellectual pursuits, and the intricacies of reason, Dionysus initiated them into a cult of palpitating excitement and demonic violence.

Aristarchus of Samothrace, a Homeric scholar writing in the third century B.C., puzzled publicly over Homer's failure to credit Dionysus as the giver of the vine, considering all the references there were to wine drinking in the *Iliad*.[11] Perhaps Homer's silence on the subject in the eighth century B.C. was because Dionysus was so insignificant at that time he hardly mer-

---

*The Titans were very old gods. They represented a pre-Olympian era when goddesses had exerted more power than they did in the time of the patriarchal Olympians.

ited mention. Hesiod, too, says little about the Dionysian myth. Yet by the fifth century, Plutarch reports that Dionysus was worshiped everywhere in Greece in both sophisticated city-states and in the surrounding rural countryside. Shrines to the wine god rapidly increased in synchrony with the soaring alphabet literacy rates that followed the adoption of the Ionian alphabet in 402 B.C. by mutual consent of the important Greek city-states.[12]

Despite a few isolated cases of resistance, most Greeks recognized that they must pay obeisance to the twice-born god. Failure to do so would bring madness to men and make women crazed, during which time they would mistake their children for animals, and kill and eat them. The essential nature of the human male and female had been forged during the 3,000,000 years spent as hunter/killers and gatherer/nurturers. Human females are generally considered to be more kindly, generous, nurturing, and compassionate than human males. The *Iliad*'s mortal women were patient and submissive. Given their placid nature, why were there so many Furies, Harpies, and sirens for Greek men to fear? Greek men even began to fear their own wives. Greek housewives, when called by Dionysus, threw down their shuttlecocks, slipped out the door, and abandoned their children. In the dead of night, they joined other bewitched women in a blood-spattered feast of the body parts of murdered husbands. This characterization of women is so out of the norm for prior and other contemporary societies that one is inclined to search for a galvanic new element affecting Greek culture. The change in perception brought about by alphabet literacy could be that element.

When one group prepares for war against another, whether they are tribes, nations, or ethnic groups, first they must demonize the enemy. During the period when the Greeks embraced the alphabet, women became the enemy. Surely, after millions of years, women had not suddenly undergone some sinister transmogrification. But to convince the average Greek citizen that his wife was capable not only of murdering him but also of eating their offspring, the Greeks imputed to a new god the ability to drive women insane, in which state they would possess superhuman strength and diabolical power. It is doubtful that the cult of Dionysus produced any women who actually ate men. But the very thought of it inspired visions of ordinary housewives transmuted into blood-swilling vampires. The terrible truth concerning the Dionysian cult is that the women did not go mad—the men did. The powerful drug they imbibed was not the fermented grapes of the vine, it was the distilled letters of the alphabet.

The name of Dionysus's mother, Semele, can be traced linguistically to a Thracian and Phrygian name meaning Earth Goddess.[13] Every Earth Goddess prior to Semele could perform the fundamental act of giving birth. By falling into the trap Hera had set, Semele brought death upon herself and near death to her fetus.* Her tragic failure as a mother was the necessary prerequisite for Dionysus's birth from his father, Zeus. Dionysus mourned the mother he never knew. After he gained admittance to Mount Olympus, Dionysus petitioned Zeus to let him resurrect Semele from Hades and bring her up to the sacred mountain. This done, Zeus conferred immortality upon her so that she might stay with the Golden Circle for eternity, and Dionysus convinced Zeus to seat her next to his throne.

This myth concerning son and mother has similarities to the older story of Demeter rescuing her daughter Persephone from Hades, god of the underworld, but for one-half of the year. The upstart Dionysus, in contrast, retrieved his mother from the land of the dead for all eternity.

For five thousand years following the advent of agriculture, people ardently believed that the Great Mother revitalized the earth, just as she resurrected her beloved son/lover/brother each spring. It is the story of Inanna and Dumuzi, Isis and Osiris, Ishtar and Tammuz, and Aphrodite and Adonis. In the most sacred ancient rite of the *hiero gamos*—the sacred marriage—the man was a mortal and the woman was a goddess. But in Classical Greece, a god arose who had the power to resurrect himself and the earth *without* the agency of the all-important mother. The son—a god—resurrected his mother who was merely mortal. A thousand years after Dionysus, this elemental myth was once again revised. Mary, the mortal mother of Christ, helplessly witnessed the death of her son in springtime. Now, only the Father could resurrect His Son. Dionysus is the crucial link between the myth of Osiris and the story of Christ.

A mother's instinct to protect her young is often greater than self-preservation. In the Dionysian myth, deranged mothers sadistically kill their children. No other human crime is so macabre, so unexpected, and so paradoxical. Nothing less than the disorienting effects of a new means of communication seems adequate to explain such an extreme change in the perception of women's nature. As if to punish them, all the women who nurture Dionysus die horrible deaths; women must suffer for loving the god who makes them mad.

In present-day Thebes, at the base of an ancient shrine's ruin is chiseled the shrine's name—Dionysos Kadmeios. Dionysus and Cadmus? What has the

---

*In another example of the Greeks revisioning of the Earth Mother's persona, Hera, the protectress of pregnant women, plotted a pregnant woman's murder.

one to do with the other? It is now time to unveil Dionysus's lineage, revealing his inextricable connection to the alphabet's arrival in Greece. We know that his father was Zeus. But on his mother's side, Semele's parents were none other than Cadmus and Harmony!

In Greek mythology, the gods pronounced maledictions upon two familial bloodlines. The more famous was the House of Atreus. Its founder, Tantalus, was a king who sacrificed his son, Pelops, serving him to the gods for dinner. When the gods, assembled around his dining table, realized what Tantalus had done to please them, they fell into silence. Zeus then angrily cursed Tantalus and all of his subsequent issue. The unfortunate heirs to this House—Agamemnon, Iphigenia, Clytemnestra, Orestes, and Electra—have become familiar names associated with tragedy. Despite its haunting theme, the Greeks renounced the practice of child sacrifice in this enlightened myth by conjuring up a potent morality tale to prevent it.

The second accursed house was the Cadmean line of Thebes. Cadmus had committed no sin: quite to the contrary, he not only brought the Greeks an invaluable gift from Phoenicia, but he intervened in a crucial drama and rescued the Olympians. Yet the Fates inflicted on the heirs of Cadmus and Harmony a terrible destiny: each of their four daughters suffered a tragic calamity that bound her closely to the cult of Dionysus.

Autonoë, Cadmus's and Harmony's oldest daughter, had a son, Acteon, who was a skilled hunter. When he inadvertently stumbled upon the place where the virgin goddess Artemis was bathing, she angrily cast a spell over his dogs and they attacked and tore him to pieces.

Agave, the second daughter, killed and ate her son while participating as a maenad in a Dionysian rite. Io, the third daughter, cared for Dionysus immediately after Semele's death. Hera drove her mad. Descending into intractable savagery she killed her child, and then threw herself from a cliff with the dead child in her arms. Semele was the fourth daughter.

Dionysus owes his lineage to the marriage of Cadmus to the daughter of Ares, the war god. The union of the alphabet and war resulted in generations of suffering and provides a metaphor for history that is both mythic and true. Every time there has been a great advance in science and knowledge assisted by alphabet literacy, it has been associated with war. The periods that historians most admire—Classical Greece, Imperial Rome, Renaissance Italy, and Elizabethan England—were born in strife and carried within them a vein of terrible madness. Indeed, whenever the alphabet appears, so too does madness. Roman history is replete with mad rulers such as Caligula and Nero. The Renaissance and the Elizabethan Age produced tremendous advances in the arts and sciences, along with witch hunts and ferocious religious wars. The French Revolution, child of the Enlightenment, ended in the mad Jacobin Reign of Terror. In the twentieth century, the Germans, who glorified reason, produced the madmen Nazis.

More recently, we have witnessed staggering advances in exploring the frontiers of knowledge. Yet we came perilously close to destroying ourselves and the planet in a nuclear holocaust. It is fitting that the Pentagon program charged with the massive buildup of thermonuclear weapons, far in excess of what could ever be needed to destroy any enemy, was named Mutual Assured Destruction, known more familiarly by its acronym, MAD.

In the fourth century B.C., when Classical Greece was at the very height of the alphabet's triumph, its much admired democracy disintegrated. In the period between 411 and 386, Athenian turned on Athenian with a ferocity previously unseen among kinsmen because of opposing *abstract* political beliefs. This strange episode can be accurately diagnosed as cultural madness. It was during this craze that Socrates was condemned to death for his *ideas* (399) and Euripides wrote *The Bacchae* (406), the story of King Pentheus's resistance to the strange god, Dionysus.

Pentheus was a good king who believed that law was the very foundation of social order. He personified the Apollonian ideal of a regent. At first, news of an unwelcome visit to his kingdom by Dionysus annoyed him. When he learned that Dionysus and his boisterous retinue had begun converting some of his subjects to this new cult and that Pentheus's wife and mother had been seen slipping out of the castle at night to join in the rituals, he ordered the young rabble-rousing god arrested.

Despite warnings from the wise old seer, Tiresias, Pentheus ordered Dionysus thrown into the castle's dungeon, but Dionysus's chains and the prison bars themselves turned into tendrils of ivy. The sensible Pentheus dismissed this divine sign as a trick. Again, Tiresias cautioned the king that Dionysus was genuine and should be honored. Unconvinced, Pentheus ordered the poseur brought before him.

In the dialogue that followed, Pentheus stubbornly reiterated to Dionysus that he would never believe he was a god. Nevertheless, he confided to Dionysus that he was most curious to know what possessed his mother and wife. Like one pleading with a magician to explain his tricks, Pentheus asked the god to tell him what the women were doing out in the forest all night.

Dionysus, slyly smiling, responded that he could not reveal such secrets, but he could arrange for the king to observe the rites for himself. The god led Pentheus to a clearing and instructed him to climb to the highest limb of a tall, branched tree.

Dionysus's assembled maenads began their frenzied dance. Pentheus's mother and his wife, the queen, soon joined them. Pentheus watched wide-eyed and increasingly apprehensive as the women fell into a deepening trance. Then at the peak of their madness, one of them spied Pentheus in his perch. Snarling, the women circled the tree and began clawing away pieces of bark. Now in fear for his life, Pentheus called out for help, but no one could hear him because he was too far from the city.

The feral maenads began to shake the tree. Pentheus lost his grip and fell. As they pounced on him, he called out to his mother, but in her glassy-eyed state, she could not recognize him. With the strength of a wild creature, his mother tore his arm from his body and impaled his head on her thyrsus wand. The other women tore his body apart and consumed his flesh.

The story takes on added relevance when we learn that Pentheus's mother was Agave, the second of the four daughters of Cadmus and Harmony. Pentheus and Dionysus were first cousins. This myth is an allegory: everyone has a masculine and feminine nature, and each of these complementarities is further split into a light and a dark side. To ignore the messages that come to us from the dark side of either nature is to invite destruction. The price exacted for not recognizing Dionysus is, like Pentheus, to be psychologically *torn apart*. There are two aspects to our psyches—reason and madness—and we deny either at great peril.

The Bacchae takes place in Thebes, where, according to myth, the alphabet first came to Greece. It was in Thebes that Cadmus so brutally defeated the power of the serpent replacing it with a new order, based on written laws born of mortals' highest faculty: their reason. It is fitting that Cadmus's grandsons should be Dionysus and Pentheus. The one, a stranger and an outcast, brings down the other, who represents the best of the written word. Euripides' play contains themes still relevant today.*

The tragedy of the house of Cadmus does not end with Pentheus's death. Pentheus's crown devolved to his son Menoeceus, and then on to his daughter, Jocasta. In a convoluted tale of mistaken identity, Oedipus, the son of Queen Jocasta and King Laius, killed a stranger on the road, unaware that the man was his father, Laius. Then, like Cadmus, Oedipus outsmarted a female monster, the Sphinx, and by so doing, won the right to marry Jocasta and become king of Thebes.

*Euripides also presciently anticipates the conversion of the Roman Empire to Christianity: both Christ and Dionysus were outcast charismatic leaders accompanied by scruffy followers. Both represented the mystic side of human nature. Both triumphed over conventional rationality and pragmatism.

In the first play of the Sophocles' Theban trilogy, *Oedipus Rex*, Oedipus's relentless search for his father's murderer led him to the terrible discovery that it was none other than himself. Jocasta, his wife, realized she had married her son who was both the father of their children and the murderer of her husband. She hanged herself. Upon confronting the truth, Oedipus blinded himself with the brooches taken from his mother's lifeless body and wandered away into self-imposed exile. The second play, *Oedipus at Colonus*, concerns the internecine strife between Oedipus's two sons, Eteocles and Polynices, and the terrible toll it took on their blind father.

The third play, *Antigone*, recounts the demise of the last female in the Cadmean line, Oedipus's loving daughter. Antigone's dictatorial uncle, Creon, seized the Theban throne after his sister Jocasta's death and Oedipus's disgrace. He passed an edict forbidding anyone to bury the body of Polynices, because the youth had attacked the city with a rival army. Polynices died within sight of the city's walls. Creon wanted his bones picked clean by vultures to serve as a lesson for other would-be usurpers. Knowing that Creon's edict was unjust, Antigone buried her brother. Her disobedience infuriated her uncle, who ordered her put to death.

Laws are the most precious legacy of Cadmus's alphabet. However, they must be tempered with justice, a faculty that has long been associated with the female. The image of Justice is a blindfolded goddess holding scales. Mercy, fairness, and compassion are qualities primarily associated with the right side of our psyche. Although the law represents order and is the best institution to prevent civic chaos, it fails when based exclusively on masculine values. Then, it often becomes the instrument of tyranny.

Antigone closed the circle that began with Cadmus's journey to Greece in search of his abducted sister, Europa. His quest led him to fame and good fortune, and he brought the Greeks what the Roman poet Nonnus called "gifts of the mind"—tiny scratchings that, when linked together, created an "etched model of a silence that speaks."[14]

The House of Cadmus suffered a curse as ghastly as the one that dogged the House of Atreus. All the Cadmean women, and many of the men, suffered terrible tribulations through six generations. The founder of the House of Cadmus killed the many-toothed serpent, the feminine symbol of power and wisdom, and was responsible for the Greeks having the instrument to initiate a society ruled by law. It was poetic justice that the last female of this line should sacrifice her life because the law had lost its soul. The alphabet was a vast gift. Women paid the price of its curse.

CHAPTER 16

ATHENS/SPARTA

We are heirs to the Greek intellectual tradition, one of single file logic and rational analysis. And it is not only the formal arguments of Aristotle that have passed down, it is the *alphabet itself* that may play an unexpected role in our brain organization. —Robert Ornstein[1]

Laws play a dominant role in any society acquiring an alphabet; non-alphabetic societies rely more on custom and taboo. The Egyptians and Chinese, for example, made many seminal contributions to the storehouse of human culture. Written canons of law were not among them.

The Israelites memorialized their acceptance of the Ten Commandments as *the event* of their cultural heritage. Although the Greeks, too, were extremely proud of their laws, they did not have a myth of comparable status at the outset of their cultural renaissance. But by the fifth century B.C., Athenians had developed tragedy into an art form that explained, retroactively, their traditions. Playwrights embellished myths to educate as well as entertain. In the *Oresteia* trilogy (458 B.C.), Aeschylus told how the Greeks acquired a judicial system. His work is pervaded with a misogyny that dramatizes the conflict between the alphabet and the Goddess.

The *Oresteia* details the blood feuds and misfortunes that consumed the House of Atreus. The gods let slip this generational avalanche of woe because Tantalus served his son, Pelops, to them for dinner. Tantalus's two other sons, Atreus and Thyestes, were bitter rivals. Atreus murdered his brother's son and cooked him in a vat. He then invited his brother to a banquet and served the unsuspecting father tender parts of his son's flesh. In the next generation, Atreus's son, Agamemnon, sacrificed his daughter, Iphigenia. Clytemnestra, his wife, avenged her daughter's murder by killing Agamemnon with his axe upon his triumphant return from the sack of Troy. This regicide is the subject of the trilogy's first play, *Agamemnon*. In the second, *The Libation Bearers*, their son, Orestes, murders his mother to avenge his father. The third play, *The Eumenides*, recounts how Apollo interceded on Orestes's behalf and rescued him from the Furies. These goddesses relentlessly pursued anyone guilty of the heinous crime of matricide. Hounded and terrorized, Orestes sought refuge in Apollo's sanctuary at Delphi since it was Apollo, archetype of the masculine influence in culture, who had ordered Orestes to kill his mother.

In the opening scene, the Furies are in a deep sleep due to a spell cast by Apollo. Orestes clings to a column, beseeching the god to save him. Apollo walks lightly among the recumbent goddesses, hissing his revulsion:

> Now look at these—
> These obscenities!—I've caught them,
> beaten down with sleep.
> They disgust me.
> These ancient children never touched
> by god, man or beast—the eternal virgins.
> Born for destruction only, the dark pit,
> they range the bowels of Earth, the world of death,
> loathed by men and the gods who hold Olympus.[2]

Apollo's antipathy stems from the Furies' archaic status. Because they belong to the oldest stratum of deities, they are beyond the control of the newer, younger race of Olympians. Virgins by choice, the Furies personify female power that has not yet been brought under the yoke of male control.* Daughters of the night, the shrieking Furies gave vent to the awesome anger of the tellurian "Mother Snake" that coiled in an unbroken spiral back through Mesopotamian and Egyptian mythology, to disappear into the miasmic bogs of the Neolithic Age. The Furies' hegemony over the dispensation of justice exasperated Apollo, the champion of the left brain. He was responsible for providing mortals with the means to subdue and defeat the wild forces of nature, and he craved to defeat them.

When the Furies awake and demand Orestes, Apollo challenges the "Old Ones" to submit to a trial judged by Athena. She represents the new Apollonian order. The Furies are reluctant to defer to a third party, even though she is a woman. But smooth-talking Apollo convinces them and they grudgingly agree, assuming Athena will side with them.

---

*The Furies were the Greek counterpart to the Jewish Lilith. Although not mentioned in the Torah, later Jewish writers (second century A.D.) began to write about the mysterious woman before Eve who refused to acknowledge Adam's authority.

Athena empanels a jury of twelve Athenians, over which she presides. The Furies obtain Orestes' confession of murder. They rest their case, confident that the court will find him guilty. Orestes whines, "But am I of my mother?" The Furies spit back, "Vile wretch, she nourished you in her own womb. Do you disown your mother's blood?"

Pleading for the defense, Apollo claims that Orestes should not be punished because his duty to his father must supersede any loyalty he might have felt toward his mother. Apollo argues, mothers play a very minor role:

> Here is the truth I tell you—see how right I am.
> The woman you call the mother of the child
> is not the parent, just a nurse to the seed
> the new-sown seed that grows and swells inside her.
> The *man* is the source of life—the one who mounts.
> She like a stranger for a stranger, keeps
> the shoot alive unless god hurts the roots.[3]

The man's sperm, according to Apollo, is the active principal, the woman, merely a passive vessel. Therefore, a mother is not related to her son by blood, and if a son kills his mother, the act should be considered no more serious than killing a stranger.

When the jury returns with a split verdict six for and six against, Athena breaks the tie by siding with Orestes. She claims that respect for motherhood is misplaced because she herself emerged fully grown from the brow of Zeus. Conveniently omitting the fact that she was initially sheltered in the womb of Metis, Zeus's first wife, Athena disingenuously denies that she had a mother. Apollo and Athena were the two most intelligent deities. If both regarded mothers as interchangeable, the audience of Aeschylus's masterpiece would be inclined to conclude that there must be something to the notion. Free to go home, a jubilant Orestes leaves the stage with Apollo.

Having defeated the chthonic power of the Furies, Athena urges them to abandon their role as forces of retribution against mother-murder and instead join her as upholders of the law. The Furies, effectively defanged by the trial's judgment, reluctantly submit. Those who formerly avenged injustices against women are silenced, tamed by a smart goddess who bought into the male system. The Furies will now serve patriarchal culture.

This play explained to the Greek populace how they came to live by the rule of law, and in the course of doing so, denigrated women and belittled motherhood. Like men, women were susceptible to this manipulation because the alphabet exerted a potent effect on them as well. Illiterate women were at an obvious disadvantage in dealing with literate men. Those few women who did become literate surrendered a considerable portion of what power they had because they were now using a method of perception that reinforced *their* masculine side at the expense of their feminine. And instead of becoming more aggressive, they became disoriented, cut off from the true roots of their strength, and they deferred to the male element in the society. They became passive spectators of events and decisions that intimately affected them. The Furies' indecision and ineffectiveness when they had to perform in the alphabet's arena, the court of law, foreshadowed female submission in subsequent centuries. The taming of the Furies tells poetically how women lost their power.

From the eighth century B.C. on, coincident with the spread of the written word, women were pushed to the periphery of Greek culture. This marginalization is nowhere better illustrated than in the disparity of women's roles in two diametrically opposing cultures: Sparta and Athens.

Sparta was a militaristic society that had little use for literacy. It produced not a single playwright, philosopher, or historian whose words or ideas are meaningful to us today. As Edith Hamilton points out, "The Spartans have left the world nothing in the way of art, literature, or science."[4] Lycurgus, who formulated their law, did not commit it to writing. He ordered everyone to memorize it. Plutarch writes that there was even a Spartan law against committing any law to writing.[5] The Spartan code of conduct glorified deprivation and cruelty; their government was oligarchic, with fascist leanings.

Athens, in contrast, produced history's greatest concentration of thinkers. Fortunately for posterity, they committed their ideas to writing. Athenians loved drama, literature, and philosophy. They were the first to debate the merits of aesthetics, and they espoused many values that we associate with the feminine. The city was the home of the first extended experiment in democracy. Their visual arts set a standard for Western art.

Given these contrasts between the two rivals, one would assume that women fared better in Athenian society. The opposite was true. In Athens, women were excluded from education, government, and public affairs. Solon, the Athenian lawgiver, denied women the right to buy or sell land.[6] As in the Old Testament, his code placed women under men's guardianship.[7] An Athenian father retained the right to dissolve his daughter's marriage.[8]

The Muses of the arts may have all been women, but they did not inspire their mortal sisters in fifth century Athens to create any art that has survived. We may never know if female artists existed and men suppressed their works or took credit for them, or whether the prejudices against women were so extreme that few even tried to express their talents.

For all its state-sanctioned hardships and brutality, Sparta was more egalitarian. Spartans educated girls in nearly the same manner as boys. Spartan girls wore loose-fitting short tunics called *peplos*. They had more freedom of movement than Athenian women, who wore the restrictive Athenian *chiton*.[9] Spartan women competed in athletic games.

Spartans honored women's life-giving role and considered it equal to that of their warriors. To immortalize his name by having it inscribed on his tombstone, a Spartan man had to die in combat; to win the same honor a Spartan woman had to perish in childbirth.[10]

Spartan women ruled in the absence of their men, who were frequently away at war, and they owned their own property and could dispose of it as they pleased. By the fourth century B.C., women owned two-fifths of all Spartan land.[11] Virginity, chastity, and fidelity were virtues demanded of Athenian women, but these strictures did not apply in the same degree for Spartan women. They were free to bear children with more than one man, providing the father belonged to the proper social class.[12]

Athens and Sparta provide a unique opportunity to test the hypothesis of this book. Both were Greek. Both worshiped the same deities. They spoke and wrote a common language. They were contemporaneous. Both were bellicose. And yet the difference in the status of their women was pronounced. One notable difference distinguishing the two city-states was their contrasting attitudes toward the alphabet.

Examining the attitudes toward writing and women's rights of Athens' three most famous philosophers—Socrates, Plato, and Aristotle—will highlight the masculinizing effect of literacy. Socrates preferred the bimodal communication of speech and did not commit his ideas to paper. We know of them because of the writing of his pupil, Plato. Socrates dismissed writing, identifying it as a mere mechanism "to remind him who knows [about] the things that have been written."[13] Socrates engaged both of his hemispheres in his search for truth. He was confident that the one-on-one give-and-take of debate was a better path to wisdom than sitting alone arguing only with himself and a pot of ink.

Writing's greatest drawback, according to Socrates, was that one could not ask a question of a written document. In Plato's *Protagoras*, Socrates derides many contemporaneous speakers, "They are just like papyrus rolls, being able neither to answer your questions nor to ask themselves."[14]

As dialogue was Socrates' principal mode of teaching and learning, it is not surprising that he was favorably disposed to the tenets of feminism. He acknowledged the priestess Diotima as his mentor.[15] Plato has Socrates say in the *Republic*,

> Then if men or women as a sex appear to be qualified for different skills or occupations, I said, we shall assign these to each accordingly; but if the only difference apparent between them is that the female bears and the male begets, we shall not admit that this is a difference relevant for our purpose, but shall still maintain that our male and female Guardians ought to follow the same occupations.[16]

After watching a talented young acrobat's performance at one of the many banquets held in Athens, Socrates mused:

> Not only from this girl, my friends, but from other things, too, we can infer that a woman's talent is not at all inferior to a man's.[17]

Plato also engaged in debates, but he preferred solitary inner dialogues to the imprecision of speech, and became history's earliest great prose writer. Ironically, although Plato was the beneficiary of writing's subtle prod toward abstract thought, he was too immersed in the new way of communicating to recognize it as the inspiration for his own brilliance. Like Socrates, Plato remained suspicious of writing. In *Phaedrus*, he pointed out that writing is the symbol for the spoken word, which itself is a symbol once removed from thought itself; therefore, the written word is twice removed from the truth in the mind of "one who knows."[18] Plato was a transitional figure, standing on the threshold between orality and literacy. His written dialogues are not quite speech and not quite prose, but contain elements of both.

"How did the Greeks ever wake up?" asks Eric A. Havelock, a classical historian. How did a tradition-bound, superstitious people come to see themselves as individuals with Free Will, who could make choices to determine their own destinies? Havelock answers, "The fundamental answer must lie in the changing technology of communication. Refreshment of memory through written signs enabled a reader to dispense with most of that emotional identification by which, alone, the acoustic record was sure of recall."[19] In other words, the left brain was able to discard the right brain's way of perceiving information and did not seem hampered in the least.

Like Socrates, Plato expounded on the subject of gender roles, but the student was not as magnanimous as his mentor. Although Plato's opinions

on women changed over the course of his long life, mostly he was condescending and believed that women should play a subservient role in society.
In the *Republic*, he agrees with Socrates that women could be guardians of
the State. But he stratified his guardians, putting the men over the women.[20]
In *Laws*, Plato accuses women of being less trustworthy than men.[21]

While proposing that prospective women guardians should be well educated, he advocated diminishing their roles as mothers. In his ideal society,
mother-love was expendable, to be replaced with State-organized day care.
Adults were to treat all children the same, regardless of their biological relationship. "Men and women are to have a common way of life . . . common
education, common children, and they are to watch over the citizens in
common."[22] Plato believed that the richness and textures that form the
rough weave of kith and kin were at the root of many of society's ills; his
solution was to masculinize women by truncating their most elemental role
as nurturers. Where this idea has been tried, it has failed miserably, which is
why Plato's *Republic* is deemed by all, including Plato, to be a "utopia."

Plato was homosexual, and in his *Symposium*, he glorified homoerotic
love. He did not write a companion piece praising conjugal relations. While
his gender preference would not make him a misogynist, it is worth noting
that although he pontificated on the dispensability of mothers, Plato never
had a wife, a child, or the responsibilities of parenting and family.

Accompanying Plato's condescending views on women was his most
un-Athenian attitude toward images. He lived during the very acme of
Greek art. Yet in his theory on art in Book 10 of the *Republic*, Plato railed
against those who created concrete images, calling them "charlatans." He
banned artists from his Utopia:

> The art of representation is therefore a long way removed from truth, and
> it is able to reproduce everything because it has little grasp of anything,
> and that little is of a mere phenomenal appearance. For example, a painter
> can paint a portrait of a shoemaker or a carpenter or any other craftsman
> without understanding any of their crafts; yet, if he is skillful enough, his
> portrait of a carpenter may, at a distance, deceive children or simple peo-
> ple into thinking it is a real carpenter.[23]

Plato's convictions regarding images put him at odds with the Paleolithic cave-painting cultures, nor were similar views advocated, so far as we
know, by anyone in the Egyptian, Mesopotamian, Minoan, or Phoenician
cultures. The majority of Greek citizens did not share his opinions. Only one

other people, the Hebrews, subscribed to the stricture against images, and they were also the only other significant alphabet users.*

The philosopher who held the most malevolent view of women was Plato's pupil, Aristotle. His many well-reasoned arguments have dominated Western thought. But, Aristotle cloaked his misogyny in a pseudo-scientific mantle. Frederic G. Kenyon, a classical scholar, wrote, "It is not too much to say that with Aristotle, the Greek world passed through oral instruction to the habit of reading."[24] Aristotle justified slavery by declaring that men were not created equal, so that it was natural for some to be born masters and others slaves. He also championed male domination of females. "The male is, by nature, superior and the female inferior; and the one rules and the other is ruled; this principle, of necessity, extends to all mankind."[25] If a thinker of Aristotle's stature had concluded that women were subhuman, who would come forward to rebut him?

The slide from egalitarianism to misogyny, represented by the views of these three successive philosophers, compressed into a few years the gradual degradation of women that took place over the centuries that Greek culture passed from an oral tradition to an alphabetic written one.

Another Greek contribution deeply influenced the course of world events— their invention of currency. In the seventh century B.C., the king of Lydia, a prosperous Asiatic city-state, authorized the minting of coins. The king promised he would uphold their value. Greek city-states soon followed his example. In the fifth century B.C., Athens carried this innovation one step further. Besides their trusted, silver drachma, they put into circulation lesser change that for the first time did not represent its value in gold or silver.

"Value" is the fuzziest of concepts, and those who accepted the Athenians' copper money in exchange for goods were forced to rise to a level of abstract thinking that required a willing suspension of disbelief as extreme as what the dramatist demanded of his audience in the amphitheater. Greeks endowed their new copper money with worth that was *not* intrinsic to the small, round slices of metal.

Animals do not engage in barter. With the exception of the flesh and sinew housing life itself, there is nothing tangible that one animal desires of another. The primates' opposing thumb made it possible not only to grasp vines and hold fruit, but, later, to conceive the meaning of the verb "to grasp" and "to hold." "Mine" would become the most contentious word in any language. That a creature could claim personal "ownership" of an inan-

*Plato was also one of the first Greek monotheists.

imate object it could clutch was the crucial factor that allowed the hominid line to master the slippery subject of greed.

There are four ways to obtain something from another: ask its owner to give it as a gift, claim it by killing its owner, steal it, or barter for it. The fairest and least disruptive is the last. Trading with others, object for object, became commonplace. Barter was the only mode of commerce for most of the human experiment. As it became more complex, those engaged in barter sought something that would substitute for value. Preliterate tribes used everything from cattle to cowry shells as mediums of exchange, but the medium always possessed some utility. Cows could be eaten and shells worn for adornment.

Beginning with the agricultural revolution, surplus production greatly increased the quantity of wealth. Traders needed a more efficient means of transacting business than mere swap. Archaeologist Denise Schmandt-Besserat proposes that Neolithic Mesopotamian traders invented different-shaped clay tokens to keep track of trades.[26] These became the precursors of writing. The peoples of antiquity took the next important step by identifying something that all longed to possess and was easily portable. The scarcity and durability of gold and silver made these metals ideal. Grains of raw ore served admirably as a substitute for sheaves of grain. Goaded by the necessity to standardize, early merchants invented a system of weights and measures, enabling them to translate the worth of ten caskets of olive oil into numeric quantities of gold and silver.

The shekel was a unit of silver and gold weight used in ancient Mesopotamia and Egypt; the Old Testament makes many references to shekels as units of barter. But the shekel was still a *commodity* with its own intrinsic value, because shekels *were* the payment. Athenian copper rounds were a logarithmic jump to a higher level of abstraction. A unit of *currency* was a *promise* to pay the owner *at a later date,* and most likely *in a different location,* an agreed-upon weight of gold. Further, someone unconnected with the original transaction would complete the redemption. Similar to the invention of writing, currency projected its owner through time and space.

While many people have either discoursed on the benefits of having money or railed against it as an evil, few have correctly classified precisely what it is. Money, first and foremost, is a form of communication. Old saws such as "Money talks" or "Put your money where your mouth is" reveal that money is truly a metaphorical language.

Nothing resembles monotheism as much as moneytheism. Because they are so closely joined, moneytheism and monotheism have had a tempestuous relationship throughout Western history. Interrupted by periods of intense conflict, alphabet cultures have usually found a way to accommodate the twin aspirations of wanting to be nearer to both *Gott* and *Geld*. The Puritan ethic encouraged guiltless devotion to both. Profits and prophets coexist. Although different in content and value, the abstract mental *process* by which people believe in an imageless deity is close to the one by which they place faith in the worth of abstract monetary equivalencies.

A clear sense of linear time is a prerequisite for the convention of currency. Possessors of coin understand that they have only *postponed* to a later time the pleasure of holding gold in their palm. Inherently, "worthless" coinage such as copper rounds represents delayed gratification. Only a populace immersed in a linear alphabet culture could have conceived of the equation "Time is money."

Both businessmen and monotheists possess an abiding faith in an ineffable, invisible force that will settle all accounts equitably in the end. Economists explain how prices respond to mysterious market forces in terms as arcane as any that one can hear in a seminary. The alleged ability of the stock market—an entity that exists nowhere and everywhere—to predict future trends has a parallel in the omniscience of the Creator. Redemption, an economic term, is a central concept of religion. Americans felt compelled to stamp their currency with the phrase "In God we trust," conjoining their faith in both God Almighty and the Almighty Dollar.

Because abstraction, numeracy, and linearity are left-brained functions, money has traditionally been the purview of men. For millions of years, the male hunted game to eat. Writing allowed him to segue from meat to money. The alphabet further refined his level of abstract thinking. Today, the man in the three-piece suit has substituted dollars for woolly mammoths. "Bringing home the bacon" no longer requires a shield and spear; a briefcase and a computer will do. Because the perceptual strategy of women is holistic and concrete, the intricacies of high finance are not as attractive to them. This, of course, is a sweeping generalization and there are and have been many astute women who manipulated the abstractions surrounding money as well as, or better than, most men. In the main, however, women have a different relationship toward monetary value than men. Until modern times, they were far more likely to prefer the tangible and concrete to the ethereal and abstract. Women, more than men, preferred to store their money where they could see and feel it, such as real estate or diamonds, rather than invest in highly abstract speculative schemes. The gulf of misunderstanding between the sexes over money reflects the markedly different split-brain modes each employs to perceive the world.

CHAPTER 17

LINGAM/YONI

A faithful wife must serve . . . her lord as if he were a god, and never do ought to pain him, whatsoever be his state, and even though he is devoid of every virtue.   —Manu Code (ca. 300 B.C.)[1]

T he word *hemisphere,* meaning one-half a sphere, has only two common uses: to describe the hemispheres of the brain and to describe
the hemispheres of the planet. Earth has two complementary yet
antipodal dominant cultures: the East and the West. Their distinguishing
features mirror the lateralized hemispheric functions of a single human's
cortex. Traditionally, the West has been outer-directed and dualistic; the
East, inward-seeking and monist. The West sees its history as a series of
events; the East tends to perceive patterns that recur. Western medicine
tends toward being mechanistic; Eastern medicine embraces a holistic
approach. The West's aspects predominately personify the left brain; the
East's predominately characterize the right. This book focuses on Western
culture, but a discussion of the relationship between the acquisition of writing and the change in the status of women would be incomplete without an
overview of Eastern traditions. The place to begin is India.

In the ancient Indian ritual of *sati,* a widow was expected to join her
husband's corpse on his funeral pyre. *Bride burning* is the infrequent modern practice in which an Indian husband sets fire to his wife ostensibly to
express his dissatisfaction with her, but often his motive is to acquire her
dowry. Female infanticide has been a recurring problem throughout Indian
history. *Purdah* is the Hindu practice of segregating women from men.

Long ago, before Indian culture evolved the customs of sati, bride burning, female infanticide, and Purdah, there was a place called Mohenjo-Daro.
Situated on the rich alluvial plain of the Indus River high in the northwest
corner of India, this ancient urban complex, excavated in the 1920s, stands as
mute testimony to a highly advanced culture that flourished from 2500 B.C.

to 1500 B.C. Composed of sturdy brick buildings laid out along handsome wide avenues, the city was more than three miles in circumference and was home to more than thirty-five thousand inhabitants. This ancient culture is called Harappan; named after Harappa, Mohenjo-Daro's twin city.

Although they flowered about five hundred years later than either Egypt or Mesopotamia, the Indus Valley cities rank as one of the progenitor civilizations of modern society. The citizenry was well versed in craft and metallurgy. The Harappans built a complex network of irrigation channels to carry the waters of the Indus River to distant fields. Their sailors made trade voyages to Sumer and Egypt as early as 3000 B.C.[2]

Surrounding the Harappan cities were lesser settlements, whose natives called themselves Nagas or "serpent worshipers." Beautifully crafted representations of hooded snakes coiled about each other have been found there in abundance.[3] Toward the southern tip of India, known as the Deccan Plain, lived the dark-skinned Dravidians. Inherited property passed through their female line; a custom that persists in a few present-day pockets.[4] Many pre-historic Dravidian sites have yielded the same bull-horned sacrificial altars found at Çatal Hüyük and Knossos. Central to all the indigenous cultures of India was a deep reverence for trees and, by extension, all vegetation.

An intriguing feature of the Indus Valley cities is the absence of grand palaces and temples. The largest civic structure was a brick-lined public bath. Harappan graves for men and women tended to be similar.[5] Harappan excavations have unearthed the first *Lingam* and *Yoni*: abstract sacred stone images of a phallus and vulva that represent the generative life force. The large majority of artifacts resembling humans appear to be statues of a Mother Goddess. From the archaeological record and present anthropological studies of customs in remoter areas of the subcontinent, a picture has emerged suggesting that all across India there once flourished relatively egalitarian, Goddess-worshipping cultures.[6]

The Harappans most likely spoke a language that was a form of early Sanskrit. The word *sanskrit* means "sacred and pure." The advanced people who built the Indus Plains irrigation systems and sailed to Sumer most likely composed the epic poems known as the Vedas, works that contain sophisticated insights about religion and philosophy. The early Indians did not, as far as we know, transcribe the Vedas, and the oldest sections make no reference to writing. This seems a peculiar omission because the inhabitants of Mohenjo-Daro and Harappa had invented a unique form of writing containing over five hundred pictographic characters. Harappan script stubbornly resists decoding. The complexity of Harappan script suggests that it would have been difficult to learn and use.

Around 1500 B.C., Harappan culture waned. In its place, sturdy warriors of Aryan stock, under the sway of the civilizations of the Fertile Crescent, slipped over the mountains that separate the Indian subcontinent from the West and descended upon the citizens of the Indus plains. Over the next two hundred years the Aryans conquered most of the subcontinent of India and subjugated those who survived.

Accompanying these warriors would have been the rudimentary letters of the alphabet. Martin Bernal estimates that the alphabet arrived in Greece as early as the eighteenth century B.C. The *Iliad* appeared one thousand years later. Since the Aryan Hittites wrote diplomatic letters to Akhenaton in 1450 B.C. from what is now Persia and Turkey, the Aryans who conquered India must have been familiar with writing and probably the alphabet. Although the majority of invaders may have been unlettered, even a few literate priests among them could have effected change. As it is said, in the valley of the blind, the one-eyed man is king. Aryan invaders subsequently adapted the Semitic alphabet to the Sanskrit they found in India.* The resultant Brahmi script matured, and after a thousand years, it, too, was ready to express literature. The oldest extant documents in Brahmi are from the third century B.C., though older writings might have existed.

It seems likely that during the transitional period from Harappan self-rule to Aryan domination, the Vedas passed from the lips of one generation to the next. The Aryans grafted onto these ancient poems their own version of cosmic events, as victorious cultures often do, superimposing their values on the Harappans. A careful reading of the Vedas, however, suggests the takeover of a barely literate, agricultural, but highly sophisticated, egalitarian society by a militaristic, patriarchal alphabetic one. Stories within the Vedas that stress militaristic and heroic themes, such as the Mahabharata and the Ramayana, are likely Aryan additions.

The Rig-Veda is India's oldest epic poem and contains glimpses of the culture as it existed before the arrival of the Aryan warriors and alphabet literacy. Women held considerable power and possessed the all-important right to own property. They participated freely at feasts and rituals. Widows could remarry.[7] Drapaudi, a heroine in the Mahabharata, was married to five brothers simultaneously.[8] Although a latter text than the Rig-Veda, the fact that polyandry is mentioned at all suggests that in the transitional Indian Epic Age (2000–1000 B.C.) women enjoyed many prerogatives.[†]

*The Aryans developed the Aramaic alphabet, an offshoot of the Semitic.
†Polyandry continued in Ceylon (Sri Lanka) until 1859, and still exists in remoter villages of the Himalayan foothills and in Tibet.

The Upanishads, the philosophical section of the Vedas, were written by known authors. Among the wisest were a man, Yajnavalkya, and a woman, Gargi. The presence of a woman sage is of signal importance, since patriarchal societies rarely permit a woman to achieve such an exalted position.

The multiplicity of Vedic creation myths suggests that the Vedas cover two distinct cultures. The prevailing myth sounds as if an unimaginative Aryan lifted the Creation story straight from the Babylonians, changing only the names. Indra (Marduk) is the god of storm and rain. He slays the water serpent Vritas (Tiamat), the primordial mother who controls the cosmic waters, and hacks her dead body into pieces.

Another version confers the creation honor upon Agni, the god of fire. Another claims that the god Soma, the spirit of a plant that contained an intoxicating drug, was responsible. There is one Vedic creation story, however, that by its very gentleness has all the markings of a pre-Aryan tale. It attributes the world to a single, irrepressible Pro-creator.

This original Being was a fusion of male and female and, in form, resembled "a woman and a man closely embraced." Desiring companionship, it split itself into two pieces.

... therefrom arose a husband (*pati*) and a wife (*patni*). Therefore ... one's self is like a half fragment; ... therefore this space is filled by a wife. He copulated with her. Therefore humans beings were produced. And she bethought herself: "How, now, does he copulate with me after we have come from each other? Come let me hide myself." She became a cow. He became a bull. With her he did indeed copulate. Then cattle were born. She became a mare, he a stallion ... Then horses were born.

The female and the male continue this charming dance, populating the world with all living beings. The original being then proudly proclaims, "I, indeed, am this creation, for I emitted it all from myself."[9]

Nice story. No sin, no guilt, no blame, no disobedience, no fall from grace, and no punishment meted out. Little children will not fidget in their seats upon hearing it. The serpent is not cursed, woman is not the root of all evil, and no one is expelled from a heavenly place. Best of all, there are no murders. The female is coequal with the male.

The Vedas emphasize that all living things are not just *creations* of a god, they are the very *manifestations* of god, implying that there is no duality. In India, the universe *is* the deity. The Hindu formula for spirituality is "I *am* Thou." In Western culture, God is something so enormous He is beyond comprehension and exists distinct from, and is the cause of, His creation. While the West reifies a monotheistic God, its formula is the dualistic "I *and* Thou." Hinduism posits that the entire visible world, *Samsara,* is like a mesmerizing providential cinema show. People must not be dazzled by its profusion of forms, for behind the screen is the One; the One is the All. While the Western deity manifests Himself primarily through His *logos,* the godhead of Hinduism appears everywhere in the world of *image.*

The Vedas also legitimize a unique feature of the Indian social system: the castes. Over centuries, these divisions mortised into social strata from which no one could escape. In circular fashion they confirmed what the culture believed: one's destiny was determined at birth. The Kshatriyas, the warrior caste, originally capped the top of the pyramid, and they thought of themselves as so fierce that they considered it a disgrace for any of their number to die in bed.[10] Initially, Kshatriyas controlled the conduct of religious rituals, but they soon created a subsidiary class of priestly assistants, called the *Brahmins.** The Brahmins steadily gained control over the precious art of writing. The Vaisyas were the farmers, merchants, and artisans. The Shudras were the working class. The lowest were the "outcasts," the Pariahs; they constitute the Untouchables present in India today.

After conquering most of India by 1250 B.C., the warrior caste settled down to a life of tillage and herding. The Hindu religion proliferated into a complex pantheon with many different gods and goddesses, and its rituals became ever more complex. Brahmins controlled the education of the young and they elevated the priestly caste to a superior position. They exaggerated their status at the expense of the warriors, and by 1000 B.C. had displaced the Kshatriyas as the premier caste. The clique that controls the flow of information in any given culture inevitably gains mastery over the other classes. History would subsequently provide repeated examples of the quill's superiority over the blade.

From early on, there were striking differences between the two cultures, East and West. In contrast to the Israelites and the Greeks, Aryan priests, recognizing the power inherent in alphabet words, tightly controlled who could learn to read and write. The Old Testament commanded ordinary Israelites to read scripture, and every male Greek was expected to have read the *Iliad.* Hindu Brahmins had strict laws forbidding others from contact with writ-

---

*Note: Brahman is a philosophical concept. This should not be confused with the name of the priestly caste, the Brahmins.

ing. Should a member of the Shudra class be convicted of reciting the Vedas, he would have his tongue split; if he possessed a written text, he would be cut in two.[11]

As literate Brahmins steadily gained control over important aspects of Indian life, the many liberties previously enjoyed by women began to disappear. The incidence of sati became commonplace, and as practiced, was different from the earlier culture. The older Rig-Veda mentioned sati, but asked only that a widow lie on her husband's pyre for a few moments before his cremation.[12] The later Mahabharata strictly enforced the wife's ritual suicide.* Brahmins discouraged women from pursuing an education and did not permit them to read and write. The Mahabharata states, "For a woman to study the Vedas indicates confusion in the realm."[13] The practice of purdah began during the Heroic Age, and widows were no longer free to remarry.[14]

The Hindu civilization evolved for two thousand years without a written code of law. The Vedas and the Upanishads contain aphorisms and ritual instructions, but these cannot properly be called a law code. Once all the wrinkles in the Brahmi script had been ironed out, the priestly class composed an alphabetic civil code, called the Laws of Manu, sometime around 300 B.C. Reflecting their Aryan origins, the code contains striking similarities to Hammurabi's earlier code. The Laws of Manu stressed the lex talionis of "an eye for an eye and a tooth for a tooth," and also tirelessly promoted Brahmin prerogatives to the detriment of the other castes. One edict claims, "All that exists in this universe is the Brahmin's property."[15]

While containing many passages honoring mothers and goddesses, the Law of Manu also has denigrating statements concerning women that were not present in the older Vedic texts. For example, "The source of dishonor is woman; the source of strife is woman; the source of earthly existence is woman; therefore avoid woman."[16] Many of the Manu's laws appeared designed to control women's power.

Every religion addresses the question: Where do we go when we die? Virtually all have answered in the same manner: a mirror world on the other side of life awaits those who leave this one. Some called it Hades, some called it Valhalla, and some called it the Land of the Dead. The Hindu doctrine of *karma*—the transmigration of souls—provided a unique answer to the

---

*The Greek historian Strabo, visiting India during Alexander's brief incursion in the third century B.C., reported that sati was commonplace. In a telling commentary on the state of conjugal relations in India at that time, Punjab Brahmins justified the practice as insurance that wives would not poison their husbands.

question. The dead did not travel on to another world, they came back in this one. Instead of an afterlife, everyone received a second chance, and also a third, a fourth, a fifth, and a sixth ad infinitum. One's earthly reassignment as fortunate prince or despised pariah depended solely on one's past behavior. The woe one suffered in this life was the result of misdeeds in previous incarnations. The law of karma, though couched in the language of fatalism, permitted the choice between acts of goodness and impiety. The Hindu notion that one will return, perhaps in improved conditions, was a powerful incentive to do better. But it also served as a potent soporific to prevent people from trying to change their positions in this life.* For example, a Shudra, condemned to a life of poverty, was sustained by the belief that if he was steadfast, he might be reborn as the Raja. To further embellish this attractive possibility, the Shudra imagined the Raja returning as a Shudra. Resolutely, the poor Shudra accepted this mortal coil as endurable.

Belief in the idea of karma deterred women from protesting their lot. The doctrine of transmigration of souls held out the promise that they could come back as men. Brahmins warned women that a wife who disobeyed her husband would be reincarnated as a jackal.[17]

The first known migration, or invasion, into India occurred ten thousand years ago when Indo-Aryans made their first forays into India. Archaeologists believe their descendants became the agricultural Harappans. The second wave of Indo-Aryans pushing through the same Western mountain passes in 1500 B.C., from the direction of Mesopotamia, were also agricultural, but they brought with them a warlike culture and male sky gods. A distinguishing trait between the first and second wave of Indo-Aryans was that the latter was more facile with the written word.

The least influential incursion into India was Alexander the Great's sortie in 327 B.C. He brought with him, however, real Cadmean reinforcements—Greek letters and Greek grammar. Still another wave of invasions began around A.D. 700, when Muslim invaders carried out a harsh, patriarchal, alphabet-based subjugation of India. The effects on Hindu customs and beliefs by this third wave, spread over five hundred years, were considerable. Yet despite the virtual suffocation of the older, egalitarian culture of early India by warrior Aryans, misogynist Greeks, and anti-iconic patriarchal Muslims, Hindu culture, especially in the south, somehow managed to retain many feminine characteristics.

---

*The Buddha compared comprehending karma to understanding the origin of Time. My explanation is an attempt to convey in a few words the essence of an exceedingly complex and mysterious subject.

India was one of the last of the major ancient cultures to adopt alphabetic writing, and, not unexpectedly, images remain profuse in its religion.
Both men and women honor the goddesses Kali, Durga, and Parvati; Indians credit the goddess Sarasvati with teaching them literacy.[18] Shiva, the lord
god who destroys and creates the world during the cycles of time, is a dancer,
unlike the God of Abraham, Moses, or Luther. In contradistinction to Western religions, Hindu art contains representations of sinuous goddesses and
exotic gods laughing and copulating. The Kamasutra and tantric yoga
unabashedly celebrate sexual union. Kundalini sexual energy, beginning in
the left toe, spirals like a snake up to the right brain. In many examples of
Hindu art, women are fully committed participants in the sexual act. The
Hindus hallow the normal.

Hindu divine couple
embracing

The most telling totem left over from the earlier Harappan culture is the
Hindu worship of the cow, an animal capable of giving sustenance without
being slaughtered. A genderless Brahman, sexually explicit art, important
goddesses, the worship of nature, and the practice of yoga to attain spirituality, all suggest a culture with strong right-brain values. Hindus venerate

the lingam and yoni, sculptural forms that represent, respectively, the equality of the male and the female generative forces. Despite the Aryans', Greeks', and Muslims' attempts to impose masculine left-brain values on Indian culture, they were only partially successful. One can only wonder what kind of culture would have developed in India had the Himalayas isolated it from the West, instead of from the North and East.

CHAPTER 18

BIRTH/DEATH

On ignorance depends karma; on karma depends consciousness; on consciousness depend name and form; on name and form depend the five organs of sense; on the five organs of sense depends contact; on contact depends sensation; on sensation depends desire; on desire depends clutching; on clutching depends existence; on existence depends birth; on birth depend old age and death, sorrow, lamentation, misery, grief and despair.

—The Buddha's twelvefold concatenation of cause and effect[1]

The East has many mysteries. Here is one concerning the Buddha. After achieving enlightenment in 533 B.C., the Buddha began preaching his doctrine. Nobles, Brahmins, women, and the working classes all flocked to hear him. Buddhism spread rapidly throughout India in the ensuing centuries. Never before had the world witnessed a new religion gain so many new converts in so short a span. But after enjoying a breathtaking rise, Buddhism went into a parabolic decline in the country of its origin. By A.D. 500, without a Hindu Torquemada, without persecutions or heretic burnings, Buddhism was almost extinct. When the Muslims invaded India, they found that the religion had all but died out among the people. Today, Buddhists comprise less than one percent of India's population.

As Buddhism shriveled into a desiccated husk in its native India, it burst like a monsoon, drenching the rest of the East. China, Laos, Tibet, Burma, Korea, Japan, Ceylon, Taiwan, Vietnam, Thailand, Cambodia, Mongolia, Indonesia, and Singapore all embraced it, each adding a slightly different interpretation of the Master's teaching. How could this have happened? How could a religion, founded by an Indian whose devotees were among the best and the brightest of his countrymen, be eradicated from its country of origin within a thousand years? What extraordinary circumstances fueled such a meteoric rise and precipitous plummet? And what factors were responsible for this doctrine finding such a hospitable reception everywhere else in the East? Mystery of mysteries. Before speculating on the answers to these questions, the story of the Buddha must be told.

Due to its quarantine by Brahmin priests, Sanskrit became a dead language by 500 B.C.; thereafter, it served as the reliquary of the Vedas' holy word. The people, meanwhile, spoke many different regional dialects. These transformations of language coincided with a significant new development in Indian society: increased alphabet literacy.

All religions are organic entities that change and evolve with the needs of society. After a thousand years, hundreds of nameless Brahmin priests had embroidered Hinduism with a melange of esoteric rituals, deities, superstitions, and competing philosophies. Some Hindu services became rites of tortured complexity. Hinduism was headed for its Reformation.

The sixth century B.C. also saw the rise of rational philosophers, who used withering arguments to discredit Vedic rites and beliefs. Paralleling the surge in logic was the appearance of super-rigorous practices whose aim was to help the individual achieve union with the god-head by bypassing the priesthood. The *Jains* were an ascetic sect that advocated the denial of all bodily wants as the highest form of spirituality. The more extreme adherents believed it was a triumph to die of starvation.[2] Despite its austere creed, Jainism gained many followers. Counterbalancing the ascetics was the increasingly popular *Bhakti* cult, which proclaimed that a communion with the divine could be only achieved through the senses. Worshipers chose a god or goddess upon whom to project their feelings, then used right-brained experiential pathways to achieve a state of ecstasy. Dance, chanting, shouting, and unbridled sexuality accompanied Bhaktic rituals. The hypertrophy of reason that results from the introduction of alphabet literacy inevitably galvanizes a countermovement that seeks to exalt the wisdom of the senses. I would suggest that alphabet literacy was the impetus behind Rationalism, Jainism, and Bhakti in India. It also prepared the ground for a new religion—Buddhism.

In 563 B.C., Siddhartha Gautama was born into a noble family near the base of the Himalayas. As a young prince, he availed himself of many earthly pleasures, then married a beautiful princess who loved him. They soon had a son on whom Siddhartha doted. His father, the Raja, beamed with pride at having such a son to whom his kingdom would one day pass.

But this idyllic existence was not to last. When he was twenty-nine years old, Siddhartha increasingly began spending his days outside the royal compound, observing the plight of ordinary people. The pain, poverty, sickness, old age, and suffering he saw troubled him deeply, and a great sadness overcame the handsome prince. He asked himself over and over again until it became like a mantra he could not still: "Why is there suffering in the world?" After much internal turmoil, he decided that he must find the answer, so late one night he slipped away while his wife and son slept peacefully.

Siddhartha traveled to the forest and there encountered a group of ascetics. Confident that these holy men must know the answer, Siddhartha immediately posed his question. They responded with abstruse replies, and hinted that to learn the answer he would have to join them and become an untiring pupil. Siddhartha shucked his royal garments and eagerly adopted the life of a wandering mendicant. Believing that the swiftest route to truth would be to deprive his body more rigorously than anyone else, he embarked on a descent into masochistic excess by sleeping among rotting human corpses that had been left for scavengers. In Siddhartha's own words,

> I thought, what if now I set my teeth, press my tongue to my palate, and restrain, crush and burn out my mind with my mind. (I did so.) And sweat flowed from my arm-pits. . . . Then I thought, what if I now practice trance without breathing. So I restrained breathing in and out from mouth and nose. And as I did so there was a violent sound of winds issuing from my ears. . . . just as if a strong man were to crush one's head with the point of a sword. . . . Then I thought, what if I were to take food only in small amounts, as much as my hollowed palm would hold. . . . My body became extremely lean. The mark of my seat was like a camel's foot-print through the little food. The bones of my spine, when bent and straightened, were like a row of spindles through the little food. . . . When I thought I would ease myself I there upon fell prone through the little food. To relieve my body, I stroked my limbs with my hand, and as I did so the decayed hairs fell from my body through the little food.[3]

A young woman found him in this moribund state and patiently nursed him until his strength returned.

As extreme self-mortification failed to reveal the answer he sought, Siddhartha tried another approach. He sat down beneath a bodhi tree to meditate and promised himself that he would not leave until he discovered the reason for suffering. One tradition has him sitting immobile for seven years, through the rains of winter and under the scorching sun of the summer. Potential disciples, eager to hear what, if anything, this unusual personage would say, kept vigil at a respectful distance.

When most people try to meditate, they become acutely aware of the mind's chattering monkeys vying for attention. Siddhartha reported that he vanquished these distracting inner voices through sheer force of will. When all was still, he reported that he serenely observed an endless cycle of rein-carnations. Birth, pain, loss, and death; birth, pain, loss, and death; birth, pain, loss, and death each paraded past his stillpoint inner eye in endless succession. He realized that the agent mandating the soul's invariable return to what he later called this "ocean of tears" was the impersonal Law of Karma. Craving led inevitably to selfishness, which in turn led to more crav-ing and suffering—a perpetual cycle of life, death, and rebirth. Each person who commits even the slightest misdeed predestines his or her own rebirth. All are condemned to ride the karmic wheel forever.

Appalled by this chain of suffering, Siddhartha focused on how to break the cycle. He concluded that its ultimate source was birth, which initiates each round of craving. Once people are deposited in the world, they want to remain. The vast majority does not *want* life to end. Despite terminal cancer, hopeless poverty, and the infirmities of old age, they cling tenaciously to life. The agent responsible for this drive is the self. Individuals passionately believe that they are distinct and separate from others. The unshakable cer-tainty of the idea of *a-partness* creates this delusion. Once this phantasm—"self"—encases itself in its self-serving armor, it dedicates every waking moment to taking care of number one: itself-I-me-ego.

Siddhartha came to see the ego as a selfish brat that will stop at nothing to continue breathing. To maintain the body, it demands food and drink. To ease its existence, it covets possessions; to reaffirm its identity, it hungers for human relationships. Of all desires, lust is the most pernicious because sex-ual union inevitably feeds the karmic cycle by providing the never-ending stream of carnal bodies that returning souls must use as vehicles to reenter this vale of woe. The ego, in short, prevents one from combining the soul of the world within each of us with the soul of the world at large. Wedged between them, the self-righteous ego blocks the individual from recognizing that the two are really one.

To achieve the state of bliss that would come from this union, Sid-dhartha recognized that the ego would have to agree to self-destruct—no small task. Its disappearance would allow an individual to achieve enlight-enment. Such an "Awakened one" would appreciate that there are no divi-sions between selves, that every individual is a seamless part of one indivisible unity. Hate would automatically disappear, because the enlight-ened would proffer love to every other living thing once they apprehended that, at the deepest level, they are one. The suffering that the ego generates out of craving and ignorance would dissipate. The karmic wheel would slow.

The fortunate selfless one would be spared that most vainglorious concept, rebirth, and would be released from the karmic wheel, having achieved the state of *nirvana,* a Sanskrit word meaning "extinguished."

Siddhartha was transformed into a *Buddha,* an "Awakened One." Although he was now free of the inexorable chain of reincarnation, Siddhartha acknowledged the obligation to share with others his insight, so he chose to stay and teach them as a *Boddhisattva:* a Buddha who decides to remain in this world. One tradition relates that when he returned from his inner sojourn, he stood up and acknowledged the hushed throng that surrounded him by holding up a small flower, smiling enigmatically, and bowing.

Despite Siddhartha's silence, news quickly spread of his mute attainment of enlightenment, and soon large groups came to hear his teachings. Never had a religious leader faced a more perplexing paradox. If his insight was ineffable and could only be gained by intense, silent, self-examination, then how was he to transmit it? Reluctantly, the Buddha began to preach.

The reason people suffer, the Buddha patiently explained, is because everything changes. Everyone lives in a fleeting, transitory world, but all stubbornly refuse to admit it. They cling to that which is impermanent: parents try to hang on to their children; women attempt to preserve their beauty; men worry about keeping their status. Love, fame, money, youth, health, fortune, reputation, and ultimately, life itself, are all subject to decay and permutation. Suffering would cease if we could achieve indifference to pain and loss. If only people did not desire, then they could be free. The price, which the Buddha considered modest, was that the enlightened would be indifferent to the joy of relationships and passion as well.

He founded the first atheistic religion, in that there was no deity to revere. He dismissed the gods and goddesses of Hinduism's supernatural domain, explaining that they were mere poltergeists in a vast delusional system constructed by humans. He taught that rituals, priests, prayers, demons, angels, devotions, sacrifices, supplications, and incantations were all worthless. He claimed that religious hierarchies were designed to benefit only priests. He resisted the temptation to promulgate a code of law, believing that all laws imposed by an authority eventually degenerate into tyranny.

Like Socrates, the Buddha was contemptuous of the written word, and he discouraged his disciples from transcribing his words. In an age when literacy was a revolutionary innovation, he preferred spoken parables and dialogue, prodding his followers to memorize his sayings and pass them on to future generations orally. The Buddha's doctrine was notable for its simplicity. He began by elaborating Four Noble Truths. He then proposed Five

Moral Rules. These five were the bedrock substrate for those committed to the path to enlightenment. For those whose circumstances did not permit them to leave their station in life for the life of a monk, he offered the Eight-fold Path: eight aphoristic guides to a righteous and pious life. The Buddha's spare creed replaced the Vedas, Upanishads, Ramayana, and the many other sesquipedalian names of Hindu works.

Let us now pause and examine this doctrine in light of the thesis of this book. To prevent confusion, we will consider *only* the doctrine of the Buddha, as he is purported to have said it, and not the refinements and embellishments that scholars have identified as later additions. Growing up in a regal compound, Siddhartha would have had access to the new technology of writing, and as eager for knowledge as he was it seems likely that he became literate at an early age. Even if he later disdained writing, the linear cognition that literacy induces would have strongly influenced his perception of the world. After his enlightenment, the Buddha's doctrine flowed from his personal experience of nirvana; mere literary narrative could never hope to convey the authenticity of his experiential insight. However, like all great teachers of antiquity, the Buddha used metaphors and straightforward talk to explain the nature of his revelation.

The Buddha believed one way to convey his insights was through his actions—if he were courteous, others would be moved to emulate him. He was kind, gentle, gracious, and courageous. He counseled returning hate with love. Nonviolence was one of the cornerstones of his creed. The Buddha championed the doctrine of equality. While he never actually proposed dismantling the hierarchical caste system, he offended the Brahmin priests by making his teachings available to anyone. He once scandalized his disciples by sharing dinner with a courtesan.[4] To the Buddha, there were no "chosen" people, no privileged castes, no divine rights of kings. His liberating universal message was that each individual, through intense personal work, could attain enlightenment, just as he himself had done. He was, he told his disciples, a mere mortal who had discovered a great truth.

Despite his courteousness, the Buddha suffered no one to ask him unanswerable questions. He dismissed speculations about creation, the nature of the soul, and the meaning of the infinite as distractions from the real work at hand: rejoining the One through a life of inner contemplation. He called such questions "the jungle, the desert, the puppet show, the writhing, the entanglement of speculation."[5] In the humid hothouse that was the Hindu religion, his message was sere in the extreme.

The Buddha's original teachings included many feminine motifs: nonviolence, equality for all, universal love, the horizontal layering of society, and the stripping of power from the male priesthood. The watchwords of all Buddhist sects are Wisdom and Compassion, two concepts traditionally associated with the feminine principle.* But the Buddha also taught that sexual desire, which resulted in new births, kept the karmic wheel turning. In his own words, "What if I, being myself subject to birth, were to seek out the nature of birth, . . . and having seen the wretchedness of the nature of birth, were to seek out the unborn, the supreme peace of Nirvana?"[6] The danger inherent in sexuality was the first issue addressed in his very first sermon, or *sutra*. Ananda, Buddha's favorite disciple, concerned about the proper stance he should adopt when conversing with women, asked:

"How are we to conduct ourselves, Lord, with regards to womankind?"
"As not seeing them, Ananda."
"But if we should see them, what are we to do?"
"No talking, Ananda."
"But if they should speak to us, Lord, what are we to do?"
"Keep wide awake, Ananda."[7]

The ranks of the Buddha's disciples excluded women, and his monks took vows of celibacy. The message that women were connected with craving and ignorance was being floated on a lotus leaf by a gentle man who was the soul of compassion. His syllogism equating the end of suffering with the negation of birth eviscerates the very essence of womanhood.

The birth of a child is the single most intensely joyous event most people will ever experience. For many mothers, despite the physical pain, the birth of her child is an almost mystical event. Who has not been enthralled at the miracle of a Lilliputian hand curling about one's little finger? What is more blissful than carrying a sleepy, freshly bathed infant, cocooned in flannel, nestled in one's arms? How could the Buddha see the journey that constitutes the panorama of life as so inherently painful and terrible that it would be best to "never have been born?"[8] Could birth, the quintessential female gift, really be the source of all the world's pain?

The Buddha began his melancholic questioning because he was struck by his insight that life, despite its pleasures, was primarily about recurring loss and separation. But what of the joys? Where is the pain and sorrow associated with walking along a surf line early in the morning? What of the sight

---

*Jewish commentators believed that wisdom could best be achieved through knowledge of God's written word. The Buddha believed that wisdom could best be achieved through direct experience and intuition.

of crocuses in springtime or the smell of a Thanksgiving dinner surrounded by family? What of the pleasures of a job well done, a book well read, or a leisurely lunch with a good friend? How could he hold repugnant the oceanic feeling one experiences, limbs entwined, in the aftermath of love-making with someone one loves?

His followers are quick to point out that the Buddha was not an unhappy man. They insist he said that it was *attachment* that causes suffering. Commitment without attachment, however, is a paradox so supremely difficult to achieve that it prevents the vast majority of people from attaining enlightenment. There is no mention of joy in the Buddha's Four Noble Truths; they all concern *dukkha*—suffering: what it is, why it is, and how to avoid it. Commonly misunderstanding his position, some disciples advocated suicide.* Despite its disappointments and unpleasant surprises, most people would vote yes on the proposition that the joys of living outweigh its sorrows.

By his own insistence, the Buddha was a man, not a god. It would not be sacrilegious, therefore, to speculate on the source of his sadness. In terms of emotional development, the greatest single loss any infant can sustain is to become separated from his or her mother. This loss can create a wound so deep that it may never heal. While there are many versions of the Buddha's birth, one fact appears consistently: his mother died as a result of it.

He was raised, we are told, by his aunt and father. His life fits the profile of an individual who has suffered the ultimate birth trauma—the loss of one's mother. Siddhartha grew into manhood surrounded by wealth, privilege, and family. Only a man with an incurable sadness corroding the center of his soul would leave a loving wife, a doting father, and an adoring son (whom he himself loved) to embark on a life of masochistic excess in search of the answer to the question of suffering. One result of his quest was his conclusion that birth was a cause of human suffering. The loss of a mother, at birth, is a tragedy immense enough to ignite such an intense desire to know the reason for suffering and may in part account for the answer at which he arrived. A clue supporting this speculation: Siddhartha's mother's name was Maya—also the Sanskrit word for illusion. To a child who never knew her, Siddhartha's mother was indeed a phantasm. The man who lost his mother in childbirth developed a system of belief that had as one of its principal tenets an extremely negative stance toward birth.

*When asked by a disciple whether suicide would be a clever strategy, the Buddha replied that it would be useless, since the soul, unpurified, would be condemned to return for another ride on the wheel.

The Buddha lived to be eighty, and his teachings had a significant impact both during his lifetime and after. Stories abound of his kindliness to every living thing. Assessing his character from his sayings, he seems to have been the gentlest and wisest of human beings. The one discordant note was his initial refusal to allow women to take orders in his new sect.

The aunt who had suckled him, having fulfilled her familial obligations, wanted to join the Master's group of disciples traveling from village to village. In a rude rejection, the Buddha told her bluntly that she could not join his band. She wept and beseeched him, but he ignored her and turned away to continue walking. She followed him to the next town, and there asked Ananda to intercede on her behalf. Ananda asked the Buddha if women could join the order. The Buddha refused. He asked again, and again the Buddha refused. Exasperated with his Master's stubbornness, Ananda reproved the Buddha while pointing to the woman who had raised him, standing outside the door, stooped with age, her feet swollen from traveling. Finally, with great reluctance, the Buddha relented, but only if she agreed to eight conditions. The first one states that a nun must rise to acknowledge a monk's presence, even if she has been in the order for years and the monk is a new initiate. Female subordination inform the other seven as well: women could join, but they must accept second-class status.

Something seems awry in this recounting. Was this the same man who proclaimed that all human beings are valuable, and made equality the centerpiece of his doctrine? Is this the same Buddha who scorned the pretensions of the Brahmin priests? The Buddha would not have treated a dog the way he allegedly spurned the woman who was his surrogate mother. The more fundamental question is, is this story true?

After the Buddha died, his disciples pledged to keep his teachings alive. An oft-repeated anecdote shows just how difficult this task would prove to be. In the days following his death, while his disciples were still mourning their loss, a rebellious monk jumped up and addressed the grieving group. "Enough, sirs! Weep not, neither lament! We are well rid of the great *Samana*. We used to be annoyed by being told, 'This beseems you, this beseems you not.' But now we shall be able to do whatever we like!"[9] The Buddha's ashes had not yet cooled and already a revisionist had appeared. The Buddha's more devoted disciples took it upon themselves to erect a hierarchy charged with guarding the purity of his teachings.

In the first generation after his death, chief monks entrusted his message to scholars who memorized the sutras and taught them to groups of initiates; they in turn recited them daily. According to this plan, the corpus of what the Buddha said was supposed to pass intact from one generation to the next; those in charge believed the participation of many monks ensured that the integrity of the Master's message would be maintained. The words of the Buddha were not put into written form until three hundred years after his death. The Pali Canon, the compiled sayings of the Master, was not canonized until five hundred years after his death. Half a millennium is a *very* long time. In the next twenty centuries, Buddhism radiated into many differing sects. If this has been the fate of his written words, might not alterations have occurred during the centuries when his message was passed along orally?

Since scholars commonly used writing in the Buddha's time, it seems unlikely that not a single monk wrote down a few mnemonics to help him remember the long sutras. As the centuries passed, and as more and more monks resorted to writing, that act imperceptibly may have changed the Buddha's message. Those who used the Brahmi script may have pushed the Buddha's teachings toward the masculine, because the use of the alphabet changes the perceptions and values of the whole culture. We cannot know what the Pali Canon would say today if women had joined men in transferring his message down through the ages, or if *only* women had passed it along. The story of the Buddha's rejection of his aunt is too dissonant with his noble character for one not to suspect this story is a later addition.

As originally set forth by the Buddha, Buddhism was a difficult religion to follow, and nirvana took a very long time to achieve. Many chose the easier and more familiar path of worshiping the Buddha as a deity. A humanistic philosopher who did not believe in gods, Buddha suffered the ignoble fate of being turned into one. One of the reasons many of his monks encouraged his deification was because it conformed to Buddhism's metamorphosis into a patriarchal religion based on an alphabetic sacred text.

Hindu polytheism has always involved a profusion of exotic images. According to the Pali Canon, the Buddha disdained images and banned them, believing they encouraged idol worship and distracted people from the self-discipline necessary to achieve enlightenment. This proscription seems odd in light of the Buddha's teaching that people should cultivate a detached indifference to reality itself, which he said was an illusion. If one could learn to be indifferent to suffering and death, could not one be indifferent to paintings and sculptures? Perhaps the Buddha's purported ban on images was attributed to him by a scribe editing much later and may have been due to the change in values that accompanies the transcription of the spoken word to written text. To perceive information in a linear, sequential form seems to engender a scorn of images. Crisp, clear alphabets entice readers to believe in spare, imageless religions. They also bring about patri-archy. Buddhism was Hinduism's "Protestant Reformation."

Buddha's doctrine is based on feminine principles but contains an abhorrence of sexuality, a suspicion of women, and a negative attitude toward birth. It was predictable that the religion that evolved from these positions would betray a considerable amount of gender confusion. I believe that Buddhism would have continued to prosper in India if it had not been an essentially feminine religion overwhelmed by the tide of patriarchy and literacy that was then sweeping the country. Its initial popularity was, I believe, related to the change in consciousness that accompanies the early stages of alphabet literacy. But its failure to embrace the alphabet was a major factor in its decline in India. When Buddhism finally reversed its posi-tion on this vital cultural innovation five hundred years later, it was too late. Every country where Buddhism subsequently found a receptive home was either largely illiterate, or used a written language that was *non-alphabetic*. Until the modern age, Buddhism had *never* succeeded in an alphabet-based society. In the Buddha's time, India was the eastward frontier of the spread of the alphabet.

In the early years of Buddhism the Brahmin priests, witnessing the rapid defection of many of their followers to the new religion, counterattacked. Within two hundred years of the Buddha's death, they outflanked his new creed with that most effective patriarchal weapon, a written set of laws. Imposed upon the people from on high, the Manu Code was in alphabetic form. Only males wrote, interpreted, administered, and judged the Laws. In the long run, Buddhism, with its themes of universal love, equality for all, and retreat from the affairs of society, was no match for this reinvigorated literate Hinduism. In the contest between the spoken word and the written one, the outcome was predictable. Buddhism accepted its mauling at the hands of the alphabet with considerable grace. The Hindus did not kill the Buddhists. Buddhism simply climbed off the karmic wheel and achieved nirvana. In the homeland of its origin, the light that was Buddhism was extinguished.

CHAPTER 19

YIN/YANG

One image is worth a thousand words.   —Chinese Proverb

The Chinese yin/yang symbol portrays the equality and complementarity of the two sexes. Consisting of two fluid teardrops nestled head to heel, each half extends deep into the hemispheric territory of the other. In the head of each half is a small circle composed of the essence of its opposite; each side contains within it the seed of its reciprocal.

Yin/yang symbol

Paradoxically, Chinese culture has been one of the world's most rigid patriarchies. For the better part of Chinese history, and especially in the last thousand years, the status of Chinese women has been abysmal. During this period, polygamy has been the norm, and many men have treated secondary wives as little better than slaves. Often, the primary function of the chief wife was to head a reproductive enterprise whose most coveted products were sons. Indoctrinated from birth to kowtow to their husband's demands, wives often had to adapt to their lowly station by effacing their own personalities.

In this man's world, a husband could divorce his wife for the most triv-ial reasons—if he decided she talked too much, for example.[1] On the other hand, she could not under any circumstances divorce him, although she could return to the house of her parents, an action viewed by others as a dis-grace that reflected poorly on her family.

Mounting archaeological evidence points to an egalitarian culture in pre-literate China and has raised the following question: does the historical condition of women represent the way things always were or was there an earlier time when Chinese women enjoyed higher status? Despite a male elite's relentless efforts to root out and destroy evidence of earlier society's gender customs, it can never do so completely. The giveaways are usually buried in myth and language, as they are in Chinese myths and folktales that refer to a time when "people knew their mothers but not their fathers," a cryptic allusion to an age of matrilineal succession.*[2] Chinese written lan-guage also contains several suggestive incongruities. For example, family names are ubiquitous in all cultures acquainted with writing. Ancient Chi-nese family names were built up from the symbol representing "woman."[3] If patriarchy had been in existence long before the recording of Chinese his-tory, why would men choose to construct their patronymics upon the spine of a maternal symbol?

Other clues abound. An ancient written Chinese character for "wife" also meant "equal."[4] The character for "roof" over the character for "woman" denotes "peace." In ancient times, a wife kept her own name after marriage.[5] These tantalizing nuggets suggest that at the outset of writing, women still enjoyed considerable equality. And then things began to change.

The nature of a spoken language exerts a powerful influence on the form of its written version. In English, there are certain identifiable, repeatable pho-netic combinations that designate nouns, verbs, adverbs, adjectives, and prepositions; they are known as "words." Although some words are homonyms (here/hear; bear/bare), each word, generally, has one meaning. The spoken word "mother" means mother and is not altered by moving its position in a sentence or inflecting it differently. "Mother?" "Mother!" and "Mother" all mean mother. The English language is versatile because its lex-icon contains over 500,000 distinct words, and combinations of these vocal-

*Even in present-day China, there remain enclaves that retain matrilineal inheri-tance customs; for example, the Nashi culture.

izations can express a broad range of thoughts. This principle is behind every language group west of the Himalayas.

Spoken Chinese differs, however, in that it has *no* distinct parts. Depending on the dialect, Chinese contains 400 to 800 monosyllabic sounds or, as linguists call them, "vocables," none of which signifies a specific word. Instead, the meaning of each syllable depends *entirely* on the place (syntax) it occupies in relation to the preceding and following vocables. The meaning of the vocalization that signifies "mother," for example, can change depending on what precedes and follows it.* There is no word for the word *word* in Chinese, because the Chinese language has no words! Besides the holistic nature of its syntax, spoken Chinese depends heavily on musicality. Each Chinese vocable has four to nine "tones." The meaning of each vocable can vary according to the singsong manner in which it is spoken.

Pattern recognition and musicality are right-brain faculties, as are deciphering the hand gestures and facial expressions that Chinese speakers liberally depend on to further enhance the nuances of their speech. By varying tone and context, a Chinese speaker can use vocables as nouns, verbs, adjectives, or adverbs. For example, the vocable *I* can have sixty-nine different meanings, *shi* fifty-nine, and so on. Thus, monosyllables, although limited in number, allow a speaker to express many diverse ideas and meanings.

The Chinese written language also differs from those used in the West. The oldest Chinese characters appeared around 1500 B.C. carved into tortoise shells and bones. Earlier scribes may have entrusted script to less durable and lasting media. This date, 1500 B.C., coincides with the emergence of the alphabet in the West, in the planet's other hemisphere.

While the Indo-Aryans and Semites found economical ways to translate the *sounds* of the voice into abstract *letters,* the Chinese transformed mental *ideas* into concrete *images.* Their use of a pictographic written language instead of an alphabetic one strongly affected their historical development. Along with ancient Hebrew, Chinese is the oldest continuously used written language. A Chinese scholar can read the most ancient script, because it does not fundamentally vary from the present writing style. Chinese dialects may so differ from region to region that neighbors might not understand each

---

*The Chinese spoken language is one vast exercise in auditory pattern recognition. Instead of keeping track of the linear sequence of words, the Chinese listen for the *whole* in order to make sense of the parts. While it is certainly true that a whole Western sentence must be heard to grasp its meaning, this relational aspect of phonemes is more critical in Chinese than in English.

other. Yet, throughout Chinese culture, all can read the written language. It is a testament to how well formed the written language was at its inception that it has undergone so few modifications over thousands of years.

Alphabets are specific to their cultures and not easily translatable even though the *principle* behind alphabets has also remained virtually unchanged after thirty-five hundred years of usage. Alphabets attempt to correlate one letter, or letter combination, with each of the forty-three distinctive sounds, or phonemes, that the human voice can easily articulate. While this feature facilitates learning an alphabet, it impedes communication between different language groups, even within the same alphabet, as any Portuguese letter writer paired with a German reader can attest.

Written Chinese has no alphabet, no parts of speech, and none of the complex rules of grammar typical of Western languages. What we refer to in the West as common nouns and verbs are represented in Chinese by symbols called "radicals." There are only 216 basic radicals. A complex Chinese ideogram, built up from as many as eight different radicals, can express sophisticated abstract ideas. The eye of the reader apprehends all the radicals *simultaneously*. To express the same set of ideas in an alphabet language requires many linear lines of exposition. Although each Chinese character can be reduced to its component radicals, the process we know as "spelling" does not exist in Chinese. The simultaneous perception of many different radicals superimposed one upon another calls forth the right brain's ability to synthesize more than it does the left brain's power to analyze.

Whether spoken, gestural, or written, every language strings one idea after another in linear fashion. Chinese characters must be read in sequence like the elements of any other written language; but unlike horizontally beaded alphabetic words, traditionally they have been arranged in vertical columns. This difference affects the way the information they convey is perceived. Consider for a moment the most common use of vertical information in alphabet writing—lists. Lists make clear the holistic interconnections of separate items. Verticality calls upon the right brain's *all-at-once* perception and allows us to organize the list's components in relation to one another. A menu in a restaurant presents the courses in a vertical layout so that the patron can perceive the concept of a dinner in its entirety. For the same reason, a theatrical performance's playbill lists its segments vertically.

Rearranging a vertical list of items horizontally makes the relationships of the parts to the whole more difficult to perceive. For example, telephone directories would be nearly impossible to use if the names were arranged across the page. A person scanning vertically can appreciate spatial relationships all at once; horizontal scanning is better for tracking time—one thing after another.* Perusing all the elements of a vertical row is primarily a right-brain function; following a horizontal line is primarily a left-brain function.

Human beings stand perpendicular to the earth. In that intense interrelational activity called "conversation" our eyes roam up and down our partner's body garnering nonverbal information. Shoes, body stance, outfit, and hairdo are elements used in the right brain's computational assessment of what is going on in the exchange. We never say we are checking someone "across," but we do look someone "over," as we "size someone up." "Over," "under," "up," and "down" refer to perpendicularity. Hunters rely on horizontal scanning, conversationalists employ vertical scrolling.

The feminine principle and Chinese writing share an emphasis on synthesis, holism, simultaneity, and concreteness. In almost every aspect, ideograms are the opposite of alphabets' linear masculine mode. Suggestive corroboration of this dichotomy is evident in the Chinese attitude toward time. The Chinese written language does not contain tenses to indicate past, present, and future; the Western grammatical quagmire called "verb conjugation" does not exist. There is no conditional pluperfect future verb tense in Chinese. And accordingly, in their culture the Chinese did not conceptualize the time frame of a week, or the notion of Sunday.

Another right-brained feature of Chinese writing is its emphasis on form. Calligraphy is a highly developed art in the East. In contrast, Western readers care little about the font displayed when they are reading. Content supersedes form in the West; form is an indispensable adjunct to content in the East. One must be artistic to write Chinese well.

Besides graphic artistry, Chinese writing depends more on poetry when expressing complex ideas than alphabets do. Combining various radicals, many constructions are exercises in appreciating metaphors. The conflation of two separate images can distill an idea of the utmost sensibility.

Ideogram for *autumn*

For example, the ideogram for "autumn" is the superimposition of the radical for "crops" upon the one for "fire."

*The power of the Vietnam Memorial in Washington, D.C., lies in the listing of the names of the deceased in the order in which they died, *by date*, reminding viewers of the impermanence of passing time.

Scientists have corroborated the right and left orientation in Eastern and Western written languages. Researchers tested a select group of Chinese- and English-speaking individuals who had learned to read and write both languages as small children and who, later in life, had experienced damage to one hemisphere or the other. Right-handed subjects who had damage to their left hemisphere lost the ability to speak either Chinese or English, and although they could not write English, they retained a limited ability to communicate in written Chinese. Those with damage to their right hemispheres could still speak Chinese and English, and although they could write English, they had difficulty writing Chinese.[6]

Despite the considerable differences between the world's two dominant writing systems, Chinese calligraphy still greatly diminishes the role of the nonverbal component of speech. Although originally based on a pictographic principle rather than a phonetic one, Chinese characters have become highly stylized and extremely abstract. Although the ideas expressed in written Chinese are presented in vertical columns, the characters must be read in sequence for the information to connect coherently.

Reading Chinese requires a certain reductionism. Although the characters are perceived *all-at-once,* a reader must pause to break down an unfamiliar one into its component parts. On the continuum that stretches from speech on one end, through pictures, pictographs, Chinese ideograms, and finally, to alphabets at the other extreme, Chinese writing is still much closer to the alphabet than it is to oral communication, and it is this proximity that makes it a masculinizing influence on culture.

Writing of any kind will realign the gender politics of any culture. A main factor promoting ancient China's patriarchy was, I believe, the change in cultural perception that accompanies the acquisition of the art of writing. Although the writing happened to be more right-brained than the style developed in the West, and produced subtle changes unique to China, the country still experienced a shift in which men appropriated power.

East and West have manifested significant differences. The left-brained alphabet cultures have been more aggressive in war, conquest, and exploration. The writers of ideographic characters built a wall around their country to keep foreigners out and discouraged exploration. Alphabet cultures, due to their extremely dualistic form of writing, are more inclined to impose their systems of belief on others and, therefore, religious persecution is commonplace, whereas religious tolerance has been the way of the gestalt-based ideographic cultures.

The snake, a female symbol, was cursed, crushed, and conquered in the alphabet cultures, yet it became an exalted, beloved, and worshiped symbol in the ideographic culture. In the West dragons were dispatched by heroes. In the East, dragons portend good fortune each new year.

The five most influential abstractions of society—imageless deities, written laws, speculative philosophy, mathematics, and theoretical science—are highly regarded and developed in alphabet cultures. Ideographic cultures, in contrast, did not conceive of imageless gods. They have relied on custom instead of law, have discouraged discussion of speculative philosophy, concentrating instead on practical issues, and have failed to see the transforming possibilities of higher mathematics and scientific hypotheses.

Due to the reductionism inherent in their written form, alphabet cultures have lacked unity. Fractured lands, fractious governments, and schismatic religions have mirrored their written languages, which have splintered into hundreds of different vernaculars and written forms. War and strife associated with intransigent political and religious ideologies have been their lot. Rarely would a single government be able to rule them all.

Ideographic cultures have formed empires uniting large numbers of people and promoting long-term cultural stability, even though ideographic lands also suffered periods of strife. Generally, they have tended to live more often under the banner of one dynasty that unified people who spoke many diverse dialects; pronunciation would never be an urgent issue in a form of writing based on images expressed poetically. The alphabet-based cultures, on the other hand, have a story about a Tower of Babel.

The alphabet users' sophisticated abstract science, combined with their bellicosity, led them to colonize the people of the patterns. In this confrontation between cultures, the ideographic-based culture has played the female's role to the alphabet's conquering male.

An important factor affecting a culture's historical development is the ability to grasp the concept of the individual. The reductionist aspect inherent in alphabets, called spelling, has encouraged users of this form to see themselves apart from nature, their deity, their governments, and each other. In contrast, the pattern recognition inherent in ideographic language has enmeshed users in a web of interpersonal relationships. The patterns in their language have kept them bound to their institutions, not separate from them. Their language has shielded them from the existential angst that parallels the actualized self, but it has also kept them straitjacketed in a conservative community stifled by etiquette, customs, and manners.

In the first round, the West has indeed bested the East, but it may have lost a significant portion of its soul in the process. Language is destiny. Which one a child learns to speak will determine how he or she thinks. The unity and continuity of Chinese script symbolizes the character of China's civilization, just as the rise and fall of Western civilizations reflect the constant flux of alphabetic written languages. Like yin and yang, these two cultures are both opposite and complementary. Like the hemispheres of the brain, each has the missing input and outlook the other needs to achieve wholeness. The integration of alphabetic and ideographic, West and East, and left and right awaits the next stage in human evolution.

CHAPTER 20

TAOISM/CONFUCIANISM

The mother principle of ruling holds good for a long time.—Lao-tzu[1]

Observe what a man has in mind to do when his father is living, and then observe what he does when his father is dead. If, for three years, he makes no changes to his father's ways, he can be said to be a good son.
—Confucius[2]

When the tentacles of literacy began to wrap around the minds of the Chinese people in the sixth century B.C., their society experienced dramatic changes. It was then that two entirely different philosophical systems emerged: Taoism and Confucianism. Their respective founders, Lao-tzu and Confucius, were contemporaries. Taoism represented an egalitarian feminine viewpoint from the past. Confucianism championed masculine dominance and became the creed of the future.

Taoism promoted Mother *nature* as the guiding force, while Confucianism touted Father *culture*. At their founding, Taoism and Confucianism both lacked a deity. Both were humanistic, practical guides to living. Both had strong opinions about women, writing, and images.

Lao-tzu transformed the mystery of the feminine spirit into his enigmatic rendering of the Tao using primarily the metaphor of horizontally flowing water. "The great Tao flows everywhere, both to the left and to the right . . . it holds nothing back. It fulfills its purpose silently and makes no claims."[3] In contrast, Confucius' system rested on a hierarchical ordering of the world. Its foundation was the family. But Confucius' idea of family values depended on a wife's obedience. The Confucian/yang need to control stands in stark contrast to the Taoist/yin admonition that the sage should never try to control anything. In Taoism, intuition was the guide to wisdom. Reason and reading the classics were the basis of Confucianism.

Taoism came first. The details of the life of its founder, if he lived at all, have been obscured by the tendrils of myth that have swirled about him. Tradition relates that Lao-tzu had been the curator of the emperor's Royal Library. In his old age, he became disgusted with the chicanery of court sycophants, and concluded that his life spent among books had been in vain. Resigning from his respected post, he planned to retire to the country to live as a recluse. He mounted a water buffalo, leaving most of his belongings behind.

On his way out of town, the guard at the gate saw Lao-tzu's packed bags and surmised that he was leaving the kingdom for good. The guard asked him if, before he left, he would please sum up what he had learned from a life spent in the quietude of the Royal Library. Lao-tzu obligingly composed his *Tao Te Ching*, history's shortest doctrinal book. The Way of Tao consisted of only 5,000 characters. Richly informed by poetry and metaphor, it had a very unusual take on all that the West holds dear.

Imagine, for a moment, that the gnarled old gnome passing through the gate was really a wrinkled right lobe of a human brain. The right hemisphere rarely has the opportunity to speak, because vocal language is not one of its functions. The boisterous left brain, stridently waving its right hand, always seems to be the one called upon by history to recite. In sixth century B.C. China, at the hinge point between non-literacy and literacy, the right hemisphere broke its natural silence to extol the qualities of the feminine.

The Tao, Lao-tzu explained, is the natural flow of movement that goes on all around us. Summer raindrops splashing on the earth to form rivulets leading to freshets are the Tao. So, too, are streams emptying into rivers that flow to the sea. The evaporating mist rising invisibly from the ocean to form clouds represents the Tao. Thunderheads that friction the air as they pass over the land are manifestations of it. Massaged by the earth to release their precious fluid, cumulus clouds contribute to it. The raindrops draining off our faces in a summer downpour coalesce, once again, into rivulets. We are ever immersed in the Tao.

Because we have layered the world with artificial categories we have obscured the Tao. If we simply let fall the veils of cultural conventions we will grasp our place in its flow. Since every cell and fiber making up our physical bodies is part of the Tao, every one of us is like seaweed gently waving to and fro in the current. Living our lives within this natural rhythm, and making no effort to resist it, would allow everything—from our institutions of government to gender relations—to float gently along as part of this river of the Way. According to Lao-tzu, it is all so easy: simply abandon all the stratagems that the left brain has so laboriously contrived, none of which exists in the natural world of the Tao.

Lao-tzu's first precept is that language is the great barrier that prevents us from knowing the Way. The opening couplet of his *Tao Te Ching*, warns:

> The Tao that can be spoken is not the real Tao.
> The Name that can be named is not the Eternal Name.

Later, Lao-tzu observes, "He who knows does not speak and he who speaks does not know." "Therefore the sage goes about doing nothing, teaching no talking."[4] Silence, in other words, is the precondition of wisdom. This Taoist maxim is what the right brain would say if only it could speak.

The Tao transcends rational thought. Knowledge, according to Lao-tzu, is not the same as wisdom. Thinking is an artifice of the mind that leads to opinions, which inevitably entangle one in disputes. Lao-tzu advised, "The wise sage does not quarrel. Therefore, no one can quarrel with him."[5] Intellectuals, because they love to argue, pose a grave threat to society.

Written codes of laws were a bane to Lao-tzu. He pointed out that as laws increase so, too, do the number of rascals. If each person managed to enter the stream of Tao, there would be no need for lawyers or laws. Pithy Taoist proverbs warned, "Sue a flea and catch a bite," and "Win your lawsuit, lose your money."[6] Laws are embroidered mental constructions that men artificially superimpose upon the natural world.

Lao-tzu cautioned people living within a city compound. He believed all aspects of culture, with its inventions, contrivances, and notions of progress, to be vexatious because they interfere with a person's contemplation of the true Way. The *Tao Te Ching* was not just a nature manual. Lao-tzu acknowledged that humans are social. His book advised those who must live together how to behave toward one another.

He addressed his book both to the guard at the gate and to the ruler of the kingdom. He taught that if leaders could intuit the Tao, they would become just, but the *Tao Te Ching* contains little practical advice as to how to govern. A wise ruler, faced with a crisis, would not try to reform society. Any action would constitute interference. Rather, he would rededicate his own life to the way of the Tao. Soon, others would emulate his behavior, and like the tines of tuning forks that begin to resonate, the entire community would be in synchrony; strife would be silenced by harmony. "If people lack knowledge and desire, then intellectuals should not try to interfere. If nothing is done, then all will be well."[7]

For communities situated close by one another, Lao-tzu advised limiting contacts. Foreign relations give rise to the need for foreign policy, and sooner or later, foreign policies degenerate into war. Lao-tzu espoused a pacifist doctrine: "Good weapons are instruments of fear; all creatures hate them. Therefore the followers of Tao never use them. The wise man prefers the left. The man of war prefers the right."[8]

Foreshadowing Thomas Jefferson by twenty-five hundred years, Lao-tzu proposed that a government that governs least governs best. Anticipating Adam Smith, Lao-tzu advocated a laissez-faire stance toward economic activity. The natural industry and self-reliance of citizenry will always correct distortions introduced by intrusive government. His Tao is what modern economists call "market forces," and passivity is the guiding principle behind both Taoism and capitalism.

Lao-tzu suggested that the yin principle was more powerful than the yang principle, that the female triumphs over the male because of her stillness. Water is the softest element and rock the hardest, yet waves will eventually wear rock away. Proud promontories, seemingly standing firm before the persistent pounding of the ocean, will eventually be reduced to granules. A walk on any sandy beach will confirm this fact.

The left brain rebels against the Tao. How, it demands, is one to understand the Tao if one can't read about it, argue about it, speak about it, or even think about it? Lao-tzu recommended relying on intuition, that most ineffable feminine principle of the right brain.

We know nothing of Lao-tzu's formative years, and there is no reference to his ever having been in love or married. These missing details suggest that Taoism predated Lao-tzu and that, just possibly, he was a woman. Perhaps he was many women, for Taoism encapsulates the philosophy that would be promulgated by the right hemisphere if it could ever get a word in edgewise. Long ago in China, it was heard and apparently heeded throughout the land.

Taoism selflessly sacrificed itself on the altar of language when Lao-tzu committed the Way to the very form of communication that would be its undoing. It is as if the right brain intuited that literacy would doom its way of knowing. There would come, however, a day in the late twentieth century when such unlikely seekers as stockbrokers, businessmen, and generals sought the wisdom of the Way by reading shelves of books with the word "Tao" in their titles. The *Tao Te Ching* was the last chance the right brain would have to ensure a hearing of its archaic values by future generations.

One historical tradition tells the following story. When the taciturn Lao-tzu was an emeritus savant retired from life, he granted an interview to Confucius, an earnest, politically ambitious young teacher from a poor family, who was traveling the land trying to convince feudal rulers to adopt his new philosophy. Lao-tzu listened quietly to Confucius' logical arguments but said little. There would have been few points upon which the two men would have agreed. The starting point of Confucian philosophy was an unbalanced relationship between the sexes. He proposed that men should learn to control their desires first, their wives second, and their children third. Without this dominant/submissive foundation in the family, he believed the greater society could not endure. Under Confucius' system, only men could control wealth, and women lost their prerogative to own property. According to Confucius, the most important familial relationship occurred between a father and his son; the second most important was between elder and younger brothers. In his subsequent teachings, Confucius spoke often of the Tao, but unlike Lao-tzu, he used the Tao as a justification for his vertical stratification of familial relationships.

Little is known about the real Lao-tzu, but historians detailed Confucius' life. Descended from the noble Fu He, Confucius' father died when he was a child; there is no mention of a mother.* Confucius married at nineteen but divorced four years later. In an omission that speaks volumes, history records the names of his sons but not the name of his wife.

Confucius must have had a sorry marriage, because after his divorce, he chose not to associate with women again. He proclaimed himself a teacher and surrounded himself with young men; they became his companions for the rest of his life. He later claimed that he had tutored over three thousand pupils, many of whom went on to important positions in government. There was not a single female among them. In one telling vignette, his disciples relate how Queen Nancia of Wei, a woman of questionable morals but an inquiring mind, desired an audience with the master. At first Confucius refused, but recognizing the potential of having such an influential personage as a friend, even if she was a woman, he consented. His disciples were displeased and demanded to know what had transpired during this meeting. Confucius assured them that he refrained from *even looking* at her.[9] He repeatedly wrote and spoke about his concept of the "superior man." "Superior to whom?" women might ask.

The signature anecdote about his life describes an encounter with a royal prospective employer. The sovereign asked the scholar what he would do first if placed in charge. Confucius replied, "First, I would rectify names."[10] By his succinct answer, Confucius identified the corruption of language as the single most pressing problem bedeviling society. Lao-tzu,

---

*She may have died in childbirth. A later tradition tells of his widowed mother selflessly subordinating her life to raising her only son. In either case we never learn her name.

remember, stated in the opening lines of his work that the first priority of society should be to *ignore* names. Naming is the principle prerogative of the left brain. Ranks, titles, and patronymics are common to all patriarchal cultures.

Confucius taught that the ideal path to wisdom was to follow the examples of the heroes described in the classics. While acquiring a thorough grounding in these texts, the superior man sharpens his wits through disputation. Reading and debating were Confucius' two principal means of preparing his superior man for a life of action and as the way to learn proper etiquette and civil behavior. Throughout the five books that he wrote or edited and the four that his disciples wrote about him, Confucius is repeatedly portrayed as a compassionate, wise man of integrity. His guiding principle, the golden rule, he couched in negative terms: "That which you would not want done to you, you should not do to another."[11]

Asked by a disciple if his philosophy could be written as one character, he answered, "Is not the character reciprocity?"[12] But his simple formulation did not extend to women. His ideal society rested on the unquestioning obedience of wives to husbands, daughters to fathers, and mothers to sons. Confucius said, "When these relationships go, chaos comes."[13]

On matters concerning sexuality, Confucius' philosophy is prim, puritan, and passionless. He warns men, "In youth when the blood and *ch'i* are still unsettled, a man should guard against the attraction of feminine beauty."[14] While he had much to say on a variety of subjects concerning human interaction, he was notably silent about that most common human emotion, love, and only addressed the subject of man-woman relations in a solitary line in his discourses. "Women and people of low birth are very hard to deal with. If you are friendly with them, they get out of hand. If you keep your distance, they resist it."[15]

Confucianism has been hailed as an ethical guide for relationships with family, Heaven, government, coworkers, friends, enemies, and ancestors. That such a system contains in its entire canon only one entry about women—and that a gratuitous set-piece of misogyny—may be because not all of what Confucius had to say has survived. As with Buddhism, very little of what we know of Confucius' teachings came from the master's own hand.

Confucius started teaching in his twenties and lived to be seventy-three. His disciples, or his disciples' disciples, waited thirty to fifty years after his death to record his conversations in a series of books called *Analects,* so what he said as a young man was not transcribed until seventy years later. Although the disciples of Confucius claim that they conscientiously recorded precisely what their teacher said verbatim, who, in 1933, could have remembered with total recall what Lincoln had said at Gettysburg seventy years earlier, in 1863? How can we be sure that these, most certainly male amanuenses, reliably recorded his message, or whether they emphasized certain teachings, editorialized others, and possibly deleted whole sections which were at odds with their own views on gender? It is both the majesty and the tyranny of the written word that it is our clearest yet narrowest window on what transpired long ago.

Like two sine waves, Taoism and Confucianism interweave throughout China's long history. Proponents of each system often disparaged followers of the other. For example, the philosopher Chuang-tzu (370 B.C.-?), who helped to revive Taoism, mocked the Confucians' rules of right living: He said, "I have heard of letting the world be; I have not heard of governing the world."[16] The Confucians mocked him by citing Confucius' desire not to "live among the birds and herds."[17] In China's history, there were periods and places where one system was ascendant over the other. Although many complex societal forces could have affected this balance, I would like to examine the relationship between Taoism and Confucianism in conjunction with only two: literacy and women's rights.

During his life, Confucius had a negligible impact on society, and for three hundred years after his death there were few outside a small loyal coterie who believed that there was anything extraordinary about his life and sayings. Then, in 200 B.C., a minister named Li Ssu standardized Chinese ideographs, making writing much easier to use. Coincident with more people becoming literate because of these reforms, the teachings of Confucius became the focus of intense interest, and soon after these two events, women's rights in China began a decline from which they have not recovered. The synchrony of these three events is striking.

Li Ssu's emperor was Shih Huang Ti, who so feared the rise of Confucianism in his realm that he ordered all the works of the master publicly burned. Fortune ebbed for Shih Huang Ti, and he was deposed. The next emperor, Wu Ti, was a follower of Confucius. He publicly anguished over the great national treasure lost to the bonfires. Hearing of the emperor's distress, eager scholars came forward, claiming that they had memorized Confucius' entire oeuvre. The emperor convened a panel of these "experts" (the record does not include any women among them) to reconstruct the conversations of a man who had lived six hundred years earlier. After working on the project for years, the committee presented Wu Ti with its version of Confucius Redux. The emperor declared Confucianism the official religion of the state and this text became the basis for all subsequent Confucian doctrine. We will never know for sure what Confucius' original views were because our lens back to the sixth century B.C. is distorted by the politics and gender relations of the first century B.C. The lens is further clouded by the ink marks of literacy that smudge its surface.

Women's status gradually declined. Slavery, a feature of societies dominated by masculine values, became a widespread and pervasive practice in China under the succeeding emperors. Women's loss of status can be inferred from the sharp reduction in the number of published biographies of high-ranking women which had been common throughout the centuries leading up to Li Ssu's extensive remake of the written language.[18] After Confucianism was proclaimed the state religion, the biographies of women (but not of men) all but disappeared.

After the initial surge in literacy that resulted from Li Ssu's labors, the dynasty dissolved. In the period of chaos and constant warfare that followed, literacy became devalued. During these Chinese "Dark Ages," the essential feminine nature of Chinese culture reasserted itself. Taoists gradually superseded the Confucians. Another factor in the decline of Confucianism was the defection of followers to Buddhism, which had arrived from India in the first century A.D. Despite the rapid growth of Buddhism in China, Taoism remained the dominant philosophical force in the early centuries of the Common Era, and it played a prominent role during the T'ang dynasty (618–906). Confucianism appeared headed for oblivion. And then, a revolution occurred.

In A.D. 923, the Chinese refined block printing, a process which had been known to them for centuries. By the middle of the tenth century Sung dynasty (960–1279), the printing press became ubiquitous. With its advent, a complex Chinese character no longer had to be fashioned painstakingly by a solitary hand holding a brush. It could be iterated repeatedly, easily, and cheaply. The emperor Li Hou-chu, impressed with this new technology of communication, commissioned printings of all the classics. The nature of Chinese writing made printing cumbersome because printers needed to have on hand a large and unwieldy inventory of blocks for the numerous individual characters. Nevertheless, within the space of a few decades, the printing press multiplied the availability of Chinese books a thousandfold.

The most common medium of Chinese writing had been thin bamboo shingles; literature therefore was quite heavy. Teachers traveled the countryside transporting their precious but hefty tomes in wheelbarrows. A "ponderous" work had two meanings, one literate and the other quite literal. A scholar often had to combine a keen mind with a strong back.

Combining strips of linen and fishnet, the Chinese had invented paper in A.D. 105. But its manufacture on a large enough scale to affect society did not occur until the Sung dynasty, when the process was perfected, expedited by the demands of the printing press. Paper and press made portable literature commonplace, and the absence of copyright laws kept it affordable. A set of all of the Chinese classics could be purchased for the modern equivalent of two dollars.[19]

Paper and printing profoundly affected Chinese culture. The Sung dynasty renaissance flowered after their introduction. As literacy rates soared, exquisite works of poetry, porcelain, and painting appeared in extravagant profusion. The combination of paper and press raised the collective level of Chinese society's abstract thinking. It was during the Sung dynasty that the Chinese put in place their first effective code of law. It was also at this point in their history that they conceived the idea of paper currency. Bills began coming off the emperor's printing presses in A.D. 970, but this new economic instrument resulted in disastrous inflation, followed by a severe depression. The Chinese derisively called their new currency "flying money," and hastily reverted back to trade and barter.

Printing, and the sharp rise in literacy that accompanied it, resuscitated Confucius' nearly moribund teachings. Confucius had been dead for seventeen hundred years, but his philosophy made an impressive comeback, and once again became the preeminent Chinese philosophical system. Chu Hsi, the Sung dynasty's great Neo-Confucian philosopher (1130–1200), completely revised Wu Ti's earlier authorized edition of Confucius' *Analects*, organizing the entries into a coherent, linear, and easily comprehensible text. In doing so, he emphasized some sections and deleted others. Chu Hsi's interpretation became authoritative, and it dominated Chinese society until Mao Zedong overthrew Confucianism in the twentieth century.

Chu Hsi put his own distinctive stamp on Confucius' ideas. He interpreted the yin and yang to be aspects of the black and white duality so characteristic of Western logic. He posited the existence of an imageless, nameless god whom he called the Absolute. The Absolute manifested itself in the world as an impersonal Law of Laws, for "Nature is nothing else than Law," Chu Hsi declared.[20] The ineffable Way had become the written Law.

The similarity between Chu Hsi's ideas and those of the Israelites are striking: the appearance of dualism, paired with a belief in an imageless deity who expresses himself in written laws. Confucian laws were literally engraved in stone, just like the Ten Commandments, and citizens were expected to read them. Chu Hsi championed Confucius' patriarchal system over the more egalitarian precepts of Taoism.

These attitudes became manifest in the customs of the culture. Around

Paleolithic campfires members of a family ate together. The word *compan-ion* is derived from Latin roots that imply breaking bread with a friend: com-*pan*-ion means just that. But Confucian views on the exalted position of men precluded husbands from even sharing a bowl of rice with their wives. A husband became so isolated that he dined alone, the rest of the family retreating to separate quarters of his house.

The most misogynist practice, epitomizing Confucian attitudes toward women, was the custom of foot-binding. Linen strips tightly wound around a young girl's growing foot deformed the bones in such a manner that the top of the forefoot bent back and under itself. A woman had to learn to walk, if she could, on what should have been the uppermost surfaces of her toes. Many adult upper class women were unable to walk and had to be carried by servants. If the binding was not carried to this extreme, a woman could walk, but only with a mincing gait. This practice began because Chinese men found this deformity sexually stimulating.

One of the distinguishing characteristics of being human is our ability to balance our weight on two narrow platforms called feet. Our upright stance is poetry in motion. Dancing, surfing, skiing, and figure skating, when skillfully performed, are marvels to behold. It is common to speak of someone who is independent as a person who "can stand on his own two feet." To deprive another human of the ability to do so creates an invalid, both physically and psychologically.

So if the binding of feet was emblematic of Chinese patriarchy at its worst, when, we might ask, did this practice begin? The first mention of foot-binding is in the annals of the court of the Sung emperor Li Hou-chu in the year A.D. 970[21]—virtually coincident with the precise moment in China's five-thousand-year history when the printing press began to domi-nate the structure of society. It was also the period when Confucianism surged past Taoism, and puritanical patriarchal values superseded egalitar-ian ones. It was the time, too, when Chinese lawmakers formulated their first effective universal code of written laws, and their first acceptance of the idea of an imageless monotheism. And it was even the same year that the Chinese experimented with paper money. Could it be coincidence that all these events clustered about one another just as men instituted a custom—for the first time in any culture anywhere and any time—based on the perception that a hobbled woman was a desirable woman?

The sudden alteration in Chinese notions of feminine beauty was so precipitous that a historian must wonder what caused such a sadistic realignment of male thinking. Perhaps one needs look no further than the invention that transformed Chinese society. The printing press, as its name implies, presses. A printer inserts a blank piece of paper between an anvil and an etched wooden block whose intaglio has been coated with ink. Then, the block and anvil squeeze the paper in a slow, crushing action until the paper absorbs the ink. Foot-binding was based on a similar principle: a slow and sustained compression over many years deformed a girl's foot. It seems extraordinary that the violence done to women so resembled the workings of the invention that spread literacy.

Another compelling coincidence: the strips of linen used to make paper were the same strips of linen used to wrap a young girl's feet. The explosion of literacy in tenth-century China crippled women in more insidious ways than anyone at the time could appreciate. Bookbinding and foot-binding, one the cultural result, I believe, of the other, occurred in tandem.

The inventions of paper and the printing press deeply affected Taoism. Also, Buddhism had keenly influenced Lao-tzu's philosophy when the latter had arrived from India. But Buddhism, too, experienced a significant transformation after it crossed the Himalayas. The Buddha, a man in India, became a deity in China; his disciples, ordinary mortals in India, became Chinese saints called *Lohars*. Taoist premises had much in common with Buddhist ones, and as time went by, the Chinese original emulated features of the new transplant.*

After being exposed to the Chinese Buddhists' sacred texts, Taoists created a sacred literature that they canonized in A.D. 1016. Hagiographies of Taoist saints and patriarchs filled volumes. A male hierarchy organized itself along Buddhist lines. Women were more and more marginalized. As a final indignity, Lao-tzu was elevated to the status of a god. Temples dedicated to him proliferated in the tenth century. Taoist priests reading from books conducted elaborate rituals in poorly lit interiors—the antithesis of the natural world. Concurrently, the most unexpected development occurred: the male hierarchy ordered Taoist priests to practice celibacy.[22]

Let us pause here to ponder this unusual turn of events. Lao-tzu began his concise book of aphorisms with the admonition to beware of language, both spoken and written. Fifteen hundred years later, young men were ruining their eyesight poring over voluminous written texts that purported to contain information about the Tao. People prayed to Lao-tzu to alleviate their suffering or to bring them solace, despite his own belief that such prac-

*It must be emphasized that despite the sharp differences between Confucianism, Taoism, and Buddhism, all three were compatible in the ecumenical Chinese mind. Thus, one could be a follower of Confucius, practice Taoist exercises, and recite a Buddhist sutra, without feeling disloyal to any one of them.

tices availed little. But of all the ways the tenth century commentaries corrupted Lao-tzu's original teaching, the one that most explicitly contradicted his message was the male hierarchy's decision to ban sex among its priesthood. The Tao is the Way. It is the flow of nature that seeks to complete itself. It is the involution of the trees in winter during the dark days surrounding the solstice. It is the tender young shoot nudging its way through the damp loam in springtime. Lao-tzu's teaching can be summed up in one phrase—"Make no dams." The symbol of Taoism is the yin/yang circle, conjoining the feminine principle to the masculine one to form a unity greater than the sum of its two parts. The most concrete example from life of this principle is the union of sperm and ovum.

How could the Taoist leadership sixteen hundred years after Lao-tzu wrote his 5,000 characters, suddenly have interpreted his aphorisms to mean, "Stop the flow!?" Taoism commends contemplating nature, and since no fish, bird, or mammal practices celibacy, no observation of nature could lead a Taoist priest to recommend bottling up sperm within the testicles so that they could waste away and die, rather than letting them go with the flow.

Altars, temples, celibacy, written texts, and a male-dominated hierarchy suggest the nefarious masculinizing effects of literacy. The printing press deflected the current of Chinese society. Malformed feet and withered sperm were but two of its sterile eddies.

As with their positions on gender, Taoists and Confucianists staked out widely divergent attitudes regarding images—especially the most ubiquitous form of representative art: the human face and body. To better understand the Chinese convention, a brief discussion of why these images have been so common across the spectrum of cultures is in order.

More than legs, breasts, beards, scents, buttocks, or ankles, the most consistently stimulating erogenous zone is the face of another human being. A languid smile, an arched eyebrow, a tongue flicked invitingly along the border of a lower lip can convey more than can an evening of conversation. Women tacitly acknowledge the centrality of their faces by expending considerable time and money caring for it and applying makeup to it, and frequently frame their visages with carefully chosen jewelry and adornments.

Almost without exception, cultures place more value on the beauty of a woman's face than on a man's, as the pairing of Beauty and the Beast and Roxanne and Cyrano attest. In general, a man falls in love through his eyes and a woman falls in love through her ears. The particular symmetry that constitutes beauty eludes definition and yet there is an unspoken consen-

sus among both men and women as to whose face is beautiful and whose
is not.

After the face, the next most important secondary sexual characteristic
for humans is their total form; that is, the male physique and the female figure. In both cases, simply looking at the various curves and angles of a particular person's chest, waist, loins, thighs, and other elements can arouse the
opposite sex. This peculiar feature of sexuality defies rational description.

The artists of many diverse cultures have attempted to render faithful
reproductions of beautiful women's faces and forms. Female statues have
been unearthed in all Neolithic cultures. Mesopotamian, Egyptian, Hindu,
Minoan, Greek, Roman, and European cultures, right up to the present
time, have made the female face and figure an enduring subject of their art.
Since woman is such a universal subject in other cultures' art, why are there
no representative images of beautiful women's faces or forms in early Chinese art and why is she virtually absent in the art that followed?

Taoists encouraged artists to create images of fish, birds, and animals.
The importance of nature in the Tao made Chinese landscape painting a
most pleasing and artful form. Occasionally, human figures appear in the
painting, but they are almost always small and insignificant. When the
viewer can discern a face, it is usually an old man's face, and the features are
never portraiture in the Western sense of the word. Taoists transformed the
beauty of the individual female into a passion for feminine nature, just as
the feminine force itself became "the Tao." The *Tao Te Ching* contains not a
single proper pronoun, and, in parallel fashion, Taoist art did not glorify the
beauty of any particular individual.

Confucianism encouraged the art of calligraphy and bamboo leaves,
two highly abstract art forms. Missing from this supremely patriarchal culture's art are images of feminine beauty either in face or figure. Men enjoy
looking at beautiful women because that is the way their nervous systems
evolved. Women, too, derive considerable pleasure from seeing other
women. A perusal of any women's magazine confirms this fact today. A culture that denies women access to these images robs them of a potent source
of self-worth. Chinese rulers did not pass explicit laws against the making of
female images, but Confucian customs dictated society's mores. Painting
images of young women's faces or their figures was not a suitable subject for
the art of this society.

Throughout the early years of Taoism and Confucianism, people worshiped a series of mature female deities represented by statues. During the
rise of Confucianism, these images began to disappear. Because the Goddess's influence had been pervasive before the spread of literacy, the Chinese

cultural dictators could not completely suppress the people's desire to acknowledge her power. As the Confucian advocates were metaphorically turning the screw on both printing presses and women's feet, she began to make a surreptitious reappearance, and soon, she became a ubiquitous image. Throughout the world, the countenance of the Great Goddess became inextricably associated with Chinese culture. Every town and city prominently displayed her image, although most would not recognize her as the Goddess, because in patriarchal China, people called her the Buddha.

The Buddha was, indisputably, a man who once lived in India. As his teaching spread throughout Asia, people dedicated statues to him in the temples and cities of every country. In those countries in which literacy did not play a dominant cultural role (Laos, Tibet, Thailand, Vietnam, and Indonesia, for example), the Buddha is depicted as a broad-shouldered, narrow-waisted, muscular man sometimes engaged in the act of dancing.

But in China, the country that invented Asian writing and had the richest literary tradition, the Buddha is almost always depicted seated and still. His shoulders are slightly stooped and rounded, his belly is protuberant, he has a hint of breasts, and he has barely any masculine muscle definition. He is heavier than Buddhas elsewhere, his girth is greater, his face is rounder and fuller, his lips are more sensual, and his countenance resembles that of the enigmatic Mona Lisa. His face radiates a benevolence more typical of a middle-aged mother than the representative stern male deities of the ancient West. He is calm, quiet, loving, passive, maternal, quiescent, protective, and contemplative. Indeed, especially after the tenth century A.D., the Chinese depiction of the Buddha looks suspiciously like a mature mother figure.

Unlike Western deities, the Buddha in his/her most typical form seldom punishes, seeks vengeance, has adventures, hurls thunderbolts, subdues monsters, or frowns. Under Confucian patriarchy at its most pronounced, the Chinese sublimated their love for the Queen of Heaven by transforming the thin, ascetic man from India into a soft, amply-fleshed, loving goddess. A precedent for this sexual crossover already existed in China in the person of Kuan Yin, Goddess of Mercy, a hermaphroditic figure who begins as a god but transforms into a goddess.

As a general rule throughout Asia, the more patriarchal the society, the more the Buddha looks like a woman; the more egalitarian the society, the more the Buddha looks like a man. Although Chinese Confucianism treated women harshly, two other sophisticated Asian cultures—Korea and Japan— surpassed the Chinese in this doleful department. These two were the *only* countries in ancient Asia to adopt a linear horizontal alphabet in addition to

LEFT: Eleventh-century *Standing Buddha,* typical of representations of the Buddha from cultures without a strong literary tradition

BELOW: *Seated Buddha* from seventeenth-century Japan, typical of representations of the Buddha from Japan, China, and Korea

their use of Chinese ideographic script. While their letters do not resemble the letters used in the West, nevertheless Japan and Korea have a written language code that approximates a phonetic alphabet. After adopting their respective alphabets, both countries also embraced unrelenting patriarchy, and it is in these two countries, along with China, that the Buddha's appearance is the most effeminate. Conversely, these same three countries are the ones in which Confucius and his teachings were most revered. Compare most statues of the Buddha from Japan or Korea with his depictions in nearby Southeast Asia, Indonesia, the Philippines, or Tibet; the differences are striking. The lands that honored the feminine and had poorly developed literary traditions retain the Buddha's masculine form. The most earnest efforts of the literate Japanese, Korean, and Chinese patriarchs could not suppress the spirit or the image of the Great Goddess, even if they disguised her as a man.

It would serve us well to now step back and survey the implications of the last twelve chapters. In the sixth and fifth centuries B.C., a number of hitherto unfamiliar schools of thought emerged suddenly, appearing in locations across a wide geographical band extending from China to Greece; they included Jainism, Asceticism, Materialism, Sophism, Rationalism, and Legalism. In addition, the cult of Bhakti in India and Dionysus in Greece imbued this period with an intensely agitated aura. The "Axial Age" is the term historians use to describe this phenomenal period, during which many of the most influential religious leaders in history were contemporaries.

Isaiah, Socrates, and Zoroaster* all gave a distinctive shape to peculiarly Western ideas. In the same brief period, Buddha, Lao-tzu, and Confucius emerged in the East. The legacies of these six men were philosophies or schools of religious thought that still claim vast numbers of adherents today. All six share certain striking similarities: each developed or refined an abstract system of thought that challenged the brains of all who attempted to understand them; all were literate. None of them had a relationship with a woman that he valued above solitude or the company of men.

Both the alphabet in the West and Chinese ideograms in the East became commonplace in the fifth and sixth century B.C. as all other antecedent scripts began to disappear. One plausible explanation for the Axial Age is that complex abstract systems of thought came into existence because literacy, the ultimate abstraction, was the impetus propelling these literate spiritual leaders to a higher level of consciousness. The question troubling feminist historians is: Why did misogyny so often accompany their message? The answer is: *There is something inherently anti-female in the written word. Men obsessed with the written word tend to be sexist.* The vast majority of men who love women and have families are not the ones who withdraw from conventional life to preach doctrines that others, similarly disposed, commit to writing.

These six highly influential religious leaders promulgated a new way to relate to the world just as the Goddess began to lose her hold on the people's imagination. Each of them proposed a new method, path, logic, Way, system, or Law to achieve spiritual awareness. Only something as powerful as literacy could have stirred up the sediment of the human condition to bring to the surface six such unique personalities. Combined, they muddied the waters, as far as women were concerned, so thoroughly that it would take twenty-five hundred years before some women, and a few men, would begin to see through the muddle again.

Now we shall return from the Far East to the West. Athens, Rome, and Jerusalem are the places, and the civilization of post-Classical Greece is the time.

---

*Zoroaster (or Zarathushtra) was the lawgiver who founded the Persian system of monotheism.

CHAPTER 21

B.C./A.D.

> But thou, O Roman, learn with sovereign sway
> To rule the nations. Thy great art shall be
> To keep the world in lasting peace, to spare
> The humbled foe and crush to earth the proud.
>
> —Virgil (*The Aeneid*, 6,848)

In every other respect these two traditions [Hebraic religion and Hellenistic philosophy], each one originating out of its own specific antecedents, and in its own terrain and time, were vastly different. In every other respect, that is, but one: they were both, from the start, profoundly informed by writing. Indeed, they both made use of the strange and potent technology which we have come to call "the alphabet."

—David Abram[1]

The Greeks passed from center stage after being defeated by the Macedonians in 338 B.C. Philip II, followed by his brilliant son, Alexander the Great, imposed a conservative regime upon their new subjects. The hyperkinetic creativity of Classical Greece was no more, but Philip was so in awe of Greece's imaginative culture that he hired Aristotle to tutor Alexander. Despite the sage's presence in his retinue, Alexander's reign was sadly lacking in memorable poets, playwrights, historians, or philosophers. The unique spark that had ignited Greece's Golden Age could not be struck against the northern conquerors' metallic shields.

Bindusara, an Indian raja who hungered after Western knowledge, wrote to King Antiochus, the Alexandrine successor to the throne of Syria, requesting the services of a Greek philosopher in exchange for a handsome finder's fee as well as a munificent sum for the philosopher himself. After a diligent search, an embarrassed Antiochus reported that there were no philosophers in his kingdom that he could recommend.[2]

This decline in influence of the written word coincided with a dramatic improvement in the fortunes of women. The largely illiterate agrarian Macedonians dispensed with Athenian notions of democracy and reasserted a kingship. Women reacquired the right to own and manage their own wealth and property. They mingled freely with men and advanced in professions that had been denied to them in Periclean Athens.

After Alexander's death at the age of thirty-three in 323 B.C., his empire disintegrated amidst the squabbling of his generals. When the tumult cleared, the boy-conqueror's huge dominion had cracked into four distinct spheres of influence. Women lived a better life under the Macedonian Ptolemies (who controlled what was left of the former Egyptian empire). An Alexandrine marriage contract from 100 B.C. illustrates women's near-equal status:

In the 7th year of the reign of Alexander, son of Alexander, the 14th year of Ptolemy's administration as satrap, in the month Dius.

Contract of marriage of Heraclides and Demetria.

Heraclides takes his lawful wife Demetria of Cos from her father Leptines of Cos and her mother Philotis. He is free: she is free. She brings with her to the marriage clothing and ornaments valued at 1000 drachmas. Heraclides shall supply to Demetria all that is suitable for a freeborn wife. We shall live together in whatever place seems best to Leptines and Heraclides, deciding together.

If Demetria is caught in fraudulent machinations to the disgrace of her husband Heraclides, she shall forfeit all that she has brought with her. But Heraclides shall prove whatever he charges against Demetria before three men whom they both approve. It shall not be lawful for Heraclides to bring home another woman for himself in such a way as to inflict contumely on Demetria, nor to have children by another woman, nor to indulge in fraudulent machinations against Demetria on any pretext. If Heraclides is caught doing any of these things, and Demetria proves it before three men whom they both approve, Heraclides shall return to Demetria the dowry of 1000 drachmas which she brought, and also forfeit 1000 drachmas of the silver coinage.... Demetria and those helping Demetria shall have the right to exact payment from Heraclides and from his property on both land and sea, as if by a legal judgment.[3]

This straightforward mutual pledge could not have been drawn up in the Athens of Plato.

The Macedonians' triumph was short-lived. Within a hundred years, what was to become known as Western civilization was in the callused hands of Roman warrior-farmers. Virtually invincible in combat, the Romans ultimately conquered every people who had contributed to Western tradition. They expanded the Greek notion of freedom to encompass an entity they called the Republic. The word derives from the Latin *res publica*, the "thing" of the public. The Romans, however, had a very restricted definition of what constituted a "public thing": only adult male landowners could participate in it. The Republic was such a boon to this privileged group that they reciprocated with intense loyalty.

This social contract propelled the orderly legions marching out of Rome to the far reaches of Europe, Asia Minor, and Africa. Could the vanquished have contributed to the official but biased accounts of Roman historians, they would have characterized the early Romans as merciless, brutal thugs. But they were thugs with a difference—they were literate thugs. A significant factor in the Romans' success was their enthusiastic advocacy of universal male literacy. A clean simple Latin alphabet, modeled along the lines of the Greek one, enhanced the likelihood of attaining this utilitarian goal.*

When the Romans handily defeated the rump remains of Alexander's empire, the victors recognized that the most valuable spoil of these campaigns was Greek culture, whose customs, religion, and traditions they unashamedly embraced. They even invented a myth to connect their lineage to the defeated Trojans of Homeric times.

The Romans were a pragmatic people, but to sustain a concept as abstract as democracy, a nation needs inventive citizen thinkers. Lacking the critical mass necessary to keep the idea alive, the Roman republican experiment collapsed after four hundred years. When Caesar defied the Senate and crossed the Rubicon into Rome in 49 B.C. with his army, he undermined the remaining moral authority of the corrupt Roman legislative body.

The Empire, the entity that replaced the Republic, began with the best of intentions. While history has judged Julius Caesar to have been an enlightened despot, he unleashed a tyranny of the mighty that truncated Roman law. Subsequent emperors further emasculated the legal system by raising themselves above the law. History is replete with egregious excesses that have been perpetrated by rulers who could not be held accountable for their actions. Lord Acton's aphorism, "power corrupts and absolute power corrupts absolutely" aptly describes such Roman reigns. After Caesar's assassi-

---

*In Pompeii, a Roman city preserved in time by a volcanic eruption in A.D. 79, the ubiquity of graffiti scrawled on its walls by members of society's underclass suggests that the Romans nearly achieved their goal.

nation, some emperors could be considered models for Plato's enlightened philosopher-kings, but many were not. Bloody coups punctuated imperial successions with such frequency that the populace hardly took notice. In the Empire, the Senate declared that the man who donned the purple was by this act transformed into a god, and Roman state religion required all Roman citizens to acknowledge the emperor's divine transfiguration.

Despite the Empire's often convulsive disarray at its center, the deadly efficient Roman military machine continued to rack up one success after another on the borders, and these victories flooded the capital with cheap slave labor that became the economy's substrate. To control so many slaves with so few masters necessitated a constant reign of terror. The Roman rulers resorted to highly visible displays of brutality, crucifixion being among the preferred methods. This public, painful, and humiliating torture-to-death served as an effective deterrent to anyone contemplating sedition. Rome became an empire of extremes and paradoxes. Most of the citizens who lived under Roman rule throughout its vast empire prospered through trade and entrepreneurial ventures. But if the rulers in Rome perceived a threat to their hegemony, they vigorously crushed the source.

Pax Romana lasted much longer than had the Greek experiment. Extending over a far greater landmass, the population of the Roman Empire outnumbered that of the Greeks by millions.* And yet, historians have puzzled over why the Romans initiated so few innovations. In some areas, such as law, engineering, and architecture, they substantively refined the Classical Greek ideal, but for the most part, Roman art, science, medicine, and philosophy did not achieve the standards set by the Greeks. Roman explorations into matters philosophical produced no one of the stature of Socrates, Plato, or Aristotle. Roman sculptors were shameless copycats and none reached the level of originality achieved by Pheidias, Praxiteles, or Lysippus. The works of Greek playwrights such as Aeschylus, Sophocles, and Euripides are so trenchant they are still performed today, but there are no Roman dramatists who can be compared to them. Lucretius, the only notable Roman scientist, suffers badly when compared to Euclid, Archimedes, or Eratosthenes. But despite their creative poverty (or, perhaps, because of it), the Romans possessed a skill that the Greeks sorely lacked—they were supremely efficient administrators. They can almost be said to have invented bureaucracy, imposing and skillfully administering government over a huge region for six

---

*At its height, the Roman Empire encompassed more than 1,250,000 square miles with a population of over 60,000,000 people.

centuries. A testament to their hardheaded practicality, Romans are remembered more for their roadways and aqueducts than for their theories and plays.

In religious matters, the Romans exhibited their lack of imagination by imitating Greek myth and ritual. By the fourth century B.C., they had transferred their allegiances to all the gods of Greece's Mount Olympus, changing only the deities' names. Perhaps because they had blithely co-opted another people's mythology in their early centuries, Roman authorities, to their credit, were extremely tolerant of others' beliefs.

Whereas the Greeks had maintained a strict separation between religious and secular realms, the Romans made religion an integral part of the State. This policy helped them pacify and assimilate newly conquered people by offering them citizenship. Because of the legal, mercantile, and educational opportunities accompanying such a passport, the offer became a coveted honor for people annexed into the Empire. The vanquished had only to acknowledge the Roman gods and the divinely inspired *genius* of the emperor. Officials distributed images of the current ruler throughout the empire. Subjects seeking dispensations paid obeisance to the Roman man-god by publicly bowing before his likeness. The Romans did not ask that anyone forswear his own religion. These reasonable terms made the offer difficult to refuse among the polyglot of peoples comprising the Empire. The only ones who objected to these conditions were the Jews. Acknowledging the great antiquity of the "People of the Book," the Romans made an exception for them so the Jews could maintain fealty to their solitary deity. And out of respect for the Jewish proscriptions against images, Roman governors assigned to Judea ordered their troops traveling through Judean crowds to cover up the flags emblazoned with the effigy of the emperor.

The Romans enthusiastically embraced the cult of Dionysus, renaming him Bacchus. During the transition to Roman culture, the paradoxical nature of Dionysus, so delicately balanced by the Greeks, fissured into two entirely separate cults. The old fertility god of irrational ecstasy, frenzied celebration, and priapitic sexuality enjoyed a rapid rise in popularity, especially in the decaying years of the Empire. But the Romans minimized the gory, flesh-eating part of Dionysus's nature and accentuated Bacchus's hedonistic inclinations. Increasingly, the Romans honored their version of the god in orgies of drugs, alcohol, and debauchery known as "bacchanals."

The other half of the Dionysian myth, the part that glorified the young, born again god whose "coming" promised mortals surcease from sorrow, appealed to the more spiritually inclined. Bacchus/Dionysus, was the only god in the pantheon who suffered persecution, died, and rose from the dead. Divorced from his sensual, mad half, the spiritual side of Bacchus metamorphosed into the part-mortal, part-god Orpheus.

Orpheus was a relatively new deity: Homer barely mentions him; Hesiod not at all. His cult did not become popular until the Romans appropriated him. The Greek Dionysus, who tore limb from limb, was transformed into the Roman Orpheus, the gentle poet-musician.

Orpheus personified two fundamental human emotions conspicuously absent from the character of other principal Greco-Roman deities: compassion and love. He was the pacifist shepherd whose music was so divine that it could soothe savage beasts. Expressing the kind, romantic side of human nature, Orpheus was the embodiment of feminine values at a time when brutish gladiatorial contests had largely replaced the subtleties of Greek drama in the amphitheaters. Women were drawn to the Orphic religion.[4]

Both Orpheus and Dionysus shared the ability to transport their devotees to another plane through the use of music and dance. Another striking similarity between the two handsome, young, mythical characters was the manner of their deaths. A frenzied clutch of maenads attacked Orpheus and dismembered him, a scene evocative of Dionysus's fate at the hands of the Titans. No other deities in the Greek or Roman pantheon died, and each of their deaths was distinctively gruesome.*

Romans of all classes and persuasions increasingly flocked to the beneficent Orphic cult.[5] Orphic priests encouraged members to practice a simple life filled with righteous and compassionate acts. Orphism gained adherents because of its promise of a higher and nobler morality as opposed to the libertine excesses and depravity of the cult of Bacchus, and because the populace was becoming disillusioned with the state religion in which emperors claimed to be gods but acted like demons. Orphic mystery rites emphasized salvation and the assurance of a better life in the hereafter. The principal mystic sacrament was the consumption of the flesh and the drinking of the blood of a sacrificial bull, the symbol of Dionysus, to commemorate the

---

*In Orpheus's most familiar exploit, he descended into Hades to bring back his beloved Eurydice, who had died in an accident. After securing her release, the young lover was told that she would follow closely behind him in their ascent from the Underworld, but that he must not look back to see if she was there. Orpheus turned to look back at Eurydice just as he emerged into the sunlight. The gods punished his disobedience by sending Eurydice back down to the Underworld forever. Despite his ultimate failure, the point should not be lost that Orpheus, like Dionysus, had successfully interceded with the god of the Underworld to resurrect a dead mortal.

god's suffering, death, and resurrection. Worshipers believed that by such acts they were absorbing the divine essence.[6] Orphics were often described by contemporaries as living lives above reproach. In Orphic ideology, Hades gradually underwent a makeover that made it sound like a paradise.

The Roman Empire in the first century B.C. encompassed a diverse populace, which in turn encouraged an active cross-fertilization of ideas. Learning and literacy were held in high esteem. The Greek and Latin alphabets saturated the fabric of the Roman world, subliminally encouraging dualistic, objective thinking. More and more, the human condition was viewed as a battleground between the forces of good and evil. The Classical Greeks had been careful not to label as evil the failings of their gods nor the actions of celebrants seized by Dionysian madness, but the more conservative Roman Orphists did not excuse such behavior. The complementarity that had been Dionysus's twin nature split into the polar opposites of Orpheus and Bacchus, each of whom would later share striking similarities to the dichotomy between Christ and Satan.

The general increase in sophistication and rationalism among educated Romans eroded their loyalty to tribal or local gods. Aware that most supplications before shrines went unanswered, intellectuals cast about for a better belief system to explain the capriciousness of fate. Plato's concept of abstract, imageless forms existing high above the fray of everyday life seemed to suit their needs. Aristotle's Prime Mover was the supreme deity whose only function was to stir the world awake while he remained unmoved. Such divine dispassion advanced the belief of the Stoics that the deity did not intervene in human affairs. People, they taught, should accept their destinies without complaint. The god of Plato and Aristotle, unlike the biblical Yahweh, was not listening; further, he did not care. Turning away from the fantastic in religions, the Stoics recommended that a person's moral code should be guided by the golden rule. The Stoic Epictetus advised, "What you shun to suffer, do not make others suffer."[7]

But the Greek philosophers' ideas were so cerebral that they did not satisfy the spiritual longings of most Romans. Philosophers' gods remained remote, bloodless abstractions. Many Romans tried to reconcile Neo-Platonic and Stoic notions with the cult of Orphism. They hoped that by animating such philosophical themes they could make them real. The heightened sense of spirituality associated with Orphism primed the populace for a new religion. Another new god was coming. In 40 B.C., the poet Virgil wrote, "Now ... the great line of centuries begins anew ... Only do thou, sweet Lucina, smile on the birth of a child, under whom the iron brood shall first cease, and a golden race spring up throughout the world!"[8] Another key feature differentiating Orpheus away from all other Cretan-Egyptian-Mesopotamian-Mycenaean-Greco-Roman deities was that Orpheus's worship relied on an alphabetic sacred text containing poems he was credited with having composed.

Besides Orphism, Judaism was the other religion that deeply impressed many first century Romans. Some were drawn to it because of its ethical structure. Others admired the industry and intellectual qualities of the Jews. Still others were attracted by the importance Jews attached to family, charity, and care for the sick and the unfortunate. The burgeoning number of slaves had created glaring distortions, warping the fabric of Roman society. Many non-Romans began to question the Romans' assertion that they were a master race, entitled to exercise life-and-death power over their human chattel. The Jews' regard for the dignity of every individual attracted disaffected members of the Empire.

The Jews were an integral part of the Roman administrative machinery. The historian Paul Johnson estimates that 12 percent of the Empire's citizens were Jewish. They congregated in the big cities and were a vital part of the Empire's commercial network. Jews had high literacy rates, making them ideal candidates to play prominent roles in the vast Roman bureaucracy. Further, they constituted a disproportionately high percentage of the Empire's intelligentsia. The general attitude toward these resilient foreigners who steadfastly adhered to a legalistic religion, sacred scripture, and odd dietary taboos was as it had been for centuries—a mixture of envy, respect, hatred, and curiosity.

Although Judaism was the only monotheistic system at the time, it was not, itself, monolithic. The Jews who lived outside of Judea had a more cosmopolitan outlook than the orthodox Jews living in Jerusalem. The outliers were aware that many honest, pious gentiles were hungering for a universal religion that would supersede the parochial sterility of the Roman state religion. Hopeful that Judaism would become the religion of the world, these Jews encouraged proselytizing. To enable converts to circumvent the onerous demand of circumcision, they created a separate category for converts, calling them "Godfearers." These gentiles could participate in the life of the synagogue, but it was understood that those last two centimeters of foreskin prevented them from ever really becoming one of the "chosen." Nevertheless, so many gentiles were willing to undergo the surgery that the Flavian emperors made it a capital offense for a gentile to be circumcised.[9]

Except for the Godfearers and the Jews, Romans glorified their polytheistic beliefs through the florid use of images. The Roman fascination with images, however, extended well beyond religion—images were used to express every aspect of life. Romans adorned their houses, squares, and temples with statuary, mosaics and paintings. The Greeks had rarely depicted the faces of real-life individuals on their statues, preferring to render passionless and diffident ideals. The Romans discarded this Greek convention, and the wealthy hired artists to capture their likenesses in marble. The busts adorning their houses were faithful to the point of being unflattering. In their quest to immortalize themselves in stone, the Romans supported more artists than any other culture, believing that art could capture their spirit better than the written word. Biography was not as yet a popular art form.

In general, Roman men had a high regard for motherhood: their founding story concerned a she wolf that suckled Romulus and Remus. Women's status markedly improved during the reign of the Empire. Despite their often despotic regimes, the Romans lifted the severe restrictions on women which had been imposed by the "democratic" Athenians. Increasingly, women took charge of their own lives. Divorce became more egalitarian. The courts revoked a father's right to annul his daughter's marriage.[10] Hadrian, emperor from A.D. 117 to 138, declared that women could own property and slaves, enter into contracts, and manage their own financial affairs. In the late Empire, women began to participate in the higher levels of government, and the professions opened to them. Juvenal was horrified that women competed as athletes and gladiators.[11] Martial described how women fought wild beasts, even lions, in the circus.[12] Cato became so alarmed over rights granted to women that he warned that if women achieved equality, they would turn it into mastery.[13] Roman women basked in the prerogatives granted to them by a regime enthralled by the images of its art. But the plethora of statues tended to obscure a dearth of gritty thinkers.

After a four-hundred-year reign, the Romans seemed to run out of ideas. A spiritual vacuum was hollowing out the center of the Roman Empire even as the battle standards of its legions continued to sweep outwards. This vortex would generate a new religion as all the expectant longings of the disparate classes swirling around in first century B.C. coalesced. No one then alive could have anticipated that a tornado cloud was forming over Judea. The funnel would touch down in a place called Golgotha, and when the debris settled four centuries later, the landscape would be permanently changed. An entirely new paradigm of reality would replace the

classical one; images would become objects of revulsion among the adherents of a new religion, who would turn on them on a scale unprecedented in
history. Statues, unable to run for their lives, were toppled, their noses, ears,
and limbs disfigured with such thoroughness that few escaped this artistic
holocaust. And women in the new religion would lose the short-lived, hard-
won gains they had wrested from the Roman Imperial Empire.

CHAPTER 22

JESUS/CHRIST

I am the Alpha and Omega, *the* Beginning and *the* End, the First and
the Last.   —Rev. 22:13

When thou wert in the world, Lord, thou didst not despise women,
but didst always help them and show them great compassion.
— Teresa of Avila, sixteenth-century Carmelite nun[1]

Of all the provinces Rome seized from the Macedonians, none was
more rebellious than fiercely independent Judea. In 43 B.C., Rome
appointed a local non-Jew, Herod, to oversee the recalcitrant dis-
trict. Herod combined Nero's cruel, capricious character with the talents of
the master architect-builder Hadrian. With an eye to posterity, Herod took
on the task of rebuilding the Temple in Jerusalem. First constructed by King
Solomon in 1000 B.C., it had been destroyed by the Assyrian conqueror Neb-
uchadnezzar during the sack of Jerusalem in 597 B.C. In the years following
the Babylonian exile, the Jews had longed to restore it to its original glory,
but had never possessed the resources or power to do so.

Herod built a structure so magnificent that it became one of the wonders of the ancient world. The thirty-five-acre complex, with its mile-long
perimeter wall, was Herod's bid to compete with the Temple of Zeus at Herculaneum and the Temple of Artemis at Ephesus. Unfortunately, by serving
as a magnet for thousands of Jews living outside Jerusalem, the massive
complex created a crisis for Judaism. Each Passover, pilgrims swelled the
city's population. These large crowds provided the kindling to spark an
uprising against the Roman occupation. In response, the Romans greatly
increased the numbers of guards (mostly Greek) protecting the Temple.
Combustible elements were placed in dangerous proximity.

The Temple priests overseeing the vast bureaucracy came to see themselves as an elite. The pervasive influence of Hellenic culture throughout the

Roman Empire compounded this new alignment. Hellenization had a salutary effect on most peoples because of the philosophical, aesthetic, and literary legacy that accompanied it. But the Jews were an exception. Greek ideas and rituals diluted the purity of Moses' message.*

Foreign temptations were not new to the Jewish community, but Greek ways were so intoxicating that Temple officials sanctioned forms of worship that resembled the pagan practices Judaism had long resisted. Yahweh had exhorted Moses to teach his people to worship Him through His written word, but complex rites of sacrifice performed in the Temple began to supplant reading Torah. Although Yahweh had demanded animal sacrifice in the Old Testament's Book of Leviticus, the practice burgeoned in Herod's temple and was carried out with assembly-line efficiency. An Alexandrine pilgrim, Aristeas, wrote home that he had witnessed seven hundred priests, each performing multiple sacrifices during a single day.[2] At feast times, the Temple resounded with the cacophonous blasts of horns and the lowing of terrified animals. Burnt offerings, mixed with the stench from blood-drenched floors, assaulted the eye, ear, and nose—a far cry from simpler times.

The god of Moses and Abraham had been nowhere and everywhere, but in the Herodian era He was presumed by many to dwell in the Temple's inner sanctum. This belief enabled the priesthood to wield absolute authority over religious matters. The Sadducees, the Temple's clerical upper class, dominated the Sanhedrin, the Council of Elders, and were intent on maintaining the status quo. By building this immense edifice, Herod, the non-Jew, had unwittingly changed the character of Judaism.

In the secular realm of the first century B.C., the Roman provinces were becoming restless. The disparity between the sybaritic lifestyle of the wealthy few and the misery of the numerous downtrodden had dangerously unbalanced society. Rebellion was in the air. In 4 B.C., the Romans crucified two thousand Jews in Galilee for sedition and left their rotting corpses on a forest of crosses as a warning to others.[3] The time was rife with dissent and ripe for revolt.

Increasingly, Jews began to question the direction their ancient faith was heading. Pharisees, mostly middle-class lawyers and merchants, were more liberal than the fundamentalist Sadducees and believed that reform lay in reinterpreting the Torah with new wisdom writings such as the Talmud.

---

*Philo of Alexandria, a first century B.C. Hellenized Jewish philosopher, attempted to fuse the two very different cultures. That Philo is a minor footnote in both Jewish and Western history speaks to his marginally successful efforts.

They expended considerable intellectual energy interpreting Mosaic law to make it more congruent with the realities of the times. Unfortunately, many of their legalistic explanations seemed to some like splitting hairs.

A collective longing turned many Jews to a passage written by Second Isaiah, in the sixth century B.C., in which the prophet first raised the subject of a savior.

> For unto us a child is born, a son is given; and the government shall be upon his shoulder, and his name shall be called . . . the mighty God, the Prince of Peace. (Isa. 9:6)

The Book of Daniel, written about 100 B.C., reiterated the promise, prophesying that Yahweh would send a representative, a "Son of Man," to walk among His people. The Book of Enoch repeated the prophecy. Those who longed for the arrival of Yahweh's savior, or *Messiah*, expected Him to rectify in one fell swoop all social inequities.

In the years closing out the B.C. era, this idea steadily gained force. The Essenes, a very religious Jewish sect, abandoned society to live in isolated desert communities to prepare for the coming confrontation. They re-created the austere conditions Israelites experienced during their wandering. Essenes lived a pious communal life. They believed that the Messiah would be an earthly military commander who would lead them to victory in the war against the sinful, and they trained to be Yahweh's soldiers in the battle of Armageddon, the ultimate conflict between the forces of good and evil.

The Sadducees, Pharisees, and Essenes represented only three of the many factions competing for the heart of Judaism in the closing decades of the first century B.C. Despite the varying positions each sect represented, compared to other contemporary religions Judaism was very humane. Compassion for the poor had not been a priority for the secular and religious leaders of Egypt, Mesopotamia, Greece, or Rome. None had a program to care for the disadvantaged. Jews, however, contributed funds to support widows, orphans, and the elderly.

In large part this tradition remained alive because of the periodic appearance of righteous teachers. Advocates for the unfortunate were such a recurring aspect of Jewish history that no one took much notice when a charismatic faith healer named Jesus of Nazareth began preaching to the communities around the shores of Galilee.

This littoral area traditionally spawned revolutionaries. To identify someone as being "from Galilee" was as much a statement about the person's political and religious leanings as it was about his origin. Galileans, Josephus stated, "are fighters from the cradle." Jesus, raised among the working class, had been educated in the Jewish tradition. His empathy for the disenfranchised made Him especially popular with them.

Since the invention of writing and then the alphabet, Western culture had been moving crablike toward the left hemisphere. When Jesus spoke, His words flowed in the opposite direction. Like the shepherd that He was, He turned His followers around and herded them back across the corpus callosum. He asked that they acknowledge the kind of knowing that occurs in the right hemisphere. He instructed them to *contemplate* with their rods instead of *scrutinizing* with their cones. He advised them to use their left arms to ward off blows, but never to ball their right hands into fists to strike back. Jesus' message was cryptic and mysterious. His method of teaching, with its aphorisms and parables, was more right-hemispheric than left.

Although Jesus preached only to the Jews, He articulated universal themes. In the tradition of the Hebrew prophets Isaiah, Hosea, and Amos, Jesus was indifferent to riches, power, influence, and family connections.

Jesus favored Genesis' egalitarian "E" version over the "J" one. He refers to Adam and Eve only once; Eve's transgression, never. He spoke out against the hierarchical ordering of society. In Jesus' eyes, the poor, the disabled, and women were equal to the richest male slave owner. By deed and word He exemplified a humanist credo.

Unlike many other political and religious reformers of His day, Jesus eschewed armed insurrection. "Whosoever shall smite thee on thy right cheek, turn to him the other also" (Matt. 5:39). No major Western figure had ever before suggested nonviolence as a response to aggression, but Jesus was interested in the triumph of the soul, not in the exultation of military victory.

As Homer had stressed courage, Moses the Law, and Plato knowledge, Jesus emphasized mercy and compassion. Leviticus is that section of the Old Testament that enumerates 613 laws—a complex and, at times, contradictory tangle of directives that govern every aspect of Jewish behavior. Out of all of these prescriptions and proscriptions, Jesus emphasized one.

When asked by a Pharisee lawyer to select which of the Commandments He believed was the greatest, Jesus answered, "Thou shalt love the Lord thy God with all thy heart and with all thy soul and with all thy mind. This is the first and greatest Commandment. And the second *is* like unto it. Thou shalt love thy neighbor as thyself. On these two Commandments hang all the law and the prophets" (Matt. 22:37–40). In a revolutionary move, Jesus demoted the Second Commandment of the Old Testament, the one prohibiting representative art, and replaced it with a more humane concept.[*4] No major figure who had previously relied on the written word acknowledged the notion that unconditional love for one's fellow beings was *the* paramount principle.

Every Old Testament prophet railed against the making of images. In many passages, idolatry seems to be an apostate's most heinous crime. We do not read that Jesus disparaged artists. Jesus angrily denounced "scribes" and "hypocrites" who, He believed, pander to the law. While there are other reasons for Jesus' disdain, "scribes" are people who write and He uses the term along with "hypocrites" to insult the learned talmudic scholars who called themselves Pharisees. When the Pharisees rebuked Him because His disciples did not wash their hands before eating bread as demanded by the law, Jesus admonished them for worrying about ritual instead of truth.

> The scribes and Pharisees ... put heavy loads of the Law upon men's shoulders, but they will not lift a finger to move them. . . . They ... like the best places at dinners and the front seats in the synagogues. . . . But alas for you hypocritical scribes and Pharisees ... you blind guides ... blind fools! ... You let the weightier matters of the Law go—justice, mercy, and integrity. . . . Outwardly you appear to men to be upright, but within you are full of hypocrisy and wickedness. . . . You are descended from the murderers of the prophets. Go on and fill up the measure of your forefathers' guilt! You serpents! You brood of snakes! (Matt. 15:1-20)[†]

Jesus drove the Pharisees to exasperation. How could a Jew not be interested in the Law? Jesus, however, recognized that excessive lawyering over the years had overlaid the Torah with an obscurantist veil. It kept lawyer-scholars fully occupied, forcing ordinary folk to seek advice from men trained in legal arcana as to how to live a righteous life. Jesus knew that excessive legalism empowered a select, priestly class of men. He proclaimed to His followers that He was the Truth and no person or written document should stand between His truth and its seeker. Like Antigone,

*Hillel the Elder, a contemporary of Jesus, also advanced this doctrine. When he was asked by a Pagan to summarize the Torah while standing on one foot, Hillel, accepting the challenge, lifted one foot off the ground and said, "What is hateful to you, do not do to your neighbor: this is the entire Torah. All the rest is commentary—go and study it."

†The invective in this passage has cast doubt on its authenticity, but when viewed with other passages believed to be authentic, it supports Jesus' disdain for legalism.

He reminded His disciples that they must answer to a higher calling. He entreated His followers to let go of all their preconceived notions. Shedding society's conventions would allow them to find the living knowledge that cannot be legislated.

Laws represent order and are among the most masculine manifestations of alphabet cultures. Laws force those compiling them to use language in a precise manner to avoid misunderstandings. Jesus did not speak the language of lawyers, nor did He engage in philosophers' rational debates. Jesus prescribed no legal system to help humans govern themselves: His was a ministry of the heart and soul. Instead of the lexicon of the ruling class, He used poetry to couch His pronouncements in visual and emotional aphorisms and parables easily recalled. As I discussed in Chapter 3, aphorisms and parables, rich in metaphor, originate in the right brain.

Money played no role in Jesus' life of the spirit; He declared that possessions were irrelevant, and argued against the evils of wealth. He said, "For what is a man profited, if he should gain the whole world, and lose his own soul?" (Matt. 16:26). In one of the few violent acts of His ministry, Jesus overturned the tables of the moneychangers outside the Temple.

Women were drawn to Jesus' ministry. He treated them with kindness and respect, even if they were infirm, prostitutes, or adulteresses. His message resonated within the hearts of women, who had been consigned to marginal roles in the prevailing patriarchal religions. Jesus astonished the Pharisees when they asked Him about His views on divorce.

> Have ye not read, that He which made *them* at the beginning made them male and female. And said, For this cause shall a man leave father and mother, and shall cleave to his wife: and the twain shall be one flesh? . . . What therefore God hath joined together, let not man put asunder. (Matt. 19:4–6)

At first glance, His refusal to recognize divorce seems to disadvantage women, but in the context of first century Judea, it helped them. Under Jewish law, women could obtain a divorce only with great difficulty, whereas men could leave their wives with ease. Barrenness, for example, was usually blamed on the wife, and a man could seek a divorce for this reason alone. The otherwise enlightened Hillel taught that a man could divorce his wife if she cooked a dish that displeased him.[5] The first century Ben Sirach states, "If thy wife does not obey thee at a signal or a glance, separate from her." (Sir. 25:26). Since divorce favored husbands, Jesus' inflexible position protected married women. Old women, fearful that their husbands would trump up an excuse to abandon them for a younger wife, found comfort and security in Jesus' teaching on this matter.

In His majestic Sermon on the Mount, Jesus taught that every person has the capacity and responsibility to distinguish between good and evil. Love, compassion, Free Will, and nonviolence combined with a disregard for laws, money, and power expressed a feminine agenda such as no Western religious leader had ever before espoused.

Neither Jesus nor any of His disciples committed any of His teachings to writing. The Gospel writings emerged later. Jesus instructed each disciple *to memorize* His important sermons. Given the period, His upbringing, and His culture, why would Jesus choose not to use the written word for this purpose? The Buddha wrote nothing down; neither did Pythagoras or Socrates.* Each, like Jesus, lived during a rapid rise in literacy rates. These exceptional teachers shared in common the intuition that *communication changes when it is written.* The Buddha, Pythagoras, Socrates, and Jesus also favored near-equality between the sexes.

Moses ordered the Israelites to read and obey Yahweh's written commandments. Jesus presented no written doctrine, and instead asked His disciples to believe in Him. Biblical scholars debate whether Jesus claimed He was Yahweh's Son, but the Gospels' tone implies that He believed He was.

Jesus' radical positions concerning the Law, the Temple, and His own divinity put Him on a collision course with both the Jewish religious community and the Roman authorities. His earliest followers were Jews. They accepted Yahweh's great gift—the Law. Jesus insinuated that the truth could be found not by studying the Torah but by putting one's faith in Him. "I am come a light into the world, that whosoever believeth on me should not abide in darkness" (John 12:46). If Jesus had desired to demonstrate beyond doubt that He was divine, then He might have ordered the sun to stand still. But that would make believing in Him too easy. He required that those who came in contact with Him to make their own decision based on the evidence at hand. He insisted that His spoken words and His presence were enough to convince.

---

*Pythagoras's cult was based on belief in reincarnation, cleanliness, and a scientific awareness that numbers undergird the universe. Pythagoras forbade his teachings to be written. He transmitted his sayings orally to his disciples, who called themselves *Akousmatics*, that is, followers of "the thing heard." Pythagoras encouraged women to join his sect and treated them as near equals.

The vast majority of Jews considered Jesus to be an inspired holy man. For most, believing that this humble son of a carpenter was the exalted Son of the all-powerful Yahweh whose very essence was indivisibility strained credulity.* Jesus himself warned, "Many false prophets will appear, many will be misled by them" (Matt. 19:24). The Jews who became His followers would have to forgo their religion as they knew it, because belief in Jesus took precedence over the Law of Moses. Anyone associating with Him would come under Roman scrutiny, which in turn would increase the risk of punishment. Jesus required that faith supersede all else, including the centerpiece of Jewish life: familial love and obligation. "If any one comes to me and does not hate his own father and mother and wife and children and brothers and sisters, yes, and even his own life, he cannot be my disciple" (Luke 14:26). In return for fulfilling these demands, Jesus promised His followers a place in the coming Kingdom of God. Besides this promise's appeal, it was also the most anti–left brain of all the things He said: Jesus prophesied that the end of linear time was at hand.

Time is the quintessential attribute of the left brain. All of the functions of this hemisphere proceed temporally. Everyone knows his or her personal time, this life, will end someday, but Jesus prophesied that *all of time,* everyone's life, this entire temporal world, was about to end . . . and soon. In its place would begin a qualitatively different kind of time called Eternity, which differed from ordinary time in that in it, *nothing* would ever happen. No one would have a baby, win an award, complete a project, grow old, or die. There would be nothing to anticipate in this new Kingdom of Heaven and nothing to strive for—no war, no sex, no laws, no property, and no marriage.

Religion has been an integral part of human existence since the Ice Ages, but nowhere in the spectacularly diverse range of belief systems had anyone embraced one in which time itself was coming to an end. When a few other cultures had speculated that the world would end, they presumed that a new era, similar in all respects to the one expiring, would take its place. Hindus in India believed in immensely long cycles of time called "Kalpas." The Chinese never conceived of an end of time because their belief system did not begin with the premise that time was linear. The Polynesians, Inuits, Aztecs, and Africans believed that time was cyclical. Egyptians and Mesopotamians had a theory about what happened after death, but their speculations did

---

*There are many today who hold those of yesterday responsible for Jesus' death. How many of these twentieth-century accusers would acknowledge Jesus' divinity if they were put into the milieu of first century B.C. Judea?

not include an end to the entire physical world. Eternity was a radically new concept.

The alphabet's powerful ability to reinforce the temporal sense made the Israelites and the Greeks acutely aware of linear time. The ancient Greeks had a Creation story but they did not have a story of destruction.* The linear Jews surmised that if there was a beginning and a middle, there must also be an end. The idea of an apocalypse first appeared in the visions of the prophet Ezekiel in approximately 500 B.C.

Among the Classical Greeks, Plato and Aristotle proposed that there were distinct "eras," and that each had a beginning and an end. The current world was just one such era and upon its extinction, an indeterminate length of time would pass before a new one began.

Jesus' apocalyptic vision contained a message of hope. At the interface between this world and the new Kingdom of Heaven would be a Judgment Day, during which social roles of all the subjects of the Empire would undergo a dramatic reversal. Not only would the meek inherit the earth, but also the first would be last and the last would be first. Slaves would become masters. Masters would receive their retribution. The rich would get their comeuppance. "It is easier for a camel to go through the eye of a needle, than for a rich man to enter into the Kingdom of God" (Matt. 19:24). The promise of such a cosmic redress of perceived inequities had immense appeal to the downtrodden underclass.

Earlier biblical prophets had issued similar warnings, but their parochial messages had been addressed only to the Jews. In Jesus' time a much larger audience was prepared to listen. The sheer magnitude of Pax Romana had instilled in its citizenry a more universal outlook. Many were electrified to hear that a prophet predicted that the End of the World was close at hand. This physical reality, this world, was close to demise. Time would cease. The ship was setting sail. All who jumped on board would be saved to live a placid life, forever free, in an immutable blissful heaven. All those who missed the departure would be left behind and would suffer unspeakable torments. To reserve a place on board one needed only the transformative belief that Jesus was divine. That was all; there were no other stipulations. Because the End of the World was imminent, many people who had heard (or heard of) Jesus' teachings experienced a sense of urgency to answer the riddle. Was He the Messiah or wasn't He?

---

*There were a few Greek thinkers who believed in an ultimate destruction of the universe but their ideas were not in the mainstream.

CHAPTER 23

DEATH/REBIRTH

No book, no doctrine, no doctrine, no book.   '—De Quincey[1]

When St. Paul founded Christianity in the gentile world of the Roman Empire, he insisted that the Cross of Christ and its exaltation of suffering was his principal message.   —Karen Armstrong[2]

During His life, Jesus' impact on the world was like that of a pebble skipped across the surface of a river. A stone's few transitory concentric ripples have no effect on the direction, volume, or speed of the current. His dramatic death, however, eventually redirected the entire flow of history and affected every culture. The carpenter from Nazareth who foretold the End of Time inspired the reconfiguring of almost every calendar, so that His birth marked the beginning of a New Era.

The story of Jesus' betrayal by one of His disciples, His trial and crucifixion is a key morality tale of Western culture. That one believed to be the Son of Yahweh died such a painful and humiliating death so young might well have served the Roman authorities and discredited Him. After all, everyone present at Golgotha could see how easily the profane strength of Rome shredded the sacred shield that one would expect to have protected a holy man. Instead, His death and transfiguration had quite the opposite effect, providing His disciples and subsequent converts with the elements out of which they fashioned one of the greatest stories ever told.

The disparity between Jesus' life and Christ's death created the first schism in this nascent religion. The creed evolving from His life was based on the sayings and actions of an exceedingly wise and gentle teacher; the mystical religion materializing from the spectral mists of His death and Resurrection concerned a god's demise. During His life, feminine-oriented aphorisms extolled love, mercy, equality, and compassion; the events surrounding His death congealed into a masculine dogma glorifying pain, suffering, and obedience. Beatific images of a Madonna adoring her baby and a healer capped by a halo were transmuted into a helpless mother and her dying child, the circle of light replaced by a crown of thorns. The nails, scourges, and crosses that punctuate these tableaux would disturb the sleep of centuries. A celebration of love and nurturing inspired His life; a death consciousness pervaded with pain haunted His crucifixion.

Early Christianity struggled with the contradictory implications of these opposite but complementary aspects of the human condition. At different periods throughout Christianity's two-thousand-year history, feminine creed and masculine doctrine have alternated. The factor that seemed to tilt the balance toward the masculine was a high regard for alphabet literacy and a low regard for imagery. The reverse has held true when imagery held greater sway than the written word.

Jesus' brutal manhandling by the Romans had sown doubts in the minds of His disciples about His authenticity. After the Crucifixion, they interred His body. Three days later, the man Jesus metamorphosed into the deity Christ, releasing an idea of immense power. The Resurrection, the crux of Christianity, proved to His disciples Jesus' divine lineage.

In no other major religion, despite many imaginative embellishments, has the central story been about a flesh-and-blood human being who survived death to return to life in the same human form. Prior peoples acknowledged death as the end of this life. But Christians embraced the belief that God, cloaked in the guise of a mortal, triumphed over death and returned to let His small band of followers see and talk with Him. Historian Elaine Pagels writes, "Other religions celebrate cycles of birth and death; Christianity insists that in one unique historical moment, the cycle reversed, and a dead man came back to life!"[3]

Over the next century, news of Christ's return disseminated throughout the Empire with such extraordinary alacrity that scholars have pondered the phenomenon ever since. Modern theological scholars have exhaustively explored the circumstances surrounding Christ's last days. I wish to pursue a collateral question: why did this story, about a Jewish healer whose life was barely noted by first-century historians, so move a diverse populace far from Judea's local politics—many of whom did not even like Jews? To believers, the answer is self-evident: these events embody God's revealed Truth. But perhaps there were other factors that might have helped to launch the fledgling religion so spectacularly.

One factor was the human need to retell themes that were older than civilization itself. James Frazer in *The Golden Bough* and Freud in *Totem and*

Taboo have described rituals used by surviving hunter/gatherer tribes to rid their group of guilt, and have hypothesized from these practices what might have occurred in prehistoric times. In one such reconstruction, a shaman selected a totem animal that embodied a particular tribe's spirit. Usually once a year, hunters stalked and captured a live specimen of this totem and tethered it to a stake in the center of a magic circle.* Each member of the tribe approached the straining, snarling animal. Out of earshot of everyone else, but just beyond the reach of the leash's radius, the tribesperson whispered into the totem's ear all the taboos that he or she had broken during the previous year. After the last confession, the entire tribe danced in a circle around the animal. Wild music and intoxicating substances transported them to a frenzy. The shaman then abruptly signaled the musicians to stop, and amid mad shrieks the entire tribe turned and fell upon the sacrificial animal en masse. Death was usually swift but messy. Because everyone participated and everyone came away bespattered with blood, no one individual bore sole responsibility for the totem's death.[†]

During the feast that followed, each tribe member ate the flesh and drank the blood of the sacrifice: every adult partook of the animal that had absorbed all the wrongs of the tribe. The totem's death was a divine gift. The ritual absolved all who participated, allowing them to begin a new year with a clean conscience. It also strengthened tribal ties. Participants were bound together in an awesome sacred bloodletting.

Such rituals were common across a wide spectrum of cultures; their outlines can still be discerned in many historical belief systems. The stories of Kingu (Tiamat's son), Osiris, Dionysus, and Christ are continuations of this tradition. In time, the totem animal began to assume human form. The biblical story of the scapegoat, the Jewish Yom Kippur and the Catholic confessional are bleached relics of this once-riveting rite.

In agricultural communities, this ritual was coequal with the one acknowledging the Earth Mother's revival of the fields at the vernal equinox. Since rebirth is the essence of springtime, the replenishment of the land became linked with the human longing to transcend death. To appease the Great Mother or gain Her favor, agrarians offered Her a sacrifice. In most cases it was an animal, but sometimes it was a human, often a virile youth. A

---

*A recurring choice among a diverse range of cultures was the bear.

†The senators who conspired to assassinate Julius Caesar agreed to strike simultaneously. For the same reasons, firing squads comprise many members. These are but two examples of how a group can alleviate the individual feelings of guilt for a ritual sacrifice.

human voluntarily surrendering life so the earth would yield the next year's crops was similar to the sacrificial totem animal that enabled others to be free of guilt. These two compelling strands, the *yearning for immortality* and the *vitiation of guilt*, became entwined in the person of the solitary sacrificial human victim.

In the process of awakening the earth, the Great Mother also gave back life to one who had died. His return coincided with spring. The dead totem animal became the "risen son" of the Great Mother. The myths of Tammuz, Osiris, Adonis, and Attis personified Her beloved lost brother/son/lover/husband whom She resurrected.

God sacrifice with its themes of altruism, suffering, and regeneration gripped the imagination of all early peoples. Only one religion in the entire Mediterranean region was not based on this vision: the early Israelites did not subscribe to the idea that a deity had to die so others could live.*

The Classical Greek world came into being because of its enthusiastic embrace of the alphabet's alpha-omega. Literacy greatly enhanced rationality, which in turn increased a sense of isolation and guilt. Individualism, while increasing creativity, splits one away from community ties. The leaping advances of logic, reason, and the written word correspondingly increased the collective psychic angst within the Hellenized Roman world. The Classical world not unexpectedly began to manifest its symptoms: anxiety, guilt, and madness. At the hinge between magic and logic, transitional humankind tried to hang on to that which was familiar. The dramatic rise in the popularity of Orphism in the years surrounding the Common Era was an expression of the desire of many people to believe in salvation and redemption through the death of a god.

Another factor contributing to the rapid spread of Christianity involves fish. One figure missing from Mesopotamian, Egyptian, Jewish, Greek and Roman religious symbolism is the fish: In both the Old Testament and the *Iliad*, the preferred sacrificial animals were goats, rams, lambs, and steers. In the aforementioned cultures' histories we do not read of a trout or a salmon on an altar. Given the obvious dependence on fish for the people who lived

---

*Prometheus was a prototypical martyr-god who sacrificed his welfare for the good of the many. He stole fire from Zeus and gave it to mortals. As punishment, Zeus chained him to a rock for eternity. Each day an avenging vulture pecked at his liver. At sundown, the vulture flew away leaving behind a small remnant. During the night Prometheus's liver regenerated. His ordeal began anew when the vulture returned the next day. In this myth, night is a metaphor for winter and the liver's regeneration represents the return of all the earth's bounty after it has been consumed.

on the shores of the Mediterranean, or on the banks of the Nile, Tigris, and Euphrates, why were not fish valued enough to be offered to the gods? This question is all the more puzzling, since creatures from the deep resemble land animals. Is not a shark as ferocious, fearless, and carnivorous as any leopard, eagle, or lion? Why then were there no shark-gods? In the zoological pantheon of ancient Egypt, almost every species had its divine exemplar. Perched upon the shoulders of their human bodies, Egyptian deities had the heads of birds, cows, lions, snakes, and monkeys. Given the Nile's importance to Egyptians, one would expect that at least one of their chimeras would have displayed gills. At one time or another, ancient peoples revered bees, ants, butterflies, and even dung beetles. Why not fish?

The Greeks accorded considerable respect to Poseidon, god of the sea. Why did the Greeks imagine Poseidon charging through his watery domain on horses or bulls instead of squid and manta rays? Dolphins (which are not fish) do appear sporadically in these littoral people's mythology but not the fish, a far more common marine representative. A visit today to the shores of any of these countries confirms the importance of fishing; and it was certainly vital in ancient times as well.

The attitude toward fish changed dramatically with Christianity. Jesus is often associated with fish. Peter, Andrew, James, and John earned their living as fishermen. There are multiple references to fish in His parables, from the miracle of the loaves and fishes to Christ Himself eating a piece of fish after His Resurrection. Christ is referred to as the "Fisher of men," and the Greek letters of the word *ichthyus,* or fish, form an acronym of the phrase "Jesus Christ, Son of God, Savior." Fish were such a prominent and recurrent theme in the Gospels that they became the first symbol of Christianity, replaced only many centuries later by the symbol of the Cross. The prominent place of fish in this new religion begs for an explanation.

Jesus' birth coincided with an age filled with expectation and dread. To understand why requires a little background. Virtually all early cultures projected their inner fears and yearnings out onto the empty screen of the nighttime sky. Star-dots, connected, became Star-gods. The twelve configurations of the zodiac appear to have been catalogued by Neolithic astronomers from Ireland to India. Even the Israelites held astrological beliefs. *Mazel tov* literally means "May your planet be favorable."[4]

Modern science has consigned astrology to the occult. Despite all efforts to debunk it, the popularity of astrology persists. Yet, the hold daily horoscopes have on people today is tentative compared to the iron grip these beliefs maintained in ancient times. Astrologers were often individuals of immense status, and every court had an official astrologer who counseled the monarch. Commanders canceled entire military campaigns if the alignment of the stars was unfavorable. Common people, confounded by the vicissitudes of daily life, found it reassuring to consult astrologers.

Given the belief in astrology's predictive ability, we can only imagine, then, the excitement experienced by those in the first century B.C. over a much-heralded cosmic event. For more than two thousand years the sun had been passing through the house of Aries the Ram.* At the time of Christ's coming, the sun was about to move into a new house whose sign was Pisces, the fish. An astrological event of great portent occurring only once every two millennia deeply affected people: some with dread, some with hope. Soothsayers hawked their predictions and premonitions for the new Age of the Fish. Augustus, who ruled as emperor between 27 B.C. and A.D. 14, outlawed the practice of astrology because of his concern of its subversive influence upon his subjects.[5]

Jesus' birth coinciding with the dawning of the age of Pisces may help to explain some part of the overwhelming appeal His new religion had for the multitudes that populated the Roman Empire. The ubiquity of the fish in Christian symbolism and its absence as a significant symbol from all prior major religions suggests a connection between the rise of Christianity and the dawning of the Age of Pisces.

Christianity arose out of the union of the two most dominant influences on the Roman world of the first century: Hellenism and Judaism. Because Jesus was Jewish, scholars traditionally seek the roots of Christianity in Old Testament prophecies, and neglect to note how the Christ story resonates with the pagan Orphic/Dionysian myth. One reason for this omission—the Church regarded paganism as a dangerous enemy. Christianity was, after Judaism, the second religion based on historical events. Its claim to uniqueness would be seriously undermined if earlier mythological beliefs were connected to the utter singularity of the Christ event.

Judaism and Orphism, Jew and Greek, aleph-bet and alpha-beta, are the two spiritual "parents" of Western culture. In a struggle of oedipal proportions, Christianity bested both "forefathers" to become the major religion of the West. It achieved this momentous victory by conjoining the best ele-

---

*The precession of the equinoxes due to the slight wobble of the earth's axis changes the plane of the earth's ecliptic causing it to move slowly through the twelve houses of the Zodiac. A passage through one house takes 2,160 years to complete.

ments from each of the older two into a new religion. Christianity annealed seemingly incompatible opposites into one seamless creed: numinous rite and written word, mythology and history, mystery and Law.

Each of the two older adversaries suffered from an insurmountable flaw that disqualified it from assuming the mantle of a universal religion. Judaism was hidebound by a tradition that demanded that potential male converts undergo a painful operation on their genitals. Then, the novice Jew had to follow the increasingly anachronistic letter of a law designed for a different culture from a bygone age. Many of the 613 Mosaic rules bore no relevance to modern Romans. Judaism's greatest strength was that it was written down in a book open to anyone who wanted to read it. This book had immense authority because unlike rituals and priestly pronouncements, it *never* changed. But exclusionary elitism, bred from the Jews' status as Yahweh's chosen people, prevented Judaism from laying claim to being a universal religion.

RIGHT: Orpheus among the animals, first century A.D.

BELOW: Christ as the Good Shepherd, second century A.D.

Orphism was the latest variation on an ancient theme: a gentle young man-god died to redeem others' sins. Unlike Yahweh, Orpheus promised eternal life. The catacombs in Rome date back to the early centuries of Christianity. On its walls, a visitor can see the Christ figure in postures indistinguishable from Orphic iconography. Orphism's major drawback was that it was an exclusive mystery religion. Membership was by invitation only and initiates were forbidden to tell outsiders what transpired during the secret rites. Its sacred book was a closely guarded secret. No intact version of the Orphic text has survived.

At the time of Jesus' birth, the cult of Orpheus was the most popular mystery religion in Greece and was rapidly gaining converts in many other parts of the far-flung Roman Empire. Diaspora Jews and their gentile admirers comprised the second largest evangelistic religious group in the Empire. But neither could deliver a message that appealed to all segments of society. The time was ripe for a creed that could be "all things to all men." Enter a man named Saul.

Saul was a thoroughly Hellenized Greek Jew. His father was a successful import-export businessman operating in the vast Mediterranean bazaar that constituted the Roman Empire of the first century. In this oriental emporium of ideas and goods, he most assuredly would have been exposed to the story of Orpheus. Saul was an exceptionally bright, literate, inquisitive, and god-intoxicated individual, awash in mystical Greek ideas. Fearing for the Jewish soul of his son, his father, a devout Pharisee, packed him off to a pharisaical high school in Jerusalem. Saul's intense quest for spiritual meaning and his passion for logic converted him to the jurisprudent exegeses of the Pharisees.

Saul became a tireless advocate for the Pharisee viewpoint. Leaving Jerusalem, Saul trod the rutted roads of the Judean hinterland, trying to win his fellow Jews over to this legalistic interpretation of Judaism. His activities would most likely have brought the young zealot into contact with one of the Pharisees' most vocal enemies, a group that roamed the same countryside in the company of a charismatic Galilean faith healer—Jesus.

Soon after Christ's crucifixion, Jewish insurgents rebelled against Roman rule. In the aftermath, Roman authorities adopted a hostile stance toward any suspicious doctrine. The new sect about a resurrected man fell into this category. Hired by Roman authorities to harry adherents of this new sect, Saul was present at the stoning of Stephen, one of Jesus' disciples.

One day while traveling on the road to Damascus, Saul had an epiphany so dramatic that it literally knocked him off his horse. While lying flat on his back, Christ appeared to him, hovering in midair. "Saul, Saul, why are you persecuting me?" (Acts 26:14). When he recovered from this shattering vision, he was transformed. Saul of Tarsus changed his name to Paul and converted to the religion of his former adversaries.*

Unlike Jesus, who wrote nothing down, Paul committed to writing what he considered important.† While Paul remained faithful to virtually all the values Jesus stood for, there were glaring differences in their positions concerning both women and images.

The Gospels portray Jesus as comfortable with women. His interchange with the Samaritan woman, His rescue of the adulteress about to be stoned, His ease at the wedding at Cana, His relationship with Mary Magdalene, His compassion for the prostitute seeking forgiveness, and for the woman plagued with menstrual bleeding are but a few examples.

Paul, on the other hand, seems to have had difficulties with women. The apostle hinted that he had been married, but despite all the other autobiographical material he provided, did not reveal why his conjugal relations ended. After his conversion, he dedicated his whole being to spreading the gospel according to his interpretation of Christ's mission, and spent the rest of his life traveling in the company of men. As women held important positions in the fledgling mission, Paul on occasion praised them. In general, he interacted with women only when it was necessary to advance his agenda.

The word love figures prominently in Paul's writings. God was love, Christ was love.

> If I have not love I am nothing. And though I give away everything that I am, and give myself, but do it in pride, not love, it profits me nothing. Love is patient and kind. It is not envious or boastful. . . . It does not insist on its rights. . . . It never fails. So faith, hope and love endure, these three; and the greatest of these is love. (I Cor. 13:1–13)

Love is an ambiguous word in any language; in Greek, Hebrew, and English it has many shades of meaning. It is paradoxical that men like Paul who wrote at length about Love with a big L seem to have been incapable of loving any one particular woman, a relationship far more demanding of com-

---

*After his vision, Paul left the area and traveled for three years in Asia Minor and Arabia. The worship of Cybele and Attis, her consort/son, was very popular there. Attis was tied to a tree with arms outstretched, died, and three days later returned to life through the agency of his mother.

†Most of Paul's writings did not come directly from his own hand. He dictated them, often adding a postscript in his own rough hand.

mitment than sitting alone in a room writing about Love in the abstract. Women's influence in the new movement, however, concerned him, and he tried to restrict their power.

> The head of every man is Christ, the head of a woman is her husband. (I Cor. 11:3. See Eph. 5:23–24, Cor. 14:34–35, I Tim. 2:11–12)

Former slaves, rogues, criminals, and peoples of every ethnicity receiving Christ became qualified to teach and have authority over congregations. Only women were excluded from this privilege. This exception brought Paul's doctrine into conflict with Jesus' principal teaching concerning equality. Paul justified his position by assailing Eve for her sin.

In the first decades after Jesus' death, women played a prominent role in the church, and in several of his epistles Paul pays tribute to them. But despite this pro forma chivalry, Paul's edicts concerning a woman's place in the church soon became dogma, and it became impossible for a woman to conduct so much as a minor religious ceremony in the new religion. I propose that the conversion of Jesus' oral message into the written word was an important reason women fared so poorly in Pauline Christianity. Ironically, Paul was the stereotypical Pharisaic scribe Jesus condemned.

Though Paul never said he met the living Jesus, he became a more effective proselytizer for the new sect than any of the original disciples. In a stunning rejection of the religion his own father held dear, Paul broke ranks with Jewish doctrine and mixed Hellenic myths with Torah. Paul preached that Jesus was Yahweh's only begotten Son.

Part of Paul's genius lay in recognizing that if Christianity were to be a credible religion, it would have to have a sacred text. He produced a prodigious number of letters, many of which were really essays concerning doctrine. The four Gospels were transcribed many years (A.D. 60–110) after the life of Jesus. Paul's Epistles, circa A.D. 40–50, are the earliest documents of the new religion and had an overwhelming influence on everyone who subsequently wrote about Jesus.

In the early decades after the Crucifixion, writers gleaned the sayings of Jesus from first and second-hand oral accounts. Their works circulated as unbound scrolls, and provided the raw information for the more complete Gospels. Gospel means "good news," and they were meant to tell of the miracle of Jesus to potential converts. But not a single one of Jesus' original twelve disciples wrote a Gospel. A mysterious man named Mark (not the apostle Mark) apparently followed the aging Peter and wrote down what Peter remembered of Jesus' teachings many years earlier. Peter does not come across as a pithy speaker and little that the Gospels attribute to him is quotable or trenchant. Nevertheless, the aged disciple's recollections form the basis of the Gospel according to Mark. A Jew who became a devout follower of the Jesus sect, Mark made it no secret that his Gospel had been influenced by Paul's teaching. He translated Peter's Aramaic reminiscences into Greek so that they could be used to convert gentiles. As with most translations, this one would have surely degraded the original text. Paul Johnson writes,

> He [Mark] was trying to do something which had never been done before, and his problems were not only those of an unpracticed writer but also those of an amateur theologian trying to transmit a complex message which he himself had received from the far-from-lucid Peter.[6]

As Greek copies of Mark's translation circulated among the gentiles, others attempted to reproduce it. Individuals impassioned enough to take on this tedious task must have been steadfast in their belief in Christ's mission, and would have to have been fluent in Greek. To know a language is to be influenced by its culture, and human nature being what it is, some copyists embellished Mark's version. Thus Greek myths seeped into the Jesus story. The Gospel writers were not historians pedantically fretting over the accuracy of every jot and tittle. They were inspired, if nameless, evangelists. Perhaps Jesus, like Pythagoras, Socrates, the Buddha and Lao-tzu before Him, would have been dismayed to know the scribes were taking over.

Luke and Matthew, the next two Gospel writers, relied heavily on Mark's text as a primary source for their Gospels seventy to ninety years after the events they described. The three are so similar to one another that they are known as "the synoptic Gospels."

Though Paul had died by the time these Gospels were written, the embryonic church followed Paul's unique interpretation of Christian events. A. N. Wilson, a Christian historian, writes,

> The first three Gospels in the New Testament were written by men who had learnt to look at things in Paul's way. They are not, in that sense, history. They are lenses, focussed on the person of Jesus through the eyes of Paul of Tarsus.[7]

The synoptic Gospels tell different versions regarding Jesus' birth and childhood; none reports anything about Him between the ages of twelve and thirty. For reasons not known, arguably the most famous person in all of history disappeared from all His biographers' sight for eighteen crucial years. All three recommence the story at the beginning of the last year of Jesus' earthly existence.* None seems to possess intimate knowledge concerning the signal event of Christianity, Christ's last days.

The last Gospel writer, John (another figure about whom scholars know virtually nothing) supplies many rich details about the arrest, trial, Crucifixion, and Resurrection. More than the other three, John connects the events surrounding Jesus' death to Old Testament prophecies, stories, and parables. He steers the reader away from Christ's obvious associations with Orpheus/Dionysus/Adonis/Attis/Osiris/Tammuz/Kingu.

The Gospel of John principally concerns Jesus' last days on earth. The Crucifixion was so central to Paul's thinking that Wilson refers to Pauline doctrine as a "Cross-tianity."[8] Few doubt that Paul inspired John. In Paul's letter to the Romans, he glorifies suffering claiming that it must precede joy. Paul had a dark view of human nature. "As it is written, there is none righteous, no, not one" (Rom. 3:10). The religion that Paul shaped combined oral and written traditions. The oral was about love and nurturing, the written more often concerned suffering and death. Paul was responsible for this shift. In this sense it is not hyperbole to say that Paul invented the religion called Christianity.

Paul was indispensable to the new religion because he alone among the disciples was a theoretician. Like Vladimir Ilich Lenin in another evangelical movement two thousand years later, Paul was disciplined, brilliant, resolute, and doctrinaire. He fully grasped the enormity of the Resurrection, and he single-handedly enlarged Jesus' ministry to encompass the whole world. First, however, he had to overcome a number of very serious obstacles, the first of which was the fact that Jesus was Jewish. Most Greeks disliked Jews, and the Romans glorified Greek values and deities. There is ample evidence of anti-Semitism in the Roman writings.

Not only was Torah law very demanding, but Paul also understood that few non-Jewish males would ever embrace any prophet associated with circumcision. In an age without anesthetics or antibiotics, any surgery could result in infection, gangrene, and death. With several strokes of his pen, Paul blasted the rock upon which Judaism rested. In place of the Law and circumcision, he substituted faith and the promise of a miraculous afterlife.

It was part of Paul's genius to recognize what had been missing from Jewish teachings and Greek conceptions of Hades. Paul assuaged humankind's most terrifying fear—individual death—by promising converts a personal resurrection. Christianity offered immortality to those who believed

---

*The Gospel of John begins three years before the Crucifixion.

in Christ's divinity. With the exception of Orphism, neither Judaism nor Greco-Roman polytheism could compete with such a prize.

One of Paul's most innovative constructions was his inversion of the concept of a "chosen people." He recognized that one of the chief reasons Jews had maintained their identity was their pride in their election by Yahweh. In contrast, polytheism's greatest drawback was the capriciousness with which both the gods and their partisans treated one another. A follower of Apollo could discard his allegiance to the god and easily switch it to Artemis. Later, he might sample a new mystery religion wafting in from another culture. The rejected gods and goddesses seemed not to care one whit about such fickleness.

The dilemma confronting Paul was how to retain the idea of specialness for his new converts and at the same time open up the new religion to everyone. His solution was inspired. He retained the *exclusiveness* of the "Chosen People," while making Christianity *inclusive*. A mere mortal had the opportunity to choose a god. Regardless of social status, each could "choose" Christ, thereby electing himself to become part of God's select circle. In exchange, the convert had to forswear all previous affiliations. The mostly powerless early converts experienced a tremendous sense of entitlement.

A sinner who had lived a reprobate and profligate life could, on his deathbed, obtain forgiveness for his entire past behavior if only he accepted Christ's divinity. No other past religion had ever so easily absolved an individual of past sins. Many converts, such as the emperor Constantine, postponed their baptism until they were on their deathbed.

Paul ardently believed that Christ's Second Coming would be similar to a blinding flash of lightning. In the celestial hail accompanying this event, every thing and every being would be pummeled into submission. A New Order would emerge, refulgent in a heavenly glow. All the trappings of the old order—titles, riches, and prerogatives—would lose relevance. Paul passionately believed that the End of the World was imminent.

> The appointed time has grown very short. From now on, those who have wives should live as though they had none . . . and those who buy anything as if they did not own it. . . . For the present shape of the world is passing away . . . *Maranatha!* Lord, come quickly. (Cor. 7:29–31)

In this scheme, the role of females became truncated, since procreation was a non-issue. Who could be interested in intimacy or in maintaining one's lineage when group death was the order of the day? Everyone was due to die, and some reborn in the fast-approaching cataclysm.

In presenting Yahweh to the Pagan world, Paul tampered with the concept of monotheism. Given the quasi-tribal nature of Western civilization at the time, most non-Jews would have had difficulty relating to a deity who had no relatives. Paul retained the Hebrew concept of the imageless hermit-god, but provided Him with a family. The revisioned Yahweh begat a son from Mary, a human mother. Semele, Dionysus's mother, had been inseminated by the chief deity, and she was but one of many mortal/divine matings in Greco-Roman mythology.*

After Paul converted the singular Yahweh into a nuclear Christian family, he was faced with the danger that Christianity was no longer a monotheistic religion. In one of the most complicated explanations ever contrived, Paul claimed that while Jesus was the Son of God, he was also God Himself. In the centuries to come, people actually killed each other over the issue of the consubstantiality of Jesus and His Father. The problem has never been completely resolved.

Further adding to the polytheistic dilemma, Paul invoked a new entity to join the Son and Father pairing—the Holy Spirit. An analogy may best illustrate Paul's unusual choice for this third entity. Suppose you were handed a torn photograph missing one third. The two figures that remain are a man with his arm draped protectively around the shoulders of a young boy—obviously a father and his son. There was clearly a third adult figure with them, but almost this entire figure is missing. If you were asked who might the missing figure be, you would most likely answer the boy's mother. But Paul's Trinity consists of a Father, a Son, and . . . a Holy Ghost. Father and son are masculine. *Pneuma,* the Greek noun for "spirit," is neuter. Paul's elevation of the *pneuma* to the Trinity further neutralized the power of the Goddess.† The Holy Ghost could have been the Holy Mother. In Paul's formulation, she evanesced into the ether. Outside the Trinity, and granted only a minor supporting role, stands the real, mortal mother.

---

*The Jesus Seminar, a contemporary group of biblical scholars, have examined the New Testament searching for the sayings of Jesus that the majority can agree are authentic according to their strict criteria. Of those passages that they believe to be so, none mention His divine genealogy. The few enigmatic references to His being the Son of Man (which paradoxically implied He was the Son of God) are of equivocal authenticity. Luke's solitary mention of the Annunciation is not found in the other three Gospels.

†The original Hebrew word for spirit, *Ruah* (which means breath), is a feminine noun. When it was translated from Hebrew to Greek she lost her femininity. *Spiritus,* the Latin translation of the Greek word, is a masculine noun. "Respire" and "inspire" still tie the word *spirit* to the word *breath.*

As an alternative to the stiff Roman state religion, Paul offered a personal, mystical, and universal one. The word "catholic" *means* universal. Despite this invitation and in light of their central role in Christianity's origin, women would be forced to play an ever-increasing subservient role in this new universal religion. The two parents of Christianity were Judaism and Orphism. Paul was the midwife who assisted at the birth.

CHAPTER 24

PATRIARCHS/HERETICS

Both read the Bible day and night; but you read black where I read
white.
—William Blake[1]

In the first two centuries following the Crucifixion, contentious disputes
broke out among the followers of the new religion. After a fissiparous
splitting and recombining of factions, two principal groups coalesced:
the Orthodox and the Gnostics. They espoused irreconcilable positions,
even though their basic beliefs and rituals identified them undeniably as
Christians. The Orthodox and the Gnostics fissured over the issue of the
written record of Christianity—that is, over whether or not the rapidly
accumulating Gospels contained all the relevant information about the religion. The Orthodox emphatically answered yes, the Gnostics adamantly
stated no, holding that the Gospels were an important introduction, but that
Jesus had entrusted secret knowledge to a few of his disciples that was not
intended for the general public. The Orthodox retorted that all that Jesus
had to say of any consequence had been faithfully written on sacred scrolls.
Dominant personalities in both groups exemplified the traits and attitudes
central to an issue as divisive as orality versus literacy.

In the late fourth century A.D., Gnostics must have foreseen that the
Orthodox would soon destroy their community. Someone hid an extensive
collection of Gnostic Gospels in a large earthen jar near Nag Hammadi in
the upper Nile Valley. Whoever buried the cache proved prescient, for the
Orthodox were so thorough in eradicating all traces of Gnostic writings that
until the Nag Hammadi find in 1945, almost everything historians knew
about the Gnostic movement had to be inferred from preserved anti-
Gnostic Orthodox polemics.

In its struggle to establish missions, the early Church was amorphous.
The lack of centralized leadership encouraged eclectic modes of worship

and blurred distinctions between clerics and laity. The Apostle Paul saw this disorganization as a serious malady and sought to remedy it by promulgating the Orthodox point of view. He rejected the idea that a few self-appointed cognoscenti had access to a secret teaching. He knew it would undermine his goal of making Christianity a universal religion. He urged his lieutenants to keep Christianity's message simple so that people of all backgrounds would be enticed to convert.

The fledgling Orthodox movement and its subsequent leaders denounced the Gnostics in the kind of hyperbolic language usually reserved for traitors. As Paul Johnson observed,

> There is thus a sinister Goebbels' Law about early Christian controversy: the louder the abuse, the bigger the lie.... There was a constant and depressing inflation in the vocabulary of invective during the course of the first two centuries . . . The venom employed in these endemic controversies reflects the fundamental instability of Christian belief during the early centuries.[2]

Most of the vituperation was directed by Orthodox toward Gnostics. For their part, the Gnostics could never understand why the Orthodox hated them so. After all, were they not all Christians trying, as Jesus had taught, to love their neighbors as themselves?

Compounding Paul's anxiety concerning the Gnostics was his uncertainty about the date of the impending End of Time. No one knew exactly when Gabriel's trumpet would blow. In the meantime, someone had to act in loco parentis for God. Paul advocated creating a special class of judges, called bishops, who would be charged with overseeing the laity's spiritual life. All were to serve temporarily, until the Second Coming.

Paul insisted that the church's hierarchical pyramid of command should be exclusively male. Jesus stood at the apex. Below, in the next tier, were eleven of the original twelve Apostles plus Paul, who had not been a member of Jesus' inner circle. This arrangement excluded Mary Magdalene, who had been a member. Each apostle had appointed a bishop, who in turn personally appointed a bishop for his successor. Thus, everyone in this privileged clerical class would be able to trace his "lineage" in an unbroken line to one of the original Apostles. Clement, in his first Epistle, wrote,

> Our apostles also knew, through our Lord Jesus Christ, that there would be contention over the name of bishop. For this reason, being possessed of complete foreknowledge, they appointed the above-mentioned men, and

then made a decree that, when these men died, other reliable men should take over their office.*[3]

The bishop of Rome, or pope, functioned as Christ's vicar on earth. The pope steadily consolidated his authority over Western bishops who wielded absolute authority over religious matters in their domain.

Women's spirituality, which had been undisputed for thousands of years, became suspect in this new wing of the religion based on alphabetic text. By the year A.D. 200, the Orthodox had formally relegated women to the back of the church[4] and had eliminated all imagery or references related to the Goddess from the New Testament.†[5]

The Gnostics prided themselves on their lack of distinction between male and female, rich and poor, educated and unlettered. They wanted to create an egalitarian church that conformed to Jesus' original message. Members drew lots to determine who would perform the sacraments. The Gnostics believed God's hand guided the lots, so that those chosen would be divinely inspired. Early Gnostics called their gatherings *Agapé,* or "Love Feast." Participants routinely exchanged the "Kiss of Peace," a buss on the cheek or mouth, at the close of services. Such behavior and organizational flexibility scandalized conservative Orthodox.

In general, the Orthodox championed the "J" version of creation that placed Adam as master and Eve as contrite, compliant helpmate. The Gnostics subscribed to the "E" version in which the Creator(s) made all men and women in *its* image. The Orthodox often banned dancing, believing it was inspired by the devil, while many Gnostics promoted dance as a spiritual exercise. In the Gnostic Gospel of Philip, Jesus intoned,

"To the universe belongs the dancer."—"Amen"
"He who does not dance does not know what happens."—"Amen"
"Now if you follow my dance, see yourself in Me who am speaking."—
"Amen"[6]

Another disagreement between the two factions concerned the literalness of the Christ event. The Orthodox held that a man composed of flesh died on the Cross and came back to life on the third day. Tertullian, an eloquent

---

*Occasionally, a bishop was chosen by acclamation of the faithful, e.g., Ambrose of Milan.

†Women remained as congregational singers or served in the choir. By the middle of the fourth century, congregational singing ceased and choirs were restricted to men and boys.

Orthodox writer (ca. A.D. 180) demanded that the faithful believe that the resurrected Christ was "this flesh, suffused with blood, built up with bones, inter-
woven with nerves, entwined with veins, (a flesh) which . . . was born,
and . . . dies, undoubtedly human."[7] He warned, "Anyone who denies the resurrection *of the flesh* is a heretic, not a Christian."[8] The Gnostics believed that
the Crucifixion, death and Resurrection of Jesus Christ were *symbolic* events.
They were incredulous that the Orthodox took these accounts *literally.* Contemptuous Gnostics referred to Orthodoxy as the "faith of fools," and pointed
out the obvious contradictions in Orthodox arguments.[9] For example, if Jesus
was indeed a god, then how could he have suffered mortal afflictions? To the
Gnostics the Christ story was to be used as a guide. As Elaine Pagels points out,
the Orthodox claimed that the Gospels were *history with a moral,* while the
Gnostics honored them because they contained *myths with meaning.*[10]

To the Orthodox, the *written* scriptures were divine revelation. In the
Gnostic tradition, spiritual instructions were given and received *orally.* The
ultimate achievement of Gnosis was to have an insight of such crystalline
clarity that one became a Christ. The Orthodox condemned this idea as
arrogant. The Gnostics derided the Orthodox claim that baptism by a priest
conferred instant redemption; they viewed baptism as the first station on an
arduous road to Truth.

The Gnostics believed that Christ's message was two-tiered. For simple
folk and those unfamiliar with His teaching there were the Gospels. The second tier was reserved for the initiated. The Gnostics argued that if Jesus had
wanted everyone to understand His teachings at the outset, He would not
have couched so many of them in elliptical and confusing turns of phrase.
Jesus' own saying, "Many are called and few are chosen" (Matt. 22:14)
strengthened their conviction, as did Mark 4:10–12:

> To you has been given the secret of the kingdom of God, but for those out-
> side everything is in parables; so that they may indeed see but not per-
> ceive, and may indeed hear but not understand.

Mystery religions have flourished periodically in the West. Eleusinian,
Dionysian, and Orphic cults claimed to possess a cryptic body of knowledge. The modern Elks' secret handshake and the initiation rites of present-
day Masons are pale remnants of these esoteric strands. Sufis, Kabbalists,
Rosicrucians, and other mystic traditions have always tasseled the fringes of
the West's major religions. They have never been central to any of them. A
creed written in an alphabet (Old Testament, New Testament, and Quran)
has superseded secret oral teachings.

The battle between the Gnostics and Orthodox wings of Christianity began within a generation after the Crucifixion and raged for several centuries. Both sides were evenly matched in terms of talented leaders and persuasive proselytizers. But in A.D. 313, when the Roman emperor Constantine declared that Christianity was the state religion, he chose the Orthodox to administer it.

A military man, Constantine favored the autocratic Orthodox. He believed the Orthodox could better help him reinvigorate Rome's declining military stature. On his cross was the inscription, "In this sign, conquer," a sentiment discordant with Jesus' message. When he made the army and police available to do the Orthodox's bidding, they quickly exploited their change of fortune. Within a century they had destroyed almost all the images associated with pagan shrines and closed down pagan temples. They showed little tolerance for Jews and sent the few Buddhists packing. But they reserved their fiercest attacks for their fellow Christians, the Gnostics. Mobs attacked Gnostic centers and eventually destroyed all of them. Orthodox authorities ordered all Gnostic gospels burned in A.D. 367. With the Gnostics driven out, the Orthodox leaders declared themselves the true Patriarchs of the Church. Subsequent Orthodox leaders conferred sainthood upon Orthodox followers; they also branded Gnostics as heretics.

The victory of the Orthodox over the Gnostics marked a turning point for Western civilization. Although much of the quarrel between the two factions was couched in abstruse arguments, the Orthodox/Gnostic struggle was at its core a conflict between words and images. One translation of the Greek *ortho-doxy* could be "straight thinking" or in the context of this book, "linear thinking." *Gnosis* is the Greek word for knowledge. The Greeks distinguished between *episteme*, knowledge acquired from facts, and *gnosis*, which we call "intuition." In the first schism of the nascent church, the Orthodox and the Gnostics split along the lines of the hemispheres of the brain. The linear thinkers favored left-brained, male-dominated patriarchies, heavy on guilt, dogma, obedience, and the literalness of the Christ story. The intuiters were more often egalitarian and were entranced by the mythopoesis of Jesus' life and death.

The Orthodox consistently produced writers who were unremitting misogynists. The Gnostics intermittently produced orators articulating egalitarian and feminine principles. Throughout history, the group that arms itself with a book will generally annihilate the group that depends on oral teachings. The key personalities on both sides illuminate how the Orthodox defeated their most serious threat, how women lost their hard-won gains, and how images were trampled as Orthodoxy triumphed.

.   .   .

The earliest prominent Gnostic to appear in the historical record was the charismatic Marcion, whose ministry reached its zenith between 120 and 140. He condemned the rapidly multiplying written Gospels, attributing most of them to fools and frauds. He proposed paring the Gospels down to their bare bones, and he discarded the Old Testament. Marcion intensely disliked the wrathful Yahweh. He accepted only seven Pauline Epistles as authentic, dismissed Mark, Matthew, and John, and accepted only limited portions of Luke and Acts.

Although an ascetic himself, Marcion did not insist on celibacy, nor did he ban images. Marcionites retained the sacred imagery of the serpent, attributing to the reptile in Genesis the role of a beneficent instructress. Marcion was a persuasive orator, his brand of Christianity was egalitarian, and he had many women followers. No document written in his hand remains. We know of him because the Orthodox denounced him.

Marcion's attack on the written word galvanized the Orthodox. Belatedly recognizing the need to censor the proliferating Gospels, the Orthodox moved to canonize only those texts that they approved. Since the Gnostics never placed great store in the written word, they failed to appreciate this event as the crucial turning point for them. For the next 1700 years all Christians would be taught the Orthodox version of the New Testament. Edited by mostly unknown scholars in A.D. 367, compiled from documents written 30 to 110 years after the Christ event by no one who was present at the events, and composed for the most part by unknown authors in the Greek language that Jesus never spoke, it is held up as the only true record of the Christ story.

The first significant Orthodox theoretician to oppose the Gnostic sects was Origen (185?–254?). Beginning with premises rooted in the mysteries of the Virgin Birth, the Transfiguration, and the Resurrection, Origen built complex arguments based on allegorical interpretations. Erudite and impassioned, he debated publicly with pagan philosophers, and by ingenious syllogisms, "proved" that all of his (essentially mystical) premises were irrefutably true. He proclaimed that in the new Christian paradigm the classical philosophers from whom he had learned his art were irrelevant. Arguing against the Gnostic position, Origen dismissed as untenable the idea that God would offer salvation only to the spiritually advanced. Like Paul, he was convinced that the Church must be simple and accessible to all.

Origen believed that the renunciation of all sexual urges promoted salvation. He was the first Christian theoretician to firmly link piety and celibacy. He considered sexuality merely a passing phase. Christians would transcend bestial lusts to achieve the exalted state of androgyny. This "third race," as Origen called it, was the state of souls in the coming Kingdom of Heaven.[11] The second major component of Origen's system was his glorification of martyrdom as the *ultimate* act of Free Will. He taught that denying sex and embracing death would greatly enhance a Christian's chance of redemption.

He learned Hebrew so that he could read the Bible in the original, and stayed in his library for days at a time. Origen wrote some six thousand books. So voluminous was his literary output that Jerome complained with exasperation, "Is there anyone who has ever read *all* the works of Origen?"[12]

The details of Origen's personal life suggest a social misfit. As a young man, he became obsessed with a line from Matthew praising "those who have made themselves eunuchs for the sake of the Kingdom of Heaven" (19:12). He castrated himself in the belief that by joining his "third race" he could better serve the Orthodox cause. The historian Edward Gibbon dryly remarked, "As it was Origen's general practice to allegorize Scripture, it seems unfortunate that, in this instance only, he should have adopted the literal sense."[13] Origen fasted often, slept on bare ground, wore no shoes (and sometimes no clothes), and routinely subjected himself to cold. He promoted the "J" version that subordinated Eve to her husband. His writings influenced Christian scholars for the next two centuries.

Initially, Origen's peers hailed the brilliant strategist as a champion of Orthodoxy. But, like so many intellectuals whose fiery enthusiasm fuels a revolution, he was cashiered after more conservative elements took control. Once the Church recognized that his passionate advocacy of Free Will was antithetical to its intention of overseeing the thoughts and actions of the laity, clerical authorities attacked it. Pope Anastasius I condemned Origen's "blasphemous opinions."[14] In 553, the Council of Constantinople declared the bulk of his teachings "anathema." Notwithstanding his rejection, Origen's teachings set the tone for the virulent misogyny that was to follow.

Another influential Gnostic sect were the Montanists. Montanus (ca. A.D. 150) was a charismatic prophet who denounced the increasing worldliness and growing autocracy of Orthodox bishops. He demanded a return to Christian austerity, and a restoration to the laity of the right of prophecy. He grounded his sect in the ecstatic spirituality of two women, Priscilla and Maximilla, both capable of falling into religious trances. The Montanists held a skeptical view of the written word: they did not believe that the passive act of reading a Gospel could produce an active religious experience. They compared reading the Gospels to telling someone about a meal, pointing out that reading a description of a meal was not to be confused with the actual experience of eating one. The Montanists believed that only through ecstatic states reached through speaking in tongues and ululations could one achieve the insight that was the essence of Christianity. Most of Montanus's closest followers were women, and they played prominent roles in all aspects of his ministry.

Valentinus (ca. A.D. 140) was one of the most prominent Gnostics. The Orthodox feared him because he conducted his life with integrity and had many followers. Valentinus did not believe that sexual abstinence played any role in Christianity. He married, raised children, and worked to support his ministerial activities. He was a gifted speaker, able to move large crowds with his eloquence.

Valentinus's central message was that all Christians are equals and that they should love and help one another regardless of sex, sect, or social strata. Valentinus taught that the deity was a dyad consisting of God the Father and God the Mother. He based his teachings on God's Genesis "E" pronouncement, "Let us make humanity," which Valentinus interpreted to mean dual parentage. All humankind, according to Valentinus, was the conjugal offspring of the masculine mind (*nous*) and feminine wisdom (*epinoia*). He called this couple the "Primal Father" and the "Mother of All."[15] Not unexpectedly, women were drawn to his sect.

The Valentinians believed that the Fall from the Garden of Eden described humanity's "fall" into consciousness, a sudden acquisition of worldly knowledge that caused humankind to lose touch with the divine. The role of Gnostic teachers was to help their congregations regain this sacred connection.

Valentinus incurred the ire of the Orthodox for not asking their permission to conduct Christian sacraments. Irenaeus, the Orthodox bishop of Lyon (ca. A.D. 180), was an outspoken Gnostic foe and attacked the Valentinians. He argued that the Gospels' authenticity rested on the fact that they had been written by Jesus' own disciples—a statement we now know is untrue. Irenaeus suffered acute embarrassment when the wife of one of his own deacons crossed over to join the Valentinians. Unable to explain why the "heretical" sects attracted women in such disproportionate numbers, Irenaeus accused the male Valentinian leaders of resorting to aphrodisiacs and seduction as recruitment methods. Irenaeus waxed particularly indignant over the Valentinian practice of allowing women priests to baptize.

The Gnostics' most strident opponent was the vitriolic writer Tertullian. A Carthaginian lawyer who converted to Christianity in midlife, he spewed his hatred for women in many of his sermons.

These heretical women—how audacious they are! They have no modesty; they are bold enough to teach, to engage in argument, to enact exorcisms, to undertake cures, and, it may be, even to baptize![16]

Do you not know that every one of you is an Eve? The sentence of God on your sex lives on in this age. . . . Women are the gate by which the demon enters. . . . weak women . . . it is on your account that Jesus died.[17]

He opposed images of any kind and condemned any Christian who was an artist. He demanded that all images of women be removed from public display and counseled Christian parents to veil their daughters.

Tertullian expressed contempt for philosophical inquiry and ordered his flock to renounce worldly curiosity. He asked, "What has Athens to do with Jerusalem? What has the Academy to do with the Church?"[18] He demanded unquestioning acceptance of the Orthodox position: "God's son died: it is believable precisely because it is absurd. He was buried but rose again: it is certain because it is impossible!"[19]

Tertullian was one of the most forceful voices in the Orthodox movement; his inspired writings helped convert pagans for the next several centuries. Tertullian was also a righteous man.* As he aged, he grew increasingly troubled by the ostentatious excesses and the dearth of Christian spirit he witnessed in the Orthodox clerical class. Many bishoprics were bought and sold to the highest bidder. Finally breaking with the Church he had so passionately supported, Tertullian denounced the Orthodox hierarchy and became Christianity's first Protestant. Risking the very excommunication he so often demanded for others, he called the Pope "the shepherd of adulterers."[20] In a final irony, Tertullian defected to the Montanists. He had come to believe they best exemplified the spirit of Christ.

Jerome (340–400?) championed the Orthodox position through his prolific writings. Paul Johnson calls him as the "wild man of God" and posits that "Jerome found sex an enormous difficulty."[21] In revealing autobiographic glimpses, Jerome tells of his strong lustful urges and of the self-punishment he endured to be free of such evil. To escape the temptations of the flesh, he joined an ascetic order in a desert hermitage.

> Day after day I cried and sighed, and when, against my will, I fell asleep, my bare bones clashed against the ground. I say nothing about my eating and drinking. . . . And yet he who, in fear of hell, had banished himself to this prison, found himself again and again surrounded by dancing girls! My face grew pale with hunger, yet in my cold body the passions of my inner being continued to glow. This human being was more dead than alive; only his burning lust continued to boil.[22]

While in the desert, he attracted the attention of his superiors because of his piety and brilliance. He was plucked from the monastery and appointed

---

*Righteousness is a very left-brained trait. The philosophy of "live and let live" better suits the right brain. It is, after all, Mother Mary and not Father God who inspired Paul McCartney to write "Let It Be."

papal secretary in Rome, a position of immense authority. Acclimating read-ily to the rarefied atmosphere of the Roman See, he began to disseminate his idiosyncratic interpretations of Old and New Testament stories. Jerome compared the Garden of Eden to a Paradise for Virginity, corrupted by Adam and Eve's sins. The terrible punishment to which they were con-demned was carnal knowledge leading to marriage. According to Jerome, "Marriage is only one degree less sinful than fornication."[23]

Despite his anti-sexual opinions, Jerome assiduously cultivated a follow-ing of wealthy aristocratic women whom he pursued almost with a lover's ardor. His purpose was to convince them to adopt celibacy as a way of life, and to accomplish this goal he used the language of seduction. For example, in a letter to the young woman Eustochium he wrote,

> Virginity can be lost even by a thought. . . . Wash your bed and water your couch with your tears. Always allow the privacy of your own room to pro-tect you: ever let the Bridegroom sport with you within. . . . When sleep overtakes you, He will come from behind the wall and put His hand through the hole of the door, and will touch your belly (*ventrum*). And you will awake and rise up and cry, "I am sick with love." And you will hear Him answer: A garden enclosed is my sister, my spouse; a spring shut up, a fountain sealed.[24]

Contrary to Jerome's intentions, the letter became public. Many considered it grossly inappropriate and called for his removal from office.

Matters came to a head in 384 when Jerome took under his tutelage the twenty-year-old Lady Blaesilla. Jerome spent an inordinate amount of his time in private audiences with the attractive young woman. Jerome per-suaded Blaesilla to become an ascetic. She then fell into a long swoon of self-denial. Alarmed at the dramatic decline in the young woman's disposition and health, her family became furious with Jerome's role and appealed directly to the Pope to intercede. While the Pope vacillated on an appropri-ate course of action, Blaesilla died from anorexia.

The scandal was too much, even for Jerome. He was not reappointed to his position, and he left Rome to live out the remaining thirty-four years of his life in the Holy Land. The last few, he lived in a cave. He con-vinced two aristocratic Roman women—Blaesilla's sister Eustochium and their mother—to give up their comfortable lives to come live with and care for him: Jerome commanded that neither woman wash nor comb their hair; he insisted that they dress in rags.[25] His ideas and behavior might be dis-missed as those of a solitary eccentric, but consider Jerome's influence on subsequent Christian thinkers: it was Jerome who translated the Old and New Testament into Latin. His Vulgate version became the standard until the Reformation. Translation is an art form that depends on the translator remaining faithful to the original. Jerome's attitudes toward sexuality, pregnancy, and motherhood affected his translation, which in turn influenced the thinkers following him who shaped early Christianity.

Jerome's status and the ever-increasing number of people who were reading the New Testament attentively contributed to making celibacy actually fashionable in Rome. This was the same city that Tacitus (200–275) had described as the "sink of human depravities." There had not been a requirement that priests abstain from sex. But in 386, a Roman synod issued an edict that demanded celibacy of all priests.

Another cleric who buttressed the Church's authority was a young bishop living in the distant, unprepossessing See of Hippo in North Africa. Augustine made his presence felt through his numerous treatises and books. Compared to such radiant lights as Rome, Antioch, Alexandria, and Constantinople, Hippo was but a dim star in the Christian constellation. That a bishop of this outer boondock was able to project such immense authority attests to the enormous influence of the written word in the latter fourth and early fifth centuries.

Augustine was born in 354 in Carthage, the child of a Christian mother and a libertine pagan father of modest means. Despite his mediocre education, Augustine became a prolific writer. He once wrote, "I write to make progress and I make progress because I write."[26] Augustine wrote the first truly psychological autobiography, his much-read *Confessions*. In it, he writes candidly of his sexual urges.

> In the sixteenth year of the age of my flesh . . . the madness of raging lust exercised its supreme dominion over me. My invisible enemy trod me down and seduced me. I drew my shackles along with me, terrified to have them knocked off.[27]

Augustine experienced a transformative vision at age thirty-two, while in Rome. He broke off his engagement to his betrothed and dedicated the rest of his life to the Church. He renounced the world of the flesh and left Rome to seek solitude in a desert monastery in North Africa nearby the city of Hippo. Wrestling with his sexuality, Augustine identified the Pudenda— the Parts of Shame as he called them—as a constant source of temptation. Because the sexual urge was so involuntary and troubling, he concluded, it must be controlled by Satan.

Augustine's piety, intelligence, and writing skills impressed the elderly bishop of Hippo, who convinced the recent convert to leave his austere life and succeed him. From this rustic fulcrum, using sentences as levers, Augustine moved the world. He laid out the blueprint for Christendom's expansion well into the next millennium. He also introduced several controversial extra-scriptural doctrines based on his interpretation of Christianity's canonized texts. In his *De libero arbitrio* (On Free Will), Augustine sought to reconcile the existence of evil with the benevolence of God. He concluded that Free Will was the demon. Mortals were so corrupt that when they exercised their ability to choose they more often than not chose evil. Augustine held that Eve's treachery and Adam's disobedience had crippled every mortal's judgment, rendering humankind incapable of self-government. All mortals were morally incompetent. "Humanity is sick, suffering, and helpless, irreparably damaged by the Fall."[28]

Another Augustinian doctrine destined to influence Christianity far into the future was Original Sin. According to Augustine, as punishment for Adam's act of disobedience, God had contaminated Adam's seed. During sexual union, Adam passed the infection to his partner, and Eve, in turn, polluted her fetus. Cain and Abel repeated the cycle in the next generation with their wives. Down through all the ages of humankind, Original Sin hid in men's semen and incubated in the Parts of Shame. Each newborn babe emerging into the world was inescapably contaminated and therefore born a sinner. Jesus Christ was the only exception to this plague, because he was conceived immaculately. Augustine intoned, "Semen . . . itself, shackled by the bond of death, transmits the damage incurred by sin."[29]

Augustine held that through an act of grace, God permitted a means of salvation: baptism at birth by a duly ordained priest of the Orthodox Church could remit all Original Sin. Should the baptized baby grow into an adult who backslid and committed another sin, only the sacrament of confession, again administered by an Orthodox priest, could prevent a relapse to the state of sin. Thus, Augustine secured the Church's place as the indispensable agent in charge of Christian souls. The reward for participation in this system was that Christians gained exclusive admittance to the City of God.*

In the New Testament, Jesus never mentioned Original Sin nor did He

---

*Original Sin was a thoroughly original idea. Buddha's formulation of karma was similar. But the difficult path to Enlightenment that Buddha illuminated presumed that individuals had the power to choose a righteously lived life *without any outside help.*

equate sexuality with sinfulness. He specifically dismissed the idea that a man's blindness was a punishment for the sins of his parents (John 9:1-7). Paul had said Adam's disobedience indicated that the flesh was weak, but he did not conceive of that frailty as one that would injure all future generations. It was Augustine who imputed to the Creator a brooding capacity for punishment. He essentially created a new mythology that subverted the entire feminine bent of Jesus' message. To many reasonable people Augustine's doctrine of Original Sin had loosed a dangerous, fanatical heresy into the Christian creed, but his reputation as the most influential churchman of the Western Christian world deterred those who considered coming forward against him. It was not only Augustine's withering logic with which a challenger would have to contend. The bishop of Hippo considered theological debate a no-holds-barred contest; losers often suffered more than mere bruising of their pride. Augustine was only one of countless charismatic preachers of the early centuries. He stood out because he combined articulateness with dedication to churning out hortatory written documents.

Because Original Sin became a radical linchpin of the new Augustinian formulation requiring God's grace to remit sin, several prominent Christians took the risk and challenged Augustine on this issue. Pelagius, a British monk, began with the premise that God was good: He had given mortals the Law, the Ten Commandments, and His only Son, and had bestowed upon them the cleansing waters of the baptism. Pelagius protested that He would not undo His perfect creation by making humans, alone among the animals, inherently evil. Pelagius argued that there was no such thing as Original Sin: only he or she who commits a sin is punished.

Pelagius moved to Rome and vigorously lobbied prelates and aristocrats to convince the papal hierarchy to repudiate Augustine's extremist position. Not to be out-maneuvered, Augustine sent spies to Rome to spread unsavory stories undermining the British monk's reputation. The debate over whether or not Free Will had been taken hostage by Original Sin was embraced with such fervor by both sides that, in 417, there were riots in the streets. As the vote on the issue loomed, Augustine surreptitiously shipped eighty expensive Arabian horses to Rome and had them distributed among the heads of key families and prominent clerics. His views prevailed. Pelagius was drummed out of the corridors of the Vatican, exiled, and excommunicated in 419. In 431, the Council of Ephesus condemned as heresy Pelagius's teaching that humankind could be good without the saving grace of baptism and confession. In the words of Augustine, "Rome has spoken; the debate is over."[30] Paul Johnson observed,

Augustine was the dark genius of imperial Christianity, the ideology of the Church-State alliance, and the fabricator of the medieval mentality. Next to Paul, who supplied the basic theology, he did more to shape Christianity than any other human being.[31]

To best appreciate how the concept of Original Sin has permeated culture down to the present day, one has only to scan the radio dial any Sunday morning. A cacophony of pastors representing a diversity of Christian denominations drill into their flocks the utter hopelessness of their condition due to the first couple's mistake. Augustine's idiosyncratic reading of scripture, crafted sixteen hundred years ago, has been accepted by many as spiritual fact. The religion that began by inviting prospective converts *to choose* now told Christians that they had *no* choice.

Augustine's dour doctrines cast shadows over Jesus' joyous message. Jesus preached a creed of forgiveness and mercy; Augustine sought revenge against his opponents. When the Donatists, a dissident Christian group in North Africa, defied Augustine's authority, he put down the revolt mercilessly. Jesus spoke of loving one's enemies. Concerning the use of torture for heretics, Augustine advised,

> The necessity for harshness is greater in the investigation, than in the infliction of the punishment; . . . it is generally necessary to use more rigor in making the inquisition, so that when the crime has been brought to light there may be scope for displaying clemency.[32]

Jesus said to turn the other cheek when confronted by an aggressor. Augustine wrote the earliest justification of the Church's use of force. Jesus preached transcending fear. Augustine observed, "Many Christians as well as pagans respond only to fear."[33] He used spies, police, and informers to achieve his aims. Jesus taught that the means justify the end. Augustine's writings suggest that he condoned the end justifying the means.

In the Gnostic Gospel of Thomas, the apostles ask Jesus how to achieve the Way. He answers them, "Do not tell lies. Do not do what you hate." Augustine was not above bending the truth to suit his political aims.

All of Jesus' interactions with women described in the New Testament demonstrate the compassion that made him so singular. Augustine proclaimed that women were morally weaker than men and justified their subjugation because they, like Eve, were temptresses.

In the four hundred years after Jesus began his ministry, Christianity underwent dramatic changes. What Jesus initiated, Augustine altered. The principal proponents of Orthodoxy—Paul, Origen, Irenaeus, Tertullian, Jerome, and Augustine—denigrated sex and women. All, by their own admission, struggled with their sexuality. They all railed against imagery. And all were enthralled by the written word. The principal proponents of Gnosticism—Marcion, Valentinus, Montanus, and Pelagius—favored an egalitarian Christianity. None demonized images. None claimed that sexuality was evil. Most Gnostic leaders preferred oration to writing.

Pious Christians who proselytized pagans to come over to the new religion were represented in both wings. Sincerity and righteousness motivated both. The gradual slide toward a masculine-dominator agenda from one that had begun as feminine-egalitarian illustrates, in historical detail, how patriarchy could have conquered the Goddess religions in earlier times. Correlation does not prove causality. Yet, in the period framed by Hammurabi's stylus to Augustine's quill, whenever literacy conferred its considerable largesse upon society, historical crimes against women and images occurred in tandem. The prime suspect of these crimes left ink-stained fingerprints at the scene.

CHAPTER 25

REASON/MADNESS

Bring wild beasts, bring crosses, bring fire, bring tortures. I know that as soon as I die, I come forth from the body. I rest in Christ. Therefore let us struggle, let us wrestle, let us groan. —Origen[1]

The great majority of the early martyrs were Christians of a type which the Church would later classify as heretic. —Paul Johnson[2]

Christianity is a religion of immense power and beauty. During its two-thousand-year history, it has been the frame upon which Western civilization has draped many of its most splendid vestments. It has provided laws to the lawless, succor to the sick, solace to the despairing, nourishment to the soul, answers to the perplexed, alms to the poor, protection to the dispossessed, and order to the confused. The message contained within its sacred text persuaded many followers to disavow their baser impulses. Christian rituals have suffused the prosaic with solemnity and the sacred with glory. Its art, music, and architecture have engendered throat-tightening awe. The story of the arisen god in springtime has invited multitudes to touch the hem of two of the most basic human longings: surcease of anxiety and everlasting life.

During periods in the West when civility and civilization were trampled under and left mud-caked by the hooves of warring armies, Christianity kept alive the principles of faith, hope, and charity. When learning and literacy were all but extinguished, Christianity attended the lamps with steadfastness. Yet, it was during the rise of Christianity that an aberration previously absent from human society began to manifest—group suicide.

Early in the second century, for the first time in the historical record of any culture anywhere, ordinary people willingly relinquished their lives en masse out of loyalty to cherished convictions about abstract concepts. The word *martyr* slipped into the stream of language. Martyr is the Greek word for witness. In the second century, mass martyrdom became common.

In previous ages, mothers sacrificed their lives on rare occasions so that their children might live. On occasion, warriors sometimes chose death to protect their comrades. In defense of home and hearth whole tribes, armies, and even cities willingly went to their deaths now and then. Once in a blue moon a love-sick youth might become so stricken that suicide seemed the only way to achieve relief. But these were the acts of isolated individuals. Child, comrade, lover, home, and hearth were specific things for which to die. There is no evidence from the study of preliterate tribes or archaeological digs that any early peoples chose martyrdom for the sake of philosophical or theological principles. The only exceptions to this important canon of self-preservation were the Jews and Greeks, the two alphabet cultures. They consistently defended their *ideals* to the death. The Greeks united against the invading Persian despot, Xerxes, to *preserve their freedom*, and the Jews under the Maccabees fought to the death for *the right to practice* their religion. In both instances the Jews and Greeks were also defending home and hearth. Until the Christian martyrs, there does not occur anywhere in the recorded history of Mesopotamia, Egypt, Persia, Greece, India, or China a single instance in which a substantial segment of the population accepted torture and death rather than forswear their belief in an ethereal concept. The instinct for survival, present in every living creature, is supreme. What unique circumstances, we might ask, enabled many early Christians to override the circuit breakers of this most fundamental hard-wiring?

Within a few years after Jesus' death the Jews did the unthinkable. They revolted against the Romans. As quixotic as this insurrection appeared to contemporary observers, it turned out to be the Empire's Vietnam. Roman generals grossly underestimated the tenacity of the Jewish urban guerrillas who revolted on three separate occasions (A.D. 66, 113, and 132).* The setbacks experienced by the Roman military machine in Judea shattered the idea of Roman invincibility. Once they were compelled to reinforce their legions there, the Romans never again expanded the borders of their realm.[3] As the populace became more rebellious within, the barbarians at the Empire's outer fringes became bolder. Imperceptibly, the pugnacious offensive posture that had characterized Roman rule shifted uneasily to a defensive one. Aware of their vulnerability, they became more tyrannous.

---

*Josephus, a chronicler of these wars, estimates that Romans killed one and one-half million Jews. Even if this is an exaggeration, it speaks to the sheer savagery of the conflict.

But the three revolts against Rome instigated by right-wing Jewish zealots brought death, destruction and exile to the Jews who had resided in Judea. The ferocity with which Jews fought these wars combined with the previous internecine conflicts of the Jewish Hasmonean families can also be classified as a kind of cultural madness. The Jews had enjoyed a fairly privileged position within the Roman Empire. By revolting, they very nearly destroyed themselves in what can be viewed as a sort of national suicide.

Against this background, the fledgling Christians began to organize into a movement that would reshape the world. The core of their beliefs repudiated pagan values, all things Roman, and authority in general. At first, sophisticated Romans viewed the new sect as an aberration. The Roman historian Suetonius called the Christians "depraved"[4] and Tacitus characterized Christianity as a "deadly superstition."[5] Emperor Marcus Aurelius despised them as morbid and misguided exhibitionists.[6] To Romans, the Christians were atheistic pacifists who refused to acknowledge Roman deities or to serve in the military, and who disrespected the emperor.

From the Jews, the Christians inherited the idea that living in truth was the supreme aspiration of life and they made this the fundamental tenet of their faith. They set up charitable institutions to help the poor and ministered to the sick and unfortunate. Their piety appealed to the better natures of many in the Empire disaffected with the State religion.

As had happened during the high point of Classical Greece, Rome's Golden Age of letters and rationality coincided with an outbreak of madness. During the years of the Roman Republic, madness rarely appeared in either rulers or populace. But with the advent of the Empire in the first century B.C., it became increasingly manifest. The emperor Caligula tried to have his horse declared a deity. The emperor Nero killed his mother, then ordered her abdomen slit open because he wanted to inspect the womb that had carried him. The emperor Hadrian insisted that his dead boy-lover, Antinoos, be declared a god. But these isolated episodes were only preludes to one of the most extraordinary instances of mass madness.

Emboldened by the rebellious Judeans, early Christians refused to acknowledge the divine authority of Roman gods. The Romans, for their part, were acutely aware of the political price they had already paid for not insisting upon complete compliance by the Jews. The stage was set. Although the dispute was ostensibly about the divinity of Christ versus the *genius* of Jupiter, the shadowy figure behind this confrontation was the cannibal embodiment of Dionysus. As Roman legal proceedings droned on in hushed tones in a thousand courts, his maenads picked up their thyrsus wands and began their deadly, circling dance.

After having been proscribed by the Hebrews, renounced by the Greeks, and outlawed by the Romans, human sacrifice made a dramatic reappearance. The flesh-eating, blood-drinking component of the Dionysian myth had been, for the most part, imaginary. In their rites, the Greeks *pretended* to be predatory animals who rent the flesh from a live human. In practice, they disguised themselves in lion and leopard skins and substituted a ritual animal in the human effigy's place.

But what had been fantastical in Greece became preternaturally real in the Roman coliseum. Christians were *literally* torn apart and eaten by lions and leopards in a carnival atmosphere before festive crowds. In the new popular religion, God had sacrificed his own Son, and the Son had willingly suffered and died to ameliorate the human condition. Emulating Christ's sacrifice, Christians participated willingly in this carnage.

Ignatius, writing from aboard the prison ship taking him to Rome for his martyrdom, pleaded with his friends not to interfere.

> I am writing to all the churches, and I give injunction to everyone, that I am dying willingly for God's sake, if you do not prevent it. I plead with you not to do an "unreasonable kindness" to me. Allow me to be eaten by the beasts, through whom I can attain to God. I am God's wheat, and I am ground by the teeth of wild beasts, so that I may become pure bread of Christ ... Do me this favor ... Let there come upon me fire, and the cross, and struggle with wild beasts, cutting and tearing apart, racking of bones, mangling of limbs, crushing of my whole body ... may I but attain to Jesus Christ.[7]

In A.D. 190, the Roman proconsul Antonius proceeded to Asia Minor under instructions from the emperor to eradicate Christianity. He set up a tribunal to try suspected Christians and let it be known that if they were willing to pay homage to the emperor's divinity, they could go free; if not, they faced torture and death. To Antonius's astonishment, hundreds of Christians voluntarily crowded before him begging for martyrdom. Most of them he dismissed with the words, "Miserable creatures! If you wish to die, are there not ropes and precipices?"[8] This was not an isolated event. Antonius's experience was replicated throughout the conservative Roman Empire. Court records preserved from a Roman province in North Africa tell one such story. The proconsul Saturninus worked to save the lives of nine men and three women accused of being Christian.

> If you return to your senses, you can obtain a pardon from our lord the emperor ... We too are a religious people, and our religion is a simple

one: We swear by the genius of our lord the emperor and offer prayers for his health—as you ought to do too.

Meeting their determined resistance, Saturninus asked, "You wish no time for reconsideration?" Speratus, one of the accused, replied, "In so just a matter, there is no need for consideration." In spite of this, the proconsul ordered a thirty-day reprieve, urging the Christians to think it over, but thirty days later, Saturninus was forced to give the order:

> Whereas Speratus, Narzalus, Cittinus, Donata, Vestia, Secunda, and the others have confessed that they have been living in accordance with the rites of the Christians, and whereas, though they have been given the opportunity to return to the Roman usage, they have persevered in their obstinacy, they are hereby condemned to be executed by the sword.

Speratus exclaimed, "We thank God!" Narzalus added, "Today we are martyrs in heaven. Thanks be to God!"[9]

The Church's early leaders, observing that human sacrifice paradoxically increased their numbers instead of diminishing them, encouraged potential martyrs to give up their lives for the cause. Convinced that the "blood of the martyrs was the seed of the Church," Tertullian mocked the Roman authorities' persecutions and taunted them to be more repressive.

Historians who chronicle the Roman Empire must tell two parallel stories. First, there is the panoramic sweep of the rise and fall of a mighty legal, civic, artistic, engineering, and military institution. Despite its excesses, Pax Romana provided a stability never before experienced in Western civilization. For a large segment of the Western world's population, prosperity, hygiene, and civic order were the fruits of Roman pacification.

Then there is the remarkable rise of Christianity that began when Rome was at the height of its power. This improbable movement overcame the regime's native religions and outlived Rome's expiring corpus. Edward Gibbon described the period circumscribing the birth and death of Jesus:

> If a man were called upon to fix the period in the history of the world during which the condition of the human race was most happy and prosperous, he would without hesitation name that which elapsed from the accession of Nerva to the death of Aurelius. Their united reigns are possibly the only period of history in which the happiness of a great people was the sole object of government.[10]

Examining the rise and decline of Rome and the explosive emergence of a new religion reveals several striking coincidences.

Roman culture passed through several distinct stages. Law and democracy were the hallmarks of the Republic, which marked the first four hundred years of Roman history. Rome produced only minor art during this expansive period. The Empire, the next four hundred years, witnessed an artistic renaissance. And while the Empire's ethical standards declined, Rome expressed itself creatively through the works of Cicero, Livy, Ovid, Virgil, Terence, and many others.

The success of these writers was due in no small part to the elegant simplicity of the Latin alphabet and the stability of Pax Romana. Under Rome's rule many people learned how to read and write. Papyrus from Egypt, tutors from Greece, and knowledge from every corner poured into the center. By the time of Christ, book publishing had hit highs never before experienced.[11] The great Library of Alexandria contained 532,000 works in the first century; although the largest library, it was by no means the only one. Wealthy Romans collected books with a passion, and armies of slave scribes were kept busy copying them. According to Seneca, "Private libraries had become as common as baths in the houses of the rich."[12] The first romantic novels and adventure stories in prose appeared.[13]

Among the five principal factors Gibbon listed as responsible for the rise of Christianity, one was the presence of a large, alphabet-literate population. Christianity was the first alphabet-based religion to spread in a population that was already largely alphabet-literate. The ground had been prepared. All that was needed was a sacred book to be the seed, and Paul and the Gospel writers he influenced planted it. The religion gained converts at the moment in history when many previously illiterate people were learning how to communicate in a new culture-transforming medium.

The sudden appearance of a new religion that encouraged one to give up one's life for one's belief occurred at the acme of pragmatic, sensible Rome's literary, philosophical, engineering, and legal triumphs. It is an extraordinary synchronicity that the meteoric ascent of a religion whose premise was anti-intellectual and anti-rational should occur during the period when Rome approached the zenith of its written accomplishments. A similar parallelism had occurred four hundred years earlier during the Golden Age of Greece. The burst of rationalism epitomized by the logical arguments of Socrates, Plato, and Aristotle was accompanied by the ecstatic worship of Dionysus. Both cultures, Greek and Roman, experienced a sudden pulse propelling them toward left-brain values. The engine behind this pullulation was alphabet literacy. This imbalance unhinged culture. In compensation, these cultures exhibited behavior that can only be characterized as mad. Christianity was not a mad religion, but the awful sacrifices some Christians were willing to make for it in those early years could be considered mad.* Reason and madness, yoked unwillingly to each other, must advance together like partners in a three-legged sack race.

The role of the alphabet in changing a culture's religious beliefs is best illustrated by events that occurred in Egypt. Many historians have puzzled over the rapid and enthusiastic conversion of Egyptians to Christianity in the second century.[14] Egypt was, after all, an immensely ancient culture whose principal characteristic was *resistance* to change. Despite having been conquered by diverse foreigners throughout its three-thousand-year history, Egyptians retained their fealty to Osiris, Isis, Amon, Maat, and Anubis. Contrary to expectations, the people who conquered them more often than not adopted the Egyptians' gods and attendant myths, and Egypt thus influenced every major civilization in the area. Osiris became Dionysus, Attis, and Adonis; Maat transformed into Athena and Minerva; and Isis was the model for Demeter and Cybele. Then, in the late second century A.D., the Egyptian people abruptly deserted their ancient gods and replaced them with a new religion emanating from a foreign land—and not from just any foreign land, but from Judea.

At that time, Jews were a prominent minority in Egypt. In Alexandria, they comprised one-fifth of the population.[15] The Jews' spare, imageless religion was the complete opposite of its Egyptian counterpart. There is historical evidence that the Egyptians resented them. Egyptians were familiar with the Jewish Passover, which annually celebrated the killing of Egyptian sons, the defeat and death of a pharaoh, and the Egyptian people's humiliation because of the Jewish deity. This celebration posed a serious impediment for any proselytizer of a religion whose central character was Jewish. Why then did the Egyptians abandon the rich bureaucracy of their own religion, attack their own priests, despoil their own temples, and embrace with a fervor unmatched anywhere else in the ancient world a new creed revolving about the story of a crucified Jewish prophet?

Alfred North Whitehead's contention that innovations nearly wreck the societies within which they occur applies to all forms of writing. In the second century B.C., the alphabet was in use by every Mediterranean people except the hidebound Egyptians, who stubbornly refused to accept it.

---

*If children today decided to sacrifice their lives for a new religion, parents would declare that behavior mad.

Instead, they refined their hieratic script into a sort of shorthand called *demotic,* based on the syllabary rather than on the alphabetic principle. Fighting a valiant rearguard action against that cultural wrecking ball, the alphabet, they merged elements of demotic with alphabetic principles to form Coptic, an Egyptian original. Almost overnight, the cumbersome hieroglyphics and hieratic script disappeared and Coptic replaced demotic. Was it merely coincidence that at the very moment Egypt was contending with an alphabetic writing system, the country should be swept by a new religion emanating from the Jews, the oldest alphabet culture? I submit that it is doubtful that Christianity could have ever gained a footing in Egypt if the Gospels had been written in hieroglyphics. And there are no traces of hieratic or demotic Gospels—only Coptic ones. Coptic is so intertwined with Christianity that today the term "Coptic" has two specific meanings: one refers to the Egyptian alphabet, the other to Egyptian Christians.

In Egypt, where women had enjoyed the greatest equality, Clement of Alexandria vowed to destroy their rights. The Christian cleric held in his hand a spurious gospel written in the new Coptic alphabet in which he claimed that Jesus had warned, "I have come to destroy the works of the female."[16] Clement's paraphrase was surely an adulteration inspired by a Coptic misogynist.

After Christianity became Rome's state religion, Church fathers ordered the destruction of images. Zealous believers ran amok in the streets, sledge hammers and knives in hand, attacking the painstakingly crafted statuary and paintings that represented two millennia of classical culture. They destroyed works of Praxiteles, Pheidias, and Lysippus. Impassioned Christians were probably responsible for knocking the nose off the Sphinx and the arms off the Venus de Milo.*[17] Those engaged in marble smashing and image slashing made no distinction between religious statues and the likenesses of prominent Romans. Why did the Church fathers order the landscape cleared not only of images of pagan deities but of all images of anything? For the same reason that Moses declared images subversive: in order for a left-brained written message to dominate, images, perceived by the right brain, must be effaced.

Women's rights were also attacked, even though women had comprised a majority of early Christians. In the beginning, alongside men, women had

---

*Books on the subject instructed pious worshipers that knocking off the nose or the ear of the statue could destroy the powers of an idol. This probably accounts for the fact that noses are missing from so many ancient statues.

conducted all important ceremonies and frequently led congregations in prayer. They nurtured the new Church, bequeathed their fortunes to it, proselytized for it, and even, not uncommonly, gave their lives for it. Since this new Church was based on feminine principles, it should have followed that women would continue to play a central role in it, and they did—until the spoken word of Jesus was transcribed. Once Jesus' oral message was codified in ink, women found themselves reduced to second-class status.

As the New Testament grew in stature, women's rights were curtailed and imagery was eliminated. In 380 the temple of Isis at Philoe was closed. In 391, the temple of Artemis at Ephesus was sacked. In 390, a mob under the direction of the patriarch Theophilus attacked and burned the library in Alexandria because it contained pagan classics. In 425, Theodosius II closed all the synagogues in Palestine. In 529, Justinian ordered the Academy of Athens disbanded. Christianity, a religion originally based on loving tolerance, had become tyrannically intolerant.

In the spring of 415, an episode occurred that epitomized the portentous change in women's fortunes. Hypatia was a renowned woman mathematician and the head of the Neoplatonist school of philosophy in the cosmopolitan city of Alexandria. As such, she was the leading advocate of the Orphic creed.[18] Her modesty, beauty, and eloquence attracted a large number of pupils of both sexes, and she exemplified wisdom, learning and science. Cyril, Alexandria's Christian patriarch, resented her position and influence. One day as she was passing through the streets, he had a group of Nitrian monks ambush her and drag her from her carriage. They took her to a church, where she was stripped and spread-eagled. The monks tortured her to death by scraping her flesh from her bones with oyster shells, and then tore her corpse apart. This torture and mutilation echoed the frenzy of the mythical maenads rendering their male victims. With the steep ascension of a patriarchal paradigm based on an alphabetic text, both the maenads and their sacrificial victim had changed gender.

CHAPTER 26

ILLITERACY/CELIBACY
500–1000

Take pity on those in need; be kind, generous, and humble. . . . Spare him who yields, whatever wrong he has done you. . . . Be manly and gay. Hold women in respect and love; this increases a young man's honor. Be constant—that is manhood's part. Short his praise who betrays honest love.

—Medieval writer Wolfram von Eschenbach's Chivalric Code[1]

You must fast every day, pray every day, work every day, read every day. A monk must live under the rule of one father and in the society of many brethren.   —St. Columban, A.D. 585[2]

An intergalactic observer sits alone in a darkened theater watching the human drama unfold. On stage, the flamboyant pageantry of the Roman Empire is on display. Characters dressed in togas and habits, laurel wreaths and mitered crowns move through the spotlight, center stage. In A.D. 410 the dramatic sacking of the Eternal City occurs. The stage progressively darkens as successive waves of barbarians break down and obliterate the glory that was Rome. The last discernible image is a burned-out shell of a city in which roving bands of mangy dogs outnumber the ragged human survivors. It is A.D. 476. The theater is plunged into darkness. Despite the blackout, the observer is aware of movement on stage. Props are being shifted about; the unmistakable sounds of human grunts and whispers suggest considerable activity. The intermission lasts five hundred years.

When the lights come up again, the stage is completely rearranged. Gone are the elegant architrave and soaring cupola. Roads and aqueducts have fallen into ruin. Cramped, semi-isolated cities and towns have replaced the sweep of Roman hegemony. Commerce is all but nonexistent. Travel has become exceedingly dangerous; bandits roam the countryside. There has been a near-total breakdown of civil authority. Everyone appears dirty and everything seems grimy. The characters no longer speak Latin or Greek. Instead, a polyglot of immature vernaculars impinges on the ear.

The dramatis personae are dressed in costumes of red, black, and brown. The Church has become the dominant institution and reserves black—like the ink of its vellum books—for itself. Red is for the nobility, who rule their petty fiefdoms that checkerboard the land. The vast mass of drab serfs who labor for a meager living wear brown shapeless shifts. They depend on the warrior aristocracy to protect their lives in this world and the clerics to save their souls in the next, and to each of these benefactors/oppressors, the serfs must tithe a hefty portion of their modest yield.

To the historian, the Dark Ages, as they are called, are dark for only one reason. A most unexpected turn of events occurred after the fall of Rome. The simple seeds of the ABCs, sown wherever Roman standards had flown, had somehow failed to root in the freshly turned minds of the intelligent people of western Europe. In secular culture, wracked by ceaseless invasion and chaos, alphabet literacy withered. Only the Church preserved the written word. Kenneth Clark speculates that for five hundred years, no king or nobleman could read.[3] While there were occasional exceptions in lay society, a lampblack illiteracy descended over most of Europe, unbalancing culture.

The Dark Ages was a black hole out from which not a single significant scientific, literary, or philosophical idea emerged. Without a written record, historians have had to piece together a sense of what life was like in the Dark Ages largely by inference and deduction. The diorama they have assembled is most unsettling. Barbarous practices, ignorance, and superstition apparently ruled. In the words of Thomas Hobbes, life was "nasty, brutish, and short."

One might expect that the strong subjugated the weak and that feminine values would have been suffocated in those churlish times. So it is all the more remarkable that when literacy finally reilluminated (albeit dimly) the stage of history in the tenth century, poets, bards, jongleurs, and troubadours were singing the praises of womanhood. From out of the pitch-black womb of the Dark Ages emerged the Age of Chivalry, in which the highest aspiration of a man was to protect and serve "the fair sex." In Germany, *Frauenlob*, "women's praise" informed the songs of the earliest minnesingers.[4] In France, knights in chain mail pledged themselves to uphold the honor of the women of their kingdom. The oral code, which was preserved later in writing, urged men to "serve and honor all women" and "spare no pain and effort in their service."[5]

There have been other turbulent times in Western history, but none in which concern for women's welfare was such an abiding priority. Despite the extreme disorder and gloom of the period from A.D. 500 to 1000, equality between the sexes reached near equilibrium. As historian Doris Stenton noted, "The evidence which has survived . . . indicates that women were more nearly equal companions of their husbands and brothers than at any other period before the modern age."[6]

Inspired by the Chivalric Age, a new mythology arose. Transmitted by song by traveling minstrels, the story of King Arthur and his gallant knights expressed the morality of the age. Chrétien de Troyes in the twelfth century and William of Malmsbury in the thirteenth passed along segments of the myth, if indeed it is a myth. In the fifteenth century, Thomas Malory organized the many episodes of King Arthur's reign into a unified fable.

King Arthur's reign was portrayed as one based on justice and good deeds, and Camelot as a place where egalitarian customs prevailed. The Arthurian ethic is implicit in the identifying phrase: King Arthur and his Knights of the Round Table. No one, including the king, can sit at the head of a circular table because there is no head: all seats are equidistant from the center. Concerning the code of conduct expected of men, we learn in Chrétien de Troyes' story of Lancelot that "he who is a perfect lover is always obedient and quickly and gladly does his mistress' pleasure . . ." Above all, this oral culture taught its men how to be *courteous*. Arthur's most trusted adviser was the wizard Merlin. Wizards are shamans and they were held in high regard during the time of orality. After the return of alphabet literacy wizards were demonized and their gender transposed into the much-feared witches of the sixteenth and seventeenth centuries.

To become an Arthurian knight required long and rigorous training that included the martial arts and self-mastery. But one also had to learn how to dance and play a musical instrument well. When not in battle defending their liege and the ladies of the realm, knights were expected to engage in acts of kindness, gallantry, and noblesse oblige. That not all knights lived up to this shining ideal does not diminish the uniqueness of this feminine-affirming military code.

The unlettered noblemen's love and admiration for women was expressed symbolically in the many Grail quest myths. The Grail was the cup from which Jesus drank wine at the Last Supper and in which His blood was collected at his crucifixion. The Grail excited the imagination of the illiterate Christian nobility of western Europe. Neither the literati of Byzantium (Constantinople) nor the literate hierarchy of the Church expressed enthusiasm for this object of devotion. After the Medieval Age passed, Christian culture as a whole lost interest in it.

As containers that hold liquid, cups and grails are archetypal symbols of the female. In Sumerian times the libation chalice, often in the shape of a vulva, was one of the most sacred votive objects of the Goddess; Her priestesses used it to pour offerings to Her.[7] The archaic Greeks believed that the gods had used Helen of Troy's breast to mold the first cup.[8] Unconsciously, mother's milk and female genitalia are associated with hollowed containers of any kind.

During the Dark Ages, the Grail replaced the fish as Christianity's most potent symbol. The male obsession to retrieve a lost cup reveals a reorientation in the illiterate segment of the population. Before the lights of literacy went out, the Christian Orthodox leaders—Paul, Tertullian, Jerome, and Augustine—had hammered together a religion whose central themes were sin, guilt, and suffering. When the lights came on again in the tenth century, Europeans had leavened these with an increased respect for birth and womanhood. This revised ethos changed the character of Christianity and is best illustrated by the sharp and unexpected ascendance of Marianism.

Mary was an unlikely candidate to become the fourth major figure of Christianity after the Trinity. Paul never mentions Jesus' mother, and the Gospel writers make only a few references to her. None acknowledge either her birth or her death, and in Mark 3:31–35 and Matt. 12:46–50 Jesus rebukes her. Only Matt. 1:18–25 unequivocally mentions a virgin birth. Like the Earth Goddesses before her, Mary plays a crucial role in only two events in Christ's life: His birth and His death.

By canonizing the written word in the fourth century, early churchmen were convinced they had insulated Christianity from the siren song of pagan polytheism. The triune religion as conceived by Paul consisted of a Son, a Father, and a Holy Spirit. Subsequent Church fathers were determined to crush the power of pagan goddesses. Augustine considered the worship of Earth-mother deities "obscene," "monstrous," and "wicked."[9] The creed of Christianity was decidedly not about a divine woman. Yet beginning in the Dark Ages, devotion to Mary blossomed throughout European Christendom. The Parthenon of Athena was rededicated to Mary ca. A.D. 600, as were almost all the other extant temples that had honored Pagan goddesses.

Every Mediterranean-based religion prior to Christianity built major monuments to honor its chief deity. Marduk's Ziggurat, Aton's City of the Horizon, the Temple of Zeus at Herculaneum, and Yahweh's Temple Mount in Jerusalem exemplify this seemingly universal impulse to honor the preeminent god with outsized stone structures. The signal accomplishment of the entire Medieval Age was the erection of great Gothic cathedrals that pierced the skies of Europe with a forest of spires. Nothing encapsulates the medieval *Zeitgeist* better than these immense stone edifices. But the great cathedrals were not dedicated to any of the three male Trinitarian divinities; instead, the four most magnificent cathedrals in France—Paris, Chartres, Reims, and Amiens—are all called Notre Dame: Our Lady. So too is Santa Maria del Fior in Florence, Saint Sophia in Constantinople, and the Frauenkirche in Munich. Civic and church leaders dedicated these churches to the *mortal mother* of the Christian deity. In France alone, over a hundred churches and eighty cathedrals were raised in Mary's name.[10] While most were completed after the eleventh century, the initial inspiration to build them arose at the end of the Dark Ages. While Mary may not have a gospel extolling her virtues, her rise in stature is eloquently expressed by her highly visible Bible of stone dotting the European landscape.

Although the New Testament is filled with detailed episodes of Jesus' life, not a single Gospel writer provides even the most minor detail of His appearance. We do not know if He was tall or short, thin or heavy, fair or dark, nor does this left-brain text offer any raw material to aid the right brain in imagining Jesus' facial features. Like Amon and Yahweh before Him, Jesus became the God-With-No-Face. Something as crucial as a physical description, an *image* of the God Incarnate, could not have been omitted by accident. Christians were forced to know Him only through black inked *words* arranged linearly on white paper.*

But the character of the Mary who emerged in illiterate Europe differed from the assertive woman who admonished her Son at the wedding at Cana in the New Testament. Unlike Jesus, the Dark Age Mary rarely speaks: no pithy parables or aphorisms have been attributed to her. Her subjects came to know her through her *image* that led every procession and adorned the walls of homes, shops, churches, and crossroads. The *likeness* of the Blessed Mother became ubiquitous throughout western Europe.

And a new phenomenon accompanied this change—one that had been absent during Christianity's first four centuries. People reported seeing visions of Mary, though she rarely spoke. Ignorant shepherds and unlettered peasant girls seem to have encountered the spectral Mother far more fre-

---

*Despite its many vivid metaphors and rich word imagery, the Gospels do not employ color terms. This is another omission that reinforces the left hemisphere's agenda over that of the right.

quently than learned churchmen.* It seemed that the farther removed a person was from alphabet learning, the more likely was the Church to authenticate the sighting. In the Old Testament, Yahweh's select few *heard* His voice or *read* His words; in the Medieval Age, people *visualized* her in apparitions. Despite the profusion of Mary sightings during these dark centuries, there were *no* sightings of the Father or the Holy Ghost and only rarely of the Son. Alphabet cultures know gods through their *words;* non-literate cultures see goddesses' *images.* I propose that Mary's rise was related directly to the collapse of alphabet literacy.

At the onset of the Dark Ages, secular art had all but vanished. Since imagery was forbidden by the Second Commandment, Pope Gregory the Great (590 to 604) confronted a vexing problem. How could he, as the chief priest presiding over a vast enterprise, ensure that Christian doctrine would be disseminated in a society where people could not read and illustrations were forbidden. Over the strident objections of many strict literalists, but to the immense relief of future art lovers, the Pope declared the Second Commandment null and void. "Painting," he said, "can do for the illiterate what writing does for those who can read."[11] Aware of the power of images, in 787 the Church authorities revised Gregory's edict: "It is for painters to execute; it is for the clergy to ordain the subjects and govern the procedure."[12] The very first painting that the Church commissioned was a portrait of the Pope receiving the symbols of his station. The personage bestowing these insignia of power was not God, Jesus, or Peter, but the Blessed Virgin, robed and crowned in the regalia of an empress.

Images of the adult Jesus who strides through the pages of the New Testament speaking wise words and doing courageous deeds are rarely found in Christian art. The Jesus of Catholic art was either a helpless infant or a dead man. In both cases, His mother cared for Him. As birth and death had been the province of the Goddess, so were they Mary's.

During the medieval age, the growth of a mother cult transformed the very character of Christianity. The devotion to Mary and to the saints undermined the masculine Orthodox creed set forth by Paul, Jerome, and Augustine. The empyreal regions of Greco-Roman religions had been filled with accessory deities; in the age of Mary, Heaven became crowded with saints. By the tenth century, people turned to saints who numbered in the thousands. Monotheistic, albeit triune, Christianity had struggled earlier against the polytheism of pagan religions and by the fourth century appeared to have triumphed, but in the age of illiteracy, polytheism reclaimed

---

*The Church has authenticated over twenty-one thousand sightings of Mary.

A Black Madonna,
from France

the popular imagination. In front of altars, the literate, all-male clergy prayed to the masculine Trinity; behind them, the illiterate folk, resonating to the cadences of mass, sat lost in contemplation of the images of the saints and the Mother.

At some unconscious level, the Church fathers recognized the threat Mary posed, for they denied Mary essential attributes possessed by previous goddesses: she did not preside over the functions of fertility and was split away from the soil. They granted her the honorific "Queen of Heaven," but not "Queen of the Earth" or "Queen of the Underworld." As Yahweh instructed Adam, the power to name is the power to control. The male Church hierarchy reverently hailed Mary as the Mother of God, but never as God the Mother. To further divorce her from sex and procreation, the Church emphasized two antithetical aspects of Mary: she was the Virgin Mother.

That the people persisted in honoring Mary as the reincarnation of the ancient Goddess worshiped by all preliterate agrarian civilizations is evidenced by the phenomenon of the Black Virgin. Many medieval churches, extending in a wide arc from Russia across Europe to Spain, had as their most sacred object a statue of a black Mary. The current official papal explanation posits that these representations were blackened by centuries of candle smoke. But close examination reveals that this could not be true, since the statues' clothes are not similarly stained. If soot is not the answer, what is? Why would a Caucasian population, many of whom were blue-eyed and fair-haired, depict the Mother of God as incontrovertibly black?

The colors of nature dazzle us with their infinite variety, but black is the one color missing from the spectrum. It is the color of night and the shade of soil. It cloaks midnight and blankets the depths of caves and grottos. In previous cultures, the most popular totem for a chief male divinity was the sun and, by extension, light; goddesses have been associated with the moon and, by extension, night. The words *matter, matrix,* and *mother* all derive from the Latin *materia,* which means "substance." Earth is the most primordial substance and sunlight, its antipode. In ancient Egypt, Isis personified the black loam lining the banks of the Nile Delta; Apuleius, the second century Roman dramatist, portrayed her wearing a black cape. The earthly incarnation of Cybele, the great Roman Tellus Mater, was a huge black stone. The statue of Artemis at Ephesus, the most famous shrine of a goddess outside of Egypt, was also black. As with many other aspects of the feminine, the black Mary appeared predominantly in unlettered times and among unlettered populations. Once alphabet literacy regained its hold over human communication she all but disappeared.

Water, *aqua femina,* has long been the quintessential symbol of femaleness. In virtually every Creation myth that informs the dawn of civilization, a mother goddess representing the undifferentiated waters created the universe, including Nammu and Tiamat in Sumeria, Vritas and Danu in India, and Tehom and Rahab in several Old Testament psalms. One of Isis's most popular names was Star of the Sea. Mary's name, *Maria,* means water. *La mer* (French), *maritime* (Latin), and *marine* (English) are just a few of the words that refer to the sea and share the same root.

The Church had to acknowledge Mary's rapidly rising popularity among the common folk. In medieval times the Vatican proclaimed August 15, the Feast of the Assumption, in her honor—by coincidence the same day pagans had honored the goddess Artemis in pre-Christian times. In both France and England, medieval calendars were recalibrated to begin each new year on the Day of Our Lady, March 15.

In a development contrived to counterbalance the beneficent Mary's burgeoning popularity, Church leaders subconsciously conjured up a figure to express pure malevolence—the devil. He cannot be found in the bulging pantheons of the Sumerians, Egyptians, Cretans, Greeks, or Romans. Their deities may have had a dark side, but none personified evil alone. Nor was he mentioned in the Torah's earliest books. The New Testament's Beelzebub was peripheral to both Jesus' prophecies and Paul's writings. Gospel writers refer to him sparingly. The patristic fathers began to invoke his name, but his diabolical appearance did not stabilize until the end of the Dark Ages. Since no one had actually ever *seen* the devil, his form—red color, horns, tail, triton, and cloven hooves—provides insight into the mind-set of his inventors.

Red has been the color of female sexuality ever since primates climbed the trunks of trees. High off the ground, they supplanted smell with sight as the premier sexual sense. Alone among myriad species, female primates signaled to males the onset of estrus by developing a swelling suffused with a flaming red color in their buttocks and vulva. The sight of this particular wavelength set off a cascade of neurotransmitters in the male primate's brain, exciting him with tumescent anticipation.

These atavistic sexual trip wires remain buried deep within the male human brain and are triggered by the color red. Throughout all ages and across all cultures, women overwhelmingly have preferred red for their lipstick to all other hues. From scarlet letters to hymenic defloration, red has consistently been the color associated with sex. It is also the color of blood, vitality, and passion. The only other Western deity consistently portrayed as red was Dionysus.

Horns are emblematic of animals such as the bull and the cow, and craniums with horns are a schematic for the uterus and fallopian tubes of all mammalian females. In most medieval depictions, the devil's sinuous tail has a peculiar, wedge-shaped swelling at its tip, evocative of a serpent's head.

Prior to Christianity, tritons had been associated with Poseidon and the sea (and prior to Poseidon, water had been the domain of mother goddesses). Tritons had been used for eons to spear fish. Putting one in the grip of the devil, who spends his time attending to the fires of Hell, is an awkward attempt to conflate a water symbol with flame imagery. More recently the Devil's triton has been described as a pitchfork, but the devil would have very little need for a hay-farming tool in Hell.*

The devil's cloven hooves were the masterstroke as the male propagandists who envisioned him attempted to execrate the symbols of female power. Pigs were sacred to the Goddess. The swine family's milieu is mud: their hooves make a distinctively shaped print that is a three-quarter oval, interrupted at one end by a cleft that runs up from the bottom.

Long ago, when humans were emerging into ego-consciousness, Paleolithic peoples painted on rocks and cave walls their universal symbol of the female; archeologists call it "the vulva sign." In its most common form, it is an oval with a cleft running up from the bottom. This sign has been identified in the cultures of Old Europe, early Mesopotamia, Harappa, and Crete.

*Hell is derived from the name of a Germanic goddess named Hel.

In an uncanny coincidence, the most evil deity that alphabet religions have ever conjured leaves a mark in the earth that closely resembles the ancient symbol of the Earth Goddess. The devil, although male, conflated symbols previously associated with the Goddess. A foil for Mary was now in place. I propose that during the medieval period, the Church played on the male fear of women's rising status by piecing together a thinly camouflaged, transsexual, diabolical Goddess.

Women played a central role in religious life in medieval society. In many regions they, rather than men, wielded authority in the local parishes. In the time of darkness women often officiated over the major sacraments. From the fifth to the twelve centuries Cathars and Waldensians routinely appointed women clergy. The issue of priestly celibacy, paramount in the fourth century, evaporated with the onset of the Dark Ages. Priests routinely had wives and children. During this period, the Church was quite tolerant of heresy: punishing witches or heretics in these supposedly barbaric times were rare events.

During the first four centuries of Christianity, extreme asceticism had been associated with the fringe elements of the religion. The Anchorites, for example, escaped the temptations of the flesh by retiring to remote sanctuaries in inhospitable climes to live contemplative lives.

In sixth-century Italy, a woman jilted the young noble Benedict of Nursia. As a result Benedict resolved to live a simple and celibate life on the slopes of Monte Cassino near Rome. Pope Gregory I tells how Benedict fought valiantly to forget the woman:

> the memory of whom the wicked spirit put into his mind, and by that memory so mightily inflamed with concupiscence the soul of God's servant . . . that, almost overcome with pleasure, he was of a mind to forsake the wilderness. But suddenly, assisted by God's grace, he came to himself; and seeing many thick briers and nettle bushes growing hard by, off he cast his apparel, and threw himself into the midst of them, and there wallowed so long that when he rose up all his flesh was pitifully torn; and so by the wounds of his body he cured the wounds of his soul.[13]

Benedict soon attracted others of like disposition and, in 529, he founded the Benedictine Order. This was the beginning of what was to become the distinguishing social movement of the next thousand years.

As his Order grew, Benedict realized that he could channel the energies of the large group of males he had at his disposal. Monks were unencumbered by wives or families and, unlike ordinary workers, they did not demand wages. Upon entering the Order they pledged obedience, accepted poverty, and promised to work as well as pray. All across Europe, cooperative labor pools of young, vigorous non-military men gathered. "Idleness is the enemy of the soul," wrote Saint Benedict, ordering all monks to perform at least six hours of labor a day.[14] Nothing like it had ever occurred before.

Julius Caesar recounted the tale of a man who told him he had walked from Poland to Spain without seeing direct sunlight; so carpeted with dense forests and swamps was Europe of the first century B.C. Small farmers could never hope to marshal the resources necessary to clear this dense foliage. At the start of the monastic movement, most of Europe was unsuitable for agriculture; by the end of it, the horizon was visible in many places. The monastic movement was responsible for deforestation on an unprecedented scale. Within a few hundred years, Benedict's spare aesthetic had gained an enthusiastic following. Men flocked to the monasteries, and monasticism transformed the social landscape as well as the physical one.

During the early years of monastic orders, monks were primarily motivated by spiritual considerations. Older men, weary of the grind, sought refuge in a place where they could dedicate their lives to quiet contemplation. But as the monastic movement gained influence and prestige, would-be brothers began to heed the call for different reasons. In the absence of effective secular authority, monasteries in many regions assumed the paternal role formerly played by government, and having a family member in the local cloister was politically advantageous. In the past, parents would seek arranged marriages to ally themselves, through their children, with another family; medieval parents, in effect, encouraged some of their offspring to marry an institution.

Shortly after the founding of monasteries, women asked for permission from the Church to establish similar institutions. Nuns became Brides of Christ, and nunneries flourished, often in conjunction with monasteries. The majority of these "double monasteries," especially in northern Europe, were headed by abbesses rather than by abbots.

As the patriarchal custom of providing a dowry for each daughter gained acceptance among feudal families over earlier practices that were the reverse, parents realized they could avoid this economic burden by pledging a daughter to a convent shortly after her birth. Nunneries were soon flooded with so many supernumerary daughters that the Church had to issue edicts against the practice. Parents mandated a celibate life for their offspring before the children understood the implications of the oath. Many nuns, cloistered against their will, found it impossible to behave as saints.

Monasteries, too, had their share of young boys called "oblates" whose parents had pledged them as infants to the monastic life. Some, raised entirely within the monasteries' walls, had never even *seen* a woman. Caesarius of Heisterbach tells of a young oblate who was a teenager before he first ventured outside the cloister. While riding through the countryside accompanied by his abbot, he nearly fell off his horse, so transfixed was he by the sight of a young maiden walking along the road. He turned to his chaperon in wonderment and asked, "What is that?" "Pay no attention to her," the older abbot replied, "for she is a demon." Turning wistfully in the direction of her vanishing form while pondering this unexpected reply, the youth muttered, "Strange, I thought she was the fairest thing I ever saw."[15]

For the lower classes, monasteries provided an escape route from the drudgery of the serf's life. Many peasant men joined orders to avoid conscription into the local militia. But there was still one other very significant incentive monasteries offered to men who were willing to give up the pleasures of the secular world. Lowly birth denied the most intelligent serfs the possibility of upward mobility. The aristocracy owned all the land, and the moat separating the classes was all but uncrossable. The Church, however, was a meritocracy in which ambitious young men could advance.

Literacy was the indispensable key to advancement in the Church hierarchy and a monastery was the only institution capable of conferring literacy, because monasteries possessed all the books there were in Europe. The price for acquiring literacy, then, was celibacy—a strange tuition indeed! Nowhere is the antithesis between the written word and sexuality better illustrated than in this peculiar quid pro quo.

The most creative force in the world is the one that commands living things to strive to continue their species. Salmon swim thousands of miles upstream and leap high rapids in order to spawn. Male elephant seals engage rivals in near-mortal combat over the right to copulate with the cows of the herd, and the male praying mantis will urgently mate with a female even as she is busy devouring him. The sexual drive powerfully influences human behavior too.

Buddhist monks were celibate but lived as mendicants. The Old Testament ostracized those who remained celibate; the Greeks frowned on the practice, and the Romans legislated against it. Among the barbarians, celibacy was considered repugnant. The vast majority of medieval priests and bishops were not celibate. By all accounts the medieval age was a lusty age. Nonetheless, the literate in monasteries demanded celibacy of initiates.

From a eugenic point of view, the Church's decision to prevent its brightest and most curious members from passing on their genes was a calamity that ensured the Dark Ages would remain dark for much longer than they would have if the Church had encouraged its intelligentsia to "be fruitful and multiply." Nature had tinkered for untold eons to develop a harsh but extremely sophisticated system that ensured the most intelligent humans would survive in order to pass along their superior genes. The principal premise of the monastic movement, celibacy, nullified the system. By culling out of the gene pool the noblest, most altruistic, and most intelligent men and women, this anti-evolutionary, eccentric social engineering scheme undoubtedly delayed the Renaissance. Nineteenth-century male Victorian anthropologists condescendingly referred to archaic goddess civilizations as "fertility cults"; twentieth-century female anthropologists, in an appropriate riposte, have characterized the medieval monastic orders as "sterility cults." The harsh patriarchy and anti-sexuality of the monastic movement can be seen, however, as the alphabet-literate minority's response to the illiterate majority's extreme feminism, embodied in the myths of King Arthur, the devotion to Mary, and the ethic of chivalry.

Four defining aspects of monastic life—time, speech, laughter, and hair—underscore the left brain's role in the monastic movement. The Fourth Commandment sacralized the sequential nature of time. Monasteries went further and created *the* most characteristic feature of Western culture—repeatable, linked segments of time. It was in Christian monasteries that the seamlessness of a day first fragmented into hours and minutes. By spacing prayer services at precisely punctuated intervals, abbots compelled their monks to acclimate to man-made units of time.

Most animals can use the angle of the sun as a reasonably accurate guide for the time of day. Night is more problematic. Monasteries divided the night up into identical segments, training monks to calculate the exact hour without the aid of daylight or starlight. With Pavlovian precision, midnight *matins* and 3:00 A.M. *lauds* summoned sleepy-eyed monks from their cells, reinforcing the left brain's time coordinate.*

Monasteries' vows of silence neutralized the right hemisphere's contribution to communication. Ostensibly, this rule prevented novitiates from dwelling on mundane matters so they might redirect their thoughts toward the divine. But silence, combined with reading and writing, encouraged new monks to rely on left-brain faculties. Also, novitiates were required to lower their eyes during the rare conversations they were allowed. To further

---

*The first cog-and-gear clock that could divide an hour into minutes was installed at the Monastery at St. Albans in 1348. It was used to call monks to prayer.

repress the right brain, novitiates were forbidden to laugh. Jesting, jokes, mirth, or playful behavior were banned.

Monastic authorities were also aware of the associations between hair and sexuality. Upon entering an order, male novitiates were immediately tonsured. This strange hairdo shaved only the top of their heads, leaving tufts at the sides. The effect was to rob a vital male of his virile crown and all young men now resembled old men whose baldness nominally (but with many exceptions) signified their failing sexual capacity. Nunneries treated hair more repressively. Outlandish designs were employed by various orders to disguise a nun so that it appeared she did not have any hair at all. A starched, white, angular, stiff wimple not only completely hid her hair, its characteristics were the antithesis of a feature of humanhood that is naturally soft, dark, wavy, and lustrous. The extremes to which monastic authorities went in neutralizing the sexuality implicit in hair is an indication of just how dangerous exposed hair is to the controlling left hemisphere. Behavioral psychology came into its own in the twentieth century. And yet, almost a thousand years earlier, those in charge of monasteries had developed sophisticated techniques that revealed a deep understanding of split-hemispheric functions.

Monasticism did more to undermine the position of medieval women than any other social institution. Nature has meticulously titrated the birth ratio of females to males to be equal. This ensures that each could find one of the other. Wars removed from circulation a large number of eligible men. Mothers' deaths in childbirth grimly but efficiently rebalanced the equation. The proliferation of monasteries added an unexpected new drain. For every male who opted for the religious life, a female could not form a family. But the sexual urge was too strong to be simply subordinated to mere oath. Many who entered monasteries did so for uninspired reasons, and not all had the fortitude to forego sex. Monks frequently formed clandestine liaisons with local women whom they euphemistically called their "cleaning ladies," provoking clerics to write strident rebukes castigating the uncontrolled "venery" of the monasteries.

Putting aside the question of sin, these new living arrangements made a mockery of the sanctity of Christian marriage. Women were still cohabiting with men, and the sexual urges of both sexes were still being satisfied. Children still played on the stoops of doorways as they had in all previous human societies. However, these "cleaning ladies" differed from homemakers in every other culture since the dawn of time because they *had no rights*. A monk who sired a child out of wedlock had no legal obligation to provide support, although many did, and since the rule of monastic orders prohibited a monk from owning personal wealth, his concubine was not entitled to an inheritance if he died. Monasteries spawned so many illegitimate children that, in exasperation, the Council of Pavia decreed in 1018 that all children born to clerics were to be condemned to perpetual slavery and disbarred from any inheritance.[16] "From this practice," said Photius, a chronicler (820–891), "we see in the West so many children who do not know their fathers."[17]

If concubinage was commonplace in the institution that was supposed to be the model of virtue for the rest of society, commoners felt few qualms imitating the practice. The institution of marriage suffered a disastrous decline. Further, the presence of vast numbers of illegitimate children destabilized medieval culture. Born without legal status, many misbegotten boys who grew into manhood felt they had no other option but to try to seize power by force. Medieval history is filled with the names of bastards: Arthur, Gawain, Roland, William the Conqueror, and many a knight in Froissart's *Chronicles* among them. Many became brigands or, like their fathers, joined monasteries. For girls born out of wedlock, menial jobs, poverty, or slavery was their lot. Some emulated their mothers and became concubines; others turned to prostitution, creating a social malaise that frequently overwhelmed local authorities. In the penitentials preserved from the late Dark Ages there were no penances for prostitution. One may infer from their absence in the roster of sins that prostitution was not a significant problem for Dark Age society. Then in the Middle Ages, many towns including Toulouse, Avignon, Frankfort, and Nuremberg, were forced to legalize the practice. Without some controls, one churchman opined, "good women could not venture safely into the streets." In 1177, Henry, the abbot of Clairvaux agonized, "Ancient Sodom is springing up from her ashes."[18] Like many other indignant prelates, he failed to connect the Church's austere position on celibacy with the problem of prostitution in society. Prostitution and bastardy subverted public morality.

In the centuries after the fall of Rome the role of the image in society changed profoundly. By the sixth century, Christendom had fissured into an eastern Orthodox branch led by a Patriarch centered at Byzantium, and a western Catholic Church headed by the Pope in Rome. The two camps eyed each other with increasing suspicion, finally rupturing in the Great Schism of 1054. While Western Europe languished in the Dark Ages, Byzantium continued the literary and artistic traditions inherited from Greece and Rome. In the eighth century, a sect arose from within the ranks of its highly literate clergy that so despised images that its members declared an all-out war against statues and paintings. They called themselves the *iconoclasts*, which means image-destroyers. One of its sympathizers became the Patriarch in 726. Leo III ordered all church murals covered with plaster and all likenesses of the Virgin effaced.

The people of Byzantium revolted against these arbitrary edicts and armed conflict broke out. Pious Christians attacked the soldiers desecrating their cherished images of the Holy Family, and many soldiers mutinied rather than carry out their orders. The iconoclasts regrouped into roving bands, their ranks swollen with hoodlums who relished vandalism. At first, they sought out only religious images to smash. Church mosaics, painted icons, and stained-glass artistry fell to their savage assaults. Later their targets also included painters, sculptors, and craftsmen. They even murdered those whose crime it was to love art. Monks who resisted were blinded and had their tongues torn out. The iconoclasts beheaded the Patriarch of the Eastern Church in 767 for refusing to support their cause.

The iconoclast movement never spread to illiterate western Europe; its madness consumed only the segment of Christendom that boasted the highest literacy rate. Artists fled for their lives from Byzantium, heading for the western court of Charlemagne whose largely illiterate courtiers welcomed them with open arms. The iconoclast movement raged for fifty years and was finally extinguished when Irene became empress in 797. With popular sentiment firmly behind her, she reversed Leo III's edict.

A few years later, on Christmas Day in 800, Charlemagne, the most powerful monarch in Europe, was crowned king of the hastily cobbled together Holy Roman Empire. This event marked the beginning of the end of the Dark Ages. Of Teutonic origin, Charlemagne was a fit, tall, handsome paragon of regal virtue. Besides being a courageous fighter, he was an intelligent statesman and a judicious administrator. Although personally opposed to divining and prophecy, he decreed that no sorcerers could be harmed in his kingdom. He established poorhouses for widows and orphans. He hired many of the artists fleeing from the turmoil in Byzantium and decorated his kingdom with their labors. Not wishing to be parted from the daughters he loved, he encouraged them to indulge their sexual desires rather than marry (he himself had several wives), as long as they did not leave his side. They consoled themselves accordingly and presented him with many illegitimate, well-loved grandchildren.

Charlemagne differed from all the Dark Age kings who had preceded him in that he alone recognized that his kingdom was held hostage by a priestly class who kept secret the arcane skill of writing. He brought from faraway York one of Europe's most learned men, the monk Alcuin, to institute educational reforms. For the first time since Roman rule, secular schools opened their doors and the bright sounds of children trooping to the schoolhouse filled the morning air.

Believing that he should set an example for his lay subjects by becoming literate, Charlemagne managed to acquire a cursory knowledge of reading, but the skill of writing eluded him entirely. An apocryphal story relates how each day when he finished his court duties he retired to his chambers accompanied by his most esteemed clergy with instructions to teach him the art. But after many frustrating attempts he threw up his hands and declared the task impossible. If Charlemagne could not learn literacy, how was he to convince his less motivated subjects that they could? He ordered the clergy to convene an assembly of the most educated minds in Christendom to reform writing. The result was the Carolingian reforms, which fundamentally simplified and clarified reading and writing.

Our English word *text* comes from the German *textura,* meaning "tapestry." Early medieval manuscripts bear a closer resemblance to a medieval tapestry than to a modern page of writing. Gothic writers scrunched all the letters of all the words together in one mass of script. The Carolingian reforms called for placing a single space between each letter, two spaces between each word, and three spaces between each sentence. Paragraphs were to be indented, and punctuation marks, such as the period and comma, signaled the reader when to pause and when to breathe. The committee also invented lowercase letters, which contrasted with and set off capital letters. The Carolingian reforms, instituted twelve hundred years ago, were the last substantive modifications to the alphabet.

These improvements made reading easier and stimulated a renewed interest in literacy throughout Europe. Unfortunately, Viking raids in the ninth and tenth centuries destroyed most of the fledgling institutions of learning, and unusually severe climatic variations led to extreme cold, floods, and drought that all but erased the Carolingian renaissance that had been slowly building after Charlemagne. Meanwhile, a perturbation occurred in the southeastern corner of the Mediterranean that was to affect Western history momentously. Its tale must now be briefly told.

CHAPTER 27

MUSLIN VEILS/
MUSLIM WORDS

Never have you [Mohammed] read a book before this, nor have you ever transcribed one with your right hand. Had you done either of these the unbelievers might have justly doubted. —Quran (Sura 29:48)

Nomads roaming the deserts of Arabia remained unaffected by the classical world's meteor shower lighting up the sky along their northern frontier. Close-knit extended families formed the basis of their society, competing with other tribes for scarce resources in an inhospitable terrain. There was no central government, very little art, and pandemic illiteracy. Roving troubadours entertained with songs of valor and romance. The annual convening of the tribes was a major event. Besides the usual contests of skill and mettle, there were poetry competitions. Winners were adulated. Women moved freely about, owned property, and the tribes practiced matrilineal inheritance customs. Images, though sparse, were appreciated.

In 1000 B.C., at the time when the Israelites began transcribing the Old Testament, Sabaean kings in the southern Arabian deserts were building an advanced civilization, complete with grand irrigation works, monumental buildings, and a distinctive alphabet. But a literary tradition did not take root and the shifting sands subsequently buried the Sabaeans' culture. Epigraphers and archaeologists know of it only from the barest of fragments. The only Sabaean historical figure to survive the anonymity of these centuries was the powerful Queen of Sheba.

Interestingly, the first thousand years of western European history, from the birth of Christ amidst the splendor of the Roman Empire up through the plunge into the Dark Ages, is almost the reverse of the story of the first thousand years of Arab history. The defining event in both cultures occurred midway: one lost, and the other gained, the knowledge of the written word.

While Europe slumbered, the prophet Mohammed was born in 569 in Mecca, a dusty city on the desiccated plateau of the Arabian Peninsula. An orphan, he grew into an intelligent but illiterate young man. Traveling far beyond his home while working for his uncle, a camel caravaneer, he had the opportunity to observe different cultures. He learned well the ways of a merchant. When he was twenty-five, Khadija, a widow fifteen years his senior with five children, chose him to be her husband. Mohammed was a devoted family man, and loved children so much that he routinely took in orphans. Khadija was a very resourceful woman who ran her own business. She became Mohammed's best friend, business adviser, and soul mate. In a society in which polygamy was acceptable, Mohammed remained monogamous until she died twenty-six years later. By all accounts, he loved, respected, and cherished her. With the exception of Abraham, no other religion can make a similar claim about its founder.

Prior to Mohammed's birth, the Arabs had evolved a polytheistic religion based on the worship of megaliths. The central object of veneration was a large black cube called the *Kaaba,* embedded in the earth at Mecca. Long before Mohammed's birth, Mecca was the Arabs' holiest city. Perhaps Mecca's association with agriculture accounted for the preponderance of female deities in a culture principally informed by manly virtues. Four main stone idols ringed the shrine at Mecca. Al-Lah and al-Lat were the divine male and female consorts who together ruled the supernatural world. The two others were the goddesses al-Uzza (which means the Mighty One) and Manah (the goddess of fate).[1] But we know little of these deities' traits, exploits, or character because almost nothing of their mythology has survived. Goddess veneration, however, was a very old Arab custom. Herodotus, writing a thousand years before Mohammed, identified the Sun Goddess al Lat as a major Arab deity.[2] Attesting to her high status, al Lat's other name was al-Rabba, the Sovereign. Even after the rise of Islam, the priests who attended the shrine at the Kaaba were known as "the sons of the Old Woman."[3] After Islam became established, Muslims referred to the period before the coming of the Prophet as the "Age of Ignorance." So eager were they to erase all traces of what they regarded as a span of shame that very little evidence of the antecedent religion has survived.

Mohammed's travels brought him into contact with the many Jews and Gnostic Christians who had settled in the area. He observed that both groups enjoyed a cohesiveness that the Arabs lacked. He attributed this enviable trait to the spiritual fortitude each group drew from its respective sacred text. Compared with these two faiths, the Arabs' preliterate state, idolatrous worship, and political disunity seemed hopelessly backward to Mohammed, who was becoming ever more cosmopolitan in his outlook.

As Mohammed approached forty, he increasingly turned away from mundane matters to retire to a cave on Mount Hira, where he meditated for long stretches at a time. One night in 610, alone in the cave, he had an epiphany. In the Prophet's own words,

> Whilst I was asleep, with a coverlet of silk brocade whereon was some writing, the Angel Gabriel appeared to me and said "Read." I said, "I do not read." He pressed me with the coverlets so tightly that methought 'twas death. Then he let me go and said "Read!" . . . So I read aloud, and he departed from me at last. And I awoke from my sleep, and it was though these words were written on my heart. I went forth until, when I was midway on the mountain, I heard a voice from heaven saying, "O Mohammed! Thou art the messenger of Allah and I am Gabriel."[4]

Shaken and terrified by this *mysterium terribile et fascinans*, Mohammed realized that he had been chosen by Allah to transmit the Arabs' own revelation. Mohammed reported to those willing to listen that Allah's revelation existed in its entirety in the heavens and that the angel Gabriel let Mohammed, a man of the people, read one fragment at a time. He recited before a growing number of converts, who were initially attracted by the obvious authenticity of his mystic experience and the beauty of his godinspired words. Those few who could write began the slippery task of capturing on parchment the poetry of the Prophet's unique phraseology.

Mohammed's message was radical. He informed his listeners that Allah was supreme, solitary, and omniscient, and he said that all Arabs must disavow allegiance to any other divinities—principally goddesses at that time. In return for repudiating goddesses, Mohammed promised converts the crucial aspect missing from their older religion: life after death. Allah would admit to Paradise anyone who believed solely in him. Infidels who persisted in venerating any other deity would be consigned to Hell.

Besides swearing fealty to Allah, Muslims had to read or recite passages from the Prophet five times a day, contribute to the care of the poor by giving alms, fast, and make a yearly pilgrimage to Mecca, known as the *hajj*. These tasks constitute the five pillars of Islam. *Islam* means "surrender"; *Muslim* means "one who surrenders."

. . . .

The Prophet taught his fellow Arabs that in Allah's eyes every mortal was equal. A woman could own property, enter any legitimate profession, manage her own earnings, and was an equal in legal cases (Sura 4:4&32).

Mohammed anathematized imagery. Targeting the impassive stone figures ringing the Kaaba, he condemned their worship. In a concession to his potential converts, he retained the site of the Kaaba as a holy place for Allah and allowed Arabs to continue the pre-Islamic practice of kissing the black stone. But the heart of his message was that Arabs must abandon iconic gender-neutral polytheism for the revelation of an imageless, monotheistic god who had initiated His contact with Mohammed through the medium of alphabetic writing.

In terms of its effect on the world, Mohammed's epiphany is one of the most momentous events in history. The central miracle at the heart of his encounter with the angel Gabriel was his instantaneous acquisition of literacy enabling him to read the sacred words. Later Islamic commentators would point to this lightning bolt of apprehension as confirmation of the divine nature of his experience: an unlettered man was given the gift of literacy by the grace of God.

The alphabet's preeminence is made clear in Allah's prefatory message to Mohammed.

> Read in the name of thy Lord who created!
> He createth man from a clot of blood.
> Read: and thy Lord is the Most Bountiful
> He who hath taught by the pen
> taught man what he knew not.* (Sura 96:1)

The first line refers to Allah's creation of the universe, the second to His creation of humankind, and the third to the creation of nature in its entirety. Rounding out this prodigious list is . . . literacy.

According to tradition, the Prophet himself committed nothing to parchment. How his words subsequently found their way onto the pages of a book is, therefore, of paramount interest. Who were his amanuenses? When did they accomplish this task? What were their qualifications? Who and what influenced them before they embarked on such a delicate assign-

---

*The word read has also been translated as "recite" or "proclaim."

ment? The Prophet has always projected such an immense shadow that these questions have not consumed Islamic scholars with the same urgency that has fired their Christian counterparts.

During Mohammed's life a few literate Arabs began to write down his sacred recitations. These 114 suras, as they are called, form the Quran (or Koran), which means "the Recitation" or "the Reading." Mohammed dictated his revelations to various scribes, who wrote them down on scraps of parchment, leather, palm leaves, and the bone-white flat shoulder blades of dead camels. The writers had neither archives nor libraries nor did they possess the most rudimentary filing system. Predictably, what they transcribed suffered from disorganization. This disarray presented such an insurmountable problem for subsequent Arabic scholars that they abandoned any hope of ever sorting out each sura's precise sequence, so they arranged them according to length, rather than by date of transmission. Thus, the oldest sections of the Quran (believed by many scholars to be the briefest suras) appear at the end, while the more recent begin the book. To Western readers accustomed to a linear narrative, this aspect of the Quran continues to confuse and confound. Compounding the problem, several different textural versions of what Mohammed said circulated during his lifetime. His life was so filled with drama and action, however, that he had little time to edit and correct the texts personally.

His principle amanuensis was Zaid ibn Thabit, who was one of the Prophet's earliest and most loyal converts. It is not known how Zaid came to be skilled in the intricacies of Arabic grammar. Nor do we know what primers he read to prepare himself for the complex mission of translating the poetry of Mohammed's speech (usually uttered while in a trance) into a text that future Arabic speakers would praise as a work of unsurpassing beauty. Zaid had no models because in the sixth century there was no literature written in Arabic prose. The sparse written materials that did exist were poems extolling romance and adventure. The Quran was the very first, and remains to this day in the opinion of virtually all Muslims, the very best example of Arabic prose writing.

In spite of the efforts of Zaid and other scribes, the written records of the Prophet's words were not deemed as important as his dedicated reciters, called *qurra*. These men and women committed each new revelation to memory and then went out among the people to amplify Mohammed's voice a hundredfold. Qurras became venerated holy persons, and were greatly esteemed compared to the haphazardly stored written records.

In 632, the Prophet died. The qurra instantly became the most important repository for the transmission of the Quran. Zaid, meanwhile, quietly

began to assemble the diverse texts and spoken traditions that had accumulated in the previous twenty-five years. Lore recounts how he culled this
information from date leaves, white stones, and the "breasts of men." He
then began the daunting task of editing this material. Because of Zaid's close
association with the Prophet, the manuscript resulting from his labors supplanted all others. His version of the Quran was the first complete one and
the most authoritative. Unfortunately, it did not survive.

As the qurras who had been contemporaries of the Prophet began to die
of old age, Zaid's Quran moved from the periphery to the center of the new
religion. The written testament began to rival in importance those who had
memorized it by listening to the qurras. The ability to read, therefore,
became paramount. Inspired by the presence of a sacred text in their very
own language, growing numbers of Muslims hungered to become literate.

However, the mechanics of the written language made the task difficult.
Sixth-century Arabic was still in the process of evolving, and Zaid did not
employ any vowels in his writing. Furthermore, Arabic did not contain the
diacritical marks necessary to distinguish between feminine and masculine
nouns, or between passive and active verbs.[5] The Arabic alphabet contained
several consonants whose shape was ambiguous; spelling, therefore, was
often a matter of interpretation. All of the above shortcomings left the
meaning of some words and phrases up to the individual reader. Both readers and writers unwittingly interjected their biases into what the Prophet
had actually said.

In 651, the caliph Uthman, alarmed over the obvious corruptions
appearing in the many proliferating Qurans, commissioned four scholars to
revise it. Joining the now aged Zaid were three men about whom historians
know next to nothing, other than that they were not members of
Mohammed's original inner circle. Undoubtedly, they were selected for both
their religious zeal and their literary skills.

When their long labor was finished, Zaid's commission presented the
caliph with their version of what the prophet had said. The caliph ordered
all other texts destroyed and then sent copies of the new scroll to all the great
Islamic cities with instructions that his sanctioned version superseded all
others. To ensure against further changes, Uthman canonized the commission's work in 651. The beauty of the Quran, along with its novelty and
integrity, strongly suggests that it was the product of one extraordinarily
inspired individual. But there is no evidence that its editors were as Godinspired as the man whose words they were revising. While attempting to
reconstruct the exact words of a prophet who had declaimed his first sura
forty-one years earlier, their personal view of women may have been

adversely affected by their passion for theological writing, as the thesis of this book has consistently maintained. It is at this critical juncture that the seeds of patriarchy could have been planted in Mohammed's divine speech. I do not suggest this subtle alteration was done consciously, but rather that it was inevitable since the redactors were four writers enraptured by the beauty of abstract calligraphy and abstract theology.

Albert Hourani, a modern Arab historian, writes,

> Most scholars would agree that the process by which different versions were collected and a generally accepted text and arrangement established did not end until after Muhammad's death. The traditional account is that this happened during the time of his third successor as head of the community, Uthman (644–56), but later dates have been suggested, and some Muslim sects have accused others of inserting into the text material not derived by transmission from the Prophet.[6]

The Arabs venerated the written words of Allah, Mohammed had said that those who read the Quran firsthand were especially favored in Allah's eyes. "He who leaves his home in search of Knowledge walks the path of God" and "The ink of the scholar is holier than the blood of the martyr."[7] Bedouins who previously had no incentive to learn literacy were suddenly electrified. Schools opened all over the Islamic realm dedicated to the transmission of this singular book.

The alphabetic book extolling monotheism gave the Arabs monocular purpose. Combining warlike intentions and religious zeal, the Muslims began a campaign of conquest and conversion that would carry them to the ends of the earth. Evidence of the new religion's appeal can be gauged by the large number of its converts in such diverse locales as Asia Minor, Persia, Egypt, Spain, southern France, India, Indonesia, and Afghanistan, many of whom converted within a few hundred years of Mohammed's first revelation.

In most cases conquered peoples were given a simple choice—decapitation or conversion. Few lost their heads. But for many others, the choice was truly voluntary. Whole populations came over to Islam without hesitation. For polytheists who had remained outside the combat arena and were trying to decide between Christianity and Judaism, the commotion swirling from out of the south gave them a third choice. Many concluded that God must be on the side of the audacious Arabs, whose new faith had won obvious victories against the devotees of the two older religions. Early Islam's appeal lay in its democratic institutions and virtual lack of a priestly hierarchy, and because its tenets were tolerant, egalitarian, and remarkably easy to follow. It was a religion of the people; clergy or imams were married, had families, and engaged in secular occupations.

As more people came into the fold, the desire of Muslims to read increased. One more development speeded the process. In 712, Arab armies captured the city of Samarkand, situated strategically astride China's silk route, and came across the most valuable of spoils—paper. The combination of a sacred text written in their own vernacular and a readily available medium proved felicitous, and made possible the efflorescence of an Islamic Golden Age. Camel scapulas were no longer necessary to supply white, flat writing surfaces. Books soon became so plentiful that every mosque was also a library. Within a hundred years of its first paper mill in 794, Baghdad boasted over a hundred booksellers and several dozen libraries.

Ascending the caliphate in 786, Harun ar-Rashid (766–809) was Charlemagne's counterpart in the Islamic world. A judicious ruler committed to learning, he inaugurated a Golden Age. For the next five hundred years, poetry, science, medicine, mathematics, architecture, and philosophy began a magic carpet ride, levitated by a tolerant religion that held the acquisition of knowledge to be one of the highest ideals. Every aspect and group within Islamic society benefited from this Golden Age, with two notable exceptions: representative art and women's rights.

Due to the Muslims' unprecedented military successes, the complexity of Islamic society made it unrecognizable from the one in which Mohammed had taught his people the love of Allah. Governing vast tracts of land containing large foreign populations in the ninth and tenth centuries was a far remove from the intertribal frictions of sixth-century Islam. Disputes proliferated with Islam's growing hegemony. Each party turned for adjudication to the Quran. This unique document, propounded in an earlier age for a different society, did not always provide litigants with clear-cut answers. Like the Jewish invention of the Talmud to answer new questions that could not be readily resolved by reference to the Torah, so, too, did the Arabs create a second, later, sacred book to clarify the Quran.

Beginning in the earliest days, a rich oral tradition concerning the life of Mohammed had evolved. These stories, called hadith, recounted details about the Prophet, his wives, friends, relatives, enemies, and children. Further, many hadiths corroborated, embroidered, and clarified some of the Quranic suras. Few of these oral traditions were committed to writing for the first century and a half of the Islamic era.

Although the Quran contained many sections concerning civil justice, Islamic society's need for a code of law became imperative. Abu Hanifa ibn

Thabit (d. 767) compiled the first comprehensive set of civil laws, called the shari'a. The shari'a did not completely satisfy the Islamic society's need for conflict resolution. In courts throughout the Islamic realm, claimants increasingly resorted to citing oral hadiths to bolster their cases. As a result, hadiths multiplied with astonishing speed, until one could be found to justify just about every point of view. The practice had become so rampant that Ibn Abi al-Awja was executed in 722 at Kufa after confessing that he had fabricated four thousand hadiths to serve his purposes.[8] Caliphs, frustrated by the proliferation of stories about the Prophet, tried without success to stem the tide.

In 870, a hundred fifty years after Mohammed's epiphany on Mount Hira, the religious scholar al Bukhari sought to transcribe many of these lively tales, which had been lovingly retold from generation to generation. Imbued with a zealous attachment for both the written word and the religion of Islam, he claimed to have collected 600,000 oral traditions. He authenticated only 7,275, which he set forth in his *Sahih* or *Correct Book*, also known as the hadith. His test of authenticity was whether or not a story could be traced directly to the Prophet or to one of his close associates.

A modern editor would want to know how an impassioned al Bukhari decided what to discard and what to include a century and a half after the fact. Was he able to keep his own biases out of the editing process? His written hadith contains many statements that seem to contradict the Prophet's basically egalitarian attitude toward women. Would the man who cherished Khadija and tousled the hair of his beloved daughter, Fatima, declare, as one hadith states he did, that women were the supreme calamity?[9] Tradition has it that Mohammed so empathized with the needs of young mothers that if their babies started to cry during his services he would shorten his sermon for their benefit.[10] Aisha, the most influential wife after Khadija, quoted Mohammed as saying that the three most precious things in the world "are women, fragrant odors, and prayers."[11] In another tradition, he is purported to have said, "The most valuable thing in the world is a virtuous woman."[12] Is this the same man who states in a companion hadith that most women will go straight to hell for their perdition?

While al Bukhari's hadith contains some stories that support the Prophet's essentially egalitarian attitude toward women, it differs from the Quran in that it is more patriarchal and, not surprisingly, it takes a much harder line on the subject of images. For instance, the Quran does not proscribe painting, but the hadith states that Mohammed added a proscription against painting to the one concerning sculpture during a conversation.

Many Islamic scholars, both ancient and modern, suspect that some of these sayings attributed to Mohammed were slipped into the hadith later by lawyers-writers-theologians. The 592,725 oral traditions al Bukhari discarded may have contained many that honored women more than those al Bukhari retained.

Over a period of many years, al Bukhari's hadith grew in stature. For most in the Sunni Muslim sect, the authenticity of al Bukhari's hadith is beyond dispute. Hourani comments, "Most western scholars, and some modern Muslims, would be more skeptical than Bukhari . . . and regard many of the hadiths which they took to be authentic as being products of polemics about authority and doctrine."[13]

As increasing numbers of Arabs became surrounded by the constructs of literacy, they could not see its pernicious side effects. Coincident with the period when the written versions of the hadith began to supersede Islam's oral tradition around the late ninth century, the prestige of women and the importance of images rapidly eroded. Soon after the introduction into Islam of paper, a code of Law, and the *Correct Book*, literate men made it a custom to veil their women. This idiosyncratic practice, unknown to non-literate cultures, spread in conjunction with the Arabic alphabet. It became so ingrained in the Arabic female psyche that a Muslim woman who practiced this custom would, if surprised at her bath, instinctively cover her face first.[14]

The human face is perceived by the right brain. Obscuring the faces of women so that even they could not see each other's visages diminished their collective power because their collective right hemispheres were, in effect, also veiled. Spouses ceased to be com-*pan*-ions, as husbands stopped dining with their wives. The practice of sequestering women in the *harem*—a word that means "forbidden"—gradually spread among the upper and middle classes after 750. Despite the open generosity of Islamic society in general, women alone would have to contend with a whole new list of "forbiddens."

In the Prophet's time, women and men had prayed together in a mosque. Later, the women were segregated from their men by a screen and relegated to the back of the mosque. Still later, they were removed altogether, and allowed to pray only when the men were not present. Finally, some sects prevented women from ever entering mosques.[15] Women, whose spirituality had been beyond dispute for untold millennia, were deprived of the basic right to conduct, participate in, or even to attend services. In the early years of Arab literacy, both men and women learned to read and write. By 750, with a few exceptions, women were denied this education in a society where knowledge of written Arabic was fast becoming an indispensable skill. But womanhood reached a nadir when literate Arab males prevented their women from shopping.

To better understand the significance of this unusual restriction, a survey of shopping is in order. Long ago, when the hominid line was beginning to differentiate from other primates, females engaged in the daily activity of gathering while their men hunted. With an independence commensurate with her egalitarian status, a woman ranged freely around the home base, gathering nuts, fruits, vegetables, and other found objects that might enhance and beautify her family's cave, lean-to, or tent. For millions of years, every adult female in every hominid society gathered. With the arrival of cities and the invention of currency, tradespeople simplified the gathering process by setting up stalls to hawk their wares. Gathering evolved into shopping, but it remained a vital daily activity that consumed a major segment of most women's time.

After millions of years of freedom, how then, are we to explain eighth-century Arab men abruptly abrogating this basic female function? Since shopping was an activity that could not simply be dropped, Arab men needed a substitute. Thus began the widespread Islamic practice of castrating male slaves, so that eunuchs instead of wives rummaged through the *souks* and *casbahs* to provide Arab homes with the staples of day-to-day living. Nowhere in the Quran does it state unequivocally that a woman cannot go out of her own house, and in pre-Islamic Arabic society, no such restriction existed. Mohammed himself, in one tradition, said to women, "It is permitted for you to go out for your needs."[16] By the fourteenth century, the status of women had sunk so low that an Egyptian jurist of the Maliki School, Ibn al-Haji (b. 1336), could write,

> Some of the pious elders (may God be pleased with them) have said that a woman should leave her house on three occasions only: when she is conducted to the house of her bridegroom, on the deaths of her parents, and when she goes to her own grave.[17]

The conflict between word and image and between the alphabet and the Goddess can be gleaned from the variations in the practice of Islam. Generally speaking, in societies in which the letters reigned supreme, representative art and women fared poorly. And while these cultures created sumptuous filigreed designs on rugs, grille work, and calligraphy, images of things were missing. They tended toward patriarchy and in their worship did not honor the divine feminine. Here, women were veiled, sequestered and exercised few rights.

Societies that did not subscribe to the admonitions against images, such as Persia, India, and the Mongol kingdom, were more tolerant of other religions, extended rights to all of their citizens, and produced beautiful examples of representative art. Here, women were more educated, made contributions to society, and their faces were not veiled. Fatima, the daughter of Mohammed, became a much-loved divine presence.

After about two hundred years, Islam split into two dominant sects: Sunnis and Shiites. The issues separating them were similar to those that divided the Gnostics from the Orthodox Christians within two hundred years of Christianity's founding. The Sunnis are strict literalists who hold that the Quran and hadiths are the ultimate arbiters of truth. The Shiites believe that there are people in each generation that can interpret the Quran and pass along an oral wisdom not necessarily confined to the pages of a book; they trace their lineage through descendants of Fatima. As one would expect, the Sunnis restrict women's rights far more than the Shiites do; it is the latter who have erected impressive architectural monuments to honor women.

Before returning to European culture, one last gender aspect of Islam must be examined. Increasingly, a growing segment of Islamic society began to inflict genital mutilation on their girls. The desire to change the appearance of the sexual display organs was not new. Primitive tribes had adorned their genitalia with everything from copper rings and ivory bones to elaborate scars and tattoos. The bedizened endured these modifications in the name of vanity, believing that the changes served to lure the opposite sex. The Egyptians had practiced male circumcision, confirmed in their wall paintings at Saqqara, as long ago as 2200 B.C. The Hebrews and the Muslims made it a central condition of their Covenant with Yahweh and Allah, respectively.

Sacrificing the prepuce of the penis does not interfere with the pleasure of the sexual act. Female genital tailoring, in contrast, cuts away the tissue containing the nerve endings that contribute to women's pleasure. In some cases, only the labia minora are removed; in others, the labia majora as well as the clitoris are amputated. In extreme cases, all external tissue rich in sexual arousal nerve endings is excised and the vagina sutured closed to be opened forcefully on the hapless girl's wedding night. For females so afflicted, sexual advances are unwanted and the act itself becomes a kind of rape. Since urination is intimately associated with the genital system in both sexes, these culture-imposed deformities often led to recurrent urinary tract infections, and eventually to kidney failure. The lassitude experienced by uremic women further ensured their compliance.

The single most powerful sexual organ humans possess is their brain. Sights, smells, sounds, and thoughts are all capable of tickling the procreative apparatus into a heightened state of readiness. The brain's ability to be awakened by sexual stimuli depends also on adequate levels of estrogen or testosterone hormones. This complex process, refined by nature over millions of years, secures the continuation of the species.

In male castration, the testicles are removed, thereby abolishing most of the male brain's response to sexual stimuli. In female genital mutilation, the estrogen-producing ovaries are unaffected, and the female brain continues to be aroused by thoughts of sexual pleasure that cannot be physically fulfilled. The result is far crueler than castration.

Today, female genital mutilation is practiced predominantly in Islamic countries—Pakistan, the Middle East, and among sub-Saharan African tribes. It is virtually nonexistent in countries under the sway of other major world religions. Psychoanalyst Bruno Bettelheim wrote of the phenomenon of subjugated people adopting the customs of their oppressors. A survivor of the Nazi concentration camps during World War II, he noted that it was not uncommon for some inmates to emulate Nazi behavior as a psychological defense against overwhelming helplessness. Some prisoners adopted their tormentors' swagger, mimicked the insignia of guards, and went out of their way to intimidate their fellow inmates. Bettelheim surmised that this domination of the helpless by the slightly less helpless served to bolster the latter's ego. Such bullying conduct has since been recorded in prisons and among other oppressed groups.

Arabs were a dominant force in Africa after their military triumphs of the seventh and eighth centuries. Unlike the other conquered peoples the Arabs absorbed into their society on a relatively egalitarian basis, African tribes were often treated as fodder for a burgeoning slave trade with the north. When the Europeans became involved in the African slave trade in the fifteenth century, they purchased their wares more often than not from experienced Arab slavers. In some cases, a tribe's adoption of Islam was due to conditions similar to what Bettelheim observed. African men, helpless against the advanced Arabs, delegated the actual task of genital mutilation to their women, thus shoving the female spirit a further rung down the ladder of debasement.*

Some anthropologists claim that the custom of female genital mutilation predated Islam. But there is no mention of it in the historical accounts of antiquity, nor does it appear among the scenes of daily life and ritual

---

*Another example of this phenomenon is that which occurred in ancient China: it was a mother's responsibility to bind her young daughter's feet to conform to male erotic standards.

painted or carved on vases, temples, and tomb walls of the ancient civilizations of Sumeria, Crete, Egypt, Etrusca, or India. Had Herodotus, Strabo, Tacitus, or other early historians heard of the custom, they would surely have noted it. The available evidence suggests that female genital mutilation is a relatively recent practice.

With the exception of a few isolated pockets, this practice has made its appearance primarily in societies in which males learned to *read* the Quran, even though there is nothing in the Quran that justifies it. Some Islamic scholars trace it back to a hadith that a majority of other scholars believe is of questionable authenticity. Mohammed was a fair, kind, loving man who dedicated his life to protecting the helpless against the predations of the strong. An orphan himself, he especially had a soft spot in his heart for children. A careful reading of the Prophet's words makes it seem unlikely that he would have ever given instructions to hurt children.

Support for my thesis that alphabet religiosity was behind the practice can be garnered by examining the pattern of the mutilation's geographical distribution. It is practiced more regularly, and with more thoroughness, among the strict literalists (Sunnis) than among the oralists (Shiites). It is more common among those peoples who have recently become literate (African tribes) than among those for whom literacy has been a cultural heritage for centuries—for example, former Carthaginians (Tunisia), Mesopotamians (Iraq), Persians (Iran), and Egyptians. It is most common and most severe in East African tribes closest to the Arabian Peninsula. The farther away from the horn of Africa a tribe is, the less chance there is that members will practice the custom; for example, it is almost nonexistent among the southernmost tribes in Africa such as the !Kung. A coincidence? Perhaps, but once again, an anti-evolutionary aberrant custom, diabolical in its effect on women's sexuality, seems to have come into existence and is practiced only in those societies newly acquainted with alphabet literacy.

As horrible as it is to contemplate female genital mutilation, Islamic society cannot claim to have mistreated its women the worst. Many miles to the north and several centuries away, something far more terrible was about to break upon the unsuspecting heads of women, in another culture that was upended by the alphabetic written word.

CHAPTER 28

MYSTIC/SCHOLASTIC
1000–1300

In these days God made manifest His power through the frail
sex . . . handmaidens whom he filled with prophetic spirit.
                                        —German Chronicle, A.D. 1200[1]

Lord God, what art is this that an old woman better understands than
a man of wit?   —Lamprecht von Regensburg, A.D. 1250[2]

A pervasive sense of doom settled over Christendom at the close of the
first millennium. The imminent Second Coming, so passionately
anticipated by Paul, had not arrived during the ensuing centuries
despite repeated warnings by those expert on such matters. As the years
slipped by, the populace, anxiously scanning the sky, continued to conduct
the business of everyday life. Since End of the World eschatology was a main
tenet of Christianity, many became convinced that their reprieve was running out and expected the blast from Gabriel's horn to sound on New Year's
Eve, A.D. 1000. These Millenarians, as they came to be called, urgently
warned all to prepare for Judgment Day. The turn of the new millennium,
however, came and went uneventfully. As the reverberations from all the
bells' tolls grew fainter, consternation set in among the prognosticators.
Once again, they had to recalibrate the dreaded date of the Day of Doom.
The Millenarians did not suspect that the dramatic event that was approaching was not the end of Time, but rather the resurrection of Literacy.

Many factors converged to renew interest in this nearly defunct art.
After the fall of Rome, secular learning declined dramatically. Priests
sequestered Latin from the common people and it lost the vitality with
which daily usage imbues any language. Necessity bred new local vernaculars that took centuries to come of age. All of the mellifluous Romance lan-

guages were born in the dark of European illiteracy. English and German, too, became supple media that also could express subtle emotions, as well as describe objective reality. Just as the lexicons and oral grammars of these languages stabilized, ninth-century Carolingian writing reforms were conveniently put in place to refine them.

The appearance of paper further advanced literacy. After the rise of Islam in the sixth century, trade between the opposite shores of the Mediterranean came to a virtual standstill. Papyrus from Egypt, the preferred writing material of the Greco-Roman culture, disappeared from western Europe, and was replaced by the far more expensive parchment, made from dried animal skins. The first paper mills in Christendom appeared in Italy in the twelfth century. Paper's appearance coincided with a rise in commerce. Buyers and sellers had to be versed in arithmetic and bookkeeping. Simple Arabic numerals replaced the clumsy Roman counting system in the twelfth century. In the early centuries of the second millennium, the pace of life was quickening and the vital fluid pulsing through Western culture's arteries and veins was ink. Increased literacy, as it always does, changed the perceptions of the culture.

The Crusades tore down the barrier between the erudite world of Islam and the ignorant one of Christendom. When the first Crusade began in 1096, Europeans resembled an adopted child unaware of his real parentage. Few in western Europe knew of the incredibly rich legacy of the classical world. In an ironic twist, fate had entrusted Islam, the West's sworn enemy, with its birth records.

An unexpected spoil of these holy wars was that the Christians gained access to their precious archives. European interest in Greek and Hebrew soared. Great debates blossomed forth and a new open-mindedness informed Europe's eleventh and twelfth centuries. It was as if secular Europe emerged from a deep sleep. Literacy had kissed it awake.

As literacy increased, the extreme emphasis on feminine values that had inspired the ethics, customs, and mythology of the Dark Ages lingered on. Between 1000 and 1300, during the period known as the High Middle Ages, Europe enjoyed a Golden Age during which feminine values enhanced by orality teeter-tottered into relative equilibrium with masculine ones encouraged by literacy. Eclipsed in memory by the glories of the subsequent Renaissance, it was in fact a memorable period.

There was relative peace throughout Europe. Borders were fluid. Learning advanced. Practitioners of all the arts gained an understanding of basic principles that provided planks for the plinth upon which the Renaissance tower would later be erected. Science began to link concrete observations with abstract theories. Medicine inched ever so slowly away from the blood-suckers toward the fact-seekers. The Western Church lacked the centralized authority of the eastern Byzantine Empire. At the beginning of this period, men of vision and tolerance directed the Church in the patchwork society of the West that embodied the spirit of a wild frontier. Local control of both secular and sacred realms invited diversity and experimentation.

The early stage of the High Middle Ages was singular because virtually no witches were accused, rarely was a heretic burned at the stake, and religious wars among western European Christians did not occur. Jews were accepted as necessary, albeit outlander, members of the community. Christians and Muslims often mingled at the borders where their cultures met, treating one another with admirable civility. Scholars were eager to learn about other cultures' beliefs. Of course there were still the usual skirmishes between age-old enemies, and the occasional snarling outburst from the ever-present beast pacing back and forth within the human soul, but, all in all, for the poor, the restless, the creative, the spiritual, the intelligent, the learned, and for most women, it was an invigorating time to be alive.

There was an impetuosity about these centuries, as if this was the adolescence of Western culture. A wide-eyed curiosity coupled with freedom of thought, movement, and belief contributed to the aura of springtime. A thousand troubadours warbled the chivalric code in praise of women; romantic novels were all the rage; the cult of Mary continued to gain disciples, and ordinary people embraced religious ideals that were pious and altruistic. Saint Francis of Assisi founded his order based on gentleness, spirituality, and poverty in 1209. His was but one of the many mystical movements that suffused the age with religiosity. Women mystics such as Margery Kempe, Hrotsvitha, Beatrice of Nazareth, Marguerite d'Oingt, Mechthild of Magdeburg, Bridget of Sweden, and Dorothy of Montan were acknowledged by an enlightened papacy and a respectful populace.

As one would expect during such an era, women's spirituality was an accepted fact of life. So many women sought entrance into religious orders that the rapidly proliferating convents could not accommodate them all. Those left out formed secular quasi-religious societies called *Beguines*. These women dedicated themselves to visiting the old, aiding the infirm, tending to the sick, feeding the hungry, and generally improving the sorry lot of that ragged segment of society perched precariously on the edge of subsistence. No one seemed to mind that the burgeoning Beguines' movement operated outside the auspices of the Church.

Abbesses in Saxony ruled vast tracts of lands. Some even minted their own coins.[3] Expressing themselves in the new vernaculars, women writers were widely read. Christine de Pisan was successful enough to write for a living and became a prominent figure of French literature from 1395 to 1405. Some convents became famous for the quality of their scriptoria. Queens ruled their subjects, noblewomen managed their estates, aristocratic women entrepreneurs bought and sold their lands, women bankers engaged in high finance,[4] working women flexed their economic muscles in the new commercial guilds, and women voters helped to choose local officials in an increasing number of regions.[5] Women warriors led their troops into battle,[6] and women at many levels quietly reassumed sacramental duties long denied them. The most remarkable aspect of this period was that men, for the most part, gracefully accepted women doing and women knowing.

Then, originating from within the Church, a small group of highly educated and determined men began to wrestle this dynamic medieval culture away from its feminine orientation toward masculine values. They focused on two seemingly unrelated activities: sexuality and literacy. Gregory VII (1020–1085), assuming the papacy in 1073, fulminated over corruption within the Church. Simony, the practice of selling benefices to the highest bidder, was rampant. Gregory was convinced that the venality was the result of priests breaking their vows of celibacy. Determined to rid the church of what he called the "foul plague of carnal contagion," Gregory took the unprecedented step of authorizing the laity to withdraw support from any priest who did not renounce his wife and children.[7]

Gregory's edict precipitated a social revolution. Especially in Italy and France, the laity and many bishops protested and tried to protect their parish priests. The bishops comprising the Council of Paris nullified the Pope's reforms, lambasting them as "unbearable and therefore irrational." When reformer Peter Damian went on a mission to Milan, he was rebuffed so vehemently that a chronicler wrote, "He barely escaped with his life, his saintly dignity came near being enhanced by the horrors of martyrdom."[8]

The reforms ultimately carried the day because of superior arms. The Pope shrewdly enlisted foreign nobility by promising them lands in return for their enforcement of his radical program. Married priests throughout Europe were forced to separate from their wives and children or face severe retribution. Many suddenly found themselves fighting for their livelihoods and, in some cases, their very lives. And while the reforms discomfited priests, their wives and children were often devastated. Husbands who chose to remain priests repudiated their wives and evicted their families; their progeny became illegitimate overnight. "Abandoned by the Church to utter destitution," historian David Noble observed, "they and their children confronted the horrors of starvation, prostitution, servitude, murder, and suicide."[9]

The misogyny of the Church reformers was blatant. Damian, one of the period's most fanatical reformers, described women as "Satan's bait, poison for men's souls, the delight of greasy pigs, inns where unclean souls turn in."[10] The eleventh-century bishop of Rennes wrote, "Of the numberless images that the crafty enemy [the devil] spreads for us . . . the worst . . . is woman, bad stem, evil root, vicious fount . . . honey and poison."*[11] Increasingly, the papal corridors were walked by men like the one who proudly claimed, "During 53 years of active calling, I never saw the face of a woman, except for that of one aged mendicant."[12] One might well have wondered whether these men had mothers. The most powerful institution in all of Europe had become a Men Only club.

The reforms also reverberated throughout the monastic system. All double monasteries were shut down and replaced by the strictly segregated Cluniac and Cistercian orders, soon followed by the militaristic Dominican friars. Abbesses were brought under the taut control of their abbots. Even the Franciscans sharply segregated women. "To be always with a woman, and not have intercourse with her," the Cistercian Bernard of Clairvaux acerbically observed, "is more difficult than raising the dead. You cannot do the less difficult; do you believe you can do what is more difficult?"[13]

At the same time that Gregory was purging heterosexual relationships from the Church, he was also passionately advocating alphabet literacy. "All bishops are to have the arts of letters taught in the churches," he proclaimed. In every major center of Europe, the papacy commissioned cathedral schools charged with educating lay and clerical males only.[14] Many of the schools—Oxford, Paris, Bologna, Pisa, and Heidelberg—were the embryos of future universities. Meanwhile, Gregory's reforms did not make the slightest dent in the practice of simony, which grew to such overweening proportions that it would precipitate the Reformation four hundred years later. One can only speculate on how the course of history might have been deflected had reformers attacked simony directly with the same vigor they used to destroy priests' marriages, the alleged cause.

Historical narrative fails to provide the human dimension to Gregory's drastic social experiment. His reforms not only curtailed women's independence but also suppressed the robust intellectual freedom that marked the early High Middle Ages. By insisting that the Church take a leading role in secular education, he believed he was combating the inevitable opposition all auto-

---

*It is noteworthy that the bishop thought of women as "images," and that images, not words, were the work of the devil.

cratic regimes confront when literacy is not monopolized by the priestly class. The tragedy of Abélard and Héloïse illustrates how the atmosphere that made the Gregorian reforms successful affected the lives of ordinary men and women.

Peter Abélard (1079–1144) was a humanist who exemplified the free-thinking of the times. Born into nobility, he declined knighthood, preferring instead a life of intellectual jousting. In 1101, he traveled to Paris where celebrated thinkers had stoked the city into a hotbed of intellectual agitation. Abelard thrived in this superheated atmosphere. Challenging his masters from the back benches with his penetrating logic, he soon stood behind the lectern himself. His wit, humor, and sharp mind attracted students from all over Europe. Elevated to Parisian Cathedral Schoolmaster by his peers, he was the spiritual founder of the University of Paris. He was also known for his poetry and love songs. Admirers hoped that the brilliant scholar might enter the Church and eventually become Pope.

In 1117, while his star was in steep ascent, a sixteen-year-old orphan girl in love with books and learning came into his life. Héloïse was the precocious niece of Fulbert, a canon of Notre Dame. She had been educated in the convent at Argenteuil, where the nuns claimed she was the brightest pupil they had ever had. Her uncle brought her to Paris to arrange an advantageous marriage and hired Abélard to tutor her privately in his quarters. (Abélard later confessed that he had heard of the young maiden's reputation and, having seen her, angled for the job.)

Cathedral Masters were expected to be chaste, but the long, lazy summer afternoons Abélard and Héloïse spent together soon worked their magic. As kisses became passionate embraces, Abélard broke his vow of chastity, and the two scholars learned a thing or two about matters not to be found in books. He later wrote that what had begun in physical desire graduated to a "tenderness surpassing in sweetness the most fragrant balm."[15]

Their love made them careless and soon tongues were wagging. As the scandal gathered force, they discovered, much to their mutual dismay, that Héloïse was pregnant. Abélard arranged for Héloïse's furtive flight from her uncle's house and sequestered her at his family estate in Brittany. There she gave birth to a son they named Astrolabe, after the navigational instrument that was changing the map of the world.

Although Abélard was honorable and proposed marriage, Héloïse refused, gravely concerned about the future of his academic career. She insisted on remaining his mistress; in part because of Gregory VII's reforms, she loathed the idea that as a cleric's wife she would be expected to enter a convent should he advance within the Church. Nonetheless, under pressure from Abélard, and seeking to appease her uncle, Héloïse relented and married him in secret. Leaving her infant in the care of Abélard's sister, Héloïse returned to Paris; there, both she and Abélard tried to resume their former lives, living apart and pretending that nothing untoward had transpired.

Their plans went awry when Fulbert, who hated Abélard for his betrayal of trust, vengefully spread the news of their secret marriage, thus seriously compromising Abélard's position at the college. Héloïse publicly denied their nuptials for Abélard's sake, essentially proclaiming that she was a harlot. Faced with an increasingly untenable situation, Héloïse slipped out of her uncle's house disguised in a nun's habit and returned to the safety of Argenteuil's convent. Fulbert, furious that Abélard had despoiled his niece and wrecked his plans to marry her to someone rich, sought vengeance.

One night while Abélard was sleeping, thugs hired by Fulbert broke into his rooms, held him down, and castrated him. News of this mutilation, like a match to pitch, spread quickly, and in shock, shame, and despair, Abélard became a monk. He persuaded Héloïse, over her protestations, to enter a nunnery. After several years of self-imposed isolation, during which he made no effort to contact his wife, Abélard, due to his repentant mien, was deemed by Church authorities to have been punished enough and he resumed teaching. Héloïse was so highly regarded in the convent that she eventually became its abbess.

Abélard later wrote of his misfortunes in his *Historia Calamitatum*, assuming the guise of consoling a friend, "so that in comparing your sorrows with mine, you may discover that yours in truth are naught." When a copy of his tale of woe fell into Héloïse's hands, she wrote what has become one of the most compelling letters in the literature of love:

To her master, nay father, to her husband, nay brother: his handmaid, nay daughter, his spouse, nay sister: to Abélard, Héloïse. Your letter written to a friend for his comfort, beloved, was lately brought to me by chance. . . . Which things I deem that no one can read or hear with dry eyes, for they renewed in fuller measure my griefs. . . . We beseech thee to deign to inform us by frequent letters of those shipwrecks in which thou still art tossed, that thou mayest have us, at least, who alone have remained to thee as partners in thy grief or joy. . . .

Thou knowest, dearest—all men know—what I have lost in thee. . . . Obeying thy command, I changed both my habit and my heart, that I might show thee to be the possessor of both my body and my mind. . . . Not for the pledge of matrimony, nor for any dowry, did I look. . . . And if the name of wife appears more sacred and valid, sweeter to me is ever the word friend, or, if thou be not ashamed, concubine or whore. . . . I call God to witness, if Augustus, ruling over the whole world, were to deem me worthy of the honor of marriage, and to confirm the whole world to me, to be ruled by me forever, dearer to me and of greater dignity would it seem to be called thy strumpet than his empress. . . .

For who among kings or philosophers could equal thee in fame? What kingdom or city or village did not burn to see thee? Who, I ask, did not hasten to gaze upon thee when thou appearedst in public . . . What wife, what maiden did not yearn for thee in thine absence, nor burn in thy presence: What queen or powerful lady did not envy me my joys and my bed.

Attend, I beseech thee, to what I ask. . . . While I am cheated of thy presence, at least by written words—whereof thou hast abundance— present the sweetness of thine image. . . . I deserved more from thee, hav- ing done all things for thee . . . I, who as a girl was allured to the asperity of monastic conversion . . . not by religious devotion, but by thy com- mand alone. . . .

And so in His name to Whom thou hast offered thyself, before God I beseech thee that in whatsoever way thou canst thou restore to me thy presence by writing to me some word of comfort. . . . Farewell, my all.[16]

The irony of Abélard's mutilation is that, to some extent, it was carried out *because* he had married Héloïse. In previous societies, revenge by a girl's family against an impregnating male was exacted because the man refused to marry. In the time of the sudden ascendance of literacy, the commonsense values that had ruled cultures for eons were stood on their head.

Despite Gregory's draconian edicts concerning clerical marriages, women continued to thrive in society at large. In Flanders, women controlled many aspects of a flourishing commerce in beer and textile. Literacy among them was common. The willful and adventuresome Eleanor of Aquitaine ruled her lands in southwestern France, where an enclave of Jews and Moors min- gled with the Christian population and, together, the three groups created a vivacious, cosmopolitan civilization. Jewish translators made the Greek clas- sics available in local tongues, while troubadours congregated there from all over Europe to sing the praises of women. People chafed under the author- ity of a distant centralized Church. Anti-clericalism was on the rise. Catharism was a movement originating among the lower classes that sought to return to the foundations of Christianity. It was particularly popular in southwestern France. In Cathar strongholds in Provence, women gathered in study groups to debate the meaning of Jesus' ministry, copies of New Testament segments open on their laps.

Albigensianism originated in Bulgaria. Like the Gnostics of the early Church, the Albigensians formed non-hierarchical communities. Their piety and simplicity appealed to people who felt that Rome was corrupt and indifferent to their spiritual well-being. We know their doctrines and rituals only through their enemies, the Orthodox, who thoroughly destroyed both the Albigensians and Cathars and their literature. Scholars have pieced together the following incomplete picture. The Albigensians based their creed on Jesus' Sermon on the Mount: love your enemies, help your neighbors, never swear, keep the peace, and refrain from violence. They also held that all priests must live in poverty. At its higher echelons, the Church violated this tenet, and some Albigensians taught that the Pope was the anti-Christ.

Albigensian fervor spread throughout western Europe but was primarily concentrated in Flanders and Provence, the two areas in which women enjoyed the greatest freedom. The audacity of these regions worried Church authorities. Emboldened by the success of Gregory's earlier reforms, Pope Innocent III (1198–1216) decided he would no longer countenance this dangerous freewheeling brand of Christianity. The Albigensian suppression began in 1208.

With a few minor exceptions, the papacy had tolerated deviations within Dark Age Christendom since the fall of Rome. In 840, the archbishop of Lyon outlawed prosecutions against witchcraft.[17] In 946, Pope Leo IX recommended that excommunication be the most severe punishment for heresy.[18] As literacy rates rose, the same stratum of male society that had demanded the destruction of clerical families a few years earlier now attacked their own people. The Albigensian Crusade was not a war about land, revenge, or even an alien religion. For the first time in human history, a governing group carried out mass genocide against its own kinsmen because of abstract theological ideas about a religion both held in common.

The twentieth century has witnessed so many instances of mass murder that we have become numbed—Kulaks in the Ukraine, Armenians in Turkey, Jews in Germany, city dwellers in China, teachers in Cambodia, Muslims in Bosnia, and Tutsis in Rwanda. We forget that there was a time when a government killing its own people was unthinkable. The Roman persecution of Christians was an early instance of this aberrant behavior, but the Romans pursued the Christians in their midst half-heartedly, sporadically, and with ambivalence. Approximately three thousand Christians were martyred in the Roman Empire. Their persecution was mild compared with the bestiality of the Albigensian campaign nine hundred years later.[19]

Friedrich Heer, the renowned medieval historian, comments,

> The war . . . was one of immense savagery and fanaticism. Even the dead were not safe from dishonor, and the worst humiliations were heaped upon women, the much-hated, much-feared and much-courted women of the South. Queen Eleanor of Aquitane's kingdom was dissolving into dust and ashes, and with it the feminine culture of the South and the "free spirit of the troubadours."[20]

Enlisting northern European nobility with promises of Cathar lands and booty, the Church sent its crusaders into the tranquil, vine-covered Dordogne Valley. As one city after another fell, rapine and unspeakable atrocities were committed. After a town had fallen, it was not uncommon for the victors to dig up the graves of known Cathars, haul the corpses to the central square, flog the decomposed bodies and then burn the flayed carcasses at the stake. Caught up in the fury was the large Jewish population, many of whom also perished. Women and children were indiscriminately slaughtered, even those that sought refuge in churches. When the large walled city of Bezier surrendered to the Crusaders after a siege, the knight in charge asked the papal legate how he was to distinguish among the prisoners between faithful Catholics and Albigensian heretics. The legate replied, "Kill them all, and let God sort them out."[21]

The proximity of historical milestones in Western culture, while not proving causality, should raise suspicions that perhaps there is a connection between them. At the same time that Pope Innocent III was perpetuating atrocities against women and freethinkers in the south of France, he was conferring official status on the University of Paris. The next Pope, Gregory IX (1227–1241), set in motion the machinery for the Inquisition. As a way to obliterate heresy, the legal scholars of the Church sanctioned the practice of torturing accused heretics to obtain confessions, a practice that went against what law codes there were in all the centuries we call the Dark Ages and denounced by the early Christians when the Romans used it against them. The men responsible for promoting literacy in medieval society were the same ones who reintroduced the rack and the thumbscrew.

When the last southern Albigensian redoubt fell in 1229, the Inquisition set up its courts in Toulouse and demanded that suspected Cathars abjure heresy. The inquisitors rounded up many accused women heretics and racked them until they confessed, then publicly burned them. While the pall of the smoke from their blackened flesh dimmed the sky, these same papal leaders laid the cornerstone for the University of Toulouse to commemorate the victory. While there have been many occasions in the history of our peculiar species when victors have chosen to commemorate their conquest with a monument, never before had a victor chosen to dedicate an institution to literacy. In an eerie coincidence, the word *ink* derives from the Greek *enkáein*, which is the verb "to burn."

Church leaders from all over Europe assembled for the occasion, taking advantage of the opportunity to hold the official Council of Toulouse. The Council decreed that no lay person could possess any scriptural text in Latin, no scripture could be translated into the vernacular, and no university text written in Latin could circulate off campus.[22] Since only males were admitted to the university, these edicts ensured that no woman could learn the language of religion, science, or philosophy. The punishment for disobedience was the stake.

The women murdered in the Dordogne River Valley were eventually avenged by one of Gregory's own reforms. The cathedral schools he had assumed would serve as supine handmaidens of the Church became instead shamanic midwives, birthing a new way of knowing that would later be called Science. Science provided an alternative belief system that eventually weakened, and in many instances broke, the spell of vested religions.

While the reimposition of celibacy on the clergy, the Inquisition, and the Albigensian Crusade were the dark side of this remarkable period, the High Middle Ages also bubbled with lusty freedom, passionate debate, and individual industry that compares favorably with any other Golden Age. During the communal age of Feudalism, artists had not signed their art works because they did not think of themselves as "individuals" in the modern sense. Emerging, blinking, into the bright light of literacy that illuminated the twelfth century, the common man and woman began to think of themselves as persons. Literacy encouraged enlightened self-interest, which in turn sparked peasant uprisings, workers' revolts, and the demand for more representative government. In 1215, King John of England was forced to sign the Magna Carta, guaranteeing his landed vassals individual freedoms that would have been unthinkable without a literate peerage breathing heavily down the neck of his ermine collar.

Scholasticism was the dominant philosophy to emerge from the increasingly literate era. This hubristic doctrine was an immiscible brew of faith and logic, feminine and masculine, and right and left. It was the concoction many intellectuals were sure could be used to prove the existence of God. Scholasticism's antipode, Mysticism, claimed that knowledge of the divine could be attained only through spiritual union with the Supreme Being. Exercises such as poverty, asceticism, silence, and prayer were the preferred channels to this experiential epiphany. The lives and thoughts of Hildegard von Bingen (1098–1179) and Thomas Aquinas (1224–1274) epitomized these two opposing philosophies.

Born into a noble family in the northern Germany city of Böckelheim, Hildegard, as she is called, was frequently ill as a child and given to seeing apparitions and shimmering lights. When only seven, her neurasthenic disposition inclined her family to pledge her to a convent. Nunneries were often refuges for female intellectuals. Hildegard's scholarly abbess, Jutta, took the eager young student under her wing. Hildegard became proficient in Latin, a rare skill for a nun, which gave her access to the accumulated knowledge of the best contemporary and ancient minds. She read voraciously. When Jutta died, the nuns and the male authorities prevailed on the shy, reluctant Hildegard to assume her mentor's position.

Soon after taking office, she began to write vividly about the visions that were to visit her for the rest of her life. She described one such episode:

A great flash of light from heaven pierced my brain, and made my heart and my whole breast glow without burning them, as the sun warms the object that it envelops with its rays. In that instant my mind was imbued with the meaning of the sacred books, the Psalter, the Gospel, and the other books of the Old and New Testament.[23]

In her first book, *Know The Ways of the Lord*, Hildegard wove strands of science, theology, and philosophy into a synthesis of the individual and cosmos, soul and nature. Her interests were eclectic and her worldview holistic. Augustinian concepts, Platonic ideas, and the most current scientific findings buttressed her arguments. For example, she envisioned the earth as spherical; she recognized that the human sexes were equal and argued that both genders contributed to the wholeness of God's divine creation. "In complete equality man beholds woman and woman beholds man."[24] Her book, circulated in 1147, was widely read, and encouraged her to write others. As she gained an ever-widening audience she also acquired a reputation as a sage and prophetess. From Germany her fame spread to Flanders, France, Italy, England, and as far away as Greece. In Rome, Pope Eugenius III warmly applauded her:

> We are filled with admiration, my daughter . . . for the new miracles that God has shown you in our time, filling you with His spirit so that you see, understand, and communicate many secret things. Reliable persons who have seen and heard you vouch to us for these facts. Guard and keep this grace that is in you.[25]

Prominent people wrote to her for advice, and the abbess became a medieval Dear Abby for rich, famous, and poor alike. Her correspondents included four popes, two emperors, several kings and queens, and the master of the University of Paris. The tone of her letters was neither condescending nor imperious, but it projected her formidable presence. She admonished King Frederick of Saxony for his arrogance and comforted Eleanor of Aquitaine on her divorce.

Although nuns were forbidden to venture outside the cloister walls, Hildegard managed to travel widely. From her prominent position, she represented untold numbers of unsung midwives, healers, and wise women who generously shared their right-brained knowledge of the world with their neighbors in an attempt to better everyone's spiritual and material well-being. The success of women like Hildegard led women to believe that a new age, an Era of Women, was dawning. Like their sisters in the late Roman Empire who thought the same, they were dead wrong.

Hildegard's final years were spent locked in a struggle over the burial of a young man whom the archbishop of Mainz had excommunicated. Ignoring what she perceived was an arbitrary edict, Hildegard ensured that the young man received last rites and a proper funeral. The archbishop placed her convent under interdict. The abbess, now eighty years old, traveled to Mainz to plead the dead man's case in person before clerical tribunals. They ordered her to submit to her archbishop. She remained steadfast.

Caught up in the arrogance of left-brain values, the Church was blind to the fact that by instituting the Inquisition and the Albigensian Crusade, it had forfeited the high moral ground. Ecclesiastical lawyers were increasingly in control, and the laws and edicts they crafted were often capricious, torturous, and unjust. Canon law, entrapped in this tomb of male literacy, lost its soul. Risking all because she intuited a higher authority, Hildegard reenacted the legendary story of Antigone, who also stood up against a soulless edict. History never quite repeats itself, but human nature unfailingly does.

As Hildegard von Bingen personified the mystic wisdom of the brain's right hemisphere, so Thomas Aquinas was the exemplar of the incisive logic of the left. While still a youth, he joined the Dominican Order. In an effort to dissuade him from what she believed was an impulsive decision, his mother conspired with two of Thomas's brothers to hold him against his will in a secluded castle. According to an oft-repeated tale, an alluring young woman was sent to his chamber to seduce him back to his senses. Thomas was so enraged by this ploy that as she began to expose her charms, he snatched a flaming brand from the fireplace and drove her from his room, then used the brand to burn the sign of the cross into the door.[26] His passionate outburst finally convinced his family to let him pursue the life of the cowl.

He studied under Albert the Great, one of the great minds of the period and Aquinas's keen intellect was noted by Church authorities. They had been looking about for some way to combat the irruption of skepticism that had broken out at the University of Paris. To better understand Aquinas's role in shaping the mind-set of his age, a brief excursion into the currents of thought flowing through his time is in order.

The European students and faculty in the twelfth and thirteenth centuries, not unlike their counterparts in 1960s America, were engaged in heady intellectual exercises.* Church elders grew increasingly alarmed because students were openly questioning, among other things, the infallibility of the Pope. In their restless pursuit of knowledge they were receptive to alternative theories and were quite taken with foreign ideas filtering into Paris by way of southwest France from across the Pyrenees. Their hero from this unlikely quarter was the Spanish Muslim Averroës (1126–98).

This Moorish physician-philosopher had rehabilitated Aristotle's rational arguments and used the Greek's methods to question some of the assumptions of Islam. But while he adopted Aristotle's methodology, the worldly Averroës disavowed the Greek's misogynist views. "The nature of women and men is of one kind," he wrote.[27] The sexes differed only in degree, and while Averroës acknowledged that women were physically weaker than men, disadvantaging them in some activities, he claimed that they were superior to men in other ways. Averroës was the original medieval Humanist. The mullahs belatedly recognized the danger that Averroës posed to their beliefs, denounced him, and had his works burned.

---

*Like most bright adolescents, the students loved to play the exciting game of reason. One University of Paris youth had studied philosophy for five years at his father's painful expense. Returning home, he proudly showed off his newly learned skills by proving to his father with relentless logic that the six eggs on the table were twelve. Thereupon, his father ate the six eggs that he could see and left the others for his son.

Averroës' thinking deeply influenced the Jewish physician Maimonides (1135-1204), also a Spaniard, whose *Guide to the Perplexed* tried to square Aristotle with the Old Testament. While many contemporaries were impressed with the clarity of Maimonides' arguments, he suffered the same fate as Averroës. Contemporary Orthodox rabbis repudiated him.*

Rome viewed the infiltration of both Averroës' and Maimonides' ideas into their flagship university with increasing alarm. Students and faculty challenged the Church by openly debating the merits of the foreign physicians' points of view. Determined to fight fire with fire, the Pope sent Thomas Aquinas to do battle with the university's logicians. This was a risky venture, as Aquinas himself was under the spell of Aristotle. He convinced his superiors that rather than repressing the ancient Greek's wisdom, they should incorporate it into Catholicism. To shrink from Aristotle, he warned, was to admit that the Christian faith could not withstand the challenges of reason. Thus was Scholasticism born.

Quoting Aristotle on nearly every page of his works, Aquinas almost single-handedly brought the pagan philosopher into the Christian fold. Aquinas believed that reason and religion could be harmonized, but only if certain mysteries of faith are placed beyond the scope of the debate. The Trinity, Incarnation, Redemption, and Last Judgment could not, he maintained, be proven by man's inadequate reason, and thus were off-limits. Aquinas discerned that *Locus ab auctoritate est infirmissimus*—"The argument from authority is the weakest." "The study of philosophy," he wrote, "does not aim merely to find out what others have thought, but what the truth of the matter is."[28] Not since Aristotle had the world seen a mind so incisive. He set as his principal task the proof of the existence of God by reason alone, using sophisticated arguments couched in a simple, direct style. *Sapientis est ordinare,* "The wise man creates order," were his watchwords.[29] Although his work lacks the passion of Augustine or the fervor of Jerome, Aquinas produced a defense of the faith tailored to his time.

He was an advocate of Free Will, believing, like Socrates, that evil flowed from ignorance rather than from malice. Ultimately, his teachings served to diminish the role of the Church. But he warned scholars and kings that they must remain directed by the Church in all things. He waxed passionate on the subject of the infallibility of the Pope, maintaining that sitting in the chair of Saint Peter conferred upon its occupant the wisdom never to err concerning Church doctrine.

---

*In those days, medics were often the most vocal skeptics. There arose an adage *ubi tres medici, duo athei*—"where there are three physicians, two of them are atheists."

· · ·

Aquinas was the most prolific writer since Origen; his published work fills 10,000 double-column folio pages. His major work, *Summa Theologica*, is twenty-one volumes long. He spent most of his life alone at his writing table. Studious, contemplative, and thoughtful, he was by everyone's description a man of immense good will. He never engaged in name-calling and did not raise his voice in debate. He treated his adversaries with courtesy and his friends with loyalty. He preached tolerance of Jews, since they bore witness to the Faith. He freely acknowledged his intellectual debt to Islam and treated people below him in social station with grace. In every respect, Thomas Aquinas was a model for his age. An inquisitive seeker of truth, he did not let the religious accretions of a thousand years obscure his life's goal, which was to understand God's revealed creation.

The mark he made on Catholicism was the most indelible since Augustine. Ignatius Loyola required the Jesuit Order to teach Thomism. Dante envisioned Thomas Aquinas as his guide to the highest stairway to Heaven. In 1545, the Council of Trent placed *Summa Theologica* on the altar alongside the Bible. Authorities, recognizing the value of Aquinas's work, elevated the philosopher to sainthood in 1323.

One persistently discordant sound interrupts the symphony of praise for Aquinas like the screeching of chalk across a blackboard: this model man vilified women. Disregarding the evidence of the senses, a theme about which he wrote extensively, Aquinas repeated many negative opinions and misogynist polemics. Unlike his other investigations, he did not subject his assertions concerning women to rigorous scrutiny.

Conflating Genesis's J and E versions, he argued that woman was inferior to man: both were made in God's image, but Eve was born of Adam's rib.[30] He swallowed the pseudo-scientific misogyny of Aristotle without a single caveat: women were merely passive vessels in the procreative process, while men contributed the entire active principle. Nature always tries to produce a male child; a female is evidence that something has gone awry, proof that "Woman is defective and misbegotten."[31] He proposed that girls were the result of either an inherent weakness in the father's generative power or else some noxious external factor such as a damp south wind. Faint-hearted, treacherous, weak, and vacuous, a woman requires everything from a man, but is needed by man only for procreation. Aquinas asserted that men can do everything better than women, including taking care of the home.[32]

Further lumbering his desolate view of womanhood, Aquinas piled on it Augustine's accusation that Eve had infected the entire human race with

Original Sin. Debating at length the fatuous question of whether women possessed souls, this otherwise gentle giant of logic argued that they did not. The salvation of nuns and widows became, therefore, a non-issue.

Written in the thirteenth century, *Summa Theologica* set an agenda the effects of which are still considerable today. It is all the more difficult to reconcile Thomas's benign persona and towering mind with his opprobrious attitudes toward women because there was a plethora of exemplary women in the age in which he lived. Since Thomas was in love with the mystery of his religion, one would have expected him to appreciate women's way of knowing. But his ever-present companions—his quill, inkpot, and alphabet—most likely tricked his left brain and right hand into leaving uncomposed anything that spoke well of 50 percent of the globe's population.

While the Church stoked the braziers of the Inquisition, believing it was incinerating a serious threat, it failed to recognize that Scholasticism was potentially far more treasonous than the most fervent Cathar. Aristotle's teachings became the stalking horse that disguised the real enemy of faith, which was reason. Due to Thomas's passion for Aristotle, logic was set loose behind the Church's high walls. It burrowed into the supports and eventually chewed at the foundations. Within a few centuries, the scholasticism Thomas was sure he could tame would undermine the entire edifice.

At age forty-seven Aquinas was overwhelmed by the brooding realization that all his writing had been for naught; so much "threshing of straw," as he put it. He never wrote again, convinced that his reason could never do justice to the Creator's inscrutable design. It is not known whether this epiphany changed his views on women.

The High Middle Ages is a problematic era for a historian to categorize. On the surface it is a confusing swirl of roiling waves and eddies. Among the many crosscurrents shaping the age was the recovery of alphabet literacy by a secular population previously dominated by a literate priestly class. As Europe emerged from the Dark Ages, for a time the feminine and the masculine and right- and left-brain values came into balance. But as the Church reasserted control, left-brain and masculine values became dominant again, and the gains women had made were lost. The years ahead would bear dramatic witness to the calamity that results when a culture's collective left hemisphere hypertrophies.

CHAPTER 29

HUMANIST/EGOIST
1300–1500

There has been discovered in Germany a wonderful new method for the production of books and those who have mastered the art are taking it out into the world. . . . The light of this discovery will spread from Germany to all parts of the earth.   —Guillaume Fichet, Paris, 1470[1]

The rise in literacy rates in the latter part of the High Middle Ages stimulated the rapid enlargement of Western culture's left hemisphere. At the same time, a mindless rage despoiled the fourteenth century. The years between 1300 and 1400 bubbled and brimmed with death and calamity. What began as a land dispute between the kings of England and France degenerated into the Hundred Years' War. By the middle of this protracted quarrel, most participants on either side could not remember its exact causes. Italy, Spain, and Germany also began to make strife a way of life. Hunter-killer values were everywhere in ascendance.

During this tumultuous time, villages were put to the torch, women raped, and the fruit trees and vines of rich farming lands were hacked down. Periodically, the armies disbanded because the kings were unable to pay them. At such times, the mercenaries formed rogue bands that perpetuated pillage and arson. A pall of smoke hovering over some ravished village in Europe symbolized the beggaring of an entire century.

Little wonder that the demoralized and pauperized populations were easy prey for another Horseman of the Apocalypse: the Plague. Striking thrice in the fourteenth century, each time like the swipe of a sharp scythe, it reduced the population of Europe by more than a third. No segment of society escaped unscathed. Archbishops, princes, doctors, and merchants— "all fall down." The invisible bacillus known as the Black Death disrupted commerce, depopulated farms, and emptied universities, and the virtuous died alongside the sinners, sorely testing belief in a just Creator.

The Age of Chivalry was among the many casualties of the Plague. King Arthur's code of honor, which had ennobled earlier generations of aristocracy, was interred when "knight" became synonymous with "thug." Fear of and respect for both clerical and secular authority slackened as familiarity with the Grim Reaper increased. The Church lost much of its luster when it became the political arm of the French monarchy. In 1305, Pope Clement VI transferred the Vatican from Rome to Avignon where it remained until 1377. Religion, the expression of humankind's longing to rise above the mundane, quickly became mired in profane politics. The decline in the moral status of both clergy and nobility in the eyes of the hard-working, over-taxed, church-going, middle and lower classes fanned dissent. Increasingly, the people demanded that the first and second estates lift the heavy yoke of unjust laws, tithes, and levies under which they labored.

As the fourteenth century drew to a close, conditions were so bleak that most citizens were both physically debilitated and spiritually emaciated. Had a pollster in the late 1390s interviewed the populace about the prospects for the coming new century, the vast majority would have been extremely pessimistic. Not a single contemporary sage, king, schoolman, philosopher, churchman, chronicler, or soothsayer predicted what lay just ahead—the Renaissance. Surely, it was one of history's most pleasant surprises.

The Renaissance was the result of an extraordinary conjunction. The Plague left behind a valuable inheritance—the tangible wealth of the deceased. Appropriating deserted farms and shops, neighbors unexpectedly acquired that most necessary ingredient for economic growth—surplus capital. As commerce surged, literacy rates followed. The more readers there were, the more books became available, which in turn encouraged readers to drift away from the crowd in the Church and be alone with themselves. These solitary acts of reading, repeated all over Europe, helped engender a new sense of self. The diffusion of books began to split the landmass of the Church into an archipelago of individual thinkers. Dirty bourgeois lucre, fertilizing the entwining skein of written words, produced the luxuriant tangle historians call the Renaissance.

In the early fifteenth century, trained copyists were in demand by the commercial "scriptoria" that copied books to sell to the public. The most sought-after books were ancient texts. Enterprising scholars scoured the dark recesses of old monasteries and unearthed many lost treasures of Greece and Rome. These long-dead literary voices were like a rejuvenating elixir, stimulating a new, ebullient self-confidence. Everyone, it seemed, became optimistic about the future.

In 1454, Johannes Gutenberg received a patent on the printing press. The Chinese and the Koreans had used a similar device many centuries earlier, but Asian printers were hampered by the complexities of printing in ideographic script. Gutenberg needed little more than twenty-six bins, each one filled with a different letter of the alphabet. He could arrange a line of type in seconds and then rapidly pull sheet after sheet of paper covered with linear text. The Chinese printing press had used wooden blocks. Movable metal type was Gutenberg's innovation.

The frenzied enthusiasm with which readers greeted this innovation is apparent in a letter a Basel scholar wrote to his friend.

> At this very moment, a whole wagonload of classics . . . has arrived from Venice. Do you want any? If you do, tell me at once, and send the money, for no sooner is such a freight landed than thirty buyers rise up for each volume, merely asking the price, and tearing one another's eyes out to get hold of them.[2]

As printing presses began to copy and disseminate ideas, there were some who decried the invention. Copyists protested that it would put them out of business. (It did.) Dismayed aristocratic bibliophiles saw the value of their manuscript libraries plummet. The more conservative elements among the nobility and clergy shifted uneasily, subconsciously aware that the printing press might be an enemy capable of spreading subversive ideas.

Erasmus ecstatically hailed printing as "the greatest of all inventions."[3] Literacy rates, which had been steadily rising, suddenly exploded. The society in which this alphabetic adventure occurred, however, was completely knocked off its pins. No society had ever had to contend with the implications of so much literacy within such a short period of time. This factor, I propose, was the central cause of the Renaissance's agony and ecstasy.

The Renaissance began in Italy in the mid fourteenth century—a full century before the advent of the printing press. It was an odd mixture of art and war, poetry and treachery, music and science, architecture and pragmatism, and sculpture and money. As gold poured into the coffers of the Church, commissions to create art flowed out. In the fourth century, the Church sent its minions into the streets of Rome to destroy all pagan art. A thousand years later the Church paid artists to re-create the lost legacy of classical art.

The nude was welcomed back and mingled in artists' ateliers with portraits of Church authorities arranged in poses of pious modesty. Images were everywhere in evidence. The Second Commandment was not.

"Renaissance" means rebirth. Dark visions of purgatory lost their hold on people's imaginations, and they began to reject the notion that life was just a cramped, tear-stained anteroom leading to a grander one. Invigorated by a new philosophy called Humanism, people began to see that they could make a difference. The Humanist Leon Battista Alberti urged his contemporaries to excel. "To you is given a body more graceful than other animals, to you powers of apt and various movements, to you most sharp and delicate senses, to you wit, reason, memory like an immortal god."[4]

The sudden surge of iconic information in the form of art should have advanced right-brain values, but such was not the case. The cult of the individual was a triumph for the left brain and for egoism. After the long, sheep-like bleating of the serfs under Feudalism, egoism was a refreshing change.

Perhaps Humanism should have been called "Masculinism." The leading proponents of Humanism did not advocate equality for women. It was a credo created by men, for men, and about men. Women of the era had to struggle with the Renaissance's predominantly macho themes, and also contend with the shift into their own left hemispheres as a result of *their* learning literacy. Few women managed to break out from beneath the suffocating cultural blanket thrown over them.

The most representative artist of the Renaissance was Michelangelo. Resembling the God he so often painted, he was solitary, difficult, and his rumbling volcanic creativity was God-like. In his *David*, a solitary youthful hero confronts a much stronger adversary and, against impossible odds, achieves victory—the Humanist credo in Carrera marble. His *Pietà* rivals the *David*. Despite its overwhelming capacity to move the viewer, it subliminally undermines the role of the Great Goddess. An arguably divine female figure holds the body of her dead son in her lap, helpless to do anything for him but grieve. While Michelangelo rendered her pain and resignation so poignantly that many people standing before it are moved to tears, a component of her sadness can also be interpreted as her loss of the power to resurrect him, which she had once possessed. Michelangelo, inspired more by the Old Testament than the New, more by the "J" version than the "E" one, also created art's most memorable rendering of Moses.

Renaissance sculptures often glorified the male obsession with rape, struggle, and death. In Benvenuto Cellini's statue *Perseus* (1554) the powerful male nude holds his blood-smeared sword at his side, where it sticks stiff and slightly upright from the level of his loins, while his other hand grasps

Michelangelo's *David*
and *Pietà*, and Cellini's
Perseus

Medusa's head by her snake-hair. A male hero on steroids has dispatched an uppity woman shaman.

The principle of perspective was one of the key developments of Renaissance art. It is the visual equivalent of left-brained dualistic thinking.* Perspective accentuates the ability to stand outside what is being viewed and look back on it "objectively." All Western alphabet religions believe that God

---

*Perspective is the illusion of depth on a flat surface. When a painting drawn in perspective is shown to people who are non-alphabet literate, they frequently cannot see the illusion. We who have been trained to read the alphabet are unaware that in order to read we focus our eyes slightly in front of a page of print. This skill is also indispensable in *seeing* a painting's perspectivist illusion.

has a perspectivist point of view, looking down on His creation from on high. People in non-alphabetic traditions believe that the deity is both of and in the world. The deity isn't on the cloud—She *is* the cloud.

The Humanist credo was behind advances in all the arts, emboldening artists to experiment. It stiffened the resolve of scientists to risk burning at the stake in their quest for truth, and it shored up sailors' courage on lonely and dangerous voyages of exploration. It also inspired people throughout Europe to demand rights that were unthinkable in preceding centuries. The Guild system protecting artisans gained strength. Parliament came into being in England. Universities became independent of the Church. A prosperous middle class burgeoned. The aristocracy, although tarnished by its convoluted wars, maintained a firm grip on their social station. Women's rights showed signs of resuscitation. During the European Renaissance, every group and category of human endeavor made gains except one. The institution that suffered a grievous regression in power and respect was, paradoxically, the one that encouraged and supported the Renaissance—the papacy.

The Popes' refusal to reform the Church ultimately precipitated the Protestant secession. I propose that another factor impeding papal reform was the anti-female policies Pope Gregory VII put in place in the eleventh century. By claiming that he had rid the Church's upper echelons of any feminine influence, Gregory VII created a flaw that contributed to leading the papacy to the brink of disaster. To obtain a perspective on the connection between the policies of a medieval pope and the desecration of the office of the Vicar of Christ in the Renaissance, a very long view of human history is required.

Long before there were cities, books, and inkwells, there were clans, caves, and middens. Human societies were shaped by the exacting rules of evolution: losers became extinct, winners survived. The crucial module guaranteeing the tribe's continuance was the family unit. All members prospered under this arrangement. A man was cared for by a solicitous woman and learned about the pleasures of playing with small children. A woman enjoyed the security she needed to devote her time to her offspring. Each gained a friend, lover, confidant, and helpmate. Children matured in a safe atmosphere guided by two caring role models. The tribe as a whole could count on the steady replenishment of both skilled hunters and pregnant mothers. This system worked better than any alternative ever tried.

A husband and wife, over time, begin to resemble one another in physical appearance. The melding of their physiognomic features is also reflected, to varying degrees, in their souls. A woman's presence in a man's life tends to soften his hard edges, just as her proximity to him tends to stiffen her central core. A mate increases the possibility that each member of the couple will exhibit that difficult-to-define quality called common sense.

Men and women often arrive at conclusions and plans of action differently. Some situations are best addressed by focused, step-by-step "masculine" logic, while holistic, "feminine" intuition comprehending many components in a complex whorl is better in others. Couples benefit from having access to each other's major hemispheric processes, which over time also strengthens their own personal minor mode. The blending of feminine knowing and masculine reason in each individual and each couple generates good sense. The wisest figure in the mythologies of ancient cultures was often a hermaphrodite—a male-female—such as Tiresias, the blind seer.

Humans belong to that class of animals called "social predators." Their hunting strategy resembles that used by wolf packs and lion prides; all members of the social unit hunt in concert to kill prey. The protracted childhoods of human young made female participation on these forays unfeasible. The all-male hunting party came into existence in only our species and with it the ethos of the left brain.

The template for all subsequent male projects remained the original hunting party, the ultimate purpose of which was to kill. Therein lay the problem. When men began to spend extensive time in each other's company, they amplified each other's hunter-killer instincts. When the hunting party became an "army," the prey became other humans. The result has been a historical record pungent with the acrid smell of fear, havoc, and death.

The greatest counterbalance to men's death-dealing impulse is to engage them in the lives of women and entangle their legs with children. The most dangerous result of these all-male cultures bereft of the input from women is the loss of common sense.* The phrase "common sense" has several meanings. In one, it is the wisdom of *all* the senses, a holistic and simultaneous grasp of multiple converging determinants. In this meaning common sense is intuitive and is often the opposite of logic. In another meaning, it is the wisdom of more than one person. It is the result of the give-and-take of face-to-face conversation with another, which allows one to "hear oneself think." In this second meaning, common sense is wisdom generated "in common."

*What follows is meant to apply to heterosexual male communities.

Confronted by a knotty problem a person often turns to a trusted adviser, not so much to receive the solution as to engage in a problem-solving dialogue. A man can resort to two entirely different advisers: his female significant other or another man. His interactions with these two most likely will be quite different.

There are certain conventions men generally obey when talking to each other. Dialogues occur in the light, with no physical contact, and both men are dressed, facing each other vertically. When a man consults his woman, it is often at night, in the dark, while both are horizontal in a position of repose, and there is frequently skin touching skin.

In both these colloquies, he talks in order to bounce his ideas off his listener and evaluate his or her response. The male adviser or woman confidante serves as his sounding board. Men, over many centuries and across a diverse range of cultures, would concur that in interpersonal matters, the best "sounding board" is often a soft pillow with a woman's head on it. Further, the syzygy of skin, night, and goose feathers is conducive to sleep. A thoughtful person when confronted by a difficult dilemma for which others demand an immediate answer will frequently withhold his reply until after he has "slept on" it. By using this common saw, he tacitly acknowledges the vital importance of talking over the problem with his mate before falling asleep and then letting the right hemisphere dream its wisdom into his response. Come morning, horizontal thinking has worked its magic and the individual has arrived at an answer that makes common sense smile.

Men need the counsel of women to help them sort out what is important from what is folly. This need is particularly acute if the man is the head of a vast enterprise. In such a situation, the other men to whom he might turn for advice—those under him—will often have their own personal agendas, which may influence the opinions they give their alpha male. The wife of the alpha male is often a truer resource—sharing his life, her fate is intimately entwined with his. And the alternative kind of wisdom she brings to his problem makes her counsel uniquely valuable to him.

Few men who have enjoyed a good relationship with a woman would disagree with the proposition that a woman's assistance in male problem solving is indispensable. Eliminating her from the process greatly increases the possibility that the man might make a wrong-headed decision about matters of import. History books are filled with such examples.

This brings us back to a flaw in the Renaissance papacy. Gregory's eleventh-century celibacy fiat ensured that no pope thereafter could acknowledge any woman as his adviser. This made the papal court the only one in the Western world where a king without a queen presided. By banning women from any positions of authority within its corridors, the Vatican created the conditions for great mischief. In conjunction with a new invention that swiftly disseminated information and changed the mind-set of a culture, conditions were in place for a debacle.

The principal Renaissance popes of the period—Sixtus IV, Innocent VII, Alexander VI, Julian II, Leo X, and Clement V—engaged in activities and made decisions that, taken as a whole, constitute one of the most dramatic examples of sustained folly in recorded history. Judging by their actions it seems that none, despite occupying the chair of Saint Peter, had the slightest inkling of his spiritual mission. One after another they embraced worldly vices that ranged from avarice, intrigue, depravity, intransigence, and pusillanimity. They conspired with assassins, blessed cannons, and sold offices. They unwaveringly preferred money, power, and personal gain and ignored repeated calls for reform. It was obvious to nearly everyone—kings, laity, and clergy—that reform was urgently needed. The popes were the only ones in a position to initiate it from within. Their failure to bring about reform led to a conflagration that nearly consumed the Church and left no one in Europe unsinged.

We know firsthand many of the popes' decisions and daily activities because they were recorded in excruciating detail by the Church's own notaries.* The reign of Pope Sixtus IV, which began in 1470, marks the beginning of the steep decline of papal authority and the appearance of the first printing press in Italy.† The freshly installed pope shocked the public by hastily appointing as cardinals two of his nephews, both in their twenties, and granting each of them benefices worth the equivalent of millions of dollars today. The nephews became notorious for their profligate spending and lavish lifestyles. Sixtus simply ignored the requirement that a cardinal be, at the very least, an ordained priest. He thoroughly secularized the college of cardinals, passing over competent clerics and conferring the second highest office in Christianity on men who had neither calling nor vision—and in many cases, questionable morals. These men were elevated to cardinals either out of cronyism and/or because of the sums they were prepared to bid for the red hat. Since many of these appointees saw themselves as "princes" of the Church, they lived in palaces with hundreds of servants, rode abroad in martial attire, and kept hounds and falcons. During his tenure, Sixtus

---

*For example, John Burchard, Master of Ceremonies of the papal court (1452–1504), was a meticulous diarist.

†The first book printed in Rome appeared in 1469; by 1500 there were 41 printers.

managed to bestow important positions on nearly every one of his male relatives, the great majority of whom were abysmally unqualified. One arch-
bishopric went to a child of eight, another to a boy of eleven.[5] Sixtus brushed
aside petitions for reform.

Innocent VIII (1484–92), Sixtus's successor, was a priest with a known
illegitimate child. It did not seem to faze the members of the college when
they put an actual father on the seat of the Holy Father, and his illegitimate
son was publicly recognized—a first in the history of the papacy. Throughout Christendom there was a groundswell of demand for reform, but the
pope ignored it. He spent considerable effort furthering the career of his dis-
reputable son, Franceschetto. This lewd youth roamed the streets of Rome at
night with a clutch of thugs, gang-raping women, including nuns. He also
invaded the homes of private citizens to rob and terrorize them, confident
that his family name made him immune from the law.[6] In 1486, Innocent
arranged Franceschetto's wedding to an heir of the Medici family and celebrated it in the Vatican with a party so lavish that he had to mortgage the
papal tiara to pay for it.[7]

To raise money for his ongoing extravagances, Innocent established a
papal bureau that dispensed favors at inflated prices. He allowed murderers
to buy pardons and walk free. When outraged reformers objected, one cardinal defended the practice on the ground that "the Lord desireth not the
death of a sinner but rather that he live and pay."[8]

The cynical Rodrigo Borgia bought enough college votes to secure the
papacy, succeeding Innocent, and took the name Alexander VI (1492–1503).
Following Sixtus's example, Alexander filled Rome with his Spanish relatives; so many that one reformer observed, "Ten papacies would not be
enough for all his cousins."[9] The calumnies and transgressions of Rodrigo,
his sinister son Cesare, and his notorious daughter Lucrezia exhibited a level
of depravity not seen in Rome since the reigns of Nero and Caligula.*[10]

---

*The mother of his children was Vanozza de Cataneis, who reputedly succeeded
her mother in that role. Many historians believe that Cesare, Lucrezia, and Alexander
were, at one point, three corners of an incestuous triangle. The eighteen-year-old
Lucrezia delivered a child who may have been either her brother's or her father's.

The evidence for these convoluted liaisons lies in two papal bulls issued by
Alexander after the boy's birth, one public, the other secret. The first legitimized the
three-year-old Giovanni, claiming he was the son of Cesare and another woman; the
private one acknowledged that Giovanni was the son of the pope and the same woman.
Since Lucrezia was the undisputed mother, these documents have given some historians the clues they believed are necessary to sort out the Borgias' sordid relationships.

At fifty-nine, just before achieving the highest office in Christendom, Alexander openly took as his mistress the beautiful nineteen-year-old Giulia Farnese. He arranged for another man to marry her, then took her to his own chamber in the Vatican on her wedding night.

Alexander's bacchanals were the talk of Christendom. To celebrate the fall of Granada to Christian forces, he once held a bullfight in the Piazza of Saint Peter.[11] He presided over one banquet remembered as the "Ballet of the Chestnuts." Burchard dispassionately recounted how fifty courtesans danced after dinner with the guests, "at first clothed, then naked." Candelabra were then placed on the floor and chestnuts scattered among them. The courtesans, still naked, crawled on their hands and knees among the burning candles to retrieve the chestnuts in inventive ways, "while the Pope, Cesare and his sister Lucrezia looked on." The climax of the evening came when the guests were invited to couple with the courtesans in front of everyone. Prizes were awarded to those "who could perform the act most often. . . ."[12] Nobles and prelates alike shucked their expensive clothing and rushed to join the competition.

A month later, Alexander and Lucrezia "watched with loud laughter and much pleasure" the mounting by stallions of mares in heat in the Vatican courtyard. On another occasion, reports Burchard, Cesare ordered condemned criminals herded into the courtyard and killed them one by one with bow and arrow.[13] While many of Burchard's entries are hard to believe, they have been corroborated by other sources.

Generally tolerant of dissent in the early years of his reign, Alexander became less so as criticism of his reign mounted. He once ordered a man's tongue torn out and his hand cut off because the miscreant had told a joke at the pope's expense.[14] Despite the fiery speeches condemning him by the passionate Savonarola in nearby Florence, Alexander did not initiate reform of the Church. When he died of an unexplained fever, no one wanted to touch his body. The populace rejoiced as a horse dragged his black-tongued, swollen corpse to his grave by a rope tied around his feet.[15]

Cardinal Della Rovere, who became Pope Julius II (1503–13), was a dour man given to tantrums. Intent on reclaiming lost papal lands seized by secular forces, he overrode the objections of his shocked cardinals and set out on horseback at the head of a mercenary army. The sight of the Holy Father, white beard peeping out from his metal visor, leading a siege against Italian forces—fellow Christians—did much to further discredit the papacy. Julius blessed the cannons that were pointed at Christian cities. And he hurled the thunderbolt of excommunication against those officers opposite him on the field, abusing and diminishing an awesome weapon that had been used only sparingly by previous popes. The leading Humanist of the day, Erasmus, lamented, "What have helmet and miter in common? What association is there between the cross and the shield? How do you dare, Bishop who holds the place of the Apostle, to school your people in war?"[16] Erasmus's discontented mutterings were echoed all over Europe. Some apologists hail Julius as the "Savior of the Church." They gloss over the harm he did.

The next pope, Leo X (1513–21), presided over the Protestant break. A Medici devoted to the arts, he was a diffident epicurean. Leo's profligate spending created a crisis.[17] The atmosphere of luxury surrounding his court is epitomized by the story that at one party given for him, the solid gold dishes used to serve the guests were not washed but simply thrown out the window into the Tiber. (Actually, the host had set up a net below to catch the plates for a repeat performance at a later date.)[18]

Leo's constant need to replenish the papal coffers necessitated his sending an army of clerical tax collectors out into the hinterlands to extract gold from the little people. Their main fund-raising device was selling indulgences. These documents, signed by the pope, expiated sins in exchange for money. One could even purchase a proxy release from purgatory for deceased relatives—or a release for transgressions the buyer might commit in the future. In 1516, Johann Tetzel, a monk notorious for his high-pressure tactics, used the slogan "As the penny in the coffer rings, the soul from purgatory springs." When he tried to sell indulgences in Martin Luther's bailiwick, it was the straw that broke the Vatican's back.

It never seemed to have occurred to Leo that reform was necessary. He believed, as did his predecessors, that threats, excommunication, and burning at the stake were the most efficient methods of dealing with critics. Erasmus, writing from the Netherlands, contemptuously observed, "As if the Church had any enemies more pestilential than impious pontiffs who, by their silence, allow Christ to be forgotten, enchain Him by mercenary rules . . . and crucify Him afresh by their scandalous life."[19] Those who were swept up in Leo's mad spending felt otherwise. One cardinal, carried away with the splendor of Leo's reign, wrote to a friend, "God be praised, for here we lack nothing but a court with ladies."[20]

This one breathless line summed up a crucial aspect of the problem. A wise wife, if he but had one, could have warned Leo that his lifestyle, and all the animosity it engendered, would bring ruin. But the all-male Vatican had eliminated the influence of women, and like his predecessors, Leo and his court continued their profligate ways. By the time he died, he had so plundered the papal treasury that Rome experienced a severe financial crash.

After the brief two-year tenure of the next pope, the college opted for a Medici cardinal who took the name of Clement VII (1523–34). The Reformation, meanwhile, was well under way. Through a series of political misjudgments, Clement angered the powerful emperor Charles V of Spain, who marched his army to the outskirts of Rome because he learned that Clement had double-crossed him in a political intrigue. Charles pledged to "revenge myself on those who have injured me, particularly that fool of a pope."[21]

Charles led his troops to within sixty miles of the Eternal City, but was too respectful to issue the order to attack. After humiliating Clement, he accepted an armistice for 60,000 ducats. But Charles's army of hungry and underpaid mercenaries smelled blood. Aided by Italian dukes hostile to Rome, they mutinied, transformed into a mob, and bolted for the prize so close to them. A vigorous counterattack by Rome's defenders was expected, but astonishingly, Charles's troops met no signs of defense. In a supreme misjudgment, Clement had simply refused to believe that a Christian army would dare to actually set foot in the sacred city. He was oblivious to the fact that Rome had become a symbol of tyranny and oppression for many Christians.

On May 6, 1527, Swiss, Dutch, German, and Spanish soldiers breached the walls. An orgy of barbarity followed. While the pope and the cardinals hastily took refuge in the fortress Sant' Angelo, the rest of the inhabitants were subjected to rape, massacre, fire, and plunder on a scale not seen since the Vandals had sacked the city eleven hundred years earlier. The soldiers went looting house-to-house, murdering and raping indiscriminately. The Tiber was filled with floating corpses, while all quarters of the city burned out of control. Christian soldiers dressed in the stolen vestments of cardinals strutted in the Piazza of Saint Peter. Churches were stripped of their treasures, and nuns were impressed into makeshift brothels for the soldiers.

The degradation of the most sacred city in Christendom was so thorough, one chronicler wrote, "It would have moved a stone to compassion."[22] Only when plague and famine descended on the city did the sated invaders finally depart. News of the sack was greeted in some parts of Europe with shock and dismay; elsewhere people rejoiced over what they saw as divine retribution for the excesses of the previous eighty years.

These six principal Renaissance popes reigned during one of the most glorious periods in human history. Yet they were at the helm during the steepest regression of papal moral authority. Taking into account the entire one thousand five hundred years of the church's existence, previous Church leaders had not exhibited behaviors so antithetical to the spirit of its founder for so many years. There is not a comparable lapse among Egyptian, Mesopotamian, Greek, Roman, Buddhist, Shinto, Hindu, Confucian, Jewish, Taoist, or Islamic priesthoods. Why did such an aberration occur at this particular time, in this particular place?

The Renaissance popes acted against the backdrop of a world being transformed by the printing press. I propose that the sudden inundation of society by alphabet letters caused a dramatic increase in left-brain hunter-killer values throughout Europe, and a diminution of the right-brain values of love, kindness, equality, respect for nature, nurturing small children, protecting the meek and weak, and common sense. These trends became exaggerated in the wealthiest, all male, most literate segment of society—the papacy. In the Renaissance Vatican, gold, gain, pride, prizes, hubris, contests, and vainglory were held in the highest regard. The occasional papal mistress present during this period was not enough to counterbalance the extreme masculine ethos of the papal court. The absence of woman wisdom was an important factor contributing to its resultant decline.

CHAPTER 30

PROTESTANT/CATHOLIC

Had the religion of Christianity been pursued according to the principles of the Founder, the states of Christianity would have been far more united and happy than they are ... Nor can there be greater proof of its decadence than the fact that the nearer people are to Rome, the head of their religion, the less religious are they. Whoever examines the principles on which Christianity is founded and sees how widely different those principles are from present practice, will judge that her ruin or chastisement is near at hand.

—Machiavelli, writing in 1513, four years before the Reformation[1]

Printing was the Reformation; Gutenberg made Luther possible.

—Will Durant[2]

T he word *Protestant* means "one who protests." Current usage reserves the word for religious contexts. ("Protester" refers to the political arena.) A protestant reformation is a wrenching reorientation in a culture's religion. There have been four lasting "protestant reformations" in the history of Western culture. They occurred in widely separated ages and under immensely different circumstances, but all shared certain features.

The first one erupted in the Sinai approximately thirty-eight hundred years ago when desert people revolted against the florid icon worship of Egyptian polytheism. They rejected the Egyptian concept of an afterlife and the idea that rites and rituals could be a substitute for individual morality. The defining event of the Israelites' reformation was the appearance of the first sacred alphabetic book. Coincident with its appearance, men sharply circumscribed women's rights, denounced the worship of goddesses as an abomination, and declared that images were profane.

The next protestant reformation occurred approximately two thousand years later in a Roman Empire that was enjoying an artistic and literary surge. Christians appeared on the scene as if from nowhere and rejected the values of the polytheistic state religion, manifested by myriad images. Like the Hebrews, the early Christians extolled the virtues of simplicity, modesty, and righteousness, and they drew their strength from the West's second significant sacred alphabetic book, the New Testament. Patristic fathers demonized goddess worship, roving bands of monks demolished images, and women's rights suffered a precipitous setback.

Several hundred years later, a third reformation occurred in the deserts of Arabia. A prophet proclaimed a new moral code transmitted to him in writing by an imageless, male deity. This writing became the West's third sacred alphabetic book, the Quran. Again, the same distinctive constellation of events accompanied this revolution. All representative images were outlawed, women's freedom was sharply curtailed, and the stone representations of previously revered goddesses were toppled.

All three of these reformations abrogated women's previously established rights to conduct religious ceremonies or pray to a goddess, and all three eroded women's property rights. Men justified this usurpation of power by citing chapter and verse from their respective sacred books.

Resembling an earthquake that suddenly releases tremendous pent-up energy, another religious seismic shock shook Europe squarely in the middle of the Renaissance.* The fourth protestant reformation began precisely at noon on October 31, 1517, when an obscure German monk, Martin Luther, nailed ninety-five refutations of the sale of papal indulgences onto the door of a Wittenberg church. Numerous tomes have explored the roots of the schism that occurred as a result of Luther's challenge. All, to varying degrees, blame the Church's leaders for abusing power. The newly invented printing press aided the reform movement's spread. Protestants were able to disperse their ideas rapidly through pamphlets and printed sermons, thwarting the Church's efforts to contain the movement. Some historians cite the rise of nationalism and the Humanist credo as playing a role. I propose that while all of the above factors influenced the overthrow of the old order, the *process* of reading alphabetic writing itself, more than the *content* of what was read, was the essential factor that precipitated the Reformation.

The crux of the Protestant revolt concerned alphabet literacy: who should be allowed to read and interpret the sacred book? The Catholic Church maintained that only a few higher echelon priests who knew Latin

*In this chapter I will discuss only Protestant doctrine at its inception.

were in a position to understand it. The pope had the final word. During the medieval period, the Church closely guarded the New Testament, which was not circulated among the faithful. More often than not, copies were chained to monastery desks or kept behind locked cabinet doors. This control over the Scriptures reinforced the Church's claim that only an ordained priest could assist one to gain entrance to the Kingdom of Heaven. As Augustine had declared, there was "no salvation outside the Church."

The Protestant position, as championed by Martin Luther, argued that no one had the right to come between an individual and God. All Christians should study the Good Book in solitude: an act that would, in itself, bring about direct communion with God. Luther refuted Augustine by declaring "Every man is his own priest"—with the ability and right to interpret the Bible according to his private judgment.[3] Luther repudiated the colorful ritual of mass, rich with icons. The nexus of the Reformation was the rekindling of the age-old conflict between written words and images.

If the Reformation had been based on a return to the content of the New Testament, one would expect it to have extolled right-hemispheric values. But I propose the Reformation was due primarily to the process of perceiving literacy, which explains why left-hemispheric values prevailed.

Average Christians were repulsed by the moral decay in the Catholic Church, the one institution they believed should provide the model for virtue. The respected Catholic historian Ludwig Pastor wrote of this period,

> A deep-rooted corruption had taken possession of nearly all the officials of the Curia. . . . The inordinate number of gratuities and exactions passed all bounds. Moreover, on all sides deeds were dishonestly manipulated, and even falsified, by the officials. No wonder that there arose from all parts of Christendom the loudest complaints about the corruption and financial extortions of the papal officials.[4]

Prior to the Reformation, numerous reformers proposed an identical solution: a return to the principles of Christianity's founder. In England, William of Ockham in 1328 did so and urged leniency for differences of religious opinion. His countryman John Wyclif urged the same reform in the late 1300s. Jan Huss was hanged in Prague in 1415 for publicly demanding it. Erasmus in 1528 said, "He commanded us nothing save love for one another, and there is nothing so bitter that affection does not soften and sweeten it.

Everything according to nature is easily borne, and nothing accords better with the nature of man than the philosophy of Christ."[5]

Reformers agreed that the necessary first step was to wrest the written text away from the elite group of priests who were holding it hostage so that people could read Christ's words for themselves. For this to happen three indispensable preconditions needed to be in place: translation of the New Testament into local vernaculars, the availability of inexpensive copies of the Scriptures, and the presence of a large literate population. The printing press achieved all three goals in a blur of mechanical wizardry.

The reformers maintained that when large numbers of lay people could examine Jesus' words for themselves, they would be transformed by them. The new social institutions they would subsequently create would elevate the lives of everyone, from kings to serfs. Reading Jesus' pithy parables and trenchant aphorisms, they anticipated, would predispose Protestants to be tolerant, nonviolent, egalitarian, generous, compassionate, and loving.

In his pivotal Sermon on the Mount (and in many other passages as well), Jesus called on people to choose between right and wrong. He declared that He was God's emissary, harbinger of the "Good News" that His Father loved them, and to show it, He would soon bring about a beneficial change in their lives.

Also significant is what Jesus did *not* say. He never mentioned Original Sin or Eve's transgression. He never advocated burning people at the stake for their beliefs. He did not proscribe images. Before comparing the ethics of Jesus with those that came to guide the Protestant Reformation, the story of the Protestant Reformation's two chief personalities must be told.

As Michelangelo was putting the finishing touches on his famous marble hero with a sling, he could not have known that a scant thirteen years later, in 1517, a flesh-and-blood David in the form of Martin Luther (1483–1546) would stand up to the mightiest institution in Europe armed only with a pen, and bring it to its knees. Thrust onto the world stage to play a great role for which he was unprepared, Martin Luther's audacity, intellect, and determination to end clerical abuse made him an outstanding figure of the sixteenth century.

Ordained as an Augustinian monk in 1506, he became a theologian at the University of Wittenberg. What began as his outrage at Tetzel's peddling of papal-sponsored indulgences to his neighborhood became a call for reforming the entire structure of organized Christianity. He eventually advocated the violent overthrow of the popes.

It was Luther's good fortune to have as his foil in this duel of wills the sybaritic Pope Leo X. Leo consistently underestimated the threat the rough, resolute Teuton posed.

After his initial confrontation with papal authorities, Luther recovered from his shock that he had not been martyred. He grasped that his call for ecclesiastical overhaul had resonated with the majority of his countrymen. Aware that he had a unique opportunity to reshape Christianity, he declared that its principles must be anchored firmly in the Bible, a work indisputably written by God. Yet the features of the new Christianity that Luther almost single-handedly shaped, and that his fellow reformers eagerly embraced as "God's Word," were not at all what one would expect from a return to a literal reading of the Scriptures.

Luther replaced the infallibility of the pope with the infallibility of God's written word. But he chose certain passages to emphasize, relying heavily on the wrathful ones of the Old Testament for his conception of the deity, and all but ignored the essence of the Gospels. An avenging Yahweh inspired him more than the merciful, loving Father described by Jesus.

Luther was deeply affected by Paul's Epistle to the Romans. In the single line "The just shall live by faith" (1:17), Luther found his lodestone. Faith alone was *the* key to salvation. Virtue played no role, and good works could not win a sinner grace. Belief in the story of how God had sacrificed His Son for humankind assured redemption.

Luther dismissed indulgences, purgatory, saints, canon law, obedience to the pope, and priests' right to perform sacraments, because they were not specifically mentioned in Scripture. But he endorsed Augustine's conception of Original Sin, even though the Scriptures never mention it. Ignoring the Old and New Testaments' many passages exhorting people to choose between right and wrong, Luther made Augustine's concept of predestination the linchpin of Protestantism.

Augustine had reasoned that God willed that all humans would be sinners and predestined the vast majority of them to hell before they were even born. Only a select few—the elect—would be saved, and God had identified before Creation who they would be. Luther was convinced of the inherent evil in each person. "We are the children of wrath," he wrote, claiming that even in the most noble, evil always far outweighs good.

Luther dismissed reason as useless in trying to counter his carefully reasoned arguments. He proposed abandoning the teaching of logic and philosophy.

Reason is the greatest enemy that faith has . . . She is the Devil's greatest whore . . . a whore eaten by scab and leprosy, who ought to be trodden underfoot and destroyed, she and her wisdom . . . Throw dung in her face . . . drown her in baptism.[6]

He disdained Thomas Aquinas and other Scholastics for making too many concessions to that "cursed, conceited, wily heathen" Aristotle.[7]

He rejected Copernicus's heliocentric theory, insisting that it must be wrong because it contradicted Scripture. He believed in witches, incubi, and evil spirits, and advanced the idea that either God or the devil was behind every natural occurrence. The concerns of Humanists were irrelevant to a man convinced that the End of the World was imminent.[8]

Luther wrote:

This is the acme of faith, to believe that God, Who saves so few and condemns so many, is merciful; that He is just Who has made us necessarily doomed to damnation, so that . . . He seems to delight in the tortures of the wretched, and to be more deserving of hatred than of love. If by any effort of reason I could conceive how God, Who shows so much anger and iniquity, could be merciful and just, there would be no need of faith.[9]

That a proposition is so seemingly absurd it *must* be true was the same illogical *credo quia incredibile* Tertullian had used to still classical critics.

Luther's anti-intellectualism shocked the Humanists, who had promoted reason as the best agent for discerning God's sometimes-scrutable design. They had hoped to bring about reform through an ever-widening web of connections within the Church and universities. Initially they applauded Luther's stance; then, one by one, they repudiated his methods as too crude. They viewed Luther and his supporters as traitors to the wisdom of the classical world which they fought hard to exhume. Most found Luther's idiosyncratic reading of the Scriptures incomprehensible.

To Erasmus, a God who punished the sins of the hapless creatures He had created to be sinners would be an immoral monster unworthy of worship. To ascribe such conduct to Christ's Father was dire blasphemy.[10] The Humanist Michael Servetus denounced Luther's notion that God would predestine souls to hell without regard for merit. "God," wrote Servetus, "condemns no one who does not condemn himself. Faith is good but love is better and God Himself is love."[11] Another cleric dismissed Luther's boast that any lay person could interpret the Bible. He warned, "The Bible is like soft wax, which every man can twist and stretch according to his pleasure."[12] Nobles, too, were uneasy over Luther's insistence that virtue played no role in gaining a favorable judgment from God, since, as one duke predicted, stressing faith rather than virtue "would only make the people presumptuous and mutinous" toward civil authority.[13] Not surprisingly, Luther's fatalism loosened the restraint of many. A youth beheaded his brother and claimed in court that his crime had been predestined. A university logician gloated as he clubbed his wife to death over some minor domestic dispute, "Now is the divine Father's will be done."[14]

Luther referred to himself as "a peasant who was the son of a peasant." His earthiness led him to reverse the Church's almost universally ignored position on clerical celibacy. He believed that all monks and nuns should marry, work for a living, and have children. The sexual urge could not be ignored. "God has provided a poultice for that sore,"[15] he noted. He still believed that copulation was a sin, even in marriage, but that, in marriage, "God covers the sin."[16]

In the process of finding husbands for the nuns of a Wittenberg convent preparatory to closing it, Luther matched all with local bachelors except the twenty-six-year-old Catherine von Bora. The young woman cast aside the names Luther suggested, one after the other. Finally, in exasperation, he asked who in her eyes would be acceptable. Catherine leveled her gaze on the most famous man in Germany and answered, "You, Herr Doktor."*[17] After the forty-two-year-old Luther recovered from his surprise, he agreed. The ex-monk and the ex-nun married. Catherine bore him six children, patiently cared for him, and inspired him to remark, "The greatest gift of God to man is a pious, kindly, God-fearing, home-loving wife."†[18]

Despite his attachment to his wife and the heartfelt love he bestowed on his daughters, Luther was not a man who held women in high regard. The ex-monk said on one occasion, "Take women from their housewifery and they are good for nothing."[19] And on another, "If women get tired and die of childbearing, there is no harm in that; let them die as long as they bear; they are made for that."[20] He believed that women should be obedient to their husbands, and he especially disliked learned women.

In a conciliatory moment, he counseled, "What defects women have we must check them in private, gently . . . for woman is a frail vessel."[21] But he also lumped women together with vermin, plagues, and wild beasts as pun-

---

*Hedging her bet, she also intimated that she would accept the other official who was present with Luther that day.

†Luther's children took notes of their father's conversations about the dinner table. They reveal a warm relationship between Luther and Catherine. In many exchanges, his wife little suffered Luther's sometimes bombastic pronouncements.

ishments God had visited upon man because of Adam's disobedience.[22] He was convinced the devil frequently mated with unmarried women to conceive malevolent incubi. He once advised drowning the infant born to one unwed local girl in order to protect the commonweal.[23]

He disliked nature, believing that venturing away from cities exposed one to diabolical influences. "Many devils are in the woods, in waters, in wilderness, and in dark pooly places, ready to hurt . . . people, some are also in thick, black clouds."[24] He attributed such natural phenomena as hail, thunder, and floods to Satan's hand.[25]

Luther was one of the most prolific writers in German history. Almost single-handedly he created a High German written script, an innovation that was much needed, as the many competing forms of the German written language had led to disarray. He translated the New Testament into High German in 1522 and the Old Testament a few years later: the German Bible became the very first printed national best-seller. By making his tracts and sermons available in the vernacular, he appealed both to a rising sense of German nationalism and a growing interest in literacy. Illiterate parents, bringing their young children to school, frequently stayed quietly in the back of the room trying to learn the art.

Luther was particularly determined to jettison the devotion to Mary. Reasoning that the New Testament never accorded Mary divinity, his new religion expunged any reference to her and banned images of a mother cradling her child. Jesus' mother ceased pleading the cases of sinners before the court of His Father.

Early on, when he was a defiant heretic hounded by the pope's agents, Luther railed against the totalitarian practices of the Inquisition. He denounced the burning of Protestants, and advised that dissidents should be "vanquished with books, not the stake."[26] He also recommended that "heathens" (Jews, Turks, and Moors, among others) be treated with respect.[27] Unfortunately, this tolerant stance gave way later in his life to splenetic bigotry, more extreme and explicit than that which the Church had practiced.

Luther thought that imagery might be useful in teaching the illiterate. The students, nobles, townspeople, and peasants who were electrified by his message, however, did not share his generous attitude about images. As happened during the first three protestant reformations, zealots wielding sledgehammers and pickaxes smashed statues, slashed paintings, and upended altarpieces. Priests or parishioners who tried to protect these images were stoned or beaten. Artists fled.

The cavernous interiors of very early Protestant churches (many of which were converted Catholic cathedrals) had whitewashed walls with no statues, crucifixes, or paintings anywhere in view. Protestants replaced the colorful Catholic mass with communal reading. Both services venerated the Trinity, but in starkly different ways. In one, worshipers surrounded by images gazed at a sumptuous spectacle conducted by resplendently dressed priests in a language the listeners could not understand, while in the other, worshipers read from open books in a visually spare environment led by ministers dressed in black and white. With the proliferation of alphabet books, images were once again overwhelmed by written words.

The printing press spread Luther's message with a celerity unknown in previous history. Within five years of the Wittenberg nailing, Erasmus wrote to a friend that "Luther's books [are] everywhere . . . and in every language. No one would believe how widely he has moved men." In Paris in 1520, Luther outsold every other single author. Luther's German New Testament sold more than 100,000 copies in his lifetime, an extraordinary number in a society recently largely illiterate. Never before had a culture been flooded by so many written words in such a short time.

Luther's influence was greatest in German-speaking lands where his Protestantism had a distinctively nationalistic flavor. The man to whom the Protestant movement would owe its widespread appeal was John Calvin, who gave it a manifesto, an organization, and a spiritual backbone stiffening the resolve of Scottish Presbyterians, French Huguenots, English Puritans, Scandinavian Protestants, and American Pilgrims.

Calvin was born in 1509 in Noyon, France, into a family closely aligned with the Catholic Church. His mother died when he was an infant. He was raised by his strict father and stepmother, and studied to be a lawyer. While in Paris, Calvin read some of Luther's sermons and was stunned by their audacity. Poring over the Scripture, he became convinced of its divine Authorship. Soon thereafter, he rejected his family's faith. In 1535, the twenty-six-year-old Calvin published his *Principles of the Christian Religion*, known as the *Institutio*, which he expanded throughout his life until it filled 1,118 pages. It became the most influential book of the Reformation.

Despite his thorough grounding in the classics, Calvin repudiated them and preached the centrality of the Scriptures. He wrote:

The revealed word must be our final authority, not only in religion and morality, but in history, politics, everything. We must accept the story of

Adam and Eve; for by their disobedience to God we explain man's evil nature and his loss of Free Will.[28]

He held a deeply pessimistic view of the human capacity for altruism, sharing, and friendly cooperation.

> that the mind of man is so entirely alienated from the righteousness of God that he cannot conceive, desire, or design anything but what is wicked, distorted, foul, impure, and iniquitous; that his heart is so thoroughly envenomed by sin that it can breathe out nothing but corruption and rottenness; that if some men occasionally make a show of goodness, their mind is ever interwoven with hypocrisy and deceit, their soul inwardly bound with the fetters of wickedness.[29]

Like Luther, Calvin accepted without question Augustine's concept of Original Sin, but he took the "Horrible Decree" of predestination one step further—not only was humankind restrained in its straitjacket, but so, too, was God. According to Calvin's reasoning, God knew the future in advance because He had preordained everything. Yet, hostage to His own omniscience, God was helpless to change anything. Calvin believed he knew why God exhibited so little mercy when He condemned the vast majority of souls to Hell before they were even born: it was God's way of demonstrating to puny humankind His awesome justice. Terrified and duly humbled, His creatures could do nothing for Him but offer their unquestioning faith.

Calvin dismissed as futile the efforts of those who performed good works because he believed that the drama of everyone's life had been scripted, far in advance, down to the smallest details. He exhorted the people to have faith: God had sacrificed His Son to redeem fallen humankind, and because of this act, a select few would be saved.

Calvin proscribed images of everything—including the crucifix. Nothing, he taught, should distract from the purity of reading the Word of God.[30] Women were tainted, according to Calvin, because of Eve's precipitation of the Fall; as Eve's descendants, they were to submit without complaint to the rule of their fathers and husbands. He strictly forbade devotion to Mary. With Calvin's *Principles of the Christian Religion*, we see once again the triad of no images, no goddess, and a curtailing of women's rights. *Principles* was a turgid, abstract theological tome created by a man intoxicated with the sound of his scratching pen.

Calvin gave Protestantism a hard, masculine edge. He preached draconian intolerance; anyone who refused to accept his version of God sacrifice would be denied salvation. He all but ignored Jesus' teaching that His Father was merciful and loving, and he appears to have skipped past most of the Gospels that resonate with Jesus' profound phrases. Calvin rejected Humanist concerns with earthly excellence and directed his followers to think of the afterworld. He wrote, "If heaven is our country, what is the earth but a place of exile?"[31]

Calvin introduced little that was original. He simply appropriated the harshest ideas from Judaism and Catholicism, excluded many wise, conciliatory words of the Jewish prophets, and negated all the mitigating and compensatory images, rituals, and sacraments of Catholicism. When this shredding was over, the religion that remained was dark, gothic, and forbidding. Calvin, along with other Reformation figures, stalled the Humanist movement and ended the glory of the Renaissance. He turned the clock back by several centuries with his medieval views, and he delayed the Enlightenment. Summing up his dour outlook, he wrote, "The best is not to be born, one should mourn and weep at births and rejoice at funerals."[32]

In his *Ordonnances Ecclésiastiques*, written in 1542, Calvin laid out his vision of how the new Church should be organized. His hierarchy of all-male ministers, deacons, and elders became the blueprint for the reformed churches of the Presbyterians, Puritans, and Huguenots; it is still in use today. Women played virtually no role in the upper echelons.

The most dramatic difference between Calvin and Luther was the Frenchman's rejection of the German's belief that every baptized Christian could interpret the Bible. Calvin believed that a male elite, knowledgeable concerning the Bible's "real" meaning, must lead the Protestant movement. Since the Word of God was also to be the Law of the Land, civil governments existed solely to carry out celestial law. The early Elders of Calvin's Church exercised almost absolute power over their congregants' lives. Calvin renewed the claims that Popes had advanced for the clergy's supremacy over kings, but he left vague the details of how a Protestant theocratic state would mesh the secular arm with the clerical. The world would soon have an opportunity to observe his theories in action.

In the 1520s, Catholic authorities in France were persecuting Protestants, and young Calvin's high profile made him a target. Tipped off that he was about to be arrested, he fled to Basel, Switzerland. There he met the forty-five-year-old William Farel. Acknowledging that sexual desire was a low priority, Calvin asked the older man to select a wife for him, requiring that she be "chaste, obliging, fastidious, economical, patient, and careful for my health."[33] At the age of thirty-one, he married one of Farel's choices, Idelette de Bure, an older widow with five children. She bore him a child who died in infancy, and died herself nine years later. Calvin never remarried.

Meanwhile, Calvin and Farel had gained the confidence of the elders of Geneva and had begun putting into practice Calvin's ideas regarding a theocratic state. Their reign was so harsh that the locals quickly voted to banish them. Genevans joyously celebrated their exit.[34] After several years, however, as the Reformation raged, the city elders reconsidered and invited Calvin, alone, to return. What powers they did not grant him he appropriated by the sheer force of his religious zeal. Beginning in 1541, he founded his ideal City of God, and Geneva became notorious as the most repressive police state in the history of religious movements.

Calvin ordered the Church elders to visit every household and compile dossiers on people's beliefs, practices, and private lives. Children were encouraged to spy on their parents. Everyone was ordered to attend services. No one was allowed to come late. Stern remonstrations were issued for first offenders, and those who were tardy more than three times faced banishment or death. Genevans who wished to worship in other ways were driven from the community for life.

As the elders tightened their grip, all dancing, singing (other than hymns), bells, incense, playing cards, entertainment, drunkenness, profanity or boisterous behavior (such as laughter) were proscribed. Laws regulated how many dishes (only a few) could be used at a meal and what color clothes (drab) people were allowed to wear. Gamblers were put in public stocks.[35] All children had to be given biblical names. One man was jailed for four days because he refused to name his child Abraham, choosing Claude instead.[36]

Women were harshly regimented. They were forbidden to wear lace, rouge, jewelry, or fine, colorful clothes. One woman was imprisoned for styling her hair too high.[37] Others were jailed for wearing improper hats.[38] These punishments, however, were among the trivial ones.

Fornication (sexual relations before marriage) was punishable by exile or drowning. Adultery—death; blasphemy—death; idolatry—death; sodomy—death; bestiality—death; heresy—death; witchcraft—death. Abortion was not an issue since any single woman discovered to be pregnant was summarily drowned.[39] Torture was routinely employed to extract confessions. Catholicism was declared a heresy. Anyone caught with a rosary or an image of the Virgin was hauled before a court of the elders.[40] Fourteen women were accused of consorting with the devil and bringing the plague to Geneva. All of them were convicted and burned at the stake.[41] Calvin's own stepson and his daughter-in-law were convicted of adultery in separate incidents. All four miscreants involved were executed.[42]

The obsessively kept records of the tribunals reveal that numerous illegitimate children were born, many of whom were abandoned. Unwed mothers, in fear for their lives, hid their pregnancies and then either furtively left their infants in the fields to die or placed them, at great personal risk, on the church's doorstep. Other young women undoubtedly perished attempting to abort themselves rather than face the unforgiving justice of the all-male tribunals.[43] The brutality of the regime reached its peak when the elders ordered the beheading of a child accused of striking his parents.[44]

The regime controlled the press and criticism of Calvin was punishable by death. An anonymously affixed placard attached to Calvin's lectern accused him of crimes worse than any ever perpetrated by the popes. Calvin suspected Jacque Gruet, a Humanist, and had him arrested. Though Gruet denied any knowledge of the offense and no proof was produced against him, he was tortured twice daily for thirty days until a dubious confession was extracted from him. He then was dragged to the public square, his feet nailed to a stake, and he was beheaded.[45] Calvin also ordered the death of his former friend, Michael Servetus, a renowned polymath who had discovered the secret of human pulmonary circulation. Servetus had made the mistake of criticizing Calvin publicly; he was burned at the stake.[46] Calvin justified his atrocious punishments:

> Whoever shall maintain that wrong is done to heretics and blasphemers in punishing them makes himself an accomplice in their crime. . . . There is no question here of man's authority; it is God who speaks, and it is clear what law He would have kept in the Church even to the end of the world. Wherefore does He demand of us so extreme severity if not to show us that due honor is not paid Him so long as we set not His service above every human consideration, so that we spare not kin nor blood of any, and forget all humanity when the matter is to combat for His glory?[47]

In other words, Calvin's God demanded nothing less than human sacrifice.

Calvin's intolerance of dissenters inspired Reformers in other countries. For example, Martin Bucer, one of his associates, demanded that after heretics were burned at the stake, their wives and children should also be killed, their livestock slaughtered, and their houses and barns razed.

Calvin was a workaholic who rarely took a day off or asked for a holiday. He praised hard work as a defense against the devil's schemes. An intense, brooding man, he lacked a sense of humor, saw art as an enemy, did not seem to have a sense of beauty or to care for nature, and had no sympathy or tolerance for human imperfection.

Calvin believed in class distinctions. He considered ambition and pride evil. He preached a philosophy of wealth that, in later times, would be called Communism. He banned begging and discouraged excessive charity, as he believed it weakened moral fiber. While acknowledging Calvin's immense impact, Will Durant wrote, "But we shall always find it hard to love the man who darkened the human soul with the most absurd and blasphemous conception of God in all the long and honored history of nonsense."[48]

After shilly-shallying for centuries on the issue of clerical reform, the Vatican was staggered to its knees by the force of the Reformation's blow. Just seventeen short years after Luther hammered in his nail, the inconceivable had happened. The Church had lost England, Denmark, Scotland, Sweden, Switzerland, and half of Germany to the Protestants. And France, the Netherlands, and even some parts of Italy were seething with discontent. In 1545, still recovering from the sack of Rome but galvanized at last by the prospect of extinction, the pope and his sobered cardinals finally agreed that the long-avoided clerical reform was urgently needed. The Council of Trent in 1563 declared that clerics must end their abuses of wealth and privilege. Similar exhortations had been made before, but this time they were accompanied by a new attitude of moral rectitude.

Ignatius of Loyola, a Spanish Catholic and former military officer, was the most influential figure in the reinvigoration of Catholicism, known as the Counter-Reformation. Zealous, dedicated, and politically savvy, Loyola founded the Society of Jesus in 1540, and structured it along military lines. Its head was called the General, and strict obedience to one's superior was the overriding rule. The Jesuit Order spread rapidly throughout what lands remained under Catholic hegemony. Italian Catholics were so influenced by these pious men in plain cassocks that black clothing became fashionable in the previously colorful meeting places of Rome.

Loyola convinced the pope to abruptly reverse a thousand years of Church policy. The reformer correctly intuited that the printing press had changed everything, and that spectacle, images, and rituals could not compete with printed books in holding the loyalty of the restless faithful. Fighting fire with fire, he advised the pope that Catholics immediately be taught the content of the Scriptures. It was a supreme irony that the Jesuit Order's most effective defense against the onslaught of Protestantism proved to be alphabet literacy.

The Jesuits rapidly founded and staffed first-rate schools and universities in all of Europe's intellectual centers. Providing religious education for the Catholic masses, they competed directly with secular universities by offering all prospective students (except women) a free education. The excellence of Jesuit facilities prompted Francis Bacon, a leading Protestant intellectual, to remark almost wistfully, "Such as they are, would that they were ours."[49]

Along with the standard fare taught in most secular universities, the Jesuits included in their curriculum readings that Loyola and his successors believed essential to combating Protestant preachers: Paul's Epistle to the Romans, Augustine's doctrines, and the works of Thomas Aquinas. They ignored Catholicism's strong tradition of mysticism, and sought to win souls instead through logic and the written word. Like Luther and Calvin, Loyola believed in the infallibility of the Bible.

So, in the end, the Catholics came around to the Protestant position that studying Scripture would reform the religion. Calvin, likewise, endorsed the Catholic views concerning the hegemony of the theocratic state and that only religious leaders could interpret the Bible. There were so many doctrinal similarities in the Protestant Reformation and the Catholic Counter-Reformation that it was difficult for an unbiased observer to understand why the two groups despised each other so. But the two camps were too busy flailing about in the perceptual backwash left by the tidal wave of press-generated alphabet literacy to notice their commonalities.

Though its leaders proclaimed the primacy of the Scriptures, the Reformation so contradicted the spirit of the Scriptures that some other factor must have been at work. It is not mere coincidence that Luther and Calvin were both prolific writers. Predestination has mesmerized *only* the alphabet literate. It has not been a belief of any non-alphabetic society. The archaic Greeks' notion of fate depended on the capricious whims of the gods. Yahweh expected each individual to choose correctly between right and wrong. A Hindu or a Buddhist's karma can be influenced in future reincarnations by personal decisions made in this one. Lao-tzu's concept of the Tao is the antithesis of predestination.

The left brain is the seat of logical thought processes. That one thing follows another forms the basis of linear cause-and-effect thinking. The practice of alphabetic reading and writing over long periods will subliminally reinforce the user's belief that the world is a chain-linked tessellation of events that occur in linear time. Cultures that experience a sudden rise in alphabet literacy will collectively embrace the concept of predestination.

Mysticism is primarily associated with right-brain processes. A creed that extols predestination tends to denigrate right-brain values. Mysticism had *no* role in the early Protestant Reformation; both Luther and Calvin depended wholly on the persuasiveness of their carefully composed inked syllogisms. All founders urged their followers to have "faith," but the underpinnings of Protestantism were actually written, torturously logical constructions that were presented in long, dense, imageless tomes.

Calvin's influence was greater than Luther's. His teachings converted millions and forged what would later be called the Protestant Ethic: a personal and social order based on simplicity, modesty, hard work, self-reliance, moral rectitude, and an abiding faith in the majesty of the Lord—and in the incorruptibility of words written in books fourteen hundred years earlier by, for the most part, unknown authors. In every European country martyrs came forward clutching Bibles, eager to fight and die for Calvin's vision. And die they did. The religious convulsion that wracked Europe was one of the morbid factors that have shaped modern Western culture. The Catholic versus Protestant wars that still smolder in Ireland remain as one example of the Reformation's legacy.

The values that typify the right brain include empathy with the plight of one's companions, generosity toward strangers, tolerance of dissent, love of nature, nurturance of children, laughter, playfulness, mysticism, forgiveness of enemies and nonviolence. These aspects, in both men and women, express the feminine gatherer/nurturer side of human nature.

In contrast, people tend to exhibit left-brain attributes when absorbed in work, goals, focus, power, and money. Cruelty, argument, violence, a disregard for nature, and lack of concern for the lame and the halt round out the list—in short, all those attributes that tend to make a man or woman a successful hunter/killer. The Gospels that contain the words of Jesus Christ *overwhelmingly* accentuate the values of the right brain. There is not a single incident in which Jesus or His Apostles ever murdered, banished, burned, or imprisoned anyone. Why did the leaders of the Reformation, whose tocsin sounded a return to the Book, so ignore the teachings of the very book they passionately defended as the Revealed Truth?

Part of the answer may lie in the backgrounds of the movement's two most influential figures, Luther and Calvin. Luther reported that his father was a choleric peasant who thrashed his young son with such regularity that Luther came to hate him, and, by his own account, entered the monastery to escape from him. His mother was similarly disposed and, in one episode he recounted, beat him almost senseless because he stole a nut. Alone in his cell in the monastery, Luther routinely flagellated himself.[50]

In modern psychological terms, Luther was an abused child. His maltreatment made him extremely sensitive to injustice and undoubtedly forged the defiant personality that served him well in his standoff with the pope and the emperor. A theology based on retribution and damnation is what one would expect from someone who, as a small child, cowered in fear.

John Calvin was a very private person known for his cool, intellectual reserve. Unlike Luther, he was not forthcoming about his childhood, but historians know that his mother died when he was young. A small child's loss of a loving mother is a wound that never quite heals. His rejection of feminine values and his lack of compassion for sinners was so complete, one wonders if her death was not the key force that shaped him.

The childhoods of Calvin and Luther might shed light on their dark views of human nature, but it does not explain why so many others embraced a religion of fear and trembling. Nor does it explain why the Reformation had no figures like Frances of Assisi, Hildegard, Abélard, Catherine of Siena, Meister Eckhart, Joan of Arc, or Jakob Böhme, or why there was not a single important female Protestant Reformer. The men who surrounded Luther and Calvin were, for the most part, very severe and dictatorial. Collectively, they instituted a very harsh patriarchy. Women were almost nonexistent in the organization and in the conduct of the new Protestant Church. Calvin explicitly prohibited women from baptizing.

What was sorely lacking in the Protestant Reformation was joy, love, mercy, laughter, and beauty. The Age of Chivalry in the eighth century, the devotion to Mary in the ninth, the mysticism of the tenth, the curiosity of the eleventh, the open-mindedness of the twelfth, the lustiness of the thirteenth, the individual ingenuity of the fourteenth, and the Humanism of the fifteenth stand in stark contrast to the sixteenth century's grim doctrine of abject helplessness.

Why did millions of people rush to embrace an immensely dour doctrine? Why did thousands willingly die for it? Why did it capture the imagination of people who had just glimpsed new human capabilities in the false dawn of the Renaissance? The Reformation was supposed to be a liberation movement bent on overthrowing a perceived tyranny. Why, then, did the Protestants eagerly slip into manacles that had predestination engraved on them? If the longing to be free was so strong, why would they embrace a belief that held that the vast majority of God-fearing people were damned in advance, and that nothing they could do would change their sentence? And why did this dogma of futility produce so many strong personalities?

The Protestant Reformation was not a worldwide phenomenon. It only occurred in western European societies, and *only* in those cultures transformed by the art of printing. The Protestant Reformation was clearly not a return to the *content* of the New Testament; but, I submit, a wrenching sociological shift wrought by a new information technology dependent on users being alphabet-literate. This, in turn, changed the collective perception of culture. The printing press made the Reformation's rigid and repressive self-discipline possible.

CHAPTER 31

ҒAITH/HATE

To so many evils has religion persuaded men.   —Lucretius[1]

The Reformers banned . . . the cult of the Virgin Mary and the saints,
and so took these images away. Christianity became more of a male
world than ever. Not only did it deprive the Christian imagination of
powerful images and myths and thus made it a cerebral, emotionally
impoverished and narrowly masculine affair, on a more basic level the
only important people and "gods" now were all men.

—Karen Armstrong[2]

A "reign of terror" is the systematic persecution of one group by
another using sadistic and violent means, with the purpose of either
exterminating the targeted group or intimidating it into submission. So far as we know, there had never been a known reign of terror based
on differing religious beliefs until the appearance of sacred, alphabetic texts.
Prior to the fifteenth century, a historian can cite only a handful of examples
of religious reigns of terror: the Roman persecutions of Christians, sporadic
Christian attacks on Jews, and the Albigensian Crusade that the Vatican
waged against the Cathars.* Then, suddenly, violent religious persecution
erupted all over Europe and reached as far as the colonies in the New World.
These religious conflagrations ignited in the late 1400s and raged for 150
years. After consuming people, resources, and wealth, they burned themselves out in all but a few cases. Historians tend to lump these reigns of terror together, calling them the "religious wars."

---

*The Christian Crusades to win back the Holy Land and the Moslem zeal to erad-
icate Hinduism in India were driven primarily by territorial aspirations.

Few plausible explanations have emerged as to why this constellation of persecutions should have clustered in the same cultures that gave us the Renaissance, the birth of science, global explorations, and many other pivotal events. Most have ascribed the phenomenon to the unsettling times that accompanied the Reformation, but this explanation is inadequate. Judaism, Christianity, and Islam had been in existence for many centuries, and quite a few of those centuries were filled with dread and angst, yet religious persecutions did not dominate. Buddhism challenged Hinduism in India, Confucianism eclipsed Taoism in China, and Zen superseded Shintoism in Japan, but none of these revolutions was accompanied by a reign of terror. I propose that the sixteenth century European nightmare was brought on by Gutenberg's press and the widespread literacy that resulted from it. Before we examine the root causes of those times of terror, let us first grasp the enormity of the evil committed in the name of faith. The following montage of events, not presented in chronological order, will suffice.

The Anabaptists were one of the first Protestant denominations to emerge from the early years of the Reformation. The movement was born among the peasants of southern, German-speaking lands and they dedicated themselves to the precepts of Jesus. Their name derived from their belief that infant baptism was meaningless, as the individual so blessed was too young to have any memory of the event. The Anabaptists—or *again*-Baptists— held that only a mature adult could comprehend the enormous implications in deciding "to live in Christ." Once inducted by submersion, Anabaptists pledged to live by the teachings of Jesus. They advocated religious tolerance, pacifism, and nonviolence. Although they were monogamous, they brought up their children in common. They avoided politics, finance, commerce, and litigation, preferring self-sustaining agricultural communities in which each member was "their brother's keeper." They tithed a portion of their wealth to the community and shared tools, labor, and land. Their disregard for private property raised the eyebrows of the nobility, who, as absentee landlords, suspected that the Anabaptists posed a threat to the social structure based on hereditary land ownership.

Instead of applauding these gentle Protestants as true Christians, the Reformation's leaders sided with the landed gentry and denounced them. The clergy who attended the Diet of Speyer in 1529, for example, passed a resolution ordering that Anabaptists should be killed on the spot like wild beasts wherever they were captured, because their heresy was too heinous to merit trials.[3] Early on, when Luther himself was in physical danger, he had advocated leniency for the Anabaptists. As their movement continued to spread and began to challenge his own, however, he reversed himself and urged the princes to kill them. He justified this new position by claiming that anyone who refused to perform infant baptism committed blasphemy against God. But it was politically expedient on his part—he was anxious to retain the support of the princes in his own fight against the Church. Luther's position was untenable. He had begun his own challenge to Catholicism with the demand that anything relating to Christianity not specifically described in the Scriptures be jettisoned. Neither Testament mentions infant baptism.

Despite Calvin's sympathies with their communist ideals he, too, condemned the Anabaptists to death.[4] Martin Bucer, Calvin's lieutenant, called Anabaptists "worse than murderers" and urged the authorities to kill every Anabaptist man, woman, and child.[5] Among the Catholic hierarchy, Humanists such as Erasmus considered these industrious tillers as having strayed from the flock, and recommended leniency. But the papacy saw them as heretics and ordered the secular authorities to deal with them harshly. There were a few temperate aristocrats who welcomed them to their lands, recognizing that they were conscientious farmers who caused little trouble. But in 1528, the Holy Roman Emperor Charles V decreed that the practice of adult baptism was a capital offense.

As a result of this hysteria, the baying against Anabaptists rose ever shriller. One Anabaptist chronicler reported:

> Some were racked and drawn asunder; others were burnt to ashes and dust; some were roasted on pillars.... Others were hanged on trees, beheaded with the sword.... Some starved or rotted in darksome prisons.... Some who were deemed too young for execution were whipped with rods and many lay for years in dungeons.... Numbers had holes burnt into their cheeks.... The rest were hunted from one country and place to another. Like owls and ravens, which durst not fly by day, they were often compelled to hide and live in rocks and clefts, in wild forests, or in caves and pits.[6]

Despite these persecutions, the tenacious Anabaptists continued to found communities in the Netherlands, England, and Germany. The Amish, Quakers, and Mennonites trace their roots back to the Anabaptists.

The New Testament was a revelation for peasants. They read how Jesus sided with the poor and prophesied that they would inherit the earth. Many Germans interpreted Luther's repudiation of the Church as a call for social reform. They transformed the Bible into a revolutionary manual and they hailed Luther as the champion of their cause. At the start of the Reformation, the Church owned more than one-third of all the land in Germany; the nobility and a few wealthy families owned the remainder. The Peasants' War (1524–26) was an uprising of workers and farmers against a social structure that kept them impoverished. All over Germany, peasants and workers armed with pikes and pitchforks marched on cathedrals and castles to confront clergy and princes. By the end of 1524, thirty thousand peasants were refusing to pay taxes.

Tyrannical princes were deposed. One, Count Ludwig von Helfenstein, was especially hated for his cruel treatment of his serfs. The rebels forced him and his retainers to walk a gauntlet of his subjects who were armed with clubs and daggers. As the count staggered past, they hurled long-pent-up epithets while prodding him along: "You thrust my brother in a dungeon because he did not bare his head as you passed by;" "You cut off the hands of my father because he killed a hare in his own field;" "Your horses, dogs, and huntsmen trod down my crops." The count died of his wounds.[7]

The revolt spread like a hay fire. "Nowhere," says a cleric's letter of 1525, "do the insurgents make a secret of their intention to kill all the clerics who do not break with the Church."[8] Luther, frightened by this release of anarchy and aware that his Reformation was being blamed for it, threw his support to the princes. In 1525, he published a pamphlet entitled *Against the Robbing and Murdering Hordes of Peasants.* Although Luther cast himself as just a peasant, he had little sympathy for the plight of real peasants. He contemptuously called them *Herr Omnes*—Mr. Crowd.

> Let everyone who can, smite, slay, and stab, secretly or openly . . . nothing can be more poisonous, hurtful, or devilish than a rebel. It is just as one must kill a mad dog; if you do not strike him he will strike you.[9]

The inflammatory pamphlet went into circulation just as the secular and clerical forces had recovered from the first shock wave of peasant attacks.

The peasants, forced to retreat, turned their fury on the Reformation, calling Luther "Dr. Lügner"—Dr. Liar—and "toady of the princes."[10] Luther became so hated that he dared not venture forth from Wittenberg. "All is forgotten that God hath done for the world through me," he anguished. "Now lords, priests, and peasants are all against me and threaten my life."[11] Never one to back down, he continued to attack the peasants. "My opinion is that it is better that all peasants be killed than that the princes and magistrates perish, because the rustics took the sword without divine authority." Further exacerbating the peasant's antipathy toward him, he continued:

> If they think this answer is too hard, and that this is talking violence and only shutting men's mouths, I reply that this is right. The answer for such a mouth is a fist that brings blood from the nose. The peasants will not listen . . . their ears must be unbuttoned with bullets till their heads jump off their shoulders. Such pupils need such a rod. He who will not hear God's Word when it is spoken with kindness must listen to the headsman when he comes with his axe . . . Of mercy I will neither hear nor know anything, but give heed to God's will in His word. . . . If He will have wrath and not mercy, what have you to do with mercy?[12]

The destruction of life and property in Germany during the peasant wars was staggering. Some 130,000 died in battle or after surrender; 10,000 of these were publicly executed. As the retaliations continued, one fretful noble warned, "If the rebels are all killed, where shall we get peasants to provide for us?"[13] Hundreds of monasteries, churches, and castles were burned to the ground, and innumerable works of art desecrated or destroyed. Peasant homes were razed, leaving more than 50,000 homeless people hiding in the forests and mountains. Widows and orphans lined the roads, but little charity was forthcoming from any quarter. Despite having recently read the New Testament for the first time, many people on both sides behaved in a manner antithetical to the spirit of the Gospels.

But the horrors of the Anabaptist persecutions and the peasant wars were mere gasps compared to the death rattle of Germany's Thirty Years' War (1618–48), which began with Lutherans and Calvinists killing each other over hair-splitting doctrinal disputes. Then Protestants and Catholics faced off in a deadly thirty-year struggle. Over one-third of Germany's population perished in this senseless carnage, and the destruction of the country's economic base was so extensive that a full recovery was not achieved until the next century.

Since the time of the Roman Empire, Spain had been an erudite, civilized Catholic society. A deeply spiritual people, the Spaniards were early converts to Christianity, and they prospered, protected by their mountains and by the beneficence of their climate. By the time of the Renaissance, Spain's navy was the envy of Europe, and her continental army consistently influenced events in other European countries. Because of Spain's proximity to northern

Africa, it was host to a large Moorish enclave of industrious Muslims. In addition, many Jews had settled in Spain and over the centuries had built a Sephardic community considered by other Diaspora Jews to be their spiritual and intellectual center. In Spain, Jewish ministers, financiers, and physicians rose to positions of prominence. The tolerant attitudes that, for the most part, had prevailed in Spain in earlier times had already persuaded large numbers of Jews to convert to Catholicism. Many of these *conversos* then achieved distinction in the government and Church. Catholic landowners remained firmly in control of the aristocracy.

In the 1470s, German printers set up shop in Spain with the able assistance of Spanish apprentices. Printed material proliferated as literacy rates soared. In 1476, Pope Sixtus IV granted King Ferdinand and Queen Isabella permission to establish their own Inquisitorial office answerable only to themselves. This was an ominous development. The Inquisition had been tightly leashed by papal authorities in the preceding century. Few heretics had been burned during the Hundred Years' War or in the Plague years; by the beginning of the Renaissance, the office had become nearly inactive.

Ferdinand and Isabella appointed an especially cruel Dominican friar, Torquemada, to be Chief Inquisitor in 1483. He expanded a preexisting campaign of innuendo and lies aimed at convincing the king and queen that the *conversos* posed a serious threat to the throne, arguing that they still secretly practiced their Hebrew faith and were traitors who planned to usurp power. On his instructions, priests inflamed the Spanish population against the *conversos*, calling them *marranos*—swine.*

In an era when peace, security, and prosperity burnished the Spanish landscape, the throne experienced a paroxysm of paranoia and concluded that Torquemada was right. They ordered agents of the Inquisition to investigate all deviations from the Catholic faith, unleashing a Spanish reign of terror. Widening his mandate, Torquemada swept up in his dragnet anyone who protested his methods or behaved in a manner he thought seditious.

The Inquisition's tribunal met behind closed doors to hear accusations that they had solicited. On the basis of these sessions they arrested victims and charged them with heresy, that convenient catchall crime against God. The defendants, who were often held incommunicado languishing in rat-infested prisons, were eventually brought to trials that were conducted in secret. The defendants had to swear never to reveal the proceedings. The accused did not know the identity of their accusers or the exact nature of the

---

*Genealogical records indicate that Torquemada was himself a *marrano* (as were many other high officials of the Inquisition).

charges. Judged guilty before their Kafka-esque trials, they were burdened with having to prove their innocence.

Torture was routinely used to exact confessions. To make it appear respectable, it could only be applied in the presence of a court-appointed physician, a notary, and members of the Inquisitorial board. Few prisoners, including women, were exempt. Girls as young as thirteen and women in their eighties were subjected to the rack and *strappado.** One inquisitor, apparently offended by the idea of Church-sanctioned torture of a pregnant woman, recommended, "We must wait until she is delivered of her child," but agreed that the torturemaster could bring the postpartum mother to the chamber immediately thereafter.[14]

Once confessions were wrung from the accused, most were sentenced to die by burning. The Church confiscated their possessions, and 20 to 50 percent of the take was given as a bounty to the anonymous accuser; the rest was divided between the Church and the crown. Creative accusers began to point fingers at the dead. Claiming that a prominent dead person had secretly been a heretic obviated the need for a prolonged trial, and if they were found guilty (most were), their bequests could be appropriated.

Although Madrid was its headquarters, the Inquisition was essentially a traveling roadshow. Some towns attempted to lock their gates, but the Inquisition had the weight of the State behind it. Those who obstructed its proceedings were themselves deemed heretical and dealt with accordingly.

Upon the conclusion of the trials, the sentenced awaited their fate in dank dungeons. To impress the locals, the Inquisition then arranged what was euphemistically called an *auto-da-fé* (an act of faith), staged with great pomp and circumstance. Elevated viewing stands were erected for Inquisitors and honored guests while the public crowded around the square. Absence was viewed as evidence of sympathy for the accused; attendance, therefore, was high. The victims were led out in a chained coffle. Boxes containing the exhumed bones of heretics punctuated the dolorous van and heightened the eeriness of the scene. These were destined for burning along with the living, who were fastened to waiting stakes. An elaborate religious ceremony followed. Finally, the fires were lit. After a short time, the screams of the victims faded and the glowing embers were banked. The shaken locals returned to their shuttered homes to contemplate the danger of making a careless remark in front of a child or to a close friend. The psychological

---

Strappado victims were hoisted by their wrists, which had been tied together behind their backs, by a pulley. Weights were added to their ankles. They would then be dropped from a height in short jerks, resulting in the dislocation of their shoulders.

repression was deadening. The Inquisitors, for whom this was just another performance, yawned and went off to dinner. *Autos-da-fé* flared all over Spain. They had no parallel in history—human sacrifice had never before been practiced on such a large scale in such an allegedly civilized society.

Juan Antonio Llorente, a general secretary of the Inquisition from 1789 to 1801, estimated that beginning in 1480, forty thousand heretics had been burned at the stake and another four hundred thousand had suffered "heavy penance." Some historians claim his figures are exaggerated, but there can be no dispute that in the years immediately following the introduction of the printing press, Spain was seized by fiery madness.

In an irony not lost on either Jews or Catholics, the segment of the Jewish community that had been singled out for punishment consisted only of those who had been baptized. For those who remained loyal to the faith of Abraham, their turn was next.

Torquemada insisted that all Jews be expelled from Spain. Goaded by the prospect of appropriating Jewish wealth, Ferdinand and Isabella agreed to this "ethnic cleansing." The king and queen signed the Edict of Exile on March 30, 1492, banishing permanently all unbaptized Jews. They had ninety days to leave the country. Anyone who remained faced death. Jews who had worked in often-adverse conditions to build a proud community over centuries saw their efforts melt away in days. Many eager Spanish Catholics, taking advantage of the Jews' duress, exploited their former neighbors: a house, for example, could be purchased for a donkey. Pirates, tipped off in advance, set upon the emigrant ships and sold their human spoils to slavers. With the exception of Italy and Portugal, the ports of European countries refused entry to the ships of the exodus. Many Jews died at sea from disease, starvation, and shipwreck. It was a lamentable chapter in Jewish history and an infamous one in Spain's. One ship sailing from Spain that same year, not part of the exodus, was captained by Christopher Columbus, who would bring Spain wondrous wealth appropriated from the New World. Adding an ironic arabesque to the whole episode is the mounting evidence that he was of Jewish ancestry.

After expelling the Jews, Ferdinand and Isabella turned on the *Moriscos,* Muslims who had converted to Catholicism. The Muslim community protested, claiming that when they ruled Spain, Christians enjoyed religious freedom, but the Crown ignored them. When the Inquisition ran out of *Moriscos* to torture and burn, they went after the 3,000,000 Spanish Moors. Ferdinand issued an edict expelling them. On February 12, 1502, all Muslims were given until April 30 to leave the country. Mandating a vast exodus in so short a time guaranteed panic and untold hardship. Cardinal Richelieu of France called the forced exile of the Moors "the most barbarous edict in history." Friar Bleda, a prominent Spanish cleric, thought it "the most glorious event in Spain since the time of the Apostles."[15]

Columbus's serendipitous discovery of a "New World" sandwiched between Asia and Europe was a momentous event. An entire hemisphere, isolated by two oceans, had escaped the influences of the rest of the world, and it contained an exotic diversity of religions, languages, and wisdom. Many of its cultures were still in the hunter/gatherer stage of evolution, but quite a few had adopted agriculture and husbandry.

The Iroquois Nation, in the northeastern North American continent, encompassed thousands of smaller social units spread over millions of square miles. Their system of government was so advanced that Benjamin Franklin recommended that many of their provisions be incorporated into the American Constitution.[16] At the southern end of the landmass, Inca architects had mastered complex engineering problems that continue to stymie present-day experts. The glyphs discovered among the Mayans' formidable ruins attest to their cultural sophistication, and the Aztecs' astronomical tables contain some highly advanced mathematics. Several New World cultures (Aztecs, Mayans, and Incas) had developed forms of writing, and not unexpectedly, these were the most patriarchal cultures. In general, the non-literate agrarian societies manifested a high degree of gender equality. Among North American Plains Indians, the election of chiefs in some tribes was the exclusive responsibility of the mature women. Wise women were honored, and virtually all of the native cultures worshiped some version of the Great Mother. A deep reverence for nature and an abiding belief that all things both animate and inanimate were interconnected undergirded their beliefs.

Initial contacts between Europeans and the first Americans were for the most part friendly. The various peoples of the New World had much to teach the explorers who landed on their shores. But engulfed in a haze of alphabet-generated, monotheistic dementia, the Europeans categorized their reunited brothers and sisters as subhuman savages, largely because they were not Christians. (Meanwhile, the "civilized" Europeans back home were busy hacking and broiling each other in a frenzy of unparalleled savagery.) What followed was genocide on a scale unprecedented in world history. More than 80 million people are estimated to have been living on the southern and northern continents of the Americas in 1492; within three hundred years, the "explorers," "conquistadors," "colonists," "settlers," and "pioneers"—exterminated the majority of the native population: their current number is approximately 10 million.[17]

Most natives died from such Old World diseases as measles and smallpox, but large numbers were enslaved and worked or beaten to death on plantations or in the insane pursuit of shiny metals. Native resistance to European control was dealt with harshly. For minor infractions, men had their penises, hands and/or feet amputated in public; women's breasts were cut away. One priest noted that the native men stayed away from their wives, lest women become pregnant and supply another generation of slaves to the white devils. Life was so cruel under Spanish rule that thousands of American Indians committed suicide.[18] The Europeans treated Native American women and the pristine New World landscape as wild enemies to be subdued and conquered; the rape of both was commonplace.

Smug in their certainty that there was nothing to be learned from the indigenous population, the Europeans set about destroying every vestige of these cultures, so different from their own. Priests thought only of "saving" the heathen by conversion. Following closely on the heels of the invaders, missionaries began to teach the natives the alphabet to enable them to read the sacred Christian book.

Montaigne, the French Humanist, composed his essay "Of Cannibals" after reading reports of the New World. "I find nothing in that nation [Indian America] that is either barbarous or savage, unless we call barbarism that which is not common among themselves." Eating dead people, Montaigne asserted, was less barbarous than torturing live ones. He noted that natives were rarely sick, nearly always happy and content, and lived peaceably without laws. He indignantly condemned his fellow colonizers:

> So many goodly cities ransacked and razed; so many nations destroyed or made desolate; so many infinite millions of harmless people of all sexes, status and ages massacred, ravaged, and put to the sword; and the richest, the fairest, the best part of the world topsy-turvied, ruined, and defaced for the traffic of pearls and peppers! Oh mechanical victories, oh, base conquest![19]

Had the discovery and invasion of the New World been undertaken by a culture *other* than sixteenth-century Europeans driven mad by the printing press, a different scenario might have ensued. In the fourth century B.C., Alexander the Great made peace treaties with Dravidian tribes in India and Scythians in Thrace; people that were as exotic as any he would have encountered in the Americas. Unencumbered by the intolerance that comes with alphabet monotheism, Alexander did not feel compelled to eradicate the local religions and enslave the native populations. If Julius Caesar had discovered the New World, would he have destroyed the local population, stolen their lands, and rooted out their culture? Likely not. This wise pagan would have forged alliances, fostered trade, and treated the people he conquered with respect. Since this was his policy toward the blue-painted Celts and Picts he encountered in northern Europe, there is no reason to suspect he would have treated befeathered American Indians differently. Why was there not a single European with Herodotus's foresight and uncensored curiosity to chronicle the New World's extraordinary cultural riches?

The ethnic atrocities that Caucasians perpetrated originated in a European culture that carried a gun in one hand and an alphabetic book in the other. The supreme irony was that the *content* of the book taught a doctrine diametrically opposed to the book owner's behavior. The paradox is that Europeans were too blinded by the *process* of literacy to notice the disparity.

When eighteen-year-old Henry VIII ascended England's throne in 1509, he showed the promise of what a great king could be. He was pious, handsome, athletic, musical, and scholarly; his subjects adored him. Sir Thomas More, his closest friend and adviser, wrote, "He has more learning than any English monarch ever possessed before him."[20] Henry married Catherine of Aragon, six years his senior, and together they labored to produce a son. After several stillborns, Catherine delivered a girl they christened Mary. At the age of two, the child was betrothed to the dauphin of France. More stillborns followed. Henry (and his subjects) grew increasingly anxious: without a male heir, his throne would pass through marriage to the King of France, and England would come under the rule of its archenemy.

At the time, the English Catholic Church had grown immensely rich and powerful. Archbishop John Colet, in a 1512 address—five scant years before Luther's challenge—urged an assembly of churchmen to "Consider the reformation of ecclesiastical affairs; for never was it so necessary. . . . For the Church—the spouse of Christ—which He wished to be without a spot or wrinkle, is become foul and deformed."[21] His was not a novel request. Calls for reform had been bandied about in England as early as 1340.

Reform efforts in England sputtered along until a little-heralded but auspicious event. William Caxton brought the printing press to England in 1476. Soon thereafter, religious tracts began to multiply. The circulation of a New Testament translated into English for the first time by William Tyndale in 1525 further abetted a growing protest movement. Precursor to the majestic King James Version, Tyndale's New Testament gave English speakers their first glimpse of the book that until then few could read.*

The Reformation came to England in the form of pamphlets of Luther's translated sermons. A devout Catholic, Henry was so offended by Luther's stance against his church that he felt compelled to refute it personally. "What serpent so venomous," wrote the future rebel king, "as he who calls the pope's authority tyrannous? . . . What a great limb of the Devil he is, endeavoring to tear the Christian members of Christ from their head!"[22] Luther, no shrinking violet, responded by calling Henry a "lubberly ass . . . that frantic madman . . . that King of lies, King Heinz by God's disgrace King of England. . . . it is right for me to bespatter this English monarch with his own filth."[†23]

But Henry's attitude began to change when it became apparent that his gentle, loyal Catherine was not going to produce a royal son. Although the Church forbade divorce, Henry expected that his regal standing would procure the necessary papal dispensation. In anticipation of his expected freedom, he took as his mistress the captivating seventeen-year-old Anne Boleyn. He did not foresee the opposition his plan generated. Powerful enemies in France and Spain advised Pope Clement VII to deny Henry's petition.

The situation became especially urgent when Anne informed her king that she was pregnant. Henry's advisers proposed a solution to his predicament—one that would serve the interests of the Reformation. If Henry were to excommunicate the entire Catholic Church and replace it with a national one, with himself at its head, he could then dissolve his loveless marriage and legitimize the heir now stirring in Anne's belly. Another beneficial outcome: the Crown could confiscate all the Church lands in England.

In 1532, Henry broke with the Vatican and established the Church of England by decree. He chose the iron-willed bishop Thomas Cranmer to oversee the new Acts of Succession, which legitimized by fiat his divorce from Catherine and his marriage to Anne. Many of the faithful were appalled that a secular being could be so brazen as to think that with a stroke of his pen he could fell an institution whose roots in Britain had been planted in the Dark Ages. Henry banned Catholicism and ordered every subject to swear an oath of fealty to him as the head of the new Anglican Church. Cranmer closed English monasteries, expelled their occupants, and appropriated their lands; Henry distributed them to loyal nobles. The peas-

---

*Tyndale was burned at the stake in 1536 for heresy.

†The German word *schiez* means feces. Luther used it liberally in his curses. Here it is translated as "filth."

antry, especially in the north and in smaller villages, was angered at such a ruthless manipulation of their religion by a king in heat, and they seethed with resentment. The Catholic regents of France and Spain called for an invasion in support of the hard-pressed English Catholics.

To maintain control in the face of such diverse opposition, Henry loosed a reign of terror. He founded his own version of the Inquisition, complete with rack and brazier. The dreaded Court of the Star Chamber persecuted anyone who opposed the Acts of Succession. A group of Carthusian monks who refused to swear the Anglican oath were disemboweled and dismembered while still alive. Segments of their body parts were hung above the gate of their monastery to convince the others to sign. Many did not and suffered the same fate.[24] Sir Thomas More, scholarly Humanist, best friend of Erasmus, and the most respected man in England, refused to sign because he foresaw that anarchy would replace the Church. Henry ordered his former boyhood friend to the Tower, and when the former prime minister remained obstinate before the Star Chamber, Henry ordered More beheaded. His execution shocked the nation.

Anne Boleyn, having failed to give Henry his much sought-after male heir, was next. Jane Seymour, another court beauty, had already attracted Henry's fancy. Henry accused his young queen of infidelity. Anne was arrested, confined to the Tower, and tried on what most scholars consider to have been trumped-up charges. She was beheaded at the age of nineteen.

There was not only conflict between Catholics and Anglicans, but also an increasingly loud chorus of denunciations from Puritans and Presbyterians, who felt Henry's new creed was much too similar to the Vatican's for their liking. English Protestantism was on the rise, fueled by the circulation of Tyndale's Bibles. Adopting Calvin's hostility to images and goddesses, the Presbyterians and Puritans demanded that the new Church of England divest itself of its imagery and devotion to Mary. In addition, so many commoners came forward spouting their own idiosyncratic interpretations of Jesus' word that a chaos of creeds threatened to further fragment an England already rent by religious fractiousness. In 1530, Henry decreed that no one other than Anglican priests could possess a Bible.

When Henry died in 1547 at age fifty-five, his six serial wives had yielded but one male heir: the sickly Edward VI. Six years later, Mary, the daughter of Catherine and Henry, ascended the throne. A devout Catholic, Queen Mary reversed the Acts of Succession. Confiscated lands were confiscated from their confiscators. Exiles rushed to return home. Seeing an opportunity to regain England, the papacy poured money and agents into this volatile mixture. Mary instituted a Catholic reign of terror. So many Anglicans, Presbyterians, and Puritans were executed for having supported Henry against the papacy that his daughter earned the sobriquet "Bloody Mary." The changeover from Protestant to Catholic regents ensured that turmoil would continue to reign in the realm.

By the time Elizabeth, Anne Boleyn's only child, was crowned in 1558, England was exhausted from these eruptions of religious fanaticism belching forth from all sides. The young queen ushered in a reign of much needed peace and prosperity. "Merrie Olde England" attended the plays of Shakespeare, defeated the Spanish Armada, and colonized the New World. It seemed as if religion had burned itself out as a divisive issue.

But like a peat bog fire that smolders under the surface, religious strife flared up again. The forces of King Charles I, who aligned himself with those who yearned to reinstate the Roman Church, opposed the Puritans and Presbyterians, who objected to the Anglican Church's retention of imagery and devotion to Mary. Full-scale war between Catholics and Protestants erupted in 1642. The heirs of the culture that had originated the Chivalric Code committed unspeakable atrocities in the name of Christ. Prisoners were tortured to death. Civilian women were raped as punishment for their husbands' heresies, and children were killed indiscriminately. Puritans beheaded Jesuits. Anglicans killed Presbyterians. Catholic Scots and Irish razed and pillaged Protestant settlements. All factions murdered Anabaptists. Puritans, Anglicans, Presbyterians, and Catholics seemed to share one grotesque belief in common—their God demanded human sacrifice.

King Charles was eventually taken prisoner after being defeated on the field. He was put on trial and convicted of "treason to God's cause." Fifty-nine Puritan judges, including their leader, Oliver Cromwell, signed the king's death sentence. In 1649, Charles ascended the stairs to the block and his head was severed with one blow. "There was such a groan by the thousands present," wrote one eyewitness, "as I never heard before and desire to never hear again."[25] Historians call this English bloodbath a "civil" war, but in truth, it was a religious reign of terror.

The rapid rise in literacy rates wrought by the printing press was a boon to European science, literature, poetry, and philosophy. And yet it seemed no country could escape the terrible religious upheaval that inevitably followed the march of the metal letters. France was no exception. Soon after the first printing presses arrived in the 1470s, Luther's sermons were put to press, and the Reformation took hold in France's intellectual centers. The cautious peasantry, however, remained staunchly Catholic, finding in the whitewashed churches and stern predestination of Calvinism a pallid substitute for the comforting forms and festivals of the older faith. In 1535 King Francis I ordered his ministers to suppress the growing heresy. Protestants, called Huguenots in French, were arrested in droves in Catholic strongholds. The king's prosecutors demanded death so often, both for heretics themselves and for anyone failing to report a Huguenot to the authorities, that his court chamber became known the "Burning Room." In spite of the represssion, the Huguenot movement grew steadily.

Protestants had enclaves in every major province and were especially well represented in the old Cathar stronghold in the southwest. And although economic and political factors played a role leading to the standoff between the two opposing branches of Christianity, it was at heart an ideological struggle; many nobles and former Catholic clerics went over to the Huguenots for purely doctrinal reasons.

After King Henry II died in 1559, Catherine de Médicis became the power behind the throne, as her son, King Charles IX, was too young to rule. The Queen Mother, a nominal Catholic, was an heir of the Italian Humanist house of Médici. Influenced more by the Renaissance than by religion, she counseled tolerance and reconciliation. Despite her efforts, murderous rancor between Catholics and Protestants persisted. In one incident, the Catholic Duke of Guise stopped with his retinue to hear mass in Vassy. When the psalm singing of a nearby Huguenot assembly disturbed the Catholic ceremony, the duke's agents ordered the Protestants to stop the music. Words were exchanged, swords were drawn, and when it was over, the Massacre of Vassy had claimed the lives of hundreds of men, women, and children. The Huguenots sought to avenge the slaughter and plotted to assassinate the perpetrators, but their plans were discovered at Amboise. The cardinal, a Guise, called in the royal troops. He was determined to set an example to discourage further sedition. "For a whole month," one chronicler wrote, "there was nothing but hanging and drowning folks." To accelerate the killing, groups of people were condemned at a time, stuffed en masse into large sacks and thrown into the Loire River. The river downstream was littered with corpses.[26]

Appalled by the growing fury, Catherine appointed a conciliatory chancellor in 1570. Michel de L'Hôpital opened Parliament with these words: "You say your religion is the better. I say mine is. Is it any more reasonable that I should adopt your opinion than that you should adopt mine? . . . Let us end these diabolical names . . . Lutherans, Huguenots, Catholics; let us change our name to Christians!"[27] He shepherded through Parliament Catherine's gift to the French people, the Edicts of Toleration.

The response from the parties involved was not ecumenical. The chairman of the University of Paris's theology department demanded the reinstatement of the death penalty for all heretics, and the papal nuncio urged Catherine to burn any Huguenot delegates who dared to assemble. The Huguenots, meanwhile, succeeded in gaining control of several outlying civil governments. Soon afterwards they ordered all citizens to attend Protestant services, seized Catholic churches, smashed all images, and drove nuns, monks, and priests out of town.[28] The social fabric of France was unraveling.

The respected leader of the Huguenots was the aristocratic admiral Gaspard de Coligny. A friend of the king, he came to Paris accompanied by bodyguards to petition the throne. While walking near the Louvre, Coligny's elbow was shattered by an assassin's bullet. On hearing of the attempt on the admiral's life, King Charles exploded. "Am I never to have any peace?"

Convinced that the Guises were behind the assassination attempt, Coligny's men circulated around the Louvre all day, shouting for revenge. Paris seethed with rumors; the sound of red-hot irons being hammered on anvils filled the humid summer air as each side increased its arsenal. The Catholics warned the king and his mother that the influx of armed Huguenots into Paris was the prelude to kidnapping him and the Queen Mother. The Duke of Guise urged the king to let him deal with the plotters and finish off Coligny. No proof of a plot was given, and the king vacillated between the advice of the Catholic nobles and that of the Protestant delegation who, despite their religious affiliation, were still his loyal subjects.

The high-strung twenty-three-year-old king was wracked with indecision. Finally, toward midnight, the Catholic partisans persuaded him to arrest Coligny and six other Huguenots on charges of conspiring against the Crown. Not satisfied, they persisted in haranguing the king. In a fit of nervous exhaustion, Charles screamed, "By the death of God, since you choose to kill the Admiral, I consent! But then you must kill all the Huguenots in France, so that not one shall be left to reproach me . . . Kill them all! Kill them all!" Shouting obscenities, he fled from his councilors and shut himself up in his chambers.

The next day was Sunday, August 24, 1572—Saint Bartholomew's Day. The Duke of Guise sent word to his militias, strategically placed around Paris, that on his signal they should close and lock the city's gates to prevent anyone's escape, then seek out and kill every Protestant.

At 3:00 A.M., a preemptory contingent broke into Coligny's apartments and stabbed the admiral while he was kneeling in prayer. They threw his body out the window to crowds waiting below. Then Guise issued the order, "*Tuez! Tuez!* Kill! Kill! The king commands it!" Royal soldiers began the slaughter of Paris's Huguenots. Mobs of Catholic citizenry, caught up in the frenzy, joined soldiers in hunting down Huguenots. Thousands died at the hands of their next-door neighbors. Bakers killed bakers, doctors killed doctors, and children killed their former friends. Crowds knocked in the doors of houses suspected of harboring Huguenots. Families found within were slain in gruesome sequence—first the husband, then his wife, then their children. Embryos were torn from dying pregnant women and smashed against the walls.[29] The streets were littered with corpses. "As I write," the excited Spanish ambassador reported while leaning out his window, "they are killing them all, they are stripping them naked . . . sparing not even the children. Blessed be God!"[30]

The Queen Mother, apprised of the king's order, tried to reverse it, but the duke told her that it was too late. Toward midday, a delegation of citizens, sickened by the carnage, petitioned the king. Emerging sheepishly from his bedroom, he ordered the killing to cease. Huguenots were taken into police custody for their own protection and the slaughter abated.

The next day, Monday, a hawthorn tree unexpectedly bloomed out of season in the middle of the Cemetery of the Innocents. A few Catholic clergy took this as a clear sign of God's delight at the previous day's activities on His behalf. Someone ordered the church bells to be rung all over the city in thanks. The populace, however, mistook the clangor as a call to renew the butchery, and the murderous rage erupted again. It took several days for the authorities to regain control.

Inspired by news of what was happening in Paris, the Catholics of Lyon, Dijon, Orléans, Bloise, Tours, Troyes, Meaux, Bourges, Angers, and Rouen, rose up and murdered their Huguenots by the thousands. When the news reached Rome, the city resonated with salvos. Bells rang joyously. Pope Gregory XIII celebrated a special mass thanking God for "this signal favor shown to Christian people."[31] Back in Paris, Coligny's body was handed over to the mob. His head was cut off and staked on the gate of the Louvre, his genitals and fingers severed and sold as souvenirs. "Praise God," Catholics exulted, "France has been saved for Catholicism."

Italy, the originator of the Humanist movement, was not spared its reign of terror. As the Reformation raged, seventy-nine-year-old Giovanni Caraffa became Pope Paul IV (1555–59). He had previously been the Grand Inquisitor, during which time he laid down the following rules:

When faith is in question, there must be no delay in prosecution.
No consideration is to be shown any prince or prelate.
Extreme severity is to be exercised.
There can be no toleration toward heresy, above all toward Calvinists.[32]

Paul turned the Inquisition into an instrument that could strike terror into Italian hearts. As one cardinal wrote, in awe of Paul's severity, "Due to the pope's superhuman rigor, the Inquisition acquired such a reputation that from no other judgment seat on earth were more horrible and fearful sentences to be expected."[33] A chill settled over Rome. Besides instigating religious persecution, Paul ordered Vatican censors to remove paintings and statues of nude figures. Scaffolds were erected in the Sistine Chapel so that hired painters could touch up Michelangelo's indiscretions. Loincloths incongruously appeared on marble masterpieces. In 1559 Paul ordered thousands of books burned—ten thousand in one day in Venice. The spirit of the Renaissance went up in that smoke and the decline of Italy was assured.

A priest and boy found guilty of homosexual relations were burned alive in the piazza. A nun convicted of fornication was punished along with her lover in the same manner. The stern pontiff thought nothing of imprisoning cardinals or even his own relatives. "Even if my own father were a heretic," he said, "I would gather wood to burn him." The historian Pastor commented:

> The hasty and credulous pope lent a willing ear to every denunciation, even the most absurd. . . . The inquisitors . . . scented heresy in numerous cases where a calm and circumspect observer would not have discovered a trace of it. . . . An actual reign of terror began, which filled all Rome with fear.[34]

One reign of terror lasted nearly a century, during which the Protestant Dutch freed themselves from the Catholic Dutch, who were backed by the Spanish Crown. At the beginning of the Reformation, the Netherlands was one of Europe's most vital centers of commerce. In Antwerp and Brussels, the clack-clack of hundreds of printing presses provided a constant background din. Protestantism spread rapidly and the Spanish Inquisition hastily set up shop to begin its relentless burning of heretics. Hardly a day passed without an execution. Whole towns were ravaged.

The rebel Protestants had the good fortune to have the aristocratic William of Orange become their leader. The level of ferocity exhibited by both sides can be gleaned from a Dutch chronicler's report:

On more than one occasion men were seen hanging their own brothers, who had been taken prisoners in the enemy's ranks. . . . A Spaniard had ceased to be human in their eyes. On one occasion, a surgeon at Veer cut the heart from a Spanish prisoner, nailed it on a vessel's prow, and invited the townsmen to come and fasten their teeth in it, which many did with savage satisfaction.[35]

The increasingly victorious Protestants soon faced a new problem. A small group of zealous Calvinists accused William of Orange of being insufficiently pious. They noted that William had attended services only once in a year when he was prosecuting the war. Although fanatical Calvinists comprised only 10 percent of the rebels, through stealth and dogged determination they gradually managed to gain control of the Dutch Reformation. The majority of the Dutch Protestants, then as now, had tolerant dispositions, and they believed they were fighting the Catholics to expel the Spanish and establish religious freedom. But they soon found themselves disparagingly referred to as "Libertines" by the fundamentalist Calvinist minority, and

LEFT: French Catholics murdering Huguenots

RIGHT: Spanish Catholic troops torturing Dutch Protestants

their advocacy of an Erasmian Humanist attitude of forbearance earned them the scornful epithet "secret papists." In 1618, the Calvinists declared anyone who disagreed with them guilty of heresy. They prohibited the preaching of the doctrines of any other Protestant denominations on pain of death.[36] Fierce fighting between the two Protestant camps erupted, and the same dreary litany of sadistic punishments was repeated, all in the name of Christ. William mourned to see his years of labor end in chaos, hatred, and division. When the father of Dutch independence was assassinated, the captured Catholic assassin confessed that he had pledged to the Virgin Mary the bounty the Spanish king had offered for William's death.[37]

The heart of Africa was one place printing press–generated madness might not have been expected to reach. But members of preliterate tribes living there in the sixteenth century would soon discover that strings of written words have immensely long tentacles. The agents of literacy, bearing nets and chains, were the English. How ironic. Britain had been the first country in Europe to disavow slavery. It was an idea repugnant to King Arthur, the monk Alcuin, and Henry V, to name only a few. The country that gave the world the Chivalric Code, the Magna Carta, Parliament, Milton, Donne, and Shakespeare, and was the most democratic, was the unlikeliest candidate to reestablish a trade in human cargo, which had been almost completely eradicated from Europe for a thousand years.

The New World natives had been harshly worked and many died. As a result, calls went out from colonists for sturdier slaves. English captains, a notoriously self-righteous, God-fearing, Bible-thumping lot, discovered that there was a profit to be made by filling their ships' holds with African captives on the trip west and apparently thought nothing of enslaving fellow humans. English behavior in this episode seems deeply at odds with their cultural traditions. Could the process of becoming literate have affected their thinking?

At the rosy dawn of the Renaissance, many freethinkers—Humanists and scientists—had declared themselves on the side of tolerance and common sense. None could have anticipated that within a few years their public statements would be used against them by zealous "thought police." Giordano Bruno was burned at the stake in 1600 for suggesting that Copernicus was right about the earth orbiting the sun rather than vice versa. Petrus Ramus, the foremost philosopher of the age, was murdered during the Saint Bartholomew's Massacre by a jealous professor at the Sorbonne.[38] The ailing Galileo was ordered to recant or face the rack. Calvin enjoyed forcing professors to burn their incriminating works with their own hands in humiliating public ceremonies. Unfortunately, the list of victims goes on and on, and we are left to ponder behavior that is inexplicable. Taken as a whole, the religious wars that wracked Europe in the 150 years after the printing press had transformed European culture can be viewed as a sort of mass madness. They occurred *only* in those lands impacted by the printing press; the steeper the rise of literacy rates the more ferocious the religious wars were. This connection could be the long-overlooked factor that fueled these bizarre aberrations in human behavior.

CHAPTER 32

SORCERY/SCIENCE

Yet none of the recent literature definitively explains the strange and tragic events that historians call the "witchcraft persecutions." Why they happened at all, why they occurred when and where they did, and why European society turned against certain groups of its own women remain unanswered questions.   —Anne Llewellyn Barstow[1]

Schizophrenia may be a necessary consequence of literacy.
—Marshall McLuhan[2]

Humans are by nature a curious lot. Our expansive sense of time and space stimulates us to ponder our place in the scheme of things. Many of us have had experiences in which we seemed to glimpse other dimensions, or realities, and these epiphanies inspire the belief that there is an existence greater than the one commonly described. Attempts to discern the supernatural and experience the transcendent have been part of virtually every culture. All spiritual traditions share certain common denominators. All have developed exercises and rituals to alter everyday consciousness to transcend an individual's feelings of alienation and reconnect (*religare*) that person to "the source." The inner peace so generated enables a person to see oneself embedded in the matrix of a grander entity, and to intuit connections to all other living things. This insight engenders in the soul of the one so graced both wisdom and compassion, two attributes that characterize every prominent ancient religious leader.

What, then, are we to make of religious "leaders" who claim that they alone have access to the "truth," and sanction the murder of those who disagree with them? How could men incite hatred, practice torture, and foul the air with their invective, and still be considered spiritual pillars? What level of demonic violence and mayhem must be attained before the judgment of history steps in and strips such zealots of their clerical camouflage?

Were the sadists who perpetrated the Inquisition and other persecutions, enslavements, and genocidal atrocities "religious worthies" entitled to the respect we traditionally render the collar and cowl?

Most history books teach that the Reformation and Counter-Reformation were great "moral cleansings." Was burning men and boys in the public square for having homosexual relations a moral victory? Was killing the newborn of an unwed mother a step forward? Was touching up Michelangelo's works or burning books a cultural advance? How did hounding intellectuals and Humanists ennoble anyone's spirit? Did beheading, hanging, and drowning vast numbers of people improve human conduct? Was the gibbet really better than the maypole? Was the most memorable Saint Bartholomew's Day in French history a more civilized ritual than the joyous Festivals of Artemis celebrated in ancient times? Is there a more feral image than Dutch burghers gnawing on a Spaniard's heart?

Unlike the many territorial wars of the preceding centuries, the conflicts of the Reformation (1517–1648) were characterized by the murder of neighbor by neighbor. The most technologically advanced society humans had ever created—sophisticated Europe, the only culture that dined with a fork and spoon—suffered the equivalence of a collective, left-hemispheric epileptic fit. Why there? Why then?

Visitors to the court of the "savage" Mongol emperors in the fourteenth century reported, with astonishment, that all religions were tolerated there. Jews and Christians living under the "beastly" Ottoman Turks experienced halcyon days compared to the homicidal battles raging among European Christians at the same time. Muslims never engaged in the volume and the degree of internecine doctrinal bloodletting that soaked the soil of Germany, France, and England. In China, India, and Japan, such large-scale religious fratricides were unknown. The "primitive" natives of the New World did not engage in widespread religious torture and murder. The factor unique to European culture was a massive injection of a left brain–enhancing method of communication. Europe, alone among the world's many cultures, experienced a logarithmic rise in alphabet literacy rates.*

This profound change was due primarily to the printing press. While the idea that typography played a sinister role in Western culture might seem counterintuitive, I submit one final piece of evidence: one last, breathtaking horror story—the torture, mutilation, and incineration of untold

*Sir Thomas More estimated that about 40 percent of his English contemporaries were literate. Three hundred years later, Alexis de Tocqueville marveled that he found it nearly impossible to locate a North American who could not read and write.

numbers of women during the European witch craze that flared from the late fifteenth through the early seventeenth centuries.

Witch hunting was *woman* hunting. A chronicler in 1600 wrote, "Demons take no account of males . . . and among a hundred witches, there's scarcely a man to be seen."[3] Over 80 percent of accused "witches" were female; in German-speaking lands the percentage often was close to 100 percent. Historians have been at a loss to explain this bizarre episode. One theory proposes that the witch hunts were used by secular and clerical authorities to seize the wealth that women controlled. Another theory is that the condemned women were much-respected healers, herbalists, and magicians, and that the newly organized medical/scientific community, in conjunction with fretful clerics, conspired to destroy the populace's faith in them in order to further their own standing. This assumes that these women possessed and exercised authority among the people. But many that suffered came from the class noted for its *lack* of power. Most witches were poor and friendless. Cultures always pay in coin for what they consider valuable; women healers, in general, had meager savings concealed under their straw mattresses.

Other historians attempt to explain the witch craze by linking it to anxiety associated with the religious wars that erupted after the Reformation, but in fact the witch hunts began in earnest in 1460, in the very glory of the Renaissance. They were well under way many years before Luther drove in his famous nail. Besides, "anxiety" had been present in many other centuries and cultures, and in no other instance had this caused men to murder their women. Economic conditions were not worse in the gilded Renaissance than they were during the famines, blights, and invasions of earlier periods. If the purpose of the witch hunts had been to be rid of burdensome old people, the poor would have been in the vanguard of exterminating useless elder women from their midst. But it was not the poor who did the killing. Ermine-cloaked prelates, shiny-armored police, and well-fed magistrates were the instigators and perpetrators of the purge.

None of these explanations are adequate. I propose that the witch craze was the result of the ballooning up of the left hemisphere's hunter-killer attributes, which was inflated by the rapid expansion of printing press–generated alphabet literacy.

The myths and customs of most societies provide ample evidence that men have feared the innate power of women. Still, murdering vast numbers of them was a practice unknown to history until the European witch craze. In ancient cultures, sacrificing a virgin was a rare event. Neither Egyptians, Mesopotamians, nor Phoenicians burned witches. The Old Testament's Yahweh was the first deity to issue the command, "Ye shall suffer no witch to live"; yet, Jewish history is devoid of memorable witch hunts. The Greeks honored and feared the power of Cassandra, Hecuba, and Circe, but they never lit fires under their women. Horace, Tibullus, Lucretius, and other Roman authors believed in the power of sorceresses. None recommended exterminating them. Muslims, Hindus, and Chinese may have mistreated their women, but they did not persecute, torture, and burn them alive in large numbers. If any hunter-gatherer tribespeople or early agrarians were informed about a culture that murdered their wise women, they would stare at the reporter with astonished disbelief.

Early Christians did not sanction witch hunts. Neither Gnostics nor Orthodox ever engaged in one, and the people who lived through the Dark Ages honored their "shamanic women" rather than despised them, as evidenced by the high status of female Christian mystics. In A.D. 643 Rathari, king of the Lombards, issued edicts expressly protecting his realm's wise women.[4] In 800 Charlemagne made killing a person for witchcraft a capital crime. In the ninth century both Boniface and Agobard relegated the belief in witchcraft to a minor sin. In 1173 Pope Gregory IX forbade agents of the newly formed Inquisition from prosecuting women sorcerers, and dismissed as ridiculous the notion that old women caused storms or plagues. In the Middle Ages the Church declared the sighting of witches flying through the air as hallucinations. Three hundred years later, during the witch craze, those who denied that witches could fly through the air were accused by the Church of aiding sorcery. Even the baleful fourteenth century, with its multiple calamities, did not lead hard-pressed men to take out their considerable anxieties on women. At the height of the Plague, when whole cities were dropping dead in their tracks, women were not blamed. Why then, in a time of relative prosperity and no serious outbreaks of disease, did the witch craze burst forth? Why did the culture bequeathing to posterity the likes of Galileo, Leonardo, Shakespeare, Newton, and Bach suddenly start foaming at the mouth like a rabid dog?

Before 1454, hardly any women were lashed to the stake for witchcraft. Then, in the very midst of the great Humanist Renaissance, at nearly the precise moment the printing presses began to churn, the madness began. In 1460, a few miles and six years distant from Gutenberg's Frankfurt plant, twelve "sorceresses" were burned in Heidelberg's public square. In 1468, the papacy, in an extraordinary legal ruling, declared witchcraft a *crimen exceptum*, a crime for which those accused could be officially tortured prior to trial. In 1484, Innocent VIII became the first pope in the fifteen-hundred-year history of the Church to declare that witchcraft posed a genuine threat to Christendom. Thirty-five years *before the Reformation,* he commissioned Inquisition agents to actively pursue those whose evil machinations supposedly blighted the fruit of both wombs and fields. His agents lost little time. In 1485, forty-one accused women were burned alive in the northern Italian lake town of Como.

The witch craze soon received a major boost from the widespread circulation of a book that, like the Bible, became a Renaissance best-seller. In 1487 two Dominican friars, Jakob Sprenger and Heinrich Kramer, compiled *Malleus Maleficarum* (The Hammer of Witches), a Church-commissioned guide for eradicating witches. Its popularity far exceeded expectation. Maximillian I, the Holy Roman Emperor, enthusiastically endorsed the work, and Innocent VIII ordered mass printings so that it could be read by the many witch hunters he continued to appoint. The printing press made possible the wide circulation of the most scurrilous attack on womanhood since writing began. As Erica Jong, a novelist who studied the period, comments, "But when we remember that this book was used for centuries as a how-to book for witch hunters, we can only despair that the printing press has as often been a tool of oppression as of liberation."[5] But I propose that it was not only the rapid dispersion of this book's content, but also the psychological alterations brought on by the process of reading that afflicted a newly literate print generation and stoked the witch fires to such a white-hot intensity.

The Hammer's authors quickly got to the heart of the matter: "All witchcraft comes from carnal lust, which is in women insatiable . . . wherefore for the sake of fulfilling their lust, they consort even with devils."[6] Women were more susceptible to the devil's advances than men, the learned clerics asserted, because women as a gender were frivolous and gullible. Sprenger and Kramer declared as fact that a witch's look alone could cause sickness and death, shrivel crops, and induce abortions; her *image* was her most dangerous weapon. Witches, they asserted, kidnapped Christian children and tore out their hearts, which they then roasted and ate as part of their satanic rituals. Associated with dance, night, nature, the moon, sexuality, and procreation—witches possessed all the attributes previously accorded the Goddess. In the joyous ancient fertility rites of field and forest women could worship one of their own. The two authors made such rituals seem to be sinister cabals worshiping the anti-Christ.

Had Sprenger and Kramer's book been published at any other time, it might have moldered quietly in obscurity. But many newly literate men snapped up copies of *The Hammer,* and its authors became celebrities. European bishops, suddenly alert to a hitherto unrecognized threat within their communities enthusiastically sought their "expertise," and Kramer and Sprenger became exceedingly successful witch hunters themselves. Before the onset of the Reformation, hunting witches had superseded hounding heretics, and it became the Inquisition's principal preoccupation for nearly half a century.

A witch was qualitatively different from a heretic. The latter deviated from Church dogma. Witches, however, possessed supernatural powers and carried out the devil's bidding. Although their form remained human, the Prince of Darkness had captured their souls. Church authorities, convinced that witches had infiltrated their parishes, became obsessed with rooting them out. *The Hammer* explained in detail how to distinguish a witch from a God-fearing Christian. Upon arriving in a village, witch hunters hired informers to report mysterious illnesses, deaths, misfortunes (hail storms, crop failures, death of livestock), or the sudden onset of impotence (a favorite). Widows, spinsters, sexually attractive women (the ones who could *really* cast a spell over men), healers, and magicians, as well as "scolds," "crones," and "hags," were then arrested as prime suspects.

The "trials" that followed differed from other legal proceedings. The principal damning evidence was not testimony but rather the presence of a witch's teat, called the "devil's mark." The terrified accused, often restrained, was stripped of her clothes and roughly fondled by an examiner, called a "pricker," in the presence of other strange men. The pricker painstakingly inspected the woman's genitalia and breasts for any mole, wart, skin tag, hemorrhoid, or slight vaginal deformity (such as might be caused by a difficult childbirth). If the pricker found a suspicious excrescence, he then jabbed a small needle he had hidden in his hand into it. If the woman did not cry out in pain, this was proof that she was a witch. The examination usually took place in a torture chamber furnished with menacing instruments. The shock of being undressed against her will in such an eerie setting, and then blindfolded, so frightened the victim that many were numb, and failed to react to the faint stab of the pricker's needle. This predictable physiological response was disastrous under the circumstances, and sealed her fate. Since prickers were paid according to their skill at identifying witches, and most were rogues, some carried retractable needles. Many accused women did not feel the pricker's jab because the needle never pierced their skin. To onlookers, however, her failure to cry out was credible enough evidence of guilt to fuel gossip in the market for days.

All female mammals have two mammary ridges that begin at each shoulder, and run down across the chest and abdomen to end in the groin.

Nipples are aligned along these two ridges. In creatures that give birth to large litters, such as pigs, cats, and dogs, females have anywhere from eight to twelve nipples. Because human females usually give birth to only one baby at a time, they have only two. But many women have supernumerary nipples that can be identified anywhere along either mammary ridge. Sometimes they take the form of nipples complete with aureolae, but more often they resemble moles. The witch hunters became expert at finding these vestigial nipples, which were identified as the dreaded "devil's mark."

The human female breast serves not only as the source of mother's milk for nursing babies, but also as a secondary sexual feature that attracts the male. It is the single most visible aspect of a woman's femaleness. In the time of the witch craze, the witch's teat, believed to succor imps, goblins, and succubi, became the most evil appendage a human could have.

Once a witch's guilt was confirmed, the next step, according to *The Hammer*, was to obtain the names of her accomplices, as every witch was believed to belong to a coven. The hideous tortures devised to extract this information frequently involved the mutilation and burning of sexual organs. Even the bravest woman could not help but eventually blurt out the names of her innocent friends and companions, who were then arrested and the cycle repeated. After a hard day's torture, the clerics involved often congratulated themselves over a beer on their ability to turn up so many witches in communities that had at first vehemently denied their presence.

After the interrogations and confessions came the burnings. In some communities witches were strangled before being staked; more often they were burned alive, since inquisitors believed this form of execution left a deeper impression on the public. The tornado of gender terror and sadism that indiscriminately sucked women up into its vortex during the European witch craze has no parallel in human history.

This grotesque gender-specific pogrom gathered support from every stratum of the intelligentsia. Many Humanists, including Erasmus and Thomas More, accepted the reality of witches. The scientist Nicholas Oresme believed in the power of the evil eye. Francis Bacon, the father of experimental science, actively supported the purge. William Harvey, physician to the English king and discoverer of the secret of blood circulation, participated in witchcraft trials. Some intellectuals remained skeptical. Montaigne, with his characteristic sardonic wit, wrote, "It is rating our conjectures highly to roast people alive for them."[7] Such public expressions of doubt were rare. Many university professors hurried to produce convoluted justifications of *The Hammer*. Legal scholars consumed untold numbers of candles drafting laws for the prosecution of witches. Many physicians, still

secretly unsure of the efficacy of their new science and jealous of their prerogatives, applauded the elimination of their competition.

When the Catholic Church began to persecute Protestants, voices from both
within and outside of the Church were raised in the Protestants' defense.
Nothing equivalent occurred in the witch craze. In 1584 Reginald Scot
described witches as poor old women who could harm no one: to ascribe
miracles and extraordinary acts to them, he argued, was an insult to those
performed by Our Savior. Few in authority paid any attention to Scot.

In earlier times, men and women alike acknowledged the skills of female
shamans. The wise woman had tucked in her bag of tricks both ergot root
for inducing abortion, and belladonna for preventing miscarriage. Many
men readily acknowledged the superiority of the medicine practiced by
women healers. Paracelsus (1493–1541), the greatest physician of his age,
acknowledged that he "had learned from the Sorceress all that he knew."[8]
The male chauvinist philosopher Thomas Hobbes admitted that, personally,
he would rather take "the advice or physic from an experienced old woman"
than see a Harley Street physician.[9]

Some witches may have been followers of *Wicca*, an archaic form of
goddess worship that emphasizes the beauty and bountifulness of the
earthly world rather than the hellfire and punishments of a next one. The
profound repression of women's rights and values during the Reformation
offered little that was life-affirming or nature-loving. The old ways of worship may have seemed crucial enough to some women that they were willing
to risk horrific punishment to keep alive the ancient traditions.

The Hammer continued to strike crushing blows like the clang of iron on
anvil. In 1510, 140 witches were burned at Brescia, a few miles south of
Como. The Medici pope Leo X ratcheted up the depravity. Three hundred
more witches were burned at Como four years later. At the time, this small
lake community probably could not claim more than five thousand inhabitants, so this spasm of misogyny constituted a holocaust for the females of
Como. The peasants in the area became so outraged at the Church that they
took up arms to stop the killing. In 1518, the year after Luther's call for
reform (which Leo barely acknowledged), the pope's attention was riveted
by a tale making the rounds in Rome of a "witch's sabbath" attended by over
twenty-five thousand devil worshipers on a broad plain outside Brescia.
More concerned by the sudden multiplication of witches than calls by
reformers, Leo ordered the area exorcised. Seventy more witches lost their
lives and thousands filled prisons. The small community watched helplessly

as Church agents, ears bent by paid informers, dragged local innocents from their hearths. Many were not seen again until they were led out, bruised, hollow-eyed, and chained on burning day. The bishop of Brescia, under intense pressure from his parishioners, vigorously protested the Inquisition's intrusion into his realm. Leo responded by issuing a bull ordering the excommunication of anyone interfering with the persecution.

Initially, only clerics hunted, but in 1532 Charles V, the Holy Roman Emperor, issued his infamous "Carolina Code," which officially sanctioned the secular authority's use of torture for suspected witches and made witchcraft a civil crime punishable by burning. In 1541, Henry VIII ordered the death penalty for several practices ascribed to witches. Queen Elizabeth made witchcraft a capital crime in 1562, and eighty-one women were executed during her reign. In 1597, James II, the king of Scotland, proudly published one of the great horrors of literature, his *Daemonolgie*, which was but an updated *Hammer*. In this farrago, James advocated the death penalty not only for women who practiced the healing arts but also for their clients. Later, as king of England, he devised a few innovative tortures that had escaped the ingenuity of the brotherhood of executioners. In Scotland, Protestants voted to levy a tax on themselves for the express purpose of buying firewood to burn witches.[10] The General Assembly of the Presbyterian Church ordered its ministers to seek out witches in every parish, and when local churches relaxed their vigil, the Privy Council issued decrees for new hunts. Scotland was kept in a continuous uproar between 1590 and 1700.

In the duchy of Lorraine, chief judge Nicholas Remy boasted that he had sent nine hundred witches to their deaths and tortured many more. He sentenced the children of the convicted to be beaten with rods while they watched their mothers burned alive, then wondered aloud if he had been too lenient on the children.[11] In 1590, when Philip II, the king of the Netherlands, declared that witchcraft "was the scourge of the human race," the generally sensible Dutch, too, joined the howl for witch pyres. The Swiss were especially thorough and ferocious. Genevan Calvinists believed sodomy was an "unnatural act" inspired by witchcraft and vigorously prosecuted homosexuals. Even far-off America could not escape the lunacy: there, the worst excess, the Salem Witch Trials, took place in 1692.*

"Hysteria" is an unmanageable fear expressed by emotional excess. It is a type of behavior many men associate with women; the word itself derives from the Greek *hystera*, meaning womb. But no superstition that any group of

---

*The first printing press appeared in America in 1638 in Cambridge.

women has ever believed has come close to the level of credulity and psychosis that seized the most educated male elite during the witch craze. As if in a deep hypnotic spell, men accepted as fact a phantasmagoria that defies comprehension—that little girls in pigtails, pregnant women, and weak, elderly widows posed a mortal danger to society. The witch craze was an example of masculine hysteria and gullibility without a parallel in any other culture. In the light of such evidence, lexicographers might well consider coining a new word to accompany "hysteria"—"testicularia" would be appropriate.

Some have suggested that women's behavior was a contributing factor to the craze.*[12] According to this theory, some accused women believed that they were indeed witches, and thus fed the men's fears—sort of a mass *folie à deux* in which each side's madness reinforced the other side's delusions. The transcribed confessions of some witches indicate that the accused seemed convinced that they flew through the night on broomsticks. Under torture, many babbled detailed accounts of their gatherings in the woods and supplied imaginative descriptions of their sexual trysts with the devil.

During the Korean War, captured American officers were subjected to intense psychological brainwashing. A disturbing number of these highly trained professionals eventually signed confessions, admitting that they were "tools of American capitalists." They seemed to enthusiastically endorse the Communist party line, married Communist women, and settled down to live in Communist countries. The tortures these men had been subjected to were not as extreme as those suffered by women in the witch craze. Further, these officers could take heart in the hope that they might be rescued, as their side had not been defeated.

In contrast, the plight of a woman ensnared in the witch craze was hopeless. She was utterly without advocates. She could not expect a white knight to free her, because the white knights of society—her pastor, her king, her magistrate, and her pope—were her tormentors. Women who went to their excruciating deaths convinced they deserved their fate had been subjected to the most severe psychological, sexual, and physical terrors in the long, baleful history of patriarchy. Anyone who suggests that women brought it on themselves should be shut up in a dank, stone dungeon and have thumbscrews applied daily for a month, and then report back to the rest of us on how their theory is holding up.

---

*One historian, Eric Midelfort, speculated that the women brought it on themselves. He tentatively wrote, "Women seemed . . . to provoke somehow an intense misogyny at times" and that historians should study "why that group attracted to itself the scapegoating mechanism."

One might have expected that with the outbreak of the Reformation, when the two adversaries, Protestants and Catholics, finally locked horns in mortal combat, they would have concentrated on the core ideological struggle. Instead both sides committed valuable time, money, and resources to continue to hunt, capture, torture, and burn witches.

Protestants might have eschewed the killing of women to distinguish themselves from their enemy, the Catholic Church. The opposite occurred. "I would have no compassion for these witches," announced Luther; "I would burn them all."[13] Calvin said, "The Bible teaches us that there are witches and they must be slain . . . this law of God is a universal law."[14] Latecomers to the frenzy, the Protestants joined the witch hunts with gusto. Though lacking the well-oiled machinery of the Inquisition, they nevertheless managed to rack up a significant tally of cruelty. The worst witch terror in English history occurred between 1645 and 1647, during the two years the Puritans controlled Parliament. Two hundred witches were dispatched. In Germany, Protestants, entering the fray much later than the Catholic authorities, nevertheless managed to burn one witch for every three their opponents burned.

It was in Germany, the birthplace of the printing press and home to the fastest rise in literacy rates, that the witch craze assumed its most monstrous proportions. A sense of the madness can be conveyed through an abbreviated roll call of statistics. The reader is left to imagine what each one of these numbers represents. In Quenlinburg, 133 witches were executed *in one day* in 1589. At Ellwangen, 390 witches were burned between 1611 and 1618. At Eichstätt, 274 witches were burned in one year, 1629. This besieged town suffered three waves of persecution, in 1590, 1603–30, and again in 1637.[15] Women lived like hunted animals. Whole lifetimes were consumed in abject terror of the coming of the witch hunter with his chains. In Offenburg and its environs, 102 witches were burned. One woman died of the torture, another, after her breasts were torn with hot pincers, committed suicide; another went mad. In two of the villages surrounding Trier, the Jesuit Peter Binsfeld was so thorough that only one woman was left alive after he and his inquisitors had departed. All the other mothers, wives, grandmothers, aunts, cousins, daughters, and sisters were exterminated. The new orphans and widowers were left to cope with their shock as best they could.

At the outset of the craze, witch hunters did not torture pregnant prisoners. This restraint ended in 1576 in Nuremberg. In some places, after the women most vulnerable to accusation had been executed, the inquisitors turned on children, convinced that witches passed their dark art on to their daughters. In the crowning grotesquerie of the entire episode, the prince-bishop of Würzburg executed forty-one girls, ages seven to eleven, between 1623 and 1631.[16] There is no other incident in all of recorded history in which a community was seized with a psychosis so extreme that it tortured and killed its own children.

The printing press made a minimal impact on the Muslim countries bordering European ones because the Muslims preferred calligraphy to print. The Islamic Balkans, adjacent to Christian lands in central Europe, did not experience a witch craze. The European Christian nations least affected by the printing press were Finland, Estonia, Norway, and Iceland, and in these cultures there were few accusations of witchcraft and fewer death penalties. And while Germany, France, and Switzerland set the night ablaze with burning pyres, the superstitious and illiterate Russians remained virtually untouched by the madness. When considering Europe as a whole, the greater the impact of the press upon a given society, the higher the ratio of accused women to men *and* of executions to convictions.

Anne Llewellyn Barstow, in her book *Witchcraze*, estimated from court records she examined that over a hundred thousand people were exterminated. Some recent investigators claim that the number was in the millions. The truth can never be completely ascertained. The last witch was "officially" executed in Poland in 1782.

ABOVE: A German witch-burning, 1555

RIGHT: A witch-hanging in Scotland, 1571

It is impossible to conceive of the irreparable damage done to the women who survived this protracted reign of terror. No woman alive in the Western world could have been unaware of what was happening. Anyone who actually *witnessed* a burning would have been severely traumatized. No friendship between women was safe. If a friend was arrested, there could be no guarantee against betrayal under the duress of torture.

The vast majority of women had no protection. Conducting oneself in a docile, silent, and unobtrusive manner, avoiding female friendships, and sticking close to home and husband was the only way to avoid the glowing pincer's grasp. Modern men have been known to ask why so few women in the last centuries made stellar contributions to the arts and sciences. Most men have never had to fear sticking out from the crowd far enough to elicit the heart-stopping accusation of "Witch!" Ancient female wisdom—medical and otherwise—accumulated painstakingly over eons went up in flames along with the "witches." How to calculate and comprehend how much European civilization lost when its men nearly annihilated its wise women?

The military tallies its casualties during wars in three categories—dead, wounded, and missing in action. If one hundred thousand expired during the witch craze, then two to three times as many were accused, tortured, and then either imprisoned for life or released. For these victims, death may have been a kinder fate. If they moved to another community, the stigma of their ordeal followed them, impeding their family's ability to make a living. Children of accused witches were believed by many to have inherited the art, and they too suffered. Husbands of accused wives frequently abandoned their families when the pressure became unbearable. Social pariahs, many of these women slid into abject poverty; still others committed suicide.

Missing in action was the feminine spirit. The misogyny behind the hunts was so devastating that women and the men who supported female values were completely vanquished. Sex crimes against women dramatically increased; perpetrators knew that if a woman pressed charges, they need only claim bewitchment to have the accusation turned against her. In England, rape trials dramatically declined during the height of the craze, although contemporary chroniclers reported an increase in the crime. It was open season on women and deviants had a field day. For the first and only time in recorded history, the majority of prisoners awaiting trial for crimes against society were women. Overcrowded dungeons groaned with the weeping and keening of terrified females.

In the wake of every war, there are those whose bodies bear no marks but whose psyches have been scarred so terribly that they fear sleep because of its inevitable nightmares. The slumber of countless women was no doubt restless and troubled, filled with remembered or imagined fiends coming at them with instruments of torture. This anxiety, penetrating deep into the psychic female marrow, cannot be accounted for in dry, statistical analysis.

The eerie conjunction of the printing press, steeply rising literacy rates, religious wars, and the witch craze seems significant. Another major synchrony must also be beaded on the line. No endeavor personifies the essence of the left brain better than science. Blackboard and white chalk, science is linear, dispassionate, rational, abstract, and cerebral. It is the world of words, symbols, and numbers. When exactly, we must ask, did science come of age?

During the height of the witch craze, women were killed for being women; women's rights and values plunged to their all-time nadir. Concurrently, Mary, the only surrogate Mother Goddess in all of Western culture, was under fierce attack by male members of Protestantism, a new, alphabet-based religion which called for destroying every image of her they could find. It was at this proximate moment in the five-thousand-year history of Western civilization that science came into its own.

Actually, science began to crown unrecognizable in the midst of the twelfth century, besmeared with the juices of alchemy and astrology. Four hundred years of incremental and sustained logic patiently wiped away the obscuring film. Francis Bacon added one new absolute condition: theory must be consistent with observed fact. Gradually, theoreticians behind the movement that had begun as a grand attempt to merge God and syllogisms realized that logic did not require the link to the divine. Scientists began making stunning advances that were mutually reinforcing.

The man most responsible for curing logicians of their obsession with trying to explain the spiritual world was René Descartes. In 1629, during the witch killings and religious frenzies, the twenty-eight-year-old youth sat in deep thought in an empty room. Throughout most of Europe, Protestants were congregating in whitewashed churches, repeating over and over again the mantra of Luther and Calvin—faith, faith, faith. For Catholics, the operative word was believe, believe, believe. Uttering the single word that would reverberate for the next four centuries, Descartes exclaimed "Doubt!" This word was the gauntlet thrown down by the Scientific Age. "The chief cause of our errors is to be found in the prejudices of our childhood," Descartes later wrote, "principles of which I allowed myself in youth to be persuaded without having inquired into their truth."[17]

A Catholic, Descartes had received a thorough Jesuit education. But he realized that had he been raised in a Muslim household, he would have been an ardent Muslim; in a Jew's family, a passionate Jew; the son of Protestants, a pious Protestant. An innocent mixup in the nursery could determine an individual's fervently held beliefs for a lifetime. How could that be? How could religious certainty, he wondered, be a mere accident of birth?

Staring into the same dark, yawning chasm of ignorance as so many philosophers and religious leaders had before him, Descartes determined to jettison all he had been taught and evolve a new system of thought shaped by doubt. Determined to begin with one certainty, he expressed his great insight in the phrase *Cogito ergo sum*—I think, therefore I am.

Descartes ordered logic and spirituality to stay on their respective sides of the corpus callosum and mind their own business. Rather than viewing nature as a whole, he broke it down into its component parts using mathematical precision that required reductionist and mechanical thinking. When he was finished, he had split mind from body and, ultimately, religion from science. This extensive, invasive surgery was necessary to stop the madness that was destroying the body politic of seventeenth-century Europe. If Descartes, in his quiet room, listened carefully enough, he could hear the screams of burning women consigned to their fate by men who believed too much. And he could hear the sickening crunch of broken bones as Protestant Christians and Catholic Christians hurled themselves against each other in a mad contest of wills over minor doctrinal differences. Much later, Western culture would have to rectify the overreach of Cartesian thinking: reductionism, scientific determinism, and a mechanical perception of the universe. But due in large part to Descartes and the scientific method he championed, over the next century the witch hunts slowly abated and became a disturbing repressed cultural memory. The religious war between Protestants and Catholics petered out but lay smoldering, like a root fire capable of flaring up even after it seems to have been extinguished.

Science provided people with an alternative explanation to the one espoused by religion. The world is governed by natural laws, scientists proclaimed, and God gave humans the gift of intelligence to discover what they are. With each new mathematically proven revelation, science chipped away at the power of the ecclesiastics. The volume of discord between credos diminished as literacy gained its proper context.

Unfortunately, science, the prim, non-excitable child of the left brain, did not like women. Evolving from the all-male priesthood that had preceded it, the early scientific community allowed no women within its hallowed halls. Science did not have much use for beauty, either, and it treated nature as an enemy. Francis Bacon, author of the scientific masterpiece *Novum Organum*, consistently used metaphors derived from the witch hunt torture chamber to describe how scientists should force nature to relinquish her secrets. In the most powerful demonstration of the new scientific paradigm, Nicolaus Copernicus displaced Mother Earth from the center of the universe and replaced her with Father Sun. Copernicus consigned the planet that was once the hub of wheeling constellations to a lonely orbit with only her barren lunar satellite to pay her homage. Science dismissed spirituality, disdained discussions of ethics and philosophy, and demonstrated a disturbing tendency to ally itself with contemporary hunter-killers—the military. Still, science was a significant improvement over the superstitious thought systems that had generated the witch craze atrocities.

To summarize the last few chapters in the context of this book's thesis, literacy is a salutary, exhilarating stimulant to human progress. Ingenious inventions, innovative new systems of thought, crisp literature, and sparkling new styles of art follow its introduction and sudden acquisition in any society. Newly literate people conceive new ways to interact with each other, formulate new forms of government, and initiate religious enlightenments. But like any strong stimulant, literacy has the potential to produce undesirable side effects.

Due to its exceedingly short learning curve, every society that has acquired alphabet literacy has become violently self-destructive a short time afterward. This madness has been associated with a virulent misogyny and spelled trouble for images, women's rights, goddesses, and right-brain values. Nothing in history accelerated alphabet literacy as much as the invention of the printing press; the spread of both coincided with the one period when women and feminine values suffered most. As a tool for hacking away at the tangle of superstitions that impedes humankind, literacy is indispensable. But societies must recognize that the process of writing and reading initially reinforces left-brain values to the detriment of right-brain values. Forewarned is forearmed.

CHAPTER 33

POSITIVE/NEGATIVE
1648-1899

I want to become a mother with the paternity unknown.
—Pauline Roland, early feminist, 1832*[1]

The single individual who best epitomized the dramatic ascent of rationality in a time shot through with madness was Isaac Newton (1642–1727). His scientific discoveries convinced a majority of educated Europeans that the universe consisted of quantifiable objects and measurable forces obeying immutable laws. The left brain's faculties of reason and mathematical skills were crucial in discovering and proving these laws.

Economists, philosophers, and political theorists soon grafted Newton's natural law onto all aspects of life. The late eighteenth century's Enlightenment, a culmination of triumphs for the left hemisphere, celebrated in advance the inevitable taming of both wild nature and irrational behavior. These, many thinkers believed, would inevitably be brought to heel by the sustained application of linear thinking. These same thinkers deemed anything that could not be comprehended by reason was "other"; by which they meant it was secondary, insignificant, not namable, less than real.

For many men, women fell into the category of "other." "Natural law" reinforced their conviction that they were "naturally" superior to women. Using "irrefutable" logic, they "proved" beyond doubt that the male was the standard and the female a defective version of him.† Women's rights and the attributes associated with the right brain suffered accordingly. Thus, European civilization passed from a patriarchal society based on laws handed

---

*She had four children by four different fathers.
†"Scientists" measured the skulls of women and men and because of their relative disparity in size claimed with scientific certainty that they had proved that men were more intelligent than women.

down three thousand years earlier by a male deity into a new version of patriarchy founded on "natural laws" discovered by male scientists.

Each successive scientific discovery persuaded more people that science was a credible belief system. Unfortunately, the faithful arrived at the joyless conclusion that the world was devoid of spontaneity. Newton and the scientists who followed him described a world in which every effect was due to a previous cause. The Age of Miracles was officially over, replaced by a new age and a new metaphor: that of the Majestic Clockwork. A dispassionate Creator fashioned it, wound it, set it ticking and then withdrew to become a non-participant in both the daily affairs of humans and the operation of the clock. This spiritual black hole was dubbed "scientific determinism."

Newton's mechanics imprisoned Free Will by proving that planets and billiard balls must follow the laws of mass and motion. If they seemed to deviate, it was only because the scientist did not yet know all the variables. There was no such thing as luck, chance, or the unexpected. Voltaire put it this way: "It would be very singular that all nature and all the planets should obey eternal laws, and that there should be a puny animal, five feet high, who, in contempt of these laws, could act as he pleased."[2]

Later, in 1859, the left brain received what could be seen as its ultimate scientific validation. Charles Darwin published *On the Origin of Species*. Darwin's view reduced the vaunted Homo sapiens from the pinnacle of creation to just one species among many. This revolutionary displacement of Man challenged the Bible's claim that God had given Adam dominion over the animal kingdom.

Women should have, but did not, benefit from this demotion of Adam. The social philosophers of the day pounced on the phrase "survival of the fittest," coined by Herbert Spencer. Spencer postulated that the havoc and mayhem of war were necessary forces that periodically pruned the human species of deadwood. Had not Darwin explained that natural selection required strife in order for the alpha male (not uncommonly the strongest and most aggressive) to rise above the pack? In a dog-eat-dog world, love, nurturance, and cooperation were perceived as signs of weakness. Henceforth, the Robber Baron could turn to natural law to justify his crass grasp for power. But this is getting ahead of the story. Earlier, there was another social change that profoundly affected the relationship between the sexes.

The Enlightenment and the scientific discoveries that underpinned it paved the way for a far greater drama—the Industrial Revolution. This event had a profound effect on human relationships; comparable in impact only to the changes previously wrought by the development of agriculture and writing. Two key factors precipitated the Machine Age: the depletion of Europe's forests, and human inventiveness. By the mid-1700s, swarming humankind, thick as termites, had chewed its timber stock to stumps. The dense canopy of trees that had once shaded Europe had been relentlessly clear-cut. Firewood, the fuel of preference, became increasingly expensive as axemen had to venture ever farther from the king's hearth to find virgin stands to fell. It was the first energy crisis since the discovery of fire 750,000 years earlier. One can just imagine the scene repeated from Bavaria to England: court ministers tentatively showing His Majesty a lump of sooty, black rock, then apologetically explaining that although coal did not burn with the clean snap and crackle of fire logs, and tunnels had to be dug in the earth to get at it, coal would keep the populace warm in winter and cook their food.

Once coal, a cheap, seemingly inexhaustible source of energy, had been identified, human inventiveness came into play. Together they were a momentous combination. Scientific discoveries bubbled forth from one laboratory after another. By 1725, science had surpassed organized religion as the chief influence shaping European and American culture. In the early nineteenth century, scientists discovered the secrets of heat energy, which led to the invention of the steam engine, which in turn gave new meaning to the word *power*.*

The Industrial Revolution aggressively increased the sum total of tangible wealth and made possible many advances unimaginable in the preceding century. One technological marvel after another contributed to a rapidly rising standard of living. But these innovations came with a price. The exploitation of children and a widening disparity between the rights and prerogatives of the sexes were just two of them.

As the eighteenth century ticked to a close, no one had the slightest inkling of the titanic force that was about to crash into his or her lives. And after the debris from the Industrial Revolution had been swept away, society would be unrecognizable from what it had been. Whole populations migrated from farms to mills and as the population of cities soared; their inadequate infrastructures groaned under the weight. Family bonds splintered as former farmers disappeared into mines and factories, and mothers labored endless hours in sweatshops. Owning the means of production began to supplant owning land as the premier source of wealth.

The new era reeked of male sweat and engine oil. The left brain was boss. The Industrial Revolution was a combination of science, brawn, finance,

*The Greeks had discovered the principle of the steam engine two thousand years earlier, but subsequent ages lost the knowledge.

mathematics, and competition and it was pursued without much concern for its effects on family life or community. The dark clouds of soot belching forth from factory smokestacks and the unearthly glow of slag heaps lit by Bessemer furnaces were considered by entrepreneurs as proud symbols of progress. These men raped Mother Nature with nary a concern for the future, ignoring the lesson of the clear-cut tree trunks.

Inspired by a small number of women who made their mark as authors, nineteenth-century women began to pull themselves up by their own boot-laces. Literacy rates for women had risen steeply. The brilliance of accom-plished literate women began to subvert the notion that women were intellectually inferior. Women increasingly contributed to the culture's liter-ature and, in a few cases, to its science.

Fiction and poetry writers create images with words through the use of similes, metaphors, description, and analogies and magically illuminate a scene or action in the reader's mind. There was a blossoming of literary luminaries, including Jane Austen, Louisa May Alcott, Elizabeth Barrett, George Sand, the Brontë sisters, Germaine de Staël, and Mary Shelley. Lon-don in the 1830s was a literary mecca, and a third of its published writers were women.[3] The literary scene in Paris was supported by many women both as writers and readers.

In the late eighteenth and early nineteenth centuries, intellectuals fissured into two opposing camps. Voltaire, Diderot, Kant, Hume, and Locke con-tributed to the intellectual heft of the times as the Age of Reason's linear thinkers segued effortlessly into the Enlightenment. Their views on matters of importance generated a strong reaction from those representing the right brain, whose champions initiated the Romantic movement. Rousseau, Keats, Byron, Goethe, and Shelley, repulsed by the Industrial Revolution's heavy-handed abuse of the earth's resources, extolled love, nature, and beauty. Enlightenment enthusiasts claimed reason was superior to emotion; to the Romantics, feelings were the surer guide to truth.

To the Enlightenment crowd, the Romantics seemed to be tilting at windmills. The ear-splitting, smoke-spewing Industrial Revolution and the left-brained values it represented appeared as unstoppable as a barreling locomotive. But two innovations provided a major assist to the values of the right brain: the invention of photography and the discovery of the electro-magnetic field. They appeared in culture simultaneously, and together they would eventually reconfigure every aspect of human interaction. Photogra-phy and electromagnetism elevated the importance of images at the expense of written words, and in so doing began to bring balance back to the left-brain-leaning European-language-speaking peoples. Before we examine how this came about, a telling of two stories is in order.

Leonardo da Vinci had described the principle of the *camera obscura* in the Renaissance. In 1837, Jacques Mandé Daguerre developed a technique of "fixing" images on metal and he named his invention "daguerreotypes." Daguerre's innovation became a household word almost overnight. With a flash of magnesium and the click of a shutter, the camera recorded a slice of visual space, preserving one moment out of the linear sequence of time. *Photo-graphy* can be read as meaning "writing with light." Opposite in nearly every respect from writing with ink, photography illuminated Europe like a bolt of lightning. It seemed that by the second half of the nineteenth century just about everyone had sat for his or her photograph at least once. Old photographs of American Indians who sometimes traveled hundreds of miles just to have their likenesses preserved in silver nitrate salts attest to the daguerreotype's seductive draw.

Philosopher José Argüelles observed, "Photography is one of those technical devices which has so drastically altered our senses and upon which we have developed such a profound dependence that it is difficult, indeed impossible, for us to think about it with any degree of detachment."[4] The right brain's face-pattern-comprehension abilities received a major boost as people became enthralled with photographs. Virtually all people were aware that photography depended on a negative transparency being transformed into positive image, which reinforced the concept of the complementarity of opposites.

Chief Joseph of the Nez Perce

If someone in the centuries immediately following Gutenberg's revolution asked a sampling of people, "If your house were on fire and you had only enough time to retrieve one personal item, what would it be?," the vast majority of Europeans and Americans would have answered: "the family Bible." Handed down from generation to generation, this book served as the family's memory bank, often containing genealogies, wedding contracts, and deeds. If you asked the same question a few decades after the introduction of photography, the answer changed to "the family photo album." A collection of images had become the most precious of possessions. The invention of photography began to shift culture from written word back to perceived image.*

Photography did for images what the printing press had done for written words: it made their reproduction easy, quick, and relatively inexpensive. An illustration of photography's iterative power: the single-most-reproduced art image is Vincent van Gogh's *Sunflowers* (1888). It is estimated that more than 17 million copies have adorned sundry hotel, parlor, and dormitory rooms. While alive, van Gogh received little monetary recompense or recognition. Due to photographic reproduction, his oeuvre is familiar to the average citizen from Maine to Borneo, and originals that *he could not give away* presently command stratospheric prices at art auctions.

Before the advent of photography, an elite audience appreciated painters. After photography, art became a common language that permeated every stratum of society and subtly changed the very nature of human intercourse. Mention the name Dali to a group from any segment of the population and someone will surely say "melting watches." Key art images have indelibly imprinted the psyche of Western culture.

Photography liberated artists from the goal of replicating nature realistically. Many great art innovations, such as Impressionism, Pointillism, Cubism, and Fauvism were the result of artists' newfound freedom. Because photography faithfully reproduced visual reality, painting and sculpture could serve new functions—to respond to the world in a variety of ways, and address the scientific, cultural, and industrial transformations buffeting the times. And as I proposed in *Art & Physics*, art increasingly intuited the shape of the future. The visionary artist is the first person in a culture to *see* the world in a new way. Sometimes simultaneously, sometimes later, a visionary physicist has an insight so momentous that he discovers a new way to *think* about the world. The artist uses images and metaphors and the physicist

*Lithography, the reproduction of images by means of engraving, was perfected in the 1820s virtually at the very moment photography superseded it in importance.

uses numbers and equations. Yet when the artist's antecedent images are superimposed on the later physicist's formula, there is a striking fit. For example, Monet's haystack series, the representation of an object in both three-dimensional in space and changing time preceded Minkowski's formulation of the fourth dimension—the space-time continuum.

As the nineteenth century progressed, people increasingly obtained information about the world through images. The camera and the newly refined art of lithography tilted culture away from the printed word and toward the visual gestalt. Political cartoons began to appear regularly in the newspapers of the day and were often more to the point than the wordy editorials that accompanied them.

Daguerre was responsible for one half of the Iconic Revolution. Michael Faraday (1791–1867) initiated the other. The circumstances of his childhood made him an unlikely candidate to be a scientific innovator. Faraday's working-class parents believed their child was retarded because he did not speak until the age of five. As a young man, he worked as a bookbinder's apprentice, a blue-collar job that afforded him the opportunity to read the books he was binding, many of which concerned science. During these years, Faraday spent his evenings attending public lectures by Sir Humphry Davy, the director of England's prestigious Royal Institute of Science. He interviewed to be Davy's assistant, showing the meticulous notes and masterfully drawn technical illustrations he had made from Davy's lectures. Davy saw in the raw twenty-two-year-old bookbinder a superior intelligence and, much to the chagrin of Ph.D. applicants from Oxford and Cambridge, he appointed "Mike," as Faraday came to be known, to the coveted position.

In the 1820s, building on the work of an international group of scientists—Ampère in France, Volta and Galvani in Italy, Ohm in Germany, and Oersted in Denmark—Faraday intuited the existence of a force field that humans could neither see, hear, smell, touch, nor taste. A few years earlier, the poet Samuel Coleridge had written, "The universe is a cosmic web woven by God and held together by the crossed strands of attractive and repulsive forces."[5] Faraday invited people to imagine the spectral lines of force that make up an electromagnetic field.

After discovering features and principles of this "cosmic web" throughout the 1820s, Faraday invented the electric dynamo in 1831. Humankind could now generate this crackling power. Just as the Mechanical Age of gears and pistons was gathering its full head of steam, Faraday and the other pioneers in electromagnetic research logarithmically increased human possibilities. Ultimately, the electric dynamo would transform culture even more than the initial stages of the Industrial Revolution had. It would also bring about a subconscious adjustment of the existing female/male equation.

Electromagnetism is not confined to one bounded locus in space. It is not mechanistic as it has no moving parts. It is not reducible and can only be apprehended in its totality. It is a pattern rather than a point, insubstantial rather than material, more a verb than a noun, more a process than an object, more sinuous than angular. Since it is invisible, one has to imagine it in order to grasp it. Early researchers conjured it using feminine metaphors. The words used to describe it, such as "web," "matrix," "waves," and "strands," are all words etymologically and mythologically associated with the feminine. A "field," which has proved to be electromagnetism's most common synonym, is a noun borrowed from agriculture and nature. Electromagnetism had an organic interdependence, and it supplanted the Mechanical Age's independent steps, sequence, and specialization with holism, simultaneity, and integration. The great principle at the heart of electromagnetism is that tension exists between polar opposites: positive and negative. An electromagnetic state only exists when both are present. The two poles, positive and negative, always strive to unite and it is only when they do that energy is generated.

Prior to the discovery of electromagnetism, poets and lovers usually compared their burning erotic love and desires to flames. The *spark of love,* an *electrifying kiss,* a *compulsive attraction,* a *magnetic personality,* an *aura of sensuality,* a *repulsive person,* and the *pull of polar opposites* entered the lexicon of love to the delight of anyone who ever needed a fresh way to express an archaic feeling.

The alphabet nation, inculcated with the belief that reality consists of a linear sequence of spatial events, had to pretend that electricity marched single file down a wire. In truth, nothing moves! Aspects of electromagnetism that *seemed* linear changed states at light speed, too fast for humans to appreciate. Electromagnetic events appeared to be both interdependent and simultaneous. Electromagnetism was mysterious and wave-like. Immaterial and insensate, electromagnetism resembles a spirit. Everything about it reaffirmed the validity of right-hemispheric faculties; in Faraday's time it subtly increased both men's and women's appreciation of the feminine.

Benjamin Lee Whorf, a twentieth-century linguist, put forth the idea that the language we learn profoundly shapes the universe we can imagine. If a culture's words describe a reality that is causal, linear, and mechanistic, then its members will accord more respect to the masculine left side of the corpus callosum, a mind-set that manifests in patriarchy. If, however, the features of a major new discovery force a people to employ the imagery of the right brain, then feminine values and status will be buoyed as a result.

Democritus, in ancient Greece, divided reality into Atoms and the Void. Thereafter, Western philosophers, convinced that there was little they could say about nothingness, ignored the Void and concentrated on describing matter's smallest indivisible components, the atoms. Science became the investigation of "things" and the forces that acted on them, and scientists envisioned reality, to a large extent, in terms of masculine metaphors. A world composed of objects obeying deterministic laws of causality reinforced the idea that the left brain was superior. Invisible electromagnetism, a *no-thing*, the other half of Democritus's duality, upset the Newtonian cog-and-gear perception of celestial Clockwork.

The discovery of electricity and the field it generated changed the world. The inventions it begat—the electric motor (1831), turbines and telegraph (1844), batteries and telephone (1876), electric lamp (1879), electric car (1875), microphone (1876), phonograph (1877), electric elevator (1880), X rays (1886), radio (1887/1903), and the twentieth century's television, cyclotrons, tape recorders, radio telescopes, VCRs, computers, fax machines, cellular phones, and cyberspace—pushed humankind's conception of reality into areas unimaginable to Faraday and his contemporaries. This hyperinflating perimeter is due not only to the content of information these devices enable us to access but also the reprogramming of the brain of each member of the culture who uses these new forms of information transfer.

Much has been written recently about the differing modes of communication used by each sex. Our awareness of the *process* as well as of the *content* of information exchanges should also take into account how gender relations have been affected by changing communication technologies. The return of the image, and the way electromagnetism reshaped reality from angular masculine to curvaceous feminine, are important factors contributing both to the rise of women's rights in the late nineteenth century and to the increased respect for nature in the second half of the twentieth century. These changes in perception came about, in part, because of two technologies that affirmed gatherer/nurturer values.

Numerous factors contributed to the rise of women's assertiveness and independence and the resurgence of feminine values and holistic thinking. All photographs increase the status of the image-recognition skills of the right brains of both sexes. This factor in turn reinforces a cultural interest in art, myth, nature, nurture, and poetry.

·   ·   ·

Since the invention of writing five thousand years ago, millions of forceful, intelligent, well-educated women have lived and died. Yet they rarely organized into a concerted movement to challenge patriarchal systems. The first organized women's movement that called for an *end* to patriarchy began in the latter part of the nineteenth century in England and America. It occurred in these two countries rather than on the Continent for the same reason that the witch craze was less severe in English-speaking lands than on the Continent. A single feature of the English language holds the secret: in all the major Continental tongues, most important nouns must be defined by gender articles. Because there are no masculine or feminine articles in the English language, English nouns are gender neutral. In the majority of European languages, most passive objects, such as urns, vessels, sheaths, and holsters (all waiting to be filled), along with doorways, gates, and thresholds (through and over which one passes), tend to be feminine; weapons that thrust, tools that pierce, smash, or crush, and implements that cut, saw, or divide, are almost always masculine.

While there is a certain rustic logic to these assignments when it comes to physical objects, the classification of more abstract nouns by gender suggests a misogyny deeply rooted in the languages. Continental children learn to distinguish between masculine and feminine nouns between the ages of two and four, and parenthetically they learn that there is sexual *value* associated with each noun. If nouns that are stationary, receptive, ill defined, or sinister require a female article, would not this information affect how a little girl will perceive her place in relation to boys? If nouns denoting passivity are feminine, would this not tend to encourage feminine passivity? If *pouvoir* (power) requires a *le* and *maladie* (sickness) a *la*, what are very young French children to make of these distinctions? In Italian, disability (*invalidata*) is feminine and honor (*onore*) is masculine; vacancy (*vacante*) is feminine in Spanish, while value (*valor*) is masculine; in German, mind (*Geist*) is masculine and foible (*Eigenheit*) is feminine. Although there are many counterexamples, in the main this division holds.

Toddler boys learn that active, positive, thrusting, and clearly defined nouns are associated with their sex just as they are becoming aware of the anatomical differences between themselves and little girls. Would not this information stimulate pride in being male and disdain for females whose gender nouns are, in general, ambiguous, passive, and negative? Many of the gender articles of Continental languages can be guessed simply by using sexual or patriarchal imagery.

English is also distinguished from Continental languages by its lack of variant second-person-singular pronouns. In English, one has no choice but to address another with the egalitarian *you*. In German, the intimate *du* is traditionally reserved for immediate family members, friends, or lovers, and the formal *Sie* is used for superiors and strangers. Similar distinctions are present in French, Italian, and Spanish. Pronouns are words that define the speaker's relationship to the person addressed. Any language that forces the speaker to choose between two pronouns to address another, *a decision that depends on the permission of the person addressed,* promotes a vertical layering of culture, and this in turn reinforces dominant/submissive interpersonal relations. The hierarchy of Continental language pronouns enters the consciousness of two-year-olds before they are aware of this artifice. One's own native language must be transcended in order to see the world as it is. Most European men and women, tripped up by the snares of their grammars at age three, are prisoners forever. Women in English-speaking cultures have been more able to consider themselves the equals of men. In parallel fashion, because of the gender-neutrality inherent in their language, English-speaking men have been more favorably disposed to women's aspirations for equality than their Continental counterparts.* The English language's gender neutrality and its lack of pronoun distinction foster democracy and I suggest this is one of the primary reasons why the suffragette movement began *where* it did. Photography and electromagnetism were key factors enabling it to begin *when* it did.

The first modern call for female equality was Mary Wollstonecraft's *A Vindication of the Rights of Women* published in 1792. Wollstonecraft challenged John Locke's libertarian stance that women should remain subordinate to their husbands, and disputed Rousseau's Romantic notion that women think differently from, and are therefore inferior to, men. There was no "sex in souls," she declared. But her male contemporaries in America, France, and England, while passionately espousing the cause of individual liberty for the male half of the population, paid little attention to her.

Then in the 1830s, Frances Wright, a Scotswoman, and Sarah Grimké, an American, took up Wollstonecraft's refrain. Wright, an atheist, raged against the "insatiate priestcraft" who kept women in a state of "mental bondage."[6] Grimké remained within the Christian fold but claimed that an erroneous

---

*Along with English, Swedish is another of the few European languages that does not heavily encumber its nouns with gender politics. Contrast the generally peaceful character of Swedish men and the equality of their women with their cousins of identical ethnic stock: the patriarchal, militaristic Prussians, who live only a few hundred miles south but speak a language freighted with male dominance.

view of scripture had evolved through "perverted interpretations of the Holy Writ."[7]

In the next generation, the articulate voices of Sojourner Truth, Elizabeth Cady Stanton, Harriet Taylor, and Susan B. Anthony joined the chorus. In 1848, at Seneca Falls, New York, women from all walks of life attended the first convention dedicated (albeit implicitly) to overthrowing patriarchy. After days of rousing speeches decrying centuries-old abuses, the attendees ratified a Declaration of Sentiments (drafted primarily by Stanton). Repeating almost verbatim the wording of the American Declaration of Independence, it called for a fundamental restructuring of society:

> We hold these truths to be self-evident: that all men *and women* are created equal; that they are endowed by their Creator with certain inalienable rights: that among these are life, liberty, and the pursuit of happiness; that to secure these rights governments are instituted, deriving their powers from the consent of the governed.[8]

Using the phraseology of the Founding Fathers was ironic because women, not having the vote, were disenfranchised from having a say in their own governance.

In his 1869 book, *The Subjection of Women*, their prestigious and unexpected ally, philosopher John Stuart Mill, provided welcome support. He called upon men voluntarily to end patriarchal practices: "the legal subordination of one sex by the other . . . is wrong in itself," he wrote; it "is now one of the chief hindrances to human improvement."[9] Using his now-familiar argument of the "greatest good for the greatest number," he wrote:

> But it is not only through the sentiment of personal dignity that the free direction and disposal of their own faculties is a source of unhappiness to human beings, and not least to women. There is nothing, after disease, indigence, and guilt, so fatal to the pleasurable enjoyment of life as the want of a worthy outlet for the active faculties.[10]

Large numbers of women suddenly refused to tolerate the injustices long perpetuated against their sex. They lent their money, courage, and intellect to the cause, and growing numbers of men endorsed their aspirations. Still, most nineteenth-century men disapproved. As an act of civil disobedience in 1872, Susan B. Anthony slipped into a voting booth and pulled the lever. Her arrest forced the issue of woman's suffrage into the courts. She was confident that any judge would be compelled to interpret the recently

enacted Fourteenth Amendment to the U.S. Constitution in her favor,
". . . Nor shall any State deprive any person of life, liberty, or property, without due process of law; nor deny to any person within its jurisdiction the
equal protection of the laws." All Anthony had to do was to convince the
court that as a respiring human born in America, she met the qualifications
to be considered a "person." The judge rejected her argument. He had composed his opinion *before* he heard her or her lawyer's brief.

Despite this and other setbacks, the success of the suffragette movement
seemed inevitable—change was in the air. Electromagnetism was exerting
an ever-widening influence on culture, pulling it like taffy into new and
unusual shapes. The telegraph collapsed time and space, the telephone and
phonograph transferred information with the immediacy of speech, and
photographic images continued to proliferate. The hold on people's psyche
that the linear alphabet had exercised for millennia began to loosen. And the
pendulum concerning attitudes about gender equality, so long stuck on the
masculine side, began to gradually swing back to the other side.

Signs of this shift were evident throughout the alphabet world. In Germany, Johann Bachofen (1815–87) investigated preliterate societies' practice
of *Mutterrecht,* "Mother Right" and questioned whether patriarchy was
always present. Friedrich Engels (1820–95) recommended a new economic
system that, in theory, granted women greater equality. In America, Ralph
Waldo Emerson (1803–82) promoted the egalitarian Transcendentalist philosophy, while William James turned his readers' attentions to the possibilities of experiential spirituality.

When Nietzsche proclaimed "God is dead!" the God he had in mind was
the singular masculine patriarch who ruled from a heavenly throne. In 1854,
a few years before Nietzsche's declaration, the Catholic Church proclaimed
that Mary had been conceived by Immaculate Conception, which meant
that Mary had not been tainted by Original Sin. She ceased to be an ordinary
mortal. The first tentative recognition in Western culture by male ecclesiastics of a Goddess in one thousand five hundred years occurred in conjunction with the putative death of God.

The nineteenth century was a period of intense religious feelings. Gnostic experiential revelations came to be valued over dogmas dispensed by figures of authority. Two of the most influential individuals were Mary Baker
Eddy, who founded Christian Science, and Helena Blavatsky, the founder of
Theosophy. Both disciplines attracted many male adherents. Adding to the
century's ferment, ashrams and Zen centers sprang up in Paris, London, and
New York, as Eastern thought systems were embraced by Occidentals. Mys-

tic traditions such as Sufism, Kabbalah, alchemy, astrology, and Rosicrucia-niam flourished. Each emphasized personal exercises that would help the individual achieve union with God, and each taught that both complementary masculine and feminine principles constituted the cosmos.

By the latter half of the nineteenth century, when images were everywhere ascendant, art became mainstream. The Impressionists awoke the general public to new ways of envisioning the world. Composers such as Ravel, Debussy, and Rimsky-Korsakoff strove to create pictorial music. Symbolist poets used words to conjure images, and some, like Stéphane Mallarmé, arranged their words on a page to create a visual pattern that resembled the animals or objects about which they wrote.

Science was also affected by these radical changes in the culture. During *La Belle Époque,* the last decade of the nineteenth century, the physicist Ludwig Boltzmann so despaired over his inability to convince his peers that reality had a significant component of randomness and disorder that he would commit suicide. He should have been more patient. Dangerous cracks were beginning to appear in Newton's mechanistic edifice and the sharp edges of Descartes' dualistic black-and-white opposites were blurring.

Politically, democracy was in the air. Kings shifted uneasily on their thrones, natives became restless, servants surly, and women dissatisfied. Communists demanded the overthrow of the ruling class and a redistribution of the wealth, while capitalists insisted that governing authorities end all interference in commerce and adopt a *laissez-faire* stance. Everywhere, paternalism was in retreat.

One of the new machines invented in the late nineteenth century profoundly affected writing. Ever since the first Sumerian had pressed a pointed stick into wet clay five thousand years ago, one dominant hand, controlled exclusively by the dominant hemisphere, had dictated the mechanics of writing. It made no difference whether the implement used was a stylus, a chisel, a brush, a quill, a crayon, a pen, or a pencil, the hunter/killer left lobe of the brains of *both* men and women directed the muscles of the aggressive right hand to write. Then, in 1873, an American, Philo Remington, invented the typewriter.

Within a generation of his patent, the sound of tap-tapping could be heard in offices and homes across the Western world. Typewriters fundamentally changed the way people created the written word. Skilled typists engaged both their dominant and their non-dominant hands, connected to both sides of their brains, and the content of typewriter-generated words was indirectly influenced. Right-brained values and attributes began to leak onto the page. The typewriter had a negligible impact on gender relations at first because at the end of the nineteenth century, secretarial pools were comprised mostly of young women transcribing letters dictated by their male bosses. The full impact of the typewriter keyboard on human communication—and on gender equality—would not be felt until the following century, when another new invention would entice men to join the world of q-w-e-r-t-y (more about this later).

In 1887, Thomas Edison's prolific laboratory developed a technology that combined electromagnetism and photography. An electric motion picture projector unspooled a series of negatives past an intense light, which shone through them. At flicker fusion the projected individual frames merged into a motion picture. Film made it possible to tell a linear story, and people were hypnotized and fascinated, eagerly congregating in darkened rooms to watch the plots of novels unfold on screen. Movies, as the new medium was eventually called, began to compete with books for the public's attention. Movie attendance first challenged and then easily surpassed church attendance. As the century turned and film technology improved, the public's enthusiasm for movies began to erode the hegemony of the written word.

At the end of the nineteenth century, thoughtful inhabitants of Europe and America looked back in wonder at the amazing changes wrought by technology. A United States government official seriously proposed closing the Patent Office because he was convinced that the next century would bring forth nothing of interest—everything, he said, had already been invented. In Paris, a major newspaper convened a panel of distinguished art critics and asked them what they foresaw for the twentieth century. To a man, they claimed that the profusion of art styles in the late nineteenth century had exhausted the reservoirs of human creativity. The art of the next century, they declared, would simply provide a filigree here and an arabesque there. In military academies everywhere, generals pored over their contingency plans and fed their horses. Few people were aware that evolving methods of communication would transform their culture yet again and that every aspect of society, including the relative status of men and women, would be reconfigured. The century just over the horizon would soon supply ample evidence of the power inherent in communication technologies to change the world.

CHAPTER 34

ID/SUPEREGO
1900–1945

As soon as we start putting our thoughts into words and sentences everything gets distorted, language is just no damn good—I use it because I have to, but I don't put any trust in it. We never understand each other.
—Marcel Duchamp[1]

It is in vain that we say what we see; what we see never resides in what we say.
—Michel Foucault[2]

The new century began like no other. A series of dramatic intellectual movements, radical art "isms," brilliant scientific discoveries, electrified inventions, and disruptive social trends—rolled like dislodged pebbles down the mountainside of Western civilization. Together, they triggered an avalanche that altered human existence. At first, these developments seemed unrelated to women's status, images, nature, and the Goddess, but subliminally they favorably inclined Westerners toward all four.

In 1900, Sigmund Freud published *The Interpretation of Dreams*. Descending deeper into the dark unexplored interior of the human psyche than anyone before him, he shined a flashlight into its subterranean caverns. There he saw and identified the poltergeist that had so often gummed up "the best laid plans of mice and men." The treacly enemy was us. Freud explained that human conduct was in part beholden to what he called the Id, a primal agent that rattled about in the right hemisphere, making things go bump in the night. No matter how diligently the left brain applies itself to solving scientific puzzles, Freud implied, it is never completely independent. The Id, operating in the Unconscious, has a way of jerking on the reins of Will when Reason least expects it. Men who were proud of their cool rationality had to confront the reality that they were not as far removed from their primate ancestors as they had so smugly thought. Further, Freud emphasized that aspects of the Unconscious—what could be called irrationality, intuition, or the sixth sense—have a wisdom that could exceed the calculus of reason. Poets, mystics, and women acknowledged this power for centuries, but the scientific community gave the notion little credence. Freud's work elevated the importance of myth, trance, and dream.

Also in 1900, physicist Max Planck stumbled upon a strange feature of the atomic world that greatly upset Newton's schema. Instead of the seamless linearity so long imagined to be at the heart of sequence, Planck discovered a ragged discontinuity. This minute jerkiness began to uncouple cause-effect, the concept supporting so many cherished Western notions including linear sequence, the core principle of alphabets. Average people needed little prompting to integrate Planck's weird quantum dictum concerning discontinuity. They were flocking to see flickering images of film, the burgeoning new communication medium.

Spontaneity, randomness, and the unexpected erupted in the new century like the guffaw following the punch line of a joke. All three attributes found their exemplar in the single most famous personage of the era—Charlie Chaplin. In previous ages, a person so renowned would most likely have been a conqueror, a king, or perhaps a philosopher or religious figure. Individuals achieving such fame have generally embodied left-brain values.

Chaplin, in contrast, was the showman of the incongruous, genius of the jerky gesture, and master of the bellylaugh. A clown who poked fun at the serious endeavors of the left brain, he did so without using a single word. With pantomime, facial expressions, and a signature waddle, Chaplin showcased the communicative power of the right hemisphere. In the company of history's other luminaries—for example, Pericles, Julius Caesar, Charlemagne, Gregory the Great, Martin Luther, and Napoleon—Chaplin sticks out like a sore thumb. Before Chaplin, had a jester ever even been included in any encyclopedia or history text? The tenor of any age is epitomized by its most celebrated resident. The prominence of Chaplin's persona signified the rapid erosion of the left brain's stature.

Just before Chaplin began lampooning the Mechanical Age in films such as *City Lights*, a major discovery in physics further challenged the supremacy of sequence in science. In 1905, Albert Einstein, an obscure twenty-six-year-old patent official in Bern, published his Special Theory of Relativity. The young genius posited that at very fast speeds reality did not obey Newton's laws.

Sequence is a vital component of speech, and it is the very crux of alphabetic written languages. A theory that struck at the heart of this principle could not help but punch another hole in the taut fabric that supports all written alphabets.

There were other harbingers of the written word's decline. Beginning in 1907, Pablo Picasso and Georges Braque began to insert pieces of words into their paintings. These alphabetic bits and tailings served as decorative icons integrated into the larger pattern of their compositions. The only other time the alphabet had assumed a similar function was in the Dark Ages when monks, illuminating manuscripts, converted letters into works of art more to be admired as patterns than to be used as tools of thought.

Since Giovanni Boccaccio invented the novel in the fourteenth century, writers based their works on the fundamental principle of linear sequential narrative. No matter how complex its plot, each story had a beginning, a middle, and an end. In the twentieth century, writers broke free of this convention. Novelist Virginia Woolf invited readers to view the events in her protagonists' lives as tiles in a mosaic rather than as beads on a line. James Joyce in *Finnegans Wake* used the physical configuration of letters as iconic forms. Aware of the influence on culture of a phonetic alphabet, he warned readers that they were in danger of becoming "abcdminded." He scrambled spelling in ingenious ways, giving words multiple, simultaneous meanings so that his alphabet resembled Chinese ideograms. Puns, double entendres, and palindromes are word games best appreciated by the right hemisphere. Joyce's *Wake* was a prescient wake for the anticipated demise of left-brain hegemony. William Faulkner, e. e. cummings, and other writers continued to loosen the knots binding causality.

As the century edged into its third decade, a new branch of physics called quantum mechanics came into its own. Quantum turned science and common sense upside down by introducing into its equations the mathematics of chance. Niels Bohr, a quantum mechanics pioneer, put forth the heretical idea that the mental decisions of an investigator influenced the outcome of the experiments the investigator performed and thus the observer, to some extent, created the reality the observer observed. Classical Newtonians knit their brows. If Bohr was correct (he was), science would have to admit its nemesis—subjectivity—into its calculations. The strict separation between object and observer, a cherished tenet of science, was, under certain circumstances, abrogated.

Bohr's work led him to the conclusion that everything in the universe is mysteriously interconnected—no event happens anywhere that does not affect events everywhere else. This insight was not a revelation to the right brain's aesthetic sensibilities. Landscape painters understand that if they change even one small feature in the background, they will likely have to make adjustments throughout the composition. The concept of an invisible "web" (already favored as an image because of the earlier discovery of electromagnetism) became the operating metaphor for reality, and supplanted the Majestic Clockwork that had been Descartes' and Newton's model. The perceptual changes wrought by the two new fields of physics (relativity and quantum) enhanced the idea of gender equality as feminine metaphors supplanted masculine ones.

Bohr challenged another scientific shibboleth in 1927 by proposing that opposites were not necessarily *either/or*, as all earlier Western dualistic thinkers had assumed, but rather might be *both/and*. He said that the opposite of a shallow truth is a falsehood, but that the opposite of a profound truth was another profound truth. In his Theory of Complementarity, Bohr posited that opposites were two different aspects of a higher unity existing just beyond our limited perceptual apparatus. When the Danish king knighted him for his pioneering work, Bohr chose the Chinese yin/yang icon of the Tao for his heraldic coat of arms. Aware that his discovery had implications beyond the specialized world of quantum physics, Bohr chose to publish his Complementarity Theory in a philosophy journal, and it did not contain a single equation.

Psychiatrist Carl Jung's work reflected Bohr's description of the subatomic realm. In his Theory of Synchronicity concerning human interactions, Jung proposed that the ligatures of causality were not the only means of suturing life's events together. Some inexplicable happenings in our lives are connected in another dimension by *meaning*. Uncanny coincidences too rich to be explained by mere statistical chance, key decisions correctly made with insufficient information, and paranormal phenomena happen, Jung said, for reasons beyond our ken. Jung translated Bohr's hypothesis concerning physics into the biological realm, proposing that all living things are interconnected in a web that cannot be scientifically quantified.

Jung was the first man of science to propose that we are all born with an extensive foreknowledge of the world. Previously, Western rationalists had accepted with few caveats Locke's concept of a newborn's brain as a *tabula rasa*, a clean slate upon which culture could write. Jung disagreed. He named his ancient knowing the "Collective Unconscious" and envisioned it as an inherited extra-corporeal net holding bits of experience filtered down through the consciousness of our forebears, both human and non-human. Like Freud's hypothetical Id, the Collective Unconscious presupposed that human awareness was thoroughly grounded in its animal nature. To support his idea, Jung cited the fact that widely separated and isolated peoples invent the same myths, just as individuals in disparate cultures assign the same meanings to certain dream symbols. To account for this, he proposed the existence of universal archetypes to which peoples of all cultures, past and present, respond. Archetypes are buried deep in the strata of our minds and appear most often in the form of images; their close association with myths, dreams, and emotions localizes them to the right of the corpus callosum. Poets, playwrights, and religious figures have long intuitively understood the immense power of these mysterious, half-conscious, half-spectral icons.

Jung, Freud, Joyce, Planck, Einstein, Picasso, Chaplin, and many others shifted the intellectual climate of the West. Each in his own way added heft to the appreciation of the faculties of the right hemisphere.

There were so many alogical features of the new world of quantum that the two most common words scientists blurted out in half-wonder and half-exasperation to describe them were "weird" and "absurd." Weirdness and absurdity also came to characterize art. "Make the world strange," the poet Ezra Pound urged other artists.[3] Dadaism, arising coincident with the mud-and-blood *danse macabre* of World War I, championed nonsensical art. One of its leaders, the poet Tristan Tzara, cut the daily newspaper into scraps of partial sentences. He dropped the pieces into a bag, shook it, dumped the contents on a tabletop, and declared that the arrangements into which the scraps fell were "Dada poems." Dada artists passed long evenings together at the Cafe Voltaire in Zurich, laughing at each other's crazy performances. Simultaneously in 1916, a few blocks distant, Albert Einstein was putting the finishing touches on his second great scientific contribution: the General Theory of Relativity. In this work, Einstein laid before us a vision of reality that was queerer than we could imagine.

Surrealism, the child of the Dada movement, explored the unconscious and jarred the viewer with such juxtapositions as fur-lined teacups and locomotives that floated in midair. *Sur-real* means "over-reality," and the surrealist vision further validated the dreamscape of the right hemisphere at the expense of the correct-perspectivist left one.

A new breed of philosophers and logicians zeroing in on the cause of the confusion in the culture agreed that it lay in language: the very words we use to communicate with each other, they proposed, constrain our imaginations. For centuries, language itself was an all-but-invisible hand that struc-tured thought. In the late nineteenth century, C. S. Peirce and Ferdinand de Saussure founded the field of semiotics, the study of the nature of lan-guage. Building on their work, the Viennese philosopher Ludwig Wittgen-stein called language a "cage." After years of exploring the intricacies of syntax and grammar, he reached the startling conclusion that language was so limited that it was inadequate for conveying the nature of reality, observ-ing, "What can be shown cannot be said."[4] Resembling the stance taken by quantum physicists and the dadaists, Wittgenstein, too, challenged the linear thinking necessary for logic and writing. Wittgenstein retired from philoso-phy at the height of his career and became a hospital orderly. Later, Edward Sapir and Benjamin Lee Whorf proposed that the form of the language we learn as children shapes our ability to imagine the world.

Under the combined weight of all the aforementioned movements, the left-brained substrate of Western philosophy and sensibility cracked. West-erners in the new century confronted mounting evidence, evident in every discipline, that something was fundamentally wrong with the dominant paradigm that had ruled for so long.

The many advances flooding the twentieth century should have made it a shining century. But they were overwhelmed by two world wars, a severe economic depression, a protracted Cold War, and the outbreak of ethnic conflicts that have left historians at a loss to explain how a society, with so much promise, could have descended into such dark times. Few have inter-preted these chilling realities within the context of the era's inundation by new media of communication.

In the five hundred years following Gutenberg, nationalism became the scourge that excoriated Western culture. Before nationalism, mercenaries on the payroll of one Renaissance Italian city-state fought their counterparts on another's, and the prince of one German principality warred with the prince of another German principality. Soldiers belonged to a professional class whose principal aspirations were to get paid and to not get killed. Few mer-cenaries died in battle and, by common consent, most skirmishes broke off at five o'clock, in time for a beer and dinner. After the appearance of the printing press, Europeans saw themselves belonging to larger entities made up of all the people who spoke and wrote as they did. Loyalty to one's "nation" suddenly became a noble cause for which to die. French-speaking people became Frenchmen—*Vive la France!* German-speaking people became Germans—*Deutschland über Alles!* And so on.

The wars fought because of jingoistic fervor are too numerous to list; most schoolchildren have groaned over having to memorize the ever-shifting national alliances of European history. The nationalistic war that was supposed to end all wars, World War I, was wholly a product of print-saturated cultures. Outside Europe and America, the mental constructions necessary to imagine nationhood did not exist. Tribesmen in Africa, though dressed in the military garb of their colonialist oppressors, rarely grasped why it was honorable to die for someone else's king and country.

Alphabet letters, like soldiers ceaselessly marching off the presses, made Europeans and Americans peculiarly vulnerable to chauvinism. People of all the alphabet nations read avidly the "Great Novels" that issued from their best authors, the theme (*content*) of which emphasized the universality of the human experience. Yet at the same time, the *process* of book reading reinforced readers' delusions that their fellows just across the river, who claimed a different nationality, were a subhuman or despicable species.

When all the wars fought for flag and country were over, France remained essentially the France of the past thousand years, Germany encompassed an area where most German-speaking people lived as they had for a thousand years, Italians still inhabited the peninsula that was their ancient home, and Englishmen still cultivated the "sceptered isle" their ancestors had tilled for a millennium. All the previous centuries' hoarse-throated charges, clanging saber swipes, and fields of young men screaming for help in many languages had accomplished little.

Hardly noticed during all the shouting and mayhem, the right brain was at work quietly behind the scenes. In America, women received the right to vote in 1920, in England, 1936. In most of Europe and America, the fanaticism that had characterized patriarchal religions was imperceptibly fading. Protestantism softened, became more egalitarian, and even inspired mystics, beginning with Sören Kierkegaard (1813-55). Protestant women wore lipstick without fear of retribution. Large numbers of Jews abandoned Orthodoxy and turned to the Reform Movement, while many Catholics, in defiance of the reigning dogma, practiced birth control in the dark.

As we have seen, the written word, introduced into a previously illiterate population, initially drives it mad. A prime example is what happened after the appearance of the *Communist Manifesto*, Western culture's fourth "sacred" alphabetic book (after the Old Testament, New Testament, and Quran.) I use the word "sacred" because the *Communist Manifesto* precipitated yet another "religious" revolution. Karl Marx's imageless tome called for the repudiation of the existing God so that another—history—could be raised in His place. Marx saw history as an unseen force that determines the lives of humans, yet history, quintessentially masculine and emanating from the left brain, is nothing more than the linear, sequential ordering of male events. In his hermetically sealed system of thought, Marx's "Force of History" replaced Yahweh's wrath, Zeus's thunderbolts, and Christ's mercy. According to his new gospel, man is first and foremost an economic animal. After Newton's impersonal "scientific determinism," Marx's concepts were not difficult for nineteenth- and twentieth-century intellectuals to assimilate. Although he addressed the concerns of the male economic animal and wrote extensively about society's natural division of labor, Marx failed to give credit to the role or contribution of women in his analysis of history.

With the self-assurance of a zealot, Marx predicted that his quasi-religious revolution would occur first in the most advanced industrial states. Voluble ideologues, gathering in coffeehouses, argued interminably about whether the first rotten fruit to fall would be France, America, England, or Germany. Much to the Marxists' surprise, their guru's turgid theories found their only Western success in Russia, the most backward of all the major Western nations.

The reason for this unexpected development, I believe, lies in Russia's extremely delayed acquisition of literacy. By the time most of Europe and America had recovered from the madness stirred up by the press, Russia was still an essentially oral society. Prior to the nineteenth century, Russia had yet to produce a national literature. In the year 1800, there were only two bookstores in all of Moscow, and there were more universities in England, France, and Germany than there were university students in all of Russia.[6] Despite the fact that Gutenberg's revolution took place on Russia's very doorstep, its citizens participated minimally in the Renaissance, the Reformation, the Age of Reason, or the Enlightenment. They contributed little to scientific and global explorations, artistic innovation, or humanistic philosophy. But they were spared the orgy of religious wars, doctrinal persecutions, and witch hunts that rent the fabric of Continental society during the early phase of European print acquisition.

When the Russians finally embraced the printing press in the nineteenth century, a great awakening occurred: schools and universities burgeoned and the education of the masses began in earnest. Russian scientists began making world-class discoveries, and by the second half of the nineteenth century, a borealis glow illuminated the Russian literary scene. Besides the awesome international twin talents of Tolstoy and Dostoevsky, Gogol, Pushkin, Chekhov, Turgenev, and many others, were all churning out one masterpiece after another as if to make up for lost time. Russian literacy rates skyrocketed, as reading and writing became a matter of national pride.

It was in this same period that the Russian national character began to undergo a change. Historically, Russians had been tolerant of others' religions. Prior to the nineteenth century, there had never been a purely religious war fought on Russian soil. (Those that involved religion were more about territorial conquest than ideology.) Almost no Russians participated in the Crusades, and Russia's mass conversion to Christianity in the tenth century was notable for its tranquility. The high number of blond, blue-eyed Ashkenazi Jews attests to wholesale Slavic conversions to Judaism somewhere between the fifth and the ninth centuries. (These physiognomic features were conspicuously absent in the Semitic Jews who left Judea in the second century.) In fact, nineteenth-century Russia possessed the single largest Jewish population in the world. The benign Slavic attitude toward religious diversity had been one of the primary reasons millions of European Jews had fled to Russia in the first place.

In the nineteenth century, a murderous anti-Semitism began to boil the Russians' blood, a development that has never been adequately explained. Russian Jews were industrious and law-abiding. They wielded little power, owned very little land, and threatened none of the major social structures. The Russian Orthodox Christian hierarchy was not in any danger from them; a minuscule number of Russians had converted in the preceding five centuries, and the aristocracy lost no sleep worrying over a possible Jewish takeover. But, paralleling the paranoia that occurred in Spain in 1492, the rapid spread of literacy in Russia was accompanied by large numbers of people turning viciously on a minority who happened to practice a religion different from their own.* The 1880s saw the Jewish communities in Russia savaged by pogroms that left many dead.

The pogroms of the nineteenth century were but a prodrome to a more malignant delirium that seized Russia in the twentieth. In 1917, the West's fifth "protestant reformation" violently overthrew the Russian aristocracy and Church. This Russian "religious transformation," coming so late after the European Reformation, was not easily recognized for what it was because it went under the alias of "Communism." Its Bible was the *Commu-*

---

*Russian Christian men considered Jews and women as "Other" and therefore interchangeable. Russia's preoccupation with persecuting her Jews, I surmise, probably spared her "babushkas" in the nineteenth century from the misogynist witch hunts that had seized so many print cultures in sixteenth-century Europe.

nist Manifesto. As it unfolded, the now-familiar litany of left-hemispheric assaults against right-sided values began. The worship of Sophia (Mary's name in Russia) was execrated. Images came under assault. The Eastern Orthodox brand of Christianity practiced by Russians invested painted *ikons* with spiritual power. Communists relentlessly targeted them for destruction. Their hatred of images soon extended to include all twentieth-century Western art. The images Communists denounced as "decadent" were similar to the ones the Hebrews had called "abominations," the fourth-century Orthodox Christians had repudiated as "pagan," and the Protestants had railed against as "idolatry." Communist thugs destroyed paintings and statues, and many artists were murdered or packed off to the gulag. Repeating the pattern of the earlier protestant movements, the Communists purged art, color, gaiety, and laughter from society. Clothing became drab, buildings gray, and smiles disappeared as people pored over their new black-and-white text. Dogma replaced rational discussions. Communists murdered Kulaks, who were productive agrarians, by the millions for an abstract principle called "collectivism." Zealots protecting the purity of the new dogma condemned doctors, scientists, and humanists as "heretics" in public trials that aped the rituals, torture sessions, and "confessions" of earlier religious persecutions. A shot to the temple at 3:00 A.M. in the KGB's Lubjianka prison replaced the burning stake in the public square.

Communism severely oppressed women. Extreme patriarchy was the rule. But it was Mother Nature that suffered the most grievous wounds at the hands of the Communists, who irretrievably despoiled much of Russia's pristine landscape. Lichen in the tundra, fish in Lake Baikal, and children around Chernobyl were condemned to death as a result of this anti-feminine assault in the name of "industrialization."

Most alphabet-based religions demonized the ones they supplanted. During the rise of patriarchy in Europe, the Goddess was turned into the anti-Christ (in the form of the devil). In the twentieth century, Communists blamed Christianity for Russia's ills. Russian Orthodox Christianity had depended on rich spectacle and mystic ritual, but the new "protestants," like those in the earlier Reformation, announced that since the citizens could read the new sacred book for themselves, they no longer needed Church patriarchs or rituals. Clutching dog-eared copies of the *Manifesto*, Communists tore down the structure of organized religion, which Marx called "the opiate of the people." Converted churches became political assembly halls. Priests were imprisoned and worship of the Trinity was forbidden.

An economic theory presented in written form by a dead white male became, essentially, a religion. Those who embraced it were as zombie-like in their unquestioning obedience to its tenets as any fanatical religious convert. Because "history" was not a proper god per se, adherents and foes alike called Communism an "ideology," but its passionate proselytizers differed little from religious zealots. The Communists instituted a reign of terror whose scope and ferocity could match any that harrowed sixteenth-century Europe. Perhaps if Russia had become literate at the same time as the rest of Europe, the twentieth century would have been spared the dark passage called the Cold War.

While the oral Russians were deeply agitated by the first stages of literacy, another "communication" phenomenon was discombobulating the highly literate Germans. In the nineteenth and twentieth centuries, Germany boasted one of best educational systems in the world. Its scrub-faced students, sitting alert in neat rows, were a teacher's dream. American doctors, English scientists, and French industrialists made regular pilgrimages to Germany to learn about the latest developments in their respective fields. The Germans took immense pride in their poets, composers, industry, and technology. Efficient, polite, and law-abiding to a fault, they constructed a model of what a literate society could achieve.

How did Germany, arguably the most cultured nation in the world, transmogrify into the most bloodthirsty ogre ever to stalk the halls of history? Where were the spirits of Schiller, Leibniz, and Goethe at Babi-Yar, Auschwitz, and Buchenwald? Perpetrators of atrocities took pleasure in reciting Heine's poetry, Mann's prose, and Mozart's music. If literacy is the key to civilizing the uncivilized, how then to explain the monstrosity called Nazi Germany? How could the cultured Germans have so thoroughly lost their collective moral compass? Why did not their refined educations protect them? After fifty years, these dark unanswered questions continue to cast a pall over all of the twentieth century's accomplishments.

It was, after all, the God-fearing, Church-going Germans who gave the world the Reformation. They were the Teutons who successfully resisted Roman rule and who were so fractious that for thousands of years they would not follow any one leader. The bristling forest of straight-armed *Sieg Heils!* was evidence that they had forsaken God and transferred that faith to *der Fürher.* Why were the cultured, twentieth century Germans so susceptible to an uncouth rabble-rouser? The usual explanations include the legacy of World War I, humiliation over reparations, and the dishonor of surrender. But neither crushing military defeats nor tribute bitterly rendered to a conqueror are unique in history. The Nazi response to them, however, was singular. An extremely powerful new factor may have been at work to overcome Germany's religious rectitude, moral education, and the Germans' identification with the best of ancient classical culture.

The crucial factor in Hitler's Svengali act was his use of radio, a relatively new technology that he manipulated with sinister effect. Radio is a medium of speech. It is sensuous, immediate, and very personal, like someone whispering into your ear in the dark. It can communicate nuance and intonation. Because the radio listener cannot *see* the speaker, radio is orality raised to the highest pitch of intensity. Because the Germans were extremely literate, they were particularly vulnerable to a demagogue with a microphone.

Prior to microphones and radio, a single speaker could only address a few hundred people. With radio, one speaker could address an entire nation at once, casting a wide, seductive net, invoking in listeners a sense of tribal unity and singleness of vision. Period photographs of mesmerized Germans gathered on street corners staring intently at outdoor radio speakers blaring Hitler's voice tell the story. McLuhan observed:

> That Hitler came into political existence at all is directly owing to radio and public address systems. . . . Radio provided the first massive experience of electronic implosion, that reversal of the entire direction and meaning of literate Western civilization.[5]

In Germany in the 1930s, Hitler used the radio to weld the German people into a fanatic Teutonic tribe entranced by his messianic Aryan message that *they* were *his* "chosen people." If Germans had only *read* Hitler's speeches, they would not have fallen under his spell.* In a radio speech, Hitler once said, "I go my way with the assurance of a somnambulist."[6] He perverted the new medium and turned a whole nation into sleepwalkers.

At the time, few grasped why Hitler, a modern day Pied Piper, had such appeal. The content of Hitler's message was and is repugnant to virtually everyone, including modern Germans who cannot fathom how their grandparents were taken in by such a farrago. The irony is that Germany was *so* highly literate that it had few defenses against a new medium that blasted it with booming spoken words. Certainly the evil that was Nazi Germany cannot be explained away simply as the result of a new technology of communication, but I believe it has been minimized as a key factor that propelled the Austrian paperhanger to the pinnacle of German political power.

Mein Kampf, his personal addition to fanatical leaders' books, was not as widely known as his radio speeches and image.

A man who originally had artistic aspirations, Hitler understood the power of spectacle and icons. He personally chose the swastika as the Third Reich's emblem, and hired entertainment professionals to stage his dramatic rallies. Aware of the critical importance of media, Hitler and Goebbels *invented* the concept of propaganda, creating the first propaganda ministry. Brilliantly manipulating the powers of both visual image and spoken language, Hitler seduced the cultured Germans into suspending their highly developed rational and moral faculties. His success seared the most ghastly images of the twentieth century into the memories of generations.

Fascism, the "ideology" of Nazi Germany, was not really about the abstract "ideas" of some theorist: it was the distillation of one man's charismatic voice into a hypnotic movement. The two rogue "ideologies" of the twentieth century, Fascism and Communism, were actually atheistic religions that unexpectedly gained huge followings during the turbulence that accompanies the changeover from one medium to another. They were also polar opposites. In *Mother* Russia, literacy supplanted orality. In the German *Fatherland,* orality upended literacy. Little wonder that the two "ideologies" were such implacable enemies.

I have asserted that the left brain's domination of the right, through its acquisition of literacy, and especially print technology, unbalanced society. This is not to say that the world has nothing to fear from the sudden expression of all right-sided attributes. The irrational right hemisphere has its dark side too. Hitler's voice burrowed into the depths of the right hemisphere, resurrecting tribal myths and rituals. The Germanic people and their language had been distinctive much earlier than Caesar's time. Germanic culture has been one of the great contributors to world civilization. And yet, in the two thousand years since the Romans first wrote about them, there have been only two dramatic Germanic deviations from the norms of human behavior: the witch craze and the Holocaust. Each occurred at the interface between one form of communication and another.

The power of the new medium was not lost on Franklin Roosevelt or Winston Churchill. The American president inaugurated his "fireside chats" during the Depression, and millions of Americans gathered around their radios to hear his reassuring voice. Later, Churchill used the radio to stiffen the spirit of resistance to the Nazis. During the darkest days of World War II, his electronically amplified voice staved off defeatism and kept hope alive among those in the conquered European countries. And, as any World War II buff knows, the weapon the Germans feared most was the shortwave radio; anyone caught possessing one faced the direst punishments.

Although it was not apparent at the outset, World War II was the *Götter-dämmerung* of the Mechanical Age. Mechanized tank divisions executed maneuvers that epitomized the uniformity and linearity of the alphabet. Calibrated artillery pieces hurled missiles along Newtonian trajectories. At the zenith of these left-brained calculations everything changed. On August 6, 1945, a blinding flash that physicist Robert Oppenheimer described as "brighter than a thousand suns" signaled the end of the war. Few people realized that the advent of the Atomic Age was also the beginning of the end of patriarchy, the return of the Goddess, and the triumph of the image over written words. A new era was dawning.

CHAPTER 35

PAGE/SCREEN
1945–2000

Competition between media contributes to the flowering of culture.
—Harold Innis[1]

We must once again accept and harmonize the perceptual biases of
both (the left and right brain) and understand that for thousands
of years the left hemisphere has suppressed the qualitative judgment
of the right, and the human personality has suffered for it.
—Bruce Powers[2]

In the aftermath of World War II, a nihilist philosophy called existential-
ism weighed like a wet blanket on the spirit of depressed intellectuals.
The war had exposed a terrible truth about human nature and even the
most sanguine were forced to admit that education and cultural sophistication were no guarantee against barbarity. Earlier national armies had more
or less subscribed to the articles of the Geneva Convention. Not since the
religious wars of the sixteenth century had combatants indulged in depravities like those perpetrated by the "civilized" Axis powers.

World War II was a firestorm for modern civilization, but the conflict
also marked the beginning of yet another massive shift in global consciousness. The combining of two "feminine" influences, photography and electromagnetism, was chiefly responsible for this change. In 1939, Philo T.
Farnsworth invented television. After the war ended, television spread
rapidly—literally house to house. One after another, living rooms were illuminated by the glow of fuzzy electronic pictures. The tube was an overnight
sensation, and soon the amount of time people spent watching images flit
on and off the front of the glowing box began to surpass the amount of time
people spent reading linear rows of black letters.

Comprehending television required an entirely different hemispheric strategy than that used in reading. Viewers called forth their pattern-recognition skills to decipher the screen's low-definition flickering mosaic mesh. The retina's cones need bright light to scan a static page of print, but television brings the eye's rods into play. They see best in dim surroundings and can detect the slightest movements. As people watched more and more television, the supremacy of the left hemisphere dimmed as the right's use increased. For 750,000 years, families had gathered around lit hearths whose flames supplied warmth, illuminated darkness, encouraged camaraderie, and encouraged storytelling. Campfires had been an essential ingredient for the evolution of oral epics. In 1950, a new kind of fire replaced the hearth; and it encouraged a different set of social qualities.

Previously, alphabetic print had exploded Western culture into millions of hard-edged shards of individualistic shrapnel. Both reading and writing are, in most cases, solitary endeavors. Television abruptly reversed the process, and the centripetal implosion not only pulled together individual families but also began to enmesh the entire human community into what McLuhan called "one vast electronic global village." Television was so startlingly original that many other adjustments in perception were necessary for the brain to make sense of it.

The electroencephalogram (EEG) brain wave patterns of someone reading a book are very different from those of the same person watching television. So fundamentally different, in fact, that there is little deviation in those patterns even when the content of the book or television program is varied.[3] A network program about adorable koala bears elicits essentially the same brain wave pattern as a program containing violence or sexuality. Watching television and meditating generate the identical slow alpha and theta waves. These EEG patterns denote a passive, receptive, and contemplative state of mind. Reading a book, in contrast, generates beta waves; the kind that appear whenever a person is concentrating on a task.[4]

Corroborating evidence concerning the perceptual differences between these two modes comes from sophisticated brain PET (position emission tomography) scanners that demonstrate the circuits in the left hemisphere lighting up when the subject is reading (while the right hemisphere remains relatively dark). When the subject looks up from his or her book and begins to watch television, the right hemisphere switches on and the left begins to idle. Task-oriented beta waves activate the hunter/killer side of the brain as alpha and theta waves emanate more from the gatherer/nurturer side. Perhaps Western civilization has for far too long been stuck in a beta mode due to literacy, and striking a balance with a little more alpha and theta, regardless of the source, will serve to soothe humankind's savage beast.

A clue to this reorientation: men, who traditionally favor logic over intuition, often engage in "surfing" when they watch television—that is, they watch many programs simultaneously. They would never try to read chapters of various books simultaneously. A hunter trying to stalk multiple animals simultaneously would go hungry. A man is much more susceptible to this adult "attention deficit disorder" behavior than a woman, because television, being a flickering image-based medium, derails the masculine-left-linear strategy, just as in parallel, the written word had earlier disoriented the gestalt-feminine-right one.*

The printing press disseminates written words. Television projects images. As television sets continue to proliferate around the world, they are redirecting the course of human evolution. The fusing of photography and electromagnetism is proving to be of the same magnitude as the discovery of agriculture, writing, and print. While most social commentators wring their hands over the dismal nature of much of television programming's *content*, they fail to accord the *process* of perceiving television's information its due as a factor reconfiguring society in a positive way. Similarly, when the printing press appeared, commentators were caught up in debating the content of books being printed. No one then appreciated the effects brought about by the process of becoming literate. While a medium's content surely is significant, the more important story is *how* the medium itself affects people's perception of reality. Fiercely loyal to the literate mode of the previous medium, many critics of television have missed the *frisson* of the present age.

Television's popularity greatly increased the power of images. Iconic information has superseded alphabetic information as the single most significant cultural influence. The first modern image to achieve universal recognition was the atomic bomb's mushroom explosion. The phallic cloud billowing up over Hiroshima symbolized the unbalanced masculine. It was the climactic end result of thousands of years of left-brain dominance. The world stared slack-jawed and wide-eyed at the awesome power of hunter/killer values carried to their farthest extreme. For all their virtues, abstract science, linear words, and sequential equations had led the world to the brink of extinction.

The eerie photographic sequence of the bomb's signature plume was shown over and over in theaters and on television screens until hardly anyone was unfamiliar with it. A great warning shock wave surged through the

*While it is true that women also engage in "surfing," the practice is far more prevalent among men and, in general, they do it more mindlessly.

nervous systems of peoples of all nations. The arms race, consuming much of the left brain's talent for thousands of years, had reached an absurd zero-sum stalemate: to "win" all-out war meant to make the planet uninhabitable for all humans, as well as for most other species.

For the next fifty years, the superpowers bluffed and feinted, but managed somehow not to initiate Armageddon. If a *written* description of the atomic explosion's aftermath were all that had been available, the bomb *would* surely have been used. But the *image* of the bomb's destructive power was universally disseminated and that picture (worth many thousands of words) saved the world.

The ominous mushroom cloud warned humankind of collective death. The first photograph of Earth taken from space flashed around the world in 1968, celebrating the interconnectedness of life. Like a Chinese ideograph, NASA's photograph of our blue marble conveyed multiple values simultaneously, values more intuitive than rational. The masculine perception of nature and the Earth itself as "things" to be conquered made the space program possible. The photo it generated began to instill in everyone who saw it an understanding that the Earth must be honored, protected, and loved. That many environmentalists are men confirms this change in orientation. NASA's photograph of the Earth floating in space provided people with "the big picture." One sees the big picture with the entire retina and the combined hemispheres. The inviting, mute image of the home planet floating in dark space did more to change the consciousness of its residents than the miles of type concerning the subject generated by the world's writers.

Over the course of history, humankind has been profoundly influenced by the periodic emergence of powerful books. From the tablets Yahweh presented to Moses to the works of Homer, Plato, Aristotle, Paul, Augustine,

The two most indelible images
of the twentieth century

Mohammed, Aquinas, Galileo, Calvin, Descartes, Newton, Kant, Jefferson, Hegel, Darwin, Marx, and Freud—each stamped their age with a unique imprimatur. Since the atomic blast in 1945 and the Earth image that followed, not a single book has come close to the degree of impact these two photos have had. The written word's influence has been declining for the last fifty years, counterbalanced by the increasing power of the image.

The shift in orientation toward perceiving information with the right hemisphere instead of the left had significant ramifications for women's rights. The suffragette movement was just beginning to catch its second wind in the "flapper era" of the 1920s when it was overshadowed by two life-threatening events: the worldwide Depression of the 1930s threatened the survival of individual families; World War II threatened the survival of whole nations.

Authorities drafted able-bodied men to bear arms. Women were called upon to build war machines. "Rosie the Riveter" flexed her muscles as women took over technical positions and mastered dangerous tasks that previously men had performed. Women savored their paychecks and realized that an independent income was the hacksaw blade hidden in the cake that would help them gain their freedom by loosening their dependence on male breadwinners. Yet, when the men returned from the war and elbowed them aside, most women once again donned their aprons. Gender relations might have reverted back to prewar conditions, except for one new factor—television.

It was not mere coincidence that the most explosive feminist movement in the five-thousand-year history of patriarchy occurred during the first television generation. Certainly the birth control pill, with its power to disconnect sex from pregnancy, played an important role, but the advent of the pill does not explain why so many young men of the era were inclined to support their sisters' and girlfriends' aspirations. Boys who spent many hours of their childhood engrossed in the *Howdy Doody* show grew up to become the first generation of men that included many who applauded the aims of the women's movement. And what a movement—bold, courageous women of every age, color, and class altered the gender equation permanently. The meteoric rise of the image, resulting in an infusion of right-brained values into culture, was like a booster rocket that propelled the women's movement into stable orbit. Very few of society's prophets saw it coming. Looking to the past for models, they also missed clues that foretold cultural shifts that were to blast 1950s society to smithereens.

In 1958, a few years before the first generation weaned on television was about to enter college, the president of Harvard, James Conant, castigated the buttoned-down psyches of that year's graduating class in *Time* magazine. He labeled the college students the "Silent Generation" and blamed their apathy on the mind-numbing pabulum of the seditious new medium. Pundits predicted that when the first *really* "television-addled" generation entered college in the 1960s, it would be catatonic from all the hours this cohort had spent staring at the cathode tube; pontificating sages predicted that these youngsters would behave even *more* passively than the transitionally literate generation of the late 1950s.

But the counterculture ran counter to all conventional wisdom. The supposedly inert, troglodyte young people saw only too clearly the flaws in such hallowed phrases as "unquestioning patriotism," "trustworthy government," and "infallible military." A psychedelic-image-besotted, back-talking, tie-dyed, pot-smoking cadre of hirsute dancing fools forced the older alphabet generation to reassess their own cherished beliefs. The right-brained word *fun*, never before used to characterize a print-dominated era, epitomized the age. Beatlemania swept up the young in an ecstatic frenzy that Western culture had not witnessed since religious flagellants whipped themselves raw in the streets of medieval cities.

Demographic bulges, the Vietnam War, and affluence have all been cited as contributing causes for the outrageous phenomenon that was the sixties. However, the never-blinking, ubiquitous cyclopean television eye was the most overarching influence behind that generation's passionate involvement in Civil Rights marches, the anti-war movement, psychedelic experimentation, the Native American rights movement, the Peace Corps, ecology awareness, the back-to-the-earth movement, reinvigoration of the democratic process, communal living, the human potential movement, and women's equality. Despite fake wrestling matches, boring test patterns, inane sitcoms, and mindlessly violent Saturday cartoons, the first rugrats-turned-couch-potatoes sallied forth and brought about a societal change bearing all the hallmarks of a true Renaissance. Entirely new forms of art, music, dress, morals, and attitudes toward war, love, and sexuality bubbled up effervescently. No one confronted with the business end of a rifle had *ever* thought to respond by placing a flower in its barrel.

The victory of television images over printed words was so sudden that society had little time to adjust. The bulwarks of written-word-based authority were repudiated. The black-and-white literalness of the Bible, the gray work ethic of corporate capitalism, and the bloodless white lab coat dispassion of science were all scrutinized and criticized as never before. The right brain, suppressed for so long, burst forth with an exuberance not seen since Dionysus cavorted with his retinue in the forests. The hippie god would have applauded the credo "sex, drugs, and rock 'n' roll."

But radical change does not occur without social upheaval. While previous populations had endured wars between tribes, empires, religions, classes, and nations, there had *never* been a war between generations. "Don't trust anyone over thirty" was the rallying cry of the image-tribe in its battle with the print-nation.

There were other indicators that something dramatic was afoot. Suddenly, Johnny couldn't read and a previously unrecognized affliction called dyslexia (nonexistent in ideographic China) broke out at alarming rates in classrooms all across Eurocentric TV-land. Dyslexic children, predominantly male (9:1), have difficulty deciphering the alphabet. One credible theory proposes that it is due to a failure of hemispheric dominance. Ninety percent of the language centers traditionally reside in the left hemisphere of right-handed people.* In the right-handed dyslexic, the distribution of language centers may be more on the order of 80/20 or 70/30. Although we cannot be sure that dyslexia was not always among us, it seems to have erupted at the very moment that an entire generation was devaluing the left hemispheric mode of knowing. Perhaps television is the agent equilibrating the human brain's two differing modes of perception.

The very concept of "brain dominance" is presently under scrutiny, as many dyslexics are talented artists, architects, musicians, composers, dancers, and surgeons. The idea that logical, linear thinking is better than intuition and holistic perception was a script written by left-brainers in the first place. Our culture has classified dyslexia as a disability. But as culture becomes more comfortable with its reliance on images, it may turn out that dyslexia will be reassessed as another of the many harbingers that announced the arrival of the Iconic Revolution.

As the influence of the written word declined after World War II, images rode a crest of ever-increasing popularity. Although more books are being published in the 1990s than ever before, a larger number of them contain illustrations. Books once stood at attention on shelves, straight-up and spine-out. Now many rest supine on the coffee table, face-up, revealing their beautiful covers. These kinds of books are not meant to be read so much as perused, like the superb decorative works of the Dark Ages.

At the same time that attendance levels have fallen at libraries in the countries that embraced television, museums have enjoyed an unprece-

---

*This does not apply to the 8 percent of the population who are left-handed. Nor is it true in all right-handers. Further, women's speech centers are less likely than men's to reside so predominantly in their left lobes.

dented surge in membership applications. Tickets to traveling exhibits of the work of masters like van Gogh and Monet are in such demand that they must be purchased far in advance, and visitors at these exhibitions walk about with the same attitude of hushed reverence that pilgrims displayed reading the Bible five centuries ago. On Times Square in New York (as in other cities), the early reliance on word-text billboards has given way to neon displays of eye-catching, rapidly changing images. Business presentations, legal cases, medical conferences, scientific meetings, and military briefings increasingly rely on colorful charts and graphics.

Police routinely use cameras, and the line-up, mug shots, and finger-prints are familiar icons of our culture. In a recent turnabout demonstrating how deeply photography and electromagnetism have penetrated society, citizens now use camcorders to monitor the police.

The effect of this image bombardment is everywhere in evidence. Dinner conversations, water-cooler schmoozing, and car-pool chit-chat are riddled with the lingo of TV, ads, sporting events, movies, and computers. References to poets and authors, common a century ago among the educated, are increasingly rare. The right brain is the home of puns, jokes, and double entendres. One of North America's premier literary magazines, The New Yorker, has elevated cartoons to an art form. From bumper stickers to T-shirts, coffee mugs to aprons, we are surrounded by clever word play.

In recent years, homogenous print cultures that had boasted high literacy rates prior to World War II have discovered that an alarming percentage of their populations have become functionally illiterate. Educators are aghast; finger pointing and accusations are traded back and forth in the media. Most involved in the debate are unwilling to consider that in the age of the image, literacy will inevitably decline. While this is a source of concern, it must be balanced with awareness that intelligence is not declining.*[5] Human society lived for 2,995,000 years without the benefit of writing, and there is considerable evidence that many preliterate cultures behaved in a more humane manner toward one another and toward their environment than the literacy-based cultures that followed.

Not since the jousting tournaments of the oral Age of Chivalry have sporting events played such a prominent role in culture. For entire centuries, hunter-killer values informed the most popular (and atavistic) sport of all— the hunt. Following the invention of Gutenberg's press, few people "played."

---

*Recent research indicates that worldwide, the IQ of all peoples, as measured by IQ tests, has risen steadily in the last fifty years.

During the period of Newton's influence, croquet, with its linear, sequential application of force on balls, enjoyed a boom among the genteel. In the heyday of America's print literacy, baseball—a sport characterized by one event following another, from the batting order to the way in which a player rounds the bases—became the country's national pastime. It was the perfect sport to complement alphabet literacy.*

After television sets filled the corner bar, baseball began to lose ground to sports that are more involving for the eye, such as football, basketball, and hockey—all sports in which multiple interactions between players occur simultaneously. Fans track the mosaic, jerky movements of these events with their right brains, grasping the gestalt of the overall field or court.

In the entertainment industry the symbolism of the right hemisphere pervades the language. Popular stars of film and television are referred to as "icons." Adoring, "worshipful" fans describe movie "idols" in mythological terms: "sirens," "sorceresses," and "enchantresses." Even the word *goddess*, so long forbidden in alphabet cultures, resurfaced. Nineteenth-century admirers of prominent female authors and poets rarely, if ever, used this terminology. The deeply felt connection to Princess Diana as evidenced by the amazing worldwide reaction to her death is another example of the power of the image. Her fame became widespread because of photographers. Those eulogizing her made constant reference to mythology, referring to her life as a "fairy tale" and a "Greek tragedy." The values she projected were compassion, kindness, vulnerability, style, and nurturing—all of which, along with mythopoesis, issue primarily from the right hemisphere.

Unlike photographs or film, television images can be simultaneous with the events they report. People watched the space walks and the standoff at Waco, Texas, as they were happening. Instead of reading about leaders' speeches, viewers could observe how they spoke. Nonverbal visual assessments of politicians' sincerity enhanced people's ability to evaluate them. The camera eye has affected the democratic political process more than any other invention since the ballot box. Photo-ops and sound bites have superseded backroom deals and smoky cigars. While many features of the changeover from print to television have been deleterious, many are not. A healthy distrust of all politicians immunizes a populace against the disastrous possibility that they will become mesmerized by the words of a demagogue.

*I believe this is the reason why baseball has inspired so many writers to eloquence whereas football, basketball, and hockey have not.

Today advertising icons have become ubiquitous, while written copy has receded into the background to become clever word play. It would be difficult to find anyone unfamiliar with McDonald's golden arches or the shape of a Coca-Cola bottle. In classical times, the Greek *logos* meant "the word"; in the twentieth century, it contracted into *logo,* the icon.

The daily newspaper, which became commonplace in the nineteenth century, initially relied exclusively on text. With the rise of photography, a newspaper's written words increasingly shared the pages with images. Today, largely in response to television, newspapers are filled with photos, color charts, weather maps, political cartoons, and comics.

Twenty years before the implosion of American culture by television, iconography was already present in the form of comic books. (Note that the generic word to describe these books—comic—is a right-hemispheric trait.) Like the crude wood-block engravings of the early Middle Ages, comics told a story using low-resolution pictures. Comics books were the province of children who were thereby prepared for their later meeting with the electromagnetic comics called television. Today, comic book characters have left the page and taken on lives of their own. Superman, Dick Tracy, and Batman have gone from static images to film and television. The Disney theme park phenomenon attests to comics' characters' pervasive, international popularity. In a sense, all left hemispheres must be checked at the gates of the Magic Kingdom, where right-hemispheric myth and fairy tale come alive.

Television's photographic images are supplanting the headline and the essay. It seems as though each week brings news that another newspaper has folded or that another bookstore has gone out of business just as another television station becomes the target of a telecommunication bidding war. Film has replaced the novel as the principal means to entertain and videos are increasingly used as educational tools. The last scene from *Casablanca* is familiar to more people than the last page of *A Tale of Two Cities.*

While culture was still reeling from the introduction of television, another marriage of photography and electromagnetism reinforced the perceptual mode of the right brain. The personal computer has greatly increased the impact of the iconic revolution and continues to do so. A major criticism of television has been that it encourages viewer passivity.* The first television generation's intense social activism and the current craze for individual derring-do sports would seem to provide presumptive evidence to the con-

*Plato and Socrates disdained book reading for the same reason.

trary. The computer, however, converted the television screen from a mono-logue to a dialogue by making it interactive. And features peculiar to computers shifted the collective cultural consciousness of the men and women who used them toward a right-hemispheric mode, which in turn has further diminished male dominance.

The computer was originally designed to aid scientists, most of whom were male. Since the 1970s, therefore, males have rushed in droves to learn what their fathers and grandfathers contemptuously dismissed as a skill for women and sissies—typing. Unlike all the scribes of past cultures, men now routinely write using both hands instead of only the dominant one. The entry into the communication equation of millions of men's left hands, directed by millions of male right brains tapping out one half of every computer-generated written message, is, I believe, an unrecognized factor in the diminution of patriarchy.

Another feature of the computer that revolutionized how men and women relate to the written word was the cursor. The "mouse," the device that controls the cursor, liberated the right hand's need to stay within the confines of the lane markers on lined paper while writing. Computer-literates use a hand-eye coordination more spatial than linear: the mouse scurries across the corpus callosum, and invites right-brain pattern skills to participate in the maneuvers necessary to generate the written word.

The computer's unique word-processing programs added still another right-brained talent. The geometrical moving about of phrases, sentences, paragraphs, and whole passages increased the right hemisphere's influence on the *composition* of writing. And there are no pages to turn in a computer, which further discourages linear thinking. "Scrolling," with its reliance on rods and right-brain pattern-recognition skills, is more akin to deciphering vertical Chinese ideograms than reading horizontal alphabet text.* In another trend boosting gestalt perception, computer designers increasingly build in iconic commands accessed by clicking on them. "Window"-formatted information has become the worldwide standard. The picture of a trashcan has replaced the word t-r-a-s-h.

---

*In the typographical revolution that followed Gutenberg's invention, Protestants routinely started their day by reading a passage from the Bible. In the Iconic Age, millions turn to the business pages of their morning newspaper to learn how their net worth fared at the previous close. Eager investors separate out their stock "symbols" from myriad other acronyms in the hard-to-read vertical columns. While conducting their scrolling search over coffee, they are exercising their right hemispheres, as if the elite of the alphabet-literate read a little Chinese before going off to work.

Five thousand years ago, writing initiated a long, painstaking process of converting images into letters. Since the invention of the computer, users have taken delight in ignoring the letters' phonetic values and instead have arranged them decoratively (confirming Picasso's and Braque's prescience). For example, Snoopys, Christmas trees, and other familiar cultural icons are assembled as a mosaic of alphabet letters, most commonly the letter *A*.

The computer's *processes* have unwittingly advanced the cause of women and images, even though these aspects of computer operation have nothing to do with the computer's *content*, which is the manipulation of information. The world of cyberspace is a computer-generated extension of the human mind into another dimension. The computer has carried human communication across a threshold as significant as writing, and cyberspace's reliance on electromagnetism and photographic reproduction will only lead to further adjustments in consciousness that favor a feminine worldview. Irrespective of content, the processes used to maneuver in cyberspace are essentially right hemispheric. The World Wide Web and the Internet are both metaphors redolent of feminine connotations.

Some fret that the computer is a dehumanizing machine that so mesmerizes its aficionados that they lose their ability to emote, but as has happened repeatedly in the past, contemporary critics are at a disadvantage when trying to gauge the effects of the technological revolutions of their age. Trapped in the center of a spinning washing machine, it is difficult for anyone so positioned to appreciate that the clothes tumbling violently about are becoming cleaner.

Today, CNN geopolitical bulletins assault the eye like an artillery barrage, flashing and exploding in our living rooms. Talking heads proffer facile explanations that do not satisfy our yearning to make sense of our century. Just as the inhabitants of one patch of the globe achieve the temperament of a helpful, tail-wagging Saint Bernard, another previously dormant swatch lunges behind the wire fence, snarling like a junkyard dog. The stately Nobel Peace Prize ceremony in Stockholm shares the same news programs with fist-waving rebels shouting unintelligible slogans from a former tranquil paradise. Perhaps some pattern can be discerned from these surrealistically juxtaposed events if we were to view them in the context of massive intrusions of unfamiliar mediums of communication into unprepared societies.

One of the disconcerting aspects of the present is the uneasy feeling one has that, as Shakespeare said of a different era, "time is out of joint." There remain many cultures still living in earlier stages of development. Unfortu-

nately, they must make the passage into the approaching twenty-first century by first having to recapitulate the sublimity and mayhem that Eurocentric cultures experienced in their journey through these ages.

The rolling advance of the printing press, which has rear-ended diverse
countries, tribes, and nations in different centuries, has complicated attempts
to identify history's patterns. Just as one country recovers from the alphabet's
whiplash and begins to enjoy its benefits, another caroms toward madness. It
is as if some parts of the world are currently experiencing their Dark Age,
some their Renaissance, some their Reformation, while others their Enlightenment. Religious wars and witch hunts consume the energies of many
others. Further obfuscating matters is the fact that the Iconic Revolution has
already arrived in countries which have still not fully integrated literacy into
their societies. While books took five centuries to permeate world culture,
television images have penetrated to the same depth in only five decades. An
examination of a brief selection of current events will help to illuminate why,
to paraphrase Joyce's protagonist in *Ulysses*, recent history is a dreadful nightmare from which we are all trying to awake.

Mao Zedong, the leader of the 1948 Communist victory in China, suspected
that a major cause of traditional Chinese passivity was the culture's reliance
on ideographic writing. Although no academician, Mao intuited that the
Roman alphabet somehow conferred a different, more aggressive, mind-set
on peoples who used it. For corroboration, he had only to compare the character and fortunes of those Chinese who had left the mainland to those who
had remained behind. In Singapore, San Francisco, and Hong Kong, over-
seas Chinese (and especially their children) had to learn an alphabet language. Once they did, these Asians behaved like shrewd Yankee traders.
Within a few generations, their offspring were bursting with artistic, scientific, and literary excellence. Without so much as a backward glance at the
religions of their ancestors, most converted to the one based on an alphabetic sacred book. Chinese students claimed top awards in Western schools
because children who knew how to read both vertical icons and horizontal
letters are better able to integrate their two cortical hemispheres and thus
bridge the two global hemispheric cultures.

Unfortunately, as we have seen repeatedly, a culture's first contact with
the alphabet drives it mad. Hunter-killer values thrust to the fore, and
nationalism, imperialism, and bloody religious revolution follow. In 1952,
Mao took a drastic corrective step attempting to make over the Chinese
character: he declared by fiat that the Chinese should immediately begin

learning and using the Romanized alphabet. China's fatal romance with Cadmean letters began with the abrupt conversion of proper names and place names—Peking, for example, became Beijing overnight and Mao Tse-Tung became Mao Zedong.*

Everything that had bedeviled sixteenth-century Europe now afflicted the previously conservative Chinese. China's written language, customs, and religions had demonstrated a remarkable ability to resist sudden change until this point. But in the late 1950s, China experienced its own convulsive "protestant reformation," which Mao called "The Great Leap Forward." The previously venerated religions of Confucianism, Taoism, and Buddhism were violently swept away by mobs of chanting young people who clutched in their waving hands—a little Red Book. They were devotees of a new deity—Mao himself. Like those of the earlier biblical prophets, his written sayings were transcribed—into letters as well as ideographs—and they became a new sacred testament. No one dared question its merits, and the little Red Book became instant dogma.

No one leader in the country's five-thousand-year history had been able to so mesmerize the conservative Chinese that they would be willing to cut the anchor lines of their culture. In a country that traditionally equated age with wisdom, Communist youths beat their elders and forced them to wear dunce caps. An anti-intellectualism similar to that which had seized the Greek Dionysians, early Christians, and the first Protestants now gripped the converted. The godless Chinese Communists exhibited a religiosity more closely resembling the fanatical Puritanism of sixteenth-century Europe than any other movement in Asian history. The Great Leap Forward featured witch hunts to root out heretics, complete with torture, elaborate public trials, and humiliating "confessions" eerily reminiscent of what took place four hundred years earlier during the European collision of man and alphabet print.

Chinese Communists discouraged spontaneous dancing, singing, and laughter. Drab shapeless clothing replaced traditionally bright and stylish garments. Taking a leaf from the Calvinist handbook concerning mandatory attendance at services on pain of death, the new regime attempted to regulate even the thoughts of their terrified subjects and required compulsory attendance at "education" meetings.

*The Wade-Giles system of Romanizing Chinese written language was developed in 1912 in the West. Initially it was used primarily to help academics translate Chinese into Roman alphabet language. Mao pushed for the Chinese to use the Western language and the Chinese developed their own system, called Pinyin, which they officially adopted in 1979.

Artists were rounded up, denounced as dangerous heretics, and imprisoned. Chinese goddesses, worshiped before the revolution, were banned overnight, and children were encouraged to spy on parents. The control of women's reproductive organs became a top priority.

Despite a history containing many notable generals, Chinese warlords had expressed virtually no interest in large-scale foreign adventures. Quite to the contrary, the greatest monument to Chinese insularity and xenophobia is their Great Wall, whose purpose was to keep foreigners *out*. Immediately after the widespread infiltration of alphabet letters, China became an imperialist power intent on expanding its territory and conquering its neighbors. Its army's incursions into India; its brutal conquest of Tibet; its army's deployment in Korea; its menacing of Taiwan; and its abrupt repudiation of its ideological twin, Russia, showed a new, outer-directed bellicosity previously not evident in the pre-alphabetic, inner-directed Chinese dynasties.

Southeast Asians lived primarily in a tribal manner until the English, French, and Dutch carved out arbitrary "Spheres of Influence" in the eighteenth century, which mortised into colonies Westerners named Laos, Burma, Vietnam, Thailand, and Cambodia. Early accounts by European settlers described the agrarians on this lush peninsula as graceful, "childlike," and generally peaceful. They loved art, worshiped goddesses, and practiced a form of nature worship. Females owned property and actively participated in religious sacraments. There was virtually *no* literary tradition in this region, and, accordingly, it had produced no significant philosophers, theologians, or scientists. Compared to the literate Korean, Chinese, and Japanese cultures nearby, the peoples of Southeast Asia had made few innovative contributions to "progress."

By the middle of the nineteenth century, Christian missionaries had adapted a form of Indian script to Southeast Asian vernaculars, as if they understood that reading and writing were the stalking horses necessary to convert the locals to a religion based on a book. In the second half of the nineteenth century, literacy rates among the indigenous population increased rapidly, and, coincidentally, a madness erupted and began to destroy this idyllic land.

Karl Marx rarely ventured forth from his cramped corner in the British Museum where he labored on his dense economic tome that railed against the excesses of the Industrial Revolution in capitalistic Western nations. It is doubtful that he had much awareness of a culture as remote from Europe as Southeast Asia. Yet here he found a loyal following. Could anything have been more improbable than an Asian farmer pondering the meaning of the "Dialectic of History" while plodding behind the swaying rump of his ox, looking up from his copy of the *Communist Manifesto* to apply his switch? Nevertheless, the tenets of Marxism became fervently held beliefs among many Southeast Asians. Imbued with Marxist ideology as though it were a new religion, and with a zealous sense of nationalism as well, the Vietnamese overthrew their ancient traditions and their French colonialist masters at the same time as they entered the fanatical, blindly doctrinal stage of early alphabet literacy.

Unbeknownst to them, the most advanced country in the world, the United States, was at that precise moment undergoing a wrenching reversal of print values. Television promotes multicultural tribalism and subverts nationalism. In an image culture, potential recruits question sacrificing their lives for an abstract concept. Separated by 10,000 miles, Vietnam and the United States were at vastly different stages of technological evolution. Nevertheless, in a fateful encounter beginning in the 1960s, the two protagonists faced off. Rarely has history witnessed a clearer David and Goliath contest. But one army was at the height of alphabet-induced determination and the other was bewitched by a new communication medium that ultimately sapped its will to win. The decisive issue was not numbers of sorties flown or tonnage of napalm dropped, but the degree of unquestioning patriotism. Despite the volumes that have been written about this conflict, the underlying role of communication technology has never been clearly stated. The Vietnamese were resolute print Minutemen, while the Americans were metaphorically busy tearing off their uniforms to go native: they were the newest members of the ancient image tribe.

After each of the other Southeast Asian nations adopted their new alphabetic language, they became haunted by extremes in human behavior. Journalists called Cambodia's Pol Pot's regime "ideological," but the murderous zeal of his adherents, determined to cleanse society of its Western (read feminine) influences, had all the earmarks of the worst aspects of the sixteenth century's extreme religiosity. Neighbor murdered neighbor over a suspected lack of zeal while the Cambodian killing fields were thoroughly sown with human bones and skulls.

In Thailand, women's status fell precipitously and prostitution became a national industry. Burma, once a self-sufficient country rich in natural resources, fell into economic decay because the only segment of society that accumulated power was the military, whose inexperienced officers mismanaged the economy of a once-thriving country.

Although other factors have been implicated as the cause of these dramatic national collective nervous breakdowns, I submit that the essential character of the twentieth-century Southeast Asian was utterly transmuted by the rapid spread of alphabet literacy in the nineteenth century.

Once a bright source of innovation in mathematics and philosophy, India entered a mild thousand-year Dark Age after the Muslim conquest in the eighth century, following which the skill of reading was lost to the majority. During this long period India was all but spared the strife that accompanies religious wars. With few exceptions, in the period between 1300 and 1900, Muslims and Hindus were tolerant of each other's beliefs. The Indian brand of Islam acknowledged the Divine Feminine. Many major Muslim architectural triumphs, such as the Taj Mahal, were dedicated to women, and Fatima, the Prophet's daughter, figured prominently.

After the conquering British began uncrating their imported printing presses throughout the nineteenth century, alphabet literacy rates among Indians soared. Within a century, they developed a keen enough sense of nationhood to rebel against the British, and as quickly as they achieved independence in 1947, a ferocious religious war tore the new nation apart. Like Protestants of sixteenth-century Europe, the Indian Muslims became extremely patriarchal and puritanical, and championed the written word over goddesses, images, and women's rights. A well-entrenched priesthood of Brahmins ministered to the Hindus. They worshiped images and goddesses in elaborate rituals resembling Catholic mass. Hindus played the counter-role of Europe's sixteenth-century Catholics in twentieth-century India's religious Reformation drama.

The savage mass murders of one group by the other and vice versa so destroyed civic comity that the Indian subcontinent, *populated by people of identical ethnic stock,* had to be divided into a Muslim Pakistan and a Hindu India. Why, we might ask, if the Hindus and Muslims had lived side by side in relative peace and harmony for nearly a thousand years, would they suddenly become so profoundly intolerant of each other's religion just as nationalism reared its head?

Not until the nineteenth and twentieth centuries, when they finally embraced the printing press, did the majority of Muslims outside India attain the high literacy rates that had distinguished the great Muslim renaissance occurring between the eighth and eleventh centuries. This recent and rapid acquisition of alphabet literacy has coincided with the sudden eruption of the Muslim protestant reformation that Westerners call "fundamentalism." Many modern Muslims insist on a stricter, more literal inter-pretation of the Quran than had been expected of followers in previous Muslim societies. In countries long associated with literacy, such as Tunisia (ancient Carthage), Iraq (ancient Mesopotamia), and Egypt, women con-tinue to enjoy greater rights, than those in other Islamic nations. Generally, the more recently a Muslim nation experienced its print revolution, the more patriarchal it is.*

The rapid rise of Muslim fundamentalism has been in reaction to the perceived threat of a foreign siren goddess with a captivating big eye: televi-sion. Beginning in the 1960s, television images of Western music, culture, and morals pervaded the Casbah. In response, Islamic extremists in Algeria gunned down TV announcers and women wearing Western clothing—a strange coupling—as well as families living in houses with TV antennas. In Iran, harsh punishments await anyone in possession of a TV satellite dish. The Taliban in Afghanistan, the most recently literate Islamists, are the most extremely patriarchal. Resembling a new generation of Cadmean warriors, the fundamentalists are fighting desperately to prevent images of any kind from invading their society; at some deep level, they understand that iconic information is the carrier of feminine cultural values.

Alas, their efforts are reminiscent of the mythical King Canute, who ordered the tide to not come in. No group in any country can successfully restrict the flow of image information. Television, more powerful than Asherah, Astarte, or Athena, has doomed all fundamentalist movements, and their extremism is the rearguard action of an army in retreat. But that does not preclude this dangerously wounded organism from inflicting severe harm on societies that are trying to grant women more equality. Ear-lier fundamentalist movements—the Hebrews, the Orthodox Christians, and the Protestants—succeeded because behind them all was the new tech-nology of alphabet literacy. Television has reversed this process, and as a result, religious fanatics who believe that the only truth is contained in a book will, in the end, be bypassed, and will become curious relics.

Other societies that tried to control image information have recently pro-vided unforgettable images—on television. The dismantling of the Berlin Wall symbolized the piercing of the Iron Curtain, which had been a

---

*This proposition would predict that the extreme fundamentalism of present-day Iran is an anomaly. Iranians are descendants of the ancient civilization of Persia, which since antiquity has had a strong literary tradition. I predict that Iran will lose its fun-damentalist ardor and return to a more centrist position in the near future.

metaphorical blockade erected to prevent electromagnetic information from inundating the authority of the totalitarian print culture of Communist Eastern Europe. The Russians feared the television image of Ed Sullivan more than the writings of Thomas Jefferson. The communists, through the use of jamming, almost succeeded in keeping their people ignorant. But in the 1980s the new VCR technology circumvented state-controlled airwaves, and smuggled videotapes of Western movies circulated in a huge black market. The computers that began to appear in the Soviet Union delivered the coup de grace. No culture can successfully shut out pictorial information for long anymore. The Iconic Revolution, surfing along on electromagnetic waves, will ultimately crest any man-made obstacle. When a culture shifts its emphasis from written words to iconic information, it will experience tumult. The reverse is also true. We live in a time when these two counter-trends are occurring simultaneously in different cultures of the world. This is the subtext behind many of this century's fractious headlines.

Throughout the world, diverse groups of people are repudiating nationalism and proclaiming loudly, through the use of car bombs and ballot boxes, that they want *out* of the current system of nationhood. Many of the entities proposed by rebels make no economic or geopolitical sense, but that in no way has dampened their advocates' tribal fervor. Ethnic groups, clamoring for independence, beset the former Soviet Union. Tribes in Africa routinely make a mockery of the colonialists' maps. Even the recent war in the former Yugoslavia was driven by ethnic and religious tribalism. Most commentators, confronted by these seemingly inexplicable occurrences, claim that the Cold War had held these passions in cold storage for fifty years. But the Cold War does not explain why northern Californians want to break away from southern Californians. It doesn't explain why the Basque separatists want to separate from Spain, or why the Quebecois clamor to pull out of Canada. The Realpolitik of the Cold War is not the reason the people of the modern world seek to shake the restraints of paternalism and return to the way of the native: the reason is that television has wrought a global change in human perception.

The shift from the word on the page to the image on the screen has also blurred the distinctions between men and women as roles, dress, hairstyles, and even language undergo ongoing revisions that serve more to unite the sexes than to separate them. In sharp contrast to the styles that dominated print eras, Victorian dandies and Renaissance fops would never have been mistaken for members of the opposite sex. Unisex is a concept that began with television.

The ascendancy of iconic information over written words seems to encourage lifestyles less encumbered by the stiff uniforms of print people. The starched shirt collar with a tie hanging down between its two pointed tabs—an abstract representation of male genitalia—has long been a symbol of patriarchal dominance. It has given way to shirts with no starch and no collar, and no ties. The tribal mode is suddenly in style. Western young people pierce themselves with metal studs and wear rings in their noses, lips, eyebrows, navels, and nether places. Most of the metal is worn on or around the face. This tellurian attention to a feature recognized by the right hemisphere points to the right's rising importance. Similarly, tattooing was once reserved chiefly for those members of the culture distinguished by their lack of interest in the alphabet. Now, among the television generation, it is increasingly acceptable to adorn one's body with—images. Young white people sport hairdos that more resemble those of the tribes of American Indians than those of the Protestants of Europe. For hundreds of years in America, African Americans tried in vain to emulate the looks of Caucasians. Since the advent of television, Caucasians increasingly try to emulate African Americans by imitating their slang, styles of dress, and musical forms, because they have intuited that African Americans are closer to their tribal ancestry and therefore are better guides to this preliterate wisdom than are any of the European American print people.

The environment, human rights, education, health care, child care, and welfare are all concerns of the gatherer/nurturer. Governments, long ruled by hunter/killers, are becoming increasingly responsive to these issues. The current backlash to this trend makes it easy to forget that neither the Greek city-states, the Roman Empire, nor European nations during the Enlightenment had a coherent plan to deal with poverty, health, or universal education. Childhood itself was an all but ignored stage of development.

The contemporary age has seen a sharp rise in violence against women. This is a reaction by men who are threatened by their correct perception that they are rapidly losing power. Women and the men sympathetic to their cause should see that the rapists' and batterers' violent outbursts are the symptoms of a group reluctant to relinquish power willingly. Lost among the rape and domestic violence statistics is the trend among most men to interact with women in a more egalitarian manner than their fathers did and to be better fathers to their children than were their recent forebears.

Many have expressed concern over the pervasiveness of sex in contemporary society. The rows of pornographic magazines in the corner convenience store seem to refute the idea that images advance women's equality.

The flood of smut is, however, but another indication that the right hemisphere is rapidly achieving freedom from the left's priggishness. The repression of sexuality by the written word for the last three thousand years has created so great a longing for release that a marked reaction toward the other direction is to be expected. It will not last. The Hebrew, Orthodox Christian, Protestant, Islamic, and Communist reformations all frowned on sexuality. Our present culture, relishing in its release by the image, is overindulging in it. After a time, I predict, culture will adjust, and sexuality's place in culture will eventually reach a healthy equilibrium.

It is very difficult to discern the pattern of the present, but one can dimly perceive that we are privileged (or damned) to live in the middle of a social revolution of unprecedented proportions. If the 1960s were the West's contemporary mini-Renaissance, then the 1990s are our mini-Reformation. The pendulum that had swung far toward liberating right hemispheric values is now swinging back toward those of the prim, grim left—as it shall swing again. But a lesson from history needs to be repeated: a small but determined minority can impose its will on a silent majority. Women saw the gains they had made in the late Roman Empire evaporate after the Orthodox Christian takeover in the fourth century. The same sequence of events occurred in the sixteenth-century Protestant Reformation. A similar threat exists today. Television, fortunately, with all its faults, often exposes the flaws in the literalists' messages as no other medium can.*

Toward the end of the last century, a number of linguists decided that there should be a universal language. They ardently believed that one tongue and a single written language would ameliorate the horrors of nationalistic wars. Being alphabet people, they tried to merge elements of the major European alphabets into one homogenized hybrid.† They hailed the invention of their new language: Esperanto.

The men and women behind the universal language movement could not have known that English, television, and computers would make Esperanto unnecessary. After World War II, the world community of scientists, businessmen, and scholars bowed to the reality of the American century and began to use English as the international language. It was a fortuitous choice for the future, as the English language's gender neutrality will incline world culture toward egalitarianism.

---

*For example, the scandals that have rocked the televangelists' ministries.

†A few protested, seriously advocating Chinese ideograms as better suited for international communication because these figures would not be dependent on phonetic pronunciation, as are all alphabet languages.

But a universal spoken and written language was just one half of the equation: the other is visual images. The sign on the men's room door no longer spells out m-e-n but instead displays an icon of a male figure. In airports and hospitals, directions are presented in symbols rather than words. Highway departments have replaced their text signage with standardized icons. Each day, it seems another complex concept, noun, or verb has been translated into a universal stick figure. We are achieving Esperanto in cartoon form.

Since World War II, the technologies of information transfer have transformed the foundations of world culture and, in the process, helped it balance feminine and masculine. Iconic information proliferating through the use of television, computers, photocopiers, fax machines, and the Internet have enhanced, and will continue to enhance, the positions in society of images, women's rights, and the Goddess.

The word *spell* has a variety of meanings. One refers to the sequence of letters in a word; another is about magic and possession. "To cast a spell" means to interfere with the reality perception of the one entranced. The alphabet's thirty-eight-hundred-year "spell" has prevented those who have used it from recognizing the price it has exacted.

Linearity, sequence, abstraction, and analysis are the mental processes used in alphabet spelling. They are also the processes that undergird the left hemisphere's most representative functions—language, logic, causality, and math computation. The left is the hemisphere principally responsible for the hunting-and-killing human survival strategy. Literacy preferentially reinforces the left's dominance over the right hemisphere, home of the gathering-and-nurturing human survival strategy. The values of the right hemisphere have suffered for millennia because literacy has literally held cultures that learned spelling "spellbound."

In the culture at large, this trance has manifested as misogyny, harsh patriarchy, and a distrust of images that periodically erupts into a destructive anti-art frenzy. I propose that alphabets are the principal reason cultures have reviled goddesses, banned women from conducting religious ceremonies, and ignored or devalued the beauty and beneficence of nature.

For the most part, women in alphabet cultures have suffered these indignities with minimal protest because they, too, were susceptible to spelling's spell, albeit in a different way. When a young girl was inducted into the alphabet's arcana, her hunter-killer lobe hypertrophied, causing her to lose trust in her intuition. Unknowingly, the girl became a victim of a Cadmean military pincer movement—one arm coming at her from within her own left brain, the other from the outside values of the surrounding culture. Further, there has often been a stratification concerning literacy. In those frequent instances when women were purposely kept outside the spelling circle their ignorance consigned them to second-class status.

Learning to spell occurs at such a young age that people are unaware of the changes in perception it causes. Once a person learns an alphabet, alphabet mental processes will influence their every assumption and decision for the rest of their lives. A culture that uses an alphabet as its primary communication tool hugs less and laughs less than those that do not. Repressed sexual urges bulge out in unexpected forms, most commonly presenting as perversion, fetishism, and a male obsession to control all aspects of female sexuality and reproduction. (Currently, the issue is abortion. At any pro-life rally a man can inevitably be observed railing against a woman's right to choose while brandishing an alphabetic book in his right hand.)

One valuable insight to emerge from modern psychology is that unconscious motivations can cause an individual to engage repeatedly in unhealthy and counterproductive behavior. Such a cycle is ordinarily not broken unless the individual somehow becomes aware of the underlying mechanism that is driving his or her behavior; only then can a person initiate corrective action.

This insight applies to cultures as well as to individuals. Only because we have recently shifted to an alternative method of processing information have we been able to gain a perspective on the alphabet's role in the repression of women. Iconic information has allowed us to disengage from the linear aspects of literacy, and to look back on them. This insight will prepare us for the *next* great communication revolution, in which we are already deeply engaged.

Reading and writing are such valuable tools in world culture that virtually all governments want their citizens to acquire them. The benefits of alphabet literacy are magnificent and life-changing. Even when we become aware that literacy has a downside, no reasonable person would throw the baby out with the bathwater and recommend that people should *not* become literate. Instead, we seek a renewed respect for iconic information, which, *in conjunction with* the ability to read, can bring our two hemispheres into greater equilibrium and allow both individuals and cultures to become more balanced.

EPILOGUE

Beauty will save the world.

—Dostoevsky

I n laying out the considerable circumstantial evidence implicating the written word as the agent responsible for the decline of the Goddess, I have sought to convince the reader that when cultures adopt writing, particularly in its alphabetic form, something negative occurs. Because of literacy's overwhelming benefits, this pernicious side effect has gone essentially unnoticed. My methods differed from most historical analyses in that I gave little weight to the content of the works of any period, and focused instead on the perceptual changes wrought by the processes used to learn an alphabet. Throughout, as a writer, as an avid reader, and as a scientist, I had the uneasy feeling that I was turning on one of my best friends.

All of my adult life I have lived in two worlds—one dictated by the exigencies of being a surgeon and the other inspired by the imaginary realm of literature. I am amazed at and humbled by the sheer volume of words in the medical textbooks I have read in order to learn my profession. I know that each written statement represents the accumulated wisdom of earlier physicians who had to endure the inevitable blind alleys associated with the imperfect process of trial and error. Without a means to organize, clarify, classify, and pass on this gleaned knowledge—not only in medicine, but in all fields—how far advanced would our culture be? But the neatly alphabetized indices appearing in our textbooks and encyclopedias represent only part of the great gift of literacy. There exists another dimension also: the sheer aesthetic pleasure that accompanies reading. Breaking the confines of the shell that more or less encases each individual, literature allows readers' minds to merge into the imaginations of the most thoughtful writers who have ever lived. I, personally, feel deeply grateful, privileged, and ennobled to count Yeats, Plato, Shakespeare, and Dostoevsky among my mentors. I am who I am because of alphabet literacy. To bring this charge against the written word, I had to use the written word to assist me in solving this complex whodunit—an irony not lost on me.

I acknowledge the analytic, linear, sequential skills of my own left brain without which I could never have kept track of the narrative arrow that aligns this work. My left hemisphere's gift of abstraction has permitted me to discern the connections among seemingly disparate historical events. My scientific side has persisted in badgering me like a pesky gadfly protesting, "yes but" throughout, and that skepticism resulted in a better book.

Perhaps in my zeal to make my points I have overstated the right/left, feminine/masculine, nurturer/killer, and intuiter/analyzer dualities. In individuals, the divisions are not so sharp, and there are dualities within each duality. Nevertheless, I believe overlaying these templates upon human history has helped clarify many complex currents and has made certain patterns apparent that otherwise would have remained murky.

I am aware that I have expended considerable ink bashing the left brain, whose wondrous achievements are celebrated on library shelves filled with the works of geniuses of logic, science, philosophy, and mathematics; I did not think it necessary to extol their contributions further here. The left brain's essential expression—masculine energy—has crafted many of humankind's great moments, but it has also informed the worst ones. For every Newton, there has been a Jack the Ripper. A subtheme of this book is that a lopsided reliance on the left side's attributes without the tempering mode of the right hemisphere initially leads a society through a period of demonstrable madness. It is only after this initial phase passes that literacy begins to work its salutary wonders for a culture.

I have tended to characterize the right-hemispheric attributes as purely positive. But it is no less true that relying on them without the ordering balance which is the forte of the left hemisphere leads to a different kind of disarray and can result in mindless anarchy and sensuous excess. Emphasis on one hemispheric mode at the expense of the other is noxious. The human community should strive for a state of complementarity and harmony.

Another reason compelling me to write this book: I have been troubled since my youth by a question that surfaced as I became entranced by Greek mythology. I do not remember at what point it occurred, but I became aware that the Greeks did not engage in religious wars. Instead, they treated one another's belief systems with admirable tolerance and civility. What then, I asked myself, had changed in human culture? Presently, to be a Jew, Muslim, Catholic, or Protestant seems to inspire suspicion and in many cases hatred of the other three. Growing up during World War II and the Holocaust made finding an answer to my question seem urgent. Nearly everyone in the Western world believes in one God. How could the adherents of the presumably lofty monotheistic belief system despise each other so since they all freely acknowledge that they worship the *same deity*?

If there had been a time in the historical past when people did not kill each other over religion, then why did they start? What factor, I asked myself, could have exerted such a powerful influence upon culture? That I suspect it was the alphabet resonates with the quote from Sophocles I cited on page 1: "Nothing vast enters the life of mortals without a curse." Writing was indeed vast and it was accompanied by a curse.

I began my inquiry intent on answering the question Who killed the Great Goddess? My conclusion—that the thug who mugged the Goddess was alphabet literacy—may seem repugnant to some and counterintuitive to others. I cannot prove that I am right. I have had to rely on the doctrine of competitive plausibility, arranging the tesserae chips of historical events into a mosaic of many periods and cultures. Any individual chip's texture and design can be (and has been) explained by local conditions, but when all of them are viewed juxtaposed together, I think a pattern can be discerned showing the shaping influence on culture of writing and particularly the alphabet. The rise and fall of images, women's rights, and the sacred feminine have moved contrapuntally with the rise and fall of alphabet literacy.

I am convinced we are entering a new Golden Age—one in which the right-hemispheric values of tolerance, caring, and respect for nature will begin to ameliorate the conditions that have prevailed for the too-long period during which left-hemispheric values were dominant. Images, of any kind, are the balm bringing about this worldwide healing. It will take more time for change to permeate and alter world cultures but there can be no doubt that the wondrous permutations of photography and electromagnetism are transforming the world both physically and psychically. The shift to right-hemispheric values through the perception of images can be expected to increase the sum total awareness of beauty.

Long before there was Hammurabi's stela or the Rosetta stone, there were the images of Lascaux and Altamira. In the beginning was the image. Then came five millennia dominated by the written word. The iconic symbol is now returning. Women, the half of the human equation who have for so long been denied, will increasingly have opportunities to achieve their potential. This will not happen everywhere at once, but the trend is toward equilibrium. My hope is that this book will initiate a conversation about the issues I have raised and inspire others to examine the thesis further.

NOTES

CHAPTER 1
IMAGE/WORD

1. Giorgio de Santillana and Hertha Von Dechand, *Hamlet's Mill: An Essay Investigating the Origins of Human Knowledge and Its Transmission Through Myth*, 10.
2. William Irwin Thompson, *The Time Falling Bodies Take to Light*, 134.
3. *The Complete Plays of Sophocles*, 131.
4. Robert Logan, *The Alphabet Effect*, 24.
5. Georges Charbonnier, *Conversations with Claude Lévi-Strauss*, 29–30.
6. Marshall McLuhan, *Understanding Media: The Extensions of Man*, 84.

CHAPTER 2
HUNTERS/GATHERERS

1. Solly Zuckerman, *The Social Life of Monkeys and Apes*, 98.
2. Gerda Lerner, *The Creation of Patriarchy*, 29.
3. Donald Symons, *The Evolution of Human Sexuality*, 138.

CHAPTER 3
RIGHT BRAIN/LEFT BRAIN

1. Virginia Woolf, *A Room of One's Own*, 98.
2. Joseph Bogen, "The Other Side of the Brain: An Appositional Mind," 111.

3. Robert E. Ornstein, *The Nature of Human Consciousness*, 104.
4. Sandra F. Witelson, "Hand and Sex Differences in the Isthmus and Anterior Commissure of the Human Corpus Callosum," 799–835.
5. *The Complete Writings of William Blake*, 614.
6. Ann Moin and David Jessel, *Brain Sex*, 18.
7. Deborah Blum, *Sex on the Brain: The Biological Differences Between Men and Women*, 65.

CHAPTER 4
MALES: DEATH/FEMALES: LIFE

1. Ernest Becker, *The Denial of Death*, 87.
2. Lucretius, *On the Nature of Things*, 235.
3. Roberto Calasso, *The Marriage of Cadmus and Harmony*, 311.
4. Anne Baring and Jules Cashford, *The Myth of the Goddess: Evolution of an Image*, 6.
5. Ibid., 39
6. Joseph Campbell, *The Way of the Animal Powers*, 73.
7. Mircea Eliade, *A History of Religious Ideas*, 1:40–41.
8. Anne Baring and Jules Cashford, 55.
9. Riane Eisler, *The Chalice and the Blade*, 17–18.

10. Anne Baring and Jules Cashford, 56.

11. James Mellaart, *Excavation at Hacilar*, 249.

12. Interview of Professor Jean-Phillippe Rigand, *National Geographic*, 448.

13. Elinor W. Gadon, *The Once and Future Goddess*, 213.

14. Marija Gimbutas, *The Language of the Goddess*, xx.

15. Claude Lévi-Strauss, *The Elementary Structures of Kinship*, 115.

16. Sherry B. Ortner, "Is Female to Male as Nature Is to Culture," 67–88.

CHAPTER 5
NONVERBAL/VERBAL

1. Harold Innis, *The Bias of Communication*, 105.

2. Robert Ornstein, *The Right Mind*, 40.

3. G. W. Hewes, "Current Status of the Gestural Theory of Language Origin," in *Origins and Evolution of Language and Speech*, 280:495.

4. Ibid., 498.

5. Jacques Derrida, *Of Grammatology*, 35.

CHAPTER 6
CUNEIFORM/MARDUK

1. R. Patton Howell, ed., *Beyond Literacy: The Second Gutenberg Revolution*, 25.

2. Gerda Lerner, *The Creation of Patriarchy*, 63.

3. C. B. F. Walker, "Cuneiform," in *Reading the Past*, 21.

4. Ibid., 47.

5. Homer Smith, *Man and His Gods*, 72.

6. Ibid., 73.

7. Anne Baring and Jules Cashford, *The Myth of the Goddess: Evolution of an Image*, 278.

8. Tikva Frymer-Kensky, *In the Wake of the Goddesses*, 79.

9. Harold Innis, *The Bias of Communication*, 12.

CHAPTER 7
HIEROGLYPHS/ISIS

1. Sir Alain Gardner, *Egypt of the Pharaohs*, 91.

2. W. V. Davis, "Egyptian Hieroglyphics," in *Reading the Past*, 81.

3. Ibid., 85–87.

4. Carolyn Larrington, ed., *The Feminist Companion to Mythology*, 24–25.

5. Cyrus Gordon, *The Common Background of Greek and Hebrew Civilization*, 118–19.

6. Donald Redford, *Akhenaton: The Heretic King*, 72.

7. Lise Manniche, *Sexual Life in Ancient Egypt*, 51.

8. R. Robert Briffault, *The Mothers*, 1:384.

9. E. M. White, *Woman in World History*, 46.

10. Merlin Stone, *When God Was a Woman*, 35–38.

CHAPTER 8
ALEPH/BET

1. Eric Havelock, *The Muse Learns to Write: Reflections on Orality and Literacy from Antiquity to the Present*, 112.

2. William H. Stiebing Jr., *Out of the Desert*, 53.

3. Herodotus, *The Histories*, 361.

4. Will Durant, *The Story of Civilization*, vol. 3, *Caesar and Christ*, 42.

5. A. R. W. Green, *The Role of Human Sacrifice in the Ancient Near East*, 182–83.

CHAPTER 9
HEBREWS/ISRAELITES

1. Robert Logan, *The Alphabet Effect*, 87.

2. Martin Bernal, *Black Athena*, 1:143.

3. Elaine Pagels, *Adam, Eve, and the Serpent*, xxii.

4. Anne Baring and Jules Cashford, *The Myth of the Goddess*, 418.

5. Robert Logan, 81.

6. Homer, *Odyssey*, chap. 13, 289.

7. Robert W. Funk, Roy W. Hoover, and The Jesus Seminar, *The Five Gospels: What Did Jesus Really Say*, 28.

CHAPTER 10
ABRAHAM/MOSES

1. Eric McLuhan and Frank Zingrone, eds., *The Essential McLuhan*, 175.

2. Tikva Frymer-Kensky, *In the Wake of the Goddess*, 158–59.

3. Sigmund Freud, *Moses and Monotheism*, 39.

CHAPTER 11
THERA/MATZAH

1. Merlin Stone, *When God Was a Woman*, xxiv.

2. Plato, *The Collected Dialogues*, 1212–24.

3. Martin Bernal, *Black Athena*, 2:274–319.

4. Ibid., 2:277.

5. Ibid., 2:297.

6. Immanuel Velikovsky, *Ages in Chaos*, 43–49.

7. Sigmund Freud, *Moses and Monotheism*, 5

8. C. M. Bowra, *The Greek Experience*, 116.

CHAPTER 12
ADAM/EVE

1. John Phillips, *Eve: The History of an Idea*, 57.

2. Anne Baring and Jules Cashford, *The Myth of the Goddess: Evolution of an Image*, 493.

3. Will Durant, *The Story of Civilization*, vol. 1, *Our Oriental Heritage*, 336.

4. Anne Baring and Jules Cashford, 492.

5. Elaine Pagels, *The Gnostic Gospels*, 30.

6. Anne Baring and Jules Cashford, 458.

7. Tikva Frymer-Kensky, *In the Wake of the Goddesses*, 158.

8. Ibid.

9. Anne Baring and Jules Cashford, 476.

10. Tikva Frymer-Kensky, 181.

CHAPTER 13
CADMUS/ALPHA

1. Marti Lu Allen and T. Keith Dix, *The Beginning of Understanding: Writing in the Ancient World*, 1.

2. Roberto Calasso, *The Marriage of Cadmus and Harmony*, 136.

3. Merlin Stone, *When God Was a Woman*, 198–214.

4. Hesiod, *Theogonis*, 42.

CHAPTER 14
SAPPHO/GANYMEDE

1. Kenneth James Dover, *Greek Homosexuality*, 65.

2. Achilles Tatius, *The Adventures of Leucippe and Cleitophon*, 2:38, 3–4.

3. Edmond O. Wilson, *On Human Nature*, 147–53.

4. Roberto Calasso, *The Marriage of Cadmus and Harmony*, 85.

CHAPTER 15
DIONYSUS/APOLLO

1. Walter Otto, *Dionysus: Myth and Cult*, 136.

2. Marshall McLuhan and Quentin Fiore, *The Medium Is the Massage: An Inventory of Effects*, 6–7.

3. Walter Otto, 90.

4. Walter Otto, 198.

5. Walter Otto, 144.

6. Walter Otto, 82–83.

7. Will Durant, *The Story of Civilization*, vol. 2, *The Life of Greece*, 291.

8. Walter Otto, 103.

9. Walter Otto, 104.

10. Walter Otto, 106.

11. Walter Otto, 55.

12. Harold Innis, *The Bias of Communication*, 43.

13. Walter Otto, 69.

14. Roberto Calasso, 392.

CHAPTER 16
ATHENS/SPARTA

1. Robert Ornstein, *The Right Mind*, 41.

2. Aeschylus, *The Eumenides*, 234.

3. Ibid., 260.

4. Edith Hamilton, *The Greek Way*, 119.

5. Plutarch, *Life of Lycurgus, Plutarch's Lives*, 1:28, 3–5.

6. Sarah B. Pomeroy, *Goddesses, Whores, Wives, and Slaves*, 73.

7. Ibid., 62.

8. Ibid., 73.

9. Ibid., 36.

10. Plutarch, *Life of Lycurgus*, 27.

11. Sarah B. Pomeroy, 39.

12. Sarah B. Pomeroy, 117.

13. Plato, *The Collected Dialogues, Phaedrus*, 275e.

14. Plato, *Protagoras*, 329a.

15. Plato, *Symposium*, 201–212b.

16. Plato, *Republic*, 454e.

17. Edith Hamilton, *The Greek Way*, 126.

18. Plato, *Phaedrus*, 274–78.

19. Eric A. Havelock, *Preface to Plato*, vol. 1, *A History of the Greek Mind*, xi.

20. Plato, *Republic*, 5.451–62.

21. Plato, *Laws*, 6.761b.

22. Plato, *Republic*, 5.460b.

23. Plato, *Republic*, 10.598c.

24. Marshall McLuhan, *The Gutenberg Galaxy*, 82.

25. Aristotle, *The Works of Aristotle, Politics*, 1254b:4–6, 12–16.

26. Denise Schmandt-Besserat, *How Writing Came About*, 15–37.

CHAPTER 17
LINGAM/YONI

1. Arthur Coke Burnell, trans., *Ordinances of Manu* (London: Trubner, 1884), 154–56.

2. Arthur Cotterell, "The Indus Civilization," in *The Penguin Encyclopedia of Ancient Civilizations*, 180–82.

3. S. Radhakrishnan, *Indian Philosophy*, 1:75.

4. L. D. Barnett, *The Heart of India*, 112.

5. Jonathan Mark Kenoyer, "Birth of a Civilization," *Archaeology* (February/March 1998): 58–59.

6. *The New Encyclopedia Brittanica*, ed. Phillip Goetz, *Macropaedia*, 21:2–30.

7. L. Lajpat Rai, *Unhappy India*, 151, 176.

8. Serenity Young, ed., *An Anthology of Sacred Texts By and About Women*, 283–86.

9. R. E. Hume, Brihadananyaka Upanishad, in *The Thirteen Upanishads*, 81.

10. N. K. Sidhanta, *The Heroic Age of India*, 206.

11. L. D. Barnett, 123; T. W. Rhys Davids, *Dialogues of the Buddha*, 3:285.

12. R. E. Hume, Rig Veda X, 18; Sidhanta, 165.

13. R. E. Hume, Sidhanta, 160, Mahabharata, Book 3, 33, 82.

14. August Bebel, *Women and Socialism*, 52.

15. Arthur Coke Burnell, trans., *Ordinances of Manu*, no. 100 (London: Trubner, 1884); Monier Monier-Williams, *Indian Wisdom* (Luzac & Co., London 1893), 237.

16. August Bebel, 52.

17. E. Westermark, *Origin and Development of Moral Ideas*, 2:650.

18. Merlin Stone, *When God Was a Woman*, 3.

CHAPTER 18
BIRTH/DEATH

1. Karl Jaspers, *Socrates, Buddha, Confucius, Jesus*, ed. Hannah Arendt, 29.

2. Will Durant, *The Story of Civilization*, vol. 1, *Our Oriental Heritage*, 419–20.

3. E. J. Thomas, *Life of Buddha as Legend and History*, 65.

4. T. W. Rhys Davids, *Dialogues of the Buddha*, 3:285.

5. Rhys Davids, *Dialogues*, 2:186.

6. E. J. Thomas, 50–51.

7. Rhys Davids, *Dialogues*, 3:102.

8. E. J. Thomas, 145.

9. Rhys Davids, *Dialogues*, 2:9–11.

CHAPTER 19
YIN/YANG

1. No Young Park, *Making a New China*, 133.

2. Will Durant, *The Story of Civilization*, vol. 1, *Our Oriental Heritage*, 792.

3. R. Wilhelm, *Short History of Chinese Civilization*, 59.

4. Will Durant, vol. 1, *Our Oriental Heritage*, 792.

5. Ibid., 792.

6. Ovid J. L. Tzeng, Daisy L. Hung, Bill Cotton, William S-Y Wang, "Visual Lateralisation Effect in Reading Chinese Characters," *Nature*, vol. 282: 499–501; Ovid J. L. Tzeng, William S-Y Wang, "The First Two R's," *American Scientist*, vol. 71: 238–43.

CHAPTER 20
TAOISM/CONFUCIANISM

1. Lao Tsu, *Tao Te Ching*, tr. Gia-Fu Feng and Jane English, no. 59.

2. Confucius, *The Analects*, tr. D. C. Lau, Book 1, 60–61.

3. Lao Tsu, *Tao Te Ching*, no. 34.

4. Lao Tsu, no. 2.

5. Lao Tsu, no. 22.

6. Will Durant, *The Story of Civilization*, vol. 1, *Our Oriental Heritage*, 797.

7. Lao Tsu, no. 3.

8. Lao Tsu, no. 31.

9. Serenity Young, ed., *An Anthology of Sacred Texts By and About Women*, 354.

10. Confucius, Book 13, 3.

11. Confucius, Book 12, 2.

12. Confucius, Book 15, 24.

13. James Legge, *The Chinese Clerics*, vol. 1, *The Life and Teachings of Confucius*, 106.

14. Confucius, Book 16, 7.

15. Confucius, Book 17, 25.

16. F. Max Müller, ed., *The Sacred Texts of China: The Texts of Taoism*, 2:xi, 1.

17. Confucius, Book 18, 6.

18. R. Wilhelm, *Short History of Chinese Civilization*, 194.

19. S. Wells Williams, *The Middle Kingdom*, 602.

20. R. Wilhelm, *Short History*, 249–50.

21. Will Durant, vol. 1, *Our Oriental Heritage*, 770.

22. *The New Encyclopedia Britannica, Macropaedia*, 28:404.

CHAPTER 21
B.C./A.D.

1. David Abram, *The Spell of the Sensuous*, 95.

2. E. B. Havell, *History of Aryan Rule in India*, 82.

3. Sarah B. Pomeroy, *Goddesses, Whores, Wives, and Slaves*, 127–28.

4. Plutarch, *Life of Lycurgus, Plutarch's Lives, Alexander* II.

5. Roberto Calasso, *The Marriage of Cadmus and Harmony*, 273.

6. W. K. C. Guthrie, *Orpheus and the Greek Religion*, 14; Jane Harrison, *Prolegomena to the Study of Greek Religion*, 489.

7. Epictetus, *Works*, Discourses 2, 10.

8. Martin Bernal, *Black Athena*, 2:126.

9. A. N. Wilson, *Paul: The Mind of the Apostle*, 7–8.

10. Sarah B. Pomeroy, 105.

11. Will Durant, *The Story of Civilization*, vol. 3, *Caesar and Christ*, 370.

12. Ibid.

13. Ibid.

CHAPTER 22
JESUS/CHRIST

1. Karen Armstrong, *The Gospel According to Woman*, 91.

2. Paul Johnson, *The History of the Jews*, 117.

3. Elaine Pagels, *Adam, Eve, and the Serpent*, 4.

4. Max I. Dimott, *Jews, God and History*, 44.

5. Mary Daly, *The Church and the Second Sex*, 76.

CHAPTER 23
DEATH/REBIRTH

1. Harold Innis, *The Bias of Communication*, 13.

2. Karen Armstrong, *The Gospel According to Woman*, 189.

3. Elaine Pagels, *The Gnostic Gospels*, 3.

4. Mitchell N. Carroll, *Greek Women*, 172.

5. Elaine Pagels, *The Gnostic Gospels*, 76.

6. Paul Johnson, *A History of Christianity*, 80.

7. A. N. Wilson, *Jesus: A Life*, 24.

8. Ibid., 38.

CHAPTER 24
PATRIARCHS/HERETICS

1. William Blake, *Poetry and Prose*, "The Everlasting Gospel," 33.

2. Paul Johnson, *A History of Christianity*, 51–52.

3. Ibid., 57.

4. Elaine Pagels, *The Gnostic Gospels*, 63.

5. David F. Noble, *A World Without Women*, 58.

6. Elaine Pagels, *The Gnostic Gospels*, 74.

7. Ibid., 4.

8. Ibid., 5.

9. Ibid., 11.

10. Ibid., 11–13.

11. David F. Noble, *A World Without Women*, 18.

12. Paul Johnson, *A History of Christianity*, 58.

13. Ibid.

14. Will Durant, *The Story of Civilization*, vol. 3, *Caesar and Christ*, 615.

15. Elaine Pagels, *The Gnostic Gospels*, 50.

16. Ibid., 60.

17. Serenity Young, ed., *An Anthology of Sacred Texts By and About Women*, 46.

18. Paul Johnson, *A History of Christianity*, 48.

19. Ibid., 47–48.

20. Will Durant, vol. 3, *Caesar and Christ*, 613.

21. Paul Johnson, *A History of Christianity*, 110.

22. Elaine Pagels, *Adam, Eve, and the Serpent*, 89.

23. Paul Johnson, *A History of Christianity*, 110.

24. Saint Jerome, *Selected Letters*, Letter 22.

25. Paul Johnson, *A History of Christianity*, 110.

26. Ibid., 112–13.

27. Augustine, *Confessions*, 69.

28. Elaine Pagels, *Adam, Eve, and the Serpent*, 99.

29. Ibid., 109.

30. Paul Johnson, *A History of Christianity*, 156.

31. Ibid., 112.

32. Ibid., 117.

33. Elaine Pagels, *Adam, Eve, and the Serpent*, 124.

CHAPTER 25
REASON/MADNESS

1. Karen Armstrong, *The Gospel According to Woman*, 189.
2. Paul Johnson, *A History of Christianity*, 72.
3. Elaine Pagels, *Gnostic Gospels*, 81.
4. Ibid.
5. Karen Armstrong, *A History of God*, 92.
6. Ibid., 82–83.
7. L. Friedlander, *Roman Life and Manners Under the Early Empire*, 3:192.
8. Elaine Pagels, *Gnostic Gospels*, 81.
9. Elaine Pagels, *Adam, Eve, and the Serpent*, 50.
10. Edward Gibbon, *Decline and Fall of the Roman Empire*, 76.
11. Will Durant, *The Story of Civilization*, vol. 3, *Caesar and Christ*, 234.
12. Robert Logan, *The Alphabet Effect*, 34.
13. Will Durant, vol. 3, *Caesar and Christ*, 636.
14. Martin Bernal, *Black Athena*, vol. 2, 122.
15. Anne Baring and Jules Cashford, *The Myth of the Goddess: Evolution of an Image*, 617.
16. Merlin Stone, *When God Was a Woman*, 194.
17. Ibid., 193.
18. Will Durant, vol. 3, *Caesar and Christ*, 192.

CHAPTER 26
ILLITERACY/CELIBACY, 500–1000

1. H. O. Taylor, *The Medieval Mind*, 1:8.
2. F. H. Dudden, *Gregory the Great*, 1:86.
3. Kenneth Clark, *Civilisation*, 17.
4. H. Schoenfeld, *Women of Teutonic Nations*, 162.
5. Jean de Meun, *Roman de la Rose*, 237.
6. Suzanne Wemple, *Women in Frankish Society*, 149.

7. Gerda Lerner, *The Creation of Patriarchy*, 142.
8. J. A. Symonds, *Studies of Greek Poets*, 73.
9. Augustine, *City of God*, Book 7, chap. 26, 286.
10. Anne Baring and Jules Cashford, *The Myth of the Goddess: Evolution of an Image*, 551.
11. Ernest Gombrich, *The Story of Art*, 95.
12. T. Hodgkin, *The Life of Charlemagne*, 312.
13. Bertrand Russell, *History of Western Philosophy*, 379.
14. Justin McCann, ed. and trans., *The Rule of St. Benedict.*, chap. 48, 111.
15. Helen Waddell, *The Wandering Scholars*, 210.
16. *Catholic Encyclopedia*, ed. R. C. Broderick, 3:486.
17. Will Durant, *The Story of Civilization*, vol. 4, *The Age of Faith*, 529.
18. Paul Lacroix, *History of Prostitution*, 1:733–42.

CHAPTER 27
MUSLIN VEILS/MUSLIM WORDS

1. Karen Armstrong, *Muhammad: A Biography of the Prophet*, 64.
2. Herodotus, *The Histories*, 200–201.
3. Gerda Lerner, *The Creation of Patriarchy*, 143.
4. R. A. Nicholson, *Translation of Eastern Poetry and Prose*, 38–40.
5. *The New Encyclopedia Britannica*, Macropaedia, 22:9.
6. Albert Hourani, *A History of the Arab Peoples*, 20–21.
7. Ameer Ali Syed, *The Spirit of Islam*, 331.
8. D. S. Margoliouth, *Mohammed and the Rise of Islam*, 80.
9. S. Lane-Poole, *Speeches and Table Talk of the Prophet Mohammed*, 161, 163.

10. Ali Maulana Muhammed, *The Religion of Islam*, 390.

11. Tor Andrae, *Mohammed*, 267.

12. S. Lane-Poole, *Speeches and Table Talk of the Prophet Mohammed*, 161.

13. Albert Hourani, *A History of the Arab Peoples*, 71.

14. Will Durant, *The Story of Civilization*, vol. 4, *The Age of Faith*, 221.

15. Ali Maulana Muhammed, *The Religion of Islam*, 390.

16. Ibid., 655.

17. Albert Hourani, *A History of the Arab Peoples*, 120.

CHAPTER 28
MYSTIC/SCHOLASTIC,
1000–1300

1. Emilie Zum Brunn and Georgette Epiney-Bugard, *Women Mystics in Medieval Europe*, xiii.

2. Ibid., xiv.

3. Frances Gies and Joseph Gies, *Woman in the Middle Ages*, 65.

4. Friedrich Heer, *The Medieval World*, 318.

5. Ibid., 318.

6. Frances Gies and Joseph Gies, *Woman in the Middle Ages*, 23.

7. David F. Noble, *A World Without Women*, 129.

8. Ibid., 130.

9. Ibid., 133.

10. Ibid., 132.

11. Frances Gies and Joseph Gies, *Woman in the Middle Ages*, 38.

12. David F. Noble, *A World Without Women*, 132.

13. Frances Gies and Joseph Gies, *Woman in the Middle Ages*, 87.

14. David F. Noble, *A World Without Women*, 138.

15. Will Durant, *The Story of Civilization*, vol. 4, *The Age of Faith*, 936.

16. Abélard, *Letters of Abélard & Héloïse*, 1:56–61.

17. G. Sarton, *Introduction to the History of Science*, 1:555.

18. Elphege Vacandard, *The Inquisition, a Critical and Historical Study of the Coercive Power of the Church*, 48.

19. William Manchester, *A World Lit Only by Fire*, 8.

20. Friedrich Heer, *The Medieval World*, 214.

21. George G. Coulton, *History of Life in the Middle Ages*, 1:68.

22. George G. Coulton, *Medieval Panorama*, 463.

23. Frances Gies and Joseph Gies, *Woman in the Middle Ages*, 76.

24. Emile Zum Brunn and Georgette Epiney-Bugard, *Women Mystics in Medieval Europe*, 14.

25. Frances Gies and Joseph Gies, *Woman in the Middle Ages*, 81.

26. M. C. D'Arcy, *Thomas Aquinas*, 35.

27. David F. Noble, *A World Without Women*, 157–58.

28. M. Grabmann, *Thomas Aquinas*, 44.

29. Thomas Aquinas, *Summa Contra Gentiles, Book One: God*, 1.1:1.

30. Thomas Aquinas, *Summa Theologiae*, vol. 13, 92.3:39.

31. Ibid., vol. 13, 92.1:1:37.

32. Will Durant, vol. 4, *The Age of Faith*, 976.

CHAPTER 29
HUMANIST/EGOIST, 1300–1500

1. George H. Putnam, *Books and Their Makers During the Middle Ages*, 1:359.

2. Johannes Janssen, *History of the German People at the Close of the Middle Ages*, 1:19.

3. Barbara W. Tuchman, *The March of Folly*, 68.

4. Leonard Shlain, *Art & Physics*, 57–58.

5. Barbara W. Tuchman, *The March of Folly*, 63.

6. William Manchester, *A World Lit Only by Fire*, 41.

7. Barbara W. Tuchman, *The March of Folly*, 67.

8. Ibid., 67.

9. Ibid., 78.

10. William Manchester, *A World Lit Only by Fire*, 83–84.

11. Ibid., 39.

12. Ibid., 79.

13. Barbara W. Tuchman, *The March of Folly*, 88.

14. Ibid., 87.

15. Ibid., 89.

16. Ibid., 95.

17. Ludwig Pastor, *History of the Popes, From the Close of the Middle Ages*, 8:99–100.

18. Barbara W. Tuchman, *The March of Folly*, 106.

19. Ibid., 112.

20. Ibid., 107.

21. Ludwig Pastor, *History of the Popes*, 9:271.

22. Barbara W. Tuchman, *The March of Folly*, 122.

CHAPTER 30
PROTESTANT/CATHOLIC

1. Niccolò Machiavelli, *The Prince, and the Discourses*, 151.

2. Will Durant, *The Story of Civilization*, vol. 6, *Reformation*, 368.

3. Charles Beard, *The Reformation of the Sixteenth Century*, 133.

4. Ludwig Pastor, *History of the Popes*, 8:124.

5. Preserved Smith, *The Age of the Reformation*, 58.

6. Martin Luther, *The Table Talk*, item 353; Jacques Maritain, *Three Reformers: Luther, Descartes, Rousseau*, 33; Charles Beard, *The Reformation of the Sixteenth Century*, 156.

7. Friedrich Paulsen, *German Education Past and Present*, 47.

8. Preserved Smith, *Conversations with Luther*, 250–51.

9. William Edward Hartpole Lecky, *History of Rationalism in Europe*, 1:387.

10. D. Erasmus and M. Luther, *Discourse on Free Will*, 88–90.

11. Roland H. Bainton, *Hunted Heretic: The Life of Michael Servetus*, 144.

12. Charles Beard, *Martin Luther and the Reformation*, 422.

13. Johannes Janssen, *History of the German People at the Close of the Middle Ages*, 3:89.

14. Ibid., 114.

15. Martin Luther, *The Table Talk*, item 715.

16. Jacques Maritain, *Three Reformers*, 171.

17. Roland Bainton, *Here I Stand: A Life of Martin Luther*, 287–88.

18. Philip Schaff, *History of the Christian Church*, 3:417.

19. R. de Maulde-La-Claviere, *Women of the Renaissance*, 467.

20. Jacques Maritain, *Three Reformers*, 184.

21. Martin Luther, *The Table Talk*, item 737.

22. Will Durant, *The Story of Civilization*: vol. 6, *The Reformation*, 372.

23. W. E. H. Lecky, *History of Rationalism in Europe*, 1:61–62.

24. Preserved Smith, *Conversations with Luther*, 58.

25. W. E. H. Lecky, *History of Rationalism in Europe*, 1:61–62.

26. Charles Beard, *Martin Luther and the Reformation*, 179.

27. Johannes Janssen, *History of the German People*, 3:129.

28. John Calvin, *Institutes of the Christian Religion*, vol. 1, Book 1, chap. 8, 1:75.

29. Ibid., vol. 1, Book 2, chap. 5, 19:291.

30. Charles Beard, *The Reformation of the Sixteenth Century*, 260.

31. John Calvin, *Institutes of the Christian Religion*, 1:3:9:4:780–87.

32. Ibid., 781.

33. Philip Schaff, *History of the Christian Church*, 8:414.

34. Ibid., 361.

35. Ibid., 490.

36. Ibid., 492.

37. Pasquale Villari, *The Life and Times of Girolamo Savonarola*, 491.

38. Will Durant, vol. 6, *Reformation*, 469.

39. William Manchester, *A World Lit Only by Fire*, 191.

40. Ibid.

41. Philip Schaff, *History of the Christian Church*, 8:492.

42. William Manchester, *A World Lit Only by Fire*, 191.

43. Preserved Smith, *The Age of Reformation*, 174.

44. Charles Beard, *The Reformation of the Sixteenth Century*, 250.

45. J. M. Robertson, *A History of Freethought*, 487–88.

46. Philip Schaff, *History of the Christian Church*, 8:778.

47. John William Allen, *History of Political Thought in the Sixteenth Century*, 87.

48. Will Durant, vol. 6, *Reformation*, 490.

49. Preserved Smith, *The Age of Reformation*, 666.

50. Will Durant, vol. 6, *Reformation*, 341–43.

CHAPTER 31
FAITH/HATE

1. Lucretius, *De rerum natura*, vol. 2, Book 1, 101:615.

2. Karen Armstrong, *The Gospel According to Woman*, 91.

3. Karl Kautsky, *Communism in Central Europe at the Time of the Reformation*, 187.

4. R. J. Smithson, *The Anabaptists*, 131.

5. Belfort Bax, *The Peasants War in Germany at the Time of the Reformation*, 352.

6. Karl Kautsky, *Communism in Central Europe*, 187.

7. Belfort Bax, *The Peasants War*, 118–30.

8. Johannes Janssen, *History of the German People at the Close of the Middle Ages*, 4:208.

9. Martin Luther, *The Works of Martin Luther*, 4:248–54.

10. Preserved Smith, *The Life and Letters of Martin Luther*, 164.

11. Ibid., 165.

12. Martin Luther, *The Works of Martin Luther*, 261–72.

13. *Cambridge Modern History*, 11:191.

14. Paul Johnson, *A History of Christianity*, 254.

15. Elphege Vacandard, *The Inquisition, a Critical and Historical Study of the Coercive Power of the Church*, 198.

16. Henry Steele Commager, *The Empire of Reason: How Europe Imagined and America Realized the Enlightenment*, 8.

17. Anne Llewellyn Barstow, *Witchcraze: A New History of the European Witch Hunts*, 161.

18. William Edward Hartpole Lecky, *History of European Morals*, 2:21.

19. Edward Dowden, *Michel de Montaigne*, 144.

20. J. A. Froude, *Life and Letters of Erasmus*, 141.

21. Frederick Seebohm, *The Oxford Reformers*, 230–46.

22. Philip Hughes, *The Reformation in England*, 1:202.

23. Preserved Smith, *The Life and Letters of Martin Luther*, 193.

24. E. K. Chambers, *The Medieval Stage*, vol. 2, 323–26.

25. Winston Churchill, *History of the English-Speaking Peoples*, 2:223.

26. François Gulliume Guizot and Madame Guizot de Witt, *History of France from the Earliest Time to 1848*, 3:303.

27. John William Allen, *History of Political Thought in the Sixteenth Century*, 295.

28. Louis Batiffol, *The Century of the Renaissance*, 201.

29. Jules Michelet, *Historie de France*, 3:476.

30 Ralph Roeder, *Catherine de Medici*, 463.

31. Louis Battifol, *The Century of the Renaissance*, 236.

32. Leopold Ranke, *History of the Reformation in Germany*, 1:159.

33. Ludwig Pastor, *History of the Popes*, 12:508.

34. Ibid., 12:286.

35. J. R. Motley, *Rise of the Dutch Republic*, 2:40.

36. *Cambridge Modern History*, 3:646.

37. Ibid., 3:258.

38. Thomas Carlyle, *Oliver Cromwell's Letters and Speeches*, 1:108.

CHAPTER 32
SORCERY/SCIENCE

. Anne Llewellyn Barstow, *Witchcraze, A New History of the European Witch Hunts*, 1.

. Marshall McLuhan, *The Gutenberg Galaxy*, 22.

3. Anne Llewellyn Barstow, *Witchcraze*, 23–24.

4. Will Durant, *The Story of Civilization*, vol. 4, *The Age of Faith*, 451.

5. Erica Jong, *Witches*, 69.

6. Montague Summers, ed. and trans., *Malleus Maleficarum*, part 1, question 6:47.

7. Paul Johnson, *A History of Christianity*, 311.

8. David F. Noble, *A World Without Women*, 187–88.

9. Ibid., 188.

10. Will Durant, vol. 4, *The Age of Faith*, 132.

11. Nicolas Remy, *Demonolotrie*, 94–95.

12. Anne Llewellyn Barstow, *Witchcraze*, 3.

13. William Edward Hartpole Lecky, *History of Rationalism in Europe*, 1:62.

14. Paul Johnson, *A History of Christianity*, 309.

15. Anne Llewellyn Barstow, *Witchcraze*, 49.

16. Ibid., 59.

17. René Descartes, *The Meditations and Selections from the Principles of René Descartes*, 130.

CHAPTER 33
POSITIVE/NEGATIVE
1648–1899

1. Paul Johnson, *The Birth of the Modern: World Society 1815-1830*, 479.

2. Timothy Ferris, *Coming of Age in the Milky Way*, 122.

3. Paul Johnson, *The Birth of the Modern*, 484.

4. José Argüelles, *The Transformative Vision*, 117.

5. Samuel Taylor Coleridge, *Works*, 1:50.

6. Josephine Donovan, *Feminist Theory: The Intellectual Tradition of American Feminism*, 12.

7. Sarah M. Grimké, *Letters on the Equality of the Sexes and the Condition of Woman*, 3.

8. Josephine Donovan, *Feminist Theory*, 6.

9. John Stuart Mill and Harriet Taylor Mill, *Essays on Sex Equality*, 125.

10. Ibid., 239.

CHAPTER 34
ID/SUPEREGO,
1900–1945

1. Linda Dalrymple Henderson, *The Fourth Dimension and Non-Euclidean Geometry in Modern Art*, 284.

2. Michel Foucault, *This Is Not a Pipe*, 9.

3. Richard Tarnas, *The Passion of the Western Mind*, 391.

4. Paul Johnson, *The Birth of the Modern: World Society 1815–1830*, 833.

5. Marshall McLuhan, *Understanding Media: The Extensions of Man*, 262.

6. Ibid., 260.

CHAPTER 35
PAGE/SCREEN,
1945–2000

1. Tony Lenz, *Orality and Literacy in Hellenic Greece*, 7.

2. Marshall McLuhan and Bruce R. Powers, *The Global Village*, 4.

3. Paul Johnson, *The Birth of the Modern: World Society 1815–1830*, 482–84.

4. José Argüelles, *The Transformative Vision: Reflections on the Nature and History of Human Expression*, 116.

5. Ulric Neisser, "Rising Scores on Intelligence Tests," *American Scientist*, 85 (1991):440–47.

BIBLIOGRAPHY

Abélard. *Letters of Abélard & Héloïse*. Edited by C. K. Scott-Moncrieff. 3 vols. New York: Cooper Square Publishers, 1974.

Abram, David. *The Spell of the Sensuous*. New York: Pantheon Books, 1996.

Aeschylus. *The Eumenides*. Translated by Robert Fagels. New York: Penguin, 1975.

Allen, John William. *History of Political Thought in the Sixteenth Century*. New York: Methuen and Co., Barnes and Noble, 1957.

Allen, Marti Lu, and T. Keith Dix. *The Beginning of Understanding: Writing in the Ancient World*. Ann Arbor: Kelsey Museum of Archaeology, 1991.

Andrae, Tor. *Mohammed*. Translated by Menzel. New York: Harper, 1936.

Aquinas, Thomas. *Summa Contra Gentiles, Book One: God*. Translated by Anton C. Pegis. Garden City, N.Y.: Hanover House, n.d.

———. *Summa Theologiae*. vol. 13. London: Eyre and Sottiswoode, and New York: McGraw-Hill, 1964.

Argüelles, José. *The Transformative Vision: Reflections on the Nature and History of Human Expression*. Boulder and London: Shambala, 1975.

Aria, Barbara. *The Nature of the Chinese Character*. New York: Simon and Schuster, 1991.

Aristotle. *The Works of Aristotle*. Translated by Benjamin Jowett; edited by W. D. Ross. Oxford: Oxford University Press, 1921.

Armstrong, Karen. *A History of God: The 4000-Year Quest of Judaism, Christianity, and Islam*. New York: Alfred A. Knopf, 1993.

———. *Muhammad: A Biography of the Prophet*. San Francisco: HarperCollins, 1992.

———. *The Gospel According to Woman: Christianity's Creation of the Sex War in the West*. New York: Doubleday, 1986.

Augustine. *City of God*. Translated by Henry Betterson. London: Penguin, 1972.

———. *Confessions*. Translated by William Watts. Cambridge, Mass.: Harvard University Press, 1977.

Bainton, Roland H. *Here I Stand: A Life of Martin Luther*. New York: Abingdon Press, 1950.

———. *Hunted Heretic: The Life of Michael Servetus*. Boston: Beacon Press, 1952.

Baring, Anne, and Jules Cashford. *The Myth of the Goddess: Evolution of an Image*. New York: Viking, 1991.

Barnett, L. D. *The Heart of India*. New York: Dutton, 1924.

Barstow, Anne Llewellyn. *Witchcraze: A New History of the European Witch Hunts*. New York: HarperCollins, 1994.

Batiffol, Louis. *The Century of the Renaissance.* New York: AMS Press, 1935.

Bax, Belfort. *The Peasants War in Germany at the Time of the Reformation.* London: Macmillan, 1889.

Beard, Charles. *Martin Luther and the Reformation.* Translated and edited by Frederick Smith. London: K. Paul, Trench and Co., 1889.

———. *The Reformation of the Sixteenth Century.* London: Williams and Norgate, 1907.

Bebel, August. *Women and Socialism.* Translated by Daniel DeLeon. New York: Schocken Books, 1971.

Becker, Ernest. *The Denial of Death.* New York: Macmillan, 1973.

Begg, Ean. *The Cult of the Black Virgin.* London: Arkana Penguin, 1985.

Bernal, Martin. *Black Athena.* 2 vols. New Brunswick: Rutgers University Press, 1987.

———. *Cadmean Letters.* Winona Lake: Eisenbraums, 1990.

Birnbaum, Lucia Chiavola. *Black Madonnas.* Boston: Northeastern University Press, 1993.

Blake, William. *The Complete Writings of William Blake.* Edited by Geoffrey Keynes. Oxford: Oxford University Press, 1966.

———. *Poetry and Prose.* New York: Doubleday, 1965.

Bloom, Harold. *The Book of J.* Translated by David Rosenberg. New York: Vintage Books, 1991.

Blum, Deborah. *Sex on the Brain: The Biological Differences Between Men and Women.* New York: Viking, 1997.

Bogen, Joseph. "The Other Side of the Brain: An Appositional Mind." In *The Nature of Human Consciousness,* edited by Robert E. Ornstein. San Francisco: W. H. Freeman, 1968.

Bowra, C. M. *The Greek Experience.* New York: New American Library, 1957.

Briffault, R. Robert. *The Mothers.* 2 vols. New York: Macmillan, 1927.

Brunn, Emilie Zum, and Georgette Epiney-Bugard. *Women Mystics in Medieval Europe.* Translated by Sheila Hughes. New York: Paragon House, 1989.

Bulfinch, Thomas. *The Age of Chivalry.* New York: Penguin, 1962.

Butler, Pierce. *Women of Medieval France.* New York: Gordon Press, 1908.

Calasso, Roberto. *The Marriage of Cadmus and Harmony.* Translated by Tim Parks. New York: Alfred A. Knopf, 1993.

Calvin, John. *Institutes of the Christian Religion.* Translated by John Allen. Vols. 1 and 2. Philadelphia: Presbyterian Board of Christian Educators, 1936.

Cambridge Modern History. 12 vols. New York: Macmillan, 1902–12.

Campbell, Joseph. *The Way of the Animal Powers.* New York: Harper, 1983.

Carlyle, Thomas. *Oliver Cromwell's Letters and Speeches.* 4 vols. New York: J. M. Dent, 1901.

Carroll, Mitchell N. *Greek Women.* Philadelphia: Rittenhouse Press, 1908.

Catholic Encyclopedia. Edited by R. C. Broderick. Vol. 3. Nashville: T. Nelson, 1976.

Charbonnier, Georges. *Conversations with Claude Lévi-Strauss.* London: Jonathan Cape, 1961.

Chambers, E. K. *The Medieval Stage.* 2 vols. London: Oxford University Press, 1903. Reprint, Mineola, N.Y.: Dover Publications, 1996.

Churchill, Winston S. *History of the English-Speaking Peoples.* 3 vols. New York: Dodd, Mead, 1957.

Clark, Kenneth. *Civilisation*. New York: Harper, 1969.

Coleridge, Samuel Taylor. *Works*. Edited by T. E. Sqedd. 7 vols. London, 1884.

Commager, Henry Steele. *The Empire of Reason: How Europe Imagined and America Realized the Enlightenment*. New York: Doubleday, 1977.

Confucius. *The Analects*. Translated by D. C. Lau. London: Penguin, 1979.

Cotterell, Arthur. "The Indus Civilization." In *The Penguin Encyclopedia of Ancient Civilizations*. Edited by Arthur Cotterell. London: Penguin, 1980.

Coulton, George G. *History of Life in the Middle Ages*. 4 vols. London, New York: Cambridge University Press, 1930.

————. *Medieval Panorama*. New York: Macmillan, 1944.

Daly, Mary. *The Church and the Second Sex*. Boston: Beacon Press, 1968.

D'Arcy, M. C. *Thomas Aquinas*. London: Sheed and Ward, 1930.

Davis, W. V. "Egyptian Hieroglyphics." In *Reading the Past*. Edited by J. T. Hooker. Berkeley: University of California Press, 1990.

de Maulde-La-Claviere, R. *Women of the Renaissance*. New York: Putnam's Sons, 1905.

de Meun, Jean. *Roman de la Rose*. Translated by Charles Dahlberg. Hanover: University Press of the New England, 1983.

de Santillana. Giorgio, and Hertha Von Dechand. *Hamlet's Mill: An Essay Investigating the Origins of Human Knowledge and Its Transmission Through Myth*. Boston: David R. Godine, 1969.

Derrida, Jacques. *Of Grammatology*. Translated by Gayatri Chakravorty Spivak. Baltimore: Johns Hopkins University Press, 1974.

Descartes, René. *The Meditations and Selections from the Principles of René Descartes*. Translated by John Veitch. LaSalle, Ill.: Open Court Publishing, 1968.

Dimott, Max I. *Jews, God and History*. New York: Penguin, 1962.

Donovan, Josephine. *Feminist Theory: The Intellectual Tradition of American Feminism*. New York: Continuum, 1990.

Dover, Kenneth James. *Greek Homosexuality*. Cambridge: Harvard University Press, 1978.

Dowden, Edward. *Michel de Montaigne*. New York: J. B. Lippincott, 1906.

Dudden, F. H. *Gregory the Great*. Vol. 1. London: Longmans, Green, 1905.

Durant, Will. *The Story of Civilization*. Vol. 1, *Our Oriental Heritage*. New York: Simon and Schuster, 1935.

————. *The Story of Civilization*. Vol. 2, *The Life of Greece*. New York: Simon and Schuster, 1939.

————. *The Story of Civilization*. Vol. 3, *Caesar and Christ*. New York: Simon and Schuster, 1944.

————. *The Story of Civilization*. Vol. 4, *The Age of Faith*. New York: Simon and Schuster, 1950.

————. *The Story of Civilization*. Vol. 5, *The Renaissance*. New York: Simon and Schuster, 1953.

————. *The Story of Civilization*. Vol. 6, *The Reformation*. New York: Simon and Schuster, 1957.

Eisler, Riane. *The Chalice and the Blade*. New York: Harper, 1988.

Eliade, Mircea. *A History of Religious Ideas*. Translated by Willard R. Trask. Vol. 1. Chicago: University of Chicago Press, 1978.

Epictetus. *Works*. Girard, Kans.: Loeb Library Encheiridion, n.d.

Erasmus, D., and M. Luther. *Discourse on Free Will*. Translated and edited by Ernst F. Winter. New York: Frederick Ungar, 1961.

Euripides. *Medea*. Translated by Philip Vellacott. London: Penguin, 1963.

Ferris, Timothy. *Coming of Age in the Milky Way*. New York: William Morrow, 1988.

Foucault, Michel. *This Is Not a Pipe*. Berkeley: University of California Press, 1983.

Freud, Sigmund. *Moses and Monotheism*. New York: Vintage Books, 1939.

Friedlander, L. *Roman Life and Manners Under the Early Empire*. Vol. 3. London: G. Routledge and Sons, 1928.

Froude, J. A. *Life and Letters of Erasmus*. New York: Charles Scribner's Sons, 1912.

Frymer-Kensky, Tikva. *In the Wake of the Goddess*. New York: Fawcett Columbine, 1992.

Funk, Robert W., Roy W. Hoover, and The Jesus Seminar. *The Five Gospels: What Did Jesus Really Say*. New York: Macmillan, 1993.

Gadon, Elinor W. *The Once and Future Goddess*. New York: Harper, 1989.

Galland, China. *Longing for Darkness*. New York: Penguin, 1990.

Gardner, Sir Alain. *Egypt of the Pharaohs*. Oxford: Oxford Press, 1961.

Gibbon, Edward. *Decline and Fall of the Roman Empire*. Edited by J. B. Bury. Vol. 1. London: Everyman Library, 1900.

Gies, Frances, and Joseph Gies. *Woman in the Middle Ages*. New York: Harper, 1978.

Gimbutas, Marija. *The Language of the Goddess*. San Francisco: HarperCollins, 1989.

Goetz, Phillip, ed. *The New Encyclopedia Britannica*. 29 vols. Chicago, 1990.

Gombrich, Ernest. *The Story of Art*. Oxford: Phaidon, 1972.

Gordon, Cyrus. *The Common Background of Greek and Hebrew Civilization*. New York: W. W. Norton, 1965.

Grabmann, M. *Thomas Aquinas*. Translated by Virgil Michel. New York: Russell and Russell, 1963.

Green, A. R. W. *The Role of Human Sacrifice in the Ancient Near East*. Missoula, Mont.: Scholar Press for American Schools of Oriental Research, 1975.

Grimké, Sarah M. *Letters on the Equality of the Sexes and the Condition of Woman*. 1838. New York: Burt Franklin, 1970.

Guizot, François Gulliume, and Madame Guizot de Witt. *History of France from the Earliest Time to 1848*. Translated by Robert Black. 8 vols. New York: H. M. Caldwell Co., 1909.

Guthrie, W. K. C. *Orpheus and the Greek Religion*. Princeton: Princeton University Press, 1952.

Hamilton, Edith. *The Greek Way*. New York, London: W. W. Norton, 1964.

Harrison, Jane. *Prolegomena to the Study of Greek Religion*. London: Merlin Press, 1980.

Havell, E. B. *History of Aryan Rule in India*. London: Harrap, n.d.

Havelock, Eric A. *Preface to Plato*. Vol. 1, *A History of the Greek Mind*. Cambridge: Harvard University Press, Belknap Press, 1963.

———. *The Muse Learns to Write: Reflections on Orality and Literacy from Antiquity to the Present*. New Haven: Yale University Press, 1986.

Heer, Friedrich. *The Medieval World*. Translated by Janet Sondheimer. New York: Mentor, The Penguin Group, 1962.

Henderson, Linda Dalrymple. *The Fourth Dimension and Non-Euclidean Geometry in Modern Art*. Princeton: Princeton University Press, 1983.

Herodotus. *The Histories.* Translated by Aubrey de Sélincourt. Middlesex, England: Penguin, 1954.

Hesiod. *Theogonis.* Translated by Dorothea Wender. Middlesex, England: Penguin, 1973.

Hewes, G. W. "Current Status of the Gestural Theory of Language Origin." In *Origins and Evolution of Language and Speech,* 280:495. New York Academy of Sciences.

Hodgkin, T. *The Life of Charlemagne.* New York: A. L. Burt, 1902.

Homer. *Odyssey.* Translated by A. J. Murray. 2 vols. New York: Loeb Library, 1954.

Houlihan, Patrick, and Steven M. Goodman. *The Birds of Ancient Egypt.* Cairo: American University in Cairo Press, 1986.

Hourani, Albert. *A History of the Arab Peoples.* New York: Warner Books, 1991.

Howell, R. Patton, ed. *Beyond Literacy: The Second Gutenberg Revolution.* Dallas: Saybrook, 1976.

Hughes, Philip. *The Reformation in England.* 2 vols. London: Macmillan, 1952.

Hume, R. E. "Brihadaranyaka Upanishad," in *The Thirteen Upanishads.* Oxford: Oxford University Press, 1921.

Innis, Harold. *The Bias of Communication.* Toronto: University of Toronto Press, 1951.

Janik, Allan, and Stephen Toulmin. *Wittgenstein's Vienna.* New York: Simon and Schuster, 1973.

Janssen, Johannes. *History of the German People at the Close of the Middle Ages.* Translated and edited by A. M. Christie and M. A. Mitchell. 4 vols. London: Kegan Paul, Trench, Trubner and Co., 1903.

Jaspers, Karl. *Socrates, Buddha, Confucius, Jesus.* Edited by Hannah Arendt; translated by Ralph Manheim. San Diego: Harcourt Brace, 1957.

Johnson, Paul. *A History of Christianity.* New York: Atheneum, 1976.

————. *The Birth of the Modern: World Society 1815–1830.* New York: HarperCollins, 1991.

————. *The History of the Jews.* New York: Harper, 1987.

Jong, Erica. *Witches.* New York: Harry N. Abrams, 1981.

Josephus. *The Jewish War.* Translated by G. A. Williamson. Hanmondsworth: Penguin, 1959.

Kaufman, Y. *The Religion of Israel.* Translated by M. Greenberg. Chicago: Chicago University Press, 1960.

Kautsky, Karl. *Communism in Central Europe at the Time of the Reformation.* New York: A. M. Kelley, 1966.

Kenoyer, Jonathan Mark. "Birth of a Civilization." *Archaeology* (February/March 1998):58–59.

Klapisch-Zuben, Christiane, ed. *A History of Women.* Cambridge: Harvard University Press, Belknap Press, 1992.

Labib, Pahon. *The Hyksos Rule in Egypt and Its Fall.* Augustin, New York, and Glückstadt, Germany, 1936.

Lacroix, Paul. *History of Prostitution.* Translated by Samuel Putnam. Vol. 1. New York: Covici, Fried, 1931.

Lane-Poole, S. *Speeches and Table Talk of the Prophet Mohammed.* London: Macmillan, 1882.

Lao Tsu. *Tao Te Ching.* Translated by Gia-Fu Feng and Jane English. New York: Vintage Books, 1972.

Larrington, Carolyn, ed. *The Feminist Companion to Mythology.* New York: Harper-Collins, 1992.

Lea, H. C. *History of the Inquisition in Spain.* 4 vols. New York: Macmillan, 1906.

Lecky, William Edward Hartpole. *History of European Morals.* 2 vols. New York: D. Appleton Press, 1975.

———. *History of Rationalism in Europe.* 2 vols. London: Longmans, Green, 1904.

Legge, James. *The Chinese Clerics.* Vol. 1, *The Life and Teachings of Confucius.* London: Trubner, 1895.

Lenz, Tony. *Orality and Literacy in Hellenic Greece.* Carbondale: Southern Illinois University Press, 1989.

Lerner, Gerda. *The Creation of Patriarchy.* New York, Oxford: Oxford University Press, 1986.

———. *The Creation of Feminist Consciousness.* New York, Oxford: Oxford University Press, 1993.

Lévi-Strauss, Claude. *The Elementary Structures of Kinship.* Boston: Macmillan, 1969.

Logan, Robert. *The Alphabet Effect.* New York: William Morrow, 1986.

Lucretius. *On the Nature of Things.* Translated by Willa Ellery Leonard. New York: Dutton, 1950.

Lucretius. *De rerum natura.* Translated by Cyril Bailey. 2 vols. Oxford: Oxford Clarendon Press, n.d.

Luther, Martin. *The Table Talk.* Translated and edited by William Hazlitt. London: George Bell and Sons, 1909.

———. *The Works of Martin Luther.* 6 vols. Philadelphia: Muhlenberg Press, 1943.

McCann, Justin, ed. and trans. *The Rule of St. Benedict.* London: Sheed and Ward, 1957.

Machiavelli, Niccolò. *The Prince, and the Discourses.* New York: Modern Library, 1950.

McLuhan, Eric, and Frank Zingrone, eds. *The Essential McLuhan.* New York: Basic Books, 1995.

McLuhan, Marshall. *Understanding Media: The Extensions of Man.* New York: A Mentor Book, McGraw-Hill, 1964.

———. *The Gutenberg Galaxy.* Toronto: University of Toronto Press, 1980.

McLuhan, Marshall, and Quentin Fiore. *The Medium is the Massage: An Inventory of Effects.* New York: Bantam Books, 1967.

McLuhan, Marshall, and Bruce R. Powers. *The Global Village.* Oxford: Oxford University Press, 1986.

Manchester, William. *A World Lit Only by Fire.* New York: Little, Brown, 1992.

Manniche, Lise. *Sexual Life in Ancient Egypt.* London: KPI Ltd., 1987.

Manu Code. Translated by Julian Jolly. London: Trubner, 1887.

Margoliouth, D. S. *Mohammed and the Rise of Islam.* New York: AMS Press, 1978.

Maritain, Jacques. *Three Reformers: Luther, Descartes, Rousseau.* New York: Charles Scribner's Sons, 1950.

Mellaart, James. *Excavation at Hacilar.* Edinburgh: Edinburgh University Press, 1970.

———. *The Neolithic of the Near East.* New York: Scribner's, 1975.

Michelet, Jules. *Historie le France.* 5 vols. Translated by G. H. Smith. D. Appleton, 1857.

Mill, John Stuart, and Harriet Taylor Mill. *Essays on Sex Equality.* Edited by Alice S. Rossi Chicago: University of Chicago Press, 1970.

Moin, Ann, and David Jessel. *Brain Sex.* New York: Dell, 1989.

Motley, J. R. *Rise of the Dutch Republic.* 3 vols. New York: D. McKay, 1898.

Muhammed, Ali Maulana. *The Religion of Islam.* Lahore: Ahmadiyya Anjuman Isha'at, Islam Publ. 1936.

Müller, F. Max, ed. *The Sacred Texts of China: The Texts of Taoism.* Translated by James Legge. 2 vols. Oxford: Oxford University Press, 1927.

Neisser, Ulric. "Rising Scores on Intelligence Tests," *American Scientist* 85 (1991): 440–47.

Neumann, Erich. *The Great Mother.* Translated by Ralph Manheim. Princeton: Princeton University Press, 1972.

Nicholson, R. A. *Translation of Eastern Poetry and Prose.* Cambridge: Cambridge University Press, 1921.

Noble, David F. *A World Without Women.* New York: Oxford University Press, 1992.

Ornstein, Robert E. *The Nature of Human Consciousness.* San Francisco: W. H. Freeman, 1968.

———. *The Right Mind.* New York: Harcourt Brace, 1997.

Ortner, Sherry B. "Is Female to Male as Nature Is to Culture." In *Woman, Culture and Society.* Edited by M. Z. Rosaldo and L. Lamphene. Stanford: Stanford University Press, 1974.

Otto, Walter. *Dionysus: Myth and Cult.* Translated by Robert Palmer. Dallas: Spring Publications, 1981.

Pagels, Elaine. *Adam, Eve, and the Serpent.* New York: Vintage Books, 1988.

———. *The Gnostic Gospels.* New York: Vintage Books, 1979.

Paglia, Camille. *Sexual Personae.* New York: Vintage Books, 1991.

Park, No Young. *Making a New China.* Boston: Stratford, 1929.

Pastor, Ludwig. *History of the Popes, From the Close of the Middle Ages.* 3d ed. 14 vols. Edited by R. Francis Kerr. St. Louis: Herder, 1950.

Patai, Raphael. *The Hebrew Goddess.* 3d ed. Detroit: Wayne State University Press, 1990.

Paulsen, Friedrich. *German Education Past and Present.* Translated by A. Lorenz. New York: Charles Scribner's Sons, 1912.

Phillips, John. *Eve: The History of an Idea.* San Francisco: HarperCollins, 1984.

Plato. *The Collected Dialogues.* Edited by Edith Hamilton and Huntington Cairns. Princeton: Princeton University Press, 1961.

Plutarch. *Life of Lycurgus, Plutarch's Lives.* Translated by Bernadotte Perrin. Vol. 1. New York: Macmillan, 1914.

Pomeroy, Sarah B. *Goddesses, Whores, Wives, and Slaves.* New York: Schocken Books, 1975.

Putnam, George H. *Books and Their Makers During the Middle Ages.* 2 vols. New York: Putnam's Son's, 1896.

Radhakrishnan, S. *Indian Philosophy.* Vol. 1. New York: Macmillan, n.d.

Rai, L. Lajpat. *Unhappy India.* Calcutta, 1928.

Ranke, Leopold. *History of the Reformation in Germany.* Translated by Sarah Austin. Vol. 1. New York: Dutton, 1905.

Redford, Donald. *Akhenaton: The Heretic King.* Princeton: Princeton University Press, 1984.

———. *Egypt, Canaan, and Israel in Ancient Times.* Princeton: Princeton University Press, 1992.

Remy, Nicolas. *Demonolotrie.* 1595. Translated by E. A. Ashwin. New York: University Books, 1971.

Rhys Davids, T. W. *Dialogues of the Buddha.* Vols. 2 and 3. Oxford: Oxford University Press, 1923.

Rigand, Jean-Phillippe. Interviewed in *National Geographic,* October 1988:448.

Robertson, J. M. *A History of Freethought.* 4th ed. rev. London: Watts, n.d.

Roeder, Ralph. *Catherine de Medici and the Lost Revolution.* New York: Viking Press, 1937.

Roth, Cecil. *History of the Jews.* New York: Schocken Books, 1954.

Russell, Bertrand. *History of Western Philosophy.* New York: Simon and Schuster, 1945.

Sacks, Oliver. *Seeing Voices: A Journey into the World of the Deaf.* Berkeley: University of California Press, 1989.

Saint Jerome. *Selected Letters.* Translated by Frederick Adam Wright. Cambridge: Loeb Library, Harvard University Press, 1954.

Sarton, G. *Introduction to the History of Science.* Vol. 1. Baltimore: Williams and Wilkins, 1950.

Schaff, Philip. *History of the Christian Church.* Vols. 3 and 8. Grand Rapids: William B. Eerdman's, 1950.

Schmandt-Besserat, Denise. *How Writing Came About.* Austin: University of Texas Press, 1992.

Schoenfeld, H. *Women of Teutonic Nations.* Philadelphia: G. Barrie, 1908.

Seebohm, Frederick. *The Oxford Reformers.* 3d ed. London: Longmans, Green, 1913.

Shlain, Leonard. *Art & Physics: Parallel Visions in Space, Time, and Light,* New York: William Morrow, 1991.

Sichel, Edith. *Catherine de Medici and French Reformation.* London: Dawsons of Pall Mall, 1969.

Sidhanta, N. K. *The Heroic Age of India.* New York: Alfred A. Knopf, 1930.

Smith, Homer. *Man and His Gods.* New York: Grosset and Dunlap, 1952.

Smith, Preserved. *Conversations with Luther.* New York: Pilgrim Press, n.d.

———. *The Age of the Reformation.* New York: Henry Holt, 1920.

———. *The Life and Letters of Martin Luther.* New York: Barnes and Noble, 1968.

Smithson, R. J. *The Anabaptists.* London: J. Clark, 1935.

Sophocles. *The Complete Plays of Sophocles.* Translated by Sir Richard Claverhouse Jebb. New York: Bantam Classic Edition, 1967.

Sprengling, M. *The Alphabet: Its Rise and Development from the Sinai Inscription.* Chicago: University of Chicago Press, 1931.

Stiebing, William H., Jr. *Out of the Desert.* Buffalo: Prometheus Books, 1989.

Stone, Merlin. *When God Was a Woman.* San Diego: Harcourt Brace, 1976.

Summers, Montague, ed. and trans. *Malleus Maleficarum.* New York: Benjamin Blom, 1970.

Syed, Ameer Ali. *The Spirit of Islam.* Lahore: Zahid Publications, 1992.

Symonds, J. A. *Studies of Greek Poets.* London: A. C. Black, 1920.

Symons, Donald. *The Evolution of Human Sexuality.* New York: Oxford University Press, 1979.

Tarnas, Richard. *The Passion of the Western Mind.* New York: Harmony Books, 1991.

Taylor, H. O. *The Medieval Mind.* Vol. 1. London: Macmillan, 1927.

Thomas, E. J. *Life of Buddha as Legend and History.* New York: Alfred A. Knopf, 1927.

Thompson, William Irwin. *The Time Falling Bodies Take to Light.* New York: St. Martin's Press, 1984.

Tuchman, Barbara W. *A Distant Mirror.* New York: Alfred A. Knopf, 1978.

———. *The March of Folly.* New York: Alfred A. Knopf, 1984.

Ullman, B. L. *Ancient Writing and Its Influence.* Toronto: University of Toronto Press, 1980.

Vacandard, Elphege. *The Inquisition, a Critical and Historical Study of the Coercive Power of the Church.* Translated by Bertrand Louis Conway. New York: Longmans, Green, 1908.

Velikovsky, Immanuel. *Ages in Chaos.* London: Abacus, 1973.

Villari, Pasquale. *The Life and Times of Girolamo Savonarola.* Translated by Linda Villari. New York: Charles Scribner's Sons, 1886.

Virgil. *The Aeneid.* Translated by W. J. Jackson Knight. London: Penguin, 1956.

Waddell, Helen. *The Wandering Scholars.* London: Constable and Sons, 1927.

Walker, C. B. F. "Cuneiform." In *Reading the Past.* Edited by J. T. Hooker. Berkeley: University of California Press, 1990.

Wemple, Suzanne. *Women in Frankish Society.* Philadelphia: University of Pennsylvania Press, 1981.

Westermark, E. *Origin and Development of Moral Ideas.* 2 vols. London: Macmillan, 1924.

White, E. M. *Woman in World History.* London: Jenkins, 1932.

Wilhelm, R. *Short History of Chinese Civilization.* Translated by Joan Joshua. New York: Viking Press, 1929.

Williams, S. Wells. *The Middle Kingdom.* New York: Scribner's, 1895.

Wilson, A. N. *Jesus: A Life.* New York: Fawcett Columbine, 1992.

———. *Paul: The Mind of the Apostle.* New York: W. W. Norton, 1997.

Wilson, Edmond O. *On Human Nature.* New York: Bantam, 1978.

Witelson, Sandra F. "Hand and Sex Differences in the Isthmus and Anterior Commissure of the Human Corpus Callosum." *Brain* 112 (1989):799–835.

Woolf, Virginia. *A Room of One's Own.* New York: Harcourt Brace, 1929.

Young, Serenity, ed. *An Anthology of Sacred Texts By and About Women.* New York: Crossroad, 1993.

Zuckerman, Solly. *The Social Life of Monkeys and Apes.* London: Butler and Tanner, 1932.

INDEX

A PENGUIN READERS GUIDE TO

THE ALPHABET
VERSUS
THE GODDESS

Leonard Shlain

A CONVERSATION WITH
LEONARD SHLAIN

You base your thesis on the idea that literacy—or the use of the alphabet—is primarily a left-brain activity, one that also represses right-brain activity. Can you elaborate on how the repression of right-brain activities would lead to misogynist societies?

When we speak and listen we use both sides of the brain. The left hemisphere processes the words linearly. Simultaneously, the right hemisphere evaluates speech's nonverbal clues such as body language and vocal inflection. Literacy, in contrast, depends primarily on the skills of the left hemisphere of men and women. I believe the right hemisphere (of both men and women who are right-handed) processes tasks traditionally female. The left hemisphere (of both men and women who are right-handed) processes tasks traditionally male. Literacy reinforces the masculine left hemisphere and devalues the right lobe, and this factor inflamed misogyny in literate societies. This occurred in the brains of both men and women, each of whom possesses a masculine side and a feminine side. Of course, it isn't as neat as I have explained here, but these are the bones of my thesis.

What, exactly, compelled you to research the effects of left-brain values on civilization? What came first: the thesis or the research?

I was electrified by the split brain research of the '60s. As a surgeon, I have operated on carotid arteries to the brain. I also was deeply affected by the ideas of media theorist Marshall McLuhan. In 1991, I went on an archaeological tour of Mediterranean sites and was intrigued by the overwhelming evidence of a time when both men and women worshipped goddesses. By the time Judaism, Christianity, and Islam became the West's only three religions, goddesses had disappeared.

3

It occurred to me that this event coincided with the time when people were learning to read and write. I suspected that there was something in the way people learned this new skill that reconfigured their brains. I hypothesized that the demise of the goddess was an inside job.

How do your findings about right- and left-brain values apply to your own dual careers as surgeon and writer?

Surgery is very yang and a little yin, writing is very yin and a little yang. Being both a writer and a surgeon provides a considerable balance to my life. Also, surgeons are steeped in science and are trained in a very left-brained manner early on. But the actual practice of surgery is very right-brained. It is tactile, intuitive, and very visual-spatial. Further, surgeons are the essence of hunter-killers seeking and rooting out disease literally with their hands. Very masculine. And yet, caring for patients during one of the most frightening and painful episodes of their lives requires tenderness and empathy. Surgery is caring and hunting.

Your description of the evolution of the early male and female body and brain is fascinating. If you were to make a conjecture, how would you guess that our bodies and brains are developing now?

Our success as the only truly predatory primate was primarily due to two incompatible features. One was our need to remain bipedal so we could walk on the ground and keep our hands free. The other was a constant need to increase cleverness by enlarging the brain. Babies' heads became so big that they became stuck in the mother's birth canal. Hominid females began to die in childbirth. Something had to give. Nature redesigned the human nervous system. Lacking hardly any instincts, humans are born helpless, but they possess a brain capable of acquiring incredible amounts of knowledge. A split brain simplified the wiring for a language brain. Language allows us to learn easily. We have continued to evolve by adding outside peripherals to our brain. The first was culture enhanced by spoken language. Then came writing, libraries, the printing press, photography, film, television, and now computers and the Internet. Each new technology of information transfer makes humans smarter and more knowledgeable and it is these extra-somatic pieces of our brain that are changing us even though our bodies remain the same.

Was there more of a dichotomy between men and women and left- and right-brain behavior at the dawn of civilization?

We can only make speculative assumptions concerning the structure of human societies long ago. Evidence seems to suggest that gender roles were more firmly established in hunter-gatherer societies than they are presently. We are social predators similar to lions, wolves, and killer whales that hunt in cooperative packs. In other social predators, the females play a leading role in the hunting and killing. In humans, hunting is left primarily to the males because crying babies cannot be brought along. Human offspring require more care from their mothers than the offspring of any other life form. What other female would come to the aid of its offspring if it called for help twenty-five years after the date of birth? Despite the considerable differences in the principal labors of each sex, there was a tacit recognition of the importance of one to the other. An economic and emotional interdependence fostered a greater level of equality than would exist in many more advanced empires that came later. There is evidence that we have been split-brained and split-handed since ancient times. Prehistoric artists painted outlines of their left hands in eighty percent of examples studied, suggesting that the same percentage were right-handed. Presently, the ratio is ninety-two percent right-handed people to eight percent left-handed. Some factor changed in culture to skew these ratios. I believe it was literacy.

5

Are we evolving into more integrated societies as a whole? How do literacy and other forms of communication influence this development?

Yes. I believe that McLuhan's aphorism "the medium is the message" provides the insight into the effect on culture of its principal form of communication. It isn't only the content of information that can change us, it is the process by which we perceive the information. Speaking and listening are very different activities from writing and reading. The former engages both sides of the brain but the latter relies more on one: the masculine side of both men and women. This factor bolsters patriarchy and misogyny and unbalances culture.

You state that "there is something inherently anti-female in the written word. Men obsessed with the written word tend to be sexist." Can you elaborate on this point? What does it mean to be "obsessed" with the written word? What happens to women obsessed with writing?

There is a neurological condition known as hypergraphia. Hypergraphia afflicts men disproportionately. Compulsive diarists possess a lesion in their left brain that causes them to write excessively, detailing every aspect of their life. They often endow their tedious writings with great religious significance. In general, hypergraphics are rigid, humorless, domineering, and unsympathetic. One could easily imagine how women, feminine values, and intuition would fare if one of these patients was in a position of power. This profile, however, fits many Western religious leaders. Augustine, Jerome, Luther, and Calvin spent great portions of their lives writing long religious tracts. These men were "obsessed" with the importance of their written words. Using fear and threats to carry out their aims, they were all misogynists whose writings turned people away from the goddess, nature, and the feminine.

Poets and novelists use metaphors, a right hemispheric form of language. They "paint" images with words and differ from writers of

6

abstract works. As an exercise, try to come up with the name of a significant male writer who wrote long dense tomes about religion and philosophy and who also was not a misogynist.

Women are generally not as affected by the masculinizing tendencies of the written words because the brains of women are not nearly as sharply divided as the brains of men. Women in general do not as often as men express extremes. Women who write feminist polemical books tend to express themselves more in their masculine modes.

You discuss at length the horrors visited upon the aboriginal peoples living in the New World by its conquerors—sixteenth-century Europeans "driven mad by the printing press"—and you wonder how such an invasion would have been different if the conquering culture had been more tolerant, such as the early Romans under Julius Caesar. How exactly does pre-literacy impact on a culture's tolerance? Weren't ancient and modern invaders of non-Western lands equally bloodthirsty and destructive?

Belligerency appears to be a fairly universal human trait. Nevertheless, the least warlike societies seem to be pre-literate agricultural societies. Iroquois Indians, for example, maintained the Great Peace in the Northeast for over three hundred years. Hunter/gatherer, pastoral, and nomadic cultures tend to be more "bloodthirsty." There is no evidence that Neolithic agricultural people ever fought organized wars. The most contentious periods in Western history were those characterized by high literacy rates: Classical Greece, Imperial Rome, the Renaissance, and Europe of the nineteenth and twentieth centuries. The roots of mayhem are complex but I feel that alphabet literacy has been an overlooked factor.

How does the Internet fit in with your hypothesis? Like the printing press, it duplicates type, and must be read. And yet it also sends out an image, making use of right-brain skills. Is the Internet an example of the

7

kind of unifying trend you see as part of current civilization's makeup? Or will it present its own problems for historians and anthropologists of future centuries to analyze and discuss?

The computer and the Internet will once again reconfigure the brains of those that use them. Typing is a two-handed activity that requires input from both sides of the brain. Writing requires only the dominant hand. The use of a mouse by the right hand necessitates the activation of right-hemispheric visual-spatial skills. The World Wide Web and the Internet are not linear, they are holistic. All ancient deities associated with webs and nets were goddesses. Many of the processes we use to operate a computer are inherently feminine.

What criticisms have your theories elicited? How would you address them?

The main criticism stems from people hearing about the theory but not reading the book and misinterpreting what I have proposed. I am not saying that men read better than women or that men's left brains are better than women's. I am not saying that people shouldn't read or that television is an unqualified benefit. Some feminists resent that a man has written a book about the goddess. Mea culpa. Some academics are appalled that a non-specialist has wandered through their turf. Mea culpa. And some reviewers believe that interpreting all history through a narrow lens is too simplistic. To write a book of such sweeping scope, I had to leave out a lot of alternative possibilities. This does not mean that I am unaware of them. In general, the book has been very favorably reviewed and many people are excited to have a neuroanatomical hypothesis to explain a historical enigma.

You set forth an optimistic view of the present and the future, of a world in which the "right-hemisphere values of tolerance, caring, and

respect for nature" will help correct some of the damage that has been wrought over the past two millennia. What sorts of changes do you envision in terms of human behavior, technology, and communication? What, if any, dangers exist in a world dominated by right-hemisphere values?

Human advances move in fits and starts. Technology has moved us all to a global village. Tolerance has markedly increased. Religious wars are on the wane. Fundamentalism is in retreat. Dogmatic ideologies have been discredited. At the same time, human rights are moving forward. Women's status is on the upswing. And a newfound respect and love for nature is evident in the burgeoning ecology movement. There remains much work to be done but I believe that as image and word come into balance, so too will left and right hemispheres, and masculine and feminine. All extremes have dangers and too much emphasis on right-hemispheric modes could lead to superstitions, sensual excesses, and a loss of scientific advances. Despite these concerns, I think we are living in a New Renaissance fueled by the Iconic Revolution.

DISCUSSION QUESTIONS

1. Throughout the book Shlain emphasizes the dualities inherent in the experience of living—life/death, yin/yang, reason/madness. Why do you think it is important to recognize these dualities? Can you think of examples in your own life in which opposing forces work together to create both negative and positive change?

2. Shlain uses the example of Christ's teachings to illustrate the difference between the spoken word and the written word. Communication, he argues, changes when it is written. What sorts of changes is he talking about? How do you think the ideas exchanged in your own group would be altered if they were written down?

3. In his history of human civilization, Shlain recounts centuries of cruel and violent behavior carried out in behalf of religion and ethnic purity. In each case, he cites a literacy-related cause for such behavior. Using his thesis, is it possible to find similar root causes for such atrocities as the tribal massacres in Rwanda, the ethnic cleansing in Yugoslavia, or the shootings in America's schools? A century from now, how do you think historians and anthropologists will explain these incidents?

4. Shlain is optimistic for the future of mankind and is convinced that we are returning to right-hemisphere-type values that point to a more peaceful future. Do you agree or disagree with him?

5. Shlain cites a number of male figures—including Moses, Christ, Plato, Augustine, Luther, Calvin, Hitler, Einstein, and Freud—who made important and lasting (but not always beneficial) contributions to civilization. What makes their contributions so significant? How were they or their actions affected by the written word? Can you add any living people—any women—who might be added to that list?

6. Chances are, you have a television and a telephone in your home. Discuss the role these technologies play in your lives, especially with regard to communication. Likewise, how do you think computers are affecting current generations of young people? Are the impacts mostly positive or negative?

7. Discuss the right-brain/left-brain theory and explain which sides each of you favor. Then discuss how the results break down by gender in your group.

8. Shlain points to the invention of the printing press as the cause for much of the excessive behavior of the sixteenth century. Is the Internet our century's printing press? Give examples in which the Internet has played an important role, whether negative or positive, in shaping recent events.

9. "In the age of the image," writes Shlain, "literacy will inevitably decline." Even if this development does not lead to a decline in our overall intelligence, what concerns does it raise? Imagine if your children's school decided that learning to perceive and create images took precedence over reading skills. Is there a prejudice against imagery in our society? If so, is it a valid prejudice?

10. After reading *The Alphabet Versus the Goddess,* do you agree with Shlain's thesis?

For information about other Penguin Readers Guides, please call the Penguin Marketing Department at (800) 778-6425, E-mail to reading@penguinputnam.com, or write to us at:

Penguin Marketing Department CC
Readers Guides
375 Hudson Street
New York, NY 10014-3657

Please allow 4–6 weeks for delivery.
To access Penguin Readers Guides on-line, visit Club PPI on our Web site at: http://www.penguinputnam.com.